More information about this series at https://link.springer.com/bookseries/4205

Christian Rathgeb · Ruben Tolosana ·
Ruben Vera-Rodriguez · Christoph Busch
Editors

Handbook of Digital Face Manipulation and Detection

From DeepFakes to Morphing Attacks

Editors
Christian Rathgeb
Department of Computer Science
Hochschule Darmstadt
Darmstadt, Germany

Ruben Vera-Rodriguez
School of Engineering
Universidad Autonoma de Madrid
Madrid, Spain

Ruben Tolosana
School of Engineering
Universidad Autonoma de Madrid
Madrid, Spain

Christoph Busch
Department of Information Security
and Communication Technology
Norwegian University of Science
and Technology
Gjøvik, Norway

Author-funded

ISSN 2191-6586   ISSN 2191-6594   (electronic)
Advances in Computer Vision and Pattern Recognition
ISBN 978-3-030-87666-1   ISBN 978-3-030-87664-7   (eBook)
https://doi.org/10.1007/978-3-030-87664-7

This Springer imprint is published by the registered company Springer Nature Switzerland AG
The registered company address is: Gewerbestrasse 11, 6330 Cham, Switzerland

Preface

This handbook represents the first comprehensive collection of research topics in the field of digital face manipulation and detection by a wide variety of experts from various research areas including computer vision, pattern recognition, biometrics and media forensics, among others. While being of primary interest to researchers in said fields, it appeals to a broad readership by providing detailed theoretical explanations to fundamentals as well as in-depth investigations of current research topics along with comprehensive experimental evaluations.

In Part I of this handbook, the reader is provided with introductory overview chapters focusing on the topics of face image and video manipulations and detection (Chap. 1), the impact of different manipulations and alteration methods on face recognition systems (Chap. 2) and general multimedia forensics before the deep learning era (Chap. 3). These chapters serve as points of entry addressing readers wishing to gain a brief overview of the current state of the art.

Part II deals with the generation of manipulated face content and its security implications on face recognition, including DeepFakes (Chaps. 4 and 5), face morphing (Chap. 6), adversarial face images (Chap. 7) and audio-to-video face generation (Chap. 8). Subsequently, Part III elaborates on face manipulation detection techniques, containing dedicated chapters on different state-of-the-art detection methods for synthetically generated face images (Chap. 9), DeepFakes videos (Chaps. 10–14), morphed face images (Chaps. 15 and 16) and retouched face images (Chap. 17). Chapters in Part II and III delve deeper into the topics of digital face manipulation and detection and are oriented towards advanced readers.

Eventually, Part IV focuses on further topics including the use of face manipulation for privacy enhancement and the detection thereof (Chap. 18), practical challenges of face manipulation in remote scenarios (Chap. 19) as well as social and ethical issues (Chap. 20). Finally, in a concluding chapter authored by different contributors to this handbook, open research problems and future trends are summarised (Chap. 21).

We would like to express our thanks to the editors of the Springer book series Advances in Computer Vision and Pattern Recognition. We also would like to thank all of the authors for the smooth cooperation and their excellent contributions to this handbook. The work on this handbook was supported by the

German Federal Ministry of Education and Research and the Hessian Ministry of Higher Education, Research, Science and the Arts within their joint support of the National Research Center for Applied Cybersecurity ATHENE and the projects PRIMA (H2020-MSCA-ITN-2019-860315), TRESPASS-ETN (H2020-MSCA-ITN-2019-860813), BIBECA (MINECO/FEDER RTI2018-101248-B-I00) and COST CA16101 (MULTI-FORESEE). Finally, we would like to thank our families and friends for their support and encouragement while we were working on this handbook.

Darmstadt, Germany   Christian Rathgeb
Madrid, Spain   Ruben Tolosana
Madrid, Spain   Ruben Vera-Rodriguez
Gjøvik, Norway   Christoph Busch

Contents

Part III   Digital Face Manipulation Detection

Part IV   Further Topics, Trends, and Challenges

Part I
Introduction

Chapter 1
An Introduction to Digital Face Manipulation

Ruben Tolosana, Ruben Vera-Rodriguez, Julian Fierrez, Aythami Morales, and Javier Ortega-Garcia

Abstract Digital manipulation has become a thriving topic in the last few years, especially after the popularity of the term DeepFakes. This chapter introduces the prominent digital manipulations with special emphasis on the facial content due to their large number of possible applications. Specifically, we cover the principles of six types of digital face manipulations: *(i)* entire face synthesis, *(ii)* identity swap, *(iii)* face morphing, *(iv)* attribute manipulation, *(v)* expression swap (a.k.a. face reenactment or talking faces), and *(vi)* audio- and text-to-video. These six main types of face manipulation are well established by the research community, having received the most attention in the last few years. In addition, we highlight in this chapter publicly available databases and code for the generation of digital fake content.

1.1 Introduction

Traditionally, the number and realism of digital face manipulations have been limited by the lack of sophisticated editing tools, the domain expertise required, and the complex and time-consuming process involved [2–4]. For example, an early work in this topic [5] was able to modify the lip motion of a subject speaking using a

---

The present chapter is an updated adaptation of the journal article [1].

R. Tolosana (✉) · R. Vera-Rodriguez · J. Fierrez · A. Morales · J. Ortega-Garcia
Universidad Autonoma de Madrid, Madrid, Spain
e-mail: ruben.tolosana@uam.es

R. Vera-Rodriguez
e-mail: ruben.vera@uam.es

J. Fierrez
e-mail: julian.fierrez@uam.es

A. Morales
e-mail: aythami.morales@uam.es

J. Ortega-Garcia
e-mail: javier.ortega@uam.es

3

C. Rathgeb et al. (eds.), *Handbook of Digital Face Manipulation and Detection*,
Advances in Computer Vision and Pattern Recognition,
https://doi.org/10.1007/978-3-030-87664-7_1

different audio track, by making connections between the sounds of the audio track and the shape of the subject's face. However, from the original manual synthesis techniques up to now, many things have rapidly evolved. Nowadays, it is becoming increasingly easy to automatically synthesise non-existent faces or manipulate a real face (a.k.a. bonafide presentation [6]) of one subject in an image/video, thanks to: *(i)* the accessibility to large-scale public data and *(ii)* the evolution of deep learning techniques that eliminate many manual editing steps such as Autoencoders (AE) and Generative Adversarial Networks (GAN) [7, 8]. As a result, open software and mobile applications such as ZAO[1] and FaceApp[2] have been released opening the door to anyone to create fake images and videos, without any experience in the field.

In this context of digital face manipulation, there is one term that has recently dominated the panorama of social media [9, 10], becoming at the same time a great public concern [11]: DeepFakes.

In general, the popular term DeepFakes is referred to all digital fake content created by means of deep learning techniques [1, 12]. It was originated after a Reddit user named "deepfakes" claimed in late 2017 to have developed a machine learning algorithm that helped him to swap celebrity faces into porn videos [13]. The most harmful usages of DeepFakes include fake pornography, fake news, hoaxes, and financial fraud [14]. As a result, the area of research traditionally dedicated to general media forensics [15–18], is being invigorated and is now dedicating growing efforts for detecting facial manipulation in image and video [19, 20].

In addition, part of these renewed efforts in fake face detection are built around past research in biometric presentation attack detection (a.k.a. spoofing) [21–23] and modern data-driven deep learning [24–27]. Chapter 2 provides an introductory overview of face manipulation in biometric systems.

The growing interest in fake face detection is demonstrated through the increasing number of workshops in top conferences [28–32], international projects such as MediFor funded by the Defense Advanced Research Project Agency (DARPA), and competitions such as the Media Forensics Challenge (MFC2018)[3] launched by the National Institute of Standards and Technology (NIST), the Deepfake Detection Challenge (DFDC)[4] launched by Facebook, and the recent DeeperForensics Challenge.[5]

In response to those increasingly sophisticated and realistic manipulated content, large efforts are being carried out by the research community to design improved methods for face manipulation detection [1, 12]. Traditional fake detection methods in media forensics have been commonly based on: *(i)* in-camera, the analysis of the intrinsic "fingerprints" (patterns) introduced by the camera device, both hardware and software, such as the optical lens [33], colour filter array and interpolation [34, 35], and compression [36, 37], among others, and *(ii)* out-camera, the analysis of

---

[1] https://apps.apple.com/cn/app/id1465199127.

[2] https://apps.apple.com/gb/app/faceapp-ai-face-editor/id1180884341.

[3] https://www.nist.gov/itl/iad/mig/media-forensics-challenge-2018.

[4] https://www.kaggle.com/c/deepfake-detection-challenge.

[5] https://competitions.codalab.org/competitions/25228.

the external fingerprints introduced by editing software, such as copy-paste or copy-move different elements of the image [38, 39], reduce the frame rate in a video [40, 41], etc. Chapter 3 provides an in-depth literature review of traditional multimedia forensics before the deep learning era.

However, most of the features considered in traditional fake detection methods are highly dependent on the specific training scenario, being therefore not robust against unseen conditions [2, 16, 26]. This is of special importance in the era we live in as most media fake content is usually shared on social networks, whose platforms automatically modify the original image/video, for example, through compression and resize operations [19, 20].

This first chapter is an updated adaptation of the journal article presented in [1], and serves in this book as an introductory part of the most popular digital manipulations with special emphasis to the facial content due to the large number of possible harmful applications, e.g., the generation of fake news that would provide misinformation in political elections and security threats [42, 43], among others. Specifically, we cover in Sect. 1.2 six types of digital face manipulations: *(i)* entire face synthesis, *(ii)* identity swap, *(iii)* face morphing, *(iv)* attribute manipulation, *(v)* expression swap (a.k.a. face reenactment or talking faces), and *(vi)* audio- and text-to-video. These six main types of face manipulation are well established by the research community, receiving most attention in the last few years. Finally, we provide in Sect. 1.3 our concluding remarks.

1.2   Types of Digital Face Manipulations

1.2.1   Entire Face Synthesis

This manipulation creates entire non-existent face images. These techniques achieve astonishing results, generating high-quality facial images with a high level of realism for the observer. Fig. 1.1 shows some examples for entire face synthesis generated using StyleGAN. This manipulation could benefit many different sectors such as the video game and 3D-modelling industries, but it could also be used for harmful applications such as the creation of very realistic fake profiles on social networks in order to generate misinformation.

Entire face synthesis manipulations are created through powerful GANs. In general, a GAN consists of two different neural networks that contest with each other in a minimax game: the Generator G that captures the data distribution and creates new samples, and the Discriminator D that estimates the probability that a sample comes from the training data (real) rather than G (fake). The training procedure for G is to maximise the probability of D making a mistake, creating, therefore, high-quality fake samples. After the training process, D is discarded and G is used to create fake content. This concept has been exploited in the last years for the entire face synthesis, improving the realism of the manipulations as can be seen in Fig. 1.1.

One of the first popular approaches in this sense was ProGAN [44]. The key idea was to improve the synthesis process growing G and D progressively, i.e., starting from a low resolution, and adding new layers that model increasingly fine details as training progresses. Experiments were performed using the CelebA database [45], showing promising results for the entire face synthesis. The code of the ProGAN architecture is publicly available in GitHub.[6] Later on, Karras et al. proposed an enhanced version named StyleGAN [46] that considered an alternative G architecture motivated by the style transfer literature [47]. StyleGAN proposes an alternative generator architecture that leads to an automatically learned, unsupervised separation of high-level attributes (e.g., pose and identity when trained on human faces) and stochastic variation in the generated images (e.g., freckles, hair), and it enables intuitive, scale-specific control of the synthesis. Examples of this type of manipulations are shown in Fig. 1.1, using CelebA-HQ and FFHQ databases for the training of the StyleGAN [44, 46]. The code of the StyleGAN architecture is publicly available in GitHub.[7]

Finally, one of the prominent GAN approaches is StyleGAN2 [48], and Style-GAN2 with adaptive discriminator augmentation (StyleGAN2-ADA) [49]. Training a GAN using too little data typically leads to D overfitting, causing training to diverge. StyleGAN2-ADA proposes an adaptive discriminator augmentation mechanism that significantly stabilises training in limited data regimes. The approach does not require changes to loss functions or network architectures, and is applicable both when training from scratch and when fine-tuning an existing GAN on another dataset. The authors demonstrated that good results are possible to achieve by using only a few thousand training images. The code of the StyleGAN2-ADA architecture is publicly available in GitHub.[8]

Based on these GAN approaches, different databases are publicly available for research on the entire face synthesis manipulation. Table 1.1 summarises the main publicly available databases in the field, highlighting the specific GAN approach considered in each of them. It is interesting to remark that each fake image may be characterised by a specific GAN fingerprint just like natural images are identified by a device-based fingerprint (i.e., PRNU). In fact, these fingerprints seem to be dependent not only of the GAN architecture, but also to the different instantiations of it [50, 51].

In addition, as indicated in Table 1.1, it is important to note that public databases only contain the fake images generated using the GAN architectures. In order to be able to perform real/fake detection experiments on this digital manipulation group, researchers need to obtain real face images from other public databases such as CelebA [45], FFHQ [46], CASIA-WebFace [53], VGGFace2 [54], or Mega-Face2 [55] among many others.

---

[6] https://github.com/tkarras/progressive_growing_of_gans.

[7] https://github.com/NVlabs/stylegan.

[8] https://github.com/NVlabs/stylegan2-ada-pytorch.

Table 1.1 Entire face synthesis: Publicly available databases

Database	Real images	Fake images
100K-Generated-Images (2019) [46]	–	100,000 (StyleGAN)
10K-Faces (2019) [52]	–	10,000 (–)
DFFD (2019) [24]	–	100,000 (StyleGAN) 200,000 (ProGAN)
iFakeFaceDB (2019) [26]	–	250,000 (StyleGAN) 80,000 (ProGAN)
100K-Generated-Images (2020) [48]	–	100,000 (StyleGAN2)
100K-Generated-Images (2020) [49]	–	100,000 (StyleGAN2-ADA)

Fig. 1.1 Real and fake examples of the **Entire face synthesis** manipulation group. Real images are extracted from http://www.whichfaceisreal.com/ and fake images from https://thispersondoesnotexist.com

We provide next a short description of each public database. In [46], Karras et al. released a set of 100,000 synthetic face images, named 100K-Generated-Images.[9] This database was generated using their proposed StyleGAN architecture, which was trained using the FFHQ dataset [46].

Another public database is 10K-Faces [52], containing 10,000 synthetic images for research purposes. In this database, contrary to the 100K-Generated-Images database, the network was trained using photos of models, considering face images from a more controlled scenario (e.g., with a flat background). Thus, no strange artefacts created by the GAN architecture are included in the background of the images. In addition, this dataset considers other interesting aspects such as ethnicity and gender diversity, as well as other metadata such as age, eye colour, hair colour and length, and emotion.

---

[9] https://github.com/NVlabs/stylegan.

Fig. 1.2 Examples of a fake
image created using
StyleGAN and its improved
version after removing the
GAN-fingerprint information
with GANprintR [26]

(a) Fake   (b) Fake after GANprintR

Recently, Dang et al. introduced in [24] a new database named Diverse Fake Face Dataset (DFFD).[10] Regarding the entire face synthesis manipulation, the authors created 100,000 and 200,000 fake images through the pre-trained ProGAN and Style-GAN models, respectively.

Neves et al. presented in [26] the iFakeFaceDB database. This database comprises 250,000 and 80,000 synthetic face images originally created through StyleGAN and ProGAN, respectively. As an additional feature in comparison to previous databases, and in order to hinder fake detectors, in this database, the fingerprints produced by the GAN architectures were removed through an approach named GANprintR (GAN fingerprint Removal), while keeping very realistic appearance. Figure 1.2 shows an example of a fake image directly generated with StyleGAN and its improved version after removing the GAN-fingerprint information. As a result of the GANprintR step, iFakeFaceDB presents a higher challenge for advanced fake detectors compared with the other databases.

Finally, we highlight the two popular 100K-Generated-Images public databases released by Karras et al. [48, 49], based on the prominent StyleGAN2 and StyleGAN2-ADA architectures. The corresponding fake databases trained using the FFHQ dataset [46] can be found in their GitHub.[11, 12]

This section has described the main aspects of the entire face synthesis manipulation. For a complete understanding of fake detection techniques on this face manipulation, we refer the reader to Chap. 9.

1.2.2 Identity Swap

This manipulation consists of replacing the face of one subject in a video (source) with the face of another subject (target). Unlike the entire face synthesis, where manipulations are carried out at image level, in identity swap the objective is to generate realistic fake videos. Figure 1.3 shows some visual image examples extracted

---

[10] http://cvlab.cse.msu.edu/dffd-dataset.html.

[11] https://github.com/NVlabs/stylegan2.

[12] https://github.com/NVlabs/stylegan2-ada.

Fig. 1.3 Real and fake examples of the **Identity Swap** manipulation group. Face images are extracted from videos of Celeb-DF database [56]

from videos of Celeb-DF database [56]. In addition, very realistic videos of this type of manipulation can be seen on Youtube.[13] Many different sectors could benefit from this type of manipulation, in particular, the film industry.[14] However, on the other side, it could also be used for bad purposes such as the creation of celebrity pornographic videos, hoaxes, and financial fraud, among many others.

Two different approaches are usually considered for identity swap manipulations: *(i)* classical computer graphics-based techniques such as FaceSwap,[15] and *(ii)* novel deep learning techniques known as DeepFakes, e.g., the recent ZAO mobile application,[16] and the popular FaceSwap[17] and DeepFaceLab[18] software tools. In general, for each frame of the source video, the following stages are considered in the generation process of the identity swap video [57]: *(i)* face detection and cropping, *(ii)* extraction of intermediate representations, *(iii)* synthesis of a new face based on some driving signal (e.g., another face), and finally *(iv)* blending the generated face of the target subject into the source video, as shown in Fig. 1.3. For each of these stages, many possibilities could be considered to improve the quality of the fake videos. We

---

[13] https://www.youtube.com/watch?v=UlvoEW7l5rs.

[14] https://www.youtube.com/c/Shamook/featured.

[15] https://github.com/MarekKowalski/FaceSwap.

[16] https://apps.apple.com/cn/app/id1465199127.

[17] https://github.com/deepfakes/faceswap.

[18] https://github.com/iperov/DeepFaceLab.

Table 1.2 Identity swap: Publicly available databases

Database	Real videos	Fake videos
1st generation		
UADFV (2018) [58]	49 (Youtube)	49 (FakeApp)
DeepfakeTIMIT (2018) [11]	–	620 (faceswap-GAN)
FaceForensics++ (2019) [20]	1000 (Youtube)	1000 (FaceSwap) 1000 (DeepFake)
2nd generation		
DeepFakeDetection (2019) [66]	363 (Actors)	3068 (DeepFake)
Celeb-DF (2019) [56]	890 (Youtube)	5639 (DeepFake)
DFDC Preview (2019) [59]	1131 (Actors)	4119 (Multiple)
DFDC (2020) [67]	23,654 (Actors)	104,500 (Multiple)
DeeperForensics-1.0 (2020) [60]	50,000 (Actors)	1000 (DeepFake)
WildDeepfake (2020) [61]	3805 (Internet)	3509 (DeepFake)

describe next the main aspects considered in publicly available fake databases. For more details about the generation process, we refer the reader to Chaps. 4, and 14.

Since publicly available fake databases such as the UADFV database [58], up to the latest Celeb-DF, DFDC, DeeperForensics-1.0, and WildDeepfake databases [56, 59–61], many visual improvements have been carried out, increasing the realism of fake videos. As a result, identity swap databases can be divided into two different generations. Table 1.2 summarises the main details of each public database, grouped in each generation.

Three different databases are grouped in the first generation. UADFV was one of the first public databases [58]. This database comprises 49 real videos from Youtube, which were used to create 49 fake videos through the FakeApp mobile application,[19] swapping in all of them the original face with the face of Nicolas Cage. Therefore, only one identity is considered in all fake videos. Each video represents one individual, with a typical resolution of 294 × 500 pixels, and 11.14 s on average.

Korshunov and Marcel introduced in [11] the DeepfakeTIMIT database. This database comprises 620 fake videos of 32 subjects from the VidTIMIT database [62]. Fake videos were created using the public GAN-based face-swapping algorithm.[20] In that approach, the generative network is adopted from CycleGAN [63], using the weights of FaceNet [64]. The method Multi-Task Cascaded Convolution Networks is used for more stable detections and reliable face alignment [65]. Besides, the Kalman filter is also considered to smooth the bounding box positions over frames and eliminate jitter on the swapped face. Regarding the scenarios considered in DeepfakeTIMIT, two different qualities are considered: *(i)* low quality (LQ) with images of 64 × 64 pixels, and *(ii)* high quality (HQ) with images of 128 × 128

---

[19] https://www.malavida.com/en/soft/fakeapp/.

[20] https://github.com/shaoanlu/faceswap-GAN.

pixels. Additionally, different blending techniques were applied to the fake videos regarding the quality level.

One of the most popular databases is FaceForensics++ [20]. This database was introduced in early 2019 as an extension of the original FaceForensics database [68], which was focussed only on expression swap. FaceForensics++ contains 1000 real videos extracted from Youtube. Regarding the identity swap fake videos, they were generated using both computer graphics and DeepFake approaches (i.e., learning approach). For the computer graphics approach, the authors considered the publicly available FaceSwap algorithm[21] whereas for the DeepFake approach, fake videos were created through the DeepFake FaceSwap GitHub implementation.[22] The FaceSwap approach consists of face alignment, Gauss–Newton optimization and image blending to swap the face of the source subject to the target subject. The DeepFake approach, as indicated in [20], is based on two autoencoders with a shared encoder that is trained to reconstruct training images of the source and the target face, respectively. A face detector is used to crop and align the images. To create a fake image, the trained encoder and decoder of the source face are applied to the target face. The autoencoder output is then blended with the rest of the image using Poisson image editing [69]. Regarding the figures of the FaceForensics++ database, 1000 fake videos were generated for each approach. Later on, a new dataset named DeepFakeDetection, grouped inside the 2nd generation due to its higher realism, was included in the FaceForensics++ framework with the support of Google [66]. This dataset comprises 363 real videos from 28 paid actors in 16 different scenes. Additionally, 3068 fake videos are included in the dataset based on DeepFake FaceSwap GitHub implementation. It is important to remark that for both FaceForensics++ and DeepFakeDetection databases different levels of video quality are considered, in particular: *(i)* RAW (original quality), *(ii)* HQ (constant rate quantization parameter equal to 23), and *(iii)* LQ (constant rate quantization parameter equal to 40). This aspect simulates the video processing techniques usually applied in social networks.

Several databases have been recently released, including them in the 2nd generation due to their higher realism. Li et al. presented in [56] the Celeb-DF database. This database aims to provide fake videos of better visual qualities, similar to the popular videos that are shared on the Internet,[23] in comparison to previous databases that exhibit low visual quality for the observer with many visible artefacts. Celeb-DF consists of 890 real videos extracted from Youtube, and 5639 fake videos, which were created through a refined version of a public DeepFake generation algorithm, improving aspects such as the low resolution of the synthesised faces and colour inconsistencies.

Facebook in collaboration with other companies and academic institutions such as Microsoft, Amazon, and the MIT launched at the end of 2019 a new challenge named the Deepfake Detection Challenge (DFDC) [59]. They first released a preview dataset consisting of 1131 real videos from 66 paid actors, and 4119 fake videos.

---

[21] https://github.com/MarekKowalski/FaceSwap.

[22] https://github.com/deepfakes/faceswap.

[23] https://www.youtube.com/channel/UCKpH0CKltc73e4wh0_pgL3g.

Later on, they released the complete DFDC dataset comprising over 100K fake videos using 8 different face- swapping methods such as autoencoders, StyleGAN and morphable-mask models [67].

Another interesting database is DeeperForensics-1.0 [60]. The first version of this database (1.0) comprises 60K videos (50K real videos and 10K fake videos). Real videos were recorded in a professional indoor environment using 100 paid actors and ensuring variability in gender, age, skin colour, and nationality. Regarding fake videos, they were generated using a newly proposed end-to-end face-swapping framework based on Variational Autoencoders. In addition, extensive real-world perturbations (up to 35 in total) such as JPEG compression, Gaussian blur, and change of colour saturation were considered. All details of DeeperForensics-1.0 database, together with the corresponding competition, are described in Chap. 14.

Finally, Zi et al. presented in [61] WildDeepfake, a challenging real-world database for DeepFake detection. This database comprises 7314 videos (3805 and 3509 real and fake videos, respectively) collected completely from the internet. Contrary to previous databases, WildDeepfake claims to contain a higher diversity in terms of scenes and people in each scene, and also in facial expressions.

To conclude this section, we discuss at a higher level the key differences among fake databases of the 1st and 2nd generations. In general, fake videos of the 1st generation are characterised by: *(i)* low-quality synthesised faces, *(ii)* different colour contrast among the synthesised fake mask and the skin of the original face, *(iii)* visible boundaries of the fake mask, *(iv)* visible facial elements from the original video, *(v)* low pose variations, and *(vi)* strange artefacts among sequential frames. Also, they usually consider controlled scenarios in terms of camera position and light conditions. Many of these aspects have been successfully improved in databases of the 2nd generation, not only at visual level, but also in terms of variability (in-the-wild scenarios). For example, the recent DFDC database considers different acquisition scenarios (i.e., indoors and outdoors), light conditions (i.e., day, night, etc.), distances from the subject to the camera, and pose variations, among others. Figure 1.4 graphically summarises the weaknesses present in identity swap databases of the 1st generation and the improvements carried out in the 2nd generation. Finally, it is also interesting to remark the larger number of fake videos included in the databases of the 2nd generation.

This section has described the main aspects of the identity swap digital manipulation. For a complete understanding of the generation process and fake detection techniques, we refer the reader to Chaps. 4, 5, and 10–14.

Fig. 1.4 Graphical representation of the weaknesses present in **Identity Swap** databases of the 1st generation and the improvements carried out in the 2nd generation, not only at visual level, but also in terms of variability (in-the-wild scenarios). Fake images are extracted from: UADFV and FaceForensics++ (1st generation) [20, 58]; Celeb-DF and DFDC (2nd generation) [56, 59]

1.2.3   Face Morphing

Face morphing is a type of digital face manipulation that can be used to create artificial biometric face samples that resemble the biometric information of two or more individuals [70, 71]. This means that the new morphed face image would be successfully verified against facial samples of these two or more individuals creating a serious threat to face recognition systems [72, 73]. Figure 1.5 shows an example of the face morphing digital manipulation adapted from [70]. It is worth noting that face morphing is mainly focussed on creating fake samples at the image level, not

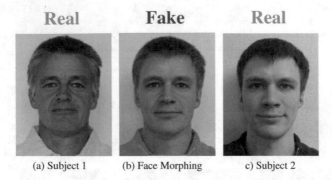

Fig. 1.5 Example for **a Face morphing** image (**b**) of subject 1 (**a**) and subject 2 (**c**). This figure has been adapted from [70]

video such as identity swap manipulations. In addition, as shown in Fig. 1.5, frontal view faces are usually considered.

There has been recently a large amount of research in the field of face morphing. Comprehensive surveys have been published in [70, 74] including both morphing techniques and also morphing attack detectors. In general, the following three consecutive stages are considered in the generation process of face morphing images: *(i)* determining correspondences between the face images of the different subjects. This is usually carried out by extracting landmark points, e.g., eyes, nose tips, mouth, etc.; *(ii)* the real face images of the subjects are distorted until the corresponding elements (landmarks) of the samples are geometrically aligned; and *(iii)* the colour values of the warped images are merged, referred to as blending. Finally, postprocessing techniques are usually considered to correct strange artefacts caused by pixel/region-based morphing [75, 76].

Prominent benchmarks have been recently presented in the field of face morphing. Raja et al. has recently presented an interesting framework in order to address serious open issues in the field such as independent benchmarking, generalizability challenges and considerations to age, gender, and ethnicity [77]. As a result, the authors have presented a new sequestered dataset and benchmark[24] for facilitating the advancements of morphing attack detection. The database comprises morphed and real images constituting 1800 photographs of 150 subjects. Morphing images are generated using 6 different algorithms, presenting a wide variety of possible approaches.

In this line, NIST has recently launched the FRVT MORPH evaluation.[25] This is an ongoing evaluation designed to obtain an assessment on morph detection capability with two separate tasks: *(i)* algorithmic capability to detect face morphing (morphed/blended faces) in still photographs, and *(ii)* face recognition algorithm resis-

---

[24] https://biolab.csr.unibo.it/fvcongoing/UI/Form/BenchmarkAreas/BenchmarkAreaDMAD. aspx.

[25] https://pages.nist.gov/frvt/html/frvt_morph.html.

tance against morphing. The evaluation is updated as new algorithms and datasets are added.

Despite these recent evaluations, we would like to highlight the lack of public databases for research. To the best of our knowledge, the only publicly available database is the AMSL Face Morph Image dataset[26] [78]. This is mainly produced due to most face morphing databases are created from existing face databases. As a result, the licenses can not be easily transferred which often prevents sharing.

This section has briefly described the main aspects of face morphing. For a complete understanding of the digital generation and fake detection techniques, we refer the reader to Chaps. 2, 6, 15, and 16.

1.2.4 Attribute Manipulation

This manipulation, also known as face editing or face retouching, consists of modifying some attributes of the face such as the colour of the hair or the skin, the gender, the age, adding glasses, etc. [79]. This manipulation process is usually carried out through GAN such as the StarGAN approach proposed in [80]. One example of this type of manipulation is the popular FaceApp mobile application. Consumers could use this technology to try on a broad range of products such as cosmetics and makeup, glasses, or hairstyles in a virtual environment. Figure 1.6 shows some examples for the attribute manipulation generated using FaceApp [81].

Despite the success of GAN-based frameworks for face attribute manipulations [80, 82–88], few databases are publicly available for research in this area, to the best of our knowledge. The main reason is that the code of most GAN approaches are publicly available, so researchers can easily generate their own fake databases as they like. Therefore, this section aims to highlight the latest GAN approaches in the field, from older to closer in time, providing also the link to their corresponding codes.

In [86], the authors introduced the Invertible Conditional GAN (IcGAN)[27] for complex image editing as the union of an encoder used jointly with a conditional GAN (cGAN) [89]. This approach provides accurate results in terms of attribute manipulation. However, it seriously changes the face identity of the subject.

Lample et al. proposed in [83] an encoder-decoder architecture that is trained to reconstruct images by disentangling the salient information of the image and the attribute values directly in the latent space.[28] However, as it happens with the IcGAN approach, the generated images may lack some details or present unexpected distortions.

---

[26] https://omen.cs.uni-magdeburg.de/disclaimer/index.php.

[27] https://github.com/Guim3/IcGAN.

[28] https://github.com/facebookresearch/FaderNetworks.

Fig. 1.6 Real and fake examples of the **Attribute Manipulation** group. Real images are extracted from http://www.whichfaceisreal.com/ and fake images are generated using FaceApp

An enhanced approach named StarGAN[29] was proposed in [80]. Before the Star-GAN approach, many studies had shown promising results in image-to-image translations for two domains in general. However, few studies had focussed on handling more than two domains. In that case, a direct approach would be to build different models independently for every pair of image domains. StarGAN proposed a novel approach able to perform image-to-image translations for multiple domains using only a single model. The authors trained a conditional attribute transfer network via attribute-classification loss and cycle consistency loss. Good visual results were achieved compared with previous approaches. However, it sometimes includes undesired modifications from the input face image such as the colour of the skin.

Almost at the same time He et al. proposed in [82] attGAN,[30] a novel approach that removes the strict attribute-independent constraint from the latent representation, and just applies the attribute-classification constraint to the generated image to guarantee the correct change of the attributes. AttGAN provides state-of-the-art results on realistic attribute manipulation with other facial details well preserved.

One of the latest approaches proposed in the literature is STGAN[31] [84]. In general, attribute manipulation can be tackled by incorporating an encoder-decoder or GAN. However, as commented Liu et al. [84], the bottleneck layer in the encoder-decoder usually provides blurry and low quality manipulation results. To improve this, the authors presented and incorporated selective transfer units with an encoder-decoder for simultaneously improving the attribute manipulation ability and the image quality. As a result, STGAN has recently outperformed the state of the art in attribute manipulation.

Finally, we would like to highlight two recent attribute manipulation approaches that are currently achieving also very realistic visual results: RelGAN and SSC-

---

[29] https://github.com/yunjey/stargan/blob/master/README.md.

[30] https://github.com/LynnHo/AttGAN-Tensorflow.

[31] https://github.com/csmliu/STGAN.

GAN [90, 91]. RelGAN improves multi-domain image-to-image translation, whereas SSCGAN injects the target attribute information into multiple style skip connection paths between the encoder and decoder in order to incorporate global facial statistics.

Despite the fact that the code of the most attribute manipulation approaches are publicly available, the lack of public databases and experimental protocols results crucial when comparing among different manipulation detection approaches, otherwise it is not possible to perform a fair comparison among studies. Up to now, to the best of our knowledge, the DFFD database [24] seems to be the only public database that considers this type of facial manipulations. This database comprises 18,416 and 79,960 fake images generated through FaceApp and StarGAN approaches, respectively.

This section has briefly described the main aspects of the face attribute manipulation. For a complete understanding of this digital manipulation group, we refer the reader to Chap. 17.

1.2.5   Expression Swap

This manipulation, also known as face reenactment, consists of modifying the facial expression of the subject. Although different manipulation techniques are proposed in the literature, e.g., at image level through popular GAN architectures [84], in this group we focus on the most popular techniques Face2Face and NeuralTextures [92, 93], which replaces the facial expression of one subject in a video with the facial expression of another subject. Figure 1.7 shows some visual examples extracted from FaceForensics++ database [20]. This type of manipulation could be used with serious consequences, e.g., the popular video of Mark Zuckerberg saying things he never said.[32]

To the best of our knowledge, the only available database for research in this area is FaceForensics++ [20], an extension of FaceForensics [68].

Initially, the FaceForensics database was focussed on the Face2Face approach [93]. This is a computer graphics approach that transfers the expression of a source video to a target video while maintaining the identity of the target subject. This was carried out through manual keyframe selection. Concretely, the first frames of each video were used to obtain a temporary face identity (i.e., a 3D model), and track the expression over the remaining frames. Then, fake videos were generated by transferring the source expression parameters of each frame (i.e., 76 Blendshape coefficients) to the target video. Later on, the same authors presented in FaceForensics++ a new learning approach based on NeuralTextures [92]. This is a rendering approach that uses the original video data to learn a neural texture of the target subject, including a rendering network. In particular, the authors considered in their implementation a patch-based GAN-loss as used in Pix2Pix [94]. Only the facial

---

[32] https://www.bbc.com/news/technology-48607673.

Fig. 1.7 Real and fake examples of the **Expression Swap** manipulation group. Images are extracted from videos of FaceForensics++ database [20]

expression corresponding to the mouth was modified. It is important to remark that all data is available on the FaceForensics++ GitHub.[33] In total, there are 1000 real videos extracted from Youtube. Regarding the manipulated videos, 2000 fake videos are available (1000 videos for each considered fake approach). In addition, it is important to highlight that different video quality levels are considered, in particular: *(i)* RAW (original quality), *(ii)* HQ (constant rate quantization parameter equal to 23), and *(iii)* LQ (constant rate quantization parameter equal to 40). This aspect simulates the video processing techniques usually applied in social networks.

In addition to the Face2Face and NeuralTexture techniques considered in expression swap manipulations at video level, different approaches have been recently proposed to change the facial expression in both images and videos. A very popular approach was presented in [95]. Averbuch-Elor et al. proposed a technique to automatically animate a still portrait using a video of a different subject, transferring the expressiveness of the subject of the video to the target portrait. Unlike Face2Face and NeuralTexture approaches that require videos from both input and target faces, in [95] just an image of the target is needed. In this line, recent approaches have been presented achieving astonishing results in both one-shot and few-shot learning [96–98].

---

[33] https://github.com/ondyari/FaceForensics.

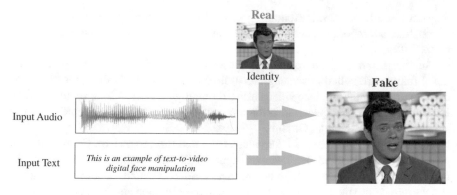

Fig. 1.8 Real and fake example of the **Audio-to-Video and Text-to-Video** face manipulation group

1.2.6 Audio-to-Video and Text-to-Video

A related topic to expression swap is the synthesis of video from audio or text. Figure 1.8 shows an example for the audio- and text-to-video face manipulation. These types of video face manipulations are also known as lip-sinc DeepFakes [99] or audio-driven facial reenactment [100]. Popular examples can be seen on the Internet.[34]

Regarding the synthesis of fake videos from audio (audio-to-video), Suwajanakorn et al. presented in [101] an approach to synthesise high-quality videos of a subject (Obama in this case) speaking with accurate lip sync. For this, they used as input to their approach many hours of previous videos of the subject together with a new audio recording. In their approach, they employed a recurrent neural network (based on Long Short-Term Memory, LSTM) to learn the mapping from raw audio features to mouth shapes. Then, based on the mouth shape at each frame, they synthesised high-quality mouth texture, and composited it with 3D pose alignment to create the new video to match the input audio track, producing photorealistic results.

In [102], Song et al. proposed an approach based on a novel conditional recurrent generation network that incorporates both image and audio features in the recurrent unit for temporal dependency, and also a pair of spatial-temporal discriminators for better image/video quality. As a result, their approach can model both lip and mouth together with expression and head pose variations as a whole, achieving much more realistic results. The source code is publicly available in GitHub.[35] Also, in [103], Song et al. presented a dynamic method not assuming a subject-specific rendering network like in [101]. In their approach, they are able to generate very realistic fake videos by carrying out a 3D face model reconstruction from the input video plus a recurrent network to translate the source audio into expression parameters. Finally,

---

[34] https://www.youtube.com/watch?v=VWMEDacz3L4.

[35] https://github.com/susanqq/Talking_Face_Generation.

they introduced a novel video rendering network and a dynamic programming method to construct a temporally coherent and photorealistic video. Video results are shown on the Internet.[36]

Another interesting approach was presented in [104]. Zhou et al. proposed a novel framework called Disentangled Audio-Visual System (DAVS), which generates high-quality talking face videos using disentangled audio-visual representation. Both audio and video speech information can be employed as input guidance. The source code is available in GitHub.[37]

Regarding the synthesis of fake videos from text (text-to-video), Fried et al. proposed in [105] a method that takes as input a video of a subject speaking and the desired text to be spoken, and synthesises a new video in which the subject's mouth is synchronised with the new words. In particular, their method automatically annotates an input talking-head video with phonemes, visemes, 3D face pose and geometry, reflectance, expression, and scene illumination per frame. Finally, a recurrent video generation network creates a photorealistic video that matches the edited transcript. Examples of the fake videos generated with this approach are publicly available.[38]

Finally, we would like to highlight the work presented in [100], named Neural Voice Puppetry. Thies et al. proposed an approach to synthesise videos of a target actor with the voice of any unknown source actor or even synthetic voices that can be generated utilising standard text-to-speech approaches, achieving astonishing visual results.[39]

To the best of our knowledge, there are no publicly available databases and benchmarks related to audio- and text-to-video fake detection content. Research on this topic is usually carried out through the synthesis of in-house data using publicly available implementations like the ones described in this section.

This section has briefly described the main aspects of the audio- and text-to-video face manipulation. For a complete understanding of this digital manipulation group, we refer the reader to Chap. 8.

1.3 Conclusions

This chapter has served as an introduction of the most popular digital face manipulations in the literature. In particular, we have covered six manipulation groups: *(i)* entire face synthesis, *(ii)* identity swap, *(iii)* face morphing, *(iv)* attribute manipulation, *(v)* expression swap (a.k.a. face reenactment or talking faces), and *(vi)* audio- and text-to-video. For each of them, we have described the main principles, publicly available databases, and code for the generation of digital fake content.

---

[36] https://wywu.github.io/projects/EBT/EBT.html.

[37] https://github.com/Hangz-nju-cuhk/Talking-Face-Generation-DAVS.

[38] https://www.ohadf.com/projects/text-based-editing/.

[39] https://justusthies.github.io/posts/neural-voice-puppetry/.

For more details about digital face manipulation and fake detection techniques, we refer the reader to Parts II and III of the present book. Finally, Part IV describes further topics, trends, and challenges in the field of digital face manipulation and detection.

Acknowledgements This work has been supported by projects: PRIMA (H2020-MSCA-ITN-2019-860315), TRESPASS-ETN (H2020-MSCA-ITN-2019-860813), BIBECA (MINECO/FEDER RTI2018-101248-B-I00), and COST CA16101 (MULTI-FORESEE).

References

1. Tolosana R, Vera-Rodriguez R, Fierrez J, Morales A, Ortega-Garcia J (2020) DeepFakes and beyond: a survey of face manipulation and fake detection. Inform Fusion 64:131–148
2. Farid H (2009) Image forgery detection. IEEE Signal Process Mag 26(2):16–25
3. Milani S, Fontani M, Bestagini P, Barni M, Piva A, Tagliasacchi M, Tubaro S (2012) An overview on video forensics. APSIPA Trans Signal Inform Process 1
4. Piva A (2013) An overview on image forensics. ISRN Signal Process
5. Bregler C, Covell M, Slaney M (1997) Video rewrite: driving visual speech with audio. Comput Graph 31(2):353–361
6. Information Technology-Biometric Presentation Attack Detection-Part 3: Testing and Reporting. Technical report, ISO/IEC JTC1 SC37 Biometrics (2017)
7. Goodfellow I, Pouget-Abadie J, Mirza M, Xu B, Warde-Farley D, Ozair S, Courville A, Bengio Y (2014) Generative adversarial nets. In: Proceedings of advances in neural information processing systems
8. Kingma DP, Welling M (2013) Auto-encoding variational bayes. In: Proceedings of international conference on learning representations
9. Cellan-Jones R (2019) Deepfake videos double in nine months. https://www.bbc.com/news/technology-49961089
10. Citron D (2019) How DeepFake undermine truth and threaten democracy. https://www.ted.com
11. Korshunov P, Marcel S (2018) Deepfakes: a new threat to face recognition? Assessment and detection. arXiv preprint arXiv:1812.08685
12. Verdoliva L (2020) Media forensics and DeepFakes: an overview. IEEE J Sel Top Signal Process 14:910–932
13. BBC Bitesize: Deepfakes: what are they and why would i make one? (2019). https://www.bbc.co.uk/bitesize/articles/zfkwcqt
14. Kietzmann J, Lee LW, McCarthy IP, Kietzmann TC (2020) Deepfakes: trick or treat? Business Horizons 63(2):135–146
15. Korus P (2017) Digital image integrity-a survey of protection and verification techniques. Digital Signal Process 71:1–26
16. Rocha A, Scheirer W, Boult T, Goldenstein S (2011) Vision of the unseen: current trends and challenges in digital image and video forensics. ACM Comput Surv 43(4):1–42
17. Stamm M, Liu K (2010) Forensic detection of image manipulation using statistical intrinsic fingerprints. IEEE Trans Inform Forensics Secur 5(3):492–506
18. Swaminathan A, Wu M, Liu KJR (2008) Digital image forensics via intrinsic fingerprints. IEEE Trans Inform Forensics Secur 3(1):101–117
19. Cozzolino D, Rössler A, Thies J, Nießner M, Verdoliva L (2020) ID-Reveal: identity-aware DeepFake video detection. arXiv preprint arXiv:2012.02512
20. Rössler A, Cozzolino D, Verdoliva L, Riess C, Thies J, Nießner M (2019) FaceForensics++: learning to detect manipulated facial images. In: Proceedinsg of IEEE/CVF international conference on computer vision

21. Galbally J, Marcel S, Fierrez J (2014) Biometric anti-spoofing methods: a survey in face recognition. IEEE Access 2:1530–1552
22. Hadid A, Evans N, Marcel S, Fierrez J (2015) Biometrics systems under spoofing attack: an evaluation methodology and lessons learned. IEEE Signal Process Mag
23. Marcel S, Nixon M, Fierrez J, Evans N (2019) Handbook of biometric anti-spoofing, 2nd edn
24. Dang H, Liu F, Stehouwer J, Liu X, Jain A (2020) On the detection of digital face manipulation. In: Proceedings of IEEE/CVF conference on computer vision and pattern recognition
25. Hernandez-Ortega J, Tolosana R, Fierrez J, Morales A (2021) DeepFakesON-Phys: Deep-Fakes detection based on heart rate estimation. In: Proceedings of 35th AAAI conference on artificial intelligence workshops
26. Neves JC, Tolosana R, Vera-Rodriguez R, Lopes V, Proença H, Fierrez J (2020) GANprintR: improved fakes and evaluation of the state of the art in face manipulation detection. IEEE J Sel Top Signal Process 14(5):1038–1048
27. Tolosana R, Romero-Tapiador S, Fierrez J, Vera-Rodriguez R (2021) DeepFakes evolution: analysis of facial regions and fake detection performance. In: Proceedings of international conference on pattern recognition workshops
28. Barni M, Battiato S, Boato G, Farid H, Memon N (2020) Multimedia forensics in the wild. In: International conference on pattern recognition. https://iplab.dmi.unict.it/mmforwild/
29. Biggio B, Korshunov P, Mensink T, Patrini G, Rao D, Sadhu A (2019) Synthetic realities: deep learning for detecting audio visual fakes. In: International conference on machine learning. https://sites.google.com/view/audiovisualfakes-icml2019/
30. Gregory S, Canton C, Leal-Taixé L, Bregler C, Farid H, Nießner M, Escalera S, Delp E, McCloskey S, Guyon I, Basharat A, Thies J, Verdoliva L, Escalante HJ, Scharfenberg C, Rössler A, Wan J, Cozzolino D, Guodong G (2020) Workshop on media forensics. In: Conference on computer vision and pattern recognition. https://sites.google.com/view/wmediaforensics2020/home
31. Raja K, Damer N, Chen C, Dantcheva A, Czajka A, Han H, Ramachandra R (2020) Workshop on Deepfakes and presentation attacks in biometrics. In: Winter conference on applications of computer vision. https://sites.google.com/view/wacv2020-deeppab/
32. Verdoliva L, Bestagini P (2019) Multimedia forensics. ACM Multimed. https://acmmm.org/tutorials/#tut3
33. Yerushalmy I, Hel-Or H (2011) Digital image forgery detection based on lens and sensor aberration. Int J Comput Vis 92(1):71–91
34. Cao H, Kot AC (2009) Accurate detection of demosaicing regularity for digital image forensics. IEEE Trans Inform Forensics Secur 4(4):899–910
35. Popescu AC, Farid H (2005) Exposing digital forgeries in color filter array interpolated images. IEEE Trans Signal Process 53(10):3948–3959
36. Chen YL, Hsu CT (2011) Detecting recompression of jpeg images via periodicity analysis of compression artifacts for tampering detection. IEEE Trans Inform Forensics Secur 6(2):396–406
37. Lin Z, He J, Tang X, Tang C (2009) Fast, automatic and fine-grained tampered JPEG image detection via DCT coefficient analysis. Pattern Recogn 42(11):2492–2501
38. Amerini I, Ballan L, Caldelli R, Bimbo A, Serra G (2011) A sift-based forensic method for copy-move attack detection and transformation recovery. IEEE Trans Inform Forensics Secur 6(3):1099–1110
39. Cozzolino D, Poggi G, Verdoliva L (2015) Splicebuster: a new blind image splicing detector. In: Proceedings of IEEE international workshop on information forensics and security, pp 1–6
40. Gironi A, Fontani M, Bianchi T, Piva A, Barni M (2014) A video forensic technique for detecting frame deletion and insertion. In: Proceedings of IEEE international conference on acoustics, speech and signal processing, pp 6226–6230
41. Wu Y, Jiang X, Sun T, Wang W (2014) Exposing video inter-frame forgery based on velocity field consistency. In: Proceedinsg of IEEE international conference on acoustics, speech and signal processing, pp 2674–2678

42. Allcott H, Gentzkow M (2017) Social media and fake news in the 2016 election. J Econ Perspect 31(2):211–236
43. Lazer DM, Baum MA, Benkler Y, Berinsky AJ, Greenhill KM, Menczer F, Metzger MJ, Nyhan B, Pennycook G, Rothschild D et al (2018) The science of fake news. Science 359(6380):1094–1096
44. Karras T, Aila T, Laine S, Lehtinen J (2018) Progressive growing of GANs for improved quality, stability, and variation. In: Proceedings of international conference on learning representations
45. Liu Z, Luo P, Wang X, Tang X (2015) Deep learning face attributes in the wild. In: Proceedings of IEEE/CVF international conference on computer vision
46. Karras T, Laine S, Aila T (2019) A style-based generator architecture for generative adversarial networks. In: Proceedings of IEEE/CVF conference on computer vision and pattern recognition
47. Huang X, Belongie S (2017) Arbitrary style transfer in real-time with adaptive instance normalization. In: Proceedings of IEEE/CVF international conference on computer vision
48. Karras T, Laine S, Aittala M, Hellsten J, Lehtinen J, Aila T (2020) Analyzing and improving the image quality of StyleGAN. In: Proceedings of IEEE/CVF conference on computer vision and pattern recognition
49. Karras T, Aittala M, Hellsten J, Laine S, Lehtinen J, Aila T (2020) Training Generative adversarial networks with limited data. arXiv preprint arXiv:2006.06676
50. Albright M, McCloskey S (2019) Source generator attribution via inversion. In: Proceedings of conference on computer vision and pattern recognition workshops
51. Marra F, Gragnaniello D, Verdoliva L, Poggi G (2019) Do GANs leave artificial fingerprints? In: Proceedings of IEEE conference on multimedia information processing and retrieval, pp 506–511
52. 100,000 faces generated by AI (2018). https://generated.photos/
53. Yi D, Lei Z, Liao S, Li S (2014) Learning face representation from scratch. arXiv preprint arXiv:1411.7923
54. Cao Q, Shen L, Xie W, Parkhi O, Zisserman A (2018) VGGFace2: a dataset for recognising faces across pose and age. In: Proceedings of international conference on automatic face & gesture recognition
55. Nech A, Kemelmacher-Shlizerman I (2017) Level playing field for million scale face recognition. In: Proceedings of IEEE/CVF conference on computer vision and pattern recognition
56. Li Y, Yang X, Sun P, Qi H, Lyu S (2020) Celeb-DF: a large-scale challenging dataset for DeepFake forensics. In: Proceedings of IEEE/CVF conference on computer vision and pattern recognition
57. Mirsky Y, Lee W (2021) The creation and detection of Deepfakes: a survey. ACM Comput Surv 54(1):1–41
58. Li Y, Chang M, Lyu S (2018) In Ictu Oculi: exposing AI generated fake face videos by detecting eye blinking. In: Proceedings of international workshop on information forensics and security
59. Dolhansky B, Howes R, Pflaum B, Baram N, Ferrer C (2019) The Deepfake detection challenge (DFDC) preview dataset. arXiv preprint arXiv:1910.08854
60. Jiang L, Wu W, Li R, Qian C, Loy CC (2020) DeeperForensics-1.0: a large-scale dataset for real-world face forgery detection. In: Proceedings of IEEE/CVF conference on computer vision and pattern recognition (2020)
61. Zi B, Chang M, Chen J, Ma X, Jiang YG (2020) WildDeepfake: a challenging real-world dataset for deepfake detection. In: Proceedings of ACM international conference on multimedia
62. Sanderson C, Lovell B (2009) Multi-region probabilistic histograms for robust and scalable identity inference. In: Proceedings of international conference on biometrics
63. Zhu J, Park T, Isola P, Efros A (2017) Unpaired image-to-image translation using cycle-consistent adversarial networks. In: Proceedings of international conference on computer vision (2017)

64. Schroff F, Kalenichenko D, Philbin J (2015) Facenet: a unified embedding for face recognition and clustering. In: Proceedings of IEEE/CVF conference on computer vision and pattern recognition
65. Zhang K, Zhang Z, Li Z, Qiao Y (2016) Joint face detection and alignment using multitask cascaded convolutional networks. IEEE Signal Process Lett 23(10):1499–1503
66. Google AI: Contributing data to Deepfake detection research (2019). https://ai.googleblog.com/2019/09/contributing-data-to-deepfake-detection.html
67. Dolhansky B, Bitton J, Pflaum B, Lu J, Howes R, Wang M, Ferrer CC (2020) The DeepFake detection challenge dataset. arXiv preprint arXiv:2006.07397
68. Rössler A, Cozzolino D, Verdoliva L, Riess C, Thies J, Nießner M (2018) FaceForensics: a large-scale video dataset for forgery detection in human faces. arXiv preprint arXiv:1803.09179
69. Pérez P, Gangnet M, Blake A (2003) Poisson image editing. ACM Trans Graph 22(3):313–318
70. Scherhag U, Rathgeb C, Merkle J, Breithaupt R, Busch C (2019) Face recognition systems under morphing attacks: a survey. IEEE Access 7:23012–23026
71. Wolberg G (1998) Image morphing: a survey. Vis Comput 14(8–9):360–372
72. Gomez-Barrero M, Rathgeb C, Scherhag U, Busch C (2017) Is your biometric system robust to morphing attacks? In: Proceedings of IEEE international workshop on biometrics and forensics
73. Korshunov P, Marcel S (2019) Vulnerability of face recognition to deep morphing. arXiv preprint arXiv:1910.01933
74. Venkatesh S, Raghavendra R, Raja K, Busch C (2021) Face morphing attack generation & detection: a comprehensive survey. IEEE Trans Technol Soc
75. Weng Y, Wang L, Li X, Chai M, Zhou K (2013) Hair interpolation for portrait morphing. Comput Graph Forum 32:79–84
76. Zhang H, Venkatesh S, Ramachandra R, Raja K, Damer N, Busch C (2021) MIPGAN-generating strong and high quality morphing attacks using identity prior driven GAN. arXiv preprint arXiv:2009.01729
77. Raja K, Ferrara M, Franco A, Spreeuwers L, Batskos I, de Wit F, Gomez-Barrero M, Scherhag U, Fischer D, Venkatesh S, Singh JM, Li G, Bergeron L, Isadskiy S, Ramachandra R, Rathgeb C, Frings D, Seidel U, Knopjes F, Veldhuis R, Maltoni D, Busch C (2020) Morphing attack detection-database. Evaluation platform and benchmarking, IEEE Trans Inform Forensics Secur
78. Neubert T, Makrushin A, Hildebrandt M, Kraetzer C, Dittmann J (2018) Extended StirTrace benchmarking of biometric and forensic qualities of morphed face images. IET Biometrics 7(4):325–332
79. Gonzalez-Sosa E, Fierrez J, Vera-Rodriguez R, Alonso-Fernandez F (2018) Facial soft biometrics for recognition in the wild: recent works, annotation and COTS evaluation. IEEE Trans Inform Forensics Secur 13(8):2001–2014
80. Choi Y, Choi M, Kim M, Ha J, Kim S, Choo J (2018) StarGAN: unified generative adversarial networks for multi-domain image-to-image translation. In: Proceedings of IEEE/CVF conference on computer vision and pattern recognition
81. FaceApp (2017). https://apps.apple.com/cn/app/id1465199127
82. He Z, Zuo W, Kan M, Shan S, Chen X (2019) AttGAN: facial attribute editing by only changing what you want. IEEE Trans Image Process
83. Lample G, Zeghidour N, Usunier N, Bordes A, Denoyer L, Ranzato M (2017) Fader networks: manipulating images by sliding attributes. In: Proceedings of advances in neural information processing systems
84. Liu M, Ding Y, Xia M, Liu X, Ding E, Zuo W, Wen S (2019) STGAN: a unified selective transfer network for arbitrary image attribute editing. In: Proceedings of IEEE/CVF conference on computer vision and pattern recognition (2019)
85. Li M, Zuo W, Zhang D (2016) Deep identity-aware transfer of facial attributes. arXiv preprint arXiv:1610.05586

86. Perarnau G, Weijer JVD, Raducanu B, Álvarez J (2016) Invertible conditional GANs for image editing. In: Proceedings of advances in neural information processing systems workshops
87. Shen W, Liu R (2017) Learning residual images for face attribute manipulation. In: Proceedings of conference on computer vision and pattern recognition
88. Xiao T, Hong J, Ma J (2018) ELEGANT: exchanging latent encodings with GAN for transferring multiple face attributes. In: Proceedings of European conference on computer vision
89. Mirza M, Osindero S (2014) Conditional generative adversarial nets. arXiv preprint arXiv:1411.1784
90. Chu W, Tai Y, Wang C, Li J, Huang F, Ji R (2020) SSCGAN: facial attribute editing via style skip connections. In: Proceedings of European conference on computer vision
91. Wu PW, Lin YJ, Chang CH, Chang EY, Liao SW (2019) RelGAN: multi-domain image-to-image translation via relative attributes. In: Proceedings of IEEE/CVF international conference on computer vision
92. Thies J, Zollhöfer M, Nießner M (2019) Deferred neural rendering: image synthesis using neural textures. ACM Trans Graph 38(66):1–12
93. Thies J, Zollhofer M, Stamminger M, Theobalt C, Nießner M (2016) Face2face: real-time face capture and reenactment of RGB videos. In: Proceedings of IEEE/CVF conference on computer vision and pattern recognition
94. Isola P, Zhu J, Zhou T, Efros A (2017) Image-to-image translation with conditional adversarial networks. In: Proceedings of conference on computer vision and pattern recognition
95. Averbuch-Elor H, Cohen-Or D, Kopf J, Cohen MF (2017) Bringing portraits to life. ACM Trans Graph 36(6):196
96. Ha S, Kersner M, Kim B, Seo S, Kim D (2020) Marionette: few-shot face reenactment preserving identity of unseen targets. In: Proceedings of AAAI conference on artificial intelligence
97. Siarohin A, Lathuilière S, Tulyakov S, Ricci E, Sebe N (2019) First order motion model for image animation. In: Proceedings of advances in neural information processing systems
98. Zakharov E, Shysheya A, Burkov E, Lempitsky V (2019) Few-shot adversarial learning of realistic neural talking head models. In: Proceedings of IEEE/CVF international conference on computer vision
99. Agarwal S, Farid H, Fried O, Agrawala M (2020) Detecting deep-fake videos from phoneme-viseme mismatches. In: Proceedings of workshop on media forensics, CVPRw
100. Thies J, Elgharib M, Tewari A, Theobalt C, Nießner M (2020) Neural voice puppetry: audio-driven facial reenactment. In: Proceedings of European conference on computer vision
101. Suwajanakorn S, Seitz S, Kemelmacher-Shlizerman I (2017) Synthesizing Obama: Learning Lip Sync From Audio. ACM Transactions on Graphics 36(4):1–13
102. Song Y, Zhu J, Li D, Wang A, Qi H (2019) Talking face generation by conditional recurrent adversarial network. In: Proceedings of international joint conference on artificial intelligence
103. Song L, Wu W, Qian C, He R, Loy C (2020) Everybody's Talkin': let me talk as you want. arXiv preprint arXiv:2001.05201
104. Zhou H, Liu Y, Liu Z, Luo P, Wang X (2019) Talking face generation by adversarially disentangled audio-visual representation. In: Proceedings of AAAI conference on artificial intelligence
105. Fried O, Tewari A, Zollhöfer M, Finkelstein A, Shechtman E, Goldman DB, Genova K, Jin Z, Theobalt C, Agrawala M (2019) Text-based editing of talking-head video. ACM Trans Graph 38(4)

Chapter 2
Digital Face Manipulation in Biometric Systems

Mathias Ibsen, Christian Rathgeb, Daniel Fischer, Pawel Drozdowski, and Christoph Busch

Abstract Biometric technologies, in particular face recognition, are employed in many personal, commercial, and governmental identity management systems around the world. The processing of digitally manipulated face images within a face recognition system may lead to false decisions and thus decrease the reliability of the decision system. This necessitates the development of manipulation detection modules which can be seamlessly integrated into the processing chain of face recognition systems. This chapter discusses the impact of face image manipulation on face recognition technologies. To this end, the basic processes and key components of biometric systems are briefly introduced with particular emphasis on facial recognition. Additionally, face manipulation detection scenarios and concepts of how to integrate detection methods to face recognition systems are discussed. In an experimental evaluation, it is shown that different types of face manipulation, i.e. retouching, face morphing, and swapping, can significantly affect the biometric performance of face recognition systems and hence impair their security. Eventually, this chapter provides an outlook on issues and challenges that face manipulation poses to face recognition technologies.

M. Ibsen · C. Rathgeb (✉) · D. Fischer · P. Drozdowski · C. Busch
Hochschule Darmstadt, Darmstadt, Germany
e-mail: christian.rathgeb@h-da.de

M. Ibsen
e-mail: mathias.ibsen@h-da.de

D. Fischer
e-mail: daniel.fischer@h-da.de

P. Drozdowski
e-mail: pawel.drozdowski@h-da.de

C. Busch
e-mail: christoph.busch@h-da.de

© The Author(s) 2022
C. Rathgeb et al. (eds.), *Handbook of Digital Face Manipulation and Detection*,
Advances in Computer Vision and Pattern Recognition,
https://doi.org/10.1007/978-3-030-87664-7_2

27

Fig. 2.1 Examples of digital face manipulation: original face image (left), a slightly retouched face image with increased eye size, slimmed nose, and cheeks (middle), and face image with a cat filter (right)

2.1 Introduction

The facial image of a subject can be altered, i.e. manipulated, in the digital domain such that the resulting digitally manipulated face image contains altered (biometric) features of the subject in a manipulated form. Digital face manipulation algorithms have advanced rapidly in recent years [50, 53]. In the scientific literature, numerous methods which can be used to alter facial images, e.g. swapping [40], morphing [43], or retouching [35], have been proposed for various application scenarios, e.g. in the film industry. Due to their popularity, face manipulation algorithms are already available in free web and mobile applications (apps). They typically allow their users to easily manipulate facial images or videos. Existing apps provide a huge variety of face manipulations ranging from funny filters to alterations in facial shape and texture; see Fig. 2.1 for examples.

Manipulated facial images which look realistic may lead to a loss of trust in digital content and can cause further harm by spreading false information [50]. Moreover, the automated processing of manipulated facial images may lead to false decisions, e.g. in a biometric system. For instance, face recognition performance might be impacted by the aforementioned manipulations. Face recognition technologies are employed for identity management in numerous application areas, e.g. mobile devices, access control, forensics, or surveillance [24, 54].

Face image manipulations might be applied for different reasons, e.g. beautification, by innocent users who have no intention of manipulating an image to impair the security of a face recognition system. However, they may also be applied by malicious users with the goal of interfering with the operation of a face recognition system. Such attacks are referred to as presentation attacks [19, 27]. Digital face image manipulation can be seen as presentation attacks in the digital domain.[1] Face recognition systems have been shown to be particularly vulnerable to presentation attacks [32], e.g. printouts of facial images or 3D masks. Presentation attacks are either performed with the aim of identity concealment, i.e. an attacker tries not to be recognized, or impersonation, i.e. an attacker tries to be recognized as somebody else (target subject). Researchers have already shown that both types of attacks are feasible with the help of digital face image manipulation [50]. In many cases, only slight alterations of original facial images are necessary to achieve alarmingly high attack success rates. This poses serious security risks to face recognition systems.

Recently, numerous methods for detecting facial image manipulations have been proposed, see [50, 53] for comprehensive surveys. Said manipulation detection methods can be applied in face recognition systems in order to protect against attacks based on manipulated face images. Moreover, detection methods may be specifically designed for integration into the processing chain of face recognition systems for different application scenarios.

This introductory chapter provides a brief overview of biometric face recognition. The potential impacts of the digital face image manipulation on facial recognition technologies are discussed, along with an empirical evaluation on a database comprising common digital face alterations using state-of-the-art face recognition systems. In addition, different face image manipulation detection scenarios and the integration of detection modules into biometric systems are described.

This chapter is organized as follows: Sect. 2.2 briefly introduces the key processes of generic biometric systems, in particular, face recognition. Subsequently, Sect. 2.3 discusses potential impacts of face image manipulation on the biometric performance of face recognition as well as detection scenarios. Experimental case studies are presented in Sect. 2.4. Finally, a summary and outlook are given in Sect. 2.5.

2.2 Biometric Systems

Biometric systems aim at establishing or verifying the identity or demographic attributes of individuals. In the international standard ISO/IEC 2382-37 [18], "biometrics" is defined as: "automated recognition of individuals based on their biological and behavioural characteristics." Humans possess, nearly universally, physiological characteristics which are highly distinctive and can, therefore, be used to distinguish between different individuals with a high degree of confidence. Prominent biometric characteristics are fingerprint, face, or iris. For a comprehensive introduction to biometrics, the interested reader is referred to [20] and the handbook series [4, 24, 26, 39, 51].

---

[1] In certain scenarios, digital face image manipulations can also be applied to perform presentation attacks at enrolment which may be referred to as backdoor attacks.

2.2.1 Processes

Generally, an automated biometric recognition system consists of: (1) a capture device (e.g. a camera), with which the biometric samples (e.g. facial images) are acquired; (2) a database which stores the biometric information and other personal data; (3) signal processing algorithms, which estimate the quality of the acquired sample, pre-process and extract the distinguishing features from it; and (4) comparison and decision algorithms, which enable ascertaining of similarity of two biometric samples by comparing the extracted feature vectors and establishing whether or not the two biometric samples belong to the same source.

During enrolment, a biometric capture device generates a reference sample of an individual, proceeds to pre-process it, and extracts a feature vector which is stored as a reference template. At the time of authentication, a probe sample is captured, processed in the same way, and the resulting probe template is compared against a reference template of a claimed identity (verification) or up to all stored reference templates (identification).[2] As a result, a (set of) biometric comparison score(s) is compared against a pre-defined threshold yielding acceptance or rejection decision. These processes are illustrated in Fig. 2.2.

In a biometric authentication attempt, two algorithmic errors may occur [17]:

- **False Match**: The comparison decision of "match" for a biometric probe and a biometric reference that belong to different biometric capture subjects.
- **False Non-Match**: The comparison decision of "non-match" for a biometric probe and a biometric reference that belong to the same biometric capture subject and of the same biometric characteristic.

The probabilities of each of these erroneous decision outcomes are defined as:

- **False Match Rate** (*FMR*): The proportion of the completed biometric non-mated comparison trials that result in a false match.
- **False Non-Match Rate** (*FNMR*): The proportion of the completed biometric mated comparison trials that result in a false non-match.

The *FMR* and the *FNMR* are measured at a certain decision threshold of the system. A change of the decision threshold usually results in a decrease of one of the error

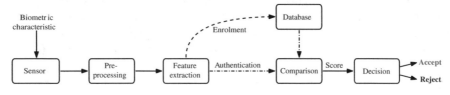

Fig. 2.2 Overview of a biometric recognition system

---

[2] This chapter focuses on biometric verification systems performing one-to-one comparisons.

rates at a cost of increasing the other. In other words, there exists a fundamental trade-off between system security (*FMR*) and convenience (*FNMR*) which is commonly illustrated by a detection error trade-off (DET) plot. The operation point where the *FMR* is equal to the *FNMR* is commonly referred to as Equal Error Rate (EER), which is often used as a single representative value to compare the biometric performance obtained by different algorithms.

2.2.2 *Face Recognition*

Face recognition systems are typically designed to process facial images captured with visible imaging sensor,[3] i.e. RGB colour cameras. In the pre-processing stage, face detection and face alignment is performed. Subsequently, face sample quality is estimated [46] and feature extraction is performed. For a long period of time, hand-crafted feature extractors, e.g. Local Binary Patterns [1] and Gabor filters [47], were predominately used. Said methods apply texture descriptors locally and aggregate extracted features into an overall face descriptor. A large variety of such systems has been proposed in the scientific literature, see [24, 25]. In contrast, current face recognition technologies utilize deep learning and massive training datasets to learn rich and compact representations of faces [15, 29]. The recent developments in Deep Convolutional Neural Networks (DCNNs) have led to breakthrough advances in facial recognition accuracy. DCNNs are usually trained using differentiable loss functions. A face embedding in the latent space is represented as a fixed-length real-valued vector. The dissimilarity of such feature vectors can be effectively estimated through simple distance measures, e.g. Euclidean distance. State-of-the-art face recognition systems have already surpassed human-level performance [34, 49] even on unconstrained (captured "in-the-wild" or with low image quality) face databases, e.g. the well-known Labeled Faces in the Wild (LFW) dataset [23].

2.3 Digital Face Manipulation in Biometric Systems

Advances in image manipulation software and machine learning technologies have made it easier to realistically manipulate face images. Some digital face manipulations are expected to impact the biometric performance of a face recognition system as they e.g. can cause severe changes in facial appearance or obscure parts of a face. Hence, methods capable of accurately detecting such manipulations are needed in order to mitigate their negative impacts on biometric systems. Development of such detection methods remains an open challenge.

---

[3] There are also face recognition systems which utilize other sensors, e.g. depth sensors for 3D face recognition.

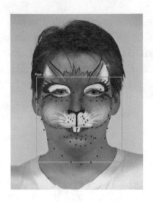 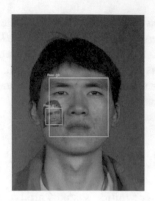

Fig. 2.3 Examples where the face of a digitally manipulated image is inaccurately detected

2.3.1 Impact on Biometric Performance

Digitally manipulated images may be introduced into a biometric system during enrolment or authentication and in systems where images are not captured live by a biometric capture device. It has been demonstrated that some manipulations (e.g. morphed images) [10, 41] can be used by attackers to circumvent the security of the system, whereas other manipulations usually carried out by bona fide users like slight retouching has little to no security implications [36]. While manipulated images can be a problem from a security-point-of-view, it can be of interest from a usability perspective, and in some applications of face recognition systems, that face recognition systems are robust to common manipulations in the digital domain. This can for instance, be relevant if images from social media are used in a face recognition system, as it is likely that users have manipulated the images without any intention of interfering with the operation of a face recognition system. Despite the intentions of digitally manipulating a face image, such images can impact different modules of a face recognition system if processed:

Face detection   Digital face manipulations which occlude parts of a face or add additional texture information (e.g. synthetic tattoos) are likely to affect a face recognition system's ability to detect a face accurately. Facial manipulations can cause detection schemes to detect multiple faces or inaccurately determine the region of interest, i.e. the face (examples are given in Fig. 2.3). If a face cannot be properly detected, reliable recognition cannot be guaranteed.

Quality estimation   It is expected that manipulations where part of a face is occluded, in general, will obtain a lower estimated face quality score than faces without occlusions. For other manipulations which aim at impersonation, it is not expected that the manipulation will have a significant effect on the quality score. If some types of digital manipulations receive a significantly lower quality score than bona fide images, quality estimation might be used to prevent the enrolment of such manipulated samples into the face recognition system database.

Comparison and feature extraction   Digital facial manipulations are expected to impact the features extracted from facial images and affect the comparison scores of mated and non-mated comparison trials. The expected behaviour depends on the type of manipulation applied. For beautification and identity concealment, it is expected that the performance significantly drops when a face is severely manipulated or when occlusions occur over key areas such as the periocular region. For manipulations that aim at impersonation, it is expected that the manipulated image becomes more similar to the target identity than the source identity. Similarly, for manipulations that aim at merging multiple identities into a single image, it is expected that the similarity score is high for all individuals contributing to the merged image.

The impact of digital face manipulations on face recognition systems depends on the type and severity of the manipulation applied. For manipulations that only alter few aspects of a facial image e.g. lighting condition and slight beautification, it is not expected that the manipulation has a big impact as modern face recognition systems are robust to such minor changes. For manipulations where a large part of a face is occluded, the *FNMR* of the system is expected to be affected significantly. For manipulations where a face is swapped with another individual's face, it is expected that the swapped face image becomes less similar to the source identity and more similar to the target identity. For high-quality morphed images, it is expected that the system will falsely accept multiple individuals.

2.3.2   Manipulation Detection Scenarios

Several detection algorithms have been proposed to improve the robustness of face recognition systems to facial manipulations and to prevent image forgery. These algorithms can be integrated into the existing face recognition systems and be used to check the authenticity and integrity of imagery. In face recognition systems, detection algorithms can be used to prevent that facial images, which have been manipulated, are stored during enrolment or used during authentication.

For detecting manipulated face images, there are two different detection scenarios:

1. No-reference detection
2. Differential detection

In no-reference detection, a single suspected image is given as input to the detection algorithm and analyzed. Thereupon, a detection score is produced and used to determine whether the image is bona fide or manipulated. In differential detection, both the suspected image and a trusted live capture are used to determine if the suspected image has been manipulated. No-reference detection is considered a

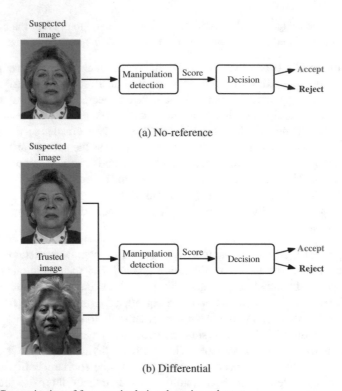

(a) No-reference

(b) Differential

Fig. 2.4 Categorisation of face manipulation detection schemes

more difficult problem and usually less accurate (see e.g. [28]). The possibility to use differential detection in face recognition systems arises due to the availability of pairs of images (reference and probe) during authentication, which is often not the case in traditional image forensics where usually only a single image or video is available. Despite the often superior performance of differential detection algorithms, no-reference detection is still important in forensic scenarios when a trusted live capture is not available. A conceptual overview of the two detection scenarios is shown in Fig. 2.4.

Several algorithms for detecting digital manipulated face images have been proposed e.g. [21, 33, 37, 40, 42, 45, 55]. In general, the existing manipulation detection schemes use (1) texture analysis, (2) digital forensics, or (3) deep-learning techniques to detect manipulated images. The use of texture descriptors has shown promising results e.g. for no-reference morphing attack detection as reported in [44]. Similarly, forensics-based detection methods, e.g. methods which analyze Photo Response Non-Uniformity (PRNU), have been shown to be useful for detecting some types of digital manipulations and have, for instance, been applied to detect retouched [36] and morphed images [7]. The features used in detection schemes based on digital forensics or texture analysis are often highly dependent on the training scenario and struggle to generalize well to unseen conditions and variations in post-processing.

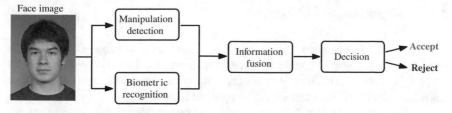

Fig. 2.5 Integration of manipulation detection and biometric recognition

Therefore, many state-of-the-art approaches utilize deep learning-based models, or features extracted from such models to detect manipulated face images. As indicated in [36] information fusion, like combining detection scores from multiple algorithms, can lead to a more robust detection system. For a more comprehensive overview of the current state-of-the-art in detecting manipulated face images, the reader is referred to [2, 35, 43, 50, 52] and to the third part of this handbook.

Figure 2.5 shows one possible integration of a manipulation detection algorithm into a face recognition system. As illustrated, the output of the manipulation detection and biometric recognition system can be fused together and used to make the final decision. Information fusion is usually based on either decision-level or score-level fusion. For decision-level fusion, the binary decision outputs of the manipulation detection and biometric system are used to determine the authentication output. For instance, a successful authentication output could be given only if neither of the systems rejects the input image. For score-level fusion, the scores produced by the two systems are combined and used together with a threshold value to determine the final authentication output. Chingovska et al. [5] investigated the impact of applying different score-level and decision-level fusion techniques for integrating a presentation attack detection algorithm with a biometric recognition system and concluded that there almost always was a trade-off between recognition and detection performance.

Another approach for making face recognition systems robust is to create algorithms capable of inverting the facial manipulations, i.e. remove the manipulation. Some authors have proposed algorithms capable of inverting specific manipulations, e.g. [11, 55].

2.4   Experiments

In this section, the vulnerability of two state-of-the-art face recognition systems towards three types of digital manipulations (retouching, morphing, and face swapping[4]) is evaluated.

---

[4] Face swapping is also some times referred to as identity swapping in the literature.

2.4.1   Experimental Setup

For the evaluation, one open-source and one commercial face recognition system are used. As the open-source system *ArcFace* [8] is used with the *MTCNN* face detector [56] for pre-processing. Due to terms of use, the used commercial system cannot be named explicitly and will henceforth be referred to as *COTS*.

To create an appropriate database, a subset of constrained facial images from the FERET [30] and FRGCv2 [31] database are manipulated using six different tools.

The changes imposed by the tools for the different manipulations are described below:

Retouching For the generation of retouched images, *InstaBeauty* [16] and *Fotorus* [14] are used. Both are proprietary software that offer features for beautifying facial images. Although the beautification operations performed by these and similar apps vary, common manipulations are smoothing of the skin, slimming of the nose, and enlargement of the eyes. Additionally, other manipulations might occur when beautifying an image e.g. enlargement of the mouth and slimming of the chin.

Morphing For the generation of morphs *FaceFusion* [9] and *UBO Morpher* [3, 12] are used. For *FaceFusion* a version which uses the landmarks of *dlib* [22] and Delaunay triangles is applied. Certain regions (e.g. eyes, nostrils, and hair) of the first face image are blended over the morph to hide potential artefacts. The *UBO Morpher* tool generates a morphed image by triangulation, warping, and blending. For finding landmarks for this tool, *dlib* are used. To avoid artefacts in the area outside of the face region, the morphed image generated by *UBO Morpher* is copied to the background of one of the original face images. Images generated by *UBO Morpher* might show artefacts at the border lines of the blended areas. In this evaluation and for both morphing tools, a single image is generated from the facial images of two different subjects and an equal weighting factor [12] of 0.5 is used for both blending and warping.

Face swap For the generation of face swapped images, *fewshot-face* [13] and *simple_faceswap* [48] are used. *fewshot-face* is a GAN-based approach capable of swapping a face using only a few target images; in the database used in this chapter a maximum of two target images was used to generate each face swapped image. *simple_faceswap* is a simple landmark-based approach which uses the landmarks detected by *dlib* to perform face swapping.

Example images generated using the above tools are shown in Fig. 2.6. For the generation of the swapped and morphed face images it was ensured that both individuals used to create the manipulated image were of the same gender. Additionally, to avoid artefacts, it was ensured that for the generation of the morphed images only one of the facial images contained glasses.

An overview of the total number of biometric comparisons in the generated database is given in Table 2.1. Note that for morphing and swapping where the manipulated image has been created from the facial images of two subjects, we only make

(a) Face swap   (b) Morphing   (c) Retouching

Fig. 2.6 Example images from the generated database

comparisons to the probe image(s) of the subject from which the area outside the face region is from. For instance, to create a mated comparison for the swapped and morphed face images in Fig. 2.6, a probe image from subject 1 is used. For the mated comparisons for retouching, morphing, and swapping, the used probe images have not been manipulated.

To evaluate the impact of the manipulations, standardized and other well-known metrics and visualizations are used. For visualizing the distributions of comparisons scores, probability density functions (PDFs) are used, and the scores produced by the algorithms are converted to similarity scores and normalized to the range [0, 1]. The degree of separation between two distributions is quantified using the decidability measure d' [6] which is calculated as follows:

Table 2.1 Number of biometric comparisons for the generated database

Scenario	Number of comparisons
Bona fide mated	2251
Retouching mated	4502
Morphing mated	4502
Face swap mated	4502
Bona fide non-mated	497,838

$$d' = \frac{|\mu_{\text{mated}} - \mu_{\text{non-mated}}|}{\sqrt{\frac{1}{2}(\sigma^2_{\text{mated}} + \sigma^2_{\text{non-mated}})}}$$

Biometric recognition performance is visualized using DET-curves which plot the *FNMR* versus the *FMR* at different decision thresholds. Furthermore, the *FNMR* at a fixed operational threshold corresponding to 0.1% *FMR* is highlighted; this security level is relevant for numerous real deployments of biometric recognition systems [38]. Finally, the equal error rate (*EER*), i.e. the point at which the *FMR* and *FNMR* are equal, is reported.

2.4.2   Performance Evaluation

This section investigates the effect of the different types of digital manipulations in the generated database (Sect. 2.4.1) on two state-of-the-art face recognition systems.

The PDFs and estimated decision thresholds at a fixed *FMR* of 0.1% for the manipulated and bona fide images in the generated database are shown in Fig. 2.7. It can be observed that the comparison scores of the manipulated images, for both *ArcFace* and *COTS*, are situated in-between the bona fide mated and non-mated score distributions. Furthermore, it can be observed that the score distribution for the retouched images is closest to the bona fide mated distribution, whereas face swapping is closest to the bona fide non-mated distribution. These observations are expected since retouching only moderately alters a face whereas for face swapping the original face identity has been replaced with the identity of another individual. From the plot, it can be observed that morphing, in general, decreases the comparison score more than retouching, but less than face swapping. Interestingly, from Fig. 2.7, it can be observed that the comparison scores for *COTS* on the swapped face images are significantly higher than the bona fide non-mated scores. When looking at the bona fide mated score distributions in Fig. 2.7 (most notable for *COTS*) two separate peaks can be observed, which is caused by using two different databases in the evaluation—the FRGCv2 database contains more unconstrained probe images than the FERET data.

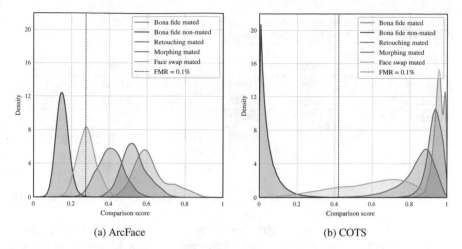

Fig. 2.7 Score distributions for manipulated and bona fide comparisons

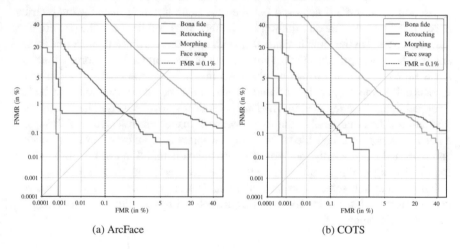

Fig. 2.8 DET-curves for performance scores of the manipulated and bona fide images

From the DET-curves in Fig. 2.8, it can be observed that face swapping has a big impact on the classification errors of both tested face recognition systems which is expected as face swapping changes the original face identity and as such makes the resulting identity less similar to the original identity. In contrast, retouching and morphing only have a moderate impact on the classification errors. For morphed images, this is a potential issue since the identity of multiple individuals contributes to a morphed image. As shown in other works, e.g. [10], morphed images can pose a security threat if accepted into a face recognition system as it is likely that the different individuals contributing to a morphed image can use the morph for authentication.

Table 2.2 Biometric performance results for ArcFace and COTS. *FNMR* is calculated at *FMR* = 0.1%. Values for *FNMR* and *EER* in the table are in %

Type	ArcFace			COTS		
	EER	FNMR	d'	EER	FNMR	d'
Bona fide	0.0004	0.0000	6.8386	0.0003	0.0000	20.4373
Retouching	0.4886	0.4887	6.7672	0.4664	0.4665	13.7155
Morphing	0.4970	1.7548	4.8792	0.1555	0.2888	10.2725
Face swap	5.8418	47.4678	2.9846	2.7765	20.7685	3.8780

Therefore, the system should ideally reject all mated comparisons where one of the images contains either a swapped or a morphed face.

In Table 2.2, the biometric performance scores are shown for *ArcFace* and *COTS*. The table shows good separability (high d') between the bona fide non-mated scores and the mated scores obtained for both the bona fide and retouched images. Least separation (lowest d') is achieved between the bona fide non-mated score distribution and the mated score distribution for the face swapped images. The performance metrics reported in the table indicate that both systems are robust to bona fide images and that face swapping has the biggest impact on the comparison scores of the systems. More specifically, it can be observed that at an operational threshold where *FMR* = 0.1%, approximately 47.5 and 20.8% of the mated comparisons for the face swapped images are rejected for *ArcFace* and *COTS*, respectively. The results show that, at best, less than half of the face swapped images are rejected, which suggest a need for algorithms capable of detecting swapped face images. For the retouched and morphed images, only moderate performance degradation can be observed. For morphed images, this means that state-of-the-art face recognition systems cannot reliably detect and reject morphing attacks. Therefore, several authors have proposed dedicated algorithms for detecting morphed images, although this remains a challenging problem [28].

2.5 Summary and Outlook

This chapter addressed the impact of digital face image manipulations on face recognition technologies. Considering the wide prevalence of face manipulation software, in particular for mobile devices and border control, face recognition systems have to cope with manipulated images. It was shown that face recognition systems can be robust to certain types of manipulations, i.e. biometric performance is maintained, while others may seriously reduce recognition capabilities. Therefore, the usability (related to the false non-match rate) and the security (related to the false match rate) of face recognition systems are impaired by digitally manipulated face images. Besides face manipulation techniques considered in this chapter, numerous face image manipulation techniques have been proposed for different fields of application. The forthcoming chapters of this book will describe many of those in detail.

Additionally, this chapter emphasized the need for reliable face manipulation detection methods to be integrated into face recognition systems. To this end, an overview of different concepts for the integration of face manipulation detection into the processing chain of a face recognition system was provided. Many of the subsequent chapters propose methods for reliable detection of different face manipulations which represent a current research challenge. Beyond that, some of the forthcoming chapters will provide more details on how to combine face recognition and face image manipulation detection effectively.

Acknowledgements This research work has been partially funded by the German Federal Ministry of Education and Research and the Hessian Ministry of Higher Education, Research, Science and the Arts within their joint support of the National Research Center for Applied Cybersecurity ATHENE and the European Union's Horizon 2020 research and innovation programme under the Marie Skłodowska-Curie grant agreement No. 860813—TReSPAsS-ETN.

References

1. Ahonen T, Hadid A, Pietikainen M (2006) Face description with local binary patterns: application to face recognition. IEEE Trans Pattern Anal Mach Intell 28(12):2037–2041
2. Akhtar Z, Dasgupta D, Banerjee B (2019) Face authenticity: an overview of face manipulation generation, detection and recognition. In: Proceedings of international conference on communication and information processing (ICCIP), pp 1–8
3. Biometric System Lab—University of Bologna. http://biolab.csr.unibo.it. Accessed 12 Mar 2021
4. Bowyer KW, Burge MJ (2016) Handbook of iris recognition. Springer International Publishing
5. Chingovska I, Anjos A, Marcel S (2013) Anti-spoofing in action: joint operation with a verification system. In: Conference on computer vision and pattern recognition workshops, pp 98–104
6. Daugman J (2000) Biometric decision landscapes. Technical Report UCAM-CL-TR-482, University of Cambridge—Computer Laboratory, January 2000
7. Debiasi L, Scherhag U, Rathgeb C, Uhl A, Busch C (2018) PRNU-based detection of morphed face images. In: 6th International workshop on biometrics and forensics, pp 1–7
8. Deng J, Guo J, Xue N, Zafeiriou S (2019) ArcFace: additive angular margin loss for deep face recognition. In: IEEE/CVF conference on computer vision and pattern recognition (CVPR), pp 4685–4694
9. FaceFusion. www.wearemoment.com/FaceFusion. Accessed 14 June 2021
10. Ferrara M, Franco A, Maltoni D (2014) The magic passport. In: IEEE International joint conference on biometrics (IJCB), pp 1–7
11. Ferrara M, Franco A, Maltoni D (2018) Face demorphing. IEEE Trans Inform Forensics Secur 13(4):1008–1017
12. Ferrara M, Franco A, Maltoni D (2019) Decoupling texture blending and shape warping in face morphing. In: International conference of the biometrics special interest group (BIOSIG), September 2019. IEEE
13. Few-shot face translation. https://github.com/shaoanlu/fewshot-face-translation-GAN. Accessed 14 June 2021
14. FotoRus (2018). https://www.apkshub.com/app/com.wantu.activity. Accessed 7 Mar 2021

15. Guo G, Zhang N (2019) A survey on deep learning based face recognition. Comput Vis Image Understanding, vol 189, pp 102805. http://dx.doi.org/10.1016/j.cviu.2019.102805
16. InstaBeauty (2017). https://www.apkshub.com/app/com.fotoable.fotobeauty. Accessed 7 Mar 2021
17. ISO/IEC JTC1 SC37 Biometrics. ISO/IEC 19795-1:2006. Information Technology—Biometric Performance Testing and Reporting—Part 1: Principles and Framework. International Organization for Standardization and International Electrotechnical Committee, March 2006
18. ISO/IEC JTC1 SC37 Biometrics. ISO/IEC 2382-37:2012 Information Technology—Vocabulary—Part 37: Biometrics. International Organization for Standardization, 2012
19. ISO/IEC JTC1 SC37 Biometrics. ISO/IEC 30107-1. Information Technology—Biometric presentation attack detection—Part 1: Framework. International Organization for Standardization, 2016
20. Jain AK, Flynn P, Ross AA (2007) Handbook of biometrics, July 2007. Springer
21. Jain A, Singh R, Vatsa M (2018) On detecting GANs and retouching based synthetic alterations. In: IEEE 9th International conference on biometrics theory, applications and systems (BTAS), pp 1–7
22. King D (2009) Dlib-ml: a machine learning toolkit. J Mach Learn Res 10(60):1755–1758
23. Learned-Miller E, Huang GB, Roy Chowdhury A, Li H, Hua G (2016) Labeled faces in the wild: a survey. In: Advances in face detection and facial image analysis. Springer, pp 189–248
24. Li SZ, Jain AK (eds) (2011) Handbook of face recognition. Springer, London
25. Liu L, Chen J, Fieguth P, Zhao G et al (2019) From BoW to CNN: two decades of texture representation for texture classification. Int J Comput Vis 127(1):74–109
26. Maltoni D, Maio D, Jain AK, Prabhakar S (2009) Handbook of fingerprint recognition, 1st edn. Springer
27. Marcel S, Nixon MS, Fierrez J, Evans N (2019) Handbook of biometric anti-spoofing: presentation attack detection, 2nd edn. Springer
28. Ngan M, Grother P, Hanaoka K, Kuo J (2021) Face recognition vendor test (FRVT) Part 4: MORPH–Performance of automated face morph detection. Technical report, National Institute of Standards and Technology, April
29. Parkhi OM, Vedaldi A, Zisserman A (2015) Deep face recognition. In: British machine vision conference (BMVC), pp 41.1–41.12
30. Phillips PJ, Wechsler H, Huang J, Rauss PJ (1998) The FERET database and evaluation procedure for face-recognition algorithms. Image Vis Comput 16(5):295–306
31. Phillips PJ, Flynn PJ, Scruggs T, Bowyer KW et al (2005) Overview of the face recognition grand challenge. In: IEEE computer society conference on computer vision and pattern recognition (CVPR), vol 1, pp 947–954. IEEE
32. Raghavendra R, Busch C (2017) Presentation attack detection methods for face recognition systems: a comprehensive survey. ACM Comput Surv 50(1):1–37
33. Raghavendra R, Raja KB, Busch C (2016) Detecting morphed face images. In: IEEE 8th international conference on biometrics theory, applications and systems (BTAS), pp 1–7
34. Ranjan R, Sankaranarayanan S, Bansal A, Bodla N et al (2018) Deep learning for understanding faces: machines may be just as good, or better, than humans. IEEE Signal Process Mag 35(1):66–83
35. Rathgeb C, Dantcheva A, Busch C (2019) Impact and detection of facial beautification in face recognition: an overview. IEEE Access 7:152667–152678
36. Rathgeb C, Botaljov A, Stockhardt F, Isadskiy S et al (2020) PRNU-based detection of facial retouching. IET Biomet 9(4):154–164
37. Rathgeb C, Satnoianu C-I, Haryanto NE, Bernardo K, Busch C (2020) Differential detection of facial retouching: a multi-biometric approach. IEEE Access 8:106373–106385
38. Research and Development Unit (2015) Best practice technical guidelines for automated border control (ABC) systems. Technical report, FRONTEX
39. Ross A, Nandakumar K, Jain A (2006) Handbook of multibiometrics. Springer

40. Rössler A, Cozzolino D, Verdoliva L, Riess C et al (2019) Faceforensics++: learning to detect manipulated facial images. In: International conference of computer vision (ICCV'19) pp 1–11
41. Sarkar E, Korshunov P, Colbois L, Marcel S (2020) Vulnerability analysis of face morphing attacks from landmarks and generative adversarial networks. arXiv e-prints, December 2020, pp 1–5
42. Scherhag U, Budhrani D, Gomez-Barrero M, Busch C (2018) Detecting morphed face images using facial landmarks. In: International conference on image and signal processing (ICISP), pp 444–452
43. Scherhag U, Rathgeb C, Merkle J, Breithaupt R, Busch C (2019) Face recognition systems under morphing attacks: a survey. IEEE Access 7:23012–23026
44. Scherhag U, Kunze J, Rathgeb C, Busch C (2020a) Face morph detection for unknown morphing algorithms and image sources: a multi-scale block local binary pattern fusion approach. IET Biomet 9(6):278–289
45. Scherhag U, Rathgeb C, Merkle J, Busch C (2020b) Deep face representations for differential morphing attack detection. IEEE Trans Inform Forensics Secur 15:3625–3639
46. Schlett T, Rathgeb C, Henniger O, Galbally J et al (2021) Face image quality assessment: a literature survey. arXiv e-prints, pp 1–29
47. Shen L, Bai L, Fairhurst M (2007) Gabor wavelets and general discriminant analysis for face identification and verification. Image Vis Comput 25(5):553–563
48. simple_faceswap. https://github.com/Jacen789/simple_faceswap. Accessed 14 June 2021
49. Taigman Y, Yang M, Ranzato M, Wolf L (2014) DeepFace: closing the gap to human-level performance in face verification. In: Conference on computer vision and pattern recognition (CVPR), pp 1701–1708
50. Tolosana R, Vera-Rodriguez R, Fierrez J, Morales A, Ortega-Garcia J (2020) Deepfakes and beyond: a survey of face manipulation and fake detection. Inform Fusion 64:131–148
51. Uhl A, Busch C, Marcel S, Veldhuis R (2020) Handbook of vascular biometrics. Springer International Publishing
52. Venkatesh S, Raghavendra R, Raja K, Busch C (2021) Face morphing attack generation & detection: a comprehensive survey. IEEE Trans Technol Soc (TTS) 2(3):128–145
53. Verdoliva L (2020) Media forensics and deepfakes: an overview. IEEE J Sel Top Signal Process 910–932
54. Wang M, Deng W (2021) Deep face recognition: a survey. Neurocomputing 429:215–244
55. Wang S, Wang O, Zhang R, Owens A, Efros A (2019) Detecting photoshopped faces by scripting photoshop. In: IEEE/CVF conference on computer vision and pattern recognition (CVPR), pp 10071–10080
56. Zhang K, Zhang Z, Li Z, Qiao Y (2016) Joint face detection and alignment using multitask cascaded convolutional networks. IEEE Signal Process Lett 23(10):1499–1503

Chapter 3
Multimedia Forensics Before the Deep Learning Era

Davide Cozzolino and Luisa Verdoliva

Abstract Image manipulation is as old as photography itself, and powerful media editing tools have been around for a long time. Using such conventional signal processing methods, it is possible to modify images and videos obtaining very realistic results. This chapter is devoted to describe the most effective strategies to detect the widespread manipulations that rely on traditional approaches and do not require a deep learning strategy. In particular, we will focus on manipulations like adding, replicating, or removing objects and present the major lines of research in multimedia forensics before the deep learning era and the rise of deepfakes. The most popular approaches look for artifacts related to the in-camera processing chain (camera-based clues) or the out-camera processing history (editing-based clues). We will focus on methods that rely on the extraction of a camera fingerprint and need some prior information on pristine data, for example, through a collection of images taken from the camera of interest. Then we will shift to blind methods that do not require any prior knowledge and reveal inconsistencies with respect to some well-defined hypotheses. We will also briefly review the most interesting features of machine learning- based methods and finally present the major challenges in this area.

3.1 Introduction

Digital image manipulation has a long history, and nowadays several powerful editing tools exist that allow creating realistic results that can easily fool visual scrutiny. Very common operations are adding, replicating, or removing objects, as in the examples

D. Cozzolino · L. Verdoliva (✉)
University Federico II of Naples, via Claudio 21, Naples, Italy
e-mail: verdoliv@unina.it

D. Cozzolino
e-mail: davide.cozzolino@unina.it

© The Author(s) 2022
C. Rathgeb et al. (eds.), *Handbook of Digital Face Manipulation and Detection*,
Advances in Computer Vision and Pattern Recognition,
https://doi.org/10.1007/978-3-030-87664-7_3

45

Fig. 3.1 Examples of image manipulations carried out using conventional media editing tools. First row: adding an object (splicing), removing an object (inpainting), and duplicating an object (copy-move). Second row: corresponding binary ground truths that indicate the pixels that have been modified in the image

of Fig. 3.1. A new object can be inserted by copying it from a different image (splicing), or from the same image (copy-move). Instead, an existing object can be deleted by extending the background to cover it (inpainting). Some suitable post-processing, like resizing, rotation, and color adjustment, can also be applied to better fit the object to the scene, both to improve the visual appearance and to guarantee coherent perspective and scale.

In the last few years, there has been intense research toward the design of methods for reliable image integrity verification [63]. Some tools discover physical inconsistencies [39, 41], regarding, for example, shadows or illumination or perspective, which may also be noticed by an attentive observer. In most cases, however, well-crafted forgeries leave no visible traces and appear semantically correct. Nonetheless, digital manipulations typically modify the underlying statistics of the original source, leaving a trail of traces which, although invisible to the eye, can be exploited by pixel-level analysis tools. In fact, each image is characterized by a number of features which depend on the different phases of its history, from the very same acquisition process to the internal camera processing (e.g., demosaicing and compression), to all external processing and editing operations (see Fig. 3.2). Therefore, by studying possible deviations of such features from their expected behavior, one can establish with good confidence whether image integrity has been violated.

Based on this general principle, a certain number of approaches have been proposed. For example, the acquisition process leaves on each image a "camera fingerprint", the photo-response non-uniformity noise (PRNU), unique for each specific device. Armed with this fingerprint, one can reliably discover and localize various types of attacks. It is also possible to use model-specific rather than device-specific features, related to manufacturing choices (like the color filter array) and in-camera processing (like the demosaicing algorithm) peculiar of each brand and model. As for external processing, the lion's share is taken by methods exploiting the proper-

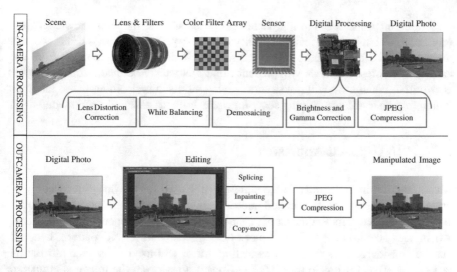

Fig. 3.2 An image is captured using an acquisition system whose basic components are represented in this figure (in-camera processing); the image can then be edited in several ways (out-camera processing)

ties of JPEG compression. Indeed, after a forgery is performed, the image is very often saved again in a JPEG compressed format. Therefore, by studying anomalies in DCT coefficients due, for example, to double quantization, or JPEG grid misalignments, integrity violation can be detected and localized. Finally, a very common form of forgery involves copy-moving image regions to duplicate or hide objects. The presence of identical regions in the image represents by itself a distinctive feature indicating manipulation, which may be discovered efficiently by several approaches, even in the presence of rotation, resizing, and other geometric distortions. Turning to videos, very simple manipulations consist in deleting or replicating entire frames. Of course, also in this case it is possible to insert or hide objects using more sophisticated editing tools [52].

This chapter will present an overview of some of the most effective tools for image forgery detection and localization that have been proposed before the rise of deep learning. In particular, we will focus on passive methods that look at the image content and disregard the associated metadata information. The most popular approaches look for artifacts related to the in-camera processing chain (camera-based clues) or the out-camera processing history (editing-based clues). These approaches often follow a model-based paradigm typically relying on statistical analyses or are based on handcrafted features and apply more classical machine learning tools. Each method relies on its own set of hypotheses, which may or may not hold for a specific manipulation, thereby limiting its applicability to a subset of cases. For example, the camera PRNU can be reliably estimated only if the camera itself is available or a large number of images taken from it. Likewise, methods thought for copy-move discovery are obviously ineffective in the presence of a splicing. Some of them are much more general, since they are based on detecting anomalies in the noise residuals.

A defining property of the approaches proposed so far is the prior knowledge they rely upon, which impacts their suitability for real-world applications. First, we will describe PRNU-based methods that require a collection of images taken from the camera of interest. Then we will present blind methods, where no prior knowledge is required. Finally, we will give a short review of machine learning-based methods which rely on a suitable training set comprising both pristine and manipulated data.

3.2 PRNU-Based Approach

Manufacturing imperfections in the silicon wafer used for the imaging sensor generate a unique sensor pattern, called photo- response non-uniformity (PRNU) noise. It is specific to each individual camera, stable in time, and independent of the scene. All images acquired by a given camera bear traces of its PRNU pattern, hence it can be considered as a sort of camera fingerprint and used for source attribution tasks, as well as for image forgery detection. If a region of the image is tampered with, the corresponding PRNU pattern is removed, which allows one to detect the manipulation.

PRNU-based forgery detection was first proposed in [49], and it is based on two main steps: *(i)* the PRNU pattern is estimated off-line from a large number of images taken from the camera, and *(ii)* the target image PRNU is estimated at test time, by means of a denoising filter, and compared with the reference (see Fig. 3.3). This approach relies on some important prior knowledge, since it assumes the availability of a certain number of images taken from the device itself. On the other hand, it is an extremely powerful approach, since it can detect every type of attack: whenever an anomaly arises due to the absence of the camera fingerprint, manipulation can be detected.

Beyond this standard methodology, there are several alternatives proposed in the literature. It is possible to model the strong spatial dependencies present in an image through a Markov Random Field so as to make joint rather than isolated decisions [16], or to rely on discriminative random fields [12] and multi-scale analysis [43]. It is worth noting that the PRNU-based approach can be also extended to blind scenarios, where no prior information about the camera is known provided a suitable clustering procedure identifies the images which share the same PRNU [20, 21]. It is even possible to recover some information about PRNU by estimating it from a single image or a group of frames in a video [51, 53, 60].

In the following, we will describe the basic approach proposed in [14]. Let y be a digital image, defined on a rectangular lattice Ω, with y_i the value at site $i \in \Omega$, observed at the camera output, either as a single color band or the composition of multiple color bands. Let us assume in a simplified model [37] that y can be written as[1]

$$y = (1 + k)x + \theta = xk + x + \theta \tag{3.1}$$

---

[1] All the operations are intended pixel-wise.

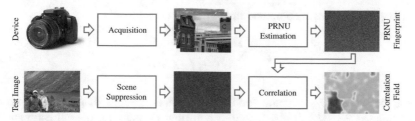

Fig. 3.3 PRNU-based forgery localization procedure. Top: the device PRNU pattern is estimated by averaging a large number of noise residuals. Bottom: the image PRNU pattern is estimated by denoising, and compared with the reference pattern: the low values in the correlation field suggest a possible manipulation

where x is the ideal noise-free image, k the camera PRNU, and θ an additive noise term which accounts for all types of disturbances. The PRNU k is the signal of interest, very weak w.r.t. both additive noise θ and the ideal image x. In this context also, the image x plays the role of unwanted disturbance, since our goal is to decide whether or not the image PRNU comes from the camera under test so as to detect possible forgeries. To increase the signal-to-noise ratio, we can subtract from y an estimate of the ideal image $\widehat{x} = f(y)$ obtained through denoising, in order to compute the so-called noise residual

$$r = y - \widehat{x} = yk + (x - y)k + (x - \widehat{x}) + \theta = yk + n \qquad (3.2)$$

where, for convenience, k multiplies the observed image y rather than the unknown original x, and the small difference term $(x - y)k$ has been included, together with the denoising error $(x - \widehat{x})$ and other disturbances in a single noise term n.

In the following, we describe in more detail the image integrity verification procedure proposed in [14] which comprises the following basic steps:

- estimation of the camera PRNU (off-line);
- computation of image noise residual and of derived statistics;
- sliding-window pixel-wise forgery detection test.

3.2.1 PRNU Estimation

As a preliminary step, the true camera PRNU pattern should be reliably estimated. This requires that either the target camera, or a large number of photos taken by it, is available. Note that the PRNU is a deterministic signal, as opposed to the other image components, and it can be easily estimated starting from the noise residuals. In addition, one can take care of using mostly uniform images (e.g., off-focus pictures of a cloudy sky) to further improve accuracy or to use fewer images to obtain the same performance. In these conditions, the maximum likelihood estimate of the PRNU from M given images is computed in [14] as

$$\widehat{k} = \sum_{m=1}^{M} y_m r_m \Big/ \sum_{m=1}^{M} y_m^2 \qquad (3.3)$$

where the weights y_m account for the fact that dark areas of the image present an attenuated PRNU and hence should contribute less to the overall estimate. Of course, this is only an estimate, however, for the sake of simplicity, we will neglect the estimation error and will assume to know the camera PRNU perfectly, that is $\widehat{k} = k$.

3.2.2 Noise Residual Computation

In the second step of the algorithm, we compute the noise residual r and suppress most of the scene content by subtracting a denoised version of the image itself:

$$r = y - f(y) = y - \hat{x} \qquad (3.4)$$

where f denotes a denoising algorithm. Even in the best case, with perfect denoising, $\hat{x} = x$, the remaining noise term is likely to dominate r which, therefore, will be only weakly correlated with the camera PRNU. In the presence of textured areas, however, denoising is typically less accurate and some signal components leak into the residual contributing to reducing the operative SNR, to the point of making detection virtually impossible. Especially in these areas, the effectiveness of the denoising algorithm becomes crucial for the overall performance.

3.2.3 Forgery Detection Test

Assuming $z = yk$, the detection problem can be formulated as a binary hypothesis test between hypothesis H_0 and H_1. Under hypothesis H_0 the camera PRNU is absent, hence the pixel has been tampered, while under hypothesis H_1, PRNU is present, hence the pixel is genuine:

$$\begin{cases} H_0 : r_i = n_i \\ H_1 : r_i = z_i + n_i \end{cases} \qquad (3.5)$$

Notice that, since we focus on the detection of forgeries, denoted by the *absence* of the PRNU, the role of two hypotheses is inverted w.r.t. what is usual. The true and estimated pixel classes will be denoted by u_i and $\widehat{u}_i$, both defined in $\{0, 1\}$, while the detection test is based on the normalized correlation index between r_{w_i} and z_{w_i}, the restrictions of r and z, respectively, to a window W_i centered on the target pixel:

$$\rho_i = \mathrm{corr}(r_{W_i}, z_{W_i}) = \frac{(r_{W_i} - \overline{r}_{W_i}) \odot (z_{W_i} - \overline{z}_{W_i})}{\|r_{W_i} - \overline{r}_{W_i}\| \cdot \|z_{W_i} - \overline{z}_{W_i}\|} \tag{3.6}$$

where $\odot$ denotes inner product, and the usual definitions hold for mean, norm, and inner product

$$\overline{x} = \frac{1}{K}\sum_{i=1}^{K} x_i, \qquad \|x\|^2 = \sum_{i=1}^{K} x_i^2, \qquad x \odot y = \sum_{i=1}^{K} x_i y_i \tag{3.7}$$

Pixel labeling is obtained by comparing the decision statistic with a threshold γ_1

$$\widehat{u}_i = \begin{cases} 0 & \rho_i < \gamma_1 \\ 1 & \text{otherwise} \end{cases} \tag{3.8}$$

To ensure the desired false acceptance rate (FAR), which is a small probability that a tampered pixel is identified as genuine, the threshold is set using the Neyman-Pearson approach. The pdf of ρ under hypothesis H_0 is estimated by computing the correlation between the camera PRNU and a large amount of noise residuals coming from other cameras, and using standard density fitting techniques. To obtain reliable estimates, rather large square blocks should be used; a dimension of 128×128 pixels represents a good compromise [14].

Once the desired FAR is fixed, the objective is to minimize the false rejection rate (FRR), which is the probability that a genuine pixel is declared tampered. This is not an easy task, since under hypothesis H_1, the decision statistic is influenced by the image content. In fact, even in the absence of forgery, the correlation might happen to be very low when the image is dark (since y multiplies the PRNU), saturated (because of intensity clipping), or in very textured areas where denoising typically does not perform well and some image content leaks into the noise residual. One possible solution to this problem is to include a "predictor" [14], which based on local images features, such as texture, flatness, and intensity, computes the expected value $\widehat{\rho}_i$ of the correlation index under hypothesis H_1. When $\widehat{\rho}_i$ is too low, indicating that, even for a genuine pixel, one could not expect a correlation index much larger than 0, the pixel is labeled as genuine, the less risky decision, irrespective of the value of ρ_i. Therefore, the test becomes

$$\widehat{u}_i = \begin{cases} 0 & \rho_i < \gamma_1 \ \text{AND} \ \widehat{\rho}_i > \gamma_2 \\ 1 & \text{otherwise} \end{cases} \tag{3.9}$$

The second threshold γ_2 is chosen heuristically by the user and separates, in practice, reliable regions from problematic ones. It is worth underlining that the refined decision test (3.9) can only reduce the false rejection rate but does not increase (actually it might reduce) the probability of detecting an actual forgery. In addition, the choice of the threshold itself is not obvious and can significantly impact the performance. Note also that the final binary map needs some post-processing operations to remove random errors and better define the shape of the forgery. This is typically done by means of morphological filtering.

3.2.4 Estimation Through Guided Filtering

As already highlighted in the previous section, a major issue with PRNU-based analysis is the impossibility to perfectly denoise the image. As a consequence, the noise residual contains traces of the image content that increase the false acceptance rates. To address this problem, it is possible to improve the denoising algorithm as done in [15], where wavelet-based denoising has been replaced by a nonlocal approach. Another possibility is to rely on the use of guided filtering [17], a strategy that turns out to be especially helpful when small forgeries are present.

In order to better understand this approach, we will elaborate some more on Eq. (3.6) and introduce some simplifications. First of all, we neglect the means (which are typically negligible) and, considering that the terms at the denominator serve only to normalize the correlation, focus on the scalar product on the numerator. Remember that $z = yk$ is the camera PRNU multiplied point-wise by the input image and, likewise, $r = hy + n$ is the noise residual, with h the observed PRNU which might or might not coincide with k. Therefore, if we divide all terms point-wise by y, we obtain the quantity

$$\tau_i = \frac{1}{|W_i|} \sum_{j \in W_i} \frac{r_j}{y_j} \frac{z_j}{y_j} = \frac{1}{|W_i|} \sum_{j \in W_i} \left(h_j + \frac{n_j}{y_j} \right) k_j \tag{3.10}$$

By defining a new noise field $\eta = nk/y$, and introducing generic weights ω_{ij}, Eq. (3.10) becomes

$$\tau_i = \sum_{j \in W_i} \omega_{ij} (h_j k_j + \eta_j) \tag{3.11}$$

This can be interpreted as the linear filtering of the image hk affected by the additive noise η. In Eq. (3.10), the weights are all equal to one $1/|W_i|$, hence, a simple boxcar filtering is carried out.

Assuming that the whole analysis window is homogeneous, either genuine ($h = k$) or forged ($h \neq k$) and, for the sake of simplicity, that y is constant over the window, so that $E[\eta_i] = \sigma_\eta^2$, we can characterize the random variable τ as

$$E[\tau] = \begin{cases} \langle k^2 \rangle_i & h = k \\ 0 & h \neq k \end{cases} \tag{3.12}$$

$$\text{VAR}[\tau] = \sigma_\eta^2 \sum_j \omega_{ij}^2 \tag{3.13}$$

where $\langle k^2 \rangle$ is the power of the camera PRNU estimated over W_i. In this condition, using uniform weights $\omega_{ij} = 1/|W_i|$ is indeed optimal, as it minimizes the variance of the estimate, and maximizes the probability of deciding correctly. However, if some of the predictor pixels are not homogeneous with the target, that is, forged instead of genuine or vice versa, the estimate will suffer a systematic bias, namely the means will not be 0 or $\langle k^2 \rangle$ anymore, but some intermediate values, heavily affecting the decision performance. In this case, the uniform weights are no more optimal, in general, and one should instead reduce the influence of heterogeneous pixels by associating a small or even null weight with them. This is exactly the problem of small-size forgeries. By using a large analysis window with fixed weights, we happen to include pixels of different nature, and the decision variable becomes strongly biased and basically useless, even in favorable (bright, smooth, and unsaturated) areas of the image. If we could find and include in the estimation only predictors homogeneous with the target, all biases would disappear, at the cost of an increased estimation variance.

The bias/variance trade-off is indeed well-known in the denoising literature. This problem has received a great deal of attention, recently, in the context of nonlocal filtering, where predictor pixels are weighted based on their expected similarity with the target. The similarity, in its turn, is typically computed by comparing patches of pixels centered on the target and the predictor pixels, respectively. This approach cannot work with our noise-like input image, rz, as it lacks the structures necessary to compute a meaningful similarity measure. However, we can take advantage of the original observed image y, using it as a "pilot" to compute similarities, and applying the resulting weights in the actual filtering of the rz field. This basic idea is implemented in [17] by means of guided filtering, a recently proposed technique which implements nonlocal filtering concepts by leveraging heavily on the use of a pilot image associated with the target image [34].

In Fig. 3.4, we show the detection performance, measured in terms of probability of detection P_D versus probability of false alarm (P_{FA}), obtained when a square forgery is placed at the center of the image. The performance obtained with the plain boxcar filter (left) and guided filtering (right) is almost the same when large forgeries are considered (128×128 pixels). However, guided filtering becomes more and more preferable as the forgeries become smaller, up to the limiting case of 48×48 pixels. This is also clear from the examples shown in Fig. 3.5, where the correlation field shows the ability of guided filtering to detect even very small forgeries, which are completely lost using boxcar filtering.

3.3 Blind Methods

Blind approaches do rely exclusively on the media asset under analysis and reveal inconsistencies with respect to some well-defined hypotheses. In particular, they look for a number of specific artifacts originated by in-camera or out-camera processing (Fig. 3.2). For example, the demosaicing algorithm is typically different for different camera models. Therefore, when a manipulation involves the composition of parts

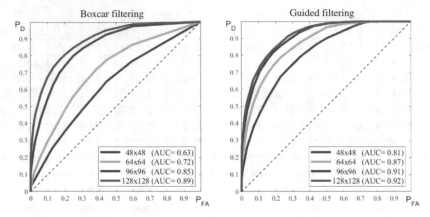

Fig. 3.4 ROCs obtained with boxcar filtering (left) and guided one (right) by varying the forgery size. Each ROC is the upper envelope of pixel-level (P_D, P_{FA}) points obtained as the algorithm parameters vary. We used a test set of 200 uncompressed 768×1024-pixel images with a square forgery at the center, drawn at random from a different image

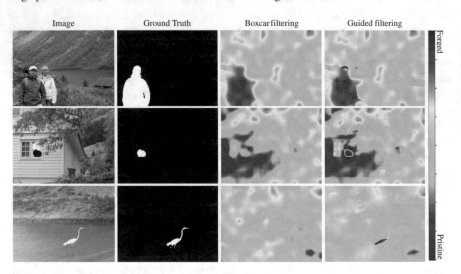

Fig. 3.5 Comparison between boxcar and guided filtering. From left to right: forged image, ground truth, and the correlation field computed using boxcar and guided filtering

of images acquired from different models, demosaicing-related spatial anomalies arise. Likewise, the out-camera editing process may introduce a specific correlation or disrupt fingerprint-like camera-specific patterns. Of course, most of these traces are very subtle and cannot be perceived at a visual inspection. However, once properly emphasized, they represent a precious source of information to establish digital integrity.

For example, most digital cameras use a color filter array (CFA), with a periodic pattern, so that each individual sensor element records light only in a certain range of wavelengths (i.e., red, green, and blue). The missing color information is then inter- polated from surrounding pixels, an operation known as demosaicing. This process introduces a subtle periodic correlation pattern in all acquired images. Whenever a manipulation occurs, this periodic pattern is perturbed. In addition, since CFA con- figuration and interpolation algorithms are specific to each camera model [8, 11], when a region is spliced in a photo taken by another camera model, its periodic pattern will appear anomalous. One of the first methods to exploit these artifacts was proposed by Popescu and Farid [57] back in 2005, based on a simple linear model to capture periodic correlations. Of course, periodic signals produce strong peaks in the Fourier domain. The problem can be also recast in a Bayesian framework, as proposed in [29], obtaining a probability map in output which allows for fine-grained localization of image tampering.

In the following, we will describe blind approaches that rely on noise patterns, compression, and editing artifacts.

3.3.1 Noise Patterns

Instead of focusing on a specific camera artifact, a more general approach is to highlight noise artifacts introduced by the whole acquisition process, irrespective of their specific origin. The analysis of *local* noise level may help reveal splicings, as shown in [50, 56], because different cameras are characterized by different intrinsic noise.

To define expressive features that are able to capture traces left locally by in- camera processing, in [23] the high-pass noise residual of the image is used and then co-occurrence-based features are extracted to capture local correlations. These features, known as rich models, are inspired by the work done in steganalysis [30], which pursue a very similar goal, i.e., detecting hidden artifacts in the signal. These features have been used successfully in a supervised learning setting for the detection task of the first IEEE IFS-TC Image Forensics Challenge [19, 20]. To form the noise residual image, r, only a linear high-pass filter of the third order has been considered of all the models proposed in [30]. In formulas

$$r_{ij} = x_{i,j-1} - 3\,x_{i,j} + 3\,x_{i,j+1} - x_{i,j+2} \tag{3.14}$$

where x and r are the original image and the noise residual, respectively, and i, j indicate spatial coordinates. The next step is to compute residual co-occurrences along the vertical and horizontal directions. First of all, residuals are quantized, using a very small number of bins to obtain a limited feature length and then truncated as

$$\widehat{r}_{ij} = \text{trunc}_T\,(\text{round}(r_{ij}/q)) \tag{3.15}$$

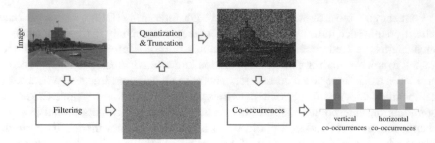

Fig. 3.6 Block diagram for computing residual co-occurrences: high-pass filtering, quantization-truncation operation, and the computation of the co-occurrence histogram

with q the quantization step and T the truncation value. Co-occurrences are computed on four pixels in a row, that is,

$$C(k_0, k_1, k_2, k_3) =$$
$$\sum_{i,j} I\left(\widehat{r}_{i,j} = k_0, \widehat{r}_{i+1,j} = k_1, \widehat{r}_{i+2,j} = k_2, \widehat{r}_{i+3,j} = k_3\right)$$

where $I(A)$ is the indicator function of event A, equal to 1 if A holds and 0 otherwise. The homologous column-wise co-occurrences are pooled with the above based on symmetry considerations. A block diagram is presented in Fig. 3.6.

Different from [30], the normalized histograms are passed through a square-root non-linearity, to obtain a final feature with unitary L2 norm. In fact, in various contexts, such as texture classification and image categorization, histogram comparison is performed by measures such as χ^2 or Hellinger that are found to work better than the Euclidean distance. After square rooting, the Euclidean distance between features is equivalent to the Hellinger distance between the original histograms. We consider two different scenarios for image forgery localization, supervised and unsupervised. In both cases, we will follow an anomaly detection rule, building a model for the host-camera features based on a fraction of the image under analysis.

- *Supervised scenario.* In this case, the user is required to select a bounding box, which will be subject to the analysis, while the rest of the image is used as a training set. In Fig. 3.7, we show some examples where some specific areas of the images are selected and then analyzed. The analysis is carried out in sliding-window modality, using blocks of size $W \times W$, from which the normalized histogram of co-occurrences, **h**, is extracted. The N blocks taken from the training area are used to estimate in advance mean μ and covariance Σ of the feature vector:

Fig. 3.7 Detecting noise artifacts in supervised modality. If a suspicion region is present, the analysis can be restricted to the region of interest (RoI), and the rest of the image is used as a reference for the pristine data

$$\mu = \frac{1}{N} \sum_{n=1}^{N} \mathbf{h_n} \qquad (3.16)$$

$$\Sigma = \frac{1}{N} \sum_{n=1}^{N} (\mathbf{h_n} - \mu)(\mathbf{h_n} - \mu)^{\mathrm{T}} \qquad (3.17)$$

Then, for each block of the test area, the associated feature $\mathbf{h}'$ is extracted, and its Mahalanobis distance w.r.t. the reference feature μ is computed

$$D(\mathbf{h}', \mu; \Sigma) = (\mathbf{h}' - \mu)^{\mathrm{T}} \Sigma^{-1}(\mathbf{h}' - \mu) \qquad (3.18)$$

Large distances indicate blocks that deviate significantly from the model. In the output map provided to the user, each block is given a color associated with the computed distance. Note that the user may repeat the process several times with different bounding boxes, implying that a meaningful analysis can be conducted even in the absence of any initial guess on the presence and location of a forgery.

- *Unsupervised scenario.* In this case, after the feature extraction phase, carried out on the whole image with unit stride, we rely on an automatic algorithm to jointly compute the model parameters and the two-class image segmentation and resort to a simple expectation-maximization (EM) clustering.

  As input, we need the mixture model of the data, namely the number of classes, their probabilities, $\pi_0, \pi_1, \ldots$, and the probability model of each class. For us, the number of classes is always fixed to two, corresponding to the genuine area of the image (hypothesis H_0) and the tampered area (hypothesis H_1). We will consider two cases for the class models:

1. both classes are modeled as multivariate Gaussian

$$p(\mathbf{h}) = \pi_0 \mathcal{N}(\mathbf{h}|\boldsymbol{\mu}_0, \boldsymbol{\Sigma}_0) + \pi_1 \mathcal{N}(\mathbf{h}|\boldsymbol{\mu}_1, \boldsymbol{\Sigma}_1)$$

2. class H_0 is modeled as Gaussian, while class H_1 is modeled as Uniform over the feature domain Ω,

$$p(\mathbf{h}) = \pi_0 \mathcal{N}(\mathbf{h}|\boldsymbol{\mu}_0, \boldsymbol{\Sigma}_0) + \pi_1 \alpha_1 \mathbf{I}(\Omega)$$

We note explicitly that the Gaussian model is only a handy simplification, lacking more precise information on the feature distribution. The first model is conceived for the case when the forged area is relatively large w.r.t. the whole image. Therefore, the two classes have the same dignity, and can be expected to emerge easily through the EM clustering. The block-wise decision statistic is the ratio between the two Mahalanobis distances.

When the forged region is very small, instead, the intra-class variability, mostly due to image content (e.g., flat vs. textured areas) may become dominant w.r.t. inter-class differences, leading to wrong results. Therefore, we consider the Gaussian-Uniform model, which can be expected to deal better with these situations, and in fact has been often considered to account for the presence of outliers, e.g., [58]. Note that, in this case, the decision test reduces to comparing the Mahalanobis distance from the Gaussian model with a threshold λ as already done in [64]. Typically, forgeries are quite small with respect to the dimension of the image and often the latter model gives more satisfying results (some examples are shown in Fig. 3.8). This idea has been extended to videos in [54] where the noise residuals of consecutive frames are analyzed and suitable features are extracted to discover traces of both intra-frame and inter-frame manipulations.

Pristine   Forged

Fig. 3.8 Detecting noise artifacts in unsupervised modality (splicebuster). A clustering algorithm is used to distinguish pristine data from forged ones

3.3.2 Compression Artifacts

Exploiting compression artifacts is a very powerful tool in image forensics. Most images are compressed using JPEG coding standard and whenever an image is edited, it will be subjected to a new compression step. An early popular approach is to exploit the so-called block artifact grid (BAG). In fact, because of the block-wise JPEG processing, discontinuities appear along the block boundaries of compressed images, giving rise to a distinctive and easily detected grid-like pattern [26]. In the presence of splicing or copy-move manipulations, the BAGs of inserted object and host image typically mismatch, enabling detection [45, 47].

Another common and very effective approach relies on double compression traces. In fact, when a JPEG-compressed image undergoes a local manipulation and is compressed again, double compression artifacts appear all over the image except in the forged region [48]. These artifacts change depending on whether the two compressions are spatially aligned or not [10, 13]. Other methods [32, 44, 55] look for anomalies in the statistical distribution of the original DCT coefficients assumed to comply with the Benford law. More specifically, this empirical law states that the probability distribution of the first digits of DCT coefficients is logarithmic:

$$p(d) = \log_{10}\left(1 + \frac{1}{d}\right) \tag{3.19}$$

If the image is modified, for example, double compressed, it will not follow anymore such distribution. In Fig. 3.9, we show an example of DCT coefficient histogram for a single compressed image and a double compressed one, together with the distribution of the first 14 AC coefficients of the DCT block.

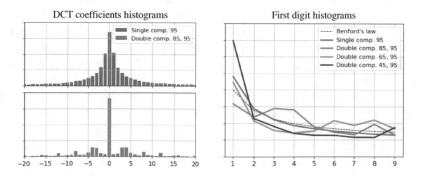

Fig. 3.9 Histograms relative to the first 14 AC coefficients in the DCT block. On the left, the histograms for single and double compression. The single compression image satisfies the Laplacian distribution; this does not happen for the double compressed image. On the right, the histograms of the first digits for single and double compressed images. In the first case, the distribution follows Benford's law, while double compressed images deviate from such distribution

Another approach relies on the so-called JPEG ghosts [27] that arise in the manipulated area when two JPEG compressions use the same quality factor (QF). To highlight ghosts, the target image is compressed at all QFs and analyzed. This approach is also at the basis of the so-called Error Level Analysis (ELA), widely used by practitioners for its simplicity. A further direction is to exploit the model-specific implementations of the JPEG standard, including customized quantization tables and post-processing steps [40]. For example, in [1] model-specific JPEG features have been defined, called JPEG dimples. These artifacts are caused by the specific procedure used when converting real to integer values, e.g., ceil, floor, and rounding operator, and represent a very discriminant clue for images saved in JPEG format.

Exploiting compression artifacts for detecting video manipulation is also possible, but it is much more difficult because of the complexity of the video coding algorithm. Traces of MPEG double compression were first highlighted in the seminal paper by Wang and Farid for detecting frame removal [65]. In fact, the de-synchronization caused by removing a group of frames introduces spikes in the Fourier transform of the motion vectors. A successive work by [62] tried to improve the double compression estimation especially in the more challenging scenario when the strength of the second compression increases and proposed a distinctive footprint, based on the variation of the macroblock prediction types in the reencoded P-frames.

3.3.3 Editing Artifacts

When an image is manipulated, for example, by adding an object, it typically needs several post-processing steps to fit the new context well. These include geometric transformations, like rotation and scaling, contrast adjustment, and blurring, to smooth the object-background boundaries. Therefore, many papers focus on detecting these basic operations as a proxy for possible forgeries. Some methods [42, 56] try to detect traces of resampling, always necessary in the presence of rotation or resizing by exploiting periodic artifacts. Other approaches focus on anomalies on the boundaries of objects when a composition is performed [25] or on blurring-related inconsistencies [3].

A very common manipulation consists in copy-moving image regions to duplicate or hide objects. Of course, the presence of identical regions is a strong hint of forgery, but clones are often modified to disguise traces, and near-identical natural objects also exist, which complicate the forensic analysis. Studies on copy-move detection date back to 2003, with the seminal work of Fridrich et al. [31]. Since then, a large amount of the literature has grown on this topic. Effective and efficient solutions are now available which allow for copy-move detection even in the presence of rotation, resizing, and other geometric distortions [18]. The common pipeline for copy-moves methods is based on three main steps (see Fig. 3.10):

- *feature extraction*: a suitable feature is computed for each pixel of interest, expressing the image behavior in its neighborhood;

Fig. 3.10 Block diagram relative to copy-move forgery detection methods. The top stream is relative to key-point-based methods, while bottom stream is relative to dense-based methods. Both methodologies have three steps: a feature extraction, a matching search, and a filtering and post-processing step

- *matching*: the best matching of each pixel is computed, based on the associated feature;
- *post-processing*: the offset field, linking pixels with their nearest neighbors, is filtered and processed in order to reduce false alarms.

Some methods [2, 61] extract image key-points and characterize them by means of suitable local descriptors, such as Scale-Invariant Feature Transform (SIFT), Speeded Up Robust Feature (SURF), Local Binary Pattern (LBP), and other variants of these local features. They are very efficient, but work only for additive forgeries, and not on occlusive ones that typically involve smooth regions. This performance gap is shown in the extensive evaluation carried out in [18] and motivates the importance to work on a block-based approach that analyzes the whole image. Of course, in this case the major problem is complexity, since all pixels undergo the three phases of feature extraction, matching, and post-processing. First of all, it is important to use features that are robust to some common forms of distortion in order to deal for example with rotated and/or rescaled duplications. Circular harmonic transforms, such as Zernike moments and polar sine and cosine transforms, are well-suited to provide rotation invariance [22, 59]. As for scale-invariance, research has mostly focused on variations of the Fourier-Mellin transform, based on a log-polar sampling.

Besides feature selection, the literature has devoted much attention to the matching step. In fact, an exhaustive search of the best matching (nearest neighbor) feature is prohibitive due to its huge complexity. A significant speed-up can be obtained by adopting some approximate nearest-neighbor search strategy, like kd-trees or locality-sensitive hashing. Nonetheless, computing the nearest-neighbor field (NNF) is too slow for the large images generated by today's cameras. A much better result can be obtained, however, by exploiting the strong regularity exhibited by the NNFs of natural images, where similar offsets are often associated with neighboring pixels, as done in PatchMatch [5], a fast randomized algorithm which finds dense approximate nearest neighbor matches between image patches. The basic algorithm described above finds only a single nearest-neighbor, and does not deal with scale changes and rotations, hence in [22] it has been proposed to add first-order predictors to the zero-order predictors used in PatchMatch, so as to deal effectively also with linear object deformations. In Fig. 3.11, we show some results of this approach that can effectively

Fig. 3.11 Examples of inpainting manipulated images with binary masks obtained using the dense-based copy-move detection algorithm proposed in [23]

deal both with additive manipulations and occlusive ones, typically carried out using inpainting methods.

Extensions to videos have been also proposed both for detection and localization [9, 24], the main issue being complexity, handled in [24] through a multi-scale processing and parallel implementation of a 3D version of the modified version of PatchMatch [22].

3.4   Learning-Based Methods with Handcrafted Features

These methods are based on machine learning and need large datasets of pristine and manipulated images. An important step is the definition of suitable features that help to discriminate between pristine and manipulated images, then a classifier is trained on a large number of examples of both types. The choice of the features depends on which type of traces one wants to discover. For example, some features have been devised to detect specific artifacts, especially those generated by double JPEG compression [14, 35, 38].

However, more precious are the *universal* features, based on suitable image statistics, which allow detecting many types of manipulations. Major efforts have been devoted to finding good statistical models for natural images in order to select the features that guarantee the highest discriminative power. In order to single out statistical fluctuations caused by manipulation operations, it is important to first remove the semantic image content, to be regarded as noise [7]. The pioneering work of Farid and Lyu [28], back in 2003, proved the potential of statistics-based features extracted from the high-pass bands of the Wavelet domain. These features capture subtle variations in the image micro-textures and prove effective in many application fields beyond image forensics. Other approaches work on residuals in the DCT domain [36] or in the spatial domain [46, 66]. Particularly effective, again, are the features extracted from the high-pass filtered version of the image and that are on the co-occurrence of selected neighbors [30] (see Fig. 3.6).

As an alternative to the two-class problem, it is also possible to learn only from pristine images and then look for possible anomalies. Since cameras of the same model share proprietary design choices for both hardware and software, they will leave similar marks on the acquired images. Therefore, in [64] it was proposed to extract local descriptors from same-model noise residuals to build a reference statistical model. Then, at test time, the same descriptors are extracted in sliding-window modality from the target noise residual and compared with the reference. Strong deviations from the reference statistics suggest the presence of a manipulation.

3.5 Conclusions

Multimedia forensics has been an active research area for a long time and many approaches have been proposed to detect classic manipulations. PRNU-based methods represent very powerful tools, however, they need a certain amount of data coming from the camera in order to reliably estimate the sensor fingerprint. In addition, it is important to note that the internal pipeline of new cameras is changing, with more sophisticated software and hardware. For example, the introduction of new coding schemes and new shooting modes makes the classic sensor noise estimation less reliable [4] and calls for new ways of detecting the camera traces.

A major appeal of blind methods is that they do not require further data besides those under test. However, methods based on very specific details depend heavily on their statistical model, and mostly fail when the hypotheses do not hold. This happens, for example, when these images are posted on social networks and undergo a global resizing and compression. The final effect is to disrupt some specific clues and impairing sharply the performance of most methods, as shown in [63]. Copy-move detectors, instead, are more reliable, even in the presence of post-processing, but can only detect cloning and some types of inpainting. On the contrary, methods based on noise patterns are quite general, and robust to post-processing, as they often do not depend on explicit statistical models but look for anomalies in the noise residual. Interestingly, many recent deep learning-based methods rely on these basic concepts [63]. For example, some of them include a constrained first layer that performs high-pass filtering of the image, in order to suppress the scene content and allow to work on residuals.

As for machine learning-based methods, they can achieve very good detection results: in the 2013 challenge the accuracy was around 94% [19]. However, performance depends heavily on the alignment between training set and test data. It is very high when training and test sets share the same cameras, same types of manipulation, same processing pipeline, like when a single dataset is split in training and test or cross-validation is used. As soon as unrelated datasets are used, the performance drops sometimes to random guesses. Lack of robustness limits the applicability of learning-based approaches to very specific scenarios.

Moreover, a skilled attacker, aware of the principles on which forensic tools work, may enact some counter-forensic measure on purpose to evade detectors [6, 33]. Therefore, the integration of multiple tools, all designed to detect the same type of attack but under different approaches, may be expected to improve performance, and especially robustness with respect to both casual and malicious disturbances. In support of this hypothesis, it is worth mentioning that the winners of the First IEEE Image Forensics Challenge resorted to the fusion of multiple tools both for the detection and the localization tasks [19, 20] and similar approaches are routinely used also for deep learning-based solutions. More in general, most of the key concepts and problems encountered in the context of AI-based forensics were already present and investigated in classical multimedia forensics, which therefore represents a necessary starting point for new advances.

Acknowledgements This material is based on research sponsored by the Defense Advanced Research Projects Agency (DARPA) and the Air Force Research Laboratory (AFRL) under agreement number FA8750-20-2-1004. The U.S. Government is authorized to reproduce and distribute reprints for Governmental purposes notwithstanding any copyright notation thereon. The views and conclusions contained herein are those of the authors and should not be interpreted as necessarily representing the official policies or endorsements, either expressed or implied, of DARPA and AFRL or the U.S. Government. This work is also supported by the PREMIER project, funded by the Italian Ministry of Education, University, and Research within the PRIN 2017 program and by a Google gift.

References

1. Agarwal S, Farid H (2017) Photo forensics from JPEG dimples. In: IEEE international workshop on information forensics and security (WIFS), pp 1–6
2. Amerini I, Ballan L, Caldelli R, Bimbo AD, Serra G (2011) A SIFT-based forensic method for copy-move attack detection and transformation recovery. IEEE Trans Inform Forensics Secur 6(3):1099–1110
3. Bahrami K, Kot A, Li L, Li H (2015) Blurred image splicing localization by exposing blur type inconsistency. IEEE Trans Inform Forensics Secur 10(5):999–1009
4. Baracchi D, Iuliani M, Nencini A, Piva A (2020) Facing image source attribution on iPhone X. In: International workshop on digital forensics and watermarking (IWDW), pp 196–207
5. Barnes C, Shechtman E, Finkelstein A, Goldman DB (2009) PatchMatch: a randomized correspondence algorithm for structural image editing. ACM Trans Graph 28(3)
6. Barni M, Stamm M, Tondi B (2018) Adversarial multimedia forensics: overview and challenges ahead. In: European signal processing conference (Eusipco), pp 962–966
7. Bayram S, Avcibaş I, Sankur B, Memon N (2006) Image manipulation detection. J Electron Imaging 15(4):1–17
8. Bayram S, Sencar H, Memon N, Avcibas I (2005) Source camera identification based on CFA interpolation. In: IEEE international conference on image processing (ICIP), pp III–69
9. Bestagini P, Milani S, Tagliasacchi M, Tubaro S (2013) Local tampering detection in video sequences. In: IEEE international workshop on multimedia signal processing (MMSP), pp 488–493

10. Bianchi T, Piva A (2012) Image forgery localization via block-grained analysis of JPEG arti-
    facts. IEEE Trans Inform Forensics Secur 7(3):1003–1017
11. Cao H, Kot A (2009) Accurate detection of demosaicing regularity for digital image forensics.
    IEEE Trans Inform Forensics Secur 4(5):899–910
12. Chakraborty S, Kirchner M (2017) PRNU-based forgery detection with discriminative random
    fields. In: International symposium on electronic imaging: media watermarking, security, and
    forensics
13. Chen YL, Hsu CT (2011) Detecting recompression of JPEG images via periodicity analysis of
    compression artifacts for tampering detection. IEEE Trans Inform Forensics Secur 6(2):396–
    406
14. Chen M, Fridrich J, Goljan M, Lukàš J (2008) Determining image origin and integrity using
    sensor noise. IEEE Trans Inform Forensics Secur 3(4):74–90
15. Chierchia G, Parrilli S, Poggi G, Sansone C, Verdoliva L (2010) On the influence of denoising
    in PRNU based forgery detection. In: ACM workshop on multimedia in forensics, security and
    intelligence, pp 117–122
16. Chierchia G, Poggi G, Sansone C, Verdoliva L (2014) A Bayesian-MRF approach for PRNU-
    based image forgery detection. IEEE Trans Inform Forensics Secur 9(4):554–567
17. Chierchia G, Cozzolino D, Poggi G, Sansone C, Verdoliva L (2014) Guided filtering for PRNU-
    based localization of small-size image forgeries. In: IEEE international conference on acoustics,
    speech and signal processing (ICASSP), pp 6231–6235
18. Christlein V, Riess C, Jordan J, Angelopoulou E (2012) An evaluation of popular copy-
    move forgery detection approaches. IEEE Transactions on Information Forensics and Security
    7(6):1841–1854
19. Cozzolino D, Gragnaniello D, Verdoliva L (2014a) Image forgery detection through residual-
    based local descriptors and block-matching. In: IEEE international conference on image pro-
    cessing (ICIP), pp 5297–5301
20. Cozzolino D, Gragnaniello D, Verdoliva L (2014b) Image forgery localization through the
    fusion of camera-based, feature-based and pixel-based techniques. In: IEEE international con-
    ference on image processing (ICIP), pp 5302–5306
21. Cozzolino D, Marra F, Poggi G, Sansone C, Verdoliva L (2017) PRNU-based forgery localiza-
    tion in a blind scenario. In: International conference on image analysis and processing (ICIAP),
    pp 569–579
22. Cozzolino D, Poggi G, Verdoliva L (2015) Efficient dense-field copy-move forgery detection.
    IEEE Trans Inform Forensics Secur 10(11):2284–2297
23. Cozzolino D, Poggi G, Verdoliva L (2015) Splicebuster: a new blind image splicing detector.
    In: IEEE international workshop on information forensics and security (WIFS), pp 1–6 (2015)
24. D'Amiano L, Cozzolino D, Poggi G, Verdoliva L (2019) A PatchMatch-based dense-field
    algorithm for video copy-move detection and localization. IEEE Trans Circ Syst Video Technol
    29(3):669–682
25. Dong J, Wang W, Tan T, Shi Y (2006) Run-length and edge statistics based approach for image
    splicing detection. In: International workshop on digital watermarking, pp 177–187
26. Fan Z, de Queiroz R (2003) Identification of bitmap compression history: JPEG detection and
    quantizer estimation. IEEE Trans Image Process 12(2):230–235
27. Farid H (2009) Exposing digital forgeries from JPEG Ghosts. IEEE Trans Inform Forensics
    Secur 4(1):154–160
28. Farid H, Lyu S (2003) Higher-order wavelet statistics and their application to digital forensics.
    In: IEEE workshop on statistical analysis in computer vision, pp 1–8
29. Ferrara P, Bianchi T, De Rosa A, Piva A (2012) Image forgery localization via fine-grained
    analysis of CFA artifacts. IEEE Trans Inform Forensics Secur 7(5):1566–1577
30. Fridrich J, Kodovsky J (2012) Rich models for steganalysis of digital images. IEEE Transactions
    on Information Forensics and Security 7:868–882
31. Fridrich J, Soukal D, Lukáš J (2003) Detection of copy-move forgery in digital images. In:
    Proceedings of the 3rd digital forensic research workshop

32. Fu D, Shi Y, Su W (2007) A generalized Benford's law for JPEG coefficients and its applications in image forensics. In: Proceedings of SPIE, security, steganography, and watermarking of multimedia contents IX, 65051L
33. Gloe T, Kirchner M, Winkler A, Böhme R (2007) Can we trust digital image forensics? In: ACM international conference on multimedia, pp 78–86
34. He K, Sun J, Tang X (2013) Guided image filtering. IEEE Trans Pattern Anal Mach Intell 35(6):1387–1409
35. He J, Lin Z, Wang L, Tang X (2006) Detecting doctored JPEG images via DCT coefficient analysis. In: European conference on computer vision (ECCV), pp 425–435
36. He Z, Lu W, Sun W, Huang J (2012) Digital image splicing detection based on Markov features in DCT and DWT domain. Pattern Recogn 45:4292–4299
37. Healey G, Kondepudy R (1994) Radiometric CCD camera calibration and noise estimation. IEEE Trans Pattern Anal Mach Intell 16(3):267–276
38. Jiang X, He P, Sun T, Xie F, Wang S (2018) Detection of double compression with the same coding parameters based on quality degradation mechanism analysis. IEEE Trans Inform Forensics Secur 13(1):170–185
39. Johnson M, Farid H (2007) Exposing digital forgeries in complex lighting environments. IEEE Trans Inform Forensics Secur 2(3):450–461
40. Kee E, Johnson M, Farid H (2011) Digital image authentication from JPEG headers. IEEE Trans Inform Forensics Secur 6(3):1066–1075
41. Kee E, O'Brien J, Farid H (2013) Exposing photo manipulation with inconsistent shadows. ACM Trans Graph 32(3):28–58
42. Kirchner M (2008) Fast and reliable resampling detection by spectral analysis of fixed linear predictor residue. In: 10th ACM workshop on multimedia and security, pp 11–20
43. Korus P, Huang J (2017) Multi-scale analysis strategies in PRNU-based tampering localization. IEEE Trans Inf Forensics Secur 12(4):809–824
44. Li B, Shi Y, Huang J (2008) Detecting doubly compressed JPEG images by using mode based first digit features. In: IEEE workshop on multimedia signal processing (MMSP), pp 730–735
45. Li W, Yuan Y, Yu N (2009) Passive detection of doctored JPEG image via block artifact grid extraction. Signal Processing 89(9):1821–1829
46. Li H, Luo W, Qiu X, Huang J (2018) Identification of various image operations using residual-based features. IEEE Trans Circ Syst Video Technol 28(1):31–45
47. Lin Z, He J, Tang X, Tang CK (2009) Fast, automatic and fine-grained tampered JPEG image detection via DCT coefficient analysis. Pattern Recognition 42(11):2492–2501
48. Lukáš J, Fridrich J (2003) Estimation of primary quantization matrix in double compressed JPEG images. In: Proceedings of the 3rd digital forensic research workshop
49. Lukàš J, Fridrich J, Goljan M (2006) Detecting digital image forgeries using sensor pattern noise. In: Proceedings of SPIE, pp 362–372
50. Lyu S, Pan X, Zhang X (2014) Exposing region splicing forgeries with blind local noise estimation. Int J Comput Vis 110(2):202–221
51. Mandelli S, Bestagini P, Tubaro S, Cozzolino D, Verdoliva L (2017) Blind detection and localization of video temporal splicing exploiting sensor-based footprints. In: European signal processing conference (EUSIPCO), pp 1362–1366
52. Milani S, Fontani M, Bestagini P, Barni M, Piva A, Tagliasacchi M, Tubaro S (2012) An overview on video forensics. APSIPA Trans Signal Inform Process 1
53. Mondaini N, Caldelli R, Piva A, Barni M, Cappellini V (2017) Detection of malevolent changes in digital video for forensic applications. In: SPIE Security, steganography, and watermarking of multimedia contents IX, pp 300–311
54. Mullan P, Cozzolino D, Verdoliva L, Riess C (2017) Residual-based forensic comparison of video sequences. In: IEEE international conference on image processing (ICIP), pp 1507–1511
55. Pasquini C, Boato G, Pèrez-Gonzàlez F (2017) Statistical detection of JPEG traces in digital images in uncompressed formats. IEEE Trans Inform Forensics Secur 12(12):2890–2905
56. Popescu A, Farid H (2004) Statistical tools for digital forensics. In: International workshop on information hiding, pp 128–147

57. Popescu A, Farid H (2005) Exposing digital forgeries in color filter array interpolated images. IEEE Trans Signal Process 53(10):3948–3959
58. Popescu A, Farid H (2005) Exposing digital forgeries by detecting traces of resampling. IEEE Trans Signal Process 53(2):758–767
59. Ryu SJ, Kirchner M, Lee MJ, Lee HK (2013) Rotation invariant localization of duplicated image regions based on Zernike moments. IEEE Trans Inform Forensics Secur 8(8):1355–1370
60. Scherhag U, Debiasi L, Rathgeb C, Busch C, Uhl A (2019) Detection of face morphing attacks based on PRNU analysis. IEEE Trans Biometr Behav Identity Sci 1(4):302–317
61. Silva E, Carvalho T, Ferreira A, Rocha A (2015) Going deeper into copy-move forgery detection: Exploring image telltales via multi-scale analysis and voting processes. J Visual Commun Image Represent 29:16–32
62. Vázquez-Padín D, Fontani M, Bianchi T, Comesana P, Piva A, Barni M (2012) Detection of video double encoding with GOP size estimation. In: IEEE international workshop on information forensics and security (WIFS), pp 151–156
63. Verdoliva L (2020) Media forensics and deepfakes: an overview. IEEE J Sel Top Signal Process 14(5):910–932
64. Verdoliva L, Cozzolino D, Poggi G (2014) A feature-based approach for image tampering detection and localization. In: IEEE international workshop on information forensics and security (WIFS), pp 149–154
65. Wang W, Farid H (2006) Exposing digital forgeries in video by detecting double MPEG compression. In: Workshop on multimedia and security, pp 37–47
66. Zhao X, Wang S, Li S, Li J, Yuan Q (2013) Image splicing detection based on noncausal Markov model. In: IEEE international conference on image processing (ICIP), pp 4462–4466

Part II
Digital Face Manipulation and Security Implications

Chapter 4
Toward the Creation and Obstruction of DeepFakes

Yuezun Li, Pu Sun, Honggang Qi, and Siwei Lyu

Abstract AI-synthesized face-swapping videos, commonly known as *DeepFakes*, is an emerging problem threatening the trustworthiness of online information. The need to develop and evaluate DeepFake detection algorithms calls for large-scale datasets. However, current DeepFake datasets suffer from low visual quality and do not resemble DeepFake videos circulated on the Internet. We present a new large-scale challenging DeepFake video dataset, *Celeb-DF*, which contains 5, 639 high-quality DeepFake videos of celebrities generated using an improved synthesis process. We conduct a comprehensive evaluation of DeepFake detection methods and datasets to demonstrate the escalated level of challenges posed by Celeb-DF. Then we introduce *Landmark Breaker*, the first dedicated method to disrupt facial landmark extraction, and apply it to the obstruction of the generation of DeepFake videos. The experiments are conducted on three state-of-the-art facial landmark extractors using our Celeb-DF dataset.

Y. Li (✉)
Ocean University of China,Qingdao, China
e-mail: liyuezun@ouc.edu.cn

P. Sun · H. Qi
University of Chinese Academy of Sciences, Beijing, China
e-mail: sunpu18@mails.ucas.ac.cn

H. Qi
e-mail: hgqi@ucas.ac.cn

S. Lyu
University at Buffalo, Buffalo, NY, USA
e-mail: siweilyu@buffalo.edu

State University of New York, Buffalo, NY, USA

© The Author(s) 2022
C. Rathgeb et al. (eds.), *Handbook of Digital Face Manipulation and Detection*,
Advances in Computer Vision and Pattern Recognition,
https://doi.org/10.1007/978-3-030-87664-7_4

4.1 Introduction

A recent twist to the disconcerting problem of online disinformation is falsified videos created by AI technologies, in particular, deep neural networks (DNNs). Although fabrication and manipulation of digital images and videos are not new [15], the use of DNNs has made the process to create convincing fake videos increasingly easier and faster.

One particular type of DNN-based fake video, commonly known as *DeepFakes*, has recently drawn much attention. In a DeepFake video, the faces of a *target* individual are replaced by the faces of a *donor* individual synthesized by DNN models, retaining the target's facial expressions and head poses. Since faces are intrinsically associated with identity, well-crafted DeepFakes can create illusions of a person's presence and activities that do not occur in reality, which can lead to serious political, social, financial, and legal consequences [10].

With the escalated concerns over DeepFakes, there is a surge of interest in developing DeepFake detection methods recently [1, 18, 29, 30, 37, 40–42, 47, 48, 61], with an upcoming dedicated global *DeepFake Detection Challenge.*[1] The availability of large-scale datasets of DeepFake videos is an enabling factor in the development of the DeepFake detection method. To date, we have the UADFV dataset [61], the DeepFake-TIMIT dataset (DF-TIMIT) [26], the FaceForensics++ dataset (FF-DF) [47][2], the Google DeepFake detection dataset (DFD) [14], and the Facebook Deep-Fake detection challenge (DFDC) dataset [12].

However, a closer look at the DeepFake videos in existing datasets reveals stark contrasts in visual quality to the actual DeepFake videos circulated on the Internet. Several common visual artifacts that can be found in these datasets are highlighted in Fig. 4.1, including low-quality synthesized faces, visible splicing boundaries, color mismatch, visible parts of the original face, and inconsistent synthesized face orientations. These artifacts are likely the result of imperfect steps of the synthesis method and the lack of curating of the synthesized videos before included in the datasets. Moreover, DeepFake videos with such low visual qualities can hardly be convincing, and are unlikely to have a real impact. Correspondingly, high detection performance on these datasets may not bear strong relevance when the detection methods are deployed *in the wild*.

In the first section, we present a new large-scale and challenging DeepFake video dataset, *Celeb-DF*,[3] for the development and evaluation of DeepFake detection algorithms. There are in total 5, 639 DeepFake videos, corresponding more than 2 million frames, in the Celeb-DF dataset. The real source videos are based on publicly available `YouTube` video clips of 59 celebrities of diverse genders, ages, and ethnic groups. The DeepFake videos are generated using an improved DeepFake synthesis method. As a result, the overall visual quality of the synthesized DeepFake videos in Celeb-DF is greatly improved when compared to existing datasets, with signifi-

---

[1] https://deepfakedetectionchallenge.ai.

[2] FaceForensics++ contains other types of fake videos. We consider only the DeepFake videos.

[3] http://www.cs.albany.edu/~lsw/celeb-deepfakeforensics.html.

Fig. 4.1 Visual artifacts of
DeepFake videos in existing
datasets. Note some common
types of visual artifacts in
these video frames,
including low-quality
synthesized faces (row 1 col
1, row 3 col 2, row 5 col 3),
visible splicing boundaries
(row 3 col 1, row 4 col 2,
row 5 col 2), color mismatch
(row 5 col 1), visible parts of
the original face (row 1 col 1,
row 2 col 1, row 4 col 3), and
inconsistent synthesized face
orientations (row 3 col 3).
This figure is best viewed in
color

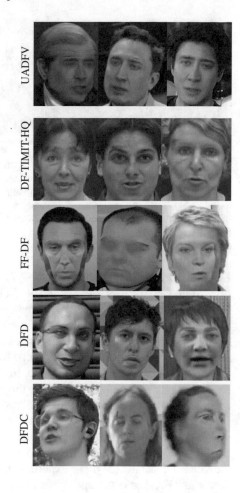

cantly fewer notable visual artifacts. Based on the Celeb-DF dataset and other existing
datasets, we conduct an evaluation of current DeepFake detection methods. This is
the most comprehensive performance evaluation of DeepFake detection methods to
date. The results show that Celeb-DF is challenging to most of the existing detection
methods, even though many DeepFake detection methods are shown to achieve high,
sometimes near perfect, accuracy on previous datasets.

In the second section, we describe a white-box method to obstruct the creation
of DeepFakes based on disrupting the facial landmark extraction, i.e., Landmark
Breaker. The facial landmarks are key locations of important facial parts including tips and middle points of eyes, nose, mouth, eyebrows as well as contours; see
Fig. 4.2. Landmark Breaker attacks the facial landmark extractors by adding adversarial perturbations [17, 54], which are image noises purposely designed to mislead DNN-based facial landmark extractors. Specifically, Landmark Breaker attacks
facial landmark heat-map prediction, which is the common first step in many recent

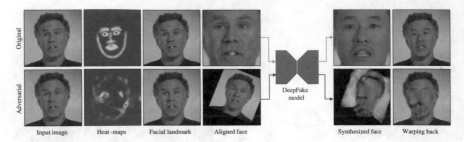

Original
Adversarial

Input image   Heat -maps   Facial landmark   Aligned face   Synthesized face   Warping back

DeepFake
model

Fig. 4.2 The overview of Landmark Breaker on obstructing DeepFake generation by disrupting the facial landmark extraction. The top row shows the original DeepFake generation, and the bottom row corresponds to the disruption after facial landmarks are disrupted. The landmark extractor we use is FAN [7] and the "Heat-maps" is visualized by summing all heat-maps. Note that training of the DeepFake generation model is also affected by disrupted facial landmarks, but is not shown here

DNN-based facial landmark extractors [7, 45, 50]. We introduce a new loss function to encourage errors between the predicted and original heat-maps to change the final locations of facial landmarks. Then we optimize this loss function using the momentum iterative fast gradient sign method (MI-FGSM) [13].

Training the DNN-based DeepFake generation model predicates on aligned input faces as training data, which are obtained by matching the facial landmarks of input face to a standard configuration. Also, in the synthesis process of DeepFakes, the facial landmarks are needed to align the input faces. As Landmark Breaker disrupts the essential face alignment step, it can effectively degrade the quality of the DeepFakes, Fig. 4.2.

We conduct experiments to test Landmark Breaker on attacking three state-of-the-art facial landmark extractors (FAN [7], HRNet [50], and AVS-SAN [45]) using the Celeb-DF dataset [31]. The experimental results demonstrate the effectiveness of Landmark Breaker in disrupting the facial landmark extraction as well as obstructing the DeepFake generation. Moreover, we perform ablation studies for different parameter settings and robustness with regards to image and video compression.

The contribution of this section is summarized as follows:

- We propose a new method to obstruct DeepFake generation by disrupting facial landmark extraction. To the best of our knowledge, this is the first study on the vulnerabilities of facial landmark extractors, as well as their application to the obstruction of DeepFake generation.
- Landmark Breaker is based on a new loss function to encourage the error between predicted and original heat-maps and optimize it using momentum iterative fast gradient sign method.
- We conduct experiments on three state-of-the-art facial landmark extractors and study the performance under different settings including video compression.

4.2 Backgrounds

4.2.1 DeepFake Video Generation

Although in recent years there have been many sophisticated algorithms for generating realistic synthetic face videos [6, 8, 11, 20, 21, 23, 27, 44, 52, 53, 55, 56], most of these have not been in the mainstream as open-source software tools that anyone can use. It is a much simpler method based on the work of neural image style transfer [32] that becomes the *tool of choice* to create DeepFake videos in scale, with several independent open-source implementations, e.g., FakeApp,[4] DFaker,[5] faceswap-GAN,[6] faceswap,[7] and DeepFaceLab.[8] We refer to this method as the *basic DeepFake maker*, and it is underneath many DeepFake videos circulated on the Internet or in the existing datasets.

The overall pipeline of the basic DeepFake maker is shown in Fig. 4.3 (left). From an input video, faces of the target are detected, from which facial landmarks are further extracted. The landmarks are used to align the faces to a standard configuration [22]. The aligned faces are then cropped and fed to an auto-encoder [25] to synthesize faces of the donor with the same facial expressions as the original target's faces.

The auto-encoder is usually formed by two convolutional neural networks (CNNs), i.e., the *encoder* and the *decoder*. The encoder E converts the input target's face to a vector known as the *code*. To ensure the encoder capture identity-independent attributes such as facial expressions, there is one single encoder regardless of the identities of the subjects. On the other hand, each identity has a dedicated decoder D_i, which generates a face of the corresponding subject from the code. The encoder and decoder are trained in tandem using uncorresponded face sets of multiple subjects in an unsupervised manner, Fig. 4.3 (right). Specifically, an encoder-decoder pair is formed alternatively using E and D_i for the input face of each subject, and to optimize their parameters to minimize the reconstruction errors (ℓ_1 difference between the input and reconstructed faces). The parameter update is performed with the backpropagation until convergence.

The synthesized faces are then warped back to the configuration of the original target's faces and trimmed with a *mask* from the facial landmarks. The last step involves smoothing the boundaries between the synthesized regions and the original video frames. The whole process is automatic and runs with little manual intervention.

---

[4] https://www.malavida.com/en/soft/fakeapp/.

[5] https://github.com/dfaker/df.

[6] https://github.com/shaoanlu/faceswap-GAN.

[7] https://github.com/deepfakes/faceswap.

[8] https://github.com/iperov/DeepFaceLab.

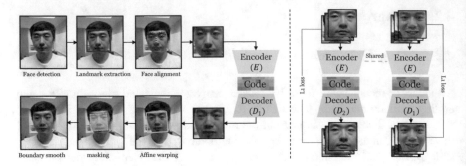

Fig. 4.3 Synthesis (left) and training (right) of the basic DeepFake maker algorithm. See texts for more details

4.2.2 DeepFake Detection Methods

Since DeepFakes become a global phenomenon, there has been an increasing interest in DeepFake detection methods. Most of the current DeepFake detection methods use data-driven deep neural networks (DNNs) as a backbone.

Since synthesized faces are spliced into the original video frames, state-of-the-art DNN splicing detection methods, e.g., [5, 33, 63, 64], can be applied. There have also been algorithms dedicated to the detection of DeepFake videos that fall into three categories. Methods in the first category are based on inconsistencies exhibited in the **physical/physiological** aspects in the DeepFake videos. The method in the work of [30] exploits the observation that many DeepFake videos lack reasonable eye blinking due to the use of online portraits as training data, which usually do not have closed eyes for aesthetic reasons. Incoherent head poses in DeepFake videos are utilized in [61] to expose DeepFake videos. In [2], the idiosyncratic behavioral patterns of a particular individual are captured by the time series of facial landmarks extracted from real videos are used to spot DeepFake videos. The second category of DeepFake detection algorithms (e.g., [29, 37]) use **signal-level** artifacts introduced during the synthesis process such as those described in the Introduction. The third category of DeepFake detection methods (e.g., [1, 18, 41, 42]) are **data-driven**, which directly employ various types of DNNs trained on real and DeepFake videos, not relying on any specific artifact.

4.2.3 Existing DeepFake Datasets

DeepFake detection methods require training data and need to be evaluated. As such, there is an increasing need for large-scale DeepFake video datasets. Table 4.1 lists the current DeepFake datasets.

Table 4.1 Basic information of various DeepFake video datasets

Dataset	# Real		# DeepFake		Release Date
	Video	Frame	Video	Frame	
UADFV	49	17.3k	49	17.3k	2018.11
DF-TIMIT-LQ	320[a]	34.0k	320	34.0k	2018.12
DF-TIMIT-HQ			320	34.0k	
FF-DF	1,000	509.9k	1,000	509.9k	2019.01
DFD	363	315.4k	3,068	2,242.7k	2019.09
DFDC	1,131	488.4k	4,113	1,783.3k	2019.10
Celeb-DF	590	225.4k	**5,639**	2,116.8k	2019.11

[a]The original videos in DF-TIMIT are from Vid-TIMIT dataset

UADFV: The UADFV dataset [61] contains 49 real `YouTube` and 49 DeepFake videos. The DeepFake videos are generated using the DNN model with `FakeAPP`.

DF-TIMIT: The DeepFake-TIMIT dataset [26] includes 640 DeepFake videos generated with `faceswap-GAN` and is based on the Vid-TIMIT dataset [49]. The videos are divided into two equal-sized subsets: DF-TIMIT-LQ and DF-TIMIT-HQ, with synthesized faces of size 64×64 and 128×128 pixels, respectively.

FF-DF: The FaceForensics++ dataset [47] includes a subset of DeepFakes videos, which has $1,000$ real `YouTube` videos and the same number of synthetic videos generated using `faceswap`.

DFD: The Google/Jigsaw DeepFake detection dataset [14] has $3,068$ DeepFake videos generated based on 363 original videos of 28 consented individuals of various genders, ages, and ethnic groups. The details of the synthesis algorithm are not disclosed, but it is likely to be an improved implementation of the basic DeepFake maker algorithm.

DFDC: The Facebook DeepFake detection challenge dataset [12] is part of the Deep-Fake detection challenge, which has $4,113$ DeepFake videos created based on $1,131$ original videos of 66 consented individuals of various genders, ages, and ethnic groups.[9] This dataset is created using two different synthesis algorithms, but the details of the synthesis algorithm are not disclosed.

Based on release time and synthesis algorithms, we categorize UADFV, DF-TIMIT, and FF-DF as the *first generation* of DeepFake datasets, while DFD, DFDC, and the proposed Celeb-DF datasets are of the *second generation*. In general, the second generation datasets improve in both quantity and quality over the first generation.

---

[9] The full set of DFDC has not been released at the time of CVPR submission, and information is based on the first-round release in [12].

4.3   Celeb-DF: the Creation of DeepFakes

The Celeb-DF dataset is comprised of 590 real videos and 5, 639 DeepFake videos (corresponding to over two million video frames). The average length of all videos is approximately 13 seconds with the standard frame rate of 30 frame-per-second. The real videos are chosen from publicly available YouTube videos, corresponding to interviews of 59 celebrities with diverse distribution in their genders, ages, and ethnic groups.[10] 56.8% subjects in the real videos are male, and 43.2% are female. 8.5% are of age 60 and above, 30.5% are between 50 and 60, 26.6% are in their 40s, 28.0% are in their 30s, and 6.4% are younger than 30. 5.1% are Asians, 6.8% are African Americans, and 88.1% are Caucasians. In addition, the real videos exhibit a large range of changes in aspects such as the subjects' face sizes (in pixels), orientations, lighting conditions, and backgrounds. The DeepFake videos are generated by swapping faces for each pair of the 59 subjects. The final videos are in MPEG4.0 format.

4.3.1   Synthesis Method

The DeepFake videos in Celeb-DF are generated using an improved DeepFake synthesis algorithm, which is key to the improved visual quality as shown in Fig. 4.4. Specifically, the basic DeepFake maker algorithm is refined in several aspects targeting the following specific visual artifacts observed in existing datasets.

Low resolution of synthesized faces: The basic DeepFake maker algorithm generates low-resolution faces (typically 64×64 or 128×128 pixels). We improve the resolution of the synthesized face to 256×256 pixels. This is achieved by using encoder and decoder models with more layers and increased dimensions. We determine the structure empirically for a balance between increased training time and better synthesis result. The higher resolution of the synthesized faces is of better visual quality and less affected by resizing and rotation operations in accommodating the input target faces, Fig. 4.5.

Color mismatch: Color mismatch between the synthesized donor's face with the original target's face in Celeb-DF is significantly reduced by training data augmentation and post- processing. Specifically, in each training epoch, we randomly perturb the colors of the training faces, which forces the DNNs to synthesize an image containing the same color pattern with the input image. We also apply a color transfer algorithm [46] between the synthesized donor face and the input target face. Figure 4.6 shows an example of the synthesized face without (left) and with (right) color correction.

---

[10] We choose celebrities' faces as they are more familiar to the viewers so that any visual artifacts can be more readily identified. Furthermore, celebrities are anecdotally the main targets of DeepFake videos.

Fig. 4.4 Example frames from the Celeb-DF dataset. The left column is the frame of real videos and the right five columns are corresponding DeepFake frames generated using different donor subject

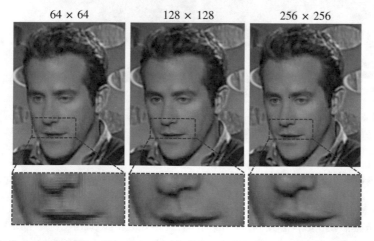

Fig. 4.5 Comparison of DeepFake frames with different sizes of the synthesized faces. Note the improved smoothness of the 256×256 synthesized face, which is used in Celeb-DF. This figure is best viewed in color

Fig. 4.6 DeepFake frames using synthesized face without (left) and with (right) color correction. Note the reduced color mismatch between the synthesized face region and the other part of the face. Synthesis method with color correction is used to generate Celeb-DF. This figure is best viewed in color

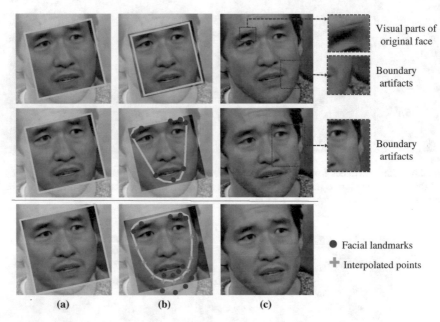

Fig. 4.7 Mask generation in existing datasets (top two rows) and Celeb-DF (third row). **a** Warped synthesized face overlaying the target's face. **b** Mask generation. **c** Final synthesis result

Inaccurate face masks: In previous datasets, the face masks are either rectangular, which may not completely cover the facial parts in the original video frame, or the convex hull of landmarks on eyebrows and lower lip, which leaves the boundaries of the mask visible. We improve the mask generation step for Celeb-DF. We first synthesize a face with more surrounding context, so as to completely cover the original facial parts after warping. We then create a smoothness mask based on the landmarks on eyebrows and interpolated points on cheeks and between lower lip and chin. The difference in mask generation used in existing datasets and Celeb-DF is highlighted in Fig. 4.7 with an example.

Temporal flickering: We reduce temporal flickering of synthetic faces in the Deep-Fake videos by incorporating temporal correlations among the detected face landmarks. Specifically, the temporal sequence of the face landmarks are filtered using a Kalman smoothing algorithm to reduce imprecise variations of landmarks in each frame.

4.3.2 Visual Quality

The refinements to the synthesis algorithm improve the visual qualities of the Deep-Fake videos in the Celeb-DF dataset, as demonstrated in Fig. 4.4. We would like to have a more quantitative evaluation of the improvement in the visual quality of the DeepFake videos in Celeb-DF and compare with the previous DeepFake datasets. Ideally, a reference-free face image quality metric is the best choice for this purpose. However, unfortunately, to date there is no such metric that is agreed upon and widely adopted.

Instead, we follow the face in-painting work [51] and use the Mask-SSIM score [36] as a referenced quantitative metric of the visual quality of synthesized DeepFake video frames. Mask-SSIM corresponds to the SSIM score [57] between the head regions (including face and hair) of the DeepFake video frame and the corresponding original video frame, i.e., the head region of the original target is the reference for visual quality evaluation. As such, low Mask-SSIM score may be due to inferior visual quality as well as changes of the identity from the target to the donor. On the other hand, since we only compare frames from DeepFake videos, the errors caused by identity changes are biased in a similar fashion to all compared datasets. Therefore, the numerical values of Mask-SSIM may not be meaningful to evaluate the absolute visual quality of the synthesized faces, but the difference between Mask-SSIM reflects the difference in visual quality.

The Mask-SSIM score takes value in the range of [0, 1] with higher value corresponding to better image quality. Table 4.2 shows the average Mask-SSIM scores for all compared datasets, with Celeb-DF having the highest scores. This confirms the visual observation that Celeb-DF has improved visual quality, as shown in Fig. 4.4.

Table 4.2 Average Mask-SSIM scores of different DeepFake datasets. Computing Mask-SSIM requires exact corresponding pairs of DeepFake-synthesized frames and original video frames, which is not the case for DFD and DFDC. For these two datasets, we calculate the Mask-SSIM on videos that we have exact correspondences for, i.e., 311 videos in DFD and 2, 025 videos in DFDC

Datasets	UADFV	DF-TIMIT		FF-DF	DFD	DFDC	**Celeb-DF**
		LQ	HQ				
Mask -SSIM	0.82	0.80	0.80	0.81	0.88	0.84	**0.92**

4.3.3 Evaluations

In Table 4.3, we list individual frame-level AUC scores of all compared DeepFake detection methods over all datasets including Celeb-DF, and Fig. 4.10 shows the frame-level ROC curves of several top detection methods on several datasets.

Comparing different datasets, in Fig. 4.8, we show the average frame-level AUC scores of all compared detection methods on each dataset. Celeb-DF is in general the most challenging to the current detection methods, and their overall performance on Celeb-DF is lowest across all datasets. These results are consistent with the differences in visual quality. Note that many current detection methods predicate on visual artifacts such as low resolution and color mismatch, which are improved in the synthesis algorithm for the Celeb-DF dataset. Furthermore, the difficulty level for detection is clearly higher for the second generation datasets (DFD, DFDC, and Celeb-DF, with average AUC scores lower than 70%), while some detection methods achieve near-perfect detection on the first generation datasets (UADFV, DF-TIMIT, and FF-DF, with average AUC scores around 80%).

In terms of individual detection methods, Fig. 4.9 shows the comparison of average AUC score of each detection method on all DeepFake datasets. These results show that detection has also made progress with the most recent DSP-FWA method achieves the overall top performance (87.4%).

As online videos are usually recompressed to different formats (MPEG4.0 and H264) and in different qualities during the process of uploading and redistribution,

Table 4.3 Frame-level AUC scores (%) of various methods on compared datasets. Bold faces correspond to the top performance

Methods↓ Datasets→	UADFV [61]	DF-TIMIT [26]		FF-DF [47]	DFD [14]	DFDC [12]	Celeb-DF
		LQ	HQ				
Two-stream [63]	85.1	83.5	73.5	70.1	52.8	61.4	53.8
Meso4 [1]	84.3	87.8	68.4	84.7	76.0	75.3	54.8
MesoInception4	82.1	80.4	62.7	83.0	75.9	73.2	53.6
HeadPose [61]	89.0	55.1	53.2	47.3	56.1	55.9	54.6
FWA [29]	97.4	99.9	93.2	80.1	74.3	72.7	56.9
VA-MLP [37]	70.2	61.4	62.1	66.4	69.1	61.9	55.0
VA-LogReg	54.0	77.0	77.3	78.0	77.2	66.2	55.1
Xception-raw [47]	80.4	56.7	54.0	**99.7**	53.9	49.9	48.2
Xception-c23	91.2	95.9	94.4	99.7	**85.9**	72.2	65.3
Xception-c40	83.6	75.8	70.5	95.5	65.8	69.7	**65.5**
Multi-task [40]	65.8	62.2	55.3	76.3	54.1	53.6	54.3
Capsule [42]	61.3	78.4	74.4	96.6	64.0	53.3	57.5
DSP-FWA	**97.7**	**99.9**	**99.7**	93.0	81.1	**75.5**	64.6

Fig. 4.8 Average AUC performance of all detection methods on each dataset

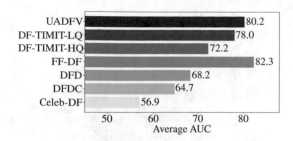

Fig. 4.9 Average AUC performance of each detection method on all evaluated datasets

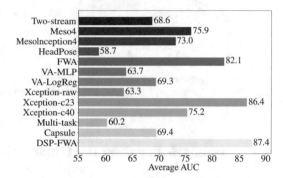

Table 4.4 AUC performance of four top detection methods on original, medium (23), and high (40) degrees of H.264 compressed Celeb-DF, respectively

	Original	c23	c40
FWA	56.9	54.6	52.2
Xception-c23	65.3	65.5	52.5
Xception-c40	65.5	65.4	59.4
DSP-FWA	64.6	57.7	47.2

it is also important to evaluate the robustness of detection performance with regards to video compression. Table 4.4 shows the average frame-level AUC scores of four state-of-the-art DeepFake detection methods on original MPEG4.0 videos, medium (23), and high (40) degrees of H.264 compressed videos of Celeb-DF, respectively. The results show that the performance of each method is reduced along with the compression degree increased. In particular, the performance of FWA and DSP-FWA degrades significantly on recompressed video, while the performance of Xception-c23 and Xception-c40 is not significantly affected. This is expected because the latter methods were trained on compressed H.264 videos such that they are more robust in this setting (Fig. 4.10).

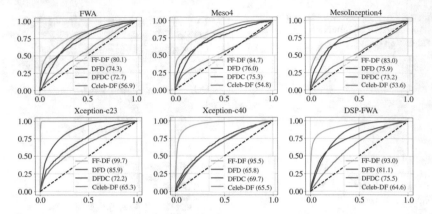

Fig. 4.10 ROC curves of six state-of-the-art detection methods (FWA, Meso4, MesoInception4, Xception-c23, Xception-40, and DSP-FWA) on four largest datasets (FF-DF, DFD, DFDC, and Celeb-DF)

4.4 Landmark Breaker: the Obstruction of DeepFakes

4.4.1 Facial Landmark Extractors

The facial landmark extractors detect and locate key points of important facial parts such as the tips of the nose, eyes, eyebrows, mouth, and jaw outline. Earlier facial landmark extractors are based on simple machine learning methods such as the ensemble of regression trees (ERT) [22] as in the Dlib package [24]. The more recent ones are based on CNN models, which have achieved significantly improved performance over the traditional methods, e.g., [7, 19, 45, 50, 58, 65]. The current CNN-based facial landmark extractors typically contain two stages of operations. In the first stage, a set of heat-maps (feature maps) are obtained to represent the spatial probability of each landmark. In the second stage, the final locations of facial landmarks are extracted based on the peaks of the heat-maps. In this work, we mainly focus on attacking the CNN -based facial landmark extractors because of their better performance.

4.4.2 Adversarial Perturbations

CNNs have been proven vulnerable against adversarial perturbations, which are intentionally crafted imperceptible noises aiming to mislead the CNN-based image classifiers [4, 17, 28, 34, 38, 39, 43, 54, 60, 62], object detectors [9, 59], and semantic segmentation [3, 16]. There are two attack settings: white-box attack, where the attackers can access the details of CNNs, and black-box attack, where the attackers do not know the details of CNNs. However, to date, there is no existing work to attack CNN-based facial landmark extractors using adversarial perturbations. Compared to the attack to image CNN-based classifiers, which aims to change the prediction of a single label, disturbing facial landmark extractors are more challenging as we need to simultaneously perturb the spatial probabilities of multiple facial landmarks to make the attack effective.

4.4.3 Notation and Formulation

Let $\mathbf{F}$ denote the mapping function of a CNN-based landmark extractor of which the parameters we have access to, and $\{h_1, \cdots, h_k\} = \mathbf{F}(\mathbf{I})$ be the set of heat-maps of running $\mathbf{F}$ on input image $\mathbf{I}$. Our goal is to find an image $\mathbf{I}^{adv}$, which can lead the prediction of landmark locations to a large error, while visually similar to as original image $\mathbf{I}$. The difference $\mathbf{I}^{adv} - \mathbf{I}$ is the adversarial perturbation. We denote the heat-maps from the perturbed image as $\{\hat{h}_1, \cdots, \hat{h}_k\} = \mathbf{F}(\mathbf{I}^{adv})$.

To this end, we introduce a loss function that aims to enlarge the error between predicted heat-maps and original heat-maps while constraining the pixel distortion in a certain budget as

$$
\begin{aligned}
\operatorname{argmin}_{\mathbf{I}^{adv}} L(\mathbf{I}^{adv}, \mathbf{I}) &= \sum_{i=1}^{k} \frac{h_i^\top \hat{h}_i}{\|h_i\| \|\hat{h}_i\|}, \\
s.t. \ \|\mathbf{I}^{adv} - \mathbf{I}\|_\infty &\leq \epsilon,
\end{aligned} \tag{4.1}
$$

where ϵ is a constant. We use cosine distance to measure the error as it can naturally normalize the loss range in $[-1, 1]$. Minimizing this loss function increases the error between predicted and original heat-maps, which will disrupt the facial landmark locations.

4.4.4 Optimization

We use the gradient MI-FGSM [13] method to optimize problem Eq.(4.1). Specifically, let t denote the iteration number and $\mathbf{I}_t^{adv}$ denote the adversarial image obtained at iteration t. The start image is initialized as $\mathbf{I}_0^{adv} = \mathbf{I}$. $\mathbf{I}_{t+1}^{adv}$ is obtained by considering the momentum and gradient as

$$
\begin{aligned}
m_{t+1} &= \lambda \cdot m_t + \frac{\nabla_{\mathbf{I}^{adv}}(L(\mathbf{I}_t^{adv}, \mathbf{I}))}{\|\nabla_{\mathbf{I}^{adv}}(L(\mathbf{I}_t^{adv}, \mathbf{I}))\|_1}, \\
\mathbf{I}_{t+1}^{adv} &= \texttt{clip}\{\mathbf{I}_t^{adv} - \alpha \cdot \texttt{sign}(m_{t+1})\},
\end{aligned} \tag{4.2}
$$

where $\nabla_{\mathbf{I}^{adv}}(L(\mathbf{I}_t^{adv}, \mathbf{I}))$ is the gradient of L with respect to the input image $\mathbf{I}_t^{adv}$ at iteration t; m_t is the accumulated gradient and λ is the decay factor of momentum; α is the step size and $\texttt{sign}$ returns the signs of each component of the input vector;

clip is the truncation function to ensure the pixel value of the resulting image is in [0, 255]. The algorithm stops when the maximum number of iterations T is reached or the distortion threshold ϵ is reached. The overall algorithm is given in Algorithm 1.

Algorithm 1 *Overview of Landmark Breaker*

Require: landmark extractor $\mathbf{F}$; input image $\mathbf{I}$; perturbed image $\mathbf{I}^{adv}$; maximal iteration number T
1: $\mathbf{I}_0^{adv} = \mathbf{I}, t = 0, m_0 = 0$
2: **while** $t \leq T$ and $||\mathbf{I}_{t+1}^{adv} - \mathbf{I}||_\infty \leq \epsilon$ **do**
3:     $m_{t+1} = \lambda \cdot m_t + \frac{\nabla_{\mathbf{I}^{adv}}(L(\mathbf{I}_t^{adv},\mathbf{I}))}{||\nabla_{\mathbf{I}^{adv}}(L(\mathbf{I}_t^{adv},\mathbf{I}))||_1}$,
4:     $\mathbf{I}_{t+1}^{adv} = \text{clip}\{\mathbf{I}_t^{adv} - \alpha \cdot \text{sign}(m_{t+1})\}$
5:     $t = t + 1$
Ensure: Adversarial perturbed image $\mathbf{I}_t^{adv}$

4.4.5 Experimental Settings

Landmark Extractors. Landmark Breaker is validated on three state-of-the-art CNN-based facial landmark extractors, namely FAN [7], HRNet [50], and AVS-SAN [45]. FAN[11] is constructed by multiple stacked hourglass structures, where we use one hourglass structure for simplicity. HRNet[12] is composed by parallel high-to-low resolution sub-networks and repeats the information exchange across multi-resolution sub-networks. AVS-SAN[13] first disentangles face images to style and structure space, which is then used as augmentation to train the network. We use implementations of all three methods trained on WLFW dataset [58].

Datasets. To demonstrate the effectiveness of Landmark Breaker on obstructing DeepFake generation, we conduct experiments on the Celeb-DF dataset [31], which contains high-quality DeepFake videos of 59 celebrities. Each video contains one subject with various head poses and facial expressions. We choose this dataset as the pretrained DeepFake models are available to us, which can be used to test our method.

In our experiment, we utilize the DeepFake method described in [31] to synthesize fake videos using original and adversarial images, respectively. We randomly select 6 identities, corresponding to 36 videos in total. Since the adjacent frames in a video show little variations, we apply Landmark Breaker to the key frames of each video, i.e., 600 frames in total, for evaluation. Since the Celeb-DF dataset does not have the ground truth of facial landmarks, we use the results of HRNet as the ground truth due to its superior performance.

---

[11] https://github.com/hzh8311/pyhowfar.

[12] https://github.com/HRNet/HRNet-Facial-Landmark-Detection.

[13] https://github.com/TheSouthFrog/stylealign.

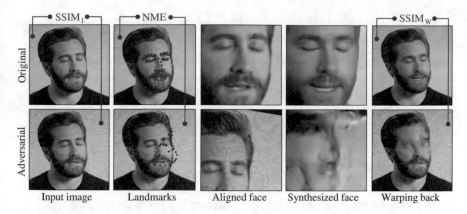

Fig. 4.11 Evaluation pipeline. $SSIM_I$ denotes the image quality of the adversarial image referred to as the original image, while $SSIM_W$ denotes the image quality of the corresponding synthesized image. NME denotes the distance of facial landmarks on adversarial image and ground truth

Evaluations. We use two metrics to evaluate Landmark Breaker, namely Normalized Mean Error (NME) [50] and Structural Similarity (SSIM) [57]. The relation of these metrics are shown in Fig. 4.11.

- NME is the average Euclidean distance between landmarks on adversarial image and the ground truth, which is then normalized by the distance between the leftmost key point in the left eye and the rightmost key point in the right eye. Higher NME score indicates less accurate landmark detection, which is the objective of Landmark Breaker.
- The SSIM metric simulates perceptual image quality. We use this indicator to demonstrate that Landmark Breaker can affect the visual quality of DeepFake. As shown in Fig. 4.11, we compute SSIM of original and adversarial input images $(SSIM_I)$[14] and then compute the SSIM of the synthesized results $(SSIM_W)$. The lower score indicates the image quality is degraded. Ideally, the attacking method should have large $SSIM_I$ such that the adversarial perturbation does not affect the quality of input image, and small $SSIM_W$ such that the synthesis quality is degraded.

Baselines. To better analyze Landmark Breaker, we adapt other two methods FGSM [54] and I-FGSM [17] from attacking image classifiers to our task. Specifically, the FGSM is a single-step optimization method as $\mathbf{I}_1^{adv} = \texttt{clip}\{\mathbf{I}_0^{adv} - \alpha \cdot \texttt{sign}(\nabla_{\mathbf{I}_0^{adv}}(L(\mathbf{I}_0^{adv}, \mathbf{I})))\}$, while I-FGSM is an iterative optimization method without considering momentum as $\mathbf{I}_{t+1}^{adv} = \texttt{clip}\{\mathbf{I}_t^{adv} - \alpha \cdot \texttt{sign}(\nabla_{\mathbf{I}^{adv}}(L(\mathbf{I}_t^{adv}, \mathbf{I})))\}$. The step size α and iteration number T of I-FGSM are set as the same in Landmark

---

[14] We employ mask-SSIM [36] to measure the quality inside a region of interest determined by face detection.

Breaker. We use these two adapted methods as our baseline methods, which are denoted as *Base1* and *Base2*, respectively.

Implementation Details. Following the previous works [35, 60], we set the maximum perturbation budget $\epsilon = 15$. The other parameters in Landmark Breaker are set as follows: The maximum iteration number $T = 20$; the step size $\alpha = 1$; the decay factor is set as $\lambda = 0.5$.

4.4.6 Results

Table 4.5 shows the NME and SSIM performance of Landmark Breaker. The landmark extractors shown in the leftmost column denote where the adversarial perturbation is from and the ones shown in the top row denotes which landmark extractor is attacked. "None" denotes no perturbations are added to the image. Landmark Breaker can notably increase the NME score and decrease the $SSIM_W$ score in white-box attack (e.g., the value in the row of "FAN" and the column of "FAN"), which indicates Landmark Breaker can effectively disrupt facial landmark extraction and subsequently affect the visual quality of the synthesized faces. We also compare Landmark Breaker with two baselines Base1 and Base2 in Table 4.6. We can observe the Base1 method merely has any effect on the NME performance but can largely degrade the quality of adversarial images compared to Base2 and Landmark Breaker (LB). The Base2 method can also achieve the competitive performance with Landmark Breaker in NME but is slightly degraded in SSIM.

Following existing works attacking image classifiers, [13, 54], which achieves the black-box attack by transferring the adversarial perturbations from a known model to an unknown model (transferability), we also test the black-box attack using the adversarial perturbation generated from one landmark extractor to attack other extractors. However, the results show that the adversarial perturbations have merely any effect on different extractors.

As shown in Table 4.5, the transferability of Landmark Breaker is weak. To improve the transferability, we employ the strategies commonly used in black-box attacks on image classifiers: (1) Input transformation [60]: we randomly resize the input image and then pad around with zero at each iteration (denoted as LB_{trans}); (2) Attacking mixture [60]: we alternatively use Base2 and Landmark Breaker to increase the diversity in optimization (denoted as LB_{mix}). Table 4.7 shows the results of a black-box attack, which reveals that the strategies effective in attacking image classifiers do not work on attacking landmark extractors. This is probably due to the mechanism of landmark extractors being more complex than image classifiers, as the landmark extractors need to output a series of points instead of labels, and only a minority of points shifted do not affect the overall prediction.

Table 4.5 The NME and SSIM scores of Landmark Breaker on different landmark extractors. The landmark extractors shown in leftmost column denote where the adversarial perturbation is from and the ones shown in the top row denote which landmark extractors are attacked

NME↑

Attacks	FAN	HRNet	AVS-SAN
None	0.03	0.00	0.09
FAN	0.87	0.05	0.09
HRNet	0.04	0.87	0.09
AVS-SAN	0.06	0.04	0.92

SSIM

Attacks	$SSIM_I$ ↑	$SSIM_W$ ↓		
		FAN	HRNet	AVS-SAN
FAN	0.81	0.68	0.89	0.89
HRNet	0.78	0.89	0.67	0.88
AVS-SAN	0.78	0.87	0.87	0.69

Table 4.6 The NME and SSIM performance of different attacking methods

NME↑

Attacks	FAN	HRNet	AVS-SAN
None	0.03	0.00	0.09
Base1	0.05	0.04	0.10
Base2	0.85	0.88	0.92
LB	0.87	0.87	0.92

$SSIM_I$ ↑ / $SSIM_W$ ↓

Attacks	FAN	HRNet	AVS-SAN
Base1	0.52/0.73	0.46/0.71	0.49/0.69
Base2	0.88/0.71	0.88/0.70	0.86/0.73
LB	0.81/0.68	0.78/0.67	0.78/0.69

4.4.7   Robustness Analysis

We study the robustness of Landmark Breaker toward three extractors under image and video compression. Note that image compression considers the spatial correlation, while video compression also considers the temporal correlation.

Image compression. We compress the adversarial images to quality 75% (Q75) and 50% (Q50) using OpenCV and then observe the variations in the performance of each method. Table 4.8 shows the NME and SSIM performance of each method under

Table 4.7 The NME and SSIM performance of black-box attack. See text for details

NME↑

Attacks		FAN	HRNet	AVS-SAN
None		0.03	0.00	0.09
FAN	LB_{trans}	0.22	0.03	0.09
	LB_{mix}	0.24	0.04	0.09
HRNet	LB_{trans}	0.04	0.10	0.09
	LB_{mix}	0.04	0.14	0.09
AVS-SAN	LB_{trans}	0.04	0.03	0.55
	LB_{mix}	0.05	0.03	0.56

SSIM

Attacks		$SSIM_I$ ↑	$SSIM_W$ ↓		
			FAN	HRNet	AVS-SAN
FAN	LB_{trans}	0.91	0.88	0.94	0.94
	LB_{mix}	0.90	0.86	0.94	0.93
HRNet	LB_{trans}	0.92	0.95	0.94	0.95
	LB_{mix}	0.90	0.95	0.91	0.94
AVS-SAN	LB_{trans}	0.89	0.94	0.93	0.82
	LB_{mix}	0.88	0.93	0.93	0.81

different compression levels. Compared to the two baseline methods, Landmark Breaker is more robust against image compression. Another observation is that the attacks on AVS-SAN exhibit high robustness, where the performance of NME and SSIM is only slightly degraded. In contrast, the attacking performance on HRNet drops quickly with compression. Figure 4.12 (left) plots the trend of each method.

Video compression. As the videos are widespread on the Internet, we also investigate the robustness against video compression. We create a video using the adversarial images using the codec in MPEG4 (denoted as C) and then separate the videos into frames to test the performance. We also perform double compression to the MPEG4 videos using the codec in H264 (denoted as C^2). Table 4.8 also shows the performance against video compression, which has the same trend as in image compression. Compared to the baseline methods, Landmark Breaker is more robust. Also, the attacks on AVS-SAN exhibit strong robustness even after double compression C^2, on the other hand, the attacks on HRNet are vulnerable against video compression; see Fig. 4.12 (right). Note the curve of Base1 and LB are fully overlapped in the last plot.

Table 4.8 The NME and SSIM performance of different attacking methods under different image compression (IC) and video compression (VC) levels

NME↑

		Attacks	FAN	HRNet	AVS-SAN
	None	Base1	0.05	0.04	0.10
		Base2	0.85	0.88	0.92
		LB	0.87	0.87	0.92
IC	Q75	Base1	0.05	0.04	0.10
		Base2	0.64	0.10	0.90
		LB	0.77	0.24	0.91
	Q50	Base1	0.05	0.03	0.10
		Base2	0.50	0.05	0.88
		LB	0.70	0.10	0.89
VC	C	Base1	0.05	0.03	0.10
		Base2	0.44	0.10	0.88
		LB	0.72	0.41	0.90
	C^2	Base1	0.05	0.03	0.10
		Base2	0.26	0.06	0.83
		LB	0.60	0.20	0.89

$SSIM_I$ ↑ / $SSIM_W$ ↓

		Attacks	FAN	HRNet	AVS-SAN
	None	Base1	0.52/0.73	0.46/0.71	0.49/0.69
		Base2	0.88/0.71	0.88/0.70	0.86/0.73
		LB	0.81/0.68	0.78/0.67	0.78/0.69
IC	Q75	Base1	0.56/0.75	0.47/0.72	0.51/0.71
		Base2	0.90/0.74	0.93/0.94	0.87/0.74
		LB	0.84/0.70	0.85/0.85	0.80/0.70
	Q50	Base1	0.59/0.76	0.55/0.75	0.52/0.71
		Base2	0.89/0.76	0.93/0.95	0.87/0.74
		LB	0.84/0.71	0.88/0.92	0.80/0.70
VC	C	Base1	0.57/0.76	0.52/0.74	0.52/0.71
		Base2	0.90/0.78	0.92/0.94	0.87/0.74
		LB	0.84/0.71	0.84/0.79	0.80/0.71
	C^2	Base1	0.58/0.76	0.52/0.74	0.53/0.72
		Base2	0.91/0.85	0.93/0.95	0.88/0.76
		LB	0.85/0.73	0.84/0.87	0.82/0.72

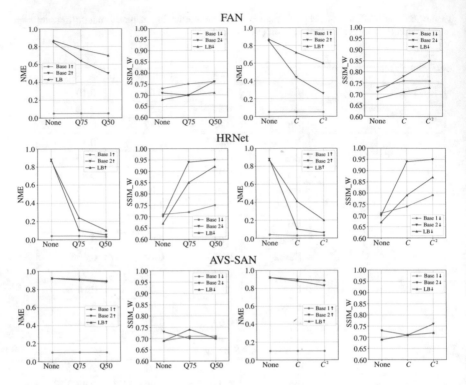

Fig. 4.12 The performance of each method on different landmark extractors under image and video compression

4.4.8 Ablation Study

This section presents ablation studies on the impact of different parameters on Landmark Breaker.

Step size. We study the impact of step size α on the performance of NME and SSIM scores. We set the step size α from 0.5 to 1.5. The results are plotted in Fig. 4.13. We observe that the NME score increases first and then decreases, which is because the small step size does not disturb the image enough within the maximum iteration number and then the large step size may not precisely follow the gradient descent direction. Moreover, a larger step size can degrade the input image quality, which also leads to the degradation of the synthesized image.

Maximum iteration number. We then study the impact of the maximum iteration number T on the performance of NME and SSIM. We vary the maximum iteration number T from 14 to 28 and illustrate the results in Fig. 4.13. From the figure, we observe that the NME score is increased and SSIM is decreased with iteration number

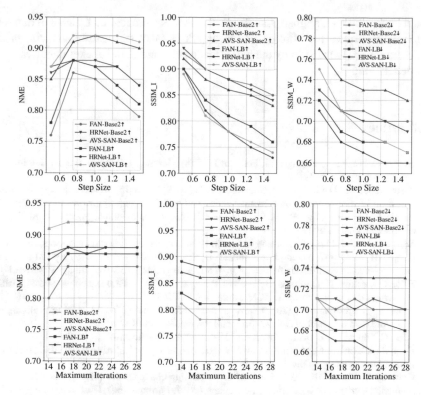

Fig. 4.13 Ablation study of Landmark Breaker regarding the performance with different step sizes and iteration numbers

increasing. Since the distortion budget constraint, the curve becomes flat after about 17 iterations. Note that several curves are fully overlapped in the plot.

4.5 Conclusion

This chapter describes our recent efforts toward the creation and obstruction of Deep-Fakes. Section 4.1 describes a new challenging large-scale dataset for the development and evaluation of DeepFake detection methods. The Celeb-DF dataset reduces the gap in the visual quality of DeepFake datasets and the actual DeepFake videos circulated online. Based on the Celeb-DF dataset, we perform a comprehensive performance evaluation of current DeepFake detection methods, and show that there is still much room for improvement. Section 4.2 describes a new method, namely Landmark Breaker, to obstruct the DeepFake generation by breaking the prerequisite step—facial landmark extraction. To do so, we create the adversarial perturbations to disrupt the facial landmark extraction, such that the input faces to the DeepFake model cannot be well aligned. Landmark Breaker is validated on Celeb-DF dataset, which demonstrates the efficacy of Landmark Breaker on disturbing facial landmark extraction. We also study the performance of Landmark Breaker under various parameter settings.

References

1. Afchar D, Nozick V, Yamagishi J, Echizen I (2018) Mesonet: a compact facial video forgery detection network. In: WIFS
2. Agarwal S, Farid H, Gu Y, He M, Nagano K, Li H (2019) Protecting world leaders against deep fakes. In: IEEE conference on computer vision and pattern recognition workshops (CVPRW)
3. Arnab A, Miksik O, Torr PH (2018) On the robustness of semantic segmentation models to adversarial attacks. In: CVPR
4. Baluja S, Fischer I (2018) Learning to attack: Adversarial transformation networks. In: AAAI
5. Bappy JH, Simons C, Nataraj L, Manjunath B, Roy-Chowdhury AK (2019) Hybrid lstm and encoder-decoder architecture for detection of image forgeries. IEEE Trans Image Process (TIP)
6. Bitouk D, Kumar N, Dhillon S, Belhumeur P, Nayar SK (2008) Face swapping: automatically replacing faces in photographs. ACM Trans Graph (TOG)
7. Bulat A, Tzimiropoulos G (2017) How far are we from solving the 2d & 3d face alignment problem? (and a dataset of 230,000 3d facial landmarks). In: ICCV
8. Chan C, Ginosar S, Zhou T, Efros AA (2019) Everybody dance now. In: ICCV
9. Chen ST, Cornelius C, Martin J, Chau DH (2018) Robust physical adversarial attack on faster r-cnn object detector. arXiv:180405810
10. Chesney R, Citron DK (2018) Deep fakes: a looming challenge for privacy, democracy, and national security. 107 California Law Review (2019, Forthcoming); U of Texas Law, Public Law Research Paper No 692; U of Maryland Legal Studies Research Paper No 2018-21
11. Dale K, Sunkavalli K, Johnson MK, Vlasic D, Matusik W, Pfister H (2011) Video face replacement. ACM Trans Graph (TOG)
12. Dolhansky B, Howes R, Pflaum B, Baram N, Ferrer CC (2019) The deepfake detection challenge (DFDC) preview dataset. arXiv:191008854
13. Dong Y, Liao F, Pang T, Su H, Zhu J, Hu X, Li J (2018) Boosting adversarial attacks with momentum. In: CVPR
14. Dufour N, Gully A, Karlsson P, Vorbyov AV, Leung T, Childs J, Bregler C (2019-09) Deepfakes detection dataset by google & jigsaw
15. Farid H (2012) Digital image forensics. MIT Press
16. Fischer V, Kumar MC, Metzen JH, Brox T (2017) Adversarial examples for semantic image segmentation. arXiv:170301101
17. Goodfellow IJ, Shlens J, Szegedy C (2015) Explaining and harnessing adversarial examples. In: ICLR
18. Güera D, Delp EJ (2018) Deepfake video detection using recurrent neural networks. In: AVSS
19. Hu T, Qi H, Xu J, Huang Q (2018) Facial landmarks detection by self-iterative regression based landmarks-attention network. In: AAAI
20. Karras T, Aila T, Laine S, Lehtinen J (2018) Progressive growing of GANs for improved quality, stability, and variation. In: ICLR
21. Karras T, Laine S, Aila T (2019) A style-based generator architecture for generative adversarial networks. In: CVPR
22. Kazemi V, Sullivan J (2014) One millisecond face alignment with an ensemble of regression trees. In: CVPR
23. Kim H, Garrido P, Tewari A, Xu W, Thies J, Nießner N, Pérez P, Richardt C, Zollhöfer M, Theobalt C (2018) Deep video portraits. ACM Trans Graph 2018 (TOG)

24. King DE (2009) Dlib-ml: A machine learning toolkit. JMLR
25. Kingma DP, Welling M (2014) Auto-encoding variational bayes. In: ICLR
26. Korshunov P, Marcel S (2018) Deepfakes: a new threat to face recognition? assessment and detection. arXiv:181208685
27. Korshunova I, Shi W, Dambre J, Theis L (2017) Fast face-swap using convolutional neural networks. In: ICCV
28. Kurakin A, Goodfellow I, Bengio S (2017) Adversarial machine learning at scale. In: ICLR
29. Li Y, Lyu S (2019) Exposing deepfake videos by detecting face warping artifacts. In: CVPR Workshops
30. Li Y, Chang MC, Lyu S (2018) In ictu oculi: exposing AI generated fake face videos by detecting eye blinking. In: WIFS
31. Li Y, Yang X, Sun P, Qi H, Lyu S (2020) Celeb-df: a large-scale challenging dataset for deepfake forensics. In: CVPR
32. Liu MY, Breuel T, Kautz J (2017) Unsupervised image-to-image translation networks. In: NeurIPS
33. Liu Y, Guan Q, Zhao X, Cao Y (2018) Image forgery localization based on multi-scale convolutional neural networks. In: ACM workshop on information hiding and multimedia security (IHMMSec)
34. Luo B, Liu Y, Wei L, Xu Q (2018) Towards imperceptible and robust adversarial example attacks against neural networks. In: AAAI
35. Luo Y, Boix X, Roig G, Poggio T, Zhao Q (2015) Foveation-based mechanisms alleviate adversarial examples. arXiv:151106292
36. Ma L, Jia X, Sun Q, Schiele B, Tuytelaars T, Van Gool L (2017) Pose guided person image generation. In: NeurIPS
37. Matern F, Riess C, Stamminger M (2019) Exploiting visual artifacts to expose deepfakes and face manipulations. In: WACV Workshops
38. Moosavi-Dezfooli SM, Fawzi A, Frossard P (2016) Deepfool: a simple and accurate method to fool deep neural networks. In: CVPR
39. Moosavi-Dezfooli SM, Fawzi A, Fawzi O, Frossard P (2017) Universal adversarial perturbations. In: CVPR
40. Nguyen HH, Fang F, Yamagishi J, Echizen I (2019) Multi-task learning for detecting and segmenting manipulated facial images and videos. In: IEEE international conference on biometrics: theory, applications and systems (BTAS)
41. Nguyen HH, Yamagishi J, Echizen I (2019) Capsule-forensics: using capsule networks to detect forged images and videos. In: IEEE international conference on acoustics, speech and signal processing (ICASSP)
42. Nguyen HH, Yamagishi J, Echizen I (2019) Use of a capsule network to detect fake images and videos. arXiv:191012467
43. Papernot N, McDaniel P, Jha S, Fredrikson M, Celik ZB, Swami A (2016) The limitations of deep learning in adversarial settings. In: EuroS&P
44. Pham HX, Wang Y, Pavlovic V (2018) Generative adversarial talking head: bringing portraits to life with a weakly supervised neural network. arXiv:180307716
45. Qian S, Sun K, Wu W, Qian C, Jia J (2019) Aggregation via separation: boosting facial landmark detector with semi-supervised style translation. In: ICCV
46. Reinhard E, Adhikhmin M, Gooch B, Shirley P (2001) Color transfer between images. IEEE Comput Graph Appl
47. Rössler A, Cozzolino D, Verdoliva L, Riess C, Thies J, Nießner M (2019) FaceForensics++: learning to detect manipulated facial images. In: ICCV
48. Sabir E, Cheng J, Jaiswal A, AbdAlmageed W, Masi I, Natarajan P (2019) Recurrent-convolution approach to deepfake detection-state-of-art results on faceforensics++. arXiv:190500582
49. Sanderson C, Lovell BC (2009) Multi-region probabilistic histograms for robust and scalable identity inference. In: International conference on biometrics

50. Sun K, Xiao B, Liu D, Wang J (2019) Deep high-resolution representation learning for human pose estimation. In: CVPR
51. Sun Q, Ma L, Joon Oh S, Van Gool L, Schiele B, Fritz M (2018) Natural and effective obfuscation by head inpainting. In: CVPR
52. Suwajanakorn S, Seitz SM, Kemelmacher-Shlizerman I (2015) What makes tom hanks look like tom hanks. In: ICCV
53. Suwajanakorn S, Seitz SM, Kemelmacher-Shlizerman I (2017) Synthesizing obama: learning lip sync from audio. ACM Trans Graph (TOG)
54. Szegedy C, Zaremba W, Sutskever I, Bruna J, Erhan D, Goodfellow I, Fergus R (2014) Intriguing properties of neural networks. In: ICLR
55. Thies J, Zollhofer M, Stamminger M, Theobalt C, Niessner M (2016) Face2face: real-time face capture and reenactment of rgb videos. In: CVPR
56. Thies J, Zollhöfer M, Nießner M (2019) Deferred neural rendering: image synthesis using neural textures. In: SIGGRAPH
57. Wang Z, Bovik AC, Sheikh HR, Simoncelli EP, et al. (2004) Image quality assessment: from error visibility to structural similarity. TIP
58. Wu W, Qian C, Yang S, Wang Q, Cai Y, Zhou Q (2018) Look at boundary: a boundary-aware face alignment algorithm. In: CVPR
59. Xie C, Wang J, Zhang Z, Zhou Y, Xie L, Yuille A (2017) Adversarial examples for semantic segmentation and object detection. In: ICCV
60. Xie C, Zhang Z, Zhou Y, Bai S, Wang J, Ren Z, Yuille AL (2019) Improving transferability of adversarial examples with input diversity. In: CVPR
61. Yang X, Li Y, Lyu S (2019) Exposing deep fakes using inconsistent head poses. In: ICASSP
62. Zeng X, Liu C, Wang YS, Qiu W, Xie L, Tai YW, Tang CK, Yuille AL (2019) Adversarial attacks beyond the image space. In: CVPR
63. Zhou P, Han X, Morariu VI, Davis LS (2017) Two-stream neural networks for tampered face detection. In: IEEE conference on computer vision and pattern recognition workshops (CVPRW)
64. Zhou P, Han X, Morariu VI, Davis LS (2018) Learning rich features for image manipulation detection. In: CVPR
65. Zou X, Zhong S, Yan L, Zhao X, Zhou J, Wu Y (2019) Learning robust facial landmark detection via hierarchical structured ensemble. In: ICCV

Chapter 5
The Threat of Deepfakes to Computer and Human Visions

Pavel Korshunov and Sébastien Marcel

Abstract Deepfake videos, where a person's face is automatically swapped with a face of someone else, are becoming easier to generate with more realistic results. The concern for the impact of the widespread deepfake videos on the societal trust in video recordings is growing. In this chapter, we demonstrate how dangerous deepfakes are for both human and computer visions by showing how well these videos can fool face recognition algorithms and naïve human subjects. We also show how well the state-of-the-art deepfake detection algorithms can detect deepfakes and whether they can outperform humans.

5.1 Introduction

Recent advances in automated video and audio editing tools, generative adversarial networks (GANs), and social media allow creation and fast dissemination of high-quality tampered video content. Such content already led to appearance of deliberate misinformation, coined "fake news," which is impacting political landscapes of several countries [3]. A recent surge of videos, often obscene, in which a face can be swapped with someone else's using neural networks, so-called Deepfakes,[1] are of a great public concern.[2] Accessible open-source software and apps for such face swapping (see Fig. 5.1 for illustration of the process) lead to large amounts of synthetically generated deepfake videos appearing in social media and news, posing a significant technical challenge for detection and filtering of such content. Some of the latest

---

[1] Open source: https://github.com/deepfakes/faceswap.
[2] BBC (Feb 3, 2018): http://www.bbc.com/news/technology-42912529.

P. Korshunov (✉) · S. Marcel
Idiap Research Institute, Martigny, Switzerland
e-mail: pavel.korshunov@idiap.ch

S. Marcel
e-mail: sebastien.marcel@idiap.ch

© The Author(s) 2022
C. Rathgeb et al. (eds.), *Handbook of Digital Face Manipulation and Detection*,
Advances in Computer Vision and Pattern Recognition,
https://doi.org/10.1007/978-3-030-87664-7_5

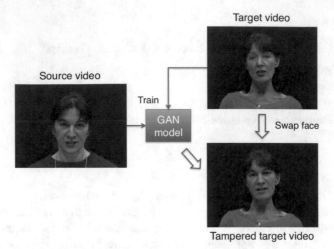

Fig. 5.1 Process of generating deepfake videos

approaches to detect deepfakes demonstrate encouraging accuracy, especially if they are trained and evaluated on the same datasets [17, 21].

At this stage, the research on deepfakes is still a relatively immature field, however the main research questions are already clear:

1. How to increase the amount of data with different types of deepfakes?
2. Can deepfakes fool automated face recognition?
3. Can deepfakes fool human visual system?
4. Can deepfakes be effectively detected?

In this chapter, we cover all the above research questions by (i) extending the pool of available deepfake datasets, (ii) demonstrating vulnerability of face recognition to deepfakes, (iii) presenting the results of subjective assessment of human ability to detect deepfakes, and (iv) showing the abilities and challenges of state-of-the-art deepfake detection approaches.

5.2   Related Work

The first approach that used a generative adversarial network to train a model between pre-selected two faces was proposed by Korshunova et al. [12]. Another related work with even a more ambitious idea was to use long short-term memory (LSTM)-based architecture to synthesize a mouth feature solely from an audio speech [24]. Right after these publications became public, they attracted a lot of publicity. Open-source approaches replicating these techniques started to appear, which resulted in the Deepfake phenomena.

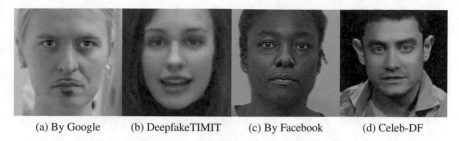

(a) By Google   (b) DeepfakeTIMIT   (c) By Facebook   (d) Celeb-DF

Fig. 5.2   Examples of deepfakes (faces cropped from videos) in different databases

Many databases with deepfake videos (see examples in Fig. 5.2) were created to help develop and train deepfake detection methods. One of the first freely available databases was based on VidTIMIT [10], followed by the FaceForensics database, which contained deepfakes generated from 1'000 YouTube videos [20] and which later was extended with a larger set of high-resolution videos provided by Google and Jigsaw [21]. Another recently proposed 5'000 videos-large database of deepfakes generated from YouTube videos is Celeb-DF [14]. But the most extensive and the largest database to date with more than 100 K videos (80% of which are deepfakes) is the dataset from Facebook [5], which was available for download to the participants in the recent Deepfake Detection Challenge hosted by Kaggle.[3]

These datasets were generated using either the popular open-source code,[4] e.g., DeepfakeTIMIT [10], FaceForensics [20], and Celeb-DF [14], or the latest methods implemented by Google and Facebook for creating deepfakes (see Fig. 5.2 for the examples of different deepfakes). This availability of large deepfake video databases allowed researchers to train and test detection approaches based on very deep neural networks, such as Xception [21], capsules networks [18], and EfficientNet [17], which were shown to outperform the methods based on shallow CNNs, facial physical characteristics [2, 13, 26, 27], or distortion features [1, 28].

5.3   Databases and Methods

Table 5.1 summarizes the databases of deepfake videos that we have used in the experiments presented in this chapter. The database by Google and Jigsaw and DF-Mobio database were split into three approximately equal in size subsets, for training, validation, and testing. The authors of Celeb-DF dataset predefined file lists for training and testing subsets but there was no validation set provided. DeepfakeTIMIT

---

[3] https://www.kaggle.com/c/deepfake-detection-challenge.

[4] https://www.kaggle.com/c/deepfake-detection-challenge/discussion/121313.

Table 5.1 Databases of deepfakes

Database	Number of swapped identities	Original videos	Deepfakes
DeepfakeTIMIT[5]	32	320	640
DF-Mobio database	72	31 950	14 546
FaceForensics	1000	1000	1000
from Google and Jigsaw	approx. 150	360	3068
from Facebook	not large	23 849	95 396
Celeb-DF	1711	590	5639

was also split only into two subsets: training and testing, due to its small size. From the Facebook dataset, we manually selected 120 videos, which we used in the subjective evaluation.

5.3.1 DeepfakeTIMIT

The DeepfakeTIMIT[5] is one of the first databases of deepfakes that we have generated by using videos from a VidTIMIT database, which contains short video clips of 43 subjects shot in a controlled environment when they are facing camera and reciting predetermined short phrases. Deepfakes were generated using open-source code[6] for 16 pairs of subjects selected based on how similar their visual appearance is, including mustaches or hair styles.

DeepfakeTIMIT contains two types of deepfakes (see examples in Fig. 5.3), the lower quality (LQ) fakes where a GAN model was trained to generate 64×64 size images and a higher quality (HQ), where GAN was trained to generate 128×128 images. The generated faces were placed in the target video using automated blending techniques that relied on histogram normalization and selective masking with Gaussian blur.

5.3.2 DF-Mobio

DF-Mobio[7] dataset is also generated by us and is one of the largest databases available with almost 15 K deepfake and 31 K real videos (see Table 5.1 for the comparison with other databases). Original videos are taken from Mobio database [15], which contains videos of a single person talking to the camera recorded with a phone or a

---

[5] https://www.idiap.ch/dataset/deepfaketimit.

[6] https://github.com/shaoanlu/faceswap-GAN.

[7] https://www.idiap.ch/dataset/dfmobio.

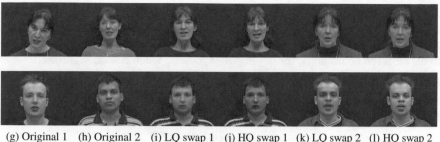

(g) Original 1   (h) Original 2   (i) LQ swap 1   (j) HQ swap 1   (k) LQ swap 2   (l) HQ swap 2

Fig. 5.3   Screenshot of the original videos from VidTIMIT database and low- (LQ) and high-quality (HQ) DeepfakeTIMIT videos

(a) Original 1   (b) Original 2   (c) Swap 1 → 2

Fig. 5.4   Screenshots of the original videos and a deepfake swap from DF-Mobio database

laptop. The scenario simulates the participation in a virtual meeting over Zoom or Skype.

The original Mobio database contains 31 K videos from 152 subjects but deepfakes were generated only for manually pre-selected 72 pairs of people with similar hairstyles, facial features, facial hair, and eyewear. Using GAN-based face-swapping algorithm based on the available code[6], for each pair, we generated videos with swapped faces from subject one to subject two and visa versa (see Fig. 5.4 for video screenshot examples).

The GAN model for face swapping was trained on face size input of 256×256 pixels. The training images were generated from laptop-recorded videos at 8 fps, resulting in more than 2 K faces for each subject, the training was done for 40 K iterations (about 24 hours on Tesla P80 GPU). The availability of this database to public is pending a publication.

5.3.3   Google and Jigsaw

To make this dataset, Google and Jigsaw [23] (see Table 5.1 for the comparison with other databases) worked with paid and consenting actors to record hundreds of videos. Using publicly available deepfake generation methods, Google then generated about

3 K of deepfakes from these videos. The resulting videos, real and fake, comprise the contribution, which was created to directly support deepfake detection efforts. As part of the FaceForensics++ [21] benchmark, this dataset is now available, free to the research community, for developing synthetic video detection methods.

5.3.4 Facebook

For construction of Facebook database, a data collection campaign [6] (see Table 5.1 for the comparison with other databases) has been carried out where participating actors have entered into an agreement to the use and manipulation of their likenesses in the creation of the dataset. Diversity in several axes (gender, skin tone, age, etc.) has been considered and actors recorded videos with arbitrary backgrounds thus bringing visual variability. A number of face swaps were computed across subjects with similar appearances, where each appearance was inferred from facial attributes (skin tone, facial hair, glasses, etc.). After a given pairwise model was trained on two identities, each identity was swapped onto other's videos.

For our experiments, we have manually looked through many videos of Facebook database and pre-selected 60 deepfake videos, split into five categories depending of how fake they look to an expert eye, with the corresponding 60 original videos (see examples in Fig. 5.5).

We use this manually selected subset of the videos in the subjective evaluations aimed to study the level of difficulty human subjects have in recognizing different types of deepfakes. We also use the same videos to evaluate deepfake detection systems and compare their performance with the human subjects.

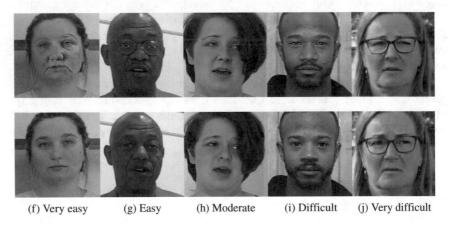

(f) Very easy   (g) Easy   (h) Moderate   (i) Difficult   (j) Very difficult

Fig. 5.5 Cropped faces from different categories of deepfake videos of Facebook database (top row) and the corresponding original versions (bottom row)

5.3.5   Celeb-DF

Celeb-DF (v2) [14] dataset contains real and deepfake synthesized videos having similar visual quality on par with those circulated online. The Celeb-DF (v2) dataset is greatly extended from the previous Celeb-DF (v1), which only contained 795 deepfake videos.

The v2 of the database contains more than 5 K deepfakes and nearly 2 K real videos, which are based on publicly available YouTube video clips of 59 celebrities of diverse genders, ages, and ethic groups. The deepfake videos are generated using an improved deepfake synthesis method [14], which essentially is an extension of methods available online[1], similar to the one used to generate both FaceForensics and DF-Mobio databases. The authors of the Celeb-DF database claim that their modified algorithm improves the overall visual quality of the synthesized deepfakes when compared to existing datasets. The authors also state that Celeb-DF is challenging to most of the existing detection methods, even though many deepfake detection methods are shown to achieve high, sometimes near perfect, accuracy on previous datasets. No consent was obtained for the videos, because the data is from the celebrities of the YouTube videos.

5.4   Evaluation Protocols

In this section, we explain how we evaluate face recognition and deepfake detection systems and what kind of objective metrics we compute.

5.4.1   Measuring Vulnerability

We use DeepfakeTIMIT database to evaluate vulnerability of face recognition. For the licit non-tampered scenario, the original VidTIMIT videos for the 32 subjects for which we have generated corresponding deepfake videos. In this scenario, we used two videos of the subject for enrollment and the other eight videos as probes, for which we computed the verification scores.

Using the scores, for each possible threshold θ, we compute commonly used metrics for evaluation of classification systems: false accept rate (FAR), which is the same as false match rate (FMR) and false reject rate (FRR), which is the same as false non-match rate (FNMR).[8] These rates are generally defined as follows:

---

[8] Strictly speaking, FRR and FNMR are not the same but are equivalent in our evaluations, since we are not concerned with such preprocessing errors like failure to enroll.

$$FAR(\theta) = \frac{|\{h_{neg} \mid h_{neg} \geq \theta\}|}{|\{h_{neg}\}|}$$

$$FRR(\theta) = \frac{|\{h_{pos} \mid h_{pos} < \theta\}|}{|\{h_{pos}\}|},$$

$$(5.1)$$

where h_{pos} is a score for original genuine samples and h_{neg} is a score for the tampered samples.

Threshold at which these FAR and FRR are equal leads to an equal error rate (EER), which is commonly used as a single value metric of the system performance.

To evaluate vulnerability of face recognition to deepfakes, in *tampered* scenario, we use deepfake videos (10 for each of 32 subjects) as probes and compute the corresponding scores using the enrollment model from the licit scenario. To understand if face recognition perceives deepfakes to be similar to the genuine original videos, we report the FAR metric computed using EER threshold θ from licit scenario. If FAR value for deepfake tampered videos is significantly higher than the one computed in licit scenario, it means the face recognition system cannot distinguish tampered videos from originals and is therefore vulnerable to deepfakes.

5.4.2 Measuring Detection

We consider deepfake detection as a binary classification problem and evaluate the ability of detection approaches to distinguish original videos from deepfake videos. All videos in DF-Mobio and Google datasets were proportionally split into training, validation, and test subsets. For Celeb-DF database, only training and test subset were provided, so the test set was used in place of validation when necessary. Similarly, DeepfakeTIMIT was also split into tow training and test subsets due to its smaller size.

The result of a deepfake detection is a set of probabilistic scores where the values close to zero correspond to deepfakes and those that are close to one correspond to genuine videos.

We define the threshold θ_{far} on the validation set to correspond to the FAR value of 10%, which means 10% of fake videos are allowed to be misclassified as genuine. Using this threshold θ_{far} on the scores of the test set will result in test FAR and FRR values. As a single value metric, we can then use the half total error rate (HTER) defined as

$$HTER(\theta_{far}) = \frac{FAR_{test} + FRR_{test}}{2}.$$

$$(5.2)$$

In addition to reporting FAR, FRR, and HTER values for the scores of the test set, we also report the area under the curve (AUC) metric, which is a popular metric for evaluation of classification system and is often used in the deepfake detection literature.

5.5   Vulnerability of Face Recognition

As examples of face recognition systems, we used publicly available pre-trained VGG [19] and Facenet [22] architectures. We used the *fc7* and *bottleneck* layers of these networks, respectively, as features and used cosine distance as a classifier. For a given test face, the confidence score of whether it belongs to a pre-enrolled model of a person is the cosine distance between the average feature vector, i.e., model, and the feature vector of a test face. Both of these systems are state-of-the-art recognition systems with VGG of 98.95% [19] and Facenet of 99.63% [22] accuracies on labeled faces in the wild (LFW) dataset.

We conducted the vulnerability analysis of VGG- and Facenet-based face recognition systems on low-quality (LQ) and high-quality (HQ) face swaps in Deepfake-TIMIT database. The results are presented in Table 5.2. In a licit scenario when only original non-tampered videos are present, both systems performed very well, with EER value of 0.03% for VGG and 0.00% for Facenet-based system. Using the EER threshold from licit scenario, we computed FAR value for the scenario when deepfake videos are used as probes. In this case, for VGG the FAR is 88.75% on LQ deepfakes and 85.62% on HQ deepfakes, and for Facenet the FAR is 94.38% and 95.00% on LQ and HQ deepfakes, respectively. To illustrate this vulnerability, we plot the score histograms for high-quality deepfake videos in Fig. 5.6. The histograms show a considerable overlap between deepfake and genuine scores with clear separation from the zero-effort impostor scores (the probes from licit scenario).

From the results, it is clear that both VGG- and Facenet-based systems cannot effectively distinguish GAN-generated and swapped faces from the original ones. The fact that more advanced Facenet system is more vulnerable is also consistent with the findings about presentation attacks [16].

5.6   Subjective Assessment of Human Vision

Since the resulted videos produced by automated deepfake generation algorithms vary drastically visually, depending on many factors (training data, the quality of the video for manipulation, and the algorithm itself), we cannot label all deepfakes into

Table 5.2 Vulnerability analysis of VGG and Facenet-based face recognition (FR) systems on low-quality (LQ) and high-quality (HQ) deepfakes in DeepfakeTIMIT database. EER value (Test set) is computed in a licit scenario without deepfakes. Using the corresponding EER threshold, FAR value (Test set) is computed for the scenario when deepfake videos are used as probes

Dataset	VGG-based FR		Facenet-based FR	
version	EER (%)	FAR (%)	EER (%)	FAR (%)
LQ deepfake	0.03	88.75	0.00	94.38
HQ deepfake	0.03	85.62	0.00	95.00

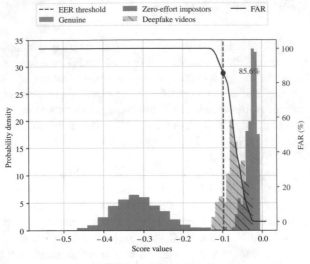

(a) VGG-based face recognition

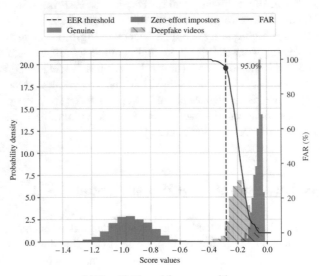

(b) FaceNet-based face recognition

Fig. 5.6 Histograms showing the vulnerability of VGG- and Facenet-based face recognition to high-quality face swapping on low- and high-quality Deepfakes

Fig. 5.7 Screenshot of one step of subjective evaluation (the video is courtesy of Facebook database)

one visual category. Therefore, we have manually looked through many videos of Facebook database[3] and pre-selected 60 deepfake videos, split into five categories depending on how clearly fake they look, with the corresponding 60 original videos (see examples in Fig. 5.5).

The evaluation was conducted using QualityCrowd 2 framework [9] designed for crowdsourcing-based evaluations (Fig. 5.7 shows a screenshot of a typical evaluation step). This framework allows us to make sure subjects watch each video fully at least once and are not able to skip any question. Prior to the evaluation itself, a display brightness test was performed using a method similar to that described in [8]. Since deepfake detection algorithms typically evaluate only the face regions cropped using a face detector, to have a comparable scenario, we have also shown to the human subjects cropped face regions next to the original video (see Fig. 5.7).

Each of the 60 naïve subjects who participated in the evaluation had to answer the question after watching a given video: "Is face of the person in the video real or fake?" with the following options: "Fake," "real," and "I do not know." Prior to the evaluation, the explanation of the test was given to the subjects with several test video examples of different fake categories and real videos. The 120 were also split in random batches of 40 each to reduce the total evaluation time for one subject, so the average time per one evaluation was about 16 minutes, which is consistent with the standard recommendations.

Due to privacy concerns, we did not collect any personal information from our subjects such as age or gender. Also, the licensing conditions of Facebook database[3] restricted the evaluation to the premises of Idiap Research Institute, which signed the license agreement not do distribute data outside. Therefore, the subjects consisted of

PhD students, scientists, administration, and management of Idiap. Hence, the age can be estimated to be between 20 and 65 years old and the gender distribution to be of a typical scientific community.

Unlike laboratory-based subjective experiments where all subjects can be observed by operators and its test environment can be controlled, the major shortcoming of the crowdsourcing-based subjective experiments is the inability to supervise participants behavior and to restrict their test conditions. When using crowdsourcing for evaluation, there is a risk of including untrusted data into analysis due to the wrong test conditions or unreliable behavior of some subjects who try to submit low-quality work in order to reduce their effort. For this reason, unreliable workers detection is an inevitable process in crowdsourcing-based subjective experiments. There are several methods for identifying the "trustworthiness" of the subject but since our evaluation was conducted within premises of a scientific institute, we only used so-called "honeypot" method [8, 11] to filter out scores from people who did not pay attention at all. Honeypot is a very easy question that refers to the video the subject just watched in the previous steps, e.g., "what was visible in the previous video?" with obvious answers that test if a person even looked at the video. Using this question, we filtered out the scores from five people from our final results, hence we ended up with 18.66 answers on average for each video, which is the number of subjects commonly considered in subjective evaluations.

5.6.1 Subjective Evaluation Results

For each deepfake or original video, we computed the percentage of answers that were "certain and correct," when people selected "Real" for an original or "Fake" for a deepfake, "certain and incorrect" (selected "Real" for a deepfake or "Fake" for an original) and "uncertain," when the selection was "I do not know." We have averaged those percentages across videos in each category to obtain the final percentages, which are shown in Fig. 5.8a. From the figure, we can note that the pre-selected deepfake categories, on average, reflect the difficulty level of recognizing them. The interesting result is the low number of uncertain answers, which means people tend to be sure when it comes to judging the realism of a video. And it also means people can be easily spoofed by a good quality deepfake video, since only in 24.5% cases "well done" deepfake videos are perceived as fakes, even though these subjects already knew they are looking for fakes. In the scenario, when such deepfake would be distributed to an unsuspected audience (e.g., via social media), we can expect the number of people noticing it to be significantly lower. Also, it is interesting to note that even videos from "easy" category were not as easy to spot (71.1% correct answers) compared to the original videos (82.2%). Overall, we can see that people are better at recognizing very obvious examples of deepfakes or real unaltered videos.

To check whether the difference between videos from the five deepfake categories is statistically significant based on the subjective scores, we performed ANOVA test with the corresponding box plot shown in Fig. 5.8b. The scores were computed

Fig. 5.8 Subjective answers
and median values with error
bars from ANOVA test for
different deepfake categories

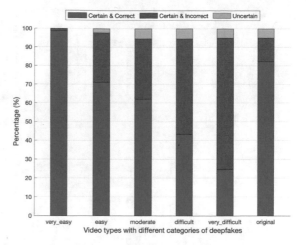

(a) Subjective answers

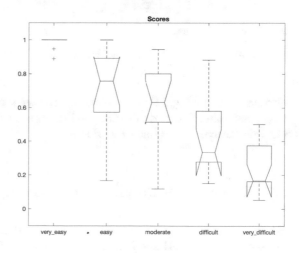

(b) ANOVA test

for each video (and per category when applicable) by averaging the answers from
all corresponding observers. For each correct answer, the score is 1 and for both
wrong and uncertain answers the score is 0. Please note that the red lines in Fig. 5.8b
correspond to median values, not average, which what we plotted in Fig. 5.8a. The
p-value of ANOVA test is below $4.7e - 11$, which means the deepfake categories are
significantly different on average. However, Fig. 5.8b shows that "easy," "moderate,"
and "difficult" categories have large scores variations and overlap, which means
some of the videos from these categories are perceived similarly. It means some
of the deepfake videos could be moved to another category. This observation is

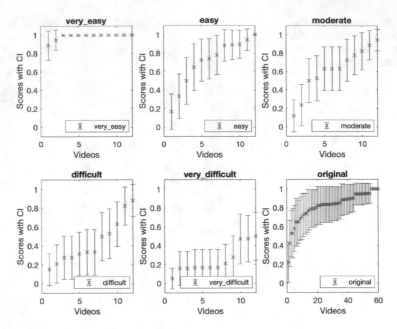

Fig. 5.9 Average scores with confidence intervals for each video in every video category

also supported by Fig. 5.9 which plots the average scores with confidence intervals (computed using student's t-distribution [7]) for each video in the deepfake category (12 videos each) and originals (60 videos).

5.7 Evaluation of Deepfake Detection Algorithms

For the example of machine vision, we took two state-of-the-art algorithms: based on Xception model [4] and EfficientNet variant B4 [17] shown to be performing very well on different deepfake datasets and benchmarks [21]. We pre-trained these models for 20 epochs each on the Google and Jigsaw dataset database [21] and Celeb-DF [14] to demonstrate the impact of different training conditions on the evaluation results. If evaluated on the test sets of the same databases they were trained on, both Xception and EfficientNet classifiers demonstrate a great performance as shown in Table 5.3. We can see that the area under the curve (AUC), which is the common metric used to compare the performance of deepfake detection algorithms, is almost at 100% in all cases.

We evaluated these models on the 120 videos we used in the subjective test. Since these videos come from Facebook database, they can be considered as unseen data, which is still an obstacle for many DNN classifiers, as they do not generalize well on the unseen data the fact also highlighted in the recent Facebook Deepfake

Table 5.3 Area under the curve (AUC) value on the test sets of Google and Celeb-DF databases of Xception and EfficientNet models

Model	Trained on	AUC (%) on Test set
Xception	Google database	100.00
Xception	Celeb-DF database	100.0
EfficientNet	Google database	99.99
EfficientNet	Celeb-DF database	100.0

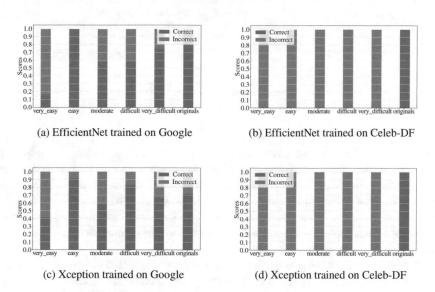

(a) EfficientNet trained on Google   (b) EfficientNet trained on Celeb-DF

(c) Xception trained on Google   (d) Xception trained on Celeb-DF

Fig. 5.10 The detection accuracy (the threshold corresponds to FAR 10% on development set of the respective database) for each video category from subjective test by Xception and Efficient models pre-trained on Google and Celeb-DF databases

Detection Challenge [25]. To compute performance accuracy, we need to select threshold. We chose the threshold corresponding to the false accept rate (FAR) of 10% selected on the development set of the respective database. We selected threshold based on FAR value as oppose to equal error rate (EER) commonly used in biometrics, because many practical deepfake detection or anti-spoofing systems have a low bound requirement on FAR value. In our case, FAR of 10% is quite generous.

Figure 5.10 demonstrates the evaluation results of pre-trained Xception and EfficientNet models on the videos from the subject test averaged for each deepfake category and originals (when using threshold corresponding to $FAR = 10\%$). In the figure, blue bar corresponds to the percent of correctly detected videos in the given category, and the orange bar corresponds to the percent of incorrectly detected. The results for algorithms are very different from the results of the subjective test (see Fig. 5.8a for the evaluation results by human subjects). The accuracy of the algorithms has no correlation to the visual appearance of deepfakes. The algorithms "see" these

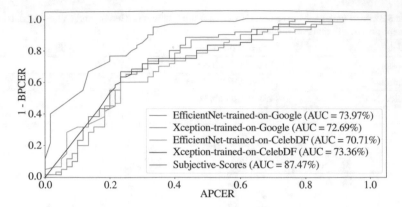

Fig. 5.11 ROC curves with the corresponding AUC value of Xception and Efficient models pretrained on Google and Celeb-DF databases evaluated on all the videos from subjective test

videos very differently from how humans perceive the same videos. To a human observer, the result may even appear random. We can even notice that all algorithms struggle the most with the deepfake videos that were easy for human subjects. It is evident that the choice of threshold and the training data have major impact on the evaluation accuracy. However, when selecting a deepfake detection system to use in practical scenario, one cannot assume an algorithm's perception will have any relation to the way we think the videos look like.

If we remove the choice of the threshold and the pre-selected video categories and simply evaluate the models on the 120 videos from the subjective tests, the receiver operating characteristic (ROC) curve and the corresponding AUC values are presented in Fig. 5.11. From this figure, we can note that ROC curves look "normal," as typical curves for classifiers that do not generalize well on unseen data, especially taking into account excellent performance on the test sets shown in Table 5.3. Figure 5.11 also shows that human subjects were more accurate at assessing this set of videos since the corresponding ROC curve is consistently higher with the highest AUC value of 87.47%.

5.8 Conclusion

In this chapter, we presented several publicly available databases of deepfake videos, including two DeepfakeTIMIT and DF-Mobio generated and provided by us. We demonstrated that the state-of-the-art VGG and Facenet-based face recognition algorithms are vulnerable to the Deepfake videos and fail to distinguish such videos from the original ones with up to 95.00% equal error rate.

We also conducted a subjective evaluation on 120 different videos (60 deepfakes and 60 originals) manually pre-selected from the Facebook database, which demonstrated that people are confused by good quality deepfakes in 75.5% of cases.

On the other hand, the evaluated state-of-the-art deepfake detection algorithms (based on Xception and EfficientNets (B4 variant) neural networks pre-trained on Google or Celeb-DF datasets) show very different perception of deepfakes compared to human subjects. The algorithms struggle to detect many videos that look obviously fake to humans, while some of the algorithms (depending on the training data and the selected threshold) can accurately detect videos that are difficult for people. The experiments also demonstrate that deepfake detection algorithm struggle to generalize to unknown set of videos, for which they were not trained for.

The continued advancements in development of face swapping techniques will result in more challenging deepfake, which will be even harder to detect by the existing algorithms. Therefore, new databases and approaches that can better generalize on unseen and realistic deepfakes need to be developed in the future. The arms race between deepfake generation and detection methods is in full swing.

References

1. Agarwal A, Singh R, Vatsa M, Noore A (2017) Swapped! digital face presentation attack detection via weighted local magnitude pattern. In: IEEE international joint conference on biometrics (IJCB), pp 659–665. https://doi.org/10.1109/BTAS.2017.8272754
2. Agarwal S, El-Gaaly T, Farid H, Lim S (2020) Detecting deep-fake videos from appearance and behavior. arXiv:2004.14491
3. Allcott H, Gentzkow M (2017) Social media and fake news in the 2016 election. J Econ Perspect 31(2):211–236. https://doi.org/10.1257/jep.31.2.211
4. Chollet F (2017) Xception: deep learning with depthwise separable convolutions. In: 2017 IEEE conference on computer vision and pattern recognition (CVPR), pp 1800–1807
5. Dolhansky B, Bitton J, Pflaum B, Russ Howes JL, Wang M, Ferrer CC (2020) The deepfake detection challenge dataset. arXiv:2006.07397
6. Dolhansky B, Howes R, Pflaum B, Baram N, Ferrer CC (2019) The deepfake detection challenge (dfdc) preview dataset. In: ArXiv
7. Hanhart P, Rerabek M, Korshunov P, Ebrahimi T (2013) Subjective evaluation of HEVC intra coding for still image compression
8. Hossfeld T, Keimel C, Hirth M, Gardlo B, Habigt J, Diepold K, Tran-Gia P (2014) Best practices for QoE crowdtesting: QoE assessment with crowdsourcing. IEEE Trans Multimed 16(2):541–558
9. Keimel C, Habigt J. Horch C, Dieopold K (2012) Qualitycrowd—a framework for crowd-based quality evaluation. https://doi.org/10.1109/PCS.2012.6213338
10. Korshunov P, Marcel S (2019) Vulnerability assessment and detection of Deepfake videos. In: International conference on biometrics (ICB 2019). Crete, Greece
11. Korshunov P, Nemoto H, Skodras A, Ebrahimi T (2014) Crowdsourcing-based evaluation of privacy in HDR images. In: Optics, photonics, and digital technologies for multimedia applications III, vol 9138. SPIE, pp 1 – 11
12. Korshunova I, Shi W, Dambre J, Theis L (2017) Fast face-swap using convolutional neural networks. In: IEEE international conference on computer vision (ICCV), pp 3697–3705. https://doi.org/10.1109/ICCV.2017.397

13. Li Y, Chang MC, Lyu S (2018) In ictu oculi: exposing ai generated fake face videos by detecting eye blinking. arXiv:1806.02877
14. Li Y, Sun P, Qi H, Lyu S (2020) Celeb-DF: a large-scale challenging dataset for deepfake forensics. In: IEEE conference on computer vision and patten recognition (CVPR). Seattle, WA, United States
15. McCool C, Marcel S, Hadid A, Pietikäinen M, Matejka P, Cernocký J, Poh N, Kittler J, Larcher A, Lévy C, Matrouf D, Bonastre J, Tresadern P, Cootes T (2012) Bi-modal person recognition on a mobile phone: using mobile phone data. In: 2012 IEEE international conference on multimedia and expo workshops, pp 635–640
16. Mohammadi A, Bhattacharjee S, Marcel S (2018) Deeply vulnerable: a study of the robustness of face recognition to presentation attacks. IET Biom 7(1):15–26. https://doi.org/10.1049/iet-bmt.2017.0079
17. Montserrat DM, Hao H, Yarlagadda SK, Baireddy S, Shao R, Horvath J, Bartusiak E, Yang J, Güera D, Zhu F, Delp EJ (2020) Deepfakes detection with automatic face weighting. In: 2020 IEEE/CVF conference on computer vision and pattern recognition workshops (CVPRW), pp 2851–2859
18. Nguyen H, Yamagishi J, Echizen I (2019) Capsule-forensics: using Capsule networks to detect forged images and videos. In: IEEE international conference on acoustics, speech and signal processing (2019)
19. Parkhi OM, Vedaldi A, Zisserman A (2015) Deep face recognition. In: BMVC (2015)
20. Rössler A, Cozzolino D, Verdoliva L, Riess C, Thies J, Nießner M (2018) Faceforensics: a large-scale video dataset for forgery detection in human faces. arXiv:1803.09179
21. Rössler A, Cozzolino D, Verdoliva L, Riess C, Thies J, Nießner M (2019) FaceForensics++: learning to detect manipulated facial images. In: International conference on computer vision (ICCV)
22. Schroff F, Kalenichenko D, Philbin J (2015) FaceNet: a unified embedding for face recognition and clustering. In: IEEE conference on computer vision and pattern recognition (CVPR), pp 815–823. https://doi.org/10.1109/CVPR.2015.7298682
23. Stanton D, Karlsson P, Vorobyov A, Leung T, Childs J, Sud A, Bregler C (2019) Contributing data to deepfake detection research. In: Blogpost
24. Suwajanakorn S, Seitz SM, Kemelmacher-Shlizerman I (2017) Synthesizing obama: learning lip sync from audio. ACM Trans Graph 36(4):95:1–95:13. https://doi.org/10.1145/3072959.3073640
25. Tolosana R, Romero-Tapiador S, Fierrez J, Vera-Rodriguez R (2020) Deepfakes evolution: analysis of facial regions and fake detection performance
26. Yang X, Li Y, Lyu S (2019) Exposing deep fakes using inconsistent head pose. In: IEEE international conference on acoustics, speech and signal processing
27. Yang X, Li Y, Qi H, Lyu S (2019) Exposing GAN-synthesized faces using landmark locations. In: ACM workshop on information hiding and multimedia security, pp 113–118
28. Zhang Y, Zheng L, Thing VLL (2017) Automated face swapping and its detection. In: IEEE international conference on signal and image processing (ICSIP), pp 15–19. https://doi.org/10.1109/SIPROCESS.2017.8124497

Chapter 6
Morph Creation and Vulnerability of Face Recognition Systems to Morphing

Matteo Ferrara and Annalisa Franco

Abstract Face recognition in controlled environments is nowadays considered rather reliable, and very good accuracy levels can be achieved by state-of-the-art systems in controlled scenarios. However, even under these desirable conditions, digital image alterations can severely affect the recognition performance. In particular, several studies show that automatic face recognition systems are very sensitive to the so-called face morphing attack, where face images of two individuals are mixed to produce a new face image containing facial features of both subjects. Face morphing represents nowadays a big security threat particularly in the context of electronic identity documents because it can be successfully exploited for criminal intents, for instance to fool Automated Border Control (ABC) systems thus overcoming security controls at the borders. This chapter will describe the face morphing process, in an overview ranging from the traditional techniques based on geometry warping and texture blending to the most recent and innovative approaches based on deep neural networks. Moreover, the sensitivity of state-of-the-art face recognition algorithms to the face morphing attack will be assessed using morphed images of different quality generated using various morphing methods to identify possible factors influencing the probability of success of the attack.

6.1 Introduction

Face morphing is generally described as a seamless transition transforming a facial image into another. Morphing was initially proposed as an image generation technique for computer graphics applications [1] or psychological studies [2, 3]. However, only in recent years it has emerged as a potential and severe security thread for Face Recognition Systems (FRS). The main risk deriving from face morphing is especially related to the adoption of automatic face-based identity verification in various

M. Ferrara (✉) · A. Franco
Department of Computer Science and Engineering, University of Bologna, via dell'Università, 50, Cesena, Italy
e-mail: matteo.ferrara@unibo.it

© The Author(s) 2022
C. Rathgeb et al. (eds.), *Handbook of Digital Face Manipulation and Detection*,
Advances in Computer Vision and Pattern Recognition,
https://doi.org/10.1007/978-3-030-87664-7_6

applications like civilian identity management, Machine Readable Travel Documents (eMRTD), or visa management. A possible attack in relation to the use of MRTD in Automated Border Control (ABC) gates has been firstly identified in [4] and later confirmed by several research works. Identity verification at an ABC relies on the comparison of a live captured probe face image with a digital face image stored in an eMRTD such as an e-passport. If a morphed image, which is similar enough to the face of the two parent subjects, can be included in an eMRTD, then two persons can share the document. In this scenario, a criminal could exploit the passport of an accomplice with no criminal records to overcome the security controls. In more details, the subject with no criminal records (i.e., the accomplice) could apply for an eMRTD by presenting the morphed face photo; if the image is not noticeably different from his/her face, the police officer accepts the photo and releases the document (see Fig. 6.1).

The attack will be successful if the morphed image contemporarily meets two conditions.

- It is able to fool the human expert, i.e., the morphed face must be very similar to the accomplice who applies for the document and no elements (e.g., morphing artifacts) of the image should raise suspicions;
- the image fools at the same time the FRS used for automatic identity verification, meaning that the morphed face can be successfully matched with both subjects (criminal and accomplice).

Some studies confirm that morphed faces can be very realistic and able to fool human experts [5–7]. It is well known, in fact, that unfamiliar face recognition is a

Fig. 6.1 The face morphing attack in the eMRTD scenario. The morphed ID photo delivered to the officer is very similar to the applicant, but also contains facial features of a different subject

hard task for humans and it becomes even harder when it has to be accomplished based on a small-size id photo such as the one used by the citizens to apply for an identity or travel document. This photo is generally obtained by printing a high-quality digital image on photographic paper (typical size is 3.5 cm × 4.5 cm) and is then scanned to be included into the document. This printing and scanning process (P&S) hides many small details of the image (e.g., artifacts introduced by the morphing process) thus making it more difficult for human examiners to spot the attack attempt.

Figure 6.2 shows two examples of morphing. In the first case (top row), the morphed image (b) is obtained with an almost equal contribution of the two subjects (a) and (c); the result is quite similar to subject (a) but a human expert could notice some differences. In the second example, the morphed image (e) has been generated from (d) and (f), but with a stronger contribution of subject (d). Visually the morphed image is almost indistinguishable from the accomplice (d) and is very unlikely that it would raise some suspicion by the officer. Both these morphed images, (b) and (d), contain enough information of the "criminal" subject to fool commercial FRSs.

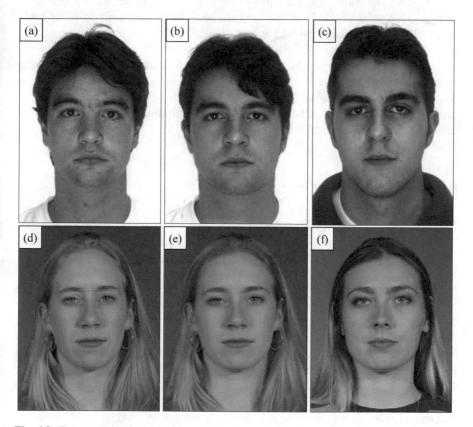

Fig. 6.2 Two example of morphed images: **b** obtained from the subjects (**a**) and (**c**); **e** obtained from the subjects (**d**) and (**f**)

It is worth noting that in case of successful attack, the document issued is perfectly regular; the attack does not consist of altering the document content but in deceiving the officer while issuing the document. The document released will thus pass all the integrity checks (optical and electronic) performed at the gates.

This attack is made possible in practice by the procedure adopted in several countries where there is no live enrolment for facial images and citizens apply for the document by providing an ID photo printed on photographic paper. The trust chain is thus broken since citizens could intentionally alter the image content by different possible digital image manipulations [5], even with criminal intents. Switching to live enrolment would certainly be the most effective solution, but its adoption by all the involved countries is very unlikely; moreover, we have to consider the huge number of documents already issued since the introduction of eMRTDs, which still represent a potential risk. In fact, governmental agencies already reported a few real morphing attack attempts and recent news confirm that the criticalities related to the morphing attack have reached a wide public audience [8–10]. Estimating the real extent of this phenomenon is hard, due to the practical impossibility of spotting the cases of successful attack. Unfortunately, the analysis of the vulnerability of FRSs to morphing attack, discussed later in this chapter, is not encouraging and confirm once again that designing effective countermeasures is quite urgent.

This chapter is organized as follows. Section 6.2 describes the face morphing generation algorithms, presenting both traditional landmark-based approaches, as well as innovative solutions based on deep learning. Section 6.3 analyzes and discusses the vulnerability of commercial FRSs to morphing attack; finally, Sect. 6.4 draws some concluding remarks.

6.2 Face Morphing Generation

Nowadays, the generation of a morphed image has become quite an easy and inexpensive task. Open-source solutions are publicly available, such as for instance general image processing software with specific plugins (e.g., the GAP plugin for GIMP [11]). Moreover, a number of free or commercial tools (e.g., FaceMorpher [12] or FantaMorph [13]), as well as applications for mobile devices or online services are available. Interested readers can refer to [14] for a comprehensive review of publicly available morphing tools. It is however worth noting that the images obtained with these fully automated systems are usually affected by the presence (more or less accentuate) of clearly visible artifacts that would probably cause a rejection of the image by the human officer during the document issuing process. As discussed later in this chapter, the creation of a high quality and credible morphed image usually requires an accurate manual intervention aimed at removing the most relevant defects and make the image undistinguishable from a bona fide one.

6.2.1 Landmark Based Morphing

Landmark-based approaches for face morphing allow synthesizing a fluid and gradual transformation from one image to another by exploiting facial landmark points in the involved images. Reference points usually correspond to prominent facial components such as mouth, nose, eyes or eyebrows, and approximately outline their shape. Such reference points can be either manually annotated or automatically determined using facial landmark detection algorithms such as Dlib [15], which is the most widely used for this purpose. Of course, the effort needed in the two cases is different, and manual annotation is a boring and time-consuming task; on the other hand, if properly executed, manual landmark labeling usually provides more precise landmark locations and achieves a better image coverage. Automatic landmark detection algorithms, in fact, usually adopt standard facial models that consider the central part of the face and the chin but ignore for instance the forehead region. As we will discuss later, the accuracy of landmark detection has a direct impact on the quality and effectiveness of the generated morphed images.

Starting from the facial landmarks, the morphing process can be generally described as follows. Let I_0 and I_1 be the two parent images to morph and let P_0 and P_1 be the two sets of correspondence points in I_0 and I_1, respectively. For most of the landmark-based approaches, the transformation between the two images is ruled by the so-called morphing factor, a parameter α representing a weighting factor for the two images. The morphing process is therefore generating a set of intermediate frames $\mathbb{M} = \{I_\alpha, \alpha \in \mathbb{R}, 0 < \alpha < 1\}$ representing the transformation of the first image (I_0) into the second one (I_1) as shown in Fig. 6.3. Note that, to obtain realistic results, the two images need to be aligned in advance (e.g., by overlaying the eye centers).

In general, each frame is a weighted linear combination of I_0 and I_1 (based on α value), obtained by combining (i) *geometric warping* [16] of the two images based on correspondence points and (ii) *texture blending*.

Formally:

$$I_\alpha(\mathbf{p}) = (1 - \alpha) \cdot I_0\big(w_{P_\alpha \to P_0}(\mathbf{p})\big) + \alpha \cdot I_1\big(w_{P_\alpha \to P_1}(\mathbf{p})\big), \qquad (6.1)$$

where

- $\mathbf{p}$ is a generic pixel position;
- α is the weight factor, representing the contribution of image I_1 to the morphing ($\alpha = 0.3$ indicates that the morphed image will be obtained for the 30% from I_1 and 70% from I_0);
- P_α is the set of correspondence points aligned according to the weight factor α;
- $w_{P_B \to P_A}(\mathbf{p})$ is a warping function.

Several warping techniques have been proposed in the literature [17]. A common approach consists in representing the two sets of points (P_A and P_B) by means of topologically equivalent (i.e., no folding or discontinuities are permitted) triangular

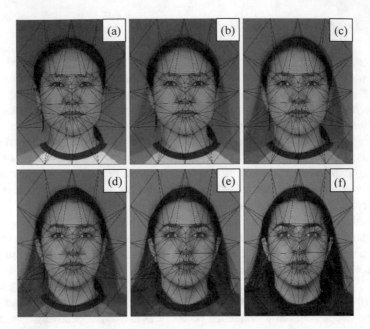

Fig. 6.3 Morphing of image I_0 (**a**) to I_1 (**f**). **b, c, d** and **e**) are intermediate frames, obtained by the morphing procedure, gradually moving from I_0 to I_1. The correspondence points and the triangular meshes are highlighted in red and blue, respectively.

meshes (see Fig. 6.3) and computing local spatial transformations that map each warped triangle to the corresponding original one [18]. Note that the meshes are constrained to cover the whole images and not to cause self-intersection (i.e., each pixel position is contained in exactly one mesh). A triangular mesh can be derived from a set of points via Delaunay triangulation [19]. Given a generic pixel position **p** in the warped image, the transformation used to map **p** onto the original image I is the local transformation corresponding to the warped triangle that contains **p** (see Fig. 6.4).

The set of aligned correspondence points P_α in Eq. (6.1) is computed as follows (see Fig. 6.5):

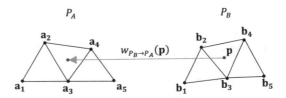

Fig. 6.4 Example of image warping using triangular meshes. The point **p** in the warped image is mapped into the original image using the inverse mapping of triangle $\triangle\,\mathbf{b_2}\mathbf{b_3}\mathbf{b_4}$ into $\triangle\,\mathbf{a_2}\mathbf{a_3}\mathbf{a_4}$

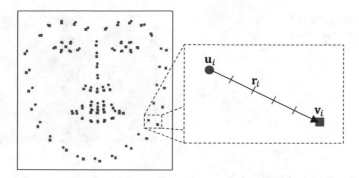

Fig. 6.5 On the left, P_0 (red circles) and P_1 (blue squares) are the corresponding points of images in Fig. 6.3a and f, respectively. On the right, the region containing points $\mathbf{u}_i$ and $\mathbf{v}_i$ is zoomed to show point $\mathbf{r}_i$ corresponding to morphed frame $I_{0.4}$ (see Eq. (6.2) and Fig. 6.3c)

$$P_\alpha = \{\mathbf{r}_i | \mathbf{r}_i = (1 - \alpha) \cdot \mathbf{u}_i + \alpha \cdot \mathbf{v}_i, \mathbf{u}_i \in P_0, \mathbf{v}_i \in P_1\}. \tag{6.2}$$

A more general formulation of the morphing process has been proposed in [20]; here geometric warping and image blending are ruled by two different factors. Equation (6.1) can be generalized as follows:

$$I_{\alpha_B, \alpha_W}(\mathbf{p}) = (1 - \alpha_B) \cdot I_0\left(w_{P_{\alpha_W} \to P_0}(\mathbf{p})\right) + \alpha_B \cdot I_1\left(w_{P_{\alpha_W} \to P_1}(\mathbf{p})\right), \tag{6.3}$$

where α_B and α_W are the blending and warping factors, respectively.

The effects of blending and warping are shown in Fig. 6.7 where two very different subjects have been selected (see Fig. 6.6) to highlight the influence of α_B and α_W. From a visual point of view, the result from different combinations is overall quite similar, but the effects produced on the probability of success of the attack by the possibility of acting separately on geometry warping and image blending have to be carefully considered. Several studies in fact show that, in the context of face recognition, humans are more sensitive to texture than to geometry [21]; the study [20] reveals that the same holds for FRSs, as confirmed by the experimental results reported in Sect. 3.2. Assigning different weighting factors to texture blending and geometry warping during the face morphing process significantly increases the chances of success, especially in the presence of look-alike subjects.

The automatic generation of morphed images can produce some visible artifacts that might be easily spotted by a human observer, thus drastically reducing the probability of success of the face morphing attack. The adoption of automatically detected facial landmarks, further increase the probability of artifacts in case of inaccurate point identification. The following visible artifacts are generally detectable:

Fig. 6.6 Images I_0 and I_1 used to generate the morphed images in Fig. 6.7

- Macroscopic ghost artifacts in the face surrounding area (see Fig. 6.8a). Facial landmarks are usually exclusively located in the facial region, and no reference points are considered for hairs, ears, and ecc. No accurate warping is therefore carried out for these regions, and the blending process produces therefore visible artifacts due to different characteristics (e.g., hair style or background) of the two contributing images.
- Minor artifacts close to the facial reference points (eyes, eye brows, mouth, nose, chin, and nostrils) mainly due to insufficient or inaccurate landmarks. Typical patterns are double edges or double reflections on irises (see Fig. 6.9a).

A widely used solution to remove the macroscopic artifacts in the face surrounding area is background substitution; the background region is typically replaced by the corresponding region of one of the parent images (the one with the highest blending factor), after a proper alignment (see Fig. 6.8b). An additional step is recommended in this case, aimed at equalizing the skin color before background substitution. In fact, due to different illumination conditions or skin color between the two face images, the retouching result could be unsatisfactory, in particular when the facial landmarks do not include the forehead region, thus causing a strong edge with the central face region. To overcome this issue, the histogram matching method described in [22] could be applied.

The second category of artifacts is more difficult to address, and no effective automatic solutions have been identified so far. At present, only a very careful manual post-processing is able to remove them, with a combination of low-level image processing operations such small region cloning from the contributing images, direct painting or edge smoothing (see Fig. 6.9b). Of course, this manual intervention is not trivial and requires some practice to achieve a good result. However, manual post-processing is a key element for the success of the morphing attack, in particular to fool human experts, which could quite easily spot morphing artifacts if not carefully removed.

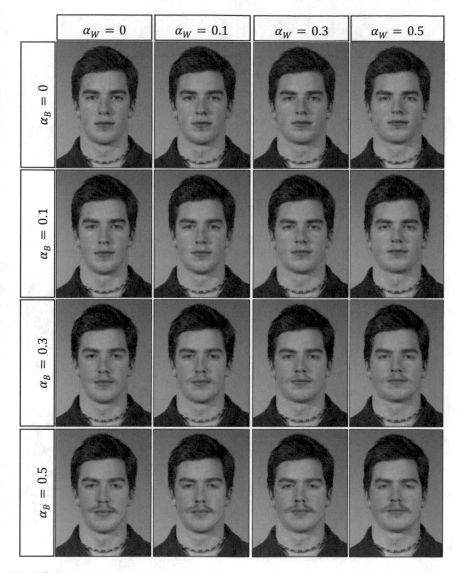

Fig. 6.7 Morphed images obtained with different blending and warping factors by combining Fig. 6.6a (I_0) and Fig. 6.6b (I_1)

6.2.2   Deep Learning-Based Face Morph Generation

The face morphing approaches presented in the previous section provide a precise control on the morphing process in relation for instance to the contribution of the two subjects in the resulting image. On the other hand, since the process relies on facial landmarks, an inaccurate detection of such reference points, as well as the lack

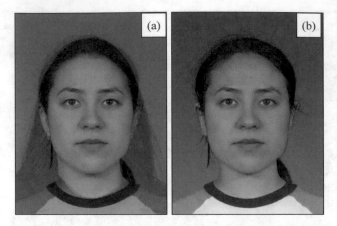

Fig. 6.8 Morphed image obtained from the two subjects in Fig. 6.3 with macroscopic artifacts in the region around face; **b** morphed image in (**a**) after automatic background substitution

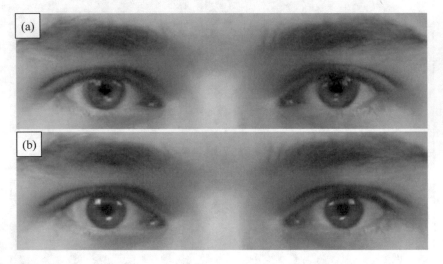

Fig. 6.9 **a** Small artifacts in the eye region, with double edge effect and multiple light reflections in the iris; **b** eye region after manual post-processing for artifact removal

of reference points in specific face regions, determine in most cases the presence of some ghost artifacts in the morphed image, which a human expert observing the image could spot quite easily. As mentioned above, the realization of an "ideal" morphed image requires a difficult and time-consuming manual post-processing aimed at removing all visible artifacts. To overcome this limitation, some innovative solutions for face morphing generation have been recently proposed, with the aim of fully automating the generation process. In particular, a few recent works in the literature exploit the potential of Generative Adversarial Networks (GAN) to synthesize morphed images by sampling the two contributing facial images in the latent space, without requiring preliminary landmark extraction and alignment.

GANs are based on the combined action of two different agents, a generator and discriminator. The first one, the generator G, produces samples from a distribution which should be ideally indistinguishable from the training distribution. The discriminator D is trained to determine if the incoming samples are drawn from the real set of training images or are fake samples generated by G. The training process gradually improves the samples produced by the generator G, which learns the most effective way to fool the discriminator.

The first approach for GAN-based face morphing generation, called MorGAN, was proposed in [23]. The network architecture is inspired by the work [24] where the Bidirectional Generative Adversarial Network (BiGAN) is introduced. In addition to the generator G from the standard GAN framework BiGAN includes an encoder E which maps data $\mathbf{x}$ to latent representations $\mathbf{z}$. The BiGAN discriminator D discriminates not only in data space ($\mathbf{x}$ versus $G(\mathbf{z})$), but jointly in data and latent space (tuples ($\mathbf{x}$, $E(\mathbf{x})$) versus ($G(\mathbf{z})$, $\mathbf{z}$), where the latent component is either an encoder output $E(\mathbf{x})$ or a generator input $\mathbf{z}$. The idea is that the BiGAN encoder E should learn to invert the generator G, even if the two modules cannot directly "communicate". This architecture is adapted by the authors of [23] to the problem of face morph generation. The generator is split into two components, complementary inverse to each other, and the discriminator is trained to distinguish between joint pairs (samples from the encoder and samples from the decoder). The main limitation of the MorGAN approach is the limited size of the generated morphed images, 64 × 64 pixels, which is quite far from the resolution needed to fulfill the ISO/ICAO quality standards (minimum inter-eye distance of 90 pixels) and to successfully fool commercial FRSs. This last aspect is confirmed in [25] where the authors evaluate the vulnerability of state-of-the-art face recognition systems to MorGAN morphed images.

The same work [25] focuses on the generation of high-quality morphed images, with the aim of overcoming the key limitation of the MorGAN approach. In particular, the authors propose the adoption of StyleGAN [26] for morphing generation. Given the latent code L_1 of the face, StyleGAN maps the inputs to an intermediate latent space through the mapping network. The mapping layer consists of 8 fully connected layers serially connected. The approach synthesizes a data-subject-specific morphed face by forcing a strategy to embed the face image into the latent space. The subject-specific embedded latent space passes through the synthesis network consisting of 18 layers, thus obtaining a representation in 18 latent spaces (dimension 512) which is further concatenated. The loss function driving the embedding measures the similarity between the input image and the reconstructed image. The images of the two contributing subjects are both processed according to the procedure described above and a weighted average (to recall the idea of morphing factor) of the corresponding latent codes is computed to obtain the morphed image latent code, which is finally passed through the synthesis network to generate the high-resolution morphed image (1024 × 1024).

The morphing approach based on StyleGAN has been successively improved by the same authors in [27] where the MIPGAN (Morphing through Identity Prior driven GAN) approach is presented. The introduction of a loss function aimed at preserving the identity of the generated morphed image, through enforced identity priors represents the main element of novelty. Given the images of the two contributing subjects, the corresponding latent vectors are first computed using a latent prediction network. The morphed image latent vector is again obtained by a weighted average of the two input vectors and is finally passed through the synthesis network to obtain a morphed image of size 1024×1024. The last step consists of a final optimization stage based on the identity preserving loss function. The authors propose two different versions of MIPGAN, obtained using two versions of StyleGAN, [26] and [28], respectively. The MIPGAN approach achieves interesting results in terms of efficacy of the attack, as shown by the results reported in the next section.

Besides image resolution, another important aspect to consider is the similarity of the morphed image to the two contributing subjects. From this point of view, the landmark-based approaches certainly allow to better preserve the identity of the two contributing subjects and to control quite easily (via the morphing factor) the similarity of the resulting morphed images to one of the two individuals. GAN-based approaches seem to have less control on this aspect, even when an identity preserving loss function is adopted. Even if the morphed images generated using GAN-based approaches can fool automatic FRSs, we believe that further work is needed to make the generated images able to fool the human expert.

6.3 Vulnerability of Face Recognition Systems to Face Morphing

In this section, we describe the experiments carried out using three commercial face recognition SDKs (referred to as SDK_1, SDK_2, and SDK_3) which provided top performance in the "Face Recognition Vendor Test (FRVT)—1:1 Verification" [29, 30]; the names of the SDKs cannot be disclosed, and the results will be therefore presented in anonymous form.

In order to simulate a realistic attack to an ABC system, the operational threshold of the face recognition software have been fixed according to the Frontex guidelines [31]. In particular, for ABC systems operating in verification mode, the face recognition algorithm has to ensure a *False Acceptance Rate* (FAR) equal to 0.1% and a *False Rejection Rate* (FRR) lower than 5%. During the experimentation, for each SDK, the security threshold indicated in the corresponding documentation to achieve FAR $= 0.1\%$ has been used. Since we focus on morphing attacks, the performance is evaluated in terms of Mated Morph Presentation Match Rate (MMPMR) [32] with the aim to quantify the percentage of morphing attacks able to fool the SDKs. To this purpose the MMPMR for all SDKs have been measured by comparing morphed face images against probe images of both subjects involved in the generation of the morphed image.

6.3.1   Data Sets

The SDKs have been evaluated on five data sets:

- BIOLAB-1.0 [5]: it contains 80 morphed images generated using the GIMP software [11, 33] after a manual labeling of the facial reference points and a first manual alignment based on eyes superimposition; a final manual retouch was carried out to remove visible artifacts. For each morphed image, it contains two probe images, one for each parent subject.
- MorphDB [34]: the aim of this dataset is to reproduce the typical scenario where the ID photo is provided by the citizens printed on photographic paper and then scanned by the officer during the issuing process. It contains 100 morphed images generated using the Sqirlz Morph 2.1 software [35] with facial landmarks automatically detected and a morphing factor in the range [0.3;0.4]. After the generation, the morphed images have been manually retouched to remove visible artifacts introduced by the morphing procedure. The P&S images have been created by printing the digital version on high quality photographic paper by a professional photographer and scanned at 300 DPI. For each morphed image, it includes a variable number of probe images of the two parent subjects.
- SOTAMD [36]: it contains 5748 high quality images for benchmarking under realistic conditions. The dataset consists of facial images from subjects of various ethnicities, age-groups, and both genders. After a careful subject pre-selection, the morphed images have been created using seven different morphing algorithms and applying manual post-processing to remove visible artifacts. Moreover, the images have been also printed and scanned. For each morphed image, it includes 10 probe images, for each contributing subject, captured under a simulated ABC gate operational scenario presenting more variations with respect to other datasets.
- AMSL [37]: a dataset containing images from the Face Research Lab London Set [38]. 2175 morphed face images were generated using the morphing approach described in [39]. All images were modified in the way to comply with the requirements of the ICAO portrait quality standard for eMRTD [40] and to fit on a chip of an eMRTD including cropping, down-scaling, and JPEG compression. For each morphed image, it contains two probe images, one for each subject.
- B&W [20]: a dataset containing morphed images automatically generated by separately varying the blending and the warping factors α_B and α_W to evaluate their importance in fooling face recognition systems. It contains 560 morphed images for each combination of α_B and α_W and for each of them, a probe image for each contributing subject.

BIOLAB-1.0, MorphDB, and SOTAMD datasets are available for testing on the Bologna Online Evaluation Platform (BOEP) [41] hosted in the FVC-onGoing framework [42, 43].

6.3.2 Results

Table 6.1 reports the single MMPMR of the three SDKs and their average on all datasets (except for B&W data set whose results are reported below).

For all SDKs, the most difficult datasets seem to be both BIOLAB-1.0 and AMSL with an average MMPMR of 95.0 and 92.7%, respectively. This is probably due to a combination of different elements:

- *morphingfactor*—both BIOLAB-1.0 and AMSL datasets contain symmetric morphed images (i.e., morphing factor equal to 0.5) while MorphDB dataset contains asymmetric morphed images generated with a morphing factor in the range [0.3;0.4] and SOTAMD dataset contains morphed images generated with two different morphing factors (0.3 and 0.5);
- *facial landmarks manually labeled*—to generate BIOLAB-1.0 morphed images, the facial landmarks have been manually selected, while automatically detected facial landmarks have been used to generate MorphDB and SOTAMD morphed images;
- *forehead landmarks*—BIOLAB-1.0 morphed images have been generated using also landmarks manually labeled on the hairline (see Fig. 11 in [5]) which have not been used to generate the other databases;
- *facial outer region substitution*—as shown in Fig. 6.3, the intermediate morphed frames could present double exposure effects outside the facial region (e.g., background, hair, shoulders, and body). To make morphed images more realistic and therefore more difficult to be detected, usually a retouching is applied. MorphDB and SOTAMD morphed images have been automatically retouched by replacing

Table 6.1 MMPMR of the three SDKs on different data sets

Database	Format	Morphed images	Probe images per parent subject	SDK_1 (%)	SDK_2 (%)	SDK_3 (%)	AVG (%)
BIOLAB-1.0	Digital	80	1	98.75	96.25	90.00	95.00
MorphDB	Digital	100	Variable	78.00	60.00	50.00	62.67
	P&S			74.00	59.00	50.00	61.00
SOTAMD	Digital	2045	10	69.10	50.81	46.41	55.44
	P&S	3703		69.89	42.07	44.64	52.20
AMSL	Digital	2175	1	99.08	94.25	84.78	92.70

the pixels outside the face region with those of the accomplice image, while BIOLAB-1.0 morphed images have been manually retouched.

- *probe images*—to simulate an ABC gate operational scenario, in the SOTAMD database, the morphed images are compared against face images acquired using ABC gates. Such images present different lighting conditions, and some of them have been acquired as grayscale images. Such differences could decrease the chance to fool the SDKs.

As the SOTAMD dataset [36] presents meta-data regarding the characteristics of the parent subjects used for morphing (e.g., gender) and of the morphing generation pipeline (e.g., morphing approach), the MMPMR of the three SDKs and their average on different subsets are reported in Tables 6.2 and 6.3 (digital and P&S versions, respectively).

Some interesting results can be observed, in relation to the main attributes characterizing the database images:

- *gender*—the chance of fooling SDKs for female subjects looks on average higher than for male subjects (about 10% better on both digital and P&S versions).
- *post-processing*—as expected manual retouching increases the probability of fooling the SDKs with respect to automatic post-processing, even if the difference is not so evident (about 5% better on both digital and P&S versions).
- *morphingalgorithm*—SDKs exhibit different behaviors as the morphing algorithm changes; algorithms C02 and C01 present a higher change to fool SDKs

Table 6.2 MMPMR of the three SDKs on digital version of SOTAMD subsets

Attribute	Subset	# Morphed images	SDK_1 (%)	SDK_2 (%)	SDK_3 (%)	AVG (%)
Gender	Female	876	71.69	58.33	53.42	61.15
	Male	1169	67.15	45.17	41.15	51.15
Post processing	Automatic	1575	67.87	49.46	45.78	54.37
	Manual	470	73.19	55.32	48.51	59.01
Morphing algorithm	C01	325	79.08	64.92	55.08	66.36
	C02	200	91.00	82.00	62.00	78.33
	C03	400	65.00	43.75	40.75	49.83
	C05	420	67.38	46.90	45.24	53.17
	C06	400	61.75	40.00	40.50	47.42
	C07	300	61.33	44.00	43.67	49.67
Morphing factor	0.3	1035	47.54	25.89	22.32	31.92
	0.5	1010	91.19	76.34	71.09	79.54
Morph quality	High	1059	89.99	76.11	66.19	77.43
	Low	986	46.65	23.63	25.15	31.81

Table 6.3 MMPMR of the three SDKs on P&S version of SOTAMD subsets

Attribute	Subset	# Morphed images	SDK_1 (%)	SDK_2 (%)	SDK_3 (%)	AVG (%)
Gender	Female	1661	71.76	49.91	50.87	57.52
	Male	2042	68.36	35.70	39.57	47.88
Post processing	Automatic	1453	66.83	37.72	45.42	49.99
	Manual	2250	71.87	44.89	44.13	53.63
Morphing algorithm	C01	500	79.80	53.00	57.60	63.47
	C02	500	95.00	79.00	57.40	77.13
	C03	1264	60.21	28.64	34.97	41.27
	C05	939	68.26	38.45	43.66	50.12
	C06	500	62.40	35.00	45.20	47.53
Morphing factor	0.3	1853	49.00	23.48	22.23	31.57
	0.5	1850	90.81	60.70	67.08	72.86
Morph quality	High	1920	90.73	64.90	63.39	73.00
	Low	1783	47.45	17.50	24.45	29.80
Image compression	Uncompressed	380	82.37	67.89	51.32	67.19
	Compressed	3323	68.46	39.12	43.88	50.49

Table 6.4 MMPMR of SDK_1 on B&W data set for each combination of α_B and α_W. Different values are represented by different blue levels (the darker, the greater)

α_B \ α_W	0	0.1	0.2	0.3	0.4	0.5
0	1.4%	1.6%	2.1%	2.7%	4.3%	4.5%
0.1	5.4%	7.7%	8.4%	9.8%	11.1%	11.6%
0.2	18.0%	20.2%	22.3%	25.0%	27.1%	29.8%
0.3	40.5%	46.4%	49.6%	55.0%	58.6%	61.8%
0.4	73.0%	79.3%	82.7%	86.4%	88.9%	90.4%
0.5	93.0%	95.2%	96.6%	97.5%	97.7%	97.9%

with respect to algorithms C06, C07, and C03. Please refer to [36] for a detailed description of the different morphing algorithms.

- *morphingfactor*—as expected symmetric morphing (morphing factor equals to 0.5) fools the SDKs more easily (more than 40% better on both digital and P&S versions) than asymmetric morphing (morphing factor equals to 0.3).
- *morph quality*—as expected high quality morphs are more difficult to detect than low quality morphs (about 45% better on both digital and P&S versions).
- *image compression*—the uncompressed images present a higher probability to fool SDKs with respect to the compressed version (about 15% better).

Tables 6.4, 6.5, 6.6, and 6.7 report the MMPMR of the three SDKs and their average on B&W data set. For all SDKs blending and warping present a very different impact on the probability of success of the attack, while geometric modifications obtained increasing the warping factor α_W do not heavily affect recognition accuracy (see ranges $\alpha_B \in [0; 0.1]$, $\alpha_W \in [0.4; 0.5]$), an opposite behavior is observed for the blending factor α_B ($\alpha_B \in [0.4; 0.5]$, $\alpha_W \in [0; 0.1]$). Hence, for a criminal it would be much more convenient to create a morphed image with $\alpha_B = 0.5$ and $\alpha_W \in [0; 0.2]$ instead of using a balanced morphing factor in the range $[0.2; 0.3]$ as

Table 6.5 MMPMR of SDK_2 on B&W data set for each combination of α_B and α_W. Different values are represented by different blue levels (the darker, the greater)

α_B \ α_W	0	0.1	0.2	0.3	0.4	0.5
0	1.4%	1.8%	2.1%	2.1%	3.0%	2.7%
0.1	3.6%	4.5%	5.7%	6.1%	7.0%	8.9%
0.2	9.3%	11.6%	15.7%	18.9%	23.8%	26.6%
0.3	27.1%	32.0%	38.4%	43.2%	47.7%	54.1%
0.4	50.9%	59.5%	66.4%	71.6%	76.3%	79.6%
0.5	72.0%	78.9%	85.0%	88.0%	91.1%	93.2%

Table 6.6 MMPMR of SDK_3 on B&W data set for each combination of α_B and α_W. Different values are represented by different blue levels (the darker, the greater)

α_B \ α_W	0	0.1	0.2	0.3	0.4	0.5
0	0.5%	0.9%	1.3%	1.1%	1.6%	2.1%
0.1	2.5%	3.0%	3.4%	4.6%	5.5%	7.0%
0.2	7.5%	9.8%	11.1%	13.2%	15.5%	18.6%
0.3	21.4%	23.9%	28.4%	33.0%	38.0%	42.5%
0.4	44.6%	51.3%	56.4%	61.1%	66.1%	69.3%
0.5	70.4%	75.5%	81.4%	85.9%	89.3%	91.6%

Table 6.7 Average MMPMR of the three SDKs on B&W data set for each combination of α_B and α_W. Different values are represented by different blue levels (the darker, the greater). The green region represents the most promising combinations of blending and warping factors to successfully perpetrate the attack

α_B \ α_W	0	0.1	0.2	0.3	0.4	0.5
0	1.1%	1.4%	1.9%	2.0%	3.0%	3.1%
0.1	3.8%	5.1%	5.8%	6.9%	7.9%	9.2%
0.2	11.6%	13.9%	16.4%	19.1%	22.1%	25.0%
0.3	29.7%	34.1%	38.8%	43.8%	48.1%	52.8%
0.4	56.2%	63.3%	68.5%	73.0%	77.1%	79.8%
0.5	78.5%	83.2%	87.7%	90.5%	92.7%	94.2%

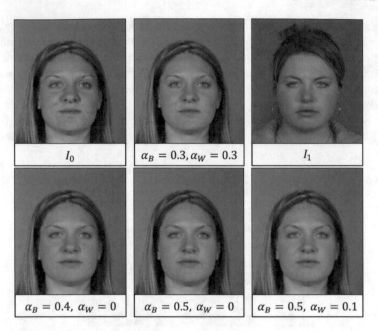

Fig. 6.10 Example images from the database used for the experiment. The morphed images are obtained combining the two images I_0 and I_1 with different blending (α_B) and warping (α_W) factors

stated in [34, 44]. This choice would increase the chances of successful attack at the border (from about 16–44 to 78–88%, on the average) keeping unaltered the chances of fooling the human officer during the document issuing process. In fact, a visual inspection of several generated morphs reveals that the difference between the two images is imperceptible, in particular when look-alike subjects are involved (see the example of Fig. 6.10). Moreover, we should always consider that human recognition capabilities are surprisingly error-prone in front of unfamiliar faces [45] and small appearance variations would probably be neglected. Finally, it is important to note that the MMPMR values could be even higher because, in a real scenario, a criminal would try to produce high quality morphed images, discarding the morphs with a low probability of success and applying manual retouching to remove unrealistic artifacts.

6.3.3 Deep Learning-Based Morphing Results

Currently no databases of morphed images generated by GANs are publicly available; therefore, the vulnerability assessment we did only focus on images generated by landmark-based approaches. However, as a reference, we think it is worth reporting the preliminary results reported by the authors of the GAN-based approaches in their paper [27].

Table 6.8 MMPMR of a face recognition system on morphed images generated by GANs as reported in [27]

Format	Morph generation type			
	Facial landmark [46] (%)	StyleGAN	MIPGAN-I (%)	MIPGAN-II (%)
Digital	100	64.68	94.36	92.93
P&S	97.64	61.72	92.97	80.56
P&S with compression	97.84	58.92	92.29	90.24

Table 6.8 compares the MMPMR of a state-of-the-art FRS on morphed images generated by (i) GANs and (ii) a landmark-based morphing method [46]. While StyleGAN generates morphed images with a low chance to fool the FRS (about 60%), the MIPGAN approach achieves interesting results in terms of efficacy of the attack (about 90%) even if lower than the facial landmark method (about 98%).

On the other hand, even if MIPGAN seems able to fool a FRS, some further efforts are necessary to improve the similarity with the contributing subjects thus increasing the effectiveness of the attack against human experts.

6.4   Conclusions

The general trust on automatic face recognition systems has recently been undermined by several possible kinds of attack, among which the face morphing is one of the most insidious and difficult to address. Dealing with face morphing is particularly complex in the context of ePassports; FRS are requested to work at fixed operational thresholds that guarantee a good trade-off between security and convenience in the use of ABC gates. Unfortunately, at these thresholds, it is very hard for FRSs to reject morphed images, thus making them quite vulnerable to the face morphing attack. This is particularly true when the morphed facial image is accurately prepared, with a manual intervention for facial landmark selection and artifact removal. Studies in the literature show that humans are easily fooled by accurate morphed images. Moreover, the high success rate measured in this chapter for landmark-based morphing techniques and the preliminary results reported in research papers for the GAN-based approaches confirm that face morphing is a real security threat. Recently, several research groups working on face recognition devoted significant efforts in designing face morphing attack detection techniques but, as discussed in a later chapter, further improvements are still needed to achieve good generalization capabilities.

References

1. Beier T (1992) Feature-based image metamorphosis. Comput Graph 26:35–42
2. Steyvers M (1999) Morphing techniques for manipulating face images. Behav Res Meth Instrum Comput 359–369
3. Jäger T, Seiler KH, Mecklinger A (2005) Picture database of morphed faces (MoFa): technical report. Experimental neuropsychology unit. Department of Psychology, Saarland University, Saarbrücken, Germany
4. Ferrara M, Franco A, Maltoni D (2014) The magic passport. In: International joint conference on biometrics, clearwater (FL), pp 1–7
5. Ferrara M, Franco A, Maltoni D (2016) On the effects of image alterations on face recognition accuracy. In: Face recognition across the imaging spectrum, pp 195–222
6. Robertson DJ et al. (2018) Detecting morphed passport photos: a training and individual differences approach. Cogn Res Princ Implic 3(27)
7. Robertson DJ (2020) Morphed passport photo detection by human observers. In: International conference on biometrics for borders. Warsaw
8. Spiegel (2021) Aktivisten schmuggeln Fotomontage in Reisepass. https://www.spiegel.de/netzwelt/netzpolitik/biometrie-im-reisepass-peng-kollektiv-schmuggelt-fotomontage-in-ausweis-a-1229418.html
9. Monroy M (2021) Laws against morphing. https://digit.site36.net/2020/01/10/laws-against-morphing/
10. The Peng! Collective (2021) Mask.ID Part II—We send our passports to Libya. https://pen.gg/campaign/mask-id-2/
11. GIMP (2021) GIMP animation package. https://www.gimp.org/news/2009/06/05/gimp-animation-package-260-released/
12. Luxand (2021) FaceMorpher. http://www.facemorpher.com/
13. Abrosoft (2021) FantaMorph. https://www.fantamorph.com/
14. Scherhag U, Rathgeb C, Merkle J, Breithaupt R, Busch C (2019) Face recognition systems under morphing attacks: a survey. IEEE Access, pp 23012–23026
15. (2021) Dlib C++ Library. http://dlib.net/
16. Wikipedia (2021) Image warping. http://en.wikipedia.org/wiki/Image_warping
17. Wolberg G (1994) Digital image warping, 1st edn. IEEE Computer Society Press, Los Alamitos, CA, USA
18. Rogers DF, Adams JA (1989) Mathematical elements for computer graphics, 2nd ed. McGraw-Hill Higher Education
19. Delaunay BN (1934) Sur la sphère vide. Bulletin de l'Académie des sciences de l'URSS, Classe des sciences mathématiques et naturelles 6:793–800
20. Ferrara M, Franco A, Maltoni D (2019) Decoupling texture blending and shape warping in face morphing. In: International conference of the biometrics special interest group (BIOSIG), Darmstadt, pp 1–5
21. Lai M, Oruç I, Barton JS (2013) The role of skin texture and facial shape in representations of age and identity. Cortex, pp 252–265
22. Gonzalez RC, Woods RE (2017) Digital image processing, 4th ed. Pearson
23. Damer N, Saladi AM, Braun A, Kuijper A (2018) Morgan: recognition vulnerability and attack detectability of face morphing attacks created by generative adversarial network. In: Internationa conference on biometrics theory, applications and systems, pp 1–10
24. Donahue J, Krähenbühl P, Darrell T (2017) Adversarial feature learning. https://arxiv.org/abs/1605.09782
25. Venkatesh S et al. (2020) Can gan generated morphs threaten face recognition systems equally as landmark based morphs?—vulnerability and detection. In: 8th International workshop on biometrics and forensics (IWBF). Porto Portugal, pp 1–6
26. Karras T, Laine S, Aila T (2019) A style-based generator architecture for generative adversarial networks. In: IEEE conference on computer vision and pattern recognition, pp 4401–4410

27. Zhang H et al. (2020) MIPGAN—generating robust and high quality morph attacks using GAN. https://arxiv.org/abs/2009.01729
28. Karras T et al. (2020) Analysing and improving the image quality of StileGAN. In: IEEE/CVF conference on computer vision and pattern recognition, pp 8110–8119
29. NIST (2021) Face recognition vendor test (FRVT) 1:1 verification. https://pages.nist.gov/frvt/html/frvt11.html
30. Grother P, Ngan M, Hanaoka K (2021) Ongoing face recognition vendor test (FRVT)—Part 1: verification. NIST, Gaithersburg, MD
31. FRONTEX—R&D Unit (2015) Best practice technical guidelines for automated border control (ABC) systems. FRONTEX, Warsaw, Poland, ISBN: 978–92–95205–50–5. https://doi.org/10.2819/39041
32. Scherhag U et al. (2017) Biometric systems under morphing attacks: assessment of morphing techniques and vulnerability reporting. In: International conference of the biometrics special interest group (BIOSIG). Darmstadt, Germany
33. GIMP (2021) GNU image manipulation program web site. http://www.gimp.org/
34. Ferrara M, Franco A, Maltoni D (2018) Face demorphing. IEEE Trans Inf Forensics Secur 13(4):1008–1017
35. Xiberpix (2021) Sqirlz Morph 2.1 web site. http://www.xiberpix.net/SqirlzMorph.html
36. Raja K et al. (2020) Morphing attack detection - database, evaluation platform and benchmarking. In: IEEE transactions on information forensics and security (TIFS)
37. (2021) AMSL face morph image data set. https://omen.cs.uni-magdeburg.de/disclaimer/index.php
38. DeBruine L, Jones B (2021) Face research lab London set. https://doi.org/10.6084/m9.figshare.5047666.v3
39. Neubert T, Makrushin A, Hildebrandt M, Kraetzer C, Dittmann J (2018) Extended stirtrace benchmarking of biometric and forensic qualities of morphed face images. IET Biometrics 7(4):325–332
40. Wolf A (2016) ICAO: portrait quality (reference facial images for MRTD), version 0.7
41. BioLab (2021) Bologna online evaluation platform web site. https://biolab.csr.unibo.it/fvcongoing/UI/Form/BOEP.aspx
42. Dorizzi B et al. (2009) Fingerprint and online signature verification competitions at ICB 2009. In: Proceedings 3rd IAPR/IEEE international conference on biometrics (ICB09). Alghero
43. BioLab (2021) FVC-ongoing web site. http://biolab.csr.unibo.it/fvcongoing
44. Robertson DJ, Kramer RSS, Burton AM (2017) Fraudulent ID using face morphs: experiments on human and automatic recognition. PLoS ONE 12(3)
45. Young AW, Burton AM (2017) Recognizing faces. Curr Dir Psychol Sci 26(3):212–217
46. Raghavendra R, Raja KB, Venkatesh S, Busch C (2017) Face morphing versus face averaging: vulnerability and detection. In: IEEE international joint conference on biometrics (IJCB). Denver, CO, USA

Chapter 7
Adversarial Attacks on Face Recognition Systems

Ying Xu, Kiran Raja, Raghavendra Ramachandra, and Christoph Busch

Abstract Face recognition has been widely used for identity verification both in supervised and unsupervised access control applications. The advancement in deep neural networks has opened up the possibility of scaling it to multiple applications. Despite the improvement in performance, deep network-based Face Recognition Systems (FRS) are not well prepared against adversarial attacks at the deployment level. The output performance of such FRS can be drastically impacted simply by changing the trained parameters, for instance, by changing the number of layers, subnetworks, loss and activation functions. This chapter will first demonstrate the impact on biometric performance using a publicly available face dataset. Further to this, this chapter will also present some strategies to defend against such attacks by incorporating defense mechanisms at the training level to mitigate the performance degradation. With the empirical evaluation of the deep FRS with and without a defense mechanism, we demonstrate the impact on biometric performance for the completeness of the chapter.

7.1 Introduction

Face recognition has been used in a large number of applications such as biometric authentication, civilian ID management and border crossing. The recent success of deep learning for recognition has led to very high biometric verification performance.

Y. Xu · K. Raja (✉) · R. Ramachandra · C. Busch
Norwegian University of Science and Technology, Trondheim, Norway
e-mail: kiran.raja@ntnu.no

Y. Xu
e-mail: xuyi@stud.ntnu.no

R. Ramachandra
e-mail: raghavendra.ramachandra@ntnu.no

C. Busch
e-mail: christoph.busch@ntnu.no

© The Author(s) 2022
C. Rathgeb et al. (eds.), *Handbook of Digital Face Manipulation and Detection*,
Advances in Computer Vision and Pattern Recognition,
https://doi.org/10.1007/978-3-030-87664-7_7

As a result, several state-of-the-art face recognition models such as VGGFace, Residual Networks (ResNet) and ArcFace have been extensively studied [2, 6]. The deeply learnt models have focused on improving the biometric performance in the presence of severe biometric sample quality degradation (i.e. face image) such as pose, illumination, expression, ageing and heterogeneity. With improved performance, the deep models can be used for identification where a subject is probed within the learnt models in a closed enrolment setting or for verification where the model is used to extract the features from two images and thereupon compare them to make a decision based on a pre-computed threshold.

In a parallel direction, a number of potential attacks have been reported on deeply learnt models for various tasks. The attacks range from simple perturbation in the input image to advanced attacks where the parameters of the model are changed. Such attacks lead to changing the robustness of the model; for instance, the changed input may lead to circumventing the identification (i.e. avoid identification from a black-list) or reaching a false match in a non-mated comparison trial. The attacks can be conducted in three different manners where an attacker is fully aware of the model's operation, partially aware of the model's operation and unaware of the model's operation, which fall under the categories white-box, black-box, and gray-box attacks [3, 4, 10, 11, 17, 21, 37, 40]. Each of these attacks can have different attack potential, and thus, not only making the deep models superior in terms of performance is needed, but demanding the robustness to be improved.

Several works have investigated the vulnerabilities of deeply learnt FRS for various attacks [1, 5, 8, 12, 16, 19, 22, 26–29, 32, 34, 35, 39, 42]. In this chapter, we provide a study on adversarial attacks on state-of-the-art deep Face Recognition System (FRS) based on ArcFace [6] in an open-set protocol setting, i.e. the testing set is unknown at the training level. We resort to such a protocol, given that most of the deeply trained FRS may be deployed in scenarios with unknown testing images. We provide a detailed analysis of the biometric implications when the attacks are successful, making the systems result in a higher False Match Rate (FMR). Specifically, when a threshold is set using a clean dataset for a fixed FMR, the attacks at the image level lead to higher FMR.

A sample illustration of such impact using two chosen attacks—Fast Gradient Sign Method (FGSM) and Projected Gradient Descent (PGD) poisoning attacks is provided in Fig. 7.1 on a trained FRS using ArcFace [6]. As noted from the Fig. 7.1, a FRS working on the pre-defined threshold (in this case $\tau = 0.4$) for a fixed $FMR = 0.1\%$ will accept a score above such defined threshold in a non-mated comparison trial. The implication of such an attack is that an attacker can use a poisoned image to circumvent the verification process and thereby be verified as another subject. Such a case can be foreseen when a person contained in a watch-list can avoid being identified, putting the biometric FRS and, thereupon, the security at risk.

In order to fully illustrate the implications of such attacks, we employ FRGC v2 dataset to generate the attacks with FGSM and PGD. We limit the focus of the work to image level attacks under the assumption that the internals of the employed network is unknown to the attacker. To validate the attack potential, we consider the black-box attack setting on trained FRS models where the adversaries can attack

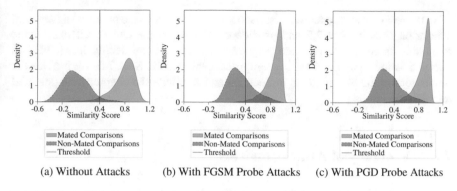

(a) Without Attacks   (b) With FGSM Probe Attacks   (c) With PGD Probe Attacks

Fig. 7.1 Illustration of increased False Match Rate due to fixed threshold based on the clean FRGC v2 Dataset

using perturbed/poisoned images[1] only at the testing/deploying stage. We use the clean version of the FRGC v2 dataset (i.e. with no poisoning) and the corresponding attack set to study the vulnerability. Further, we also re-train the model from scratch using the poisoned (attack) data as adversarial examples to make the trained model aware of such examples while learning. We further study the deep FRS models for their biometric performance with the trained models with adversarial examples. To provide an unbiased observation of the FRS, we employ disjoint training and testing sets without any subject overlap throughout the experiments in this chapter.

We conduct one study where an attacker has the full freedom to poison the probe data alone and another study where an attacker can also poison the enrolment data. In both cases, we assume that neither the trained model nor the training data set are available for the attacker to poison. Through empirical evaluations, we provide a detailed analysis and note the observations for the completeness of the chapter.

The main contributions of this chapter are

- Provides a detailed taxonomy of the potential adversarial attacks on the FRS and their applications.
- Provides empirical validation of vulnerability of the deeply learnt FRS model, which is trained from scratch. The attacks are generated through two different relevant and realizable approaches using Fast Gradient Sign Method (FGSM) and Projected Gradient Descent (PGD).
- Provides a comparative evaluation of the deeply learnt FRS model against commercial-off-the-shelf (COTS) FRS to benchmark the impact of the adversarial attack in each case.
- Provides an evaluation of the robustness of FR models when the same is trained with the adversarial examples using FGSM and PGD.

---

[1] Both perturbed and poisoned images in this chapter refer to the same kind of attacks and are used interchangeably.

In the rest of this chapter, we first list out the taxonomy of the potential adversarial attacks on FRS in Sect. 7.2 and provide the details on the chosen attacks for the evaluation in Sect. 7.3. We then provide the details of the deeply learnt FRS in Sect. 7.5 followed by the details on empirical evaluation in Sect. 7.6. We provide the discussion on the observations in Sect. 7.8 and conclude the chapter with potential research directions.

7.2 Taxonomy of Attacks on FRS

Szegedy et al. [33] illustrated the impact of small perturbations on the images for the image classification problem and defeated state-of-the-art Deep Neural Networks (DNNs) with high misclassification rates. These misclassified samples were named adversarial examples that can impact the performance of the deep models. A number of works have thereafter been proposed for creating such attacks, and the adversarial attacks can be classified by the amount of knowledge an attacker has over the model [3, 4, 10, 11, 17, 21]. Based on such knowledge, the attacks can be classified [37, 40] as:

- White-box attack—assuming the complete knowledge of the target model, i.e. its parameters, architecture, training method, and even in some cases, its training data.
- Gray-box attacks—having partial knowledge of the internal operations and parameters of the network.
- Black-box attacks—feeding a target model with the adversarial examples (during testing) created without knowing that model (e.g. its training procedure or its architecture or parameters). Despite the limited knowledge of the model, an attacker can interact with such a model by utilizing the transferability of adversarial examples.

Motivated by such adversarial attacks, several works have investigated the impact of such attacks on FRS and have provided various mitigation measures [1, 5, 8, 12, 16, 19, 22, 27–29, 32, 34, 35, 39, 42]. We provide an alternative taxonomy of such adversarial attacks by categorizing them in two dimensions such as threat model and perturbation. Figure 7.2 presents the taxonomy under two such dimensions with various sub-attacks. We provide a brief overview of the attacks for the convenience of the reader in this section.

7.2.1 Threat Model

We could break down the threat model into four perspectives, adversarial falsification, adversary's knowledge, adversarial specificity and attack frequency, making different attack examples from various kinds of adversarial attack attributes ground on different assumptions, the knowledge of the model, specificity and attack scenarios.

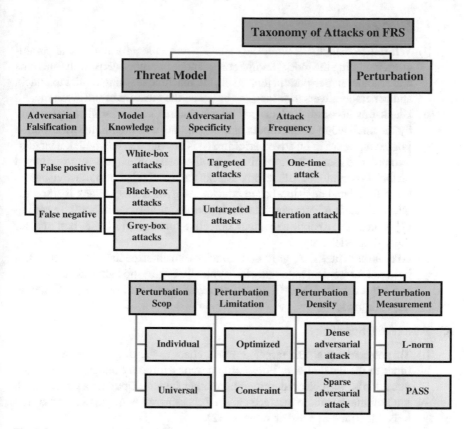

Fig. 7.2 A taxonomy of potential adversarial attacks on FRS

(A) Adversarial Falsification

(i) **False positive**: A false positive attack rejects a true null hypothesis, also called Type I Error, where a negative example is misclassified as a positive class. Within the context of FRS, this error implies a comparison decision of match for a biometric probe and a biometric reference from different biometric capture subjects. For instance, a false match is when subject A is identified or falsely verified as subject B, i.e. a zero-effort impostor accepted in a non-mated comparison trial.

(ii) **False negative**: A false negative attack makes the non-rejection of a false null hypothesis, also called Type II Error, where a positive example is misclassified as a negative class. In the context of FRS, this implies a comparison decision of "non-match" for a biometric probe and a biometric reference from the same biometric capture subject and the same biometric characteristic. Alternatively, a subject A in a mated comparison trial is rejected by the biometric system.

(B) Model Knowledge

(i) **White-box attacks**: A white-box attack gets all the information and parameters, including the model architectures, model weights, activation functions and all other hyper-parameters inside the machine learning model to attack, and generates adversarial samples based on the gradient of the given model.

(ii) **Black-box attacks**: A black-box attack generates adversarial samples only by the knowledge of the inputs and the outputs of a neural network model. For example, when an adversarial image is provided to the model, a label or a confidence score corresponding to another class of image is returned based on the chosen model. Black-box attacks can be divided into transfer-based, score-based and decision-based attacks. An evolutionary attack method for query-efficient adversarial attacks in the decision-based black-box setting [7] is proposed to optimize attack objective function in a black-box manner through queries only.

(iii) **Grey-box attacks**: A grey-box attack is an intermediate attack that lies between former and latter attacks. Typically in grey-box attacks, an attacker can exploit partial knowledge of models, inputs and outputs of a neural network model.

(C) Adversarial Specificity

(i) **Targeted attacks**: The targeted attack changes the output classification of input to the desired one. For example, many different attacks can be conducted to be verified or identified as another subject. Dodging attacks is such kind of attacks where the face can be accessorized with glasses or makeup to be identified as another subject [32].

(ii) **Untargeted attacks**: The goal of an untargeted attack is to lead the neural network to misclassify the inputs. An attacker can simply employ similar approaches of wearing a mask, glasses [32], makeup [42] or have expressions [22] to impersonate another subject, typically an enrollee within the enrolment dataset.

(D) Attack Frequency

(i) **One-time attack**: A one-time attack takes only one time to raise the adversarial examples. A number of different approaches can be used for circumventing the FRS, for instance, creating a face image through deepfakes [16, 27, 34].

(ii) **Iteration attack**: An iterative attack takes multiple times to upgrade the adversarial examples. A potential use case of such attacks can be in creating a morphed face image by combining two face images iteratively with various morphing factors until a successful verification is obtained [25, 36].

Perturbation

Adding perturbations on face images is an easy but effective attack on FRS. Adversarial examples could be generated by adding a small imperceptible perturbation to deceive both humans and the model. Although larger perturbations can be added to the face images, this will lead to producing non-human figures, and the applicability of such perceptible perturbations can only fool FRS but not the human operators if such a system is monitored by one. The perturbation could be categorized in three different sets based on factors of perturbation scope, perturbation limitation, and perturbation measurement.

(A) Perturbation Scope

  (i) **Individual perturbation**: Individual attacks produce various perturbations for each clean input. For instance, a face image may be blurred, added pixel-level noises, masked portions of the face to create the adversarial sample [1, 12].

  (ii) **Universal perturbation**: Universal attacks generate a universal perturbation for the entire data set. Although these attacks are very effective, an attacker needs to avail the entire dataset to devise a good perturbation model to fool the FRS effectively [1, 12, 19, 41].

(B) Perturbation Limitation

  (i) **Optimized perturbation**: An optimized perturbation aims to minimize the perturbation in order to prevent humans from recognizing the perturbation, in the meantime, to fool the FRS [29, 39].

  (ii) **Constraint perturbation**: A constraint perturbation, on the other hand, sets perturbation as a diminutive constraint, for instance, in a chosen area of the face [5, 24].

(C) Perturbation Density

  (i) **Dense adversarial attack**: Dense adversarial attacks perturb the image over all the pixels in one image [3]. As the perturbations are spread over the image, these attacks can be effective, but when the perturbation level is increased, the image structure may change, making them irrelevant attack samples mainly due to loss of visual fidelity.

  (ii) **Sparse adversarial attack**: A sparse adversarial attack means only partial positions are considered, regardless of those immaterial pixels. The adversarial model would choose which parts should be attacked. Perturbation factorization [8] was proposed to enable sparse, dense adversarial attacks.

(D) Perturbation Measurement

  (i) ℓ_p**-norm:** ℓ_p-norm is used to define the magnitude of perturbations which is denoted as $\|\mathbf{x}\|_p$ on a vector $\mathbf{x}$ and is defined as

$$\|\mathbf{x}\|_p = \sqrt[p]{\sum_{n}^{i=1} |v_i|^p} \tag{7.1}$$

where p defines the norm. The one-norm (also known as the L_1-norm, ℓ_1-norm, or mean norm), where p equals 1, is defined as the sum of the absolute values of its components. The two-norm (also known as the L_2-norm, ℓ_2-norm, least-squares norm or mean norm), where p equals 2, is defined as the square root of the sum of the squares of the absolute values of its components. The infinity norm (also known as the L_∞-norm, ℓ_∞-norm, max norm, or uniform norm), where p equals ∞, is defined as the maximum of the absolute values of its components.

(ii) **Psychometric perceptual adversarial similarity score (PASS)**: A novel Perceptual Adversarial Similarity Score (PASS) [28] is a new measure to quantify adversarial images. It is proposed to be more consistent with human perception than prior ℓ_p-norm measurements and to serve as a similarity measure to quantify how adversarial a misclassified image is. It supports many transformations, including small translations and rotations, which result in images that are perturbed to observable extents compared to their original counterparts while still appear to be reasonable samples of the same images.

7.3 Poisoning Attacks on FRS

Although several attacks can be found in the literature, we focus on "Adversarial Falsification" attacks under which both False Non-Match Rate (FNMR) and False Match Rate (FMR) are impacted. Further, we restrict ourselves to Black-box setting where the knowledge of the model is limited and create the attacks using perturbations (or poisoning). Two kinds of perturbations such as Fast Gradient Sign Method (FGSM) and Projected Gradient Descent (PGD) [11] attacks are considered in this chapter, mainly due to lower attack generation cost in terms of time and effort. Different variants of the same attacks can be found in the literature, but they generally take a longer time to generate, and we restrict our focus to realizable attacks in terms of the time required to generate the attack itself. We provide a brief overview of the attack generation mechanism for both attacks in this section.

7.3.1 Fast Gradient Sign Method

The Fast Gradient Sign Method (FGSM) [11] is a linear perturbation of non-linear models. It uses the gradients of the neural network to create adversarial examples. The perturbation is defined as

$$\eta = \epsilon \, sign \left(\nabla_x J \left(\theta, x, y \right) \right),$$

where θ is the parameters of a model, x and y are the input to the model and the labels associated with x respectively, $J(\theta, x, y)$ represents the cost used to train the neural network and ϵ is the perturbation factor. The optimal max-norm η is defined by linearizing the cost function around the current value of θ. The adversarial image is produced by adding η to the original input image. The neural networks are designed by leveraging the gradients to optimize the learning. The FGSM attack generation simply uses the gradient of loss of the input data and adjusts the input data in such a way that the loss is maximized.

7.3.2 *Projected Gradient Descent*

The idea of Projected Gradient Descent (PGD) [11] is essentially a saddle point problem as the composition of an inner maximization problem and an outer minimization problem. The basic formulation of PGD is denoted as

$$\min_{\theta} \mathbb{E}_{(x,y)\sim\mathcal{D}}(\max_{\delta\in\mathcal{S}} L(\theta, x + \delta, y)).$$

$\mathcal{D}$ represents an underlying data distribution over pairs of examples x and corresponding labels y. The θ is the set of model parameters and $L(\theta, x, y)$ is the loss function. The goal of PGD algorithm is to find parameters θ that minimize the empirical risk $\mathbb{E}_{(x,y)\sim\mathcal{D}}(L(\theta, x, y))$. A set of allowed perturbations $\mathcal{S}$ is introduced to formalize the manipulative power of the adversary for each data point x. $\mathcal{S}$ captures perceptual similarity between images in the classification tasks. The goal of the inner maximization problem is to find a perturbation $\delta \in \mathcal{S}$ of a given data point x that achieves the highest loss. While the outer minimization problem aims to find the model parameters to minimize the adversarial loss. PGD algorithm can start from random perturbations in the ball of interest decided by ℓ_∞-norm around a sample and repeatedly take s steps of α size till convergence. Random starts would help PGD to solve local optima within the objective.

7.4   Carlini and Wagner (CW) Attacks

The general idea of CW algorithm [3] is the typical adversarial attack which utilizes the adversarial loss and the image distance loss. The former loss ensures the adversarial images to fool the classification models while the latter one is used to control the perturbation of the adversarial examples. The CW attack could be formulated as

$$\text{minimize} \quad \|\delta\|_p + c \cdot f(x + \delta) \tag{7.2}$$

$$\text{such that} \quad x + \delta \in [0, 1]^n \tag{7.3}$$

c is a constant that differs between models. The author of CW used binary search to choose c. δ is the small change that the CW algorithm adds to mystifies the classifier. Given x_i, δ_i is defined as

$$\delta_i = \frac{1}{2}\left(tanh\left(w_i\right) + 1\right) - x_i,$$

$tanh(w_i)$ is introduced to meet the request of box constraint Eq. (7.3).

Object function f is chosen as

$$f(x') = \max(\max_{i \neq t} Z(x')_i - Z(x')_t, -k),$$

which chooses the difference of two probability values or the confidence parameter k. By setting the value of $-k$, the user could specify the confidence of the adversarial attack. This chapter focuses on open-set verification protocols by simply extracting the embeddings and comparing with cosine distance, and therefore we do not consider this attack further.

A sample illustration of FGSM and PGD perturbation is shown in Fig. 7.3. As noted from Fig. 7.3, perturbation factor ϵ directly influences the perceptual quality of the image. While higher perturbation factors may result in stronger attacks, one has to focus on visual appearance to make the attack not obvious to human perception.

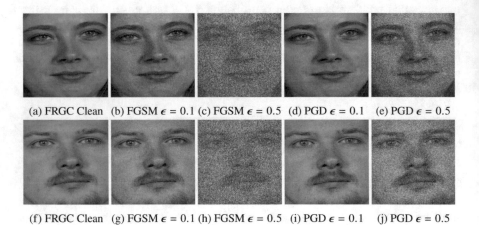

(a) FRGC Clean   (b) FGSM $\epsilon = 0.1$ (c) FGSM $\epsilon = 0.5$ (d) PGD $\epsilon = 0.1$ (e) PGD $\epsilon = 0.5$

(f) FRGC Clean   (g) FGSM $\epsilon = 0.1$ (h) FGSM $\epsilon = 0.5$ (i) PGD $\epsilon = 0.1$ (j) PGD $\epsilon = 0.5$

Fig. 7.3 Adversarial attack examples of FGSM and PGD with $\epsilon = 0.1$ and $\epsilon = 0.5$ where ϵ is the strength of the perturbation. As noted from the illustration, FGSM attack degrades the visual appearance quality of the image when the perturbation factor ϵ is increased while the visual appearance is still tolerable with the PGD even with a larger ϵ

7.5   ArcFace FRS Model

Of the number of models available for large-scale training data, both the softmax-loss-based methods [2] and the triplet-loss-based methods [30] can achieve high recognition performance. However, both the softmax loss and the triplet loss have some drawbacks for scalability issues. The size of the linear transformation matrix $W \in \mathbb{R}^{d \times n}$ increases linearly with the identities number n, and the learned features are separable for the closed-set classification problem but not discriminative enough for the open-set face recognition problem which is typical for face recognition. As for the triplet loss, the combinatorial explosion in the number of face triplets is especially for large-scale datasets, leading to a significant increase in the number of iteration steps. Semi-hard sample mining is a quite difficult problem for effective model training, which depends on the availability of large-scale data. Based on these two motivations, we choose to employ ArcFace deep FRS due to its superior performance as demonstrated in various works [6].

In this work, we choose to employ the ResNet101 architecture and Additive Angular Margin Loss (ArcFace) loss to directly benefit from the discriminative power of the face recognition model without much overhead on training process [6]. ArcFace utilizes the arc-cosine function to calculate the angle between the current feature and the target weight. ArcFace directly optimizes the geodesic distance margin under the exact correspondence between the angle and arc in the normalized hypersphere. Specifically, we extract 512 dimensional embeddings for all the experiments.

We first validate the choice of ResNet101 network and ArcFace loss using the publicly available LFW [13], CFP-FP [31], AgeDB-30 [20]. Based on the accuracy obtained on these datasets, we fix the architecture choices and then use it for all our experiments on FRGC v2 dataset [23].

7.6   Experiments and Analysis

In this section, we list the details of the dataset, attack generation and the set of FRS analysis conducted. We employ False Non-Match Rate (FNMR) at a False Match Rate (FMR) of 0.1% and Equal Error Rate (EER) to report the performance of FRS and supplement the results using the Detection Error Trade-off (DET) curves when applicable.

7.6.1   Clean Dataset

Considering the focus of this work on FRS, we choose a state-of-art FR dataset– FRGCv2 dataset [23] specifically to report the open-set verification experiments. Our choice is based on two factors (1) FRGCv2 dataset presents a mix of images that closely resemble the biometric enrolment and probe dataset and are not significantly degraded, impacting the model's performance due to noise (2) by splitting the FRGC dataset into disjoint sets, we can illustrate the performance on open-set verification protocols. We, therefore, evaluate the attack potential on the deeply learnt FRS model corresponding to the protocol known as Experiment-1 [23]. We have reorganized the dataset to have 222 subjects in the training set and validation set (randomly subsampled in each training epoch) and the rest of the non-overlapping subjects in the disjoint testing test. Care has been exercised not to overlap any subjects in the training set and testing set. The database is first processed to detect the face region, and then the facial images are aligned [6]. Each image in all three sets is further resized to 112×112 pixels for training the model and testing the model.

7.6.2 Attack Dataset

We generate the attack dataset corresponding to all three subsets, such as training, validation and testing set of FRGC v2 dataset. We generate two kinds of attacks such as FGSM attacks and PGD attacks as both of these attacks can retain the similarity of the face region despite adding the noise to the image.[2]

7.6.2.1 Attack Dataset—FGSM Perturbations

Using the clean version of the FRGC dataset (i.e. non-poisoned), we generate the FGSM attack dataset for all three subsets of training, validation and testing set. We employ Torchattack library[3] to generate the attack dataset for FGSM. We specifically use the FGSM model from Torchattack library to generate the attacks with a perturbation factor of $\epsilon = 0.1$ and $\epsilon = 0.5$.[4] Although we have experimented with various ϵ, we choose the perturbation factor of $\epsilon = 0.1$ based on the stronger attack potential while not degrading the image's visual appearance. It should, however, be noted that the $\epsilon < 0.1$ is still effective to attack FRS with a limited success rate.

7.6.2.2 Attack Dataset—PGD Perturbations

Similar to FGSM attacks, we use the clean version (i.e. non-poisoned) of the FRGC dataset to generate a PGD attack dataset for all three subsets of training, validation and testing set. We employ the Torchattack library to generate the PGD attack dataset.

---

[2] CW attacks take larger time for generation, and we do not consider CW attacks in this work as their practical applicability in our study is limited.

[3] https://adversarial-attacks-pytorch.readthedocs.io/en/latest/attacks.html.

[4] https://github.com/Harry24k/adversarial-attacks-pytorch.

In the lines of FGSM attacks, we employ generate the attacks with a perturbation factor of $\epsilon = 0.1$ and $\epsilon = 0.5$.

7.6.2.3 COTS Evaluation

In order to first understand the impact of poisoning (perturbation) attacks, we evaluate the biometric performance using the COTS system.[5] We employ testing partition of clean FRGC data and testing partition of poisoned data with FGSM and PGD attacks to verify the recognition performance. We first evaluate the performance of COTS FRS using clean FRGC data against clean data. We further evaluate the performance of COTS FRS by enrolling clean FRGC data and probed using PGD and FGSM attacks generated with $\epsilon = 0.1$. The attacks generated with $\epsilon = 0.5$ do not compromise the FRS as the FRS rejects them as Failure-to-Extract, and we do not report the error rates for such a setting.

We note from the Table 7.1 that COTS FRS[6] is not sensitive to the poisoned data and provides ideal biometric performance irrespective of clean or poisoned data. Our assertion of this observation is that the version of the COTS FRS does not employ deep networks and thus makes it robust against poisoning attacks. However, as the COTS FRS does not disclose the algorithm, we cannot fully confirm our hypothesis.

7.6.3 FRS Model for Baseline Verification

We train the ArcFace deep learning model from scratch using the training set and verify the model's performance using the disjoint validation set. We carry out the training for 100 epochs with a learning rate of 0.01 with ArcFace loss [6] to avoid overfitting due to limited sample size. The trained model is further used to extract the embedding of length 512 on the testing set, and the similarity between two images is computed using the cosine distance in our baseline performance evaluation. We employ the False Non-Match Rate (FNMR) at False Match Rate (FMR) of 0.01 for validating the model on the validation set. The performance reported in this chapter further on is only on the testing set of the FRGCv2 dataset and corresponding attack sets for FGSM and PGD attacks.

7.6.4 FRS Baseline Performance Evaluation

The trained model on FRGC v2 training dataset is first evaluated to obtain the baseline performance on the FRGC testing set, FGSM attack testing set and PGD attack

---

[5] Neurotech Verilook—Version 11.1—https://www.neurotechnology.com.

[6] We do not present the DET curves as the EER=0% for chosen COTS SDK.

Table 7.1 Performance of FRS without attacks, with FGSM attacks and PGD attacks

	EER (%)	FNMR (%) @ FMR = 0.1%	EER (%)	FNMR (%) @ FMR = 0.1%
Deep FRS	Cosine		Euclidean	
	Similarity		Distance	
FRGC Clean	4.18	13.54	6.21	42.68
FGSM probe attacks	8.08	39.44	6.59	74.04
PGD probe attacks	7.45	31.98	7.20	84.32
COTS FRS				
	EER (%)		FNMR (%)	
FRGC Clean	0		0	
FGSM probe attacks	0		0	
PGD probe attacks	0		0	

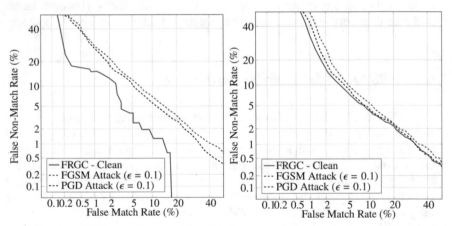

(a) DET curves - baseline performance for models trained on FRGC clean data (Cosine similarity)

(b) DET curves - baseline performance for models trained on FRGC clean data (Euclidean distance)

Fig. 7.4 Baseline DETs on FRS trained on clean FRGC, probed with FRGC clean data, FGSM and PGD attack data

testing set. The results obtained from baseline evaluation are presented in Fig. 7.4a. For reporting the performance, we extract the embedding of length 512 from the trained FRS and then employ cosine similarity to obtain the comparison score. As noted from Table 7.1 and the corresponding DET can be found in Fig. 7.4a, the trained model performs best when the data is clean (i.e. without attack), resulting in an Equal Error Rate (EER) of 4.18%.

7.6.4.1 Baseline Evaluation with Euclidean Distance

In order to study the variance of performance with distance measure on the FRS model, we also conduct the same analysis using the Euclidean distance measure to obtain the comparison scores. As it can be observed from Fig. 7.4b, there is a performance drop when the embeddings are compared using the Euclidean distance illustrating the dependence of distance measure in deep FRS. This aspect can be attributed to the training mechanism optimized for cosine similarity, and thus it is not surprising to see the drop in the performance. Table 7.1 presents the obtained error rates using the Euclidean distance with a baseline EER of 6.21% when the model is presented with no attacks.

7.6.4.2 Impact of Increased Perturbations

Further, we also study the impact of the perturbation strength on FRS by poisoning the images with a perturbation factor ϵ of 0.5. Specifically, we poison the probe images and use them to probe against clean FRGC enrolment. Figure 7.5a presets the DETs corresponding to these experiments and it can be noted from the Fig. 7.5a that such attacks lead to a significant number of false matches and false non-matches. A similar observation can be made for the comparison of embeddings using the Euclidean distance as depicted in Fig. 7.5b. Further, to illustrate the impact of such attacks with a high degree of poisoning, we present the distribution shifts Fig. 7.6. As one can note, such attacks lead to very high false rejects and a small number

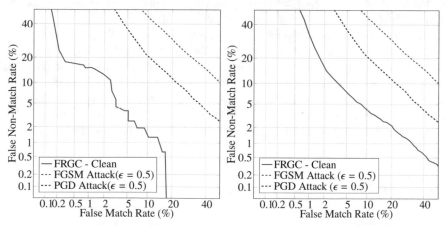

(a) DET curves - baseline performance for models trained on FRGC clean data (Cosine similarity) - Attacks FGSM ($\epsilon = 0.5$) and PGD ($\epsilon = 0.5$)

(b) DET curves - baseline performance for models trained on FRGC clean data (Euclidean distance) - Attacks FGSM ($\epsilon = 0.5$) and PGD ($\epsilon = 0.5$)

Fig. 7.5 Baseline DETs on FRS trained on clean FRGC and tested on FRGC clean data, FGSM and PGD attack data with $\epsilon = 0.5$

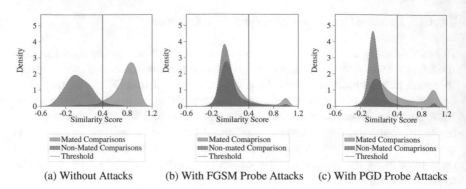

(a) Without Attacks (b) With FGSM Probe Attacks (c) With PGD Probe Attacks

Fig. 7.6 Illustration of increased False Non-Match Rate due to fixed threshold based on the clean FRGC v2 Dataset and probed with highly perturbed images $\epsilon = 0.5$

Table 7.2 Performance of FRS with FGSM and PGD attacks with larger perturbation ($\epsilon = 0.5$)

	EER (%)	FNMR (%) @ FMR = 0.1%	EER (%)	FNMR (%) @ FMR = 0.1%
	Cosine		Euclidean	
FGSM probe attacks	24.72	86.20	18.44	89.28
PGD probe attacks	15.05	65.46	24.81	74.50

of false matches. Table 7.2 presets the performance obtained in terms of EER and FNMR@FMR=0.1% to illustrate the degradation of FRS.

The attacks with such amount of poisoning may not benefit the attacker to be falsely verified against another identity, making them not highly lucrative for the attackers targeting false acceptance. However, such attempts for verification using highly poisoned images may easily help the attacker to be not identified in a watch-list where the FRS does not obtain a high enough comparison score to cross the pre-determined threshold. It can be asserted with a high degree of confidence that this kind of attacks may not be attractive as they distort the images to a high degree.

7.6.5 FRS Performance on Probe Data Poisoning

Considering that an attacker is unable to change the enrolment set, we also provide another study where the attacker can only change the data at the probe level. The critical assumption here is that an attacker can get hold of images from social media sites that may not be of optimal quality for biometric use cases. Using such images, an attacker can generate the poisoning such that the FRS can still accept the attack images. In order to achieve this, we retain the original FRGC clean data as an enrolment set and use the FGSM and PGD attacks at the probe level. Figure 7.4 presents the change in performance when the probe images are alone attacked where the poisoned data succeeds in verifying against the enrolment set. This can be both seen as the robustness of the network to noisy data and also as a weakness in distinguishing the poisoned attack images.

7.6.6 FRS Performance on Enrolment Data Poisoning

While we have assumed that an attacker is unable to access the enrolment set in the earlier set of experiments, we also consider another scenario where the attacker is fully capable of poisoning the enrolment dataset. We consider a scenario where an attacker can poison the enrolment database using FGSM attacks and probe against PGD attacks. As illustrated in Fig. 7.7a and b, under such a scenario of poisoned enrolment set, the attack succeeds in obtaining a reasonable biometric performance. However, these attacks may not be highly realistic when secure mechanisms are used to protect the enrolment data, as seen in most of the operational systems. Despite limited success, this set of experiments shows that the FRS are vulnerable if the enrolment set is compromised, and this aspect needs further investigation.

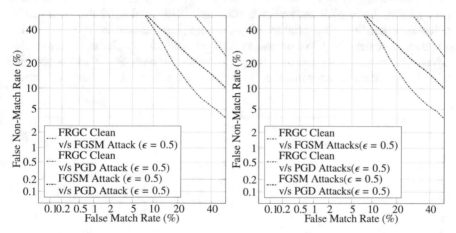

(a) Cross-poisoning evaluation of FRGC clean data v/s FGSM ($\epsilon = 0.5$) and PGD ($\epsilon = 0.5$) attack - Cosine Distance

(b) Cross-poisoning evaluation of FRGC clean data v/s FGSM ($\epsilon = 0.5$) and PGD ($\epsilon = 0.5$) attack - Eucliedean Distance

Fig. 7.7 DETs for clean FRGC enrolment poisoned with versus attack probe images with higher perturbations ($\epsilon = 0.5$)

7.7 Impact of Adversarial Training with FGSM Attacks

As the performance of the FRS under adversarial attacks can change, in this section, we analyze if training the FRS with adversarial samples can improve the accuracy. While different strategies for mitigating the adversarial attacks starting from having detection schemes [18] to training the FRS with adversarial samples [9, 38], we simply resort to train the FRS model with the adversarial samples using both perturbation factors of $\epsilon = 0.1$ and $\epsilon = 0.5$. To account for the generalisability towards both FGSM and PGD attacks, we train a FRS network by incorporating the FGSM and PGD adversarial samples into the training data.

Figure 7.8 depicts the performance obtained using the FRS trained with FGSM + PGD attacks on the various testing sets. As it can be noted, the FRS, despite having low accuracy when the adversarial samples are presented under open-set evaluation protocol, performance is restored to similar accuracy simply by incorporating the adversarial samples in the training set. It is interesting to note that the adversarially trained model performs equally well with the embeddings compared using Euclidean distance, unlike the model trained with clean data under similar settings as shown in the Fig. 7.9. Although this indicates the robustness of the trained model when adversarial samples are provided, a detailed analysis is further needed.

Further, we also evaluate the performance of the adversarially trained FRS for cross-poisoning attacks corresponding to Sect. 7.6.5. The obtained performance is presented in the Fig. 7.9 and the performance is also listed in Table 7.3. It can be evidently noted that adversarial training can help in addressing the cross-poisoning attacks to a greater extent. In the lines of previously noted results, it can be seen that the adversarial training also improves the performance for comparison scores obtained with the Euclidean distance measure for measuring the dissimilarity between embed-

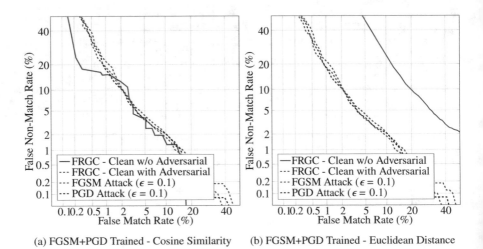

(a) FGSM+PGD Trained - Cosine Similarity   (b) FGSM+PGD Trained - Euclidean Distance

Fig. 7.8 ROC graphs for adversarial trained FRS with FGSM+PGD attack data

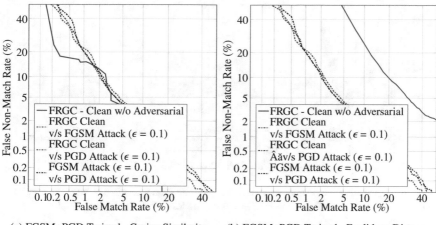

(a) FGSM+PGD Trained - Cosine Similarity   (b) FGSM+PGD Trained - Euclidean Distance

Fig. 7.9 ROC graphs for adversarial trained FRS with FGSM+PGD attack data and increased poisoning

Table 7.3 Performance of FRS trained with adversarial examples when probed with attack images from FGSM and PGD attack generation

	EER (%)	FNMR (%) @ FMR = 0.1%	EER (%)	FNMR (%) @ FMR = 0.1%
	Cosine		Euclidean	
FRGC Clean	4.18	13.54	6.21	42.68
FGSM Probe Attacks	4.65	22.20	4.37	22.04
PGD Probe Attacks	4.37	23.18	4.70	24.81

dings. Further, to illustrate the advantage of the adversarial training in observing the shift in distribution between mated and non-mated comparison scores, we also present the obtained distributions in Fig. 7.10. As it can be noted from Fig. 7.10, the distribution of mated and non-mated comparison becomes very identical to baseline system performance when no attacks are conducted, as shown in Fig. 7.1a.

7.8 Discussion

With the set of all experiments conducted in this work under the open-set protocols for biometric verification using a deep model, we observe that the FRS are generally vulnerable to poisoning/perturbation attacks. Although the deep FRS are sensitive to a different degree based on the degree of poisoning of images, both FGSM and PGD

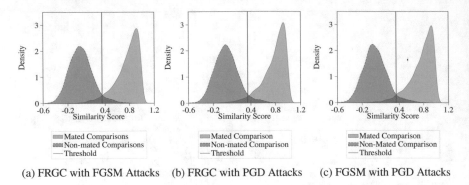

(a) FRGC with FGSM Attacks   (b) FRGC with PGD Attacks   (c) FGSM with PGD Attacks

Fig. 7.10 Distribution shift in mated and non-mated comparison scores as a result of the adversarial training in a combined manner using PGD+FGSM samples on cross-poisoning attacks

attacks can adversely affect the false match and false non-match decisions, both of which have a significant operational impact if deployed. We noted that the baseline performance of FRS degrades when the clean data alone (despite capture noises such as bad illumination, pose and expression) is used. The performance of the systems further degrades when the cross-poisoning attacks are carried out, specifically when the attacker can manipulate the images in the enrolment set and probe with images of significant attack degree. Unlike the deep FRS, we also note that the COTS FRS is insensitive to such attacks, but due to limited knowledge on the employed algorithm in COTS, one cannot conclude on what contributes to its robustness.

However, we also note that by simply retraining the entire network with adversarial examples, we can improve the baseline performance of the deep FRS and also make it robust to cross-poisoning attacks. One key benefit of such an approach is the limited overhead on the network design where one can simply reuse the network. While on the other hand, the deep FRS may still remain sensitive to the newer attacks if such examples are not seen by the network during the training phase. Alternatively, one can simply add another layer to the FRS network which can detect adversarial attacks, which is a common practice in presentation attack detection. On the downside of such design is the additional overhead of design of the network and no guarantee that these adversarial sample detection module would scale to newer and unknown attacks. In another direction, stricter constraints can be imposed to eliminate the non-conforming images according to quality standards as defined by ISO/IEC standards—29794-5 [14, 15] should such systems be deployed. Such observations and arguments lead us to critically analyze the deep FRS for various factors and study the generalizing ability to diverse adversarial attacks on FRS. This can be an interesting direction for future works for mitigating the adversarial threats on deep FRS.

7.9 Conclusions and Future Directions

Despite the impressive accuracy obtained with deep models for various face recognition tasks, they are vulnerable to various kinds of attacks. In this chapter, we have presented various adversarial attacks that can negatively impact the biometric performance of face recognition systems. Further, we have chosen two relevant adversarial attacks based on the poisoning of the images at both probe level and enrolment level. The chosen attacks were thoroughly evaluated using a state-of-art face dataset to illustrate the impact of the poisoning attacks on deep network-based face recognition. This chapter specifically illustrated the impact on biometric performance in terms of false match and false non-match decisions when such poisoned data is used for attacks. Further, this chapter also illustrated the use of adversarial examples to make the deep models robust towards such poisoning attacks.

Future works in this direction can also combine the poisoning attacks with the parameter level attacks to verify the impact on biometric performance. Another potential direction is to study the model and parameter protection mechanisms to avoid white-box attacks.

References

1. Agarwal A, Singh R, Vatsa M, Ratha N (2018) Are image-agnostic universal adversarial perturbations for face recognition difficult to detect? In 2018 IEEE 9th international conference on biometrics theory, applications and systems (BTAS). IEEE, pp 1–7
2. Cao Q, Shen L, Xie W, Parkhi OM, Zisserman A (2018) Vggface2: A dataset for recognising faces across pose and age. In 2018 13th IEEE international conference on automatic face & gesture recognition (FG 2018). IEEE, pp 67–74
3. Carlini N, Wagner D (2017) Towards evaluating the robustness of neural networks. In: Proceedings—IEEE symposium on security and privacy, pp 39–57
4. Chen W, Zhang Z, Hu X, Wu B (2020) Boosting decision-based black-box adversarial attacks with random sign flip. In: European conference on computer vision. Springer, pp 276–293
5. Dabouei A, Soleymani S, Dawson J, Nasrabadi N (2019) Fast geometrically-perturbed adversarial faces. In: 2019 IEEE winter conference on applications of computer vision (WACV). IEEE, pp 1979–1988
6. Deng J, Guo J, Xue N, Zafeiriou S (2019) Arcface: additive angular margin loss for deep face recognition. In: Proceedings of the IEEE/CVF conference on computer vision and pattern recognition, pp 4690–4699
7. Dong Y, Su H, Wu B, Li Z, Liu W, Zhang T, Zhu J (2019) Efficient decision-based black-box adversarial attacks on face recognition, pp 7714–7722
8. Fan Y, Wu B, Li T, Zhang Y, Li M, Li Z, Yang Y (2020) Sparse adversarial attack via perturbation factorization. Lecture notes in computer science (including subseries Lecture Notes in Artificial Intelligence and Lecture Notes in Bioinformatics), vol 12367 LNCS, pp 35–50
9. Goel A, Singh A, Agarwal A, Vatsa M, Singh R (2018) Smartbox: benchmarking adversarial detection and mitigation algorithms for face recognition. In: 2018 IEEE 9th international conference on biometrics theory, applications and systems (BTAS). IEEE, pp 1–7. IEEE
10. Goodfellow IJ, Shlens J, Szegedy C (2014) Explaining and harnessing adversarial examples. arXiv:1412.6572

11. Goodfellow IJ, Shlens J, Szegedy C (2015) Explaining and harnessing adversarial examples. In: 3rd international conference on learning representations, ICLR 2015-conference track proceedings, pp 1–11

12. Goswami G, Agarwal A, Ratha N, Singh R, Vatsa M (2019) Detecting and mitigating adversarial perturbations for robust face recognition. Int J Comput Vis 127(6):719–742

13. Huang GB, Mattar M, Berg T, Learned-Miller E (2008) Labeled faces in the wild: a database forstudying face recognition in unconstrained environments. In: Workshop on faces in 'Real-Life' images: detection, alignment, and recognition

14. International Organization for Standardization. ISO/IEC TR 29794-5:2010 Information technology–Biometric sample quality–Part 5: Face image data, 2020

15. International Organization for Standardization. ISO/IEC 29794-5:2020 Information technology–Biometric sample quality–Part 5: Face image data, 2020

16. Korshunov P, Marcel S (2018) Deepfakes: a new threat to face recognition? assessment and detection. arXiv:1812.08685

17. Kurakin A, Goodfellow I, Bengio S et al (2016) Adversarial examples in the physical world

18. Massoli FV, Carrara F, Amato G, Falchi F (2021) Detection of face recognition adversarial attacks. Comput Vis Image Underst 202:103103

19. Moosavi-Dezfooli S-M, Fawzi A, Fawzi O, Frossard P (2017) Universal adversarial perturbations. In: Proceedings of the IEEE conference on computer vision and pattern recognition, pp 1765–1773

20. Moschoglou S, Papaioannou A, Sagonas C, Deng J, Kotsia I, Zafeiriou S (2017) Agedb: the first manually collected, in-the-wild age database. In: Proceedings of the IEEE conference on computer vision and pattern recognition workshops, pp 51–59

21. Papernot N, McDaniel P, Goodfellow I, Jha S, Celik ZB, Swami A (2017) Practical black-box attacks against machine learning. In: Proceedings of the 2017 ACM on Asia conference on computer and communications security, pp 506–519

22. Peña A, Serna I, Morales A, Fierrez J, Lapedriza A (2020) Facial expressions as a vulnerability in face recognition. arXiv:2011.08809

23. Phillips PJ, Flynn PJ, Scruggs T, Bowyer KW, Chang J, Hoffman K, Marques J, Min J, Worek W (2005) Overview of the face recognition grand challenge. In: 2005 IEEE computer society conference on computer vision and pattern recognition (CVPR'05), vol 1. IEEE, pp 947–954

24. Qin L, Peng F, Venkatesh S, Ramachandra R, Long M, Busch C (2020) Low visual distortion and robust morphing attacks based on partial face image manipulation. IEEE Trans Biomet Behav Identity Sci

25. Raja K, Ferrara M, Franco A, Spreeuwers L, Batskos I, de Wit Marta Gomez-Barrero F, Scherhag U, Fischer D, Venkatesh S, Singh JM et al (2020) Morphing attack detection–database, evaluation platform and benchmarking. In: IEEE - TIFS

26. Ramachandra R, Busch Christoph (2017) Presentation attack detection methods for face recognition systems: a comprehensive survey. ACM Comput Surveys (CSUR) 50(1):1–37

27. Rossler A, Cozzolino D, Verdoliva L, Riess C, Thies J, Nießner M (2016) Faceforensics++: learning to detect manipulated facial images. In: Proceedings of the IEEE/CVF international conference on computer vision, pp 1–11

28. Rozsa A, Rudd EM, Boult TE (2016) Adversarial diversity and hard positive generation. In: IEEE computer society conference on computer vision and pattern recognition workshops, pp 410–417

29. Saha S, Sim T (2020) Is face recognition safe from realizable attacks? In: 2020 IEEE international joint conference on biometrics (IJCB), pp 1–8

30. Schroff F, Kalenichenko D, Philbin J (2015) Facenet: a unified embedding for face recognition and clustering. In: Proceedings of the IEEE conference on computer vision and pattern recognition, pp 815–823

31. Sengupta S, Chen J-C, Castillo C, Patel VM, Chellappa R, Jacobs DW (2016) Frontal to profile face verification in the wild. In: 2016 IEEE winter conference on applications of computer vision (WACV). IEEE, pp 1–9

32. Sharif M, Bhagavatula S, Bauer L, Reiter MK (2016) Accessorize to a crime: real and stealthy attacks on state-of-the-art face recognition. In: Proceedings of the 2016 acm sigsac conference on computer and communications security, pp 1528–1540
33. Szegedy C, Zaremba W, Sutskever I, Bruna J, Erhan D, Goodfellow I, Fergus R (2013) Intriguing properties of neural networks. arXiv:1312.6199
34. Tolosana R, Vera-Rodriguez R, Fierrez J, Morales A, Ortega-Garcia J (2020) Deepfakes and beyond: a survey of face manipulation and fake detection. Inf Fusion 64:131–148
35. Vakhshiteh F, Nickabadi A, Ramachandra R (2020) Adversarial attacks against face recognition: a comprehensive study. arXiv:2007.11709
36. Venkatesh S, Ramachandra R, Raja K, Busch C (2021) Face morphing attack generation & detection: a comprehensive survey. In: IEEE-TTS
37. Vivek BS, Mopuri KR, Venkatesh Babu R (2018) Gray-box adversarial training. In: Proceedings of the European conference on computer vision (ECCV), pp 203–218
38. Wu D, Xia S-T, Wang Y (2020) Adversarial weight perturbation helps robust generalization. Adv Neural Inf Process Syst 33
39. Xu X, Chen J, Xiao J, Wang Z, Yang Y, Shen HT (2020) Learning optimization-based adversarial perturbations for attacking sequential recognition models. In: Proceedings of the 28th ACM international conference on multimedia, pp 2802–2822
40. Zhao R (2020) Vulnerability of the neural networks against adversarial examples: a survey. arXiv:2011.05976
41. Zhong Y, Deng Weihong (2020) Towards transferable adversarial attack against deep face recognition. IEEE Trans Inf Forensics Secur 16:1452–1466
42. Zhu Z-A, Lu Y-Z, Chiang C-K (2019) Generating adversarial examples by makeup attacks on face recognition. In: 2019 IEEE international conference on image processing (ICIP). IEEE, pp 2516–2520

Chapter 8
Talking Faces: Audio-to-Video Face Generation

Yuxin Wang, Linsen Song, Wayne Wu, Chen Qian, Ran He, and Chen Change Loy

Abstract Talking face generation aims at synthesizing coherent and realistic face sequences given an input speech. The task enjoys a wide spectrum of downstream applications, such as teleconferencing, movie dubbing, and virtual assistant. The emergence of deep learning and cross-modality research has led to many interesting works that address talking face generation. Despite great research efforts in talking face generation, the problem remains challenging due to the need for fine-grained control of face components and the generalization to arbitrary sentences. In this chapter, we first discuss the definition and underlying challenges of the problem. Then, we present an overview of recent progress in talking face generation. In addition, we introduce some widely used datasets and performance metrics. Finally, we discuss open questions, potential future directions, and ethical considerations in this task.

Y. Wang · W. Wu · C. Qian
SenseTime Research, Beijing, China
e-mail: wangyuxin1@sensetime.com

W. Wu
e-mail: wuwenyan@sensetime.com

C. Qian
e-mail: qianchen@sensetime.com

L. Song · R. He
NLPR, CASIA, Beijing, China
e-mail: songlinsen2018@ia.ac.cn

R. He
e-mail: rhe@nlpr.ia.ac.cn

C. C. Loy (✉)
S-Lab, Nanyang Technological University, Singapore, Singapore
e-mail: ccloy@ntu.edu.sg

© The Author(s) 2022
C. Rathgeb et al. (eds.), *Handbook of Digital Face Manipulation and Detection*,
Advances in Computer Vision and Pattern Recognition,
https://doi.org/10.1007/978-3-030-87664-7_8

8.1   Introduction

Talking face generation aims at synthesizing a realistic target face, which talks in correspondence to the given audio sequences. Thanks to the emergence of deep learning methods for content generation [1–3], talking face generation has attracted significant research interests from both computer vision [4–8] and computer graphics [9–14].

Talking face generation has been studied since 1990s [15–18], and it was mainly used in cartoon animation [15] or visual-speech perception experiments [16]. With the advancement of computer technology and the popularization of network services, new application scenarios emerged. First, this technology can help multimedia content production, such as making video games [19] and dubbing movies [20] or TV shows [21]. Moreover, the animated characters enhance human perception by involving visual information, such as video conferencing [22], virtual announcer [23], virtual teacher [24], and virtual assistant [12]. Furthermore, this technology has the potential to realize the digital twin of real person [21].

Talking face generation is a complicated cross-modal task, which requires the modeling of complex and dynamic relationships between audio and face. Existing methods typically decompose the task into subproblems, including audio representation, face modeling, audio-to-face animation, and post-processing. As the source of talking face generation, voice contains rich content and emotional information. To extract essential information that is useful for talking face animation, one would require robust methods to analyze and comprehend the underlying speech signal [7, 12, 22, 25–28]. As the target of talking face generation, face modeling and analysis are also important. Models that characterize human faces have been proposed and applied to various tasks [17, 22, 23, 29–33]. As the bridge that joins audio and face, audio-to-face animation is the key component in talking face generation. Sophisticated methods are needed to accurately and consistently match a speaker's mouth movements and facial expressions to the source audio. Last but not least, to obtain a natural and temporally smooth face in the generated video, careful post-processing is inevitable.

Toward conversational human-computer interaction, talking face generation requires techniques that could generate realistic digital talking faces that make human observers feeling comfortable. As highlighted in Uncanny Valley Theory [34], if an entity is anthropomorphic but imperfect, its non-human characteristics will become the conspicuous part that creates strangely familiar feelings of eeriness and revulsion in observers. The requirement poses stringent requirements on the talking face models, demanding realistic fine-grained facial control, continuous high-quality generation, and generalization ability for arbitrary sentence and identity. In addition, this also prompts researchers to build diverse talking face datasets and establish fair and standard evaluation metrics.

8.2 Related Work

In this session, we discuss relevant techniques employed to address the four sub-problems in talking face generation, namely, audio representation, face modeling, audio-to-face animation, and post-processing.

8.2.1 Audio Representation

It is generally believed the high-level content information and emotional information in the voice are important to generate realistic talking faces. While original speech signal can be directly used as the input of the synthesis model [25], most methods prefer more representative audio features [7, 12, 22, 26–28]. A pre-defined analysis method or a pre-trained model is often used to extract audio features from the original speech, and then the obtained features are used as the input to the face generation system. Four typical audio features are illustrated in Fig. 8.1.

Mel-spectrum features are commonly used in speech-related multimodal tasks, such as speech recognition. Considering that human auditory perception is only concentrated on specific frequencies, methods can be designed to selectively filter the audio frequency spectrum signal to obtain Mel-spectrum features. Mel-frequency

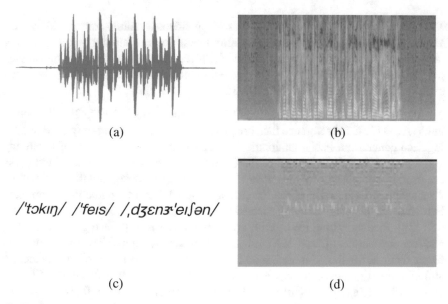

(a)   (b)

/ˈtɔkɪŋ/ /ˈfeɪs/ /ˌdʒɛnɝˈeɪʃən/

(c)   (d)

Fig. 8.1 Illustration of four commonly used audio features. **a** Original speech signal, **b** spectrum feature, **c** phoneme (English International Phonetic Alphabet (IPA)), and **d** Mel-frequency cepstrum coefficients (MFCC)

cepstrum coefficients (MFCC) can be obtained by performing Cepstrum analysis on the Mel-spectrum features. Prajwal et al. [26] used Mel-spectrum features as audio representation to generate talking face, while Song et al. [7] used MFCC.

Noise in the original audio signal could corrupt the MFCC. Some methods thus prefer to extract text features that are related to the content of the speech. These methods often borrow models from specific speech signal processing tasks such as automatic speech recognition (ASR) or voice conversion (VC). The automatic speech recognition (ASR) task aims at converting speech signals into corresponding text. For example, DeepSpeech [35, 36] is a speech-to-text model, which can transform an input speech frequency spectrum to English strings. Das et al. [27] took DeepSpeech features as the input to the talking face generation model. From the perspective of acoustic attributes, a phoneme is the smallest speech unit. It is considered that each phoneme is bounded to a specific vocalization action. For example, there are 48 phonemes in the English International Phonetic Alphabet (IPA), corresponding to 48 different vocal patterns. Quite a few methods [12, 28] use phoneme representation to synthesize talking face. The voice conversion (VC) task aims at converting non-verbal features such as accent, timbre, and speaking style between speakers while retaining the content features of the voice. Zhou et al. [22] used a pre-trained VC model to extract text features to characterize the content information in the speech.

8.2.2 Face Modeling

The human's perception of the quality of talking videos is mainly constituted by their visual quality, lip-sync accuracy, and naturalness. To generate high-quality talking face videos, the synchronization of 2D/3D facial representations with the input audios play an important role. Many geometry representations of human faces have been explored in recent years, including 2D/3D face modeling.

2D Models. 2D facial representations like 2D landmarks [17, 22, 29–31], action units (AUs) [32], and reference face images [23, 31, 33] are commonly used in talking face generation. Facial landmark detection is defined as the task of localizing and representing salient regions of the face. As shown in Fig. 8.2, facial landmarks are usually composed of points around eyebrows, eyes, nose, mouth, and jawline. As a shape representation of the face, facial landmark is a fundamental component in many face analysis and synthesis tasks, such as face detection [37], face verification [38], face morphing [39], facial attribute inference [40], face generation [41], and face reenactment [29]. Chen et al. [37] showed that aligned face shapes provide better features for face classification. The proposed joint learning of face detection and alignment greatly enhances the capability of real-time face detection. Chen et al. [38] densely sampled multi-scale descriptors centered at dense facial landmarks and used the concatenated high-dimensional feature for efficient face verification. Seibold et al. [39] presented an automatic morphing pipeline to generate morphing attacks, by warping images according to the corresponding detected facial landmarks

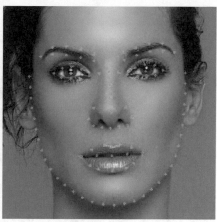

Fig. 8.2 Illustration of 106 facial landmarks. The landmarks are detected and marked in green. Best viewed zoomed in. The original pictures are obtained from the Internet

and replacing the inner part of the original image. Di et al. [41] presented that the information preserved by landmarks (gender in particular) can be further accentuated by leveraging generative models to synthesize corresponding faces. Lewenberg et al. [40] proposed an approach that incorporates facial landmark information for input images as an additional channel, helping a convolutional neural network (CNN) to learn face-specific features for predicting various traits of facial images. Automatic face reenactment [42] learns to transfer facial expressions from the source actor to the target actor. Wayne et al. proposed ReenactGAN [29] to reenact faces by the facial boundaries constituted by facial landmarks. Conditioned on the facial boundaries, the reenacted face images become more robust to challenging poses, expressions, and illuminations.

Action units are the fundamental actions of facial muscles defined in the Facial Action Coding System (FACS) system [32]. The combination of AUs can characterize comprehensive facial expression features, which can be used in expression-related face analysis and synthesis, e.g., facial expressions recognition [32], and facial animation [43]. For example, Pumarola et al. [43] introduced a generative adversarial network (GAN) [1] conditioning on action units annotations to realize controllable facial animation with robust expressions and lighting conditions.

3D Models. Some exiting methods exploit the 3D geometry of human faces like 3D landmarks [44, 45], 3D point cloud [46], facial mesh [47], facial rigs [13], and facial blendshapes [48–50] to generate talking face videos with diverse head gestures and movements.

Before the emergence of deep convolution networks (DCN) and GAN [1] in face image generation, 3D morphable face model (3DMM) is commonly deployed as a general face representation and a popular tool to model human faces. In 1999, Blanz and Vetter [44] proposed the first 3DMM that shows impressive performance. In

| shape mean | shape components 1st. (+5σ) 2nd. (+5σ) 3rd. (+5σ) | texture mean | texture components 1st. (+5σ) 2nd. (+5σ) 3rd. (+5σ) | Mask |

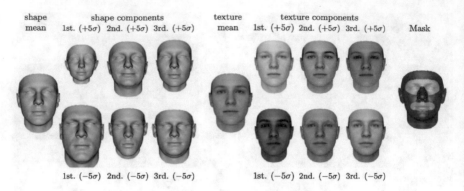

1st. (−5σ) 2nd. (−5σ) 3rd. (−5σ)   1st. (−5σ) 2nd. (−5σ) 3rd. (−5σ)

Fig. 8.3 Illustration of sampled faces of basel face model (BFM) proposed by Paysan et al. [45]. The mean together with the first three principle components of the shape (left) and texture (right) PCA model. The figure shows the mean shape and texture, along with their components with plus/minus five standard deviations σ. A mask with four manually chosen segments (eyes, nose, mouth, and rest) is used in the fitting to extend the flexibility. The image is adopted from Paysan et al. [45]

2009, the first publicly available 3DMM model, also known as basel face model (BFM), is released by Paysan et al. [45]. These face models inspire the research of 3DMM and its applications on many computer vision tasks related to human faces. For instance, Cao et al. [51] proposed the FaceWarehouse model and Bolkart and Wuhrer [52] proposed the Multilinear face model. Both models capture the geometry of facial shapes and expressions. Cao et al. [51] released a RGBD dataset of 150 subjects, each with 20 expressions. Bolkart et al. [52] released a dataset of 100 subjects, each with 25 expressions. Sampled faces of Basel Face Model (BFM) are shown in Fig. 8.3.

These methods model the facial shapes and expressions in a linear space, neglecting the nonlinear transformation of facial expressions. Li et al. [48] proposed the FLAME model that enables the nonlinear control on 3D face model by incorporating the linear blendshapes with eyes, jaw, and neck joints. To tackle the challenges like large head poses, appearance variations, inference speed, and video stability in 3D face reconstruction, Guo et al. proposed 3DFFA [49] and its improved variant, 3DFFA_V2 [50]. Apart from the 3D Face Morphable Model, other 3D models like face rigs [13], 3D point cloud [46], facial mesh [47], and customized computer graphic face model are also applied in 3D face representation.

With the advances of 3D face models, a variety of applications are enabled, such as face recognition [53], face reenactment [42], face reconstruction [54], face rotation [55], visual dubbing [56], and talking face generation [57]. Blanz et al. [53] showed that the cosine distance between two face images' shape and color coefficients estimated by a 3D face model can be used for identification. Thies et al. [58] proposed the first real-time face reenactment system by transferring the expression coefficients of a source actor to a target actor while preserving person-specificness. Gecer et al. [54] employed a large-scale face model [59] and proposed a GAN-based method for high-fidelity 3D face reconstruction. Zhou et al. [55] developed a face rotation algorithm by projecting and refining the rotated 3D face reconstructed from the input 2D face image by 3DDFA [49]. Kim et al. [56] presented a visual dubbing method that enables a new actor to imitate the facial expressions, eye movements, and head movements of one actor only from its portrait video. Thies et al. [57] presented that the learned facial expression coefficients from speech audio features extracted by DeepSpeech [36] can animate a 3D face model uttering the given speech audio. In general, these 3D models are not publicly released due to copyright restrictions.

8.2.3 Audio-to-Face Animation

To synthesize realistic and natural talking faces, it is crucial to establish the correspondence between the audio signal and the synthesized face. To improve the visual quality, lip-sync accuracy, and naturalness of talking videos, different methods have been explored in recent years, including 2D/3D-based models and video frame selection algorithm.

Audio-Visual Synchronization. Quite a few methods construct the correspondence between phonemes and visemes and use search algorithms to map audios to mouth shapes during the testing phase [12, 17, 28]. The pipeline is illustrated in Fig. 8.4. Specifically, they divide speech into pre-defined minimum audio units (phonemes), which naturally correspond to the smallest visual vocalization methods (visemes). In this way, a repository of phoneme-viseme pairs can be established from training data. After that, each sentence can be decomposed into a sequence of phonemes, correspond to a sequence of visemes during the testing phase. The video will be further synthesized from visemes by generation or rendering. The visemes here can be the facial landmarks related to the vocalization [17], or the pre-defined 3D face model controller coefficients [12, 28]. In this framework, defining phoneme-viseme pairs and finding a search-stitching algorithm are two critical steps. Considering coarticulation, Bregler et al. [17] split each word into a sequence of triphones, and established a corresponding relationship with the eigenpoint position of the lips and chin. Yao et al. [28] established the relationship between the phonemes obtained by the p2fa [60] algorithm and the controller coefficients obtained by the parameterized human head model [61]. They proposed a new phoneme search algorithm to quickly find the best phoneme subsequence combination and stitch the corresponding expression coefficients to synthesize the speaking video.

Other researchers designed an encoder-decoder structure, taking in audio and speaker images, outputting the generated target faces [5, 25, 62]. Specifically, as shown in Fig. 8.5a, the designed model is a combination of two encoders taking in audio and face images as input for two different modalities, and a decoder generating an image synchronized with the audio while preserving the identity information of the input images. In this system, two encoders are, respectively, responsible for encoding the audio content information and the facial identity information. The decoder following is responsible for decoding the fused multi-modality features into

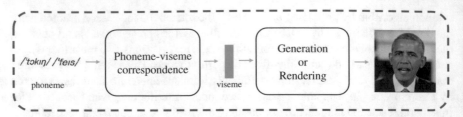

Fig. 8.4 Pipeline of phoneme-viseme correspondence method for talking face generation. Phoneme is firstly mapped to viseme according to an established phoneme-viseme correspondence. Images are further synthesized based on visemes

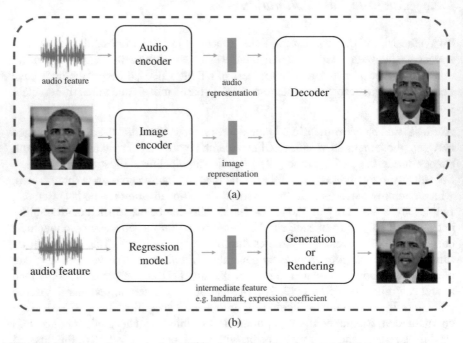

Fig. 8.5 Pipelines of two methods for talking face generation. As shown in (**a**), an encoder-decoder structure is used to generate the target face by taking in the audio features and images. As shown in (**b**), the relationship between the audio features and specific intermediate features is established first, and then the corresponding face is generated based on the intermediate features

a face image with the corresponding mouth shape and face identity. The encoders and the decoder are usually trained end-to-end simultaneously. This kind of method makes full use of encoder-decoder structure and multimodal fusion to generate target images. In this way, researchers often design specific models and losses to realize the disentanglement of speaking content and speaker identity. For example, Zhou et al. [5] used a pre-trained word classifier to force the content information to be forgotten in the identity encoding process, and the content information obtained from images and audio were constrained as close as possible.

Other methods choose to first establish the relationship between audio features and intermediate features pre-defined by face modeling methods and then generate the corresponding faces from the intermediate features [22, 31], as shown in Fig. 8.5b. The intermediate features mentioned here can be the pre-defined facial landmarks or the expression coefficients of the 3D face model.

For 2D-based generation methods, facial landmarks are often used as sparse shape representation. Suwajanakorn et al. [31] used a recurrent neural network (RNN) to map the MFCC features to the PCA coefficients of the facial landmarks. The corresponding face image is thus generated from the reconstructed facial landmarks with the texture information provided by the face images. Zhou et al. [22] mapped the voice content code and the identity code to the offset of the facial landmarks relative to a face template, and then generated the target image through an image-to-image network. For 3D-based methods, the facial expression parameters are often used as the intermediate representation. Fried et al. [12] used the facial expression parameters of the human head model as intermediate features and designed a neural renderer to generate the target video. Wiles et al. [63] established a mapping from audio features to the latent code in a pre-trained face generation model to achieve audio-driven facial video synthesis. Guo et al. [64] used a conditional implicit function to generate a dynamic neural radiance field from the audio features, and then synthesized video using volume rendering. The main difference between these methods (as shown in Fig. 8.5b) and the aforementioned phoneme-viseme search methods (as shown in Fig. 8.4) is the use of regression models for replacing pre-constructed phoneme-viseme correspondence. The former can obtain more consistent correspondence in the feature space.

Some researchers designed specific models to ensure audio-visual synchronization. Chung et al. [65] proposed a network, as shown in Fig. 8.6, taking in audio features and face images sequence as input, outputting the lip-sync error. This structure is often used in talking face model training [26, 66] or evaluation [25, 27]. A specific model was designed by Agarwal et al. [67] to detect the mismatch between phoneme and viseme to determine whether the video has been modified.

Synthesis Based on 2D Models. At the early stage of 2D-based talking face generation, videos are generated based on a pre-defined face model or composition of background portrait video and mouth images. Lewis [15] associated the recognized phonemes from synthesized speeches with mouth positions to animate a face model. Bregler et al. [17] designed the first automatic facial animation system that automatically labels phonemes in the training data and morphs these mouth gestures with the background portrait video. Cosatto and Graf [23] described a system to animate lip-synced head model from the phonetic transcripts by retrieving images of facial parts and blend them onto a whole face image.

With the popularity of the multidimensional morphable model (MMM), Ezzat et al. [68] designed a visual speech model to synthesize a speaker's mouth trajectory in MMM space from the given utterance and an algorithm to re-composite the synthesized mouths onto the portrait video with natural head and eye movement.

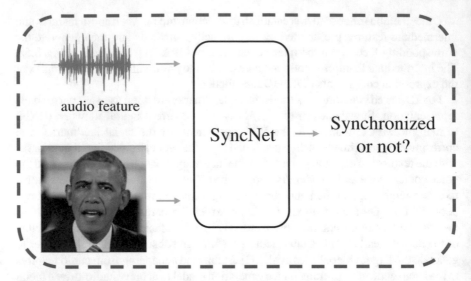

Fig. 8.6 Illustration of the pipeline of SyncNet [65]. The network predicts whether the input audio and face images are synchronized

Chang and Ezzat [69] animated a novel speaker with only a small video corpus (15 s) by transferring an MMM trained on a different speaker with a large video corpus (10–15 min).

Inspired by the successful application of the hidden Markov model (HMM) in speech recognition, many HMM-based methods, such as R-HMM [18], LMS-HMM [70], and HMMI [71], were proposed since talking face generation can be seen as an audio-visual mapping problem. Different from these HMM-based methods that use a single-state chain, a coupled hidden Markov model (CHMM) approach [19] was used to model the subtle characteristics of audio and video modalities. To exploit the capability of HMM in modeling the mapping from the audio to visual modalities, Wang et al. [72] proposed a system to generate talking face videos guided by the visual parameter trajectory of lip movements produced from the trained HMM according to the given speech audio.

Due to the advancement of using RNN and long short term memory (LSTM), HMM is gradually replaced by LSTM in learning the mapping from the audio to the visual modality. For instance, Fan et al. [24] trained a deep bidirectional LSTM to learn the regression model by minimizing the error of predicting visual sequence from audio/text sequence, outperformed their previous HMM-based models. Suwajanakorn et al. [31] trained a time-delayed LSTM model to learn the mapping from the Mel-frequency cepstral coefficients (MFCC) features of an audio sequence to the mouth landmarks of a single frame.

The quality of human face synthesis improves dramatically with the recent advances of GAN-based image generator, such as DCGAN [2], PGGAN [73], CGAN [3], StyleGAN [74] and StyleGAN2 [75]. In 2014, Goodfellow et al. proposed GAN [1] and demonstrated its ability in image generation by generating low-resolution images after training on datasets like MNIST [76], TFD [77] and CIFAR-10 [78]. Then, DCNs with different architectures are developed in GAN to generate images of higher resolution for specific domains. For instance, DCGAN [2] applied the layered deep neural network and PGGAN [73] learned to generate images in a coarse-to-fine manner by gradually increasing the resolution of generated images. In the context of image generation of human faces, a conditional CycleGAN [79] and FCENet [80] were developed to generate face images with controllable attributes like hair and eyes. While facial attributes can be precisely controlled by input condition codes, the image resolution is not high (128×128) and many facial details are missing. To generate high-resolution face images, Karras et al. proposed StyleGAN [74] and StyleGAN2 [75] to generate face images with a resolution up to 1024×1024 pixels, where coarse-grained style (e.g., eyes, hair, lighting) and fine-grained style (e.g., stubble, freckles, skin pores) are editable. To edit facial attributes more precisely, some GAN-based models [79, 80] were proposed to modify the generated high-resolution face images where fine-grained attributes like eyes, nose size, and mouth shape can be controlled by input condition codes. The design of 2D-based talking face video synthesis models is inspired by some related synthesis tasks like image-to-image translation [81, 82], high-resolution face image generation [74], face reenactment [29], and lip reading [65].

Inspired by GAN [1], many methods [4–8] improve the generated video quality from different aspects. Chen et al. designed a correction loss [4] to synchronize changes of lip and speech. Zhou et al. [5] proposed an adversarial network to disentangle the speaker identity from input videos and the word identity from input speeches to enable arbitrary-speaker talking face generation. To improve both the image and video realism, Chen et al. [6] designed a dynamic adjustable pixel-wise loss to eliminate the temporal discontinuities and subtle artifacts in generated videos. Song et al. [7] proposed a conditional recurrent generation network and a pair of spatial-temporal discriminators that integrate audio and image features for video generation. These GAN-based studies mainly concentrate on the talking face video generation of the frontal face and neutral expressions. The development of GAN-based human face generation and editing methods on head poses [83] and facial emotions [84] influences the research in talking face generation. For instance, Zhu et al. [8] employed the idea of mutual information to capture the audio-visual coherence and design a GAN-based framework to generate talking face videos that are robust to pose variations. Taking into account the speaker's emotions and head poses, Wang et al. [85] released an audio-visual dataset that contains various head poses, emotion categories, and intensities. They also proposed a baseline to demonstrate the feasibility of controlling emotion categories and intensities in talking face generation.

Synthesis Based on 3D Models. In the early days of the talking face generation, 3D representation is often used to represent the mouth or face of the driven speaker. For instance, in 1996, a 3D model of lips with only five parameters was developed to adapt lip contours of various speakers and any speech gesture [16]. Wang et al. [88]

proposed to control a 3D face model with the head trajectory and articulation movement predicted by an HMM model. Interestingly, after several years' exploration of applying deep learning in talking face generation, especially the recent advances of DCN and GAN, many methods return to 3D representation by integrating 3DMM and other 3D face models. For instance, Pham et al. [9] introduced a 3D blendshape model animated by 3D rotation and expression coefficients predicted only from the input speech. Karras et al. [10] presented a network that animates the 3D vertex coordinates of a 3D face model with different emotions from the input speech and emotional codes. Taylor et al. [11] developed a real-time system that animates active appearance model (AAM), CG characters, and face rigs by retargeting the face rig movements predicted from the given speech. Fried et al. [12] proposed a parametric head model to provide the position of retargeting the mouth images to the background portrait video. Edwards et al. [13] presented a face-rig model called JALI that mainly concentrates on the JAw and LIp movements. By making use of JALI, Zhou et al. [14] proposed a deep learning method to drive the JALI or standard FACS-based face rigs by the JALI and viseme parameters predicted from a 3-stage LSTM network. Recently, a series of methods explore the potential of deep learning techniques in learning the nonlinear mapping from audio features to facial movement coefficients of 3DMM. For instance, Thies et al. [57] introduced a small convolutional network to learn the expression coefficients of 3DMM from the speech features extracted by the DeepSpeech [35]. This method does not pay much attention to large head poses, head movements and requires a speaker-specific video renderer. Song et al. [33] presented an LSTM-based network to eliminate speaker information and predict expression coefficients from input audios. This method is robust to large pose variations and the head movement problem is tackled by the designed frame selection algorithm. Different from this method that retrieves head poses from existing videos, Yi et al. [89] tried to solve the head pose problem by directly predicting the pose coefficients of 3DMM from the given speech audio. Chen et al. [90] introduced a head motion learner to predict the head motion from a short portrait video and the input audio. To eliminate the visual discontinuity brought by the apparent head motion, a 3D face model is used due to its stability. In Fig. 8.7, representative works of talking face generation in recent years are listed in chronological order.

Video Frame Selection Algorithm. Note that the mouth texture in the training videos is abundant, video frame selection algorithms are designed to facilitate the synthesis of talking face videos by selecting frames from existing videos according to the input audios or mouth motion representations. The selected video frames can provide the texture of the whole face [31, 33] or only mouth areas [23].

Currently, generation based on 2D face representation (e.g., DCN and GAN) and 3D face representation (e.g., 3DMM) dominates the field of talking face synthesis. Before the emergence of these techniques, talking face generation mainly rely on 3D models and select video frames with matched mouth shapes. For instance, Cosatto et al. [23] introduced a flexible 3D head model used to composite facial parts' images retrieved by sampled mouth trajectories. Chang et al. [69] proposed a matching-by-synthesis algorithm that selects new multidimensional morphable model (MMM)

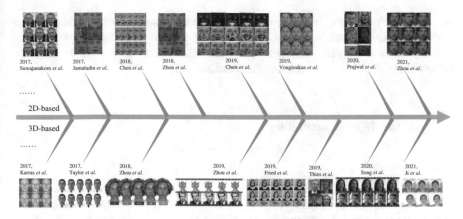

Fig. 8.7 Representative works of talking face generation in recent years (since 2017). The methods above the timeline are based on 2D models, from left to right are [4–6, 25, 26, 31, 62, 86]. The methods below the timeline are based on 3D models, from left to right are [10–12, 14, 22, 33, 57, 87]. The generated images of these methods are adopted from corresponding papers. Best viewed by zooming on the screen

prototype images from driving speaker's videos. Wang et al. [72] introduced an HMM trajectory-guided approach as a guide to select an optimal mouth sequence from the training videos. Liu and Ostermann [91] presented a unit selection algorithm to retrieve mouth images from a speaker's expressive database characterized by phoneme, viseme, and size.

The research on frame selection algorithms is still active even with the impressive talking face generation performance brought by deep learning and 3DMM techniques. For example, Fried et al. [28] introduced a dynamic programming method to retrieve expressions in the parameter space by visemes inferred from the input transcript. Suwajanakorn et al. [31] designed a dynamic programming algorithm to retrieve background video frames according to the input audio. How well the input audio volume matches the eye blink as well as head movement is considered in the frame selection algorithm.

8.2.4 Post-processing

The generated talking faces may not be of high quality or natural enough due to various reasons. This requires researchers to do introduce post-processing steps, such as refinement and blending, to further enhance the naturalness of the videos. For instance, Jamaludin et al. [62] first obtained a talking face generation model that produced blurred faces and then trained a separate CNN to sharpen the blurred images. Bregler et al. [17] pointed out the necessity to blend the generated faces into a natural background, and the importance of animate the chin and jawlines, not just the mouth region to improve realism. There exist many methods that apply a static video background [4, 5, 8, 68]. For some news program translation or movie dubbing applications [21, 26], the natural video results can be obtained by blending the generated face back into the original background.

8.3 Datasets and Metrics

8.3.1 Dataset

In recent years, increasingly more audio-visual datasets have been released, promoting the development of talking face generation. These datasets can be used for lip reading, speech reconstruction, and talking face generation. We divide these datasets into two categories according to the collection environment. (1) Indoor environment, where speakers recite the specified words or sentences. (2) In-the-wild environment, where speakers talk in the scene closer to the actual applications, such as speech video and news program video. In this section, we summarize commonly used audio-visual datasets and their characteristics.

Indoor Environment. Datasets collected in the indoor environment often exhibit consistent settings and lighting conditions, when the speakers read the specified words or sentences.

GRID [92] is a multi-speaker audio-visual corpus consisting of audio and video recordings of 1000 sentences spoken by each of 34 speakers. TCD-TIMIT [93] consists of audio and video footages of 62 speakers reading a total of 6913 phonetically rich sentences. Three of the speakers are professionally-trained lip speakers, with the assumption that trained speakers can read better than ordinary speakers. Video footage was recorded from the frontal view and 30° pitch angle. CREMA-D [94] is a dataset of 7442 original clips from 91 actors. The speakers are composed of 48 men and 43 women from different races and nationalities, ranging in age from 20 to 74 years old. They speak 12 sentences using one of six different emotions and four different emotion levels. However, all the datasets mentioned above do not consider emotional information. Wang et al. [85] released a high-quality audio-visual dataset that contains 60 actors and actresses talking with eight different emotions at three different intensity levels. All clips in MEAD are captured at seven different view angles in a strictly controlled environment.

In-the-Wild Environment. Other datasets are often derived from news program videos or speech videos. They are closer to actual application scenarios, with more abundant words, more natural expressions, and more speakers.

Suwajanakorn et al. [31] downloaded 14 h of Obama weekly address videos from YouTube for experiments. LRW [95], LRS2 [96], LRS3 [97] datasets are all designed for research on lip reading. Lip reading is defined as understanding speech content by visually interpreting the movements of the lips, face, and tongue when normal sound

Table 8.1 Summary of audio-visual datasets commonly used for talking face generation

Dataset	Environment	Identity	Hours	Year
GRID [92]	Indoor	34	27.5	2006
CREMA-D [94]	Indoor	91	11.1	2014
TCD-TIMIT [93]	Indoor	62	11.1	2015
MEAD [85]	Indoor	60	40	2020
Obama weekly address [31]	Wild	1	14	2017
LRW [95]	Wild	Hundreds of	173	2016
LRS2 [96]	Wild	Hundreds of	224.5	2018
LRS3 [97]	Wild	Thousands of	438	2018
VoxCeleb1 [98]	Wild	1251	352	2017
VoxCeleb2 [99]	Wild	6112	2400	2018

is not available. This is similar to the inverse task of talking face generation. LRW consists of about 1000 utterances of 500 words, spoken by hundreds of speakers. All videos are about 1.16 s in length, and the duration of each word is also given. LRS2 expands the content of the speech from words to sentences, consisting of thousands of spoken sentences from BBC television, where each sentence is up to 100 characters in length. LRS3 contains thousands of spoken sentences from TED and TEDx speech videos.

VoxCeleb1 [98] collects celebrity videos uploaded by users from YouTube, which contains over 100,000 utterances for 1251 celebrities. VoxCeleb2 [99] further expands the data volume, which contains over 1 million utterances for 6112 celebrities. VoxCeleb2 can be used as a supplement for VoxCeleb1 because it has no overlap with the identities in the VoxCeleb1. Datasets mentioned in this section are summarized in Table 8.1.

8.3.2   Metrics

It is challenging to evaluate the naturalness of generated talking faces. People often have very strict requirements on the quality and naturalness of the generated talking face. A slight flaw will be regarded as obviously unreal. On the one hand, this puts high demands on the models of talking face generation. On the other hand, it is crucial to develop comprehensive evaluation metrics for talking face generation. Evaluation metrics can be divided into objective quantitative evaluation and subjective qualitative evaluation.

Quantitative Evaluation. As mentioned above, people can easily find out when the generated talking faces do not speak like real people from various aspects. Thus, the quantitative evaluation also needs to measure from several different angles. In general, existing quantitative evaluation metrics mainly focus on the following aspects of the generated video. (1) The generated videos should be of high quality. (2) The mouth shape of the generated speaker should match the audio. (3) The speaker in the synthesized video should be the same as the target person. (4) Eye blinking when speaking should be natural.

Image quality evaluation metrics are commonly used in face generation tasks. Peak signal-to-noise ratio (PSNR), defined via mean squared error, can reflect the pixel-level difference between two images. However, there is still a considerable gap between human perception and PSNR. Structural Similarity (SSIM) [100] measures the similarity of two images in terms of illuminance, contrast, and structure. To evaluate the diversity of the generative model, Inception Score (IS) [101] is introduced. Fréchet inception distance (FID) [102] is calculated by comparing the mean and standard deviation of the two features produced by a pre-trained Inception-v3 model. However, these methods require reference images for evaluation. Cumulative probability blur detection (CPBD) [103] is a non-reference image evaluation metric used to evaluate the sharpness of images, while frequency domain blurriness measure (FDBM) [104] evaluates frequency domain blurriness based on the image spectrum.

Audio-lip synchronization is also an important indicator to measure the naturalness of talking face generation. Landmark distance (LMD) is defined as the mouth landmark distance between generated and real reference images to measure the generated mouth shape. As mentioned in Sect. 8.2.3, the lip reading task learns the mapping from face images to the corresponding text. Thus, the pre-trained lip reading model can be used to calculate the word error rate (WER). For example, Vougioukas et al. [105] calculated WER based on a LipNet [106] model pre-trained on GRID [92]. Syncnet [65], the model specifically designed to judge audio-visual synchronization, can also be borrowed [25, 27] to calculate Audio-Visual synchronization metrics (AV Offset and AV confidence). A lower AV offset with higher AV confidence indicates better lip synchronization. Recently, Chen et al. [107] proposed a new lip-synchronization evaluation metric lip-reading similarity distance (LRSD) from the perspective of human perception. Based on a newly proposed lip reading model, they use the distance between features of generated video clips and ground truth video clips to measure the audio-visual synchronization.

Some methods suffer from wrong or lost of speaker identity, that is, the generated speaker and the target speaker do not seem to be the same person. Therefore, some metrics that measure identity preservation are also applied in the talking face generation task. Often, a pre-trained face recognition model [108, 109] is used as an identity feature extractor. Identity preservation is quantified by measuring the distance between features. For instance, average content distance (ACD) [25, 27] is calculated by measuring the similarity between FaceNet [108] features of the reference identity image and the predicted image. Chen et al. [90] used cosine similarity (CSIM) between embedding vectors of ArcFace [109] for measuring identity mismatch.

Finally, the realisticness of blinking should also be considered. Vougioukas et al. [25] proposed that the average blink duration and blink frequency from the generated video should be similar to that of natural human blinks. In specific, they

Table 8.2 Summary of quantitative talking face metrics via four different degrees. The upward arrows (↑) indicate higher values are better for that metric, while downward arrows (↓) mean lower values are better

Degree	Metrics
Image quality	PSNR↑ SSIM↑ IS↑ FID↓ CPBD↑ FDBM↑
Audio-lip synchronization	LMD↓ WER↓ AV (Offset)↓ AV (Confidence)↑ LRSD↓
Identity-preserved	ACD↓ CSIM↑
Blink	Duration Frequency

calculated the average duration and frequency to evaluate the naturalness of blinking. Quantitative evaluation metrics mentioned in this section are summarized in Table 8.2.

Qualitative Evaluation. Although the quantitative evaluation mentioned above can provide a reference and filter out some obvious artifacts, the ultimate goal of talking face is to fool real people. Therefore, the generated talking face still needs some subjective feedback from people. Generally speaking, researchers usually design user studies to allow real users to judge the quality of the generated videos.

8.4 Discussion

8.4.1 Fine-Grained Facial Control

Even if the speaker's mouth movements naturally match the audio, one wishes to establish the relationship between audio and other facial components, such as chins, jawlines, eyes, head movements, and even teeth.

In fact, most of the current talking face generation methods do not consider the correlation between audio and eyes. Vougioukas et al. [25] designed a blink generation network, using Gaussian noise vectors as input to generate eyes keypoints, which can generate blinks of similar duration and frequency to real videos. Zhang et al. [110] took eye blink signal and audio signal together as input to generate the corresponding talking face. Zhou et al. [22] learned mapping from the audio information to facial landmarks where eye landmarks are excluded. These methods are based on the assumption that blinking is a random signal unrelated to the input audio. However, according to Karson et al. [111], listeners' blink duration is related to talking and thinking. Hömke et al. [112] also proposed that blinks are meaningfully rather than randomly paced, although no visual information is processed. When it comes to generation techniques, the movements of the eyes are generally modeled as part of the emotional coefficients in 3D-based methods and as eye landmarks in 2D-based methods. Shu et al. [113] leveraged user's photo collections to find a set of reference eyes and transfer them onto a target image. However, for now, it is still difficult to model the relationship between audio and eye movements. In other words, how to generate more flexible and informative eyes is still an open question in talking face generation task.

Another question is whether the teeth generation is related to the input audio. From the perspective of phoneme-viseme correspondence, each phoneme corresponds to a set of teeth and tongue movements. However, as described in [31], the teeth are sometimes hidden behind lips when speaking, which makes synthesis challenging. There are also no teeth landmarks in 2D landmark definition. Even in most 3D head models, the teeth are not explicitly modeled. Some researchers copy teeth texture from other frames [58] or use teeth proxy [20, 114]. However, these methods may cause blur or artifacts. Suwajanakorn et al. [31] achieved decent teeth generation by combining low-frequency median texture and high-frequency details from a teeth proxy image. Recently, some more accurate teeth models have been established, for example, Velinov et al. [115] established an intra-oral scan system for capturing the optical properties of live human teeth. Some new teeth editing methods have also been proposed. For example, Yang et al. [116] realized an effective disentanglement of an explicit representation of the teeth geometry from the in-mouth appearance, making it easier to edit teeth.

The lips, eyes, and teeth mentioned above are all part of the human face. One would also need to consider the generation of natural head movements. Most talking face methods do not consider the problem of generating controllable head movements without a pre-defined 3D model. Jamaludin et al. [62] only generated aligned faces while Zhang et al. [110] took the head pose signal as the input signal explicitly. Wiles et al. [63] can generate talking faces with different poses, but the head motion is not decoupled from other facial expression attributes. Recently, some researchers have proposed methods to generate controllable head poses. Chen et al. [90] designed a head motion disentangler to decouple the head movement in the 3D geometry space and used the head motion and audio information of the current frame to predict the head motion of the next frame. Similarly, Wang et al. [117] realized the decoupling of motion-related information and identity-specific information by learning 3D keypoint representation. Zhou et al. [86] modularized audio-visual representations by devising an implicit low-dimension pose code to generate pose-controllable talking face videos.

For a realistic talking face, the emotion of the speaker should also match the voice. For example, a voice with an angry tone should correspond to an angry face. But how to manipulate the emotion in 2D-based talking face generation is still an open question. Some researchers exploit expression information from the voice to generate talking faces [25, 118]. But they cannot explicitly control the emotional intensity of the video. MEAD [85] is a talking face dataset featuring 60 people talking with eight different emotions at three different intensity levels, which provides data support for the generation of emotional talking faces. Ji et al. [87] decomposed speech into emotion space and content space. With the disentangled features, emotional facial landmarks and videos can be deduced.

In Sect. 8.3.2, we mentioned several evaluation metrics for talking face generation, but these quantitative indicators still have limitations from the perspective of human perception. We believe that talking face integrating eyes, teeth, head pose, and emotion will be a more natural and human-like virtual person.

8.4.2 Generalization

The model generalization of a talking face system is mainly determined by the dataset used to build the system and the applied techniques in designing the modules of the system. The audio-visual datasets are contributed by two essential factors, the phonetic dictionary size of the corpus and the diversity of speakers such as gender, age, language, accent, and the speaker number. In the following, the model generalization of recent talking face generation methods is analyzed by key factors, e.g., corpus and speaker.

The small corpus size and speaker number of many audio-visual datasets might limit the model generalization. For example, the GRID dataset [92] contains very few words. Although it is designed to cover the pronunciations of every single phoneme, the limited vocabulary still lacks diverse diphones and triphones that encode surrounding phonemes. Many audio-visual datasets contain very limited speaker diversity, i.e., the speaker number of GRID [92] and RAVDESS [119] is fewer than 100 and these datasets do not contain diverse accents, head pose, movements, and emotions. To alleviate the poor model generalization brought by audio-visual datasets, Wang et al. [85] collected a large-scale dataset with different skin colors, emotions and head poses.

With the development of GAN-based image generation methods, recent methods can generate photo-realistic talking face videos with fewer and fewer portrait videos. For instance, generating a high-fidelity fake video of Barack Obama requires massive training footage up to 14 h in [31]. Though the generated videos of [31] are hard to distinguish from the real ones, the requirement on training data is inapplicable in many real-world application scenarios. Thus, many methods circumvent the training data burden at the cost of generated video quality. For example, Thies et al. [57] presented that transferring a trained model to an unseen speaker requires about only 2 min of footage. Zhou et al. [22] presented that even a single static face image is sufficient for generating talking videos with diverse head movements.

Another aspect of model generalization is the speaker's identity. Suwajanakorn et al. [31] built a speaker-specific 3D face model and trained a speaker-specific network for Barack Obama to synthesize his forged videos. The applied speaker-specific 3D face model limits its generalization for other speakers. Then, Thies et al. [57] proposed an audio-to-video pipeline that consists of a speaker-generalized network to learn the mapping from the audio to expression parameters and a speaker-specific video renderer to render photo-realistic video according to the 3D head model and learned expressions. To an unseen speaker, it still requires a 2 min portrait video to fine-tune the speaker-specific renderer. The renderer parameters only optimize for a specific speaker since it refines the speaker-specific texture rendered by 3DMM. Recent methods [22, 33, 117] can generate talking video for unseen speakers without any further finetuning and the testing set can even be as small as a short footage [33] or a single image [22, 117]. Such model generalization is realized since these methods do not optimize based on any speaker-specific prior knowledge.

8.5 Conclusion

With the advancement of face modeling methods and deep learning techniques, especially generation models, academic researchers make it possible to generate realistic talking faces. In turn, considering a wide range of practical applications, talking face generation has also attracted increasing interest from industrial developers. This chapter has summarized the development of talking face generation from different perspectives. Related work and recent progresses are discussed from the perspectives of audio representation, face modeling, audio-to-face animation, and post-processing. We have also listed commonly used public datasets and evaluation metrics. Finally, we discussed some open questions in the task of talking face generation.

Talking face generation techniques may be misused or abused for various malevolent purposes, e.g., fraud, aspersion, and dissemination of malicious propaganda. Out of ethical considerations, the government and researchers should jointly detect and combat harmful edited videos, and apply this technology without harming the public interest. We believe that with the dual attention of academia and industry, the generated videos will become more realistic with newly proposed models. In the future, there will also be more practical applications conducive to the public.

8.6 Further Reading

Interested readers are referred to the following further readings:

- Chen et al. [107] for a benchmark designed for evaluating talking-head video generation.
- Zhu et al. [120] for a survey on deep audio-visual learning.

References

1. Goodfellow I, Pouget-Abadie J, Mirza M, Xu B, Warde-Farley D, Ozair S, Courville A, Bengio Y (2014) Generative adversarial nets. In: Proceedings of the advances in neural information processing systems, vol 27
2. Radford A, Metz L, Chintala S (2016) Unsupervised representation learning with deep convolutional generative adversarial networks. In: Proceedings of the international conference on learning representations
3. Mirza M, Osindero S (2014) Conditional generative adversarial nets. CoRR arXiv:abs/1411.1784
4. Chen L, Li Z, Maddox RK, Duan Z, Xu C (2018) Lip movements generation at a glance. In: Proceedings of the European conference on computer vision, pp 520–535
5. Zhou H, Liu Y, Liu Z, Luo P, Wang X (2019) Talking face generation by adversarially disentangled audio-visual representation. In: Proceedings of the AAAI conference on artificial intelligence, vol 33, no 1, pp 9299–9306
6. Chen L, Maddox RK, Duan Z, Xu C (2019) Hierarchical cross-modal talking face generation with dynamic pixel-wise loss. In: Proceedings of the IEEE/CVF conference on computer vision and pattern recognition, pp 7832–7841
7. Song Y, Zhu J, Li D, Wang A, Qi H (2019) Talking face generation by conditional recurrent adversarial network. In: Kraus S (ed) Proceedings of the international joint conference on artificial intelligence, pp 919–925
8. Zhu H, Huang H, Li Y, Zheng A, He R (2020) Arbitrary talking face generation via attentional audio-visual coherence learning. In: Proceedings of the international joint conference on artificial intelligence, pp 2362–2368
9. Pham HX, Cheung S, Pavlovic V (2017) Speech-driven 3d facial animation with implicit emotional awareness: a deep learning approach. In: Proceedings of the IEEE conference on computer vision and pattern recognition workshops, pp 80–88
10. Karras T, Aila T, Laine S, Herva A, Lehtinen J (2017) Audio-driven facial animation by joint end-to-end learning of pose and emotion. ACM Trans Graph 36(4):1–12
11. Taylor S, Kim T, Yue Y, Mahler M, Krahe J, Rodriguez AG, Hodgins J, Matthews I (2017) A deep learning approach for generalized speech animation. ACM Trans Graph 36(4):1–11
12. Fried O, Tewari A, Zollhöfer M, Finkelstein A, Shechtman E, Goldman DB, Genova K, Jin Z, Theobalt C, Agrawala M (2019) Text-based editing of talking-head video. ACM Trans Graph 38(4):1–14
13. Edwards P, Landreth C, Fiume E, Singh K (2016) Jali: an animator-centric viseme model for expressive lip synchronization. ACM Trans Graph 35(4):1–11
14. Zhou Y, Xu Z, Landreth C, Kalogerakis E, Maji S, Singh K (2018) Visemenet: audio-driven animator-centric speech animation. ACM Trans Graph 37(4):1–10
15. Lewis J (1991) Automated lip-sync: background and techniques. J Visualization Comput Animat 2(4):118–122
16. Guiard-Marigny T, Tsingos N, Adjoudani A, Benoit C, Gascuel M-P (1996) 3d models of the lips for realistic speech animation. In: Proceedings of the computer animation, pp 80–89
17. Bregler C, Covell M, Slaney M (1997) Video rewrite: driving visual speech with audio. In: Proceedings of the annual conference on computer graphics and interactive techniques, pp 353–360
18. Brand M (1999) Voice puppetry. In: Proceedings of the annual conference on computer graphics and interactive techniques, pp 21–28
19. Xie L, Liu Z-Q (2007) A coupled HMM approach to video-realistic speech animation. Pattern Recogn 40(8):2325–2340
20. Garrido P, Valgaerts L, Sarmadi H, Steiner I, Varanasi K, Perez P, Theobalt C (2015) Vdub: modifying face video of actors for plausible visual alignment to a dubbed audio track. Comput Graph Forum 34(2):193–204
21. Charles J, Magee D, Hogg D (2016) Virtual immortality: reanimating characters from TV shows. In: Proceedings of the European conference on computer vision, pp 879–886

22. Zhou Y, Han X, Shechtman E, Echevarria J, Kalogerakis E, Li D (2020) Makelttalk: speaker-aware talking-head animation. ACM Trans Graph 39(6):1–15
23. Cosatto E, Graf HP (2000) Photo-realistic talking-heads from image samples. IEEE Trans Multimedia 2(3):152–163
24. Fan B, Wang L, Soong FK, Xie L (2015) Photo-real talking head with deep bidirectional LSTM. In: Proceedings of the IEEE international conference on acoustics, speech and signal processing, pp 4884–4888
25. Vougioukas K, Petridis S, Pantic M (2019) Realistic speech-driven facial animation with gans. Int J Comput Vis 1–16
26. Prajwal KR, Mukhopadhyay R, Namboodiri VP, Jawahar CV (2020) A lip sync expert is all you need for speech to lip generation in the wild. In: Proceedings of the ACM international conference on multimedia, pp 484–492
27. Das D, Biswas S, Sinha S, Bhowmick B (2020) Speech-driven facial animation using cascaded gans for learning of motion and texture. In: Proceedings of the European conference on computer vision, pp 408–424
28. Yao X, Fried O, Fatahalian K, Agrawala M (2020) Iterative text-based editing of talking-heads using neural retargeting. arXiv preprint arXiv:2011.10688
29. Wu W, Zhang Y, Li C, Qian C, Loy CC (2018) ReenactGAN learning to reenact faces via boundary transfer. In: Proceedings of the European conference on computer vision, pp 603–619
30. Song L, Wu W, Fu C, Qian C, Loy CC, He R (2021) Everything's talkin': Pareidolia face reenactment. In: Proceedings of the IEEE/CVF conference on computer vision and pattern recognition
31. Suwajanakorn S, Seitz SM, Kemelmacher-Shlizerman I (2017) Synthesizing Obama: learning lip sync from audio. ACM Trans Graph 36(4):1–13
32. Friesen E, Ekman P (1978) Facial action coding system: a technique for the measurement of facial movement. Palo Alto 3(2):5
33. Song L, Wu W, Qian C, He R, Loy CC (2020) Everybody's talkin': let me talk as you want. arXiv arXiv:abs/2001.05201
34. Mori M, MacDorman KF, Kageki N (2012) The uncanny valley [from the field]. IEEE Robot Autom Mag 19(2):98–100
35. Hannun AY, Case C, Casper J, Catanzaro B, Diamos G, Elsen E, Prenger R, Satheesh S, Sengupta S, Coates A, Ng AY (2014) Deep speech: scaling up end-to-end speech recognition. CoRR abs/1412.5567
36. Amodei D, Ananthanarayanan S, Anubhai R, Bai J, Battenberg E, Case C, Casper J, Catanzaro B, Cheng Q, Chen G et al (2016) Deep speech 2: end-to-end speech recognition in English and mandarin. In: Proceedings of the international conference on machine learning, pp 173–182
37. Chen D, Ren S, Wei Y, Cao X, Sun J (2014) Joint cascade face detection and alignment. In: Proceedings of the European conference on computer vision, pp 109–122
38. Chen D, Cao X, Wen F, Sun J (2013) Blessing of dimensionality: high-dimensional feature and its efficient compression for face verification. In: Proceedings of the IEEE/CVF conference on computer vision and pattern recognition, pp 3025–3032
39. Seibold C, Samek W, Hilsmann A, Eisert P (2017) Detection of face morphing attacks by deep learning. In: Proceedings of the international workshop on digital watermarking, pp 107–120
40. Lewenberg Y, Bachrach Y, Shankar S, Criminisi A (2016) Predicting personal traits from facial images using convolutional neural networks augmented with facial landmark information. In: Proceedings of the AAAI conference on artificial intelligence, vol 30, no 1
41. Di X, Sindagi VA, Patel VM (2018) GP-GAN: gender preserving GAN for synthesizing faces from landmarks. In: Proceedings of the international conference on pattern recognition, pp 1079–1084
42. Garrido P, Valgaerts L, Rehmsen O, Thormahlen T, Perez P, Theobalt C (2014) Automatic face reenactment. In: Proceedings of the IEEE/CVF conference on computer vision and pattern recognition, pp 4217–4224

43. Pumarola A, Agudo A, Martinez AM, Sanfeliu A, Moreno-Noguer F (2018) Ganimation: anatomically-aware facial animation from a single image. In: Proceedings of the European conference on computer vision, pp 818–833
44. Blanz V, Vetter T (1999) A morphable model for the synthesis of 3d faces. In: Proceedings of the annual conference on computer graphics and interactive techniques, pp 187–194
45. Paysan P, Knothe R, Amberg B, Romdhani S, Vetter T (2009) A 3d face model for pose and illumination invariant face recognition. In: Proceedings of the IEEE international conference on advanced video and signal-based surveillance, pp 296–301
46. Besl PJ, McKay ND (1992) Method for registration of 3-d shapes. In: Sensor fusion IV: control paradigms and data structures, vol 1611. International Society for Optics and Photonics, pp 586–606
47. Kalogerakis E, Hertzmann A, Singh K (2010) Learning 3d mesh segmentation and labeling. ACM Trans Graph 29(4):1–12
48. Li T, Bolkart T, Black MJ, Li H, Romero J (2017) Learning a model of facial shape and expression from 4d scans. ACM Trans Graph 36(6):1–17
49. Zhu X, Liu X, Lei Z, Li SZ (2017) Face alignment in full pose range: a 3d total solution. IEEE Trans Pattern Anal Mach Intell 41(1):78–92
50. Guo J, Zhu X, Yang Y, Yang F, Lei Z, Li SZ (2020) Towards fast, accurate and stable 3d dense face alignment. Proceedings of the European conference on computer vision 12364:152–168
51. Cao C, Weng Y, Zhou S, Tong Y, Zhou K (2013) Facewarehouse: a 3d facial expression database for visual computing. IEEE Trans Visualization Comput Graph 20(3):413–425
52. Bolkart T, Wuhrer S (2015) A groupwise multilinear correspondence optimization for 3d faces. In: Proceedings of the IEEE international conference on computer vision, pp 3604–3612
53. Blanz V, Romdhani S, Vetter T (2002) Face identification across different poses and illuminations with a 3d morphable model. In: Proceedings of the IEEE international conference on automatic face and gesture recognition, pp 202–207
54. Gecer B, Ploumpis S, Kotsia I, Zafeiriou S (2019) Ganfit: generative adversarial network fitting for high fidelity 3d face reconstruction. In: Proceedings of the IEEE/CVF conference on computer vision and pattern recognition, pp 1155–1164
55. Zhou H, Liu J, Liu Z, Liu Y, Wang X (2020) Rotate-and-render: unsupervised photorealistic face rotation from single-view images. In: Proceedings of the IEEE/CVF conference on computer vision and pattern recognition, pp 5911–5920
56. Kim H, Garrido P, Tewari A, Xu W, Thies J, Niessner M, Pérez P, Richardt C, Zollhöfer M, Theobalt C (2018) Deep video portraits. ACM Trans Graph 37(4):1–14
57. Thies J, Elgharib M, Tewari A, Theobalt C, Nießner M (2020) Neural voice puppetry: audio-driven facial reenactment. In: Proceedings of the European conference on computer vision, pp 716–731
58. Thies J, Zollhofer M, Stamminger M, Theobalt C, Nießner M (2016) Face2face: real-time face capture and reenactment of RGB videos. In: Proceedings of the IEEE/CVF conference on computer vision and pattern recognition, pp 2387–2395
59. Booth J, Roussos A, Zafeiriou S, Ponniah A, Dunaway D (2016) A 3d morphable model learnt from 10,000 faces. In: Proceedings of the IEEE/CVF conference on computer vision and pattern recognition, pp 5543–5552
60. Rubin S, Berthouzoz F, Mysore GJ, Li W, Agrawala M, Content-based tools for editing audio stories. In: Proceedings of the ACM symposium on user interface software and technology, pp 113–122
61. Garrido P, Zollhöfer M, Casas D, Valgaerts L, Varanasi K, Pérez P, Theobalt C (2016) Reconstruction of personalized 3d face rigs from monocular video. ACM Transactions on Graphics 35(3):1–15
62. Jamaludin A, Chung JS, Zisserman A (2019) You said that?: synthesising talking faces from audio. Int J Comput Vision 127(11):1767–1779
63. Wiles O, Koepke A, Zisserman A (2018) X2face: a network for controlling face generation using images, audio, and pose codes. In: Proceedings of the European conference on computer vision, pp 670–686

64. Guo Y, Chen K, Liang S, Liu Y, Bao H, Zhang J (2021) Ad-nerf: audio driven neural radiance fields for talking head synthesis. arXiv preprint arXiv:2103.11078
65. Chung JS, Zisserman A (2016) Out of time: automated lip sync in the wild. In: Proceedings of the Asian conference on computer vision, pp 251–263
66. Prajwal KR, Mukhopadhyay R, Philip J, Jha A, Namboodiri V, Jawahar CV (2019) Towards automatic face-to-face translation. In: Proceedings of the ACM international conference on multimedia, pp 1428–1436
67. Agarwal S, Farid H, Fried O, Agrawala M (2020) Detecting deep-fake videos from phoneme-viseme mismatches. In: Proceedings of the IEEE/CVF conference on computer vision and pattern recognition workshops, pp 660–661
68. Ezzat T, Geiger G, Poggio T (2002) Trainable videorealistic speech animation. ACM Trans Graph 21(3):388–398
69. Chang Y-J, Ezzat T (2005) Transferable videorealistic speech animation. In: Proceedings of the ACM SIGGRAPH/Eurographics symposium on computer animation, pp 143–151
70. Chen T (2001) Audiovisual speech processing. IEEE Signal Process Mag 18(1):9–21
71. Choi K, Luo Y, Hwang J-N (2001) Hidden markov model inversion for audio-to-visual conversion in an mpeg-4 facial animation system. J VLSI Signal Process Syst Signal Image Video Technol 29(1):51–61
72. Wang L, Qian X, Han W, Soong FK (2010) Synthesizing photo-real talking head via trajectory-guided sample selection. In: Proceedings of the annual conference of the international speech communication association0
73. Karras T, Aila T, Laine S, Lehtinen J (2018) Progressive growing of gans for improved quality, stability, and variation. In: Proceedings of the international conference on learning representations
74. Karras T, Laine S, Aila T (2019) A style-based generator architecture for generative adversarial networks. In: Proceedings of the IEEE/CVF conference on computer vision and pattern recognition, pp 4401–4410
75. Karras T, Laine S, Aittala M, Hellsten J, Lehtinen J, Aila T (2020) Analyzing and improving the image quality of stylegan. In: Proceedings of the IEEE/CVF conference on computer vision and pattern recognition, pp 8110–8119
76. LeCun Y, Bottou L, Bengio Y, Haffner P (1998) Gradient-based learning applied to document recognition. Proc IEEE 86(11):2278–2324
77. Devries T, Biswaranjan K, Taylor GW (2014) Multi-task learning of facial landmarks and expression. In: Proceedings of the Canadian conference on computer and robot vision, pp 98–103
78. Krizhevsky A et al (2009) Learning multiple layers of features from tiny images. Master's thesis, University of Tront
79. Lu Y, Tai Y-W, Tang C-K (2018) Attribute-guided face generation using conditional cyclegan. In: Proceedings of the European conference on computer vision, pp 282–297
80. Song L, Cao J, Song L, Hu Y, He R (2019) Geometry-aware face completion and editing. Proc AAAI Conf Artif Intell 33(1):2506–2513
81. Huang X, Belongie S (2017) Arbitrary style transfer in real-time with adaptive instance normalization. In: Proceedings of the IEEE international conference on computer vision, pp 1501–1510
82. Shen Z, Huang M, Shi J, Xue X, Huang TS (2019) Towards instance-level image-to-image translation. In: Proceedings of the IEEE/CVF conference on computer vision and pattern recognition, pp 3683–3692
83. Yin Y, Jiang S, Robinson JP, Fu Y (2020) Dual-attention GAN for large-pose face frontalization. In: Proceedings of the IEEE international conference on automatic face and gesture recognition, pp 24–31
84. Qiao F, Yao N, Jiao Z, Li Z, Chen H, Wang H (2018) Geometry-contrastive GAN for facial expression transfer. arXiv preprint 1802.01822
85. Wang K, Wu Q, Song L, Yang Z, Wu W, Qian C, He R, Qiao Y, Loy CC (2020) Mead: a large-scale audio-visual dataset for emotional talking-face generation. In: Proceedings of the European conference on computer vision, pp 700–717

86. Zhou H, Sun Y, Wu W, Loy CC, Wang X, Liu Z (2021) Pose-controllable talking face generation by implicitly modularized audio-visual representation. In: Proceedings of the IEEE/CVF conference on computer vision and pattern recognition
87. Ji X, Zhou H, Wang K, Wu W, Loy CC, Cao X, Xu F (2021) Audio-driven emotional video portraits. In: Proceedings of the IEEE/CVF conference on computer vision and pattern recognition
88. Wang L, Han W, Soong FK (2012) High quality lip-sync animation for 3d photo-realistic talking head. In: Proceedings of the IEEE international conference on acoustics, speech and signal processing, pp 4529–4532
89. Yi R, Ye Z, Zhang J, Bao H, Liu Y-J (2020) Audio-driven talking face video generation with natural head pose. arXiv preprint arXiv:2002.10137
90. Chen L, Cui G, Liu C, Li Z, Kou Z, Xu Y, Xu C (2020) Talking-head generation with rhythmic head motion. In: Proceedings of the European conference on computer vision, pp 35–51
91. Liu K, Ostermann J (2011) Realistic facial expression synthesis for an image-based talking head. In: IEEE international conference on multimedia and expo, pp 1–6
92. Cooke M, Barker J, Cunningham S, Shao X (2006) An audio-visual corpus for speech perception and automatic speech recognition. J Acoust Soc America 120(5):2421–2424
93. Harte N, Gillen E (2015) TCD-TIMIT: an audio-visual corpus of continuous speech. IEEE Trans Multimedia 17(5):603–615
94. Cao H, Cooper DG, Keutmann MK, Gur RC, Nenkova A, Verma R (2014) Crema-d: crowd-sourced emotional multimodal actors dataset. IEEE Trans Affect Comput 5(4):377–390
95. Chung JS, Zisserman A (2016) Lip reading in the wild. In: Proceedings of the Asian conference on computer vision, pp 87–103
96. Chung JS, Senior A, Vinyals O, Zisserman A (2017) Lip reading sentences in the wild. In: Proceedings of the IEEE conference on computer vision and pattern recognition, pp 3444–3453
97. Chung JS, Zisserman A (2017) Lip reading in profile. In: Proceedings of the British machine vision conference
98. Nagrani A, Chung JS, Xie W, Zisserman A (2020) Voxceleb: large-scale speaker verification in the wild. Comput Speech Lang 60:101027
99. Chung JS, Nagrani A, Zisserman A (2018) Voxceleb2: deep speaker recognition. In: In proceedings of the annual conference of the international speech communication association, pp 1086–1090
100. Wang Z, Bovik AC, Sheikh HR, Simoncelli EP (2004) Image quality assessment: from error visibility to structural similarity. IEEE Trans Image Process 13(4):600–612
101. Salimans T, Goodfellow IJ, Zaremba W, Cheung V, Radford A, Chen X (2016) Improved techniques for training GANs. In: Proceedings of the neural information processing systems
102. Heusel M, Ramsauer H, Unterthiner T, Nessler B, Hochreiter S (2017) GANs trained by a two time-scale update rule converge to a local nash equilibrium. In: Proceedings of the international conference on neural information processing systems, pp 6629–6640
103. Narvekar ND, Karam LJ (2011) A no-reference image blur metric based on the cumulative probability of blur detection (CPBD). IEEE Trans Image Process 20(9):2678–2683
104. De K, Masilamani V (2013) Image sharpness measure for blurred images in frequency domain. Procedia Eng 64:149–158
105. Vougioukas K, Petridis S, Pantic M (2019) End-to-end speech-driven realistic facial animation with temporal GANs. In: Proceedings of the IEEE/CVF conference on computer vision and pattern recognition workshops, pp 37–40
106. Assael YM, Shillingford B, Whiteson S, De Freitas N (2016) Lipnet: end-to-end sentence-level lipreading. arXiv preprint arXiv:1611.01599
107. Chen L, Cui G, Kou Z, Zheng H, Xu C (2020) What comprises a good talking-head video generation?: a survey and benchmark. arXiv preprint arXiv:2005.03201
108. Schroff F, Kalenichenko D, Philbin J (2015) Facenet: a unified embedding for face recognition and clustering. In: Proceedings of the IEEE/CVF conference on computer vision and pattern recognition, pp 815–823

109. Deng J, Guo J, Xue N, Zafeiriou S (2019) Arcface: additive angular margin loss for deep face recognition. In: Proceedings of the IEEE/CVF conference on computer vision and pattern recognition, pp 4690–4699
110. Zhang J, Zeng X, Xu C, Chen J, Liu Y, Jiang Y (2020) Apb2facev2: real-time audio-guided multi-face reenactment. arXiv preprint arXiv:2010.13017
111. Karson CN, Berman KF, Donnelly EF, Mendelson WB, Kleinman JE, Wyatt RJ (1981) Speaking, thinking, and blinking. Psychiatry Res 5(3):243–246
112. Hömke P, Holler J, Levinson SC (2018) Eye blinks are perceived as communicative signals in human face-to-face interaction. PloS one 13(12):e0208030
113. Shu Z, Shechtman E, Samaras D, Hadap S (2016) Eyeopener: editing eyes in the wild. ACM Trans Graph 36(1):1–13
114. Thies J, Zollhöfer M, Nießner M, Valgaerts L, Stamminger M, Theobalt C (2015) Real-time expression transfer for facial reenactment. ACM Trans Graph 34(6):1–14
115. Velinov Z, Papas M, Bradley D, Gotardo PFU, Mirdehghan P, Marschner S, Novák J, Beeler T (2018) Appearance capture and modeling of human teeth. ACM Trans Graph 37(6): 207:1–207:13
116. Yang L, Shi Z, Wu Y, Li X, Zhou K, Fu H, Zheng Y (2020) Iorthopredictor: model-guided deep prediction of teeth alignment. ACM Trans Graph 39(6):1–15
117. Wang T-C, Mallya A, Liu M-Y (2021) One-shot free-view neural talking-head synthesis for video conferencing. In: Proceedings of the IEEE/CVF conference on computer vision and pattern recognition
118. Sadoughi N, Busso C (2019) Speech-driven expressive talking lips with conditional sequential generative adversarial networks. IEEE Trans Affect Comput
119. Livingstone SR, Russo FA (2018) The Ryerson audio-visual database of emotional speech and song (ravdess): a dynamic, multimodal set of facial and vocal expressions in north American English. PloS one 13(5):e0196391
120. Zhu H, Luo M-D, Wang R, Zheng A-H, He R (2021) Deep audio-visual learning: a survey. Int J Autom Comput 1–26

Part III
Digital Face Manipulation Detection

Chapter 9
Detection of AI-Generated Synthetic Faces

Diego Gragnaniello, Francesco Marra, and Luisa Verdoliva

Abstract In recent years there have been astonishing advances in AI-based synthetic media generation. Thanks to deep learning methods it is now possible to generate visual data with a high level of realism. This is especially true for human faces. Advanced deep learning tools allow one to easily change some specific attributes of a real face or even create brand new identities. Although this opens up a large number of new opportunities, just think of the entertainment industry, it also undermines the trustworthiness of media content and supports the spread of fake identities over the internet. In this context, there is a fundamental need to develop robust and automatic tools capable of distinguishing synthetic faces from real ones. The scientific community is making a huge research effort in this field, proposing several interesting approaches. However, a universal detector is yet to come. Fundamentally, the research in this field is like a cat and mouse game, with new detectors that are designed to deal with powerful synthetic face generators, while the latter keep improving to produce more and more realistic images. In this chapter we will present the most effective techniques proposed in the literature for the detection of synthetic faces. We will analyze their rationale, present real-world application scenarios , and compare different approaches in terms of accuracy and generalization ability.

9.1 Introduction

Among the many applications of generative adversarial networks (GANs), image synthesis is one of the most investigated, and research in this field has shown a great potential. Particularly impressive are the results that can be achieved in face

D. Gragnaniello · F. Marra · L. Verdoliva (✉)
University of Naples Federico II, via Claudio 21, Naples, Italy
e-mail: verdoliv@unina.it

D. Gragnaniello
e-mail: diego.gragnaniello@unina.it

F. Marra
e-mail: francesco.marra@unina.it

C. Rathgeb et al. (eds.), *Handbook of Digital Face Manipulation and Detection*,
Advances in Computer Vision and Pattern Recognition,
https://doi.org/10.1007/978-3-030-87664-7_9

Fig. 9.1 Fully synthetic face images generated by different GAN architectures. Top, from left to right: images generated using the method proposed in [20], BEGAN [3], and ProGAN [25] at two different resolutions. Bottom, images generated by StyleGAN [27] (left) and StyleGAN2 [28] (right)

generation, with images of higher and higher resolution quality, as also shown by the examples of Fig. 9.1 which depict the evolution of synthetic faces over time. The visual appearance of the images generated by the latest GAN architectures is so realistic that it deceives even the experienced and attentive observer. This raises major concerns on the possible malicious use of such tools. For example, they can be used to create fake profiles on social networks and, more in general, they can be used to spread false information over the web. Therefore, it is urgent to develop automatic tools that can reliably distinguish real content from synthetic content.

Despite their high visual quality, GAN images are characterized by specific artifacts left from the generation process that can be used to develop effective tools for their detection. In some cases, their synthetic origin can be identified by visual inspection due to the presence of semantic inconsistencies, such as color anomalies or lack of symmetries. More generally, these images present invisible artifacts, closely linked to the architecture of the generative network, which can be extracted through appropriate processing steps. These artifacts represent very strong clues, which can be exploited even when synthetic images appear perfectly realistic. In fact, GAN-generated images have been shown to embed a sort of artificial fingerprints [36, 60], specific to each individual GAN architecture. Such patterns also show themselves as peaks in the Fourier domain, not present in the spectral distribution of natural images [16, 18, 61] (see Fig. 9.2).

Many of the detectors proposed so far for GAN-generated faces explicitly use the features described above, while others exploit them implicitly by relying on convolutional neural networks suitably trained on very large datasets [52]. Typically, these solutions show very good performance in distinguishing synthetic faces from real ones. However, they often require that the training set include a sufficient number of examples of the specific GAN architecture that generated images in the test set.

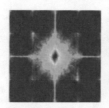

Fig. 9.2 GAN fingerprints extracted in the spatial domain (left) and traces of synthetic images in the frequency domain (right)

Hence, the limited generalization capability is a major problem for current GAN image detectors. As new AI-based models for synthesizing faces are proposed by the day, it is very important to propose solutions that can generalize to new unseen examples. Likewise, robustness is a major challenge, as images are routinely compressed and resized on social networks and valuable clues can be easily reduced or destroyed.

In this chapter, after briefly reviewing the main GAN architectures for face generation, we carry out an analysis of the state-of-the-art detection techniques. We will first present the notion of artificial fingerprints and then describe the major detection methods. We will also present an investigation on the performance of the most promising detectors by testing their generalization and robustness ability on several recent GAN architectures. Besides providing a baseline, this comparative analysis allows us to single out some key features of successful solutions, clearing the way for the design of new and more effective tools.

9.2 AI Face Generation

Progress on synthetic face generation has been possible thanks to the development of deep learning techniques especially autoencoders and generative adversarial networks [20], but also the availability of large-scale public face datasets. Early works were trained on very small face images dataset, while more recent ones rely on the CelebA dataset [33], that includes more than 200k face images of 10k identities, its extension CelebA-HQ with 30k images, and FFHQ [27] that comprises 70k high-quality images collected from Flickr.

AI face generation methods can be roughly classified in the following categories:

- *Fully synthetic faces*: generated faces are synthesized completely from scratch. Some examples have been already shown in Fig. 9.1. Beyond the availability of high resolution face images, some specific strategies have been of key importance to produce more accurate and realistic faces than those produced by the basic GAN architecture [20]. A major breakthrough came with the ProGAN architecture proposed in [25], where high resolution has been achieved by growing both the generator and discriminator progressively during the training process. Another

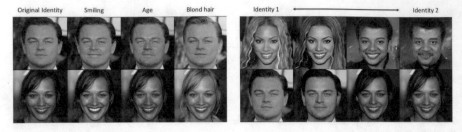

Original Identity　Smiling　Age　Blond hair　Identity 1　⟷　Identity 2

Fig. 9.3 Images manipulated by changing a face attribute (left) and images where two identities are fused together (right)

significant improvement can be found in several works that rely on style transfer to gain more control in the synthesis process and that led to several successful architectures: StyleGAN[1] [27], StyleGAN2 [28] and the recent variant adaptive discriminator augmentation (ADA) [26].

- *Face attributes modification*: beyond synthesizing faces from scratch, it is also possible to modify an attribute of a real face, such as gender, age, skin, or hair color. Conditional GANs represent a very effective tool to address this task and many different approaches have been proposed in the literature and that allow a surprisingly realistic result [32, 46, 51, 55, 62]. More sophisticated modifications let to change the pose or the facial expression [49, 58]. In Fig. 9.3 (left), some examples are shown. It is worth underlining that these manipulations do not change the original identity of the involved subject. Some of these approaches can be found in some mobile applications, such as the popular FaceApp[2].
- *Face blending*: this category comprises methods that are able to fuse the identities from two different face images. The resulting identity is neither non-existent nor preserved, but the resulting face mixes both identities in one. In Fig. 9.3 (right) some examples of face identity blending[3] are presented using the approach proposed in [30].

9.3　GAN Fingerprints

Early work on synthetic media forensics has focused on extending successful approaches and methods of real multimedia forensics to this new domain. In particular, device and model fingerprints represent formidable assets to perform a wide array of forensic tasks, from source attribution to forgery detection and localization, to blind image clustering. Device fingerprints have been first exposed in the seminal work of Chen et al. [34] and Lukas [9]. Due to sensor imperfections, each camera

---

[1] https://thispersondoesnotexist.com/.

[2] https://play.google.com/store/apps/details?id=io.faceapp.

[3] https://openai.com/blog/glow/.

presents a so-called photo-response non-uniformity (PRNU) which leaves on each acquired image traces that are unique of that device and stable in time. This image-like pattern represents therefore a device fingerprint, which can be reliably estimated from sample images of the device.

Given their potential, extending such tools to synthetic media has an obvious appeal. The existence of "artificial" GAN fingerprints was first demonstrated in [36]. These fingerprints are extracted using the very same procedure adopted for real fingerprints. More specifically, for a generic image X_i generated by a given GAN a high-pass filter, i.e., a denoiser, is used to remove the semantic image content:

$$R_i = X_i - f(X_i) \tag{9.1}$$

Then, we assume the residual to be the sum of a *non-zero* deterministic component, the fingerprint F, and a random noise component W_i

$$R_i = F + W_i \tag{9.2}$$

Accordingly, the fingerprint is estimated by a simple average over the available residuals

$$\widehat{F} = \frac{1}{N} \sum_{i=1}^{N} R_i \tag{9.3}$$

As the number of averaged residuals grows, a weak but stable pattern emerges, which characterizes uniquely the GAN architecture. The whole procedure is outlined in Fig. 9.4. Once the GAN fingerprint has been extracted from 200 to 300 GAN images, it can be compared by means of the normalized cross-correlation with the noise residual extracted from the image under test. Experiments carried out in [36] prove

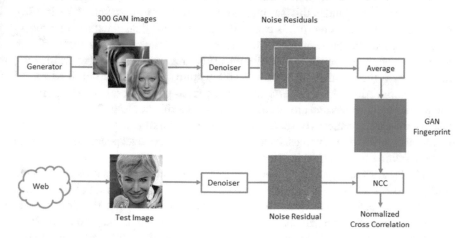

Fig. 9.4 Pipeline for GAN fingerprint extraction

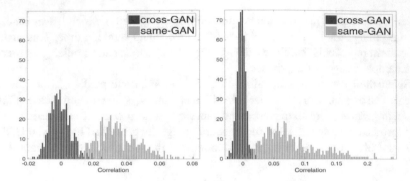

Fig. 9.5 Correlation of CycleGAN (left) and ProGAN (right) residuals with same/cross-GAN fingerprints

that such fingerprints can be used to reliably tell apart real images from synthetically generated ones, and also to attribute an image to its source GAN.

As an example, Fig. 9.5 shows the histograms of the correlation coefficients between image residuals and fingerprint of two GAN architectures. On the left, the GAN-A fingerprint is considered, with green/red colors indicating images generated from the same (GAN-A) or the other (GAN-B) network. The cross-GAN histogram is evenly distributed around zero, indicating no correlation between generated images and unrelated fingerprints. On the contrary, the same-GAN histogram is shifted around larger values, testifying of a significant correlation with the correct fingerprint. The behavior is very similar when GAN-B residuals are considered and the roles are reversed, on the right. In both cases the two distributions are well separated, allowing reliable discrimination.

In [60] fingerprint extraction is addressed by means of a supervised deep learning scheme, where the fingerprint maximizes the correlation with images generated by the same-GAN. Under this setting, both image-like fingerprints, like in [36], and compact vectorial fingerprints can be used. The sophisticated extraction process further improves the performance. Moreover, the experiments prove that different fingerprints arise not only due to different GAN architectures but also from small differences in the training of the same architecture, enabling fine-grained model authentication. Also, GAN fingerprints are shown to persist across different image frequencies and patches and are not biased by GAN artifacts. Both [36] and [60] suggest that the regular patterns observed in GAN fingerprints are due to the up-sampling operations typical of the synthesis network, while instance-level peculiarities depend on the specific filters learned in training.

In [1, 28] attribution of GAN generated images to their source is pursued through GAN inversion. The idea is to provide the test image as target to a set of generators. The likely source is the generator that ensures the minimum reconstruction error. In fact, a GAN architecture cannot perfectly generate a synthetic image that has been produced by another GAN architecture nor it can perfectly reproduce a real image. The projection-based method of [28] was used to prove that an image was synthesized

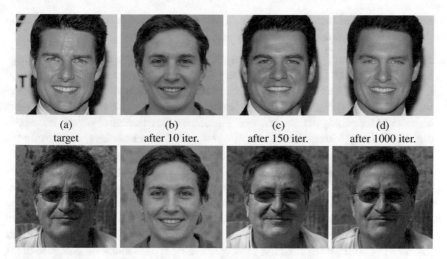

Fig. 9.6 Target face (**a**) and generated faces at different iterations (**b, c, d**). In one case (top) the GAN model is not able to perfectly reproduce the target real face, while it succeeds in perfect reconstruction (bottom) with a target image generated by the GAN itself, that is, face (**a**) is identical to (**d**)

by a specific GAN network. We show such a result in Fig. 9.6, where the target image (a) and the output of the GAN generation process at different iterations are shown. We can observe that in one case (top figure) the GAN is not able to perfectly reproduce the target face, since it is real, while in the second case the target face is perfectly reproduced by the GAN generator (bottom figure), which demonstrates that it was generated by that GAN model.

9.4 Detection Methods in the Spatial Domain

Most of the techniques that aim at distinguishing AI-generated faces from real ones rely on some sort of artifacts, either visible, such as unnatural facial traits, or invisible, like pixel-level statistical inconsistencies that suggest the presence of a generative process. In this section we present detection approaches that work in the original spatial domain. They all use a neural classifier, eventually, but differ for the nature of the features on which the classification is based, handcrafted, or data-driven.

9.4.1 Handcrafted Features

Several handcrafted discriminative features have been proposed to detect generated face images, typically based on the visual inspection of GAN imagery and on prior knowledge of the relevant architectures. In the following we describe the most common and effective ones.

- *Face asymmetries.* Synthetic faces are often characterized by unnatural asymmetries. Indeed, to the best of our knowledge, no specific constraint on symmetry is imposed in the generation phase, probably because of technical difficulties. Therefore, symmetry emerges only as a common feature of the training data and cannot be ensured for all tiny details, however significant for a human observer. For example, GAN images sometimes present eyes with different colors, or asymmetric specular reflections, different earrings, or only on earrings, or ears with markedly different characteristics (see Fig. 9.7). These artifacts are exploited in [39], where simple features are built in order to capture them, such as the correlation between the eyes in suitable color spaces. To exploit asymmetric corneal specular reflections a detector is proposed in [23] based on inconsistencies between light sources reflected in the two eyes. However, this approach needs high-resolution images in order to correctly segment the light spots in both eyes and then compare them, which is not the case of most social networks. This problem is tackled in [22], where a super-resolution module is used, trained to preserve generation artifacts. After the resolution increase, a CNN is used which pools different feature maps on the basis of facial key-points.
- *Landmark locations.* Just like for symmetry, no explicit constraint can be imposed in the generation process to ensure the correct positioning of facial landmark points. As a consequence, it may happen that all individual face parts are generated with a high level of realism and with many details, but their relative locations are unnatural. Based on this observation, the method proposed in [57] uses the locations of the facial landmark points, like the tips of the eyes, nose, and the mouth, as discriminative features for detection.
- *Color features.* GANs produce by design only a limited range of intensity values, and do not generate saturated and/or under-exposed regions. While this is a good property to ask of a photo, a large number of natural face images do present extreme-valued pixels, and their absence suggests a synthetic origin. This fact is exploited in [40] by measuring the frequency of saturated and under-exposed pixels in each image. Turning to color, current GANs are known to not accurately preserve the natural correlation among color bands. This property is exploited in [31] where the chrominance components of the image are high-pass filtered and their co-occurrence matrices are computed to form discriminative features for detection. Indeed, co-occurrences of high-pass filtered images are popular tools in image forensics since invisible artifacts are often present in the high-frequency signal components [12]. Thus, co-occurrence matrices extracted from the RGB channels are also used in [42] as the input of a CNN and, similarly, in [2] co-occurrences across color bands are computed to capture discriminative information.

Fig. 9.7 Examples of GAN synthetic faces with visible artifacts. A generated face with asymmetric earrings (left) and a face with eyes of different colors

9.4.2   Data-Driven Features

Deep networks, in particular Convolutional Neural Networks (CNNs), have proven to adapt well to multimedia forensic tasks [48]. A first investigation of detectors based on very deep networks is carried out in [35], where state-of-the-art pre-trained CNNs, like Xception, Inception, and DenseNet, are shown to ensure excellent performance for GAN image detection. In particular, they turn out to outperform CNN models specifically tailored to forensics tasks and trained from scratch, especially in the most challenging scenarios. More recently, Xception [11] has been used also in [15] as the backbone of a strategy that includes an attention mechanism.

In [53], following an approach originally proposed in Deepxplore [45], detection is based on the neurons' activity at each layer of the network. Experiments carried out on the challenging DFDC dataset show that the neurons' activity provides detailed information about the network behavior and leads to improved classification performance and higher robustness against adversarial attacks. In [24] both detection and attribution are pursued by means of a three-level hierarchical framework. The first level distinguishes real images from manipulated ones, the latter are then classified in the second level as retouched or generated from scratch, and these latter are finally attributed to the generating GAN architecture in the third level. At each level, a CNN is used for feature extraction and an SVM for classification.

GAN architectures typically includes up-sampling stages, which produce a typical checkerboard pattern. To exploit this trace, in [41] an ad hoc self-attention mechanism is proposed to replace plain global pooling in the final layers of the CNN.

9.5   Detection Methods in the Frequency Domain

The checkerboard pattern mentioned in the previous Section shows its traces very clearly in the frequency domain. In fact, the up-sampling operations give rise to quasi-periodic patterns which result in strong peaks in the image spectrum

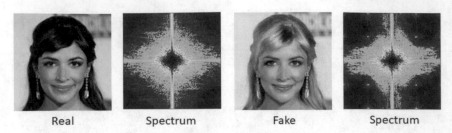

Fig. 9.8 A real image and its Fourier transform (left) a GAN image generated using starGAN [10] and its Fourier transform (right). In this last case it is possible to observe clear peaks in the spectrum

(see again Fig. 9.2 for generic images and Fig. 9.8 for faces). Based on this observation, a detector is proposed in [61] which takes the frequency spectrum instead of image pixels as input for a CNN. A frequency-domain analysis is also performed in [18] to investigate the presence of artifacts across different network architectures, datasets, and resolutions. Then, a CNN-based classifier is trained with Fourier spectra taken from both real images and their synthetic versions obtained through an adversarial autoencoder. Also [17] shows that GAN images do not faithfully mimic the spectral distributions of natural images. Various generative architectures are considered, based both on GANs and autoencoders, and the spectra of the generated images are compared with those of real ones. It results that the spectrum decay along the radial dimension is markedly different in the two cases, with fake images that exhibit higher energy at mid-high frequencies than real ones, which corresponds to small-scale correlations. To exploit these findings, a KNN classifier is trained using the energy spectral distribution as an input feature. Along the same line, in [16] a parametric model is used to fit the decay function of the Fourier spectrum and a classifier is trained on the fitting parameters. It is worth noting that both approaches propose also countermeasures to limit the appearance of such spectral artifacts by means of a simple post-processing [17] or a spectral loss to be used during GAN training [16].

Frequency analyses have been also widely used to detect generated images shared online. Indeed, images uploaded to the web are very often coded using the JPEG standard, based on the Fourier-like discrete cosine transform (DCT). For synthetic images, this compression step may reveal distinctive traces of the generation process, absent in real images, which can be used for reliable detection. As an example, for generated images, the most significant digit of the quantized DCT coefficients violates the well-known Benford's law. Based on this evidence, in [4] a compact feature vector is extracted from the DCT coefficients and used to train a random forest classifier. Frequency-aware features are learned in the DCT domain in [47] to exploit both local and global frequency clues. On one hand, the proposed approach learns the global DCT coefficients where it is easier to spot fake faces. On the other hand, block-wise DCT frequency statistics are computed as complementary features to improve detection.

9.6 Learning Features that Generalize

Fully supervised approaches are typically very effective when the GAN images under test come from a model that is also present in training. However, often they fail to generalize to data generated by new unseen models. This phenomenon has been shown both in [29] and in [14], where some interesting experiments are carried out that highlight the inability of both handcrafted and data-driven features to support cross-dataset generalization. In the following we will review some of the methods proposed so far to address this issue.

- *Few-shot and incremental learning.* In [14] a strategy based on few-shot learning is proposed to increase transferability. An autoencoder with a bipartite hidden layer is trained. Then, the input image is projected onto a latent vector where the information needed to make the real/synthetic decision is disentangled from the image representation. This allows for higher detection rates in cases where only a few training samples of an unseen GAN architecture are available. In [38], instead, an approach based on incremental learning is proposed to update the detector to new data (i.e., new GAN architectures) made available at different times. A few representative template vectors of the known architectures are kept in a compact memory. In this way, the network can be re-trained on new data of a novel architecture without forgetting the old ones. Despite the improved generalization, these methods still require some examples of the new GAN architecture, which could not be available in a real scenario.
- *Augmentation.* A different solution is proposed in [56]. The idea is to carry out augmentation by Gaussian blurring so as to force the discriminator to learn more general features while discarding noise-like patterns that impair the training. A similar approach is followed in [54] where a standard pre-trained model, ResNet50, is further trained with a strong augmentation based on compression and blurring. Experiments show that, even by training on a single GAN architecture, the learned features generalize well to unseen architectures, datasets, and training methods. The comparative analysis of [21], instead, shows that by avoiding any subsampling in the first layer of the network ensures improved detection results. This finding is also confirmed by studies on no-subsampling network architectures for more general multimedia forensics tasks [37].
- *Patch-based learning.* A different perspective is adopted in [8] where a fully convolutional patch-based classifier with limited a receptive field is proposed. The authors prove the importance of focusing on local patches rather than on the global structure of the image, and hence ensemble the patch-wise decisions to obtain the overall prediction.

9.7 Generalization Analysis

Early techniques proposed for the detection of AI-generated faces were evaluated in an ideal scenario in which both the training and testing samples were generated by the very same AI (or small variations thereof). In this setting, even a simple approach like a shallow CNN can reach almost perfect performance [2, 4, 18, 35, 42]. As already discussed in the previous section, the detection performance drops on images generated by different GAN architectures. In this chapter, we will analyze the ability of several AI face detectors to generalize on synthetic images that are not used during training.

Following the protocol proposed in [54], we train all the detection methods on a large dataset of pristine images from LSUN, while synthetic images are generated using 20 ProGAN models [25], each trained on a different category, for a grand total of more than 700k images. All images have a resolution of 256×256 pixel and a subset of 4k images are used for validation. The test dataset comprises both same-resolution and higher resolution (1024×1024) images generated by various GAN architectures: StyleGAN [27], StyleGAN2 [28], BigGAN [6], CycleGAN [62], StarGAN [10], RelGAN [55], and GauGAN [44]. Then we have a large dataset of real images both low-resolution and high-resolution ones, as specified in [21].

In this analysis, the following synthetic image detectors are considered: Xception [35], SRNet [5], Spec [61], M-Gb [56], Co-Net [42], Wang2020 [54], PatchForensics [8]. Beyond these methods that are specifically proposed for GAN image detection, we also include SRNet that was instead originally proposed for steganalysis. In fact, both steganalysis and image forensics have a very similar goal, i.e., detecting hidden traces in the image, and methods proposed for steganalysis have often shown a great potential also in forensics [52]. More specifically, to better preserve features related to noise residual, SRNet avoids down-sampling in the first layers of the network.

To manage both low- and high-resolution images in the test phase, we adopt the strategy proposed in the original papers. In particular, for M-Gb, FFD and Patch-Forensics, the image is resized to the dimension of network input, meanwhile for Spec the central clip of size 224×224 is considered. The remaining techniques are applied on the whole test image without clipping/resizing it since they include a global average pooling. The list of the analyzed approaches and their test strategy are summarized in Table 9.1.

Results are shown in Fig. 9.9 for low-resolution (top) and high-resolution (bottom) images in terms of several performance metrics: area under the receiver-operating curve (AUC), accuracy at the fixed threshold of 0.5, and probability of detection for a 5% (Pd@5%) and 1% (Pd@1%) false alarm rate (FAR). Performance in terms of AUC on low-resolution (LR) images are very good, considering that there is a misalignment between training and testing data, with several methods exceeding the 0.9 level. However, accuracy results are much less encouraging, since a fixed threshold is used. Indeed, we noticed that each GAN architecture needs a different threshold to be set. Hence, without sample images generated from a specific GAN, it is hard to set the correct threshold. Considering the Pd@FAR metric, results become

Table 9.1 List of the methods used in our analysis together with the test strategy, as proposed in the original papers

References	Acronym	Test strategy
[35]	Xception	No cropping and no resizing
[5]	SRNet	No cropping and no resizing
[61]	Spec	Central cropping (224 × 224)
[56]	M-Gb	Resizing (128 × 128)
[42]	Co-Net	No cropping and no resizing
[15]	FFD	Resizing (299 × 299)
[54]	Wang2020	No cropping and no resizing
[8]	PatchForensics	Resizing (299 × 299)

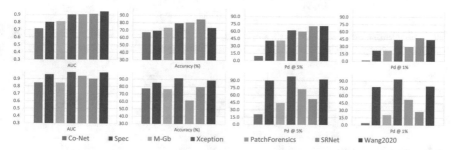

Fig. 9.9 Results of the methods under comparison in terms of AUC, Accuracy, Pd@5% and Pd@1% for all the tested methods on low-resolution (top) and high-resolution images (bottom)

worse, and only a few methods are able to ensure a good detection ability for high-resolution images. It is interesting to observe that the ranking of the methods change based on the specific metric.

9.8 Robustness Analysis

In this section we present a robustness analysis of the GAN detectors analyzed in the previous section. In fact, it is important to understand to which extent these detectors are affected by post-processing operations such as image compression or resizing that is commonly applied when images are uploaded on a social network. These operations could strongly reduce the low-level inconsistencies. For example in Fig. 9.10 it is shown the spectrum of GAN images when resizing and compression operations have been applied. One can observe that by reducing the size of the image the peaks in the Fourier domain tend to vanish, while enlarging the image further enhances those artifacts. Compression reduces the Fourier artifacts that completely disappear if the quality factor is too low (below 70).

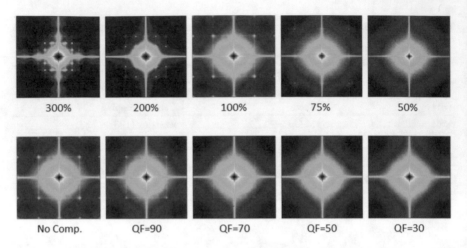

Fig. 9.10 Fourier transform of a GAN image by varying its dimensions using different resizing factors (top) and by applying JPEG compression at different quality levels (bottom)

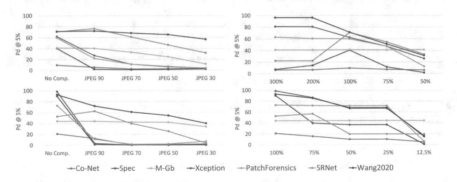

Fig. 9.11 Results of the methods under comparison in terms of Pd@5% by varying the JPEG quality compression level and by resizing the images at different factors. LR images are both enlarged and reduced in size, while HR images are only reduced

Figure 9.11 reports the Pd@5% performance for low-resolution and high-resolution images for varying compression factors and resizing scales. Several methods suffer dramatic impairments as soon as they move away from the ideal case of no compression and 100% scale. For example, we can notice that a 2x downsampling has a catastrophic effect, as justified by the fact that peaks completely disappear in the Fourier spectrum (see again Fig. 9.10). The most robust methods are those that benefit by a strong augmentation, in addition we can observe the good performance of SRNet on compressed images. Overall these experiments suggest that there is still much room for improvements with respect to the existing solutions, especially in terms of robustness to compression and resizing.

9.9 Further Analyses on GAN Detection

In this section we want to further investigate the performance of a good solution for GAN detection so as to identify the key ingredients of the most promising solutions. We consider as baseline the method proposed in [54], given the very good performance shown in the previous experiments, and introduce the following variations: remove Imagenet pre-training (no-pretrain), include an initial layer for residual extraction as often performed in image forensics strategies [52] (residual), do not perform down-sampling in the first layer as suggested by [5] (no-down), perform a stronger augmentation (strong-aug) by including Gaussian noise adding, geometric transformations, cut-out, and brightness and contrast changes. In addition, for the no-down variant, we also change the backbone network and replace ResNet50 with Xception (Xception no-down) and Efficient-B4 (Efficient no-down).

Results for the various metrics are shown in Fig. 9.12, while Fig. 9.13 shows results in terms of Pd@5% as a function of compression level and scaling factor. We can notice that the solution that avoids down-sampling in the first block of the architecture is very promising also in presence of resizing and compression. Instead no significant improvement can be observed by adopting strong augmentation or changing the backbone network. Note also the importance of the pre-training step on imagenet especially to gain robustness to resizing and compression.

Finally, in Table 9.2 we show the results for the baseline and the best variant over all the different GAN architectures, also including ProGAN that was used in the training step. We can notice that the best variant (no-down) provides an average gain of about 15% in terms of accuracy and 14% in terms of Pd@5%. Overall accuracy is always above 90% irrespective of the type of architecture. Finally, we added a further experiment by adopting 23 StyleGAN2 different models in training. In this last case performance are almost perfect with a further consistent improvement with respect to our baseline.

These experiments confirm the importance of diversity to increase robustness, like ImageNet pre-training, as already observed in steganalysis [59]. For the same

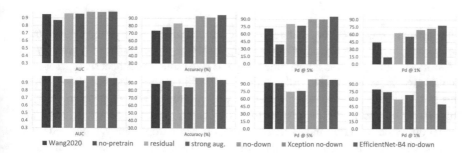

Fig. 9.12 Results of the baseline (Wang2020) and its variants in terms of AUC, Accuracy, Pd@5% and Pd@1% for variants of Wang2020 on low-resolution (top) and high-resolution images (bottom)

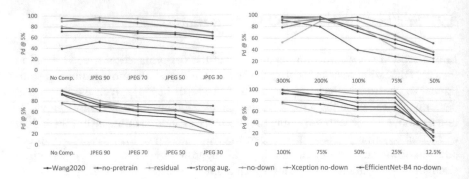

Fig. 9.13 Results of the baseline (Wang2020) and its variants in terms of Pd@5% by varying the JPEG quality compression level and by resizing the images at different factors. LR images are both enlarged and reduced in size, while HR images are only reduced

Table 9.2 Accuracy and Pd@5% for the baseline and the best variant that avoids down-sampling in the first block

Accuracy/Pd@5%		Wang2020 (baseline)	Best variant (no-down)	On StyleGAN2 (no-down)
Low res.	ProGAN	99.3/100.0	94.7/100.0	99.8/100.0
	StyleGAN	75.9/73.9	93.7/93.1	99.9/100.0
	StyleGAN2	71.5/69.0	92.2/88.8	99.9/100.0
	BigGAN	59.2/45.2	93.5/92.0	96.5/99.4
	CycleGAN	77.4/80.5	90.3/81.5	96.5/99.5
	StarGAN	84.3/89.4	94.5/97.6	99.9/100.0
	RelGAN	63.6/56.0	92.8/86.6	99.7/100.0
	GauGAN	82.5/86.3	93.6/93.5	90.8/97.1
High res.	ProGAN	99.7/100.0	97.1/100.0	99.7/100.0
	StyleGAN(Cel.)	99.3/100.0	97.1/100.0	99.7/100.0
	StyleGAN(FFHQ)	82.6/93.7	96.6/98.7	99.7/100.0
	StyleGAN2	73.2/78.1	96.9/99.6	99.7/100.0

reason, image pre-processing like resizing to match the input size of the CNN should be avoided. In fact, just like other forensics applications, the useful information lays in pixel-level patterns spread all over the image. If size reduction is necessary, cropping should always be preferred to resizing both during the training and test phase. Along this same direction, the no-down variant is very promising and suggests to work on full-resolution end-to-end processing to design better and more robust detectors, as also proposed in [37] for image forgery detection. More importantly, they shed some lights on the needs for well-designed evaluation protocols to assess the generalization capabilities of AI-generated image detectors in real-world scenarios.

9.10 Open Challenges

The advent of deep learning has given extraordinary impulse to both face manipulation methods and forensic detection tools. We have seen that successful detectors rely on inconsistencies at different levels, looking for both hidden and visible artifacts. One first important observation is that visual imperfections on faces will likely disappear soon. Newer GAN architectures [28] already improved upon this aspect by producing faces with even more details and highly realistic. Thus, relying exclusively on these traces could be a losing strategy in the long term. Turning to generic deep learning based-solutions, the main technical issue is probably the inability to adapt to situations not seen in the training phase. Misalignment between training and test, compression, and resizing are all sources of serious impairments and, at the same time, highly realistic scenarios for real-world applications. Also, to deal with the rapid advances in manipulation technology, deep networks should be able to adapt readily to new manipulations, without a full re-training, which may be simply impossible for lack of training data or entail catastrophic forgetting phenomena.

A more fundamental problem is the two-player nature of this research which is common to many security-related fields. In fact, detection algorithms must confront with the capacity of an adversary to fool them. This means that new solutions are needed in order to cope with unforeseen attacks. This applies to any type of classifier and is also very well known in forensics, where many counter-forensics methods have been proposed in the literature in order to better understand weaknesses of current approaches and help to improve them over time.

In the following, we analyze some works that have shown the vulnerabilities of GAN detectors to different types of threats.

- *Adding adversarial perturbations.* It is well known, from the object recognition field, that suitable slight perturbations can induce misclassification [50]. Following this path, in [7] it has been investigated the robustness of GAN detectors to imperceptible noise both in a white-box and in a black-box scenario. The authors show that it is possible to generate appropriate adversarial perturbations so as to misclassify fake images as real (see Fig. 9.14), but also the opposite. In addition, they show that the attack can survive JPEG compression. Interestingly, it is also possible to design an effective strategy in a black-box threat model when the adversary does not have perfect knowledge of the classifier but is aware about the type of classifier. A similar analysis is conducted in [19], where adversarial attacks are designed to fool co-occurrence-based GAN detectors.
- *Removing GAN fingerprints.* Instead of adding noise, one can take a different perspective and remove the specific fingerprints that are used to discriminate GAN images from real ones. This approach is pursued in [43], where an autoencoder-based strategy is proposed, that is trained using only real faces and is able to remove the high-frequency components that correspond to the fingerprints of the models used to generate synthetic images. At test time the autoencoder takes as input synthetic face images and modifies them so as to spoof GAN detection systems.

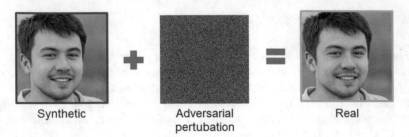

Synthetic   Adversarial   Real
pertubation

Fig. 9.14 A small and imperceptible adversarial perturbation can be added to the synthetic face image in order to fool the detector

- *Inserting camera fingerprints.* Another possible direction to attack GAN detectors is to insert the specific camera traces that characterize real images. In fact, real images are characterized by their own device and model fingerprints, as explained before. Such differences are important to carry out camera model identification from image content but can also be used to better highlight anomalies caused by image manipulations [52]. In [13] it is proposed a targeted black-box attack that is based on a GAN architecture, able to insert specific real camera traces in a synthetic images. In this way it is possible not only to fool a GAN detector without any prior information on its architecture, but also to fool a camera model identification algorithm, that will attribute the GAN image to the targeted camera under attack.

It is worth observing that all these approaches generate face images that are visually indistinguishable from real ones. This makes clear that a good GAN detector should always taken into account possible adversarial attacks and include proper strategies to face them. Another issue for forensics deep learning-based methods is interpretability. The black-box nature of these approaches makes it difficult to understand the reason behind a certain decision. Hence it is important to develop strategies that increase the level of understanding so as to improve its design and maybe also increase robustness to possible malicious attacks.

Overall, we can conclude that AI synthetic face detection is not a trivial task and, despite the huge effort made by the scientific community, we need to develop more reliable tools, that should also include anti-forensics and adversarial attacks since these techniques are widespread and can seriously impair the detection performance. It is difficult to forecast whether detection tools will be able to ensure a good defense against a bad use of synthetic content over the web or if active protection technology will become necessary. However, we believe that developing reliable detectors that possess good features in terms of generalization and robustness can represent a first step to protect our society.

Acknowledgements This material is based on research sponsored by the Defense Advanced Research Projects Agency (DARPA) and the Air Force Research Laboratory (AFRL) under agreement number FA8750-20-2-1004. The U.S. Government is authorized to reproduce and distribute reprints for Governmental purposes notwithstanding any copyright notation thereon. The views and conclusions contained herein are those of the authors and should not be interpreted as necessarily representing the official policies or endorsements, either expressed or implied, of DARPA and AFRL or the U.S. Government. This work is also supported by the PREMIER project, funded by the Italian Ministry of Education, University, and Research within the PRIN 2017 program and by a Google gift.

References

1. Albright M, McCloskey S (2019) Source generator attribution via inversion. In: IEEE/CVF conference on computer vision and pattern recognition workshops (CVPRW), pp 96–103
2. Barni M, Kallas K, Nowroozi E, Tondi B (2020) CNN detection of GAN-generated face images based on cross-band co-occurrences analysis. In: IEEE international workshop on information forensics and security (WIFS), pp 1–6
3. Berthelot D, Schumm T, Metz L (2017) BEGAN: boundary equilibrium generative adversarial networks. arXiv preprint arXiv:1703.10717
4. Bonettini N, Bestagini P, Milani S, Tubaro S (2020) On the use of Benford's law to detect GAN-generated images. In: IEEE international conference on pattern recognition
5. Boroumand M, Chen M, Fridrich J (2019) Deep residual network for steganalysis of digital images. IEEE Trans Inform Forensics Secur 14(5):1181–1193
6. Brock A, Donahue J, Simonyan K (2018) Large scale GAN training for high fidelity natural image synthesis. In: International conference on learning representations (ICLR)
7. Carlini N, Farid H (2020) Evading deepfake-image detectors with white- and black-box attacks. In: IEEE/CVF conference on computer vision and pattern recognition workshops (CVPRW), pp 2804–2813
8. Chai L, Bau D, Lim SN, Isola P (2020) What makes fake images detectable? Understanding properties that generalize. In: European conference on computer vision (ECCV). Springer, pp 103–120
9. Chen M, Fridrich J, Goljan M, Lukás J (2008) Determining image origin and integrity using sensor noise. IEEE Trans Inform Forensics Secur 3(1):74–90
10. Choi Y, Choi M, Kim M, Ha JW, Kim S, Choo J (2018) StarGAN: unified generative adversarial networks for multi-domain image-to-image translation. In: IEEE/CVF conference on computer vision and pattern recognition (CVPR), pp 8789–8797
11. Chollet F (2017) Xception: Deep learning with depthwise separable convolutions. In: IEEE/CVF conference on computer vision and pattern recognition (CVPR)
12. Cozzolino D, Poggi G, Verdoliva L (2017) Recasting residual-based local descriptors as convolutional neural networks: an application to image forgery detection. In: ACM workshop on information hiding and multimedia security, pp 1–6 (2017)
13. Cozzolino D, Thies J, Roessler A, Niessner M, Verdoliva L (2019) SpoC: spoofing camera fingerprints. In: IEEE CVPR Workshops, June 2021
14. Cozzolino D, Thies J, Rössler A, Riess C, Nießner M, Verdoliva L (2018) ForensicTransfer: weakly-supervised domain adaptation for forgery detection. arXiv preprint arXiv:1812.02510
15. Dang H, Liu F, Stehouwer J, Liu X, Jain A (2020) On the detection of digital face manipulation. In: IEEE/CVF conference on computer vision and pattern recognition (CVPR), pp 5781–5790
16. Durall R, Keuper M, Keuper J (2020) Watch your up-convolution: CNN based generative deep neural networks are failing to reproduce spectral distributions. In: IEEE/CVF conference on computer vision and pattern recognition (CVPR)

17. Dzanic T, Shah K, Witherden F (2020) Fourier spectrum discrepancies in deep network generated images. In: Conference on neural information processing systems (NeurIPS)
18. Frank J, Eisenhofer T, Schönherr L, Fischer A, Kolossa D, Holz T (2020) Leveraging frequency analysis for deep fake image recognition. In: IEEE/CVF conference on computer vision and pattern recognition (CVPR)
19. Goebel M, Manjunath B (2020) Adversarial attacks on co-occurrence features for GAN detection. arXiv preprint arXiv:2009.07456
20. Goodfellow I, Pouget-Abadie J, Mirza M, Xu B, Warde-Farley D, Ozair S, Courville A, Bengio Y (2014) Generative adversarial nets. In: Conference in neural information processing systems (NIPS)
21. Gragnaniello D, Cozzolino D, Marra F, Poggi G (2021) Verdoliva L (2021) Are GAN generated images easy to detect? IEEE international conference on multimedia and expo (ICME), A critical analysis of the state-of-the-art. In
22. Han X, Ji Z, Wang W (2020) Low resolution facial manipulation detection. In: IEEE international conference on visual communications and image processing (VCIP), pp 431–434
23. Hu S, Li Y, Lyu S (2020) Exposing GAN-generated faces using inconsistent corneal specular highlights. In: IEEE international conference on acoustics, speech and signal processing 2021
24. Jain A, Majumdar P, Singh R, Vatsa M (2020) Detecting GANs and retouching based digital alterations via DAD-HCNN. In: IEEE/CVF conference on computer vision and pattern recognition workshops (CVPRW), pp 2870–2879
25. Karras T, Aila T, Laine S, Lehtinen J (2018) Progressive growing of GANs for improved quality, stability, and variation. In: International conference on learning representations (ICLR)
26. Karras T, Aittala M, Hellsten J, Laine S, Lehtinen J, Aila T (2020) Training generative adversarial networks with limited data. In: Conference on neural information processing systems (NeurIPS)
27. Karras T, Laine S, Aila T (2019) A style-based generator architecture for generative adversarial networks. In: IEEE/CVF conference on computer vision and pattern recognition (CVPR), pp 4396–4405
28. Karras T, Laine S, Aittala M, Hellsten J, Lehtinen J, Aila T (2020) Analyzing and improving the image quality of StyleGAN. In: IEEE/CVF conference on computer vision and pattern recognition (CVPR), pp 8110–8119
29. Khodabakhsh A, Ramachandra R, Raja K, Wasnik P, Busch C (2018) Fake face detection methods: Can they be generalized? In: International conference of the biometrics special interest group (BIOSIG), pp 1–6
30. Kingma DP, Dhariwal P (2018) Glow: generative flow with invertible 1×1 convolutions. In: Conference on neural information processing systems (NIPS), pp 10236–10245
31. Li H, Li B, Tan S, Huang J (2020) Detection of deep network generated images using disparities in color components. Signal Process 174
32. Liu M, Ding Y, Xia M, Liu X, Ding E, Zuo W, Wen S (2019) STGAN: a unified selective transfer network for arbitrary image attribute editing. In: IEEE/CVF conference on computer vision and pattern recognition (CVPR), pp 3673–3682
33. Liu Z, Luo P, Wang X, Tang X (2015) Deep learning face attributes in the wild. In: International conference on computer vision (ICCV)
34. Lukas J, Fridrich J, Goljan M (2006) Digital camera identification from sensor pattern noise. IEEE Trans Inform Forensics Secur 1(2):205–214
35. Marra F, Gragnaniello D, Cozzolino D, Verdoliva L (2018) Detection of GAN-generated fake images over social networks. In: IEEE conference on multimedia information processing and retrieval (MIPR)
36. Marra F, Gragnaniello D, Verdoliva L, Poggi G (2019) Do GANs leave artificial fingerprints? In: IEEE conference on multimedia information processing and retrieval (MIPR), pp 506–511
37. Marra F, Gragnaniello D, Verdoliva L, Poggi G (2020) A full-image full-resolution end-to-end-trainable CNN framework for image forgery detection. IEEE Access 8
38. Marra F, Saltori C, Boato G, Verdoliva L (2019) Incremental learning for the detection and classification of GAN-generated images. In: IEEE international workshop on information forensics and security (WIFS)

39. Matern F, Riess C, Stamminger M (2019) Exploiting visual artifacts to expose deepfakes and face manipulations. In: IEEE winter applications of computer vision workshops (WACVW), pp 83–92
40. McCloskey S, Albright M (2019) Detecting GAN-generated imagery using saturation cues. In: IEEE international conference on image processing (ICIP)
41. Mi Z, Jiang X, Sun T, Xu K (2020) GAN-generated image detection with self-attention mechanism against GAN generator defect. IEEE J Sel Top Signal Process 14(5):969–981
42. Nataraj L, Mohammed T, Manjunath B, Chandrasekaran S, Flenner A, Bappy J, Roy-Chowdhury A (2019) Detecting GAN generated fake images using co-occurrence matrices. In: IS&T Electronic imaging, media watermarking, security, and forensics, pp 532–1–532–7
43. Neves JC, Tolosana R, Vera-Rodriguez R, Lopes V, Proena H, Fierrez J (2020) GANprintR: improved fakes and evaluation of the state of the art in face manipulation detection. IEEE J Sel Top Signal Process 14(5):1038–1048
44. Park T, Liu MY, Wang T-C, Zhu J-Y (2019) Semantic image synthesis with spatially-adaptive normalization. In: IEEE/CVF conference on computer vision and pattern recognition (CVPR), pp 2337–2346
45. Pei K, Cao Y, Yang J, Jana S (2017) Deepxplore: automated whitebox testing of deep learning systems. In: 26th symposium on operating systems principles, pp 1–18
46. Perarnau G, van de Weijer J, Raducanu B, Álvarez J (2016) Invertible conditional GANs for image editing. In: NIPS workshop on adversarial training
47. Qian Y, Yin G, Sheng L, Chen Z, Shao J (2020) Thinking in frequency: face forgery detection by mining frequency-aware clues. In: European conference on computer vision (ECCV), pp 86–103
48. Rössler A, Cozzolino D, Verdoliva L, Riess C, Thies J, Nießner M (2019) FaceForensics++: learning to detect manipulated facial images. In: International conference on computer vision (ICCV)
49. Shen Y, Luo P, Yan J, Wang X, Tang X (2018) Faceid-GAN: learning a symmetry three-player GAN for identity-preserving face synthesis. In: IEEE/CVF conference on computer vision and pattern recognition (CVPR), pp 821–830
50. Szegedy C, Zaremba W, Sutskever I, Bruna J, Erhan D, Goodfellow I, Fergus R (2014) Intriguing properties of neural networks. In: International conference on learning representations (ICLR)
51. Upchurch P, Gardner J, Pleiss G, Pless R, Snavely N, Bala K, Weinberger K (2017) Deep feature interpolation for image content changes. In: IEEE/CVF conference on computer vision and pattern recognition (CVPR), pp 7064–7073
52. Verdoliva L (2020) Media forensics and deepfakes: an overview. IEEE J Sel Top Signal Process 14(5):910–932
53. Wang R, Juefei-Xu F, Ma L, Xie X, Huang Y, Wang J, Liu Y (2020) FakeSpotter: a simple yet robust baseline for spotting AI-synthesized fake faces. In: International joint conference on artificial intelligence (IJCAI), pp 3444–3451
54. Wang SY, Wang O, Zhang R, Owens A, Efros A (2020) CNN-generated images are surprisingly easy to spot... for now. In: IEEE/CVF conference on computer vision and pattern recognition (CVPR)
55. Wu PW, Lin YJ, Chang H-C, Chang E, Liao SW (2019) RelGAN: multi-domain image-to-image translation via relative attributes. In: IEEE international conference on computer vision (ICCV)
56. Xuan X, Peng B, Wang W, Dong J (2019) On the generalization of GAN image forensics. In: Chinese conference on biometric recognition, pp 134–141
57. Yang X, Li Y, Qi H, Lyu S (2019) Exposing GAN-synthesized faces using landmark locations. In: ACM workshop on information hiding and multimedia security, pp 113–118
58. Yao G, Yuan Y, Shao T, Zhou K (2020) Mesh guided one-shot face reenactment using graph convolutional networks. In: ACM international conference on multimedia, pp 1773–1781
59. Yousfi Y, Butora J, Khvedchenya E, Fridrich J (2020) ImageNet pre-trained CNNs for JPEG Steganalysis. In: IEEE international workshop on information forensics and security (WIFS), pp 1–6

60. Yu N, Davis L, Fritz M (2019) Attributing fake images to GANs: learning and analyzing GAN fingerprints. In: IEEE international conference on computer vision (ICCV)
61. Zhang X, Karaman S, Chang SF (2019) Detecting and simulating artifacts in GAN fake images. In: IEEE international workshop on information forensics and security (WIFS), pp 1–6
62. Zhu JY, Park T, Isola P, Efros A (2017) Unpaired image-to-image translation using cycle-consistent adversarial networks. In: IEEE international conference on computer vision (ICCV), pp 2223–2232

Chapter 10
3D CNN Architectures and Attention Mechanisms for Deepfake Detection

Ritaban Roy, Indu Joshi, Abhijit Das, and Antitza Dantcheva

Abstract Manipulated images and videos have become increasingly realistic due to the tremendous progress of deep convolutional neural networks (CNNs). While technically intriguing, such progress raises a number of social concerns related to the advent and spread of fake information and fake news. Such concerns necessitate the introduction of robust and reliable methods for fake image and video detection. Toward this in this work, we study the ability of state-of-the-art video CNNs including 3D ResNet, 3D ResNeXt, and I3D in detecting manipulated videos. In addition, and toward a more robust detection, we investigate the effectiveness of attention mechanisms in this context. Such mechanisms are introduced in CNN architectures in order to ensure that robust features are being learnt. We test two attention mechanisms, namely SE-block and Non-local networks. We present related experimental results on videos tampered by four manipulation techniques, as included in the Face-Forensics++ dataset. We investigate three scenarios, where the networks are trained to detect (a) all manipulated videos, (b) each manipulation technique individually, as well as (c) the veracity of videos pertaining to manipulation techniques not included in the train set.

R. Roy
BITS, Pilani, India
e-mail: f2015842@pilani.bits-pilani.ac.in

I. Joshi
IIT Delhi, Delhi, India
e-mail: indu.joshi@cse.iitd.ac.in

A. Das (✉)
Thapar University, Patiala, India
e-mail: abhijit.das@thapar.edu

A. Dantcheva
Inria Sophia Antipolis, Valbonne, France
e-mail: antitza.dantcheva@inria.fr

© The Author(s) 2022
C. Rathgeb et al. (eds.), *Handbook of Digital Face Manipulation and Detection*,
Advances in Computer Vision and Pattern Recognition,
https://doi.org/10.1007/978-3-030-87664-7_10

213

10.1 Introduction

Manipulated images date back to the creation of the first photograph in the year 1825 [18]. Related manipulation techniques have been widely driven by profit stemming from identity theft, age deception, illegal immigration, organized crime, and espionage, inflicting negative consequences on businesses, individuals, and political entities. While forgery was associated with a slow, painstaking process usually reserved for experts, we are entering new levels of manipulation of images and video, where deep learning and related *manipulation* are streamlined to reduce costs, time, and skill needed to doctor images and videos. Automated generation and manipulation of audio, image and video bares highly exciting perspectives for science, art and video productions, e.g., video animation, special effects, reliving already passed actors.

While highly intriguing from computer vision perspective, *deepfakes* entail a number of challenges and threats, given that (a) such manipulations can fabricate animations of subjects involved in actions that have not taken place and (b) such manipulated data can be circumvented nowadays rapidly via social media. Particularly, we cannot trust anymore, what we see or hear on video, as deepfakes betray sight and sound, the two predominantly trusted human innate senses [44]. Given that (i) our society relies heavily on the ability to produce and exchange legitimate and trustworthy documents, (ii) sound and images have recorded our history, as well as informed and shaped our perception of reality, e.g., axioms and truths such as "I'll believe it when I see it." "Out of sight, out of mind." "A picture is worth a thousand words". (iii) Social media has catapulted online videos as a mainstream source of information; deepfakes pose a threat of distorting what is perceived as reality. To further fuel concern, deepfake techniques have become open to the public via phone applications such as FaceApp[1], ZAO[2] and Wombo[3]. Further, *digital identity*[4], associated to the entire collection of information generated by a person's online activity including usernames and passwords, photographs, online search activities, birth date, social security becomes highly vulnerable, with deepfakes entailing the premise to inflict severe damage. Additional social threats [12, 17] can affect domains such as journalism, education, individual rights, democratic systems and have intrigued a set of journalists[5, 6, 7, 8].

---

[1] https://apps.apple.com/gb/app/faceapp-ai-face-editor/id1180884341.

[2] https://apps.apple.come/cn/app/id146519927.

[3] https://www.wombo.ai/.

[4] https://www.indrastra.com/2018/01/Digital-Identity-Gateway-to-All-Other-Use-Cases-004-01-2018-0034.html.

[5] https://edition.cnn.com/interactive/2019/01/business/pentagons-race-against-deepfakes/.

[6] https://www.nytimes.com/2019/11/24/technology/tech-companies-deepfakes.html.

[7] https://www.theguardian.com/commentisfree/2018/jul/22/deep-fake-news-donald-trump-vladimir-putin.

[8] https://www.cnbc.com/2019/10/14/what-is-deepfake-and-how-it-might-be-dangerous.html.

We differentiate two cases of concern: the first one has to do with *deepfakes being perceived as real*, and the second relates to *real videos being misdetected for fake*, the latter referred to as "liar's dividend". Given such considerations, e.g., video evidence becomes highly questionable.

Recent research on deepfake generation proposed approaches, where forged videos are created based on a *short video* of the source person [30, 48], as well as from a *single ID photo* [5] of the source person. In addition, fully synthesized *audio-video* images are able to replicate synchronous speech and lip movement [46] of a target person. Hence deepfakes coerce the target person in a video to reenact the dynamics of the source person.

Two deepfake-schemes have evolved, corresponding to *head puppetry* (the dynamics of a head from a source person are synthesized in a target person), as well as face swapping (the whole face of a target person is swapped with that of a source person). Lip syncing (the lip region of the target person is reenacted by the lip region of a source person) falls in the first category. Currently such manipulations include subtle imperfections that can be detected by humans and, if trained well, by computer vision algorithms [3, 32, 33]. Toward thwarting such attacks, early multimedia forensics based detection strategies have been proposed [3, 4, 16, 41]. Such strategies, although essential, cannot provide a comprehensive solution against manipulated audio, images, and video. Specifically, the detection of deepfakes is challenging for several reasons: (a) it evolves a "cat-and-mouse-game" between the adversary and the system designer, (b) deep models are highly domain-specific and likely yield big performance degradation in cross-domain deployments, especially with large train-test domain gap.

The *manipulation scenario* of interest in this work has to do with a face video or expressions of a *target person* being superimposed to a video of a *source* person, widely accepted and referred to as *deepfake*.

Contributions

Motivated by the above, this work makes following contributions.

(i)   We compare state-of-the-art *video* based techniques in detecting deepfakes. Our intuition is that current state-of-the-art forgery detection techniques [1, 8, 14, 19, 39, 40] omit a pertinent clue, namely, *motion*, by investigating only spatial information. It is known that generative models have exhibited difficulties in preserving appearance throughout generated videos, as well as motion consistency [42, 51, 54, 57]. Hence, we here show that using 3D CNNs indeed outperforms state of the art image-based techniques.

(ii) We show that such models trained on known manipulation techniques generalize poorly to tampering methods outside of the training set. Toward this, we provide an evaluation, where train and test sets do not intersect with respect to manipulation techniques.

(iii) We determine the efficacy of two attention mechanisms, namely SE-block and Non-local networks by comparing the number of parameters, inference time, and classification performance for deepfake detection. We find that a non-local neural network indeed improves the classification accuracy of 3D CNNs without introducing significant computational overhead.

(iv) Lastly, we analyze the correlation matrix of learnt features, as well as activations of Seg-Grad-Cam [53] to provide insight on how attention mechanisms work.

We note that this chapter extends the work of Wang and Dantcheva [60] by contributions (iii) and (iv).

10.2   Related Work

A very recent survey has revisited image and video manipulation approaches and early detection efforts [49]. An additional comprehensive survey paper [63] reviews manipulations of images, graphs, and text.

Generative adversarial networks (GANs) [20] have enabled a set of face manipulations including identity [28, 35], facial attributes [61], as well as facial expressions [27, 34, 57–59].

10.2.1   Deepfake Detection

While a number of *manipulation-detection-approaches* are *image-based* [1, 40], others are targeted toward *video* [3, 33, 41] or jointly toward audio and video [31]. We note that although some **video-based approaches** might perform better than image-based ones, such approaches are only applicable to particular kinds of attacks. For example, many of them [3, 33] may fail, if the quality of the eye area is not sufficiently good or the synchronization between video and audio is not sufficiently natural [32].

Image-based approaches are general-purpose detectors, for instance, the algorithm proposed by Fridrich and Kodovsky [19] is applicable to both steganalysis and facial reenactment video detection. Rahmouni et al. [39] presented an algorithm to detect computer-generated images, which was later extended to detecting computer-manipulated images. However, performance of such approaches on new tasks is limited compared to that of task-specific algorithms [40].

Agarwal et al. exploited both facial identity as well as behavioral biometrics information provided by the temporal component of videos to classify a video as real or fake [2]. Cozzolino et al. used temporal facial features to learn behavior of a person and use this as an identifier to compare characteristics in the presented video and verify the claim of identity [15]. Guarnera et al. argued that deepfake videos contain a forensic trait pertaining to the generative model used to create them. Specifically, they showed that convolutional traces are instrumental in detecting deepfakes [22]. Khalid and Woo [29] posed deepfake detection as an anomaly detection problem and used variational auto-encoder for detecting deepfakes. Hernandez-Ortega [24] proposed a deepfake detection framework based on physiological measurement, namely, heart rate using remote photoplethysmography (rPPG). Trinh et al. [50] utilized dynamic representations (i.e., prototypes) to explain deepfake temporal artifacts. Sun et al. [45] attempted to generalize forgery face detection by proposing a framework based on meta-learning. Tolosana et al. [49] revisited first and second DeepFake generations w.r.t. facial regions and fake detection performance.

We show in this work that such algorithms are indeed challenged, if confronted with manipulation techniques outside of the training data.

Rössler et al. [40] presented a comparison of existing handcrafted, as well as deep neural networks (DNNs), which analyzed the **FaceForensics++** dataset and proceeded to detect adversarial examples in an *image-based* manner. This was done for (i) raw data, (ii) high quality videos compressed by a constant rate quantization parameter equal to 23 (denoted as HQ), as well as (iii) low quality videos compressed by a quantization rate of 40 (denoted as LQ). There were two training settings used: (a) training on all manipulation methods concurrently, (b) individual training on each manipulation method separately. These two settings refer to the first two scenarios of interest in this work.

We summarize for training setting (a), which is the more challenging setting (as indicated by lower related detection rates).

1. **Raw data**: It is interesting to note that the correct detection rates for all seven compared algorithms ranged between 97.03 and 99.26%. The highest score was obtained by the XceptionNet [13].
2. **HQ**: High quality compressed data was detected with rates, ranging between 70.97 and 95.73% (XceptionNet).
3. **LQ**: Intuitively low quality compressed data had the lowest detection rates with 55.98–81% (XceptionNet).

We here focus on the LQ-compression as the most challenging setting.

We note that reported detection rates pertained to the analysis of a facial area with the dimension 1.3 times the cropped face. Analyzing the full frame obtained lower accuracy.

A challenge, not being addressed by Rössler et al. has to do with the generalization of such methods. When detection methods, as the presented ones are confronted with adversarial attacks, outside of the training set, such networks are challenged. This has to do with the third scenario of interest in this chapter.

10.2.2   Attention Mechanisms

Attention mechanisms are designed to identify and focus on salient information, which can facilitate improved decisions. Deepfake videos are acquired in uncontrolled conditions and can include a number of artificially created objects in the background (e.g., news-banners). We hypothesize that attention mechanisms are instrumental in facilitating improved classification accuracy of a deepfake detector by enabling the model to focus on discriminative information. Additionally, visualization of attention maps is beneficial in interpretation of the taken decision.

The understanding about attention can be derived from Nadaraya-Watson's regression model [37, 62]. Given the paired training data $\{(x_1, y_1), (x_2, y_2)...(x_n, y_n)\}$, for a given test example x, a regression model predicts the target value $\hat{y}$ as

$$\hat{y} = \sum_{k=1}^{n} \alpha(x, x_k) y_k \qquad (10.1)$$

i.e., the target value is a weighted average of training instances. Here, the weight $\alpha(x, x_k)$ signifies the relevance of training instance x_k for making a prediction for x. Attention mechanisms in deep models are analogous to Nadaraya-Watson's regression model, as such models are similarly designed to learn a weighting function.

Attention models incorporate an encoder-decoder architecture, solving the pitfall of auto-encoder by allowing the decoder to access the entire encoded input sequence. Attention aims at automatically learning an attention weight, which captures the relevance between the *encoder hidden state*, i.e., candidate state and the *decoder hidden state* i.e., the query state. The seminal work on attention was proposed by Bahdanau et al. [6] for a sequence-to-sequence modeling task. Attention modeling has evolved to different types of attention based on the category of input and output, as well as application domain. While the input of an attention model constitute an image, sequence, graph, or tabular data and the output is represented by an image, sequence, embedding, or a scalar. We note that attention can be categorized based on the number of sequences, number of abstraction levels, number of positions, as well as number of representations [11]. We proceed to explain such types in detail.

With respect to **number of sequences**, attention can be of three types, namely, distinctive, co-attention, and self attention. While in distinctive attention candidate and query states belong to two distinct input and output sequences, in self attention [38, 52] the candidate and query states belong to the same sequence. In contrast, co-attention accepts multiple input sequences as input at the same time and jointly produces an output sequence.

Considering **number of abstraction**, attention can be divided into two types of levels, namely, single-level and multilevel. In single-level attention weights are computed only for the original input sequence, whereas in multilevel there are lower and higher level of abstraction, works can be organized in top-down or bottom-up approaches.

While considering the **number of positions**, attention can be of two types, soft/global and hard/local. Hard attention requires the weights to be binary; for instance, a model that crops the image toward naturally discarding non-necessary details [21]. A major limitation of hard attention is that it is implemented using stochastic non-differentiable algorithms [7, 36]. As a result, models employing it cannot be trained in an end-to-end manner. Deviating from this, models employing soft attention take an image or video as input and soft-weigh the region of interest [26, 55]. Soft weighing is ensured by employing either sigmoid or softmax after the

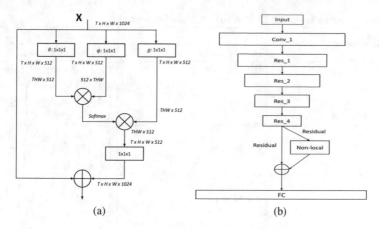

Fig. 10.1   Schematic diagrams of **a** non-local block, **b** non-local block in the backbone architecture

attention gates. This allows weights to be real valued and the objective function to be differentiable.

Based on **number of representations** we have multi-representational and multidimensional attention. While in the former different aspects of the input are considered, in the latter focus is placed on determining the relevance of each dimension of the input.

Finally, with respect to the type of **architecture**, related attention models can be implemented as encoder-decoder, transformer, and memory networks. An encoder-decoder based attention model takes any input representation and reduces it to a single fixed length, a transformer network aims to capture global dependencies between input and output, and in memory networks facts that are more relevant to the query are filtered out.

Application domains of attention include (i) natural language processing, (ii) computer vision, (iii) multi-modal tasks, (iv) graphical systems, and (v) recommender systems. Visual attention brings to the fore a vector of importance weights; in order to predict or infer one element, e.g., a pixel in an image, we estimate using the attention vector how meaningful it is. In particular in this scenario, attention modules are designed to indicate decisive regions of an input, for the task in hand. The output of an attention module is a vector, representing relative importance. This vector is then used to re-weight network parameters, so that pertinent characteristics have higher weights. Consequently, an attention module boosts the model's performance in a targeted task. For this work we introduce a self attention, soft attention, single-level, multidimensional attention for deepfake detection.

We proceed to describe two promising modules used extensively and successfully in image and video processing applications, and which we employ in this chapter, viz., *non-local block*, which is based on transformer network and *squeeze and excitation* that is based on an encoder-decoder network.

Table 10.1 Architecture of 3D ResNet-101 with non-local block

Layer name	Output size	Architecture
Conv_1	$16 \times 112 \times 112$	$7 \times 7 \times 7, 3$, stride $(1, 2, 2)$
Res_1	$16 \times 56 \times 56$	$3 \times 3 \times 3$ maxpool, stride 2 $\begin{pmatrix} 1 \times 1 \times 1, 64 \\ 3 \times 3 \times 3, 64 \\ 1 \times 1 \times 1, 256 \end{pmatrix} \times 3$
Res_2	$8 \times 28 \times 28$	$\begin{pmatrix} 1 \times 1 \times 1, 128 \\ 3 \times 3 \times 3, 128 \\ 1 \times 1 \times 1, 512 \end{pmatrix} \times 4$
Res_3	$4 \times 14 \times 14$	$\begin{pmatrix} 1 \times 1 \times 1, 256 \\ 3 \times 3 \times 43, 256 \\ 1 \times 1 \times 1, 1024 \end{pmatrix} \times 23$
Res_4	$2 \times 7 \times 7$	$\begin{pmatrix} 1 \times 1 \times 1, 256 \\ 3 \times 3 \times 3, 256 \\ 1 \times 1 \times 1, 1024 \end{pmatrix} \times 3$
Non-local block	$2 \times 7 \times 7$	Fig. 10.1a
Avg pool & FC	$1 \times 1 \times 1$	Average pool and sigmoid

Non-local Block

The architecture of a non-local block [56] is based on the observation that convolutional and recurrent operations process only a local neighborhood. Consequently, these fail to capture long-range dependencies. To overcome this limitation of CNNs, non-local block performs a non-local operation to compute feature responses (see Fig. 10.1 and Table 10.1). A non-local operation is characterized by computing the response at a position as a weighted sum of features at all positions in the input feature maps.

Given that video processing requires access to information in distant pixels in space an time, computation of long-range dependencies is necessitated. Non-local operations enable a CNN to capture long-range dependencies and thus are highly beneficial in video processing. Formally, in the context of CNNs, a non-local operation is defined as

$$o_i = \frac{1}{C(x)} \sum_{\forall j} p(x_i, x_j) \ r(x_j), \tag{10.2}$$

where x and o denote the input and output feature, respectively. p represents a pairwise function that computes a relationship (e.g., affinity) between pixels i and j. r signifies a unary function, which computes a representation of input feature at pixel j. $C(x)$ is a normalization factor and is set as $C(x) = \sum_{\forall j} p(x_i, x_j)$.

In this chapter, the default choices of p and r are used. g is a linear embedding and is defined as $g(x) = W_g \ x_j$. Pairwise function is defined as

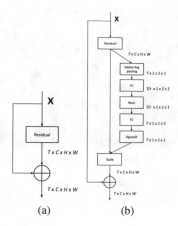

Fig. 10.2 **a** Residual block, **b** residual block after adding SE-block

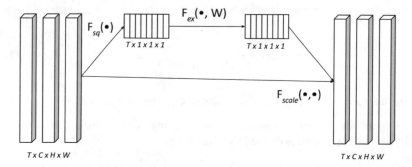

Fig. 10.3 Schematic diagram of SE-block showcasing the squeeze and excitation function

$$p(x_i, x_j) = e^{\alpha(x_i)^T \beta(x_j)}, \tag{10.3}$$

where $\alpha(x_i) = W_\alpha x_i$ and $\beta(x_j) = W_\beta x_j$ are the associated embeddings. This pairwise function is called embedded Gaussian and primarily computes dot-product similarity in the embedding space.

Squeeze and Excitation Block

The Squeeze and Excitation (SE) block [25] boosts the representational power of a CNN by modeling inter-dependencies between channels of the features learnt by it (see Fig. 10.2). As illustrated in Fig. 10.3, the SE-block comprises two operators: squeeze and excitation. While the *squeeze* operation aggregates features across spatial dimensions and creates a global distribution of channel-level feature response, the *excitation* operation is a self-gating mechanism that generates a vector of per-channel re-calibration weights. We proceed to define both operations.

Squeeze Operation. Let us assume that the input feature $X \in R^{W \times H \times C}$ is represented as $X = [x_1, x_2, \ldots x_C]$, where $x_i \in R^{W \times H}$. The squeeze operation exploits

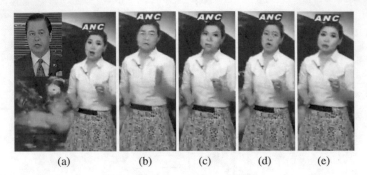

(a)   (b)   (c)   (d)   (e)

Fig. 10.4 Sample frames from the FaceForensics++ dataset. From left to right: original source (large) and target (small) images, deepfakes, face2face, faceswap, neuraltextures

global spatial information by squeezing X through global average pooling and creating a channel descriptor, $z \in R^C$ where ith element of z is calculated as

$$z_i = F_{sq}(x_i) = \frac{1}{H \times W} \sum_{j=1}^{W} \sum_{k=1}^{H} x_i(j, k). \tag{10.4}$$

Excitation Operation. Exploits information acquired through squeeze operation to model dependency among channels through gating with sigmoid activation. Formally, squeeze operation is defined the following.

$$a = F_{ex}(z, w_1, w_2) = \sigma(w_2 \delta(w_1 z)), \tag{10.5}$$

where $w_1 \in R^{\frac{C}{r} \times C}$, $w_2 \in R^{C \times \frac{C}{r}}$. In this context a denotes the modulation weights per-channel and δ denotes ReLU. The recalibrated feature is then computed as

$$\tilde{x}_i = F_{scale}(x_i, a_i) = a_i x_i$$
$$\tilde{X} = [\tilde{x}_1, \tilde{x}_2, ...\tilde{x}_C]. \tag{10.6}$$

We proceed to discuss the dataset (Fig. 10.4).

10.3 Dataset

The FaceForensics++ dataset [40] comprises 1000 talking subjects, represented in 1000 real videos. Further, based on these 1000 real videos, 4×1000 adversarial examples have been generated by following four manipulation schemes.

1. **Faceswap** represents a graphic approach transferring a full face region from a source video to a target video. Using facial landmarks, a 3D template model employs blend-shapes to fit the transferred face. FaceSwap.[9]
2. **Deepfakes** has become the synonym for all face manipulations of all kind, it origins to FakeApp[10] and faceswap github.[11]
3. **Face2face** [48] is a facial reenactment system that transfers the expressions of a source video to a target video, while maintaining the identity of the target person. Based on an identity reconstruction, the whole video is being tracked to compute per frame the expression, rigid pose, and lighting parameters.
4. **Neuraltextures** [47] incorporates facial reenactment as an example for a *Neural-Textures*-based rendering approach. It uses the original video data to learn a neural texture of the target person, including a rendering network that has been trained with a photometric reconstruction loss in combination with an adversarial loss. Only the facial expression corresponding to the mouth region is being modified, i.e., the eye region stays unchanged.

10.4 Algorithms

We select three state-of-the-art 3D CNN methods, which have excelled in action recognition. We proceed to briefly describe them.

- **I3D** [10] incorporates sets of RGB frames as input. It replaces 2D convolutional layers of the original Inception model by 3D convolutions for spatio-temporal modeling and inflates pre-trained weights of the Inception model on ImageNet as its initial weight. Results showed that such inflation has the ability to improve 3D models.
- **3D ResNet** [23] and **3D ResNeXt** are inspired by I3D, both extending initial 2D ResNet and 2D ResNeXt to spatio-temporal dimension for action recognition. We note that deviating from the original ResNet-bottleneck block, the ResNeXt-block introduces group convolutions, which divide the feature maps into small groups. We also conducted experiments with the 3D ResNet modified with squeeze-excitation blocks and non-local block, and the 3D ResNeXt modified with non-local block to investigate the effect of using self attention on these networks.

Given the binary classification problem in this work, we replace the prediction layer in all networks with a single neuron layer, which outputs one scalar value. All three networks have been pre-trained on the large-scale human action dataset Kinetics-400. We inherit the weights in the neural network models and further fine-tune the networks on the FaceForensics++ dataset in all our experiments.

---

[9] https://github.com/MarekKowalski/FaceSwap/.

[10] https://www.fakeapp.com.

[11] https://github.com/deepfakes/faceswap.

We detect and crop the face region based on facial landmarks, which we detect in each frame using the method from Bulat and Tzimiropoulos [9]. Next, we enlarge the detected region by a factor of 1.3, in order to include pixels around the face region.

10.5   Experiments

We conduct experiments on the manipulation techniques listed above with the algorithms I3D, 3D ResNet and 3D ResNext aiming at training and detecting (a) all manipulation techniques, (b) each manipulation technique separately, as well as (c) cross-manipulation techniques. Toward this, we split train, test, and validation sets according to the protocol provided in the FaceForensics++ dataset.

We use PyTorch to implement our models. The three entire networks are trained end-to-end on 4 NVIDIA V100 GPUs. We set the learning rates to $1e^{-3}$. For training, I3D accepts videos of 64 frames with spatial dimension 224×224 as input. The size of input of 3D ResNet and 3D ResNeXt are 16 frames of spatial resolution 112×112. For testing, we split each video into short trunks, each of temporal size of 250 frames. The final score assigned to each test video is the average value of the scores of all trunks.

We also investigate the impact of two attention mechanisms on 3D ResNet, namely, Squeeze-Excitation blocks and Non-local blocks. In the case of the 3D ResNet with the Squeeze-Excitation (SE) blocks, the network is trained from scratch as the SE blocks are incorporated in the bottleneck modules themselves. Despite this addition not performing at par with the original 3D ResNet pre-trained on Kinetics, training is more stable and obtains superior results compared to a 3D ResNet that is trained on the dataset from scratch. Based on the limitations and advantages we observe for the 3D ResNet, we also investigate the impact of using the non-local block in the 3D ResNeXt, which outperform the other 3D architectures in most cases after this modification. We report in all experiments the true classification rates (TCR).

10.5.1   All Manipulation Techniques

Firstly we evaluate the detection accuracy of the three video CNNs (with and without attention), and compare the results to *image*-forgery detection algorithms. For the latter we have in particular the state-of-the-art XceptionNet [40], learning-based methods used in the forensic community for generic manipulation detection [8, 14], computer-generated vs. natural image detection [39] and face tampering detection [1]. Given the unbalanced classification problem in this experiment (number of fake videos being nearly four times the number of real videos), we use weighted cross-entropy loss, in order to reduce the effects of unbalanced data. We observe that among the unmodified 3D CNNs, the detection accuracy of I3D is the highest and it is also the most computationally intense. The performance of 3D ResNet improves with

Table 10.2 Detection of all four manipulation methods, LQ. TCR = True classification rate, DF = deepfakes, F2F = face2face, FS = face-swap, NT = neuraltextures

Algorithm	Train and test	TCR
Steg. Features + SVM [19]	FS, DF, F2F, NT	55.98
Cozzolino et al. [14]	FS, DF, F2F, NT	58.69
Bayar and Stamm [8]	FS, DF, F2F, NT	66.84
Rahmouni et al. [39]	FS, DF, F2F, NT	61.18
MesoNet [1]	FS, DF, F2F, NT	70.47
XceptionNet [13]	FS, DF, F2F, NT	81.0
I3D	FS, DF, F2F, NT	87.43
3D ResNet	FS, DF, F2F, NT	83.86
3D ResNet (w/o pre-training)	FS, DF, F2F, NT	54.96
3D ResNet (with SE)	FS, DF, F2F, NT	80.0
3D ResNet (with non-local)	FS, DF, F2F, NT	85.85
3D ResNeXt	FS, DF, F2F, NT	85.14
3D ResNeXt (with non-local)	FS, DF, F2F, NT	88.28

Table 10.3 AUC values of 3D ResNet and 3D ResNeXt endowed with attention

Algorithm	AUC
3D ResNet	0.82
3D ResNet (w/o pre-training)	0.51
3D ResNet (with SE)	0.72
3D ResNet (with non-local)	0.86
3D ResNeXt (with non-local)	0.91

the introduction of the non-local block. The lack of pre-training does hamper the performance of the 3D ResNet with the SE attention, however it performs significantly better than the vanilla 3D ResNet which was initialized with random weights. Interestingly, with the addition of the non-local block to the 3D-ResNeXt, its detection accuracy becomes the highest, surpassing I3D. Related results are depicted in Table 10.2. We present the receiver operating characteristic curves (ROC curves) in Fig. 10.5 and the area under the curve (AUC) in Table 10.3.

10.5.2   Single Manipulation Techniques

We proceed to investigate the performances of all algorithms, when trained and tested on single manipulation techniques. We report the TCRs in Table 10.4. Interestingly, here the video-based algorithms perform similarly as the best image-based algorithm. This can be due to the data-size pertaining to videos of a single manipulation

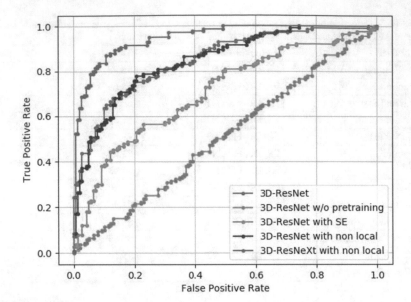

Fig. 10.5 ROC curves pertaining to 3D ResNet and 3D ResNext endowed with attention mechanisms for testing and training of all four manipulation methods

technique being smaller. I3D performed best among unmodified video-based methods. 3D ResNet with non-local block once again outperformed the pre-trained 3D ResNet and the 3D ResNet with SE attention outperformed the randomly initialized 3D ResNet that was trained from scratch. The performance of 3D ResNeXt also improved upon introduction of the non-local block, and in fact, it performed best among all video-based methods.

Our experiments suggest that all detection approaches are consistently utmost challenged on the GAN-based *neuraltextures*-approach. We note that *neuraltextures* trains a unique model for each video, which results in a higher variation of possible artifacts. While *deepfakes* similarly trains one model per video, a fixed post-processing pipeline is used, which is similar to the computer-based manipulation methods and thus has consistent artifacts that can be instrumental for deepfake detection.

10.5.3 Cross-Manipulation Techniques

In our third experiment, we train the 3D CNNs and the attention-endowed models with videos manipulated by 3 techniques, as well as the original (real) videos and proceed to test on the last remaining manipulation technique, as well as original videos. We show related results in Table 10.5. Naturally, this is the most challeng-

Table 10.4 Detection of each manipulation method individually, LQ. TCR = True classification rate, DF = deepfakes, F2F = face2face, FS = face-swap, NT = neuraltextures

Algorithm	DF	F2F	FS	NT
Steg. Features + SVM [19]	73.64	73.72	68.93	63.33
Cozzolino et al. [14]	85.45	67.88	73.79	78.00
Bayar and Stamm [8]	84.55	73.72	82.52	70.67
Rahmouni et al. [39]	85.45	64.23	56.31	60.07
MesoNet [1]	87.27	56.20	61.17	40.67
XceptionNet [13]	96.36	86.86	90.29	80.67
I3D	95.13	90.27	92.25	80.5
3D ResNet	91.81	89.6	88.75	73.5
3D ResNet (w/o pre-training)	58.80	73.60	59.20	56.50
3D ResNet (with SE)	81.70	77.00	75.90	66.25
3D ResNet (with non-local)	94.67	89.20	92.13	76.00
3D ResNeXt	93.36	86.06	92.50	80.50
3D ResNeXt (with non-local)	95.50	90.4	95.08	80.71

ing setting. At the same time, it is the most realistic one, because it is unlikely that knowledge on whether and how videos have been manipulated will be provided. Similar to the first experiment, we use weighted cross-entropy loss, in order to solve the unbalanced classification problem. For the detection algorithms, one of the more challenging settings in this experiment is when *faceswap* is the manipulation technique to be detected. We note that 3D ResNet with non-local block outperformed all other networks in this scenario.

While *face2face* and *faceswap* represent graphics-based approaches, *deepfakes* and *neuraltextures* are learning-based approaches. However, *faceswap* replaces the largest facial region in the target image and involves advanced blending and color correction algorithms to seamlessly superimpose source onto target. Hence the challenge might be due to the inherent dissimilarity of *faceswap* and learning-based

Table 10.5 Detection of cross-manipulation methods, LQ. TCR = True classification rate, DF = deepfakes, F2F = face2face, FS = face-swap, NT = neuraltextures, NL = non-local, scratch = w/o pre-training

Train	Test	3D	I3D	3D ResNeXt	3D ResNet (scratch)	3D ResNet (with SE)	3D ResNet (with NL)	3D ResNeXt (with NL)
FS, DF, F2F	NT	64.29	68.57	66.79	54.28	55.35	62.9	63.2
FS, DF, NT	F2F	74.29	70.71	68.93	51.0	53.5	68.2	69.1
FS, F2F, NT	DF	75.36	75.00	72.50	50.7	52.5	76.78	77.8
F2F, NT, DF	FS	59.64	57.14	55.71	50.3	53.5	68.2	65.71

Table 10.6 Number of parameters in 3D ResNet without and with attention

Algorithm	No. of parameters
3D ResNet	85,249,216
3D ResNet with SE	94,303,808
3D ResNet with non-local	93,647,040

approaches, as well as due to the seamless blending between source and target, different than *face2face*.

We note that *humans* easily detected manipulations affectedResNet by *faceswap* and *deepfakes* and were more challenged by *face2face* and ultimately *neuraltextures* [40]. This is also reflected in the performance of 3D ResNet and 3D ResneXt with non-local block, which were most challenged by the videos manipulated by *neuraltextures*.

10.5.4   Effect of Attention in 3D ResNets

We here analyze the correlation matrices between two layers (at the same depth) for all the three variants of the 3D ResNet—the original 3D ResNet, the 3D ResNet with squeeze-excitation and the 3D ResNet with non-local block (Fig. 10.6). The high correlation observed in distinct patches in Fig. 10.6a indicates that the original 3D ResNet without attention possibly overfits to the data. The addition of squeeze-excitation (Fig. 10.6b) improves upon this and a further improvement is seen with the introduction of the non-local block in the 3D ResNet (Fig. 10.6c).

Both attention mechanisms, squeeze-excitation, and non-local block increase the number of parameters in the 3D ResNet by around 10% (Fig. 10.6), however when trained and tested on the whole dataset, we observe an improvement of 2% in the true classification rate in case of the model with non-local block (Table 10.2). We note that the 3D Resnet with SE attention could not be initialized with pre-trained Kinetics weights, so for a fair comparison, a 3D ResNet trained on the dataset from scratch was considered. Interestingly, without pre-trained weights, the vanilla 3D-ResNet is unable to converge its training in most cases and was underfitting. The training for the 3D ResNet with SE was more stable and yielded superior results over most experiments. It is also interesting to observe that *face2face* challenges 3D ResNet with non-local block more than the vanilla 3D ResNet. The exact reason behind this was not certain, however, as pointed out before, it was one of the more challenging scenarios for humans to detect as well [40]. In summary, 3D ResNet with the non-local block outperforms predominantly all other 3D ResNet variants (Table 10.2–10.5).

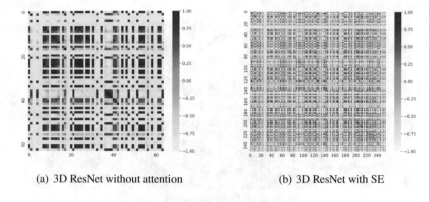

(a) 3D ResNet without attention   (b) 3D ResNet with SE

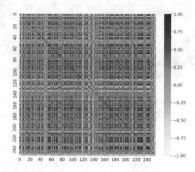

(c) 3D ResNet with non-local

Fig. 10.6 Correlation matrices for the 3D ResNets

10.5.5   Visualization of Pertinent Features in Deepfake Detection

We proceed to visualize features each of the 3D ResNet models are focusing on for detecting of deepfakes by Grad-CAM [43]. We note that Grad-CAM finds the final convolutional layer in a network and examines the gradient information flowing into that layer. The output of Grad-CAM is represented by a heat map visualization for a given class label, in our case deepfake detection. In particular, we visualize five frames from a *deepfake*-video in Fig. 10.7, for each of the three variants of 3D ResNet. Interestingly, we observe that 3D ResNet with both attention mechanisms focuses stronger on the central part of a face, as compared to the original 3D ResNet. It is also worth noting that the heat map for 3D ResNet with non-local block is located slightly higher than 3D Resnet with squeeze-excitation block, yielding the highest accuracy.

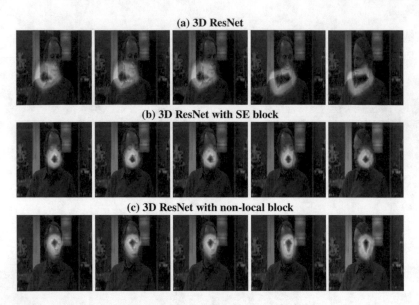

Fig. 10.7 Grad-CAM visualizations for the 3D ResNet models for the same video. The frames are taken from the same fake video with a time step of 24. Red represents higher probability of the region being manipulated

10.6 Conclusions

In this work we compared three state-of-the-art video-based CNN methods in detecting four deepfake-manipulation-techniques. The three tested methods included 3D ResNet, 3D ResNeXt and I3D, which we adapted from action recognition. In addition, we tested two attention mechanisms. Despite the pre-training of mentioned methods on the action recognition dataset Kinetics-400, the methods generalized very well to deepfake detection. Experimental results showed that 3D/video CNNs outperformed or performed at least similarly to image-based detection algorithms.

In addition, we observed that the incorporation of attention mechanisms in 3D CNNs improved related detection accuracy and were beneficial in placing focus of the models on areas of maximum manipulation in the forged videos.

Further, we noted a significant decrease in detection rates in the scenario, when we detected a manipulation technique not represented in the training set. One reason relates to the fact that networks lack an adaptation-ability to transfer learned knowledge from one domain (trained manipulation methods) to another domain (tested manipulation method). It is known that current machine learning models exhibit unpredictable and overly confident behavior outside of the training distribution.

Future work will involve the consideration of additional deepfake-techniques. Further, we plan to develop novel deepfake detection approaches, which place emphasis on appearance, motion as well as pixel-level-based generated noise, targeted to outsmart the improving generation and manipulation algorithms.

References

1. Afchar D, Nozick V, Yamagishi J, Echizen I (2018) Mesonet: a compact facial video forgery detection network. In: 2018 IEEE international workshop on information forensics and security (WIFS). IEEE (2018)
2. Agarwal S, El-Gaaly T, Farid H, Lim SN (2020) Detecting deep-fake videos from appearance and behavior. arXiv preprint arXiv:2004.14491
3. Agarwal S, Farid H, Gu Y, He M, Nagano K, Li H (2019) Protecting world leaders against deep fakes. In: IEEE/CVF conference on computer vision and pattern recognition workshops (CVPRW), pp 38–45 (2019)
4. Amerini I, Galteri L, Caldelli R, Del Bimbo A (2019) Deepfake video detection through optical flow based CNN. In: IEEE international conference on computer vision workshops (ICCVW), pp 1205–1207. https://doi.org/10.1109/ICCVW.2019.00152
5. Averbuch-Elor H, Cohen-Or D, Kopf J, Cohen MF (2017) Bringing portraits to life. ACM Trans Graph (TOG) 36(6):196
6. Bahdanau D, Cho K, Bengio Y (2014) Neural machine translation by jointly learning to align and translate. arXiv preprint arXiv:1409.0473
7. Baradel F, Wolf C, Mille J, Taylor GW (2018) Glimpse clouds: Human activity recognition from unstructured feature points. In: IEEE/CVF conference on computer vision and pattern recognition (CVPR), pp 469–478
8. Bayar B, Stamm MC (2016) A deep learning approach to universal image manipulation detection using a new convolutional layer. In: Proceedings of the 4th ACM workshop on information hiding and multimedia security. ACM, pp 5–10
9. Bulat A, Tzimiropoulos G (2017) How far are we from solving the 2D & 3D face alignment problem? (and a dataset of 230,000 3D facial landmarks). In: International conference on computer vision (ICCV)
10. Carreira J, Zisserman A (2017) Quo vadis, action recognition? A new model and the kinetics dataset. In, IEEE/CVF conference on computer vision and pattern recognition (CVPR), pp 6299–6308
11. Chaudhari S, Polatkan G, Ramanath R, Mithal V (2019) An attentive survey of attention models. arXiv preprint arXiv:1904.02874
12. Chesney R, Citron DK (2018) Deep fakes: a looming challenge for privacy, democracy, and national security. 107 California law review (2019, forthcoming); University of Texas Law. Public Law Research Paper 692:2018–2021
13. Chollet F (2017) Xception: deep learning with depthwise separable convolutions. In: Proceedings of the IEEE conference on computer vision and pattern recognition, pp 1251–1258
14. Cozzolino D, Poggi G, Verdoliva L (2017) Recasting residual-based local descriptors as convolutional neural networks: an application to image forgery detection. In: Proceedings of the 5th ACM workshop on information hiding and multimedia security. ACM, pp 159–164
15. Cozzolino D, Rössler A, Thies J, Nießner M, Verdoliva L (2020) ID-Reveal: identity-aware deepfake video detection. arXiv preprint arXiv:2012.02512
16. Dang H, Liu F, Stehouwer J, Liu X, Jain AK (2020) On the detection of digital face manipulation. In: IEEE/CVF conference on computer vision and pattern recognition, pp 5781–5790
17. Eichensehr K (2018) Don't believe it if you see it: deep fakes and distrust. Technology law; jotwell: the journal of things we like (lots), pp 1–2
18. Farid H (2011) Photo tampering throughout history. http://www.cs.dartmouth.edu/farid/research/digitaltampering
19. Fridrich J, Kodovsky J (2012) Rich models for steganalysis of digital images. IEEE Trans Inform Forensics Secur 7(3):868–882
20. Goodfellow I, Pouget-Abadie J, Mirza M, Xu B, Warde-Farley D, Ozair S, Courville A, Bengio Y (2014) Generative adversarial nets. In: Advances in neural information processing systems (NIPS), pp 2672–2680

21. Guan Q, Huang Y, Zhong Z, Zheng Z, Zheng L, Yang Y (2018) Diagnose like a radiologist: attention guided convolutional neural network for thorax disease classification. arXiv preprint arXiv:1801.09927
22. Guarnera L, Giudice O, Battiato S (2020) Deepfake detection by analyzing convolutional traces. In: Proceedings of the IEEE/CVF conference on computer vision and pattern recognition workshops (CVPRW), pp 666–667
23. Hara K, Kataoka H, Satoh Y (2018) Can spatiotemporal 3D CNNs retrace the history of 2D CNNs and imagenet? In: IEEE conference on computer vision and pattern recognition (CVPR), pp 6546–6555
24. Hernandez-Ortega J, Tolosana R, Fierrez J, Morales A (2020) Deepfakeson-phys: deepfakes detection based on heart rate estimation. arXiv preprint arXiv:2010.00400
25. Hu J. Shen L, Sun G (2018) Squeeze-and-excitation networks. In: Proceedings of the IEEE conference on computer vision and pattern recognition (CVPR), pp 7132–7141
26. Jaderberg M, Simonyan K, Zisserman A, Kavukcuoglu K (2015) Spatial transformer networks. arXiv preprint arXiv:1506.02025
27. Jiang L, Wu W, Li R, Qian C, Loy CC (2020) Deeperforensics-1.0: a large-scale dataset for real world face forgery detection. arXiv preprint arXiv:2001.03024
28. Karras T, Laine S, Aila T (2019) A style-based generator architecture for generative adversarial networks. In: IEEE/CVF conference on computer vision and pattern recognition (CVPR), pp 4401–4410
29. Khalid H, Woo SS (2020) Oc-fakedect: classifying deepfakes using one-class variational autoencoder. In: IEEE/CVF conference on computer vision and pattern recognition workshops (CVPRW), pp 656–657
30. Kim H, Carrido P, Tewari A, Xu W, Thies J, Niessner M, Pérez P, Richardt C, Zollhöfer M, Theobalt C (2018) Deep video portraits. ACM Trans Graph (TOG) 37(4):163
31. Korshunov P, Marcel S (2018) Speaker inconsistency detection in tampered video. In: 2018 26th European signal processing conference (EUSIPCO), pp 2375–2379. IEEE
32. Korshunov P, Marcel S (2019) Vulnerability assessment and detection of deepfake videos. In: The 12th IAPR international conference on biometrics (ICB), pp 1–6 (2019)
33. Li Y, Chang MC, Lyu S (2018) In ictu oculi: exposing AI generated fake face videos by detecting eye blinking. arXiv preprint arXiv:1806.02877
34. Liu Z, Song G, Cai J, Cham TJ, Zhang J (2019) Conditional adversarial synthesis of 3D facial action units. Neurocomputing 355:200–208
35. Majumdar P, Agarwal A, Singh R, Vatsa M (2019) Evading face recognition via partial tampering of faces. In: Proceedings of the IEEE conference on computer vision and pattern recognition workshops (CVPRW), pp 11–20. https://doi.org/10.1109/CVPRW.2019.00008
36. Mnih V, Heess N, Graves A, Kavukcuoglu K (2014) Recurrent models of visual attention. arXiv preprint arXiv:1406.6247
37. Nadaraya EA (1964) On estimating regression. Theory Prob Appl 9(1):141–142
38. Parmar N, Vaswani A, Uszkoreit J, Kaiser L, Shazeer N, Ku A, Tran D (2018) Image transformer. In: International conference on machine learning (ICML), pp 4055–4064
39. Rahmouni N, Nozick V, Yamagishi J, Echizen I (2017) Distinguishing computer graphics from natural images using convolution neural networks. In: 2017 IEEE workshop on information forensics and security (WIFS). IEEE
40. Rössler A, Cozzolino D, Verdoliva L, Riess C, Thies J, Nießner M (2019) Faceforensics++: learning to detect manipulated facial images. arXiv preprint arXiv:1901.08971
41. Sabir E, Cheng J, Jaiswal A, AbdAlmageed W, Masi I, Natarajan P (2019) Recurrent convolutional strategies for face manipulation detection in videos. Interfaces (GUI) 3:1
42. Saito M, Matsumoto E, Saito S (2017) Temporal generative adversarial nets with singular value clipping. In: IEEE international conference on computer vision (ICCV), pp 2830–2839
43. Selvaraju RR, Cogswell M, Das A, Vedantam R, Parikh D, Batra D (2017) Grad-cam: visual explanations from deep networks via gradient-based localization. In: IEEE international conference on computer vision (ICCV), pp 618–626. https://doi.org/10.1109/ICCV.2017.74
44. Silbey J, Hartzog W (2018) The upside of deep fakes. Md L Rev 78:960

45. Sun K, Liu H, Ye Q, Liu J, Gao Y, Shao L, Ji R (2021) Domain general face forgery detection by learning to weight. Proceedings of the AAAI conference on artificial intelligence 35:2638–2646
46. Suwajanakorn S, Seitz SM, Kemelmacher-Shlizerman I (2017) Synthesizing Obama: learning lip sync from audio. ACM Trans Graph (TOG) 36(4):95
47. Thies J, Zollhöfer M, Nießner M (2019) Deferred neural rendering: image synthesis using neural textures. arXiv preprint arXiv:1904.12356
48. Thies J, Zollhofer M, Stamminger M, Theobalt C, Nießner M (2016) Face2face: real-time face capture and reenactment of RGB videos. In: Proceedings of the IEEE conference on computer vision and pattern recognition, pp 2387–2395
49. Tolosana R, Vera-Rodriguez R, Fierrez J, Morales A, Ortega-Garcia J (2020) Deepfakes and beyond: a survey of face manipulation and fake detection. Inform Fusion 64:131–148
50. Trinh L, Tsang M, Rambhatla S, Liu Y (2021) Interpretable and trustworthy deepfake detection via dynamic prototypes. In: Proceedings of the IEEE/CVF winter conference on applications of computer vision (WACV), pp 1973–1983
51. Tulyakov S, Liu MY, Yang X, Kautz J (2018) MoCoGAN: decomposing motion and content for video generation. In: Proceedings of the IEEE/CVF conference on computer vision and pattern recognition (CVPR)
52. Vaswani A, Shazeer N, Parmar N, Uszkoreit J, Jones L, Gomez AN, Kaiser L, Polosukhin I (2017) Attention is all you need. arXiv preprint arXiv:1706.03762
53. Vinogradova K, Dibrov A, Myers G (2020) Towards interpretable semantic segmentation via gradient-weighted class activation mapping (student abstract). Proceedings of the AAAI conference on artificial intelligence 34:13943–13944
54. Vondrick C, Pirsiavash H, Torralba A (2016) Generating videos with scene dynamics. In: Advances in neural information processing systems (NIPS) (2016)
55. Wang F, Jiang M, Qian C, Yang S, Li C, Zhang H, Wang X, Tang X (2017) Residual attention network for image classification. In: Proceedings of the IEEE conference on computer vision and pattern recognition (CVPR), pp 3156–3164
56. Wang X, Girshick R, Gupta A, He K (2018) Non-local neural networks. In: Proceedings of the IEEE conference on computer vision and pattern recognition, pp 7794–7803
57. Wang Y, Bilinski P, Bremond F, Dantcheva A (2020) G3AN disentangling appearance and motion for video generation. In: Proceedings of the IEEE/CVF conference on computer vision and pattern recognition (CVPR), pp 1–10. https://openaccess.thecvf.com/CVPR2020_search
58. Wang Y, Bilinski P, Bremond F, Dantcheva A (2020) ImaGINator conditional spatio-temporal gan for video generation. In: Proceedings of the IEEE/CVF winter conference on applications of computer vision (WACV)
59. Wang Y, Bremond F, Dantcheva A (2021) InMoDeGAN interpretable motion decomposition generative adversarial network for video generation. arXiv preprint arXiv:2101.03049
60. Wang Y, Dantcheva A (2020) A video is worth more than 1000 lies. Comparing 3dcnn approaches for detecting deepfakes. In: FG'20, 15th IEEE international conference on automatic face and gesture recognition, May 18–22, 2020, Buenos Aires, Argentina
61. Wang Y, Dantcheva A, Bremond F (2018) From attributes to faces: a conditional generative adversarial network for face generation. In: International conference of the biometrics special interest group (BIOSIG), vol 17
62. Watson GS (1964) Smooth regression analysis. Indian J Stat, Ser A, Sankhyā, pp 359–372
63. Xu H, Ma Y, Liu H, Deb D, Liu H, Tang J, Jain A (2019) Adversarial attacks and defenses in images, graphs and text: a review. arXiv preprint arXiv:1909.08072

Chapter 11
Deepfake Detection Using Multiple Data Modalities

Hanxiang Hao, Emily R. Bartusiak, David Güera, Daniel Mas Montserrat, Sriram Baireddy, Ziyue Xiang, Sri Kalyan Yarlagadda, Ruiting Shao, János Horváth, Justin Yang, Fengqing Zhu, and Edward J. Delp

Abstract Falsified media threatens key areas of our society, ranging from politics to journalism to economics. Simple and inexpensive tools available today enable easy, credible manipulations of multimedia assets. Some even utilize advanced artificial intelligence concepts to manipulate media, resulting in videos known as *deepfakes*. Social media platforms and their "echo chamber" effect propagate fabricated digital content at scale, sometimes with dire consequences in real-world situations. However, ensuring semantic consistency across falsified media assets of different modalities is still very challenging for current deepfake tools. Therefore, cross-modal analysis (e.g., video-based and audio-based analysis) provides forensic analysts an opportunity to identify inconsistencies with higher accuracy. In this chapter, we introduce several approaches to detect deepfakes. These approaches leverage different data modalities, including video and audio. We show that the presented methods achieve accurate detection for various large-scale datasets.

11.1 Introduction

The rapid proliferation of easy-to-use machine learning tools contributes to an ever-increasing amount of manipulated media. These tools enable users to create realistic and believable face swaps in images and videos. They also convincingly alter or replace audio tracks in videos. Some of these tools use machine learning (ML) and deep learning (DL) techniques. Videos (with or without audio) generated with deep learning methods are collectively referred to as the term *deepfakes*. Recently, many methods have been developed to effectively detect these deepfake videos. Since most of the deepfake videos still contain the artifacts that are caused by inaccurate face swapping (i.e., splicing artifacts), [1, 2] propose to detect these manipulated videos

H. Hao · E. R. Bartusiak · D. Güera · D. Mas Montserrat · S. Baireddy · Z. Xiang ·
S. K. Yarlagadda · R. Shao · J. Horváth · J. Yang · F. Zhu · E. J. Delp (✉)
Video and Image Processing Laboratory (VIPER), School of Electrical and Computer
Engineering, Purdue University, West Lafayette, IN, USA
e-mail: ace@ecn.purdue.edu

© The Author(s) 2022
C. Rathgeb et al. (eds.), *Handbook of Digital Face Manipulation and Detection*,
Advances in Computer Vision and Pattern Recognition,
https://doi.org/10.1007/978-3-030-87664-7_11

by finding the temporal inconsistency of 3-D head pose and facial landmarks using Support Vector Machine (SVM). Most of the deepfake generation tools are based on the Generative Adversarial Networks (GANs). In [3, 4], several deep-learning-based detectors are proposed to discriminate between authentic images and GAN-generated images obtained from various GAN-based deepfake generators. In order to improve the generalizability of the detection methods, [5] uses metric learning and adversarial learning to enable to the deepfake detection method trained only with authentic videos without the requirement of manipulated videos. Please refer to [6–9] for the completed survey about the deepfake detection methods.

In this chapter, we present various methods to detect the manipulated videos by leveraging different data modalities (e.g., video, audio). We first propose an approach to detect deepfakes by utilizing spatiotemporal information present in videos. More specifically, we use Convolutional Neural Networks (CNNs) and Recurrent Neural Networks (RNNs) to extract visual and temporal features from video frame sequences to accurately detect manipulations. This technique focuses on face swapping detection by examining the visual and temporal features of facial regions in each frame. Some frames may contain blurry faces, hindering effective detection of manipulations. To solve this issue, we utilize a novel attention mechanism to emphasize reliable frames and disregard low-quality frames in each sequence.

Next, we present a method that analyzes audio signals to determine whether they contain real human voices or fake human voices (i.e., voices generated by neural acoustic and waveform models). Instead of analyzing the audio signals directly, the proposed approach converts the audio signals into spectrogram images displaying frequency, intensity, and temporal content and evaluates them with a CNN. We convert the audio signals into spectograms in order to leverage frequency information and provide a more amenable configuration of the data to a CNN. A CNN can analyze different frequency ranges more explicitly from a spectrogram, revealing artifacts in certain frequency ranges. This method can also aid in a deepfake detection task in which the audio as well as the visual content has been manipulated. Analysts can use our method to verify the voice tracks of videos and flag them as manipulated if either the audio analysis or the video analysis reveals manipulated content.

Finally, we extend the previous video-based and audio-based methods to detect deepfakes using audio-video inconsistency. As mentioned previously, ensuring semantic consistency across these manipulated media assets of different modalities is still very challenging for current deepfake tools. For a photo-realistic deepfake video, a visual analysis alone may not be able to detect the manipulations, but pairing the visual analysis with audio analysis provides an additional avenue for authenticity verification. Therefore, we also describe several existing methods to analyze the correlations between lip movements and voice signals via phoneme-viseme mismatching and affective cues. These methods incorporate both video and audio data modalities, which provide rich information for deepfake detection.

The remaining sections in this chapter are structured as follows. Section 11.2 discusses a deepfake detection method that relies only on video content. Section 11.3 presents a method that introduces audio analysis to detect manipulated audio. Finally,

Sect. 11.4 explores several methods to evaluate audio-video inconsistency for deep-fake video detection, building off of the methods presented in Sect. 11.3.

11.2   Deepfake Detection via Video Spatiotemporal Features

With the fast development of deepfake techniques, deepfake videos seem more and more realistic, causing viewers to struggle to determine their authenticity. However, current deepfake techniques still suffer from temporal inconsistency issues, such as flickering and unrealistic eye blinking. In this section, we introduce a deep learning-based method to detect deepfakes by incorporating temporal information with video frames.

Figure 11.1 shows the block diagram of our spatiotemporal-based method. A shared CNN model first encodes input video frames into deep features. CNNs have achieved success in many vision tasks, such as image recognition and semantic seg-mentation. In our case, we utilize these CNN models to extract features for deepfake detection. In recent literature [10, 11], InceptionV3 [12], EfficientNet [13], Xception model [14], or an ensemble of these models have been used to extract deepfake fea-tures. Transfer learning is also used to fine-tune these models that are pretrained on some large-scale image datasets (e.g., ImageNet [15]) to speed up training processes and improve performance. We will compare the results achieved with these CNNs in Sect. 11.2.6. A shared CNN model also reduces the number of parameters that must be trained. This technique will force the model to extract the features that are agnostic to the input video content and manipulation methods, which is important to make the model generalize better to new deepfake videos.

Then, we input the features to a temporally aware network to leverage the rela-tionship between frames. There are many types of temporally aware networks, including Recurrent Neural Networks (RNNs), Long Short-Term Memory networks

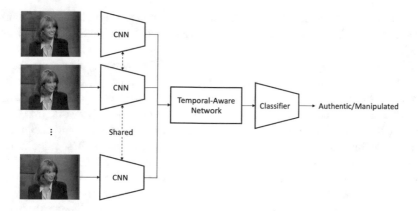

Fig. 11.1 Overview of the spatiotemporal deepfake detection system

(LSTMs) [16], and Gated Recurrent Units (GRUs) [17]. LSTMs and GRUs are special kinds of RNNs that are capable of learning long-term dependencies across sequences. For our deepfake detection task, a GRU will analyze CNN-extracted features from video frames to accumulate useful information related to deepfake artifacts. The GRU leverages temporal information implicitly to reveal deepfakes, rather then being explicitly designed to focus on temporal inconsistencies. This feature will also prepare the model to generalize better to different types of deepfakes. The result of the GRU is a new representation of the video in the latent space that contains discriminating information from the entire video.

Next, we use a classifier to label a video as authentic or manipulated. For deep learning models, people often use a multi-layer perceptron (MLP) (i.e., fully connected layers) as a classifier along with batch normalization and Rectified Linear Unit (ReLU).

11.2.1 Overview

In this section, we introduce the details of our video-based deepfake detection approach. The main workflow commences with CNN-based face detection followed by CNN-based facial feature extraction to determine a set of salient facial indicators that will aid in manipulation detection. Then, the facial features are analyzed by an Automatic Face Weighting (AFW) mechanism and a Gated Recurrent Unit (GRU) network to extract meaningful features to verify videos as authentic or manipulated. Additionally, a Boosting Network is used to aid the backbone network in learning to discriminate between authentic and manipulated videos.

11.2.2 Model Component

The next few sections detail the architecture of the main ensemble network, which consists of the CNN-based face detector, CNN-based feature extractor, AFW, and GRU.

Face Detection. For our analysis, we focus on faces, which typically are the primary target of deepfakes. This means that face regions generally contain indicators of a video's true nature. Thus, the first step in our approach is to locate faces within video frames. We use a Multi-task Cascaded Convolutional Network (MTCNN) [18] for this task since it produces bounding boxes around faces and facial landmarks simultaneously. MTCNN consists of three stages. In the first stage, a fully convolutional network, called Proposal Network, generates a large number of face bounding box proposals. In the second stage, another CNN, called Refine Network, improves the output from the first stage by rejecting a large number of false proposals. The remaining valid proposals are passed to the third stage, where the bounding boxes and facial landmark positions are finalized. Non-maximum suppression and bounding box regression are applied in every stage to suppress overlapping proposals and refine the output prediction.

To speed up face detection, we downsample each video by a factor of 4 and extract faces from 1 in every 10 frames. We also expand the margin of detected face bounding boxes by 20 pixels to include possible deepfake artifacts around the edges of faces and hairlines. After face detection, we resize all face occurrences to 224×224 pixels.

Face Feature Extraction. After detecting faces in the frames, we begin to train our deepfake detection model to identify authentic and manipulated faces. We extract features with another CNN and perform binary classification to determine if the faces contain authentic or manipulated information. Because of the large amount of video data that needs to be processed, we prioritize CNNs that are both fast and accurate for this task. In the end, we chose to use EfficientNet-b5 [13] since it was designed with neural architecture search to ensure it is both lightweight and highly accurate.

We further enhance EfficientNet by training it with the additive angular margin loss (ArcFace) [19] as opposed to softmax and cross-entropy. ArcFace is a learnable loss function that modifies the regular classification cross-entropy loss to ensure a more efficient representation. It aims to enforce a margin between each class in the latent feature space obtained from the previously mentioned CNN models. This results in features that are forced to be highly discriminative, resulting in a more robust classification.

Automatic Face Weighting. After classifying each frame as manipulated or not, we have to determine a classification for the entire video. The straightforward option is to simply average the classifications of the frames to come up with a video classification. However, this may not be the best option. Generally, face detectors are accurate, but sometimes they incorrectly categorize background regions in images as "faces", which can impact frame-level and video-level classifications in downstream applications. Additionally, there is no limit on the number of faces in a frame, of which any number can be authentic or manipulated. Faces can also be blurry or noisy, which further complicates direct averaging of frame predictions.

To address this issue, we propose an automatic face weighting (AFW) mechanism that highlights the faces that reliably contribute to the correct video-level classification while disregarding less reliable faces. This approach can be considered similar to the attention mechanisms found in transformer networks [20]. We assign a weight w_j to the output label l_j determined by EfficientNet for the jth extracted face. Using these weights, we can calculate a weighted average of all the frames' labels to obtain a final classification for the video. Both labels l_j and weights w_j are estimated by a fully connected linear layer that takes the EfficientNet features as input, meaning that the EfficientNet features are used to determine a label for how much a face has been manipulated (l_j) as well as how confident the network is of its classification (w_j). The final output probability p_w of a video being manipulated can be calculated as

$$p_w = \sigma \left(\frac{\sum_{j=1}^{N} w_j l_j}{\sum_{j=1}^{N} w_j} \right), \tag{11.1}$$

where w_j and l_j are the weight value and label obtained for the jth face region, respectively, N is the total number of frames under analysis, and $\sigma(.)$ refers to the sigmoid function. To ensure that $w_j \geq 0$, we pass w_j through a ReLU function. We also perturb the values with a small value to avoid division by 0. This process ensures we have an adaptive approach to combine frame-level classifications to obtain a video-level classification.

Gated Recurrent Unit. In this work, we choose Gated Recurrent Unit (GRU) [17] as the temporal-aware network. As previously mentioned, LSTM and GRU are special kinds of RNNs. Both of them improve the original RNN using multiple gated units to resolve the vanishing gradient issue in order to learn the long-term dependencies across sequences. Due to the less complicated structure, we choose GRU instead of LSTM to reduce the training time. GRU is used to analyze all previously computed values in a temporal manner to evaluate the information learned over time. More specifically, GRU operates on vectors describing each face detected in a video, where the vectors consist of 1,048 facial features extracted with Efficient-Net for frame j, the logit l_j, the weight w_j, and the probability of manipulation p_w computed with AFW.

The GRU consists of three stacked, bi-directional layers, and a uni-directional layer with a hidden layer of 512. The final layer consists of a linear layer with a sigmoid activation function to estimate a final probability, p_{RNN}, which describes the likelihood that the video is manipulated.

Weight Initialization. Each network of the overall ensemble is initialized with weights in a manner that will help it best succeed. We use a pretrained MTCNN for face detection. The EfficientNet face extractor is initialized with weights pretrained on ImageNet, and the AFW and GRU are initialized with random weights. Before training the entire ensemble in an end-to-end fashion, we train the EfficientNet with the ArcFace loss on 2,000 batches of cropped faces selected randomly. Although this initial training step is not necessary to increase the accuracy of the overall approach, our experiments indicated that it aided the network in faster convergence with a more stable training process. This step ensures the parameters passed onto the rest of the network are more suited to our deepfake detection task.

Loss Function. The network utilizes three different loss functions. The first is ArcFace loss, which operates on the output of EfficientNet. It is used only to update the weights of EfficientNet to extract facial features based on batches of cropped faces from randomly selected frames and videos. The second loss function is a binary cross-entropy (BCE) loss, which operates on the AFW prediction p_w. It is used to update the weights associated with EfficientNet and the AFW. The third loss function is another BCE, which operates on the GRU prediction p_{RNN}. It is used to update the weights of EfficientNet, the AFW, and the GRU. The ArcFace loss evaluates frame-level classifications, while the BCE losses evaluate video-level predictions.

11.2.3 Training Details

In this work, we train and evaluate the proposed method on the Deepfake Detection Challenge (DFDC) Dataset [21]. We split the dataset into training, validation, and testing sets with the ratio of 3:1:1. Since our approach consists of many components that rely upon each other, it is important to train each portion properly to ensure the success of the overall ensemble. We train our facial feature extractor (i.e., EfficientNet), the AFW, and the GRU ourselves, but we do not train or update the MTCNN. The entire ensemble is trained end-to-end with the Adam optimizer [22] and a learning rate of 0.001.

Our method can only afford to evaluate one video at a time during training due to the size of the network, the number of frames, and GPU computational limits. However, the network parameters are updated after processing groups of videos. EfficientNet is updated with the ArcFace loss after 256 random frames, and the entire ensemble is updated with the BCE losses after 64 videos. During training, we oversample videos that contain genuine, authentic faces to balance the dataset so that the network is presented with balanced manipulated and authentic faces during the training process.

11.2.4 Boosting Network

In order to further improve the model performance, we also utilize a boosting network. The boosting network is a duplicate of the backbone with a different objective. Instead of minimizing BCE on class predictions, the boosting network strives to predict error in the logit domain between predictions and the true classifications for both the AFW and the GRU. More specifically, the output of the AFW layer is defined as

$$p_w^b = \sigma \left(\frac{\sum_{j=1}^{N}(w_j l_j + w_j^b l_j^b)}{\sum_{j=1}^{N}(w_j + w_j^b)} \right), \tag{11.2}$$

where w_j and l_j refer to the weights and logits produced by the main network and w_j^b and l_j^b refer to the weights and logits produced by the boosting network for the jth face region. N is the total number of frames under analysis, and $\sigma(.)$ refers to the sigmoid function. In a similar manner, the output of the GRU is defined as

$$p_{RNN}^b = \sigma(l_{RNN} + l_{RNN}^b), \tag{11.3}$$

where l_{RNN} refers to the logit produced by the GRU of the main network, l_{RNN}^b refers to the logit produced by the GRU of the boosting network, and $\sigma(.)$ refers to the sigmoid function. The main network is trained on the training data, while the boosting network is trained on the validation data. The main network and the boosting network interact in the AFW layer and after the GRU.

11.2.5   Test Time Augmentation

We leverage one other technique to enhance the performance of our approach: data augmentation during testing. Data augmentation has been used in training to reduce overfitting. However, in our experiments, we discover that using the following data augmentation procedure during testing can reduce the incorrect and overconfident predictions. Once the MTCNN identifies facial regions in a desired frame, we crop the designated areas in the desired frame, in the previous two frames, and in the following two frames. We repeat this for all frames in the test sequence, resulting in five sequences of video frames depicting faces. Next, we randomly apply a horizontal flip data augmentation to each sequence and run each of the sequences through our full model. The final classification prediction for a video sequence is the average of the five predictions on the shifted sequences. This technique decreases the number of incorrect and overconfident predictions since averaging smooths out anomalous predictions.

11.2.6   Result Analysis

We train and evaluate the proposed method on the Deepfake Detection Challenge (DFDC) Dataset [21]. In addition, we make quantitative comparisons with Efficient-Net [13], Xception [14], Conv-LSTM [10], and a modified version of Conv-LSTM using the facial regions detected by MTCNN as input. For the EfficientNet [13] and Xception [14] networks, the final prediction result of each video is obtained by averaging the predictions of each frame.

We select a configuration for each model based on the validation set with balanced authentic/manipulated data. The corresponding Receiver Operating Characteristic (ROC) and Detection Error Trade-off (DET) curves are shown in Fig. 11.2. Since the Conv-LSTM method extracts the features based on the entire video frames, it cannot effectively capture the manipulations that occur in facial regions. However, when we use the detected facial regions instead of the entire frames as input, the detection performance improves significantly. The two typical CNN models EfficientNet-b5 [13] and Xception [14] have achieved good performance in manipulation detection based on video frames. The results of the proposed method indicate that performance of EfficientNet-b5 can be further improved by adding an Automatic Face Weighting layer (AFW) and a Gated Recurrent Unit (GRU).

We also evaluate how the boosting network and data augmentation affects the results in the testing phase. In order to do so, we use the log-likelihood error (the lower the better) to represent the system performance, since log-likelihood score can penalize heavily for being confident but wrong. The results are shown in Table 11.1. It demonstrates that by including both the boosting network and test augmentation at the same time, the log-likelihood can be decreased to 0.321.

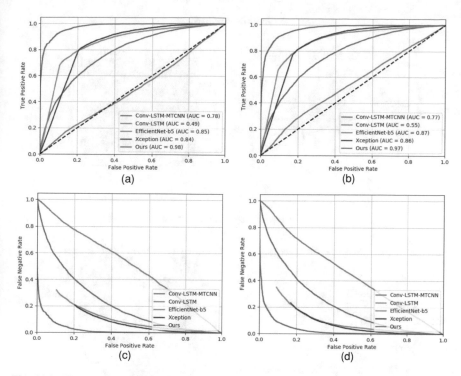

Fig. 11.2 The manipulation detection performance comparison. Figures **a** and **b** are the ROC curves obtained from validation and testing sets, respectively. Figures **c** and **d** are the DET curves obtained from validation and testing sets, respectively

Table 11.1 The log-likelihood error results

Method	Log-likelihood
Baseline	0.364
Baseline + Boosting network	0.341
Baseline + Boosting network + Test augmentation	0.321

11.3 Deepfake Detection via Audio Spectrogram Analysis

Visual content is just one data modality that can be altered. Audio attacks can be used to spoof devices to gain access to personal records. They may also be used to change the message delivered by a figure in a video. Such attacks may consist of only newly synthesized audio to achieve a nefarious objective. Other times, falsified audio may be used in deepfakes to sync with the newly generated faces (or just lips) in the videos [23]. We need methods to analyze standalone audio signals as well as signals that accompany visual content to verify the authenticity of the messages we hear.

A Genuine Audio Signal

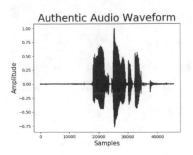
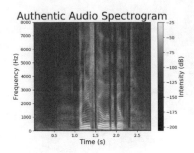

A Synthesized Audio Signal

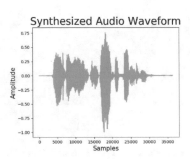
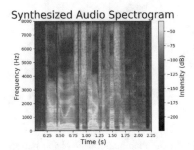

Fig. 11.3 *Left column:* Raw audio waveforms, where purple indicates an authentic audio signal and orange indicates a synthesized audio signal. *Right column:* Spectrograms corresponding to the raw audio waveforms, which serve as inputs to the CNN to classify the signals based on authenticity

In this section, we present a method that analyzes audio signals to determine their authenticity. Our approach works by analyzing audio signals in the form of spectrograms, as shown in Fig. 11.3, with a Convolutional Neural Network (CNN). This work can prevent spoofing attacks by analyzing audio signals on their own, or it can aid in the detection of deepfakes by adding audio analysis to a video analysis as shown in Sect. 11.4.

11.3.1 Overview

We present a method that analyzes a few seconds of an audio signal and identifies whether it is genuine human speech or synthesized speech. Figure 11.4 depicts an overview of our method. It consists of four main steps. First, we apply the Fourier Transform to raw audio waveforms. Then, we use the resulting Fourier coefficients to

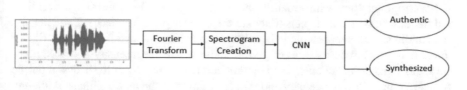

Fig. 11.4 Proposed Method. The proposed approach applies the Fourier Transform to raw audio signals to generate spectrogram "images"—the inputs to the CNN. The CNN classifies signals as *authentic* or *synthesized*

construct spectrograms of the audio waveforms. Next, we analyze the spectrograms with a CNN, and finally we classify audio signals as *authentic* or *synthesized*.

11.3.2 Dataset

For our experiments, we utilize the dataset [24] of the 2019 Automatic Speaker Verification Spoofing and Countermeasures Challenge (ASVspoof2019) [25]. This large-scale dataset contains 121,467 audio tracks. Some of the audio samples are authentic and contain recordings of humans speaking. Other samples contain audio to be used in spoofing attacks. The inauthentic audio samples were generated via voice conversion (VC), speech synthesis (SS), and replay methods. Since our ambitions focus more on deepfake detection than spoofing attacks, we only consider audio signals that have been synthetically generated to replicate human voices, which is included in the VC and SS subsets. This data was generated with neural acoustic models and Artificial Intelligence, including Long Short-Term Memory networks (LSTMs) and Generative Adversarial Networks (GANs). For training and evaluating our CNN classifier, we utilize the official dataset split of the ASVspoof2019 challenge, which divides the full dataset into 25,380 training audio tracks, 24,844 validation tracks, and 71,243 testing tracks.

11.3.3 Spectrogram Generation

The first step in our audio verification method is to apply the Fourier transform to raw audio signals. A Fast Fourier Transform (FFT) is a method that efficiently computes the Discrete Fourier Transform (DFT) of a sequence. We utilize the FFT to compute the Fourier coefficients of an audio signal under analysis. Then, we convert the Fourier coefficients to decibels. The second step in our approach is to construct spectrograms of the audio signals. We create spectrogram "images" of size 50x34 pixels to analyze with our CNN. Examples of the spectrograms created for our dataset are shown in Fig. 11.3.

Spectrograms convey information about the intensity of an audio signal over time and frequency. One axis depicts time and the other depicts frequency. The intensity of an audio signal is represented via color at a specific time and frequency. Brighter colors that are closer to shades of yellow indicate greater intensity and volume of the audio signals. On the other hand, darker colors that are closer to shades of purple or black indicate lower intensity and quieter volume of the audio signals. Although these colors assist us in seeing the differences in intensity over time and frequency of an audio signal, we do not use them in the spectrograms analyzed by the CNN. After the spectrogram images are constructed, we remove the color and convert the images to grayscale. We also normalize their values to prepare them for analysis by the CNN.

11.3.4   Convolutional Neural Network (CNN)

Since our method analyzes spectrogram "images", our CNN employs 2-D convolutions. This is in contrast to a CNN that analyzes a raw audio waveform, which would utilize 1-D convolutions across the 1-D sequence. By using 2-D convolutions to analyze spectrograms, our method incorporates intensity information over frequency and time.

Table 11.2 outlines the specifics of the network architecture. It mainly consists of two convolutional layers. Next, it utilizes max pooling and dropout to introduce regularization into the network and decrease the chances of overfitting. After two dense layers and more dropout, the CNN produces a final class prediction, indicating whether the audio signal is authentic or synthesized. We train the CNN for 10 epochs using the Adam optimizer [26] and cross-entropy loss function.

Table 11.2 CNN Details. This table specifies the parameters of the developed CNN. Each row in the table describes *(from left to right)* the function of the layer, its output shape, and the number of parameters it introduces to the CNN. (N, H, W) refers to the number of feature maps produced by the layer (N), along with their height H and width W

Layer	Output shape (N, H, W)	Parameters
$conv_1$	(32, 48, 32)	320
$conv_2$	(30, 46, 64)	18,496
max pooling	(15, 23, 64)	0
$dropout_1$	(15, 23, 64)	0
$flatten_1$	(22080)	0
$dense_1$	(128)	2,826,368
$dropout_2$	(128)	0
$dense_2$	(2)	258

Table 11.3 Results. This table presents results achieved with the baseline random classifier and our CNN approach

Method	Accuracy (%)	Precision (%)	Recall (%)	F-1 (%)
Baseline (random)	49.98	50.12	50.34	40.69
Proposed method	**82.54**	**66.00**	**81.38**	**68.93**

11.3.5   Experimental Results

Table 11.3 summarizes the results of our method. We evaluate our results based on accuracy, precision, recall, and F1-score. We also calculate Receiver Operator Characteristic (ROC), Detection Error Trade-off (DET), and Precision-Recall (PR) curves. We demonstrate the success of our method over a random classifier, which serves as a baseline for comparison. The random classifier randomly guesses whether an audio signal is authentic or synthesized according to a uniform random distribution. Results indicate that our method outperforms the baseline random classifier based on all metrics.

Figure 11.5 shows Receiver Operating Characteristic (ROC), Detection Error Trade-off (DET), and Precision-Recall (PR) curves for our results in comparison to the baseline. Our approach achieves a high ROC-AUC of 0.8975, which outperforms the baseline ROC-AUC of 0.5005. The PR-AUC exhibits similar behavior. Our method achieves PR-AUC of 0.4611, while the baseline PR-AUC settles at 0.1024. All metrics included in both the table and the figures indicate that our method accomplishes better verification of audio signals than the baseline for both the validation and testing sets.

Considering that the testing dataset contains new audio attacks which were never seen before in training and validation, these results are very promising. Analysis of audio signals in the frequency domain formatted as spectrograms is effective for an audio verification task. It can also be used as audio features for audio-video inconsistency analysis in the following section.

11.4   Deepfake Detection via Audio-Video Inconsistency Analysis

The previously mentioned audio analysis technique can aid in the detection of deepfake videos by extending the scope to include two different media modalities. For videos in which only the audio has been altered, this method will complement a pixel analysis method. For some realistic deepfakes, a visual analysis alone may not be able to detect the manipulations, but pairing the visual analysis with audio analysis provides an additional avenue for authenticity verification.

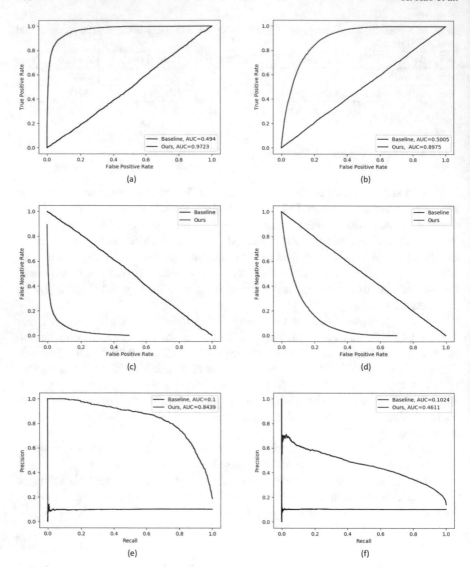

Fig. 11.5 ROC, DET, PR curves. Figures **a** and **b** show the ROC curves obtained from the validation and testing sets, respectively. Figures **c** and **d** show the DET curves obtained from the validation and testing sets, respectively. Figures **e** and **f** show the PR curves obtained from the validation and testing sets, respectively

In this section, we discuss detecting deepfakes by analyzing the natural correlations that manifest when lip movements are coherent with the voice in videos of
speaking persons. Then, the absence of such correlations in videos will point to plausible manipulations. Several works [27, 28] have explored this direction. For example,
Korshunov et al. [27] propose to use lip keypoints obtained from 68-point facial landmarks and audio Mel-frequency cepstrum to check their consistency. These lip and
audio features are concatenated together via Principal Component Analysis (PCA)
for dimensionality reduction. Then, we can use these features to train a classifier
(e.g., Gaussian mixture model, SVM, or LSTM) for deepfake detection.

However, simply concatenating the visual features and audio features does not
always work, especially due to the large variation of possible facial and head movements and individual appearance differences. In the following sections, we will
describe several deepfake detection methods based on the work [28, 29] to provide
more reliable approaches using audio and video inconsistency analysis.

11.4.1   Finding Audio-Video Inconsistency via Phoneme-Viseme Mismatching

As described earlier, current deepfake techniques are still not able to produce coherent
lip-sync manipulated videos. To exploit this, Agarwal *et al.* [28] propose to explicitly
detect the mismatch of phonemes and visemes. A phoneme is a distinct unit of human
speech, while viseme is the counterpart of a phoneme for lip movement. In their
work, they focus only on the close-mouth phoneme, such as the phoneme group of
M (e.g., mother), *B* (e.g., brother), and *P* (e.g., parent), since detecting closed lips
is more accurate than other lip movements. If the audio narrative text is available,
the closed-lip phoneme can be found directly through phonograms. If only audio
data is provided, there are tools available to transcribe the audio track into text, such
as the Speech-to-Text API from Google.[1] After finding the closed-lip phoneme, we
describe an approach to detect the viseme.

Figure 11.6 shows how we detect the closed-lip viseme. 68-point facial landmarks
are first detected given a RGB frame using an online tool.[2] As shown in Fig. 11.6,
the landmark points include both inner and outer loops of the lips. To find if the
lips are closed or open, we compute the two middle points of the upper and lower
lips and collect the intensities of the pixels along the line segment shown as the red
line in Fig. 11.6. Note that we use bilinear interpolation to obtain the pixel intensity
along the line segment. The right two plots in Fig. 11.6 show the corresponding pixel
intensity plot given the images on the left after converting to grayscale. We apply
moving average with a window size of 10 to smooth the plots. Then we find the local
maxima and local minima and their prominences, h_i and l_i, using the MATLAB
function *findpeaks* for frame i. h_i measures the intensity drop from upper lip to the

---

[1] https://cloud.google.com/speech-to-text.

[2] https://github.com/1adrianb/face-alignment.

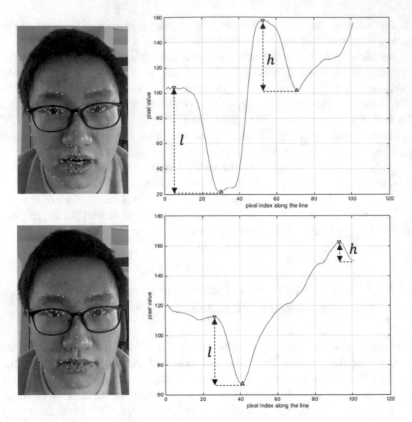

Fig. 11.6 Viseme detection. The first row shows the viseme profile of open mouth and the second row shows the case of closed mouth. The two images on the left are the original RGB images with inpainted landmarks and profile line (red line). The two plots on the right are the corresponding profile feature plots with local minima (blue triangle) and maxima (red triangle)

mouth interior, while l_i measures the intensity boost from mouth interior to lower lip. To detect a closed-lip viseme, given the reference h_r and l_r from a ground truth closed-lip frame, we measure the distance $|l_i - l_r| + |h_i - h_r|$. If the distance is smaller than a threshold value, it will be classified as a closed-lip viseme.

Given a closed-lip phoneme event at a specific event frame, we will first collect several frames before and after the event frame. If there is at least one closed-lip viseme that can be found in the selected frames, we consider the phoneme and viseme to match. Otherwise, we consider the phoneme and viseme mismatched. With this approach, we determine if the given video is deepfake or not by detecting phoneme-viseme mismatching.

This approach explicitly finds phoneme-viseme mismatching to detect audio-video inconsistency. However, it is not always necessary to explicitly find such a mismatch. In the following section, we introduce a method that uses a deep learning model to automatically detect deepfakes from audio and video data.

11.4.2   Deepfake Detection Using Affective Cues

In this section, we will introduce a method based on [29] that does not rely on the hand-designed audio and video features mentioned in Sect. 11.4.1. Instead, we will guide the model to learn a latent space that disentangles the manipulated/authentic data for both audio and video modalities. Different from the work in Sect. 11.2.1, which learns a manipulated/authentic discriminative latent space for video only, the presented work aims to find such a space for both audio and video, simultaneously.

Figure 11.7 shows the block diagram of our presented method. Given an image sequence, face features are extracted first using a CNN-based method, such as the method previously shown in Sect. 11.2.1. To extract audio features, we can use the same approach as proposed in Sect. 11.3 using spectrograms as audio features. Then, we pass the video feature f and audio feature s to two separate CNN models (i.e., video and audio modality embedders) to map input features into a latent space that is discriminative for manipulated/authentic data. Emotion features can also be extracted from f and s using a pretrained Memory Fusion Network (MFN) [30]. MFN is a deep learning model that aims to detect human emotion from different data modalities like facial expressions and speech. Similarly, we use two separate MFNs as video and audio emotion embedders to map the input features into the latent space that is discriminative for manipulated/authentic data. After obtaining the embeddings of video and audio modality features (m^f and m^s) and the embeddings of video and audio emotion features (e^f and e^s), we compute the feature distance (e.g., Euclidean distance or cosine distance) to determine if the input is a deepfake or not. There are many loss functions that are applicable to obtaining a discriminative latent space for the manipulated and authentic data, such as triplet loss [31] and ArcFace [19] (as described in Sect. 11.2.1).

As described above, we show that instead of solely relying on video modality, we can detect deepfakes using both audio and video modalities. These methods are more robust to new attacks (i.e., new deepfake techniques) because they consider more

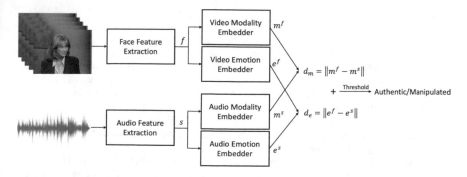

Fig. 11.7 Deepfake detection model using affective cues. The presented method extracts data modality features and emotion features from both audio and video. Then the detection result is obtained by jointly comparing the audio-video feature distances from data modality and emotion

information. As deepfakes continue to become more realistic, focusing on multiple data modalities can give us a better opportunity for accurate detection. Video and audio data modalities are not the only modalities that can assist in deepfake detection. Other data modalities (e.g., video metadata [32]) are also useful to improve the robustness of the detection algorithm. We believe that with the help of multi-modality and cross-modality analysis, detection methods will be more robust against future deepfake attacks.

11.5 Conclusion

In this chapter, we introduce several approaches that analyze deepfake features to determine their authenticity. First, we design a deepfake detection method that relies on spatiotemporal features obtained from video frames. Then, we pivot to incorporate an audio analysis to further improve our deepfake detection. We develop an audio-based method to detect synthetic speech based on spectrogram analysis. Next, we describe several methods that utilize both video frames and audio speech to detect deepfakes via audio-video inconsistency. We show that the presented approaches successfully identify deepfake videos from various large-scale datasets with high accuracy. The true potential of deepfakes is still untapped. We continue to evolve and innovate as new technology becomes available.

Acknowledgements This material is based on research sponsored by the Defense Advanced Research Projects Agency (DARPA) and Air Force Research Laboratory (AFRL) under agreement numbers FA8750-16-2-0173 and FA8750-20-2-1004. The U.S. Government is authorized to reproduce and distribute reprints for Governmental purposes notwithstanding any copyright notation thereon. The views and conclusions contained herein are those of the authors and should not be interpreted as necessarily representing the official policies or endorsements, either expressed or implied, of DARPA and AFRL or the U.S. Government.

References

1. Yang X, Li Y, Lyu S (2019) Exposing deep fakes using inconsistent head poses. In: Proceedings of the IEEE international conference on acoustics, speech and signal processing, May 2019
2. Yang X, Li Y, Qi H, Lyu S (2019) Exposing gan-synthesized faces using landmark locations. In: Proceedings of the international workshop on information hiding and multimedia security, July 2019
3. Marra F, Gragnaniello D, Cozzolino D, Verdoliva L (2018) Detection of gan-generated fake images over social networks. In: Proceedings of the IEEE conference on multimedia information processing and retrieval, April 2018
4. Gragnaniello D, Cozzolino D, Marra F, Poggi G, Verdoliva L (2021) Are GAN generated images easy to detect? A critical analysis of the state-of-the-art. In: Proceedings of the IEEE international conference on multimedia and expo, July 2021
5. Cozzolino D, Rössler A, Thies J, Nießner M, Verdoliva L (2021) Id-reveal: Identity-aware deepfake video detection. In: arXiv preprint arXiv:2012.02512, December 2021

6. Verdoliva L (2020) Media forensics and deepfakes: an overview. IEEE J Select Topics Signal Process 14(5):910–932
7. Tolosana R, Vera-Rodríguez R, Fiérrez J, Morales A, Ortega-Garcia J (2020) Deepfakes and beyond: a survey of face manipulation and fake detection. In: arXiv preprint arXiv:2001.00179, January 2020
8. Mirsky Y, Lee W (2021) The creation and detection of deepfakes: a survey. In: ACM Computing survey, vol 54, No 1, January 2021
9. Nguyen TT, Nguyen CM, Nguyen DT, Nguyen DT, Nahavandi S (2021) Deep learning for deepfakes creation and detection. In: arXiv preprint arXiv:1909.11573, April 2021
10. Güera D, Delp EJ (2018) Deepfake video detection using recurrent neural networks. IEEE international conference on advanced video and signal based surveillance, November 2018. Auckland, New Zealand, pp 1–6
11. Montserrat D, Hao H, Yarlagadda S, Baireddy S, Shao R, Horvath J, Bartusiak ER, Yang J, Guera D, Zhu F, Delp E (2020) Deepfakes detection with automatic face weighting. In: IEEE conference on computer vision and pattern recognition workshops, June 2020, pp 2851–2859
12. Szegedy C, Vanhoucke V, Ioffe S, Shlens J, Wojna Z (2016) Rethinking the inception architecture for computer vision. In: Proceedings of the IEEE conference on computer vision and pattern recognition, June 2016, Las Vegas, pp 2818–2826
13. Tan M, Le QV (2019) Efficientnet: Rethinking model scaling for convolutional neural networks. In: arXiv preprint arXiv:1905.11946
14. Chollet F (2017) Xception: Deep learning with depthwise separable convolutions. In: Proceedings of the IEEE conference on computer vision and pattern recognition, July 2017, Honolulu, pp 1251–1258
15. Russakovsky O, Deng J, Hao S, Krause J, Satheesh S, Ma S, Huang Z, Karpathy A, Khosla A, Bernstein M, Berg AC, Fei-Fei L (2015) ImageNet large scale visual recognition challenge. Int J Comput Vis 115(3):211–252
16. Hochreiter S, Schmidhuber J (1997) Long short-term memory. Neural Comput 9(7)
17. Cho K, van Merriënboer B, Gulcehre C, Bahdanau D, Bougares F, Schwenk H, Bengio Y (2014) Learning phrase representations using RNN encoder–decoder for statistical machine translation. In: Proceedings of the conference on empirical methods in natural language processing, October 2014
18. Zhang K, Zhang Z, Li Z, Qiao Y (2016) Joint face detection and alignment using multitask cascaded convolutional networks. In: IEEE signal processing letters, vol 23, April 2016
19. Deng J, Guo J, Xue N, Zafeiriou S (2019) ArcFace: additive angular margin loss for deep face recognition. In: Proceedings of the IEEE conference on computer vision and pattern recognition, June 2019, Long Beach
20. Vaswani A, Shazeer N, Parmar N, Uszkoreit J, Jones L, Gomez AN, Kaiser Ł, Polosukhin I (2017) Attention is all you need. In: Proceedings of advances in neural information processing systems, December 2017, Long Beach, pp 5998–6008
21. Dolhansky B, Howes R, Pflaum B, Baram N, Ferrer CC (2019) The deepfake detection challenge (dfdc) preview dataset. In: arXiv preprint arXiv:1910.08854
22. Kingma D, Ba J (2015) Adam: A method for stochastic optimization. In: Proceedings of the IEEE conference on international conference for learning representations, May 2015
23. Suwajanakorn S, Seitz SM, Kemelmacher-Shlizerman I (2017) Synthesizing obama: learning lip sync from audio. ACM Trans Graph 36(4)
24. Yamagishi J, Todisco M, Sahidullah M, Delgado H, Wang X, Evans N, Kinnunen T, Lee K, Vestman V, Nautsch A (2019) Asvspoof 2019: The 3rd automatic speaker verification spoofing and countermeasures challenge database. University of Edinburgh, The Centre for Speech Technology Research
25. Todisco M, Yamagishi J, Sahidullah M, Delgado H, Wang X, Evans N, Kinnunen T, Lee K, Vestman V, Nautsch A (2019) Asvspoof 2019: Automatic speaker verification spoofing and countermeasures challenge evaluation plan. In: ASVspoof consortium, January 2019
26. Kingma D, Ba J (2015) Adam: a method for stochastic optimization. In: Proceedings of the international conference for learning representations, May 2015, San Diego

27. Korshunov P, Marcel S (2018) Speaker inconsistency detection in tampered videos. In: Proceedings of the IEEE European signal processing conference, September 2018, pp 2375–2379
28. Agarwal S, Farid H, Fried O, Agrawala M (2020) Detecting deep-fake videos from phoneme-viseme mismatches. In: Proceedings of the IEEE conference on computer vision and pattern recognition workshops, June 2020, pp 2814–2822
29. Mittal T, Bhattacharya U, Chandra R, Bera A, Manocha D (2020) Emotions don't lie: an audio-visual deepfake detection method using affective cues. In: Proceedings of the ACM international conference on multimedia, October 2020, Seattle, pp 2823–2832
30. Zadeh A, Liang PP, Mazumder N, Poria S, Cambria E, Morency L-P (2018) Memory fusion network for multi-view sequential learning. In: Proceedings of the AAAI conference on artificial intelligence
31. Schroff F, Kalenichenko D, Philbin J (2015) FaceNet: A unified embedding for face recognition and clustering. In: Proceedings of the IEEE computer vision and pattern recognition. Boston, pp 815–823
32. Güera D, Baireddy S, Bestagini P, Tubaro S, Delp EJ (2019) We need no pixels: Video manipulation detection using stream descriptors. In: Proceedings of the international conference on machine learning, synthetic-realities: deep learning for detecting audiovisual fakes workshop, June 2019, Long Beach

Chapter 12
DeepFakes Detection Based on Heart Rate Estimation: Single- and Multi-frame

Javier Hernandez-Ortega, Ruben Tolosana, Julian Fierrez,
and Aythami Morales

Abstract This chapter describes a DeepFake detection framework based on physiological measurement. In particular, we consider information related to the heart rate using remote photoplethysmography (rPPG). rPPG methods analyze video sequences looking for subtle color changes in the human skin, revealing the presence of human blood under the tissues. This chapter explores to what extent rPPG is useful for the detection of DeepFake videos. We analyze the recent fake detector named DeepFakesON-Phys that is based on a Convolutional Attention Network (CAN), which extracts spatial and temporal information from video frames, analyzing and combining both sources to better detect fake videos. DeepFakesON-Phys has been experimentally evaluated using the latest public databases in the field: Celeb-DF v2 and DFDC. The results achieved for DeepFake detection based on a single frame are over 98% AUC (Area Under the Curve) on both databases, proving the success of fake detectors based on physiological measurement to detect the latest DeepFake videos. In this chapter, we also propose and study heuristical and statistical approaches for performing continuous DeepFake detection by combining scores from consecutive frames with low latency and high accuracy (100% on the Celeb-DF v2 evaluation dataset). We show that combining scores extracted from short-time video sequences can improve the discrimination power of DeepFakesON-Phys.

The present chapter is an updated adaptation of the conference paper [21].

J. Hernandez-Ortega (✉) · R. Tolosana · J. Fierrez · A. Morales
Universidad Autonoma de Madrid, Madrid, Spain
e-mail: javier.hernandezo@uam.es

R. Tolosana
e-mail: ruben.tolosana@uam.es

J. Fierrez
e-mail: julian.fierrez@uam.es

A. Morales
e-mail: aythami.morales@uam.es

© The Author(s) 2022
C. Rathgeb et al. (eds.), *Handbook of Digital Face Manipulation and Detection*,
Advances in Computer Vision and Pattern Recognition,
https://doi.org/10.1007/978-3-030-87664-7_12

255

12.1 Introduction

DeepFakes have become a great public concern recently [5, 8]. The very popular term "DeepFake" is usually referred to a deep learning-based technique able to create fake videos by swapping the face of a subject with the face of another subject. This type of digital manipulation is also known in the literature as Identity Swap, and it is moving forward very fast [46].

Currently, most face manipulations are based on popular machine learning techniques such as AutoEncoders (AE) [25] and Generative Adversarial Networks (GAN) [15], achieving in general very realistic visual results, specially in the latest generation of public DeepFakes [45], and the present trends [24]. However, despite the impressive visual results, are current face manipulations also considering the physiological aspects of the human being in the synthesis process?

Physiological measurement has provided very valuable information to many different tasks such as e-learning [17], health care [31], human-computer interaction [44], and security [29], among many other tasks.

In physical face attacks, a.k.a. Presentation Attacks (PAs), real subjects are often impersonated using artefacts such as photographs, videos, makeup, and masks [13, 29, 38, 39]. Face recognition systems are known to be vulnerable against these attacks unless proper detection methods are implemented [14, 19]. Some of these detection methods are based on liveness detection by using information such as eye blinking or natural facial micro-expressions [4]. Specifically for detecting 3D mask impersonation, which is one of the most challenging type of attacks, detecting pulse from face videos using remote photoplethysmography (rPPG) has shown to be an effective countermeasure [20]. When applying this technique to a video sequence with a fake face, the estimated heart rate signal is significantly different from the heart rate extracted from a real face [12].

Seeing the good results achieved by rPPG techniques when dealing with physical 3D face mask attacks, and since DeepFakes are digital manipulations somehow similar to them, in this chapter, we hypothesize that fake detectors based on physiological measurement can also be used against DeepFakes after adapting them properly. DeepFake generation methods have historically tried to mimic the visual appearance of real faces (a.k.a. bona fide presentations [1]). However, to the best of our knowledge, they do not emulate the physiology of human beings, e.g., heart rate, blood oxygenation, or breath rate, so estimating that type of signals from the video could be a powerful tool for the detection of DeepFakes.

This chapter analyzes the potential of DeepFakesON-Phys, which was originally analyzed in [21] for the detection of DeepFakes videos at frame level, and it is further studied in this chapter for the detection at short-term video level. DeepFakesON-Phys is a fake detector based on deep learning that uses rPPG features previously learned for the task of heart rate estimation and adapts them for the detection of DeepFakes by means of a knowledge-transfer process, thus obtaining a novel fake detector based on physiological measurement. This chapter also includes new additional experiments using DeepFakesON-Phys, comparing the accuracies of DeepFake detection based on scores from single frames and on the temporal integration of scores from consecutive frames.

In particular, the information related to the heart rate is considered to decide whether a video is real or fake. DeepFakesON-Phys intends to be a robust solution to the weaknesses of most state-of-the-art DeepFake detectors based on the visual features existing in fake videos [3, 30] and also on the artefacts/fingerprints inserted during the synthesis process [32], which are highly dependent on a specific fake manipulation technique.

DeepFakesON-Phys is based on DeepPhys [6], a deep learning model trained for heart rate estimation from face videos based on rPPG. DeepPhys showed high accuracy even when dealing with challenging conditions such as heterogeneous illumination or low resolution, outperforming classic handcrafted approaches. In [21], we used the architecture of DeepPhys, but making changes to suit the approach for DeepFake detection. We initialized the weights of the layers of DeepFakesON-Phys with the ones from DeepPhys (meant for heart rate estimation based on rPPG) and we adapted them to the new task using fine-tuning. This process allowed us to train our detector without the need of a high number of samples (compared to training it from scratch). Fine-tuning also helped us to obtain a model that detects DeepFakes by looking into rPPG-related features from the images in the face videos.

In this context, in this chapter, we:

- Perform an in-depth literature review of DeepFake detection approaches with special emphasis on physiological techniques, including the key aspects of the detection systems, the databases used, and the main results achieved.
- Describe DeepFakesON-Phys,[1] a recent approach presented in [21] based on the physiological measurement to detect DeepFake videos. Figure 12.1 graphically summarizes DeepFakesON-Phys, which is based on the original architecture DeepPhys [6], a Convolutional Attention Network (CAN) composed of two parallel Convolutional Neural Networks (CNN) able to extract spatial and temporal information from video frames. This architecture is adapted for the detection of DeepFake videos by means of a knowledge-transfer process.
- Include a thorough experimental assessment of DeepFakesON-Phys, considering two of the latest public databases of the second DeepFake generation: Celeb-DF v2 [28] and DFDC Preview [11]. We evaluated DeepFakesON-Phys doing both analysis of fake detection at frame level and also at the short-term video level. DeepFakesON-Phys achieves high-accuracy results in both evaluations, outperforming the state of the art. In addition, the results achieved prove that current face manipulation techniques do not pay attention to the heart-rate-related physiological information of the human being when synthesizing fake videos.

The remainder of the paper is organized as follows. Section 12.2 summarizes previous studies focused on the detection of DeepFakes. Section 12.3 describes

---

[1] https://github.com/BiDAlab/DeepFakesON-Phys.

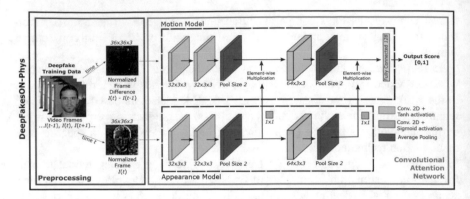

Fig. 12.1 DeepFakesON-Phys architecture [21]. It comprises two stages: (i) a preprocessing step to normalize the video frames, and (ii) a Convolutional Attention Network composed of Motion and Appearance Models to better detect fake videos

DeepFakesON-Phys. Section 12.4 summarizes all databases considered in the experimental framework of this study. Sections 12.5 and 12.6 describe the experimental protocol and the results achieved in comparison with the state of the art, respectively. Finally, Sect. 12.7 draws the final conclusions and points out future research lines.

12.2 Related Works

Different approaches have been proposed in the literature to detect DeepFake videos. Table 12.1 shows a comparison of the most relevant approaches in the area, paying special attention to the fake detectors based on physiological measurement. For each study, we include information related to the method, classifiers, best performance, and databases for research. It is important to remark that in some cases, different evaluation metrics are considered, e.g., Area Under the Curve (AUC) and accuracy (Acc.), which complicate the comparison among studies. Finally, the results highlighted in *italics* indicate the generalization ability of the detectors against unseen databases, i.e., those databases were not considered for training. Most of these results are extracted from [28].

The first studies in the area focused on the visual artefacts existed in the first generation of fake videos. The authors of [30] proposed fake detectors based on simple visual artefacts such as eye color, missing reflections, and missing details in the teeth areas, achieving a final 85.1% AUC.

Approaches based on the detection of the face warping artefacts have also been studied in the literature. For example, [27, 28] proposed detection systems based on CNN in order to detect the presence of such artefacts from the face and the surrounding areas, being one of the most robust detection approaches against unseen face manipulations.

Table 12.1 Comparison of different state-of-the-art fake detectors. Results in *italics* indicate the generalization capacity of the detectors against unseen databases. FF++ = FaceForensics++, AUC = Area Under the Curve, Acc. = Accuracy, EER = Equal Error Rate.

Study	Method	Classifiers	Best performance (%)	Databases
Matern et al. [30]	Visual Features	Logistic Regression MLP	AUC = 85.1	Own
			AUC = 78.0	*FF++ / DFD*
			AUC = 66.2	*DFDC Preview*
			AUC = 55.1	*Celeb-DF*
Li et al. [27, 28]	Face Warping Features	CNN	AUC = 97.7	UADFV
			AUC = 93.0	*FF++ / DFD*
			AUC = 75.5	*DFDC Preview*
			AUC = 64.6	*Celeb-DF*
Rossler et al. [40]	Mesoscopic Features Steganalysis Features Deep Learning Features	CNN	Acc. $\simeq$ 94.0	FF++ (DeepFake, LQ)
			Acc. $\simeq$ 98.0	FF++ (DeepFake, HQ)
			Acc. $\simeq$ 100.0	FF++ (DeepFake, RAW)
			Acc. $\simeq$ 93.0	FF++ (FaceSwap, LQ)
			Acc. $\simeq$ 97.0	FF++ (FaceSwap ,HQ)
			Acc. $\simeq$ 99.0	FF++ (FaceSwap, RAW)
Nguyen et al. [33]	Deep Learning Features	Capsule Networks	*AUC = 61.3*	*UADFV*
			AUC = 96.6	*FF++ / DFD*
			AUC = 53.3	*DFDC Preview*
			AUC = 57.5	*Celeb-DF*
Dang et al. [10]	Deep Learning Features	CNN + Attention Mechanism	AUC = 99.4 EER = 3.1	DFFD
Dolhansky et al. [11]	Deep Learning Features	CNN	Precision = 93.0 Recall = 8.4	DFDC Preview
Sun et al. [43]	Deep Learning Features	CNN	AUC = 98.5	FF++
			AUC = 61.4	Celeb-DF
			AUC = 69.0	*DFDC Preview*

(continued)

Table 12.1 (continued)

Study	Method	Classifiers	Best performance (%)	Databases
Sabir et al. [41]	Image + Temporal Features	CNN + RNN	AUC = 96.9 AUC = 96.3	FF++ (DeepFake, LQ) FF++ (FaceSwap, LQ)
Trinh et al. [47]	Image + Temporal Features	CNN	AUC = 99.2	FF++
			AUC = 68.2	Celeb-DF
Tolosana et al. [45]	Facial Regions Features	CNN	AUC = 100.0	UADFV
			AUC = 99.5	FF++ (FaceSwap, HQ)
			AUC = 91.1	DFDC Preview
			AUC = 83.6	Celeb-DF
Conotter et al. [9]	Physiological Features	–	Acc. = 100	Own
Li et al. [26]	Physiological Features	LRCN	AUC = 99.0	UADFV
Agarwal et al. [3]	Physiological Features	SVM	AUC = 96.3	Own (FaceSwap, HQ)
Ciftci et al. [7]	Physiological Features	SVM/CNN	Acc. = 94.9 Acc. = 91.5	FF++ (DeepFakes) Celeb-DF
Jung et al. [23]	Physiological Features	Distance	Acc. = 87.5	Own
Qi et al. [35]	Physiological Features	CNN + Attention Mechanism	Acc. = 100.0	FF++ (FaceSwap)
			Acc. = 100.0	FF++
			Acc. = 64.1	*DFDC Preview*
DeepFakesON-Phys[21]	**Physiological Features**	**CAN**	**AUC = 99.9**	**Celeb-DF v2 (Frame Level)**
			AUC = 98.2	**DFDC Preview (Frame Level)**
			AUC = 100	**Celeb-DF v2 (Short-Term Video Level)**

Undoubtedly, fake detectors based on pure deep learning features are the most popular ones: feeding the networks with as many real/fake videos as possible and letting the networks to automatically extract the discriminative features. In general, these fake detectors have achieved very good results using popular network architectures such as Xception [11, 40], novel ones such as Capsule Networks [33], and novel training techniques based on attention mechanisms [10]. In particular, we highlight the work presented in [43], focused on improving the generalization ability of the models to detect DeepFake videos. The authors defined a Learning-To-Weight (LTW) framework based on meta-learning that is composed of two branches: the first one performs binary detection, extracting features from the images and determining if an image is real or a fake, while the second branch aims to assign domain-adaptive weights to each sample, helping the model to extract more domain-general features.

Fake detectors based on the image and temporal discrepancies across frames have also been proposed in (DeepFake) the literature [41, 47]. In [41], the authors proposed a Recurrent Convolutional Network similar to [16], trained end-to-end instead of using a pre-trained model. Their proposed detection approach was tested using FaceForensics++ database [40], achieving AUC results above 96%.

In [47], Trinh et al. proposed a human-centered approach for detecting forgery in face images. Their approach looked for temporal artefacts within DeepFake videos, detecting them efficiently while providing explanations of DeepFake dynamics, useful for giving useful information to supervising humans.

Although most approaches are based on the detection of fake videos using the whole face, in [45], the authors evaluated the discriminative power of each facial region using state-of-the-art network architectures, achieving interesting results on DeepFake databases of the first and second generations.

We also pay special attention to the fake detectors based on physiological information. The eye blinking rate was studied in [23, 26]. Li et al. [26] proposed Long-Term Recurrent Convolutional Networks (LRCN) to capture the temporal dependencies that existed in human eye blinking. Their method was evaluated on the UADFV database, achieving a final 99.0% AUC. More recently, [23] proposed a different approach named DeepVision. They fused the Fast-HyperFace [37] and EAR [42] algorithms to track the blinking, achieving an accuracy of 87.5% over an in-house database.

Fake detectors based on the analysis of the way we speak were studied in [3], focusing on the distinct facial expressions and movements. These features were considered in combination with Support Vector Machines (SVM), achieving a 96.3% AUC over their own database.

Finally, fake detection methods based on the heart rate have been also studied in the literature. One of the first studies in this regard was [9] where the authors preliminarily evaluated the potential of blood flow changes in the face to distinguish between computer-generated and real videos. Their proposed approach was evaluated using 12 videos (six real and fake videos each), concluding that it is possible to use this metric to detect computer-generated videos.

Changes in the blood flow have also been studied in [7, 35] using DeepFake videos. In [7], the authors considered rPPG techniques to extract robust biological features. Classifiers based on SVM and CNN were analyzed, achieving final accuracies of 94.9% and 91.5% for the DeepFakes videos of FaceForensics++ and Celeb-DF, respectively.

Recently, in [35], a more sophisticated fake detector named DeepRhythm was presented. This approach was also based on features extracted using rPPG techniques.

DeepRhythm was enhanced through two modules: *(i)* motion-magnified spatial-temporal representation and *(ii)* dual-spatial-temporal attention. These modules were incorporated in order to provide a better adaptation to dynamically changing faces and various fake types. In general, good results with accuracies of 100% were achieved on FaceForensics++ database. However, this method suffers from a demanding pre-processing stage, needing a precise detection of 81 facial landmarks and the use of a color magnification algorithm prior to fake detection. Also, poor results were achieved on databases of the second generation such as the DFDC Preview (Acc. = 64.1%).

Regarding DeepFakesON-Phys originally presented in [21], in addition to the proposal of a different DeepFake detection architecture, we enhanced previous approaches, e.g. [35], by keeping the preprocessing stage as light and robust as possible, only composed of a face detector and frame normalization. To provide an overall picture, we include in Table 12.1 the results achieved with our proposed method in comparison with key related works, showing the good results on both Celeb-DF v2 and DFDC Preview databases for the frame-level analysis and on Celeb-DF v2 for the temporal integration of consecutive scores, AUC = 100%.

12.3 DeepFakesON-Phys

Figure 12.1 graphically summarizes the architecture of DeepFakesON-Phys [21], the proposed fake detector based on heart rate estimation. We hypothesize that rPPG methods should obtain significantly different results when trying to estimate the sub-jacent heart rate from a video containing a real face, compared with a fake face. Since the changes in color and illumination due to oxygen concentration are sub-tle and invisible to the human eye, we think that most of the existing DeepFake manipulation methods do not consider the physiological aspects of the human being yet.

The initial architecture of DeepFakesON-Phys is based on the DeepPhys model described in [6], whose objective was to estimate the human heart rate using facial video sequences. The model is based on deep learning and was designed to extract spatio-temporal information from videos mimicking the behavior of traditional hand-crafted rPPG techniques. Features are extracted through the color changes in users' faces that are caused by the variation of oxygen concentration in the blood. Signal processing methods are also used for isolating the color changes caused by blood from other changes that may be caused by factors such as external illumination and noise.

As can be seen in Fig. 12.1, after the first preprocessing stage, the Convolutional Attention Network (CAN) is composed of two different CNN branches:

- **Motion Model**: it is designed to detect changes between consecutive frames, i.e., performing a short-time analysis of the video for detecting fakes. To accomplish this task, the input at a time t consists of a frame computed as the normalized difference of the current frame $I(t)$ and the previous one $I(t-1)$.

- **Appearance Model**: it focuses on the analysis of the static information on each video frame. It has the target of providing the Motion Model with information about which points of the current frame may contain the most relevant information for detecting DeepFakes, i.e., a batch of attention masks that are shared at different layers of the CNN. The input of this branch at time t is the raw frame of the video $I(t)$, normalized to zero mean and unitary standard deviation.

The attention masks coming from the Appearance Model are shared with the Motion Model at two different points of the CAN. Finally, the output layer of the Motion Model is also the final output of the entire CAN.

In the original architecture [6], the output stage consisted of a regression layer for estimating the time derivative of the subject's heart rate. In our case, as we do not aim to estimate the pulse of the subject, but the presence of a fake face, we change the final regression layer to a classification layer, using a sigmoid activation function for obtaining a final score in the [0,1] range for each instant t of the video, related to the probability of the face being real.

Since the original DeepPhys model from [6] is not publicly available, instead of training a new CAN from scratch, we decided to initialize DeepFakesON-Phys with the weights from the model pre-trained for heart rate estimation presented in [18], which is also an adaptation of DeepPhys but trained using the COHFACE database [22]. This model also showed to have high accuracy in the heart rate estimation task using real face videos, so our idea is to take benefit of that acquired knowledge to better train DeepFakesON-Phys through a proper fine-tuning process.

Once we initialized DeepFakesON-Phys with the mentioned weights, we freeze the weights of all the layers of the original CAN model apart from the new classification layer and the last fully connected layer, and we retrain the model. Due to this fine-tuning process, we take the benefit of the weights learned for heart rate estimation, just adapting them for the DeepFake detection task. This way, we make sure that the weights of the convolutional layers remain looking for information relative to heart rate and the last layers learn how to use that information for detecting the existence of DeepFakes.

12.4   Databases

Two different public databases are considered in the experimental framework of this study. In particular, Celeb-DF v2 [28] and DFDC Preview [11], the two most challenging DeepFake databases up to date. Their videos exhibit a large range of variations in aspects such as face sizes (in pixels), lighting conditions (i.e., day, night, etc.), backgrounds, different acquisition scenarios (i.e., indoors and outdoors), distances from the subject to the camera, and pose variations, among others.

These databases present enough images (fake and genuine) to fine-tune the original weights meant for heart rate estimation, obtaining new weights also based on rPPG features but adapted for DeepFake detection.

12.4.1 Celeb-DF v2 Database

Celeb-DF v2 is one of the most challenging DeepFake databases up to date [28]. The aim of the Celeb-DF v2 database was to generate fake videos of better visual quality compared with the previous UADFV database [26]. This database consists of 590 real videos extracted from YouTube, corresponding to celebrities with a diverse distribution in terms of gender, age, and ethnic group. Regarding fake videos, a total of 5,639 videos were created swapping faces using DeepFake technology. The final videos are in MPEG4.0 format.

12.4.2 DFDC Preview

The DFDC database [11] is one of the latest public databases, released by Facebook in collaboration with other companies and academic institutions such as Microsoft, Amazon, and the MIT. In the present study, we consider the DFDC Preview dataset consisting of 1,131 real videos from 66 paid actors, ensuring realistic variability in gender, skin tone, and age. It is important to remark that no publicly available data or data from social media sites were used to create this dataset, unlike other popular databases. Regarding fake videos, a total of 4,119 videos were created using two different unknown approaches for fakes generation. Fake videos were generated by swapping subjects with similar appearances, i.e., similar facial attributes such as skin tone, facial hair, and glasses. After a given pairwise model was trained on two identities, the identities were swapped onto the other's videos.

12.5 Experimental Protocol

Celeb-DF v2 and DFDC Preview databases have been divided into non-overlapping datasets, development and evaluation. For the Celeb-DF v2 database, we consider real/fake videos of 40 and 19 different identities for the development and evaluation datasets, respectively, whereas for the DFDC Preview database, we follow the same experimental protocol proposed in [11] as the authors already considered this concern.

In this chapter, we followed two different strategies for DeepFake detection. First, for Celeb-DF v2 and DFDC Preview, we perform detection based on single scores obtained by DeepFakesON-Phys where the evaluation is carried out at a frame level as in most previous studies [46], not video level, using the popular AUC and accuracy metrics. Second, we also perform for Celeb-DF v2 videos temporal integration of DeepFake detection scores combining the single scores from non-overlapped temporal windows of T seconds to form a final fused DeepFake detection score. We decided to combine the individual scores following three different strategies:

- **Mean Score**: The DeepFake detection scores of individual frames from each temporal window (T seconds) are averaged to obtain the integrated score.
- **Median Score**: We computed the median of the individual DeepFake detection scores into each temporal window (T seconds).
- **Quickest Change Detection (QCD)**: This is a statistical method that first estimates match and non-match distributions of the scores, i.e., real face and DeepFakes. Then it tries to detect the specific moment in which the incoming detection scores change from one type of distribution to the other. This approach needs prior data in order to build the match and non-match distributions. Some variants of QCD also require to know the probability of a DeepFake in advance, so we decided to implement the MiniMax QCD (MQCD) algorithm from [34], which only needs the score distributions that we obtained in advance using a development data subset.

12.6 Fake Detection Results: DeepFakesON-Phys

This section evaluates the ability of DeepFakesON-Phys to detect some of the most challenging DeepFake videos of the second generation from Celeb-DF v2 [28] and DFDC Preview [11] databases.

12.6.1 DeepFakes Detection at Frame Level

Table 12.2 shows the fake detection results for the case in which we perform an analysis at frame level, following the traditional procedure in the literature [45, 46]. It is important to highlight that a separate fake detector is trained for each database. In general, very good results are achieved in both DeepFake databases. For the Celeb-DF v2 database, DeepFakesON-Phys achieves an accuracy of 98.7% and an AUC of 99.9%. Regarding the DFDC Preview database, the results achieved are 94.4% accuracy and 98.2% AUC, similar to the ones obtained for the Celeb-DF database.

Observing the results, it seems clear that the fake detectors have learnt to distinguish the spatio-temporal differences between the real/fake faces of Celeb-DF v2 and DFDC Preview databases. Since all the convolutional layers of the proposed fake detector are frozen (the network was originally initialized with the weights from the model trained to predict the heart rate [18]), and we only train the last fully connected layers, we can conclude that the proposed detection approach based on physiological measurement is successful using pulse-related features for distinguishing between

Table 12.2 Comparison of different state-of-the-art DeepFake detectors with the **frame-level detection** based on DeepFakesON-Phys. The best results achieved for each database are remarked in **bold**. Results in *italics* indicate that the evaluated database (Celeb-DF or DFDC) was not used for training

Study	Method	Classifiers	AUC Results (%)	
			Celeb-DF [28]	DFDC [11]
Yang et al. [48]	Head pose features	SVM	*54.6*	*55.9*
Li et al. [28]	Face warping features	CNN	*64.6*	*75.5*
Afchar et al. [2]	Mesoscopic features	CNN	*54.8*	*75.3*
Dang et al. [10]	Deep learning features	CNN + Attention mechanism	*71.2*	–
Tolosana et al. [45]	Deep learning features	CNN	83.6	91.1
Qi et al. [35]	Physiological features	CNN + Attention mechanism	–	*Acc. = 64.1*
Ciftci et al. [7]	Physiological features	SVM/CNN	Acc. = 91.5	–
Sun et al. [43]	Deep learning features	CNN	*61.4*	*69.0*
Trinh et al. [47]	Image + Temporal features	CNN	*68.20*	–
DeepFakesON-Phys [21]	Physiological Features	CNN + Attention Mechanism	AUC = 99.9 Acc. = 98.7	AUC = 98.2 Acc. = 94.4

real and fake faces. These results prove that the current face manipulation techniques do not pay attention to the heart-rate-related physiological information of the human being when synthesizing fake videos.

In Table 12.2, we also compare the results achieved with the single score Deep-Fake detection approach against other state-of-the-art DeepFake detection methods: head pose variations [48], face warping artefacts [28], mesoscopic features [2], pure deep learning features [10, 45], and physiological features [7, 35]. Results in *italics* indicate that the evaluated database was not used for training. Some of these results are extracted from [28]. Note that the comparison is not always made under the same datasets and protocols; therefore, it must be interpreted with care. Despite of that, it is patent that DeepFakesON-Phys has achieved state-of-the-art results. In particular, it has further outperformed popular fake detectors based on pure deep learning approaches such as Xception and Capsule Networks [45] and also other recent physiological approaches based on SVM/CNN [7].

Figure 12.2 shows some examples of successful and failed detections when evaluating the fake detection at the frame level. In particular, all the failures correspond

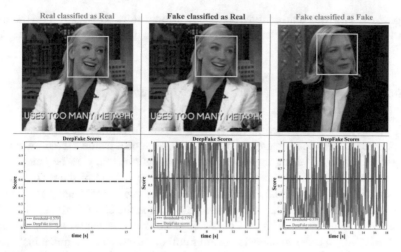

Fig. 12.2   Examples of successful and failed DeepFake detections. Top: sample frames of evaluated videos. Bottom: detection scores for each evaluated video (frame level). For the fake video misclassified as containing a real face, the DeepFake detection scores present a higher mean compared to the case of the fake video correctly classified as a fake

to fake faces generated from a particular video, misclassifying them as real faces. Figure 12.2 shows a frame from the original real video (top-left), one from a misclassified fake video generated using that scenario (top-middle), and another from a fake video correctly classified as fake and generated using the same real and fake identities but from other source videos (top-right).

Looking at the score distributions along time of the three examples (Fig. 12.2, bottom), it can be seen that for the real face video (left), the scores are 1 for most of the time and always over the detection threshold. However, for the fake videos considered (middle and right), the score of each frame changes constantly, making the score of some fake frames to cross the detection threshold and consequently misclassifying them as real.

We believe that the failures produced in this particular case are propitiated by the interferences of external illumination. rPPG methods that use handcrafted features are usually fragile against external artificial illumination in the frequency and power ranges of normal human heart rate, making it difficult to distinguish those illumination changes from the color changes caused by blood perfusion. Anyway, DeepFakesON-Phys is more robust to this kind of illumination perturbations than handcrafted methods, thanks to the fact that the training process is data-driven, making it possible to identify those interferences by using their presence in the training data.

Nevertheless, it is important to remark that these mistakes only happen if we analyze the results at frame level (traditional approach followed in the literature [46]). In case we consider the temporal information available in short-time segments of the video, e.g., in a similar way as described in [20] for continuous face anti-spoofing,

DeepFakesON-Phys could achieve better detection results. This analysis at the short-term video level (not frame level) is described in the next section.

12.6.2 DeepFakes Detection at Short-Term Video Level

With the objective of detecting the type of errors illustrated in Fig. 12.2, in this section, we perform combination of the frame-level scores inside a temporal window of variable length (T) using three different combination strategies, i.e., mean score, median score, and QCD score [34]. The output for each one of these combination methods will be an individual DeepFake detection score for each temporal window. Therefore, the analysis carried out in this section is at the short-term video level.

We evaluate these methods on Celeb-DF v2 considering values of T going from 5 to 15 seconds in order to have a relevant number of scores to combine inside each time window. In this case, a DeepFake detection decision will be generated with a Delay of T seconds (video segments are not overlapped in time in our experiments). Additionally, the QCD algorithm also needs prior data in order to build the match and non-match distributions. To compute those distributions, we use all the single scores of 50 different time windows (25 real, 25 fake) from the evaluation dataset, leaving them out of the final testing process and results included in this section.

Table 12.3 shows the results for the evaluation of the DeepFake detector when varying the duration of the temporal window T. QCD has shown to be the most accurate integration method, obtaining the highest levels of AUC and accuracy even with slightly shorter values of T than the other combination strategies.

It can be seen that, in general, the highest AUC (i.e., the best DeepFake detection performance) is not obtained when using the largest T value, but lower ones (T = 6-7 seconds). For example, for the QCD scores, we have achieved an AUC and an accuracy of 100.0% using temporal windows of 6 seconds, while using higher values of T makes performance to get slightly worse. With shorter values of T (less of 5 s.), the small amount of available frame-level scores within each decision time window may diminish the reliability of each combined score. On the other hand, the combined scores obtained with large values of T may be less reliable as they are more prone to errors due to variations inside each window.

Finally, we decided to test the evolution of the different strategies for temporal integration of scores in cases like the one shown in Fig. 12.2 (right), where the single frame-level scores vary constantly. With temporal integration of scores, we expect to avoid that changeful behavior, obtaining more stable DeepFake detection results.

Figure 12.3 shows the evolution of the different detection scores for a former fail case video, both for single frame-level scores and for mean and QCD integrated scores. The results in the figure show that the temporal integration of scores can reduce the shakiness of the single scores (both for mean and QCD combinations), what is translated into an improved AUC and accuracy rates like the ones seen in Table 12.3. Even though QCD scores have achieved the highest improvement in performance,

Table 12.3 DeepFakes Detection at Short-Term Video Level. The study has been performed on Celeb-DF v2, changing the length of the time window T of the video sequences analyzed. Values are in %. The highest values of AUC for each type of combination of score are highlighted in bold

Mean score

Window Size T [s]	5	6	7	8	9	10	11	12	13	14	15
AUC [%]	99.97	99.98	**99.99**	99.97	99.98	99.96	99.97	99.98	99.97	99.97	99.93
Acc. [%]	99.24	99.47	99.47	99.24	99.46	99.15	99.32	99.63	99.14	99.06	99.37

Median score

Window Size T [s]	5	6	7	8	9	10	11	12	13	14	15
AUC [%]	99.97	99.98	**99.99**	99.97	99.98	99.96	99.97	99.98	99.97	99.97	99.93
Acc. [%]	99.24	99.47	99.47	99.24	99.46	99.15	99.32	99.63	99.14	99.06	99.37

QCD score

Window Size T [s]	5	6	7	8	9	10	11	12	13	14	15
AUC [%]	99.97	**100.0**	99.98	99.96	99.98	99.96	99.97	99.98	99.97	99.97	99.93
Acc. [%]	99.49	100.0	99.73	99.24	99.46	99.15	99.32	99.63	99.14	99.06	99.37

the mean scores also obtain the same stability benefits with the additional advantage of not needing any previous knowledge of the real and fake scores distributions.

12.7   Conclusions

This chapter has evaluated the potential of physiological measurement to detect Deep-Fake videos. In particular, we have described the recent DeepFake detector named DeepFakesON-Phys, originally presented in [21]. DeepFakesON-Phys is based on a Convolutional Attention Network (CAN) initially trained for heart rate estimation using remote photoplethysmography (rPPG). The proposed CAN approach consists of two parallel Convolutional Neural Networks (CNN) that extract and share temporal and spatial information from video frames.

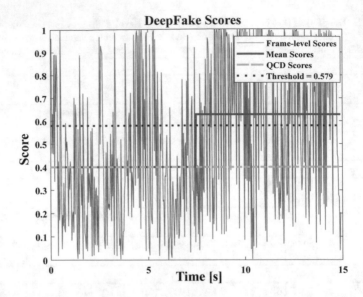

Fig. 12.3 **Examples of successful temporal integration of frame-level scores**. The figure shows the single scores, the mean scores, and QCD integrated scores ($T = 7$ sec.) for a DeepFake video of Celeb-DF v2. For the single frame-level score detection, the scores go over and under the threshold causing numerous false acceptances. For the temporal integration strategies (short-term video analysis), the mean detection score is under the threshold for the first temporal window (successful DeepFake detection), but for the second window, the score crosses the threshold causing a false acceptance. On the contrary, the QCD score is under the threshold for both temporal windows thanks to its statistical nature

DeepFakesON-Phys has been evaluated using Celeb-DF v2 and DFDC Preview databases, two of the latest and most challenging DeepFake video databases. Regarding the experimental protocol, each database was divided into development and evaluation datasets, considering different identities in each dataset in order to perform a fair evaluation of the technology.

Two different evaluations have been performed using DeepFakesON-Phys, the first one consisted in detecting DeepFakes using frame-level scores, proving the soundness and competitiveness of the detection model with Area Under the Curve (AUC) values of 99.9% and 98.2% for the Celeb-DF and DFDC databases, respectively. These results have outperformed other state-of-the-art fake detectors based on face warping and pure deep learning features, among others.

However, in some specific cases, the detection of DeepFakes using frame-level scores has shown some instability that leads to misclassified DeepFakes and real videos. To solve these issues, we have included a second evaluation on Celeb-DF v2, in which we have performed temporal integration of the scores inside a temporal window of T seconds (analysis at short-term video level). We have calculated three different integrated scores: mean, median, and Quickest Change Detection (QCD) scores. The results of this second evaluation have improved those obtained with the single scores (analysis at frame level), achieving both an AUC and an accuracy of 100% when using the QCD score with a temporal window of $T=6$ seconds. We can conclude that the experimental results of this study reveal that current face manipulation techniques do not pay attention to the heart-rate-related or blood-related physiological information.

Immediate work will be oriented to the analysis of the robustness of the proposed fake detection approach against face manipulations unseen during the training process [46], and the application of the proposed physiological approach to other face manipulation techniques such as face morphing [36].

Acknowledgements This work has been supported by projects: PRIMA (H2020-MSCA-ITN-2019-860315), TRESPASS-ETN (H2020-MSCA-ITN-2019-860813), BIBECA (MINECO/FEDER RTI2018-101248-B-I00), and COST CA16101 (MULTI-FORESEE). J. H.-O. is supported by a PhD fellowship from UAM.

References

1. Information Technology-Biometric Presentation Attack Detection-Part 3: Testing and Reporting. Tech. rep., ISO/IEC JTC1 SC37 Biometrics (2017)
2. Afchar D, Nozick V, Yamagishi J, Echizen I (2018) MesoNet: a compact facial video forgery detection network. In: Proceedings of IEEE international workshop on information forensics and security (2018)
3. Agarwal S, Farid H (2019) Protecting world leaders against deep fakes. In: Proceedings of IEEE/CVF conference on computer vision and pattern recognition workshops (2019)
4. Bharadwaj S, Dhamecha TI, Vatsa M, Singh R (2013) Computationally efficient face spoofing detection with motion magnification. In: Proceedings IEEE/CVF conference on computer vision and pattern recognition workshops (2013)
5. Cellan-Jones R (2019) Deepfake videos double in nine months (2019). https://www.bbc.com/news/technology-49961089
6. Chen W, McDuff D (2018) DeepPhys: video-based physiological measurement using convolutional attention networks. In: Proceedings of European Conference on Computer Vision, pp 349–365
7. Ciftci UA, Demir I, Yin L (2020) FakeCatcher: detection of synthetic portrait videos using biological signals. IEEE Trans Pattern Anal Mach Intell
8. Citron D (2019) How deepfake undermine truth and threaten democracy. https://www.ted.com
9. Conotter V, Bodnari E, Boato G, Farid H (2014) Physiologically-based detection of computer generated faces in video. In: Proceedings IEEE international conference on image processing
10. Dang H, Liu F, Stehouwer J, Liu X, Jain A (2020) On the detection of digital face manipulation. In: Proceedings IEEE/CVF conference on computer vision and pattern recognition
11. Dolhansky B, Howes R, Pflaum B, Baram N, Ferrer CC (2019) The deepfake detection challenge (DFDC) preview dataset. arXiv:1910.08854
12. Erdogmus N, Marcel S (2014) Spoofing face recognition with 3D masks. IEEE Trans Inf Forensics Secur 9(7):1084–1097
13. Galbally J, Fierrez J, Ortega-Garcia J (2007) Vulnerabilities in biometric systems: attacks and recent advances in liveness detection. In: Proceedings Spanish workshop on biometrics, SWB
14. Galbally J, Marcel S, Fierrez J (2014) Biometric anti-spoofing methods: a survey in face recognition. IEEE Access 2:1530–1552
15. Goodfellow I, Pouget-Abadie J, Mirza M, Xu B, Warde-Farley D, Ozair S, Courville A, Bengio Y (2014) Generative adversarial nets. In: Proceedings advances in neural information processing systems

16. Güera D, Delp E (2018) Deepfake video detection using recurrent neural networks. In: Proceedings international conference on advanced video and signal based surveillance
17. Hernandez-Ortega J, Daza R, Morales A, Fierrez J, Tolosana R (2020) Heart rate estimation from face videos for student assessment: experiments on edBB. In: Proceedings IEEE computer software and applications conference
18. Hernandez-Ortega J, Fierrez J, Morales A, Diaz D (2020) A comparative evaluation of heart rate estimation methods using face videos. In: Proceedings IEEE international workshop on medical computing
19. Hernandez-Ortega J, Fierrez J, Morales A, Galbally J (2019) Introduction to face presentation attack detection. In: Handbook of biometric anti-spoofing. Springer, pp 187–206
20. Hernandez-Ortega J, Fierrez J, Morales A, Tome P (2018) Time analysis of pulse-based face anti-spoofing in visible and NIR. In: Proceedings IEEE conference on computer vision and pattern recognition workshops
21. Hernandez-Ortega J, Tolosana R, Fierrez J, Morales A (2021) DeepFakesON-Phys: deepfakes detection based on heart rate estimation. AAAI's workshop on artificial intelligence safety (SafeAI) (2021)
22. Heusch G, Anjos A, Marcel S (2017) A reproducible study on remote heart rate measurement. arXiv:1709.00962
23. Jung T, Kim S, Kim K (2020) DeepVision: deepfakes detection using human eye blinking pattern. IEEE Access 8:83144–83154
24. Karras T et al (2020) Analyzing and improving the image quality of StyleGAN. In: Proceedings IEEE/CVF conference on computer vision and patter recognition
25. Kingma DP, Welling M (2013) Auto-encoding Variational Bayes. In: Proceedings international conference on learning represent
26. Li Y, Chang M, Lyu S (2018) In Ictu Oculi: exposing AI generated fake face videos by detecting eye blinking. In: Proceedings IEEE international workshop information forensics and security
27. Li Y, Lyu S (2019) Exposing deepfake videos by detecting face warping artifacts. In: Proceedings IEEE/CVF conference on computer vision and pattern recognition workshops
28. Li Y, Yang X, Sun P, Qi H, Lyu S (2020) Celeb-DF: a large-scale challenging dataset for deepfake forensics. In: Proceedings IEEE/CVF conference on computer vision and pattern recognition
29. Marcel S, Nixon M, Fierrez J, Evans N (2019) Handbook of biometric anti-spoofing, 2nd edn
30. Matern F, Riess C, Stamminger M (2019) Exploiting visual artifacts to expose deepfakes and face manipulations. In: Proceedings IEEE winter applications of computer vision workshops
31. McDuff DJ, Estepp JR, Piasecki AM, Blackford EB (2015) A survey of remote optical photoplethysmographic imaging methods. In: Proceedings annual international conference of the IEEE engineering in medicine and biology society
32. Neves JC, Tolosana R, Vera-Rodriguez R, Lopes V, Proença H, Fierrez J (2020) GANprintR: improved fakes and evaluation of the state of the art in face manipulation detection. IEEE J Select Top Signal Process 14(5):1038–1048
33. Nguyen HH, Yamagishi J, Echizen I (2019) Use of a capsule network to detect fake images and videos. arXiv:1910.12467
34. Perera P, Fierrez J, Patel V (2020) Quickest intruder detection for multiple user active authentication. In: IEEE international conference on image processing (ICIP)
35. Qi H, Guo Q, Juefei-Xu F, Xie X, Ma L, Feng W, Liu Y, Zhao J (2020) DeepRhythm: exposing deepfakes with attentional visual heartbeat rhythms. In: Proceedings ACM multimedia conference
36. Raja K, Ferrara M, Franco A, Spreeuwers L, Batskos I, de Wit F, Gomez-Barrero M, Scherhag U, Fischer D, Venkatesh S, Singh JM, Li G, Bergeron L, Isadskiy S, Ramachandra R, Rathgeb C, Frings D, Seidel U, Knopjes F, Veldhuis R, Maltoni D, Busch C (2020) Morphing attack detection-database. Evaluation platform and benchmarking. IEEE Trans Inf Forensics Secur
37. Ranjan R, Patel VM, Chellappa R (2017) Hyperface: a deep multi-task learning framework for face detection, landmark localization, pose estimation, and gender recognition. IEEE Trans Pattern Anal Mach Intell 41(1):121–135

38. Rathgeb C, Drozdowski P, Busch C (2020) Makeup presentation attacks: review and detection performance benchmark. IEEE Access 8:224958–224973
39. Rathgeb C, Drozdowski P, Busch C (2021) Detection of makeup presentation attacks based on deep face representations. In: Proceedings international conference on pattern recognition
40. Rössler A, Cozzolino D, Verdoliva L, Riess C, Thies J, Nießner M (2019) FaceForensics++: learning to detect manipulated facial images. In: Proceedings IEEE/CVF international conference on computer vision
41. Sabir E, Cheng J, Jaiswal A, AbdAlmageed W, Masi I, Natarajan P (2019) Recurrent convolutional strategies for face manipulation detection in videos. In: Proceedings IEEE/CVF conference on computer vision and pattern recognition workshops
42. Soukupova T, Cech J (2016) Real-time eye blink detection using facial landmarks. In: Proceedings computer vision winter workshop
43. Sun K, Liu H, Ye Q, Liu J, Gao Y, Shao L, Ji R (2021) Domain general face forgery detection by learning to weight. In: Proceedings AAAI conference on artificial intelligence
44. Tan D, Nijholt A (2010) Brain-computer interfaces and human-computer interaction. In: Brain-computer interfaces. Springer, pp 3–19
45. Tolosana R, Romero-Tapiador S, Fierrez J, Vera-Rodriguez R (2020) DeepFakes evolution: analysis of facial regions and fake detection performance. In: Proceedings international conference on pattern recognition workshops
46. Tolosana R, Vera-Rodriguez R, Fierrez J, Morales A, Ortega-Garcia J (2020) DeepFakes and beyond: a survey of face manipulation and fake detection. Inf Fusion 64:131–148
47. Trinh L, Tsang M, Rambhatla S, Liu Y (2021) Interpretable and trustworthy deepfake detection via dynamic prototypes. In: Proceedings IEEE/CVF winter conference on applications of computer vision (WACV), pp 1973–1983
48. Yang X, Li Y, Lyu S (2019) Exposing deep fakes using inconsistent head poses. In: Proceedings IEEE international conference on acoustics, speech and signal processing

Chapter 13
Capsule-Forensics Networks for Deepfake Detection

Huy H. Nguyen, Junichi Yamagishi, and Isao Echizen

Abstract Several sophisticated convolutional neural network (CNN) architectures have been devised that have achieved impressive results in various domains. One downside of this success is the advent of attacks using deepfakes, a family of tools that enable anyone to use a personal computer to easily create fake videos of someone from a short video found online. Several detectors have been introduced to deal with such attacks. To achieve state-of-the-art performance, CNN-based detectors have usually been upgraded by increasing their depth and/or their width, adding more internal connections, or fusing several features or predicted probabilities from multiple CNNs. As a result, CNN-based detectors have become bigger, consume more memory and computation power, and require more training data. Moreover, there is concern about their generalizability to deal with unseen manipulation methods. In this chapter, we argue that our forensic-oriented capsule network overcomes these limitations and is more suitable than conventional CNNs to detect deepfakes. The superiority of our "Capsule-Forensics" network is due to the use of a pretrained feature extractor, statistical pooling layers, and a dynamic routing algorithm. This design enables the Capsule-Forensics network to outperform a CNN with a similar design and to be from 5 to 11 times smaller than a CNN with similar performance.

H. H. Nguyen (✉) · J. Yamagishi
The Graduate University for Advanced Studies, SOKENDAI and The National Institute of
Informatics, Tokyo, Japan
e-mail: nhhuy@nii.ac.jp

J. Yamagishi
e-mail: jyamagis@nii.ac.jp

I. Echizen
The National Institute of Informatics, The University of Tokyo,
and The Graduate University for Advanced Studies, SOKENDAI, Tokyo, Japan
e-mail: iechizen@nii.ac.jp

© The Author(s) 2022
C. Rathgeb et al. (eds.), *Handbook of Digital Face Manipulation and Detection*,
Advances in Computer Vision and Pattern Recognition,
https://doi.org/10.1007/978-3-030-87664-7_13

275

13.1   Introduction

Ever since the invention of photography, people have been interested in manipulating photographs, mainly to correct problems in the photos or to enhance them. Technology has advanced far beyond these basic manipulations and can now be used to change the identities of the subjects or alter their emotions. The advent of deep learning has enabled high-quality manipulated images and videos to be easily created. Moreover, the popularity of social media has enabled massive amounts of data, including personal information, news reports, images, and videos, to be created and shared. The consequence is that people with malicious intent can easily make use of these advanced technologies and data to create fake images and videos and then publish them widely on social networks.

The requirements for manipulating or synthesizing videos were dramatically simplified when it became possible to create forged videos from only a short video [22, 46] or even from a single ID photo [7] of the target subject. Suwajanakorn et al.'s mapping method [42] has enhanced the ability of manipulators to learn the mapping between speech and lip motion. State-of-the-art natural speech synthesizers can be used with Suwajanakorn's method to create a fake video of any person speaking anything. Deepfakes [3] exemplify this threat—an attacker with a personal computer and an appropriate tool can create videos of a person impersonating any other person. Deepfake videos have been posted on YouTube with the challenge being to spot them. In this chapter, we use the term "deepfake" to refer to this family of manipulation techniques, not to a particular one. Several examples of high-quality computer-generated images and deepfake ones are shown in Fig. 13.1.

Several countermeasures have been developed to detect fake images and videos. Automatic feature extraction using convolutional neural networks (CNNs) has dra-

Fig. 13.1 Example computer-generated and deepfake images. Images in top row are fully computer-generated (from Digital Emily Project [6], from Dexter Studios [2], and was generated using Style-GAN [21], respectively). Images in bottom row, left to right, were manipulated using deepfake [3], Face2Face [46], and Neural Textures [45] methods, respectively

matically improved detection performance [4, 36, 38]. Several methods are image-based [4, 36, 54] while others work only on videos [5, 27, 38] or on video with voice [24]. Although some video-based methods perform better than image-based ones, they are only applicable to particular kinds of attacks. For example, some of them [5, 27] may fail if the quality of the eye area is sufficiently good or the synchronization between the video and audio parts is sufficiently natural [25]. In this chapter, we limit our scope to image-based methods since our aim is to build a general detector that can work with both generated/manipulated images and videos and does not rely on any particular kind of attack.

Conventionally, the performance of a CNN can be improved by increasing its depth [16], its width [52], and/or the number of inner connections [19]. Another solution is to use multiple CNNs as is done in Zhou et al.'s two-stream network [54] or to use feature aggregation (feature fusion) or output fusion (ensemble). The fusion approach has been used in several competitions [13, 29]. This approach not only improves network performance on seen data but also improves network performance on unseen data. This has resulted in CNNs and groups of CNNs becoming bigger and thus consuming more memory and computation power. Moreover, they may need more training data, which are not always available when new attacks emerge. Rather than making the network bigger, we took a different approach: redesign it to make it more efficient in memory usage, detection accuracy, and generalization.

We previously reported "Capsule-Forensics" [32], a proof-of-concept capsule network [39] designed especially for detecting manipulated images and videos. In this work, we focused on explaining the theoretical aspect of Capsule-Forensics, which was not fully discussed in our previous work [32]. We hypothesized that the special design of the network makes it better able to detect deepfakes than a corresponding CNN while keeping the network smaller. This special design includes:

- A feature extractor, which is part of a pretrained image classification CNN, prevents the network from overfitting and improves its performance on both seen and unseen attacks.
- A statistical pooling layer, which is used in each primary capsule of the network, greatly reduces the number of parameters compared with the original capsule network while improving performance on deepfake detection.
- A dynamic routing algorithm produces better fusion than the traditional feature aggregation approach.

To sum up, our contribution is three-fold:

1. We provide a theoretical explanation of the Capsule-Forensics network on deepfake detection by verifying our hypothesis that its special design is the reason it performs better than the corresponding CNN version.
2. We visualize the activation of each primary capsule as well as the routing weights and thereby clarify which kind of information these capsules learn and how they agree on the final decision of the entire network. This is a step toward explainability of the Capsule-Forensics network.

3. We introduce small deepfake detection benchmarks that focuses on detection performance, number of parameters, and inference time for both seen and unseen data.

The rest of this chapter is structured as follows. We first describe work related to deepfakes, deepfake detection, and the challenges in deepfake detection. We also give some background on capsule networks. Next, we describe the Capsule-Forensics network. We also visualize the features the Capsule-Forensics network learns to understand the differences between it and a conventional capsule network, which learns the hierarchical relationships between object parts. Then, we describe several experiments we performed to test our hypothesis that the special design of the network makes it better able to detect deepfakes than a corresponding CNN while keeping the network smaller. Finally, we conclude by discussing the meaning of our results and mentioning future work.

13.2 Related Work

13.2.1 Deepfake Generation

Recent achievements demonstrate that deepfakes can reach a photo-realistic level. Thies et al. demonstrated that expression transfer for facial reenactment can be performed in real time [46]. Kim et al. demonstrated the transfer of a head pose along with facial movements from an actor to another person [22]. Similarly, Tripathy et al. devised a lightweight face reenactment method using a generative adversarial network (GAN) [47]. Nirkin et al. presented a face swapping method that does not require training on new faces [33], unlike the early deepfake methods [3]. Thies et al. combined the traditional graphics pipeline with learnable components to deal with imperfect 3D contents [45].

Work on deepfakes has gone beyond only the visual part. Suwajanakorn et al. presented a method for learning the mapping between speech and lip movements in which speech can also be synthesized, enabling creation of a full-function spoof video [42]. Fried et al. demonstrated that speech can be easily modified in any video in accordance with the intention of the manipulator while maintaining a seamless audio-visual flow [15]. Averbuch-Elor et al. addressed a different problem—converting still portraits into motion pictures expressing various emotions [7]. This work greatly simplified the requirements for attackers: simply acquire a picture of the victim (usually a profile picture on a social network or an ID photo). Zakharov et al. followed up by improving the quality of videos generated using only a few input images [53]. Vougioukas et al. raised the bar by introducing a method for animating a facial image from an audio track containing speech [48].

13.2.2 Deepfake Detection

The handcrafted steganalysis-based method developed by Fridrich and Kodovsky [14] was used in early efforts to detect manipulated images. Noise residuals extracted using handcrafted linear and nonlinear high-pass filters are fed into an ensemble classifier. This approach was later implemented in a CNN by Cozzolino et al. [12]. Transfer learning is a common choice when a CNN pretrained on the ImageNet dataset [37] is used [31, 36]. Nguyen et al. [31] used part of a pretrained VGG-19 network [41] as the feature extractor for their modular network while Rössler et al. finetuned the XceptionNet network [11] on a deepfake dataset. Afchar et al. utilized inception modules [43] to build a lightweight network [4] while Wang et al. utilized a dilated residual network [49]. Bayar and Stamm presented a new convolutional layer that helps a CNN adaptively learn manipulation detection features [10]. Zhou et al. proposed using a two-stream network in which one stream takes RGB input and the other takes steganalysis features and uses a triplet loss [54].

Videos provide more information than images for detection, especially when they contain sound. Li et al. used eye blinking as a feature to detect deepfakes [27] while Agarwal et al. used facial expressions and movements [5]. Sabir et al. used a recurrent neural network to additionally learn the temporal information [38]. Korshunov and Marcel used several approaches for lip-syncing and dubbing detection to detect fake videos [24].

In addition to binary classification, another major branch in digital media forensics is locating manipulated regions in images. Besides "pure" segmentation-based approaches [9, 30, 55], binary classification approaches are also applicable by using a sliding window to locate manipulated regions [31, 36]. From a different viewpoint, Li et al. introduced a method called face X-ray to detect the blending boundary between real and fake regions [26]. They noted that blending methods have not been advancing as rapidly as manipulation methods; therefore, focusing on blending methods makes the detector more robust against unseen manipulations.

Several standardized datasets have been constructed to support deepfake detection, including the FaceForensics++ dataset [36], the Google Deepfake Detection (DFD) dataset [1], the DeepFakeTIMIT dataset [25], the Celeb-DF dataset [28], the Deepfake Detection Challenge dataset [13], and the DeeperForensics dataset [20]. We focused on the FaceForensics++ and Google DFD datasets as they cover several well-known attacks, including Face2Face [46], FaceSwap [36], deepfake [3], and Neural Textures [45] attacks (examples are shown in Fig. 13.1). We focused on the image domain and treated videos as a set of separable frames.

13.2.3 Challenges in Deepfake Detection

There are several challenges in deepfake detection. Since deepfakes have altered faces, most deepfake detection methods need to first detect and crop the face. The success of this step depends on the performance of the face detection method. Most state-of-the-art deepfake datasets have annotated face regions, so researchers may assume that cropped faces are available without considering the face detector's performance. Another challenge is the generalizability of the detector when an advanced deepfake technique is introduced. Moreover, a large amount of appropriate training data may not be available when a new attack appears, so detectors using large networks may be difficult to train. Another challenge is gaining user trust by convincing them to accept the detection results. This requires visualizing the learned features and/or focused regions of the detectors.

The performance of general CNNs can usually be improved by increasing their depth, their width, and/or the number of inner connections. Multiple CNNs are commonly used for deepfake detection, especially in competitions [13, 29]. Fusion is often used in the multiple-CNN approach, including feature aggregation (feature fusion) and output fusion (ensemble). Consequently, these networks get bigger with more parameters, consuming more memory and computation power. Since a larger number of parameters usually requires more training data, dealing with new attacks is difficult. Our Capsule-Forensics network was designed to overcome these limitations.

13.2.4 Capsule Networks

"Capsule network" is not a new term as it was first introduced in 2011 by Hinton et al. [17]. They argued that CNNs have limited ability to learn the hierarchical relationships between object parts and introduced a more robust architecture comprising several "capsules." However, they initially faced the same problem affecting CNNs—limited hardware performance—and the lack of effective algorithms, which prevented practical application of capsule networks. CNNs thus remained dominant in this research field.

These problems were overcome when the dynamic routing algorithm [39] and its variant—the expectation-maximization routing algorithm [18]—were introduced. These breakthroughs enabled capsule networks to achieve better performance and outperform CNNs on object classification tasks [8, 18, 39, 50, 51]. The agreements between low- and high-level capsules, which encode the hierarchical relationships between objects and their parts with pose information, enable a capsule network to preserve more information than a CNN while using only a fraction of the data used by a CNN.

13.3 Capsule-Forensics

13.3.1 Why Capsule-Forensics?

To overcome the weakness of conventional CNNs, we adapted the capsule network concept [39], which was originally designed for computer vision tasks, to make it well suited for deepfake detection. We named our adapted network "Capsule-Forensics." Its design takes advantage of transfer learning by using part of a pretrained CNN (trained on the ImageNet dataset [37]) as the feature extractor. This helps the network achieve high performance and have better generalizability. The feature aggregation used in conventional CNNs was replaced with a modified version of the dynamic routing algorithm. The use of a statistical pooling layer in each primary capsule reduces the number of parameters while improving performance. The next two sections describe the processing flow and architecture. We performed several experiments to verify the novelty of this design. The results are presented and discussed in the Evaluation section.

13.3.2 Overview

The Capsule-Forensics based method comprises three processing units, as illustrated in Fig. 13.2. The task performed in the pre-processing unit depends on the input. If the input is video, the first step is to separate the frames. A face detection algorithm is used to crop the facial area(s). The cropped face(s) are sent to the Capsule-Forensics unit for classification. The detection result(s) are sent to the post-processing unit, which works in accordance with the pre-processing one. If the input is an image, nothing is done here. If the input is video, the scores of all frames are averaged. This average score is the final output.

13.3.3 Architecture

The Capsule-Forensics network includes a feature extractor, several primary capsules, and two output capsules ("real" and "fake"), as illustrated in Fig. 13.3. For

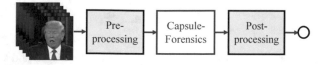

Fig. 13.2 Capsule-Forensics unit processing

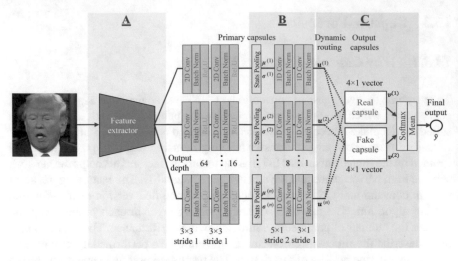

Fig. 13.3 Capsule-Forensics architecture. Blocks A, B, and C contain tunable hyperparameters

simplification, we use the same architecture for all primary capsules. Since we use random weight initialization, their behaviors are not the same after training. The number of primary capsules is a hyperparameter.

Each primary capsule has three parts: a 2D convolutional part, a statistical pooling layer, and a 1D convolutional part. The statistical pooling layer has been proven to be effective in detecting computer-generated images [31, 35] by learning the statistical differences between the real and computer-generated images. For deepfakes, when a part of a face image is swapped, the swapped face region may have different textures and color patterns. The blending region between the swapped face region and the remaining original face region may also contain artifacts. Thus, the statistics such as mean and variance of each filter are useful for differentiating the swapped region from the original one. Moreover, they help reduce the number of parameters by omitting features that are not useful for deepfake detection.

The mean and variance of each filter are calculated in the statistical pooling layer.

- Mean:

$$\mu_k = \frac{1}{H \times W} \sum_{i=1}^{H} \sum_{j=1}^{W} I_{kij}$$

- Variance:

$$\sigma_k^2 = \frac{1}{H \times W - 1} \sum_{i=1}^{H} \sum_{j=1}^{W} (I_{kij} - \mu_k)^2,$$

where k is the layer index, H and W are, respectively, the height and width of the filter, and I is a two-dimensional filter array.

The output of the statistical layer goes through the following 1D convolutional part. Then it is dynamically routed to the output capsules. The final result is calculated on the basis of the activation of the output capsules. The algorithm is discussed in detail in the next section. For binary classification, there are two output capsules, as shown in Fig. 13.3. Multi-class classification could be performed by adding more output capsules, as discussed in Sect. 13.4.3.

The Capsule-Forensics source code has been published at https://github.com/nii-yamagishilab/Capsule-Forensics-v2.

13.3.4   Dynamic Routing Algorithm

Different manipulation methods use different face regions, generating models, and blending algorithms. Therefore, each primary capsule extracts different features depending on the manipulation method, and they may work better on a particular manipulation than on others. Furthermore, since the weights of the primary capsules are initialized differently in training, the capsules learn different features for the same input. These features need to be fused correctly to predict whether the input is real or fake. For a capsule network, this fusion is done dynamically using a dynamic routing algorithm. The "agreement" between all primary capsules is calculated and routed to the appropriate output capsule (real or fake for binary classification). An example of the routing weight vectors is visualized in Fig. 13.4. Since the primary capsules may make different judgments and some of them may be wrong, this algorithm is designed to find a consensus. The output probabilities are determined on the basis of the activations of the output capsules.

Let us call the output vector of each primary capsule $\mathbf{u}^{(i)} \in \mathbb{R}^k$ and each output vector capsule $\mathbf{v}^{(j)} \in \mathbb{R}^l$. There are m primary capsules and n output capsules. $\mathbf{W}^{(i)} \in \mathbb{R}^{l \times k}$ is the matrix used to route an $\mathbf{u}^{(i)}$ to all $\mathbf{v}^{(j)}$, and r is the number of iterations. The dynamic routing algorithm is shown in Algorithm 1. A simple example is presented in the Appendix.

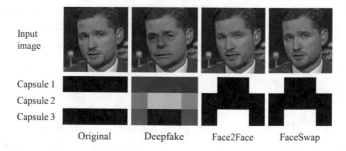

Fig. 13.4 Visualization of the routing matrix $\mathbf{C}^{(2)\top}$ used to route the outputs of three primary capsules to fake output capsule. Face2Face and FaceSwap methods are graphical based, so their routing weights are similar. Deepfake method is deep learning based, so its routing weights are different from the two graphical-based manipulation methods

---

Algorithm 1 Dynamic routing between capsules.

procedure ROUTING($\mathbf{u}^{(i)}, \mathbf{W}^{(i)}, r$)
    $\widehat{\mathbf{W}}^{(i)} \leftarrow \mathbf{W}^{(i)} + \text{rand}(\text{size}(\mathbf{W}^{(i)}))$
    $\widehat{\mathbf{u}}^{(i)} \leftarrow \widehat{\mathbf{W}}^{(i)}\text{squash}(\mathbf{u}^{(i)})$ $\triangleright\ \widehat{\mathbf{u}}^{(i)} \in \mathbb{R}^l$
    $\widehat{\mathbf{u}}^{(i)} \leftarrow \text{dropout}(\widehat{\mathbf{u}}^{(i)})$
    for all output capsules j **do**
        $\mathbf{B}^{(j)} \leftarrow 0$ $\triangleright\ \mathbf{B}^{(j)} \in \mathbb{R}^{l \times m}$
    for r iterations **do**
        for all output capsules j and all vector elements **do**
            $(c_{\_,1}^{(j)}, c_{\_,2}^{(j)}, \ldots, c_{\_,m}^{(j)}) \leftarrow \text{softmax}(b_{\_,1}^{(j)}, b_{\_,2}^{(j)}, \ldots, b_{\_,m}^{(j)})$
        for all output capsules j **do** $\mathbf{s}^{(j)} \leftarrow \sum_i^m \mathbf{c}_{:,i}^{(j)} \odot \widehat{\mathbf{u}}^{(i)}$
        for all output capsules j **do** $\mathbf{v}^{(j)} \leftarrow \text{squash}(\mathbf{s}^{(j)})$
        for all input capsules i and output capsules j **do**
            $\mathbf{B}^{(j)} \leftarrow \mathbf{B}^{(j)} + \left[\widehat{\mathbf{u}}^{(1)}\ \widehat{\mathbf{u}}^{(2)} \ldots \widehat{\mathbf{u}}^{(m)}\right] \odot \mathbf{v}^{(j)}$
    return $\mathbf{v}^{(j)}$

We slightly improved the algorithm of Sabour et al. [39] by introducing two regularizations: adding random noise to the routing matrix and adding a dropout operation. They are used **only during training** to reduce overfitting. Their effectiveness is discussed in the Evaluation section. Furthermore, a squash function (Eq. 13.1) is applied to $\mathbf{u}^{(i)}$ before routing to normalize it, which helps stabilize the training process. The squash function is used to scale the vector magnitude to unit length.

$$squash(\mathbf{u}) = \frac{\|\mathbf{u}\|_2^2}{1 + \|\mathbf{u}\|_2^2} \frac{\mathbf{u}}{\|\mathbf{u}\|_2} \tag{13.1}$$

In practice, to stabilize the training process, the random noise should be sampled from a normal distribution ($\mathcal{N}(0, 0.01)$), the dropout ratio should not be greater than 0.05 (we used 0.05 in all experiments), and two iterations ($r = 2$) should be used in the dynamic routing algorithm. The two regularizations are used along with random weight initialization to increase the level of randomness, which helps the primary capsules learn with different parameters.

To calculate predicted label $\widehat{y}$, we apply the softmax function to each dimension of the output capsule vectors to achieve stronger polarization rather than simply using the length of the output capsules [39]. The final results are the means of all softmax outputs:

$$\widehat{\mathbf{y}} = \frac{1}{l} \sum_i^l \text{softmax}(v_i^{(1)}, v_i^{(2)}, \ldots, v_i^{(n)}), \tag{13.2}$$

where $\widehat{\mathbf{y}}$ is the predicted probabilities vector. Since there is no reconstruction in the Capsule-Forensics method, we simply use the cross-entropy loss function and the Adam optimizer [23] to optimize the network.

13.3.5 Visualization

To illustrate how Capsule-Forensics works, we used a Capsule-Forensics network with three primary capsules trained on the FaceForensics++ database [36]. For visualization, we applied and modified an open-source tool [34] implementing the guided back propagation algorithm [40]. To visualize each primary capsule in this way, we chose the latent features extracted before the statistical pooling layers since they still had the 2D structure.

The activations of each capsule and of the whole network are illustrated in Fig. 13.5. The differences in activation among capsules and between each capsule and the whole network are also shown. The regions of interest mainly include the eyes, nose, mouth region, and facial contours. Some capsules missed some of these regions, and some failed to detect the manipulated input (i.e., the third capsule in Fig. 13.6). Nevertheless, the final results mostly focused on the important regions detected by all capsules due to agreement driven by the dynamic routing algorithm between the other two capsules. A CNN using only the third primary capsule would fail to detect the manipulated input.

The behavior of the Capsule-Forensics network for the deepfake detection problem differs from that of the original capsule network for the inverse graphics problem, in which the focus is on the spatial hierarchies between simple and complex objects [17, 18, 39]. In the deepfake detection problem, abnormal appearances are the key features, so each primary capsule is designed to capture them and communicate its findings to the other capsules. This behavior is similar to that of jurors during a trial, and the consensus judgment is the final detection result.

13.4 Evaluation

We conducted several experiments to test the detection performance of the Capsule-Forensics network. After describing the datasets and metrics we used (Sect. 13.4.1 and 13.4.2), we discuss the effectiveness of the improvements introduced in this chapter in comparison with our previous work [32]: larger input size, more primary capsules, and dropout in the dynamic routing algorithm (Sect. 13.4.3). We then compare several candidate feature extractors (Sect. 13.4.4) and evaluate the effectiveness of the statistical pooling layer used in each primary capsule (Sect. 13.4.5). Finally, we compare the detection performance of the improved Capsule-Forensics network with that of a CNN on both seen and unseen attacks (Sect. 13.4.6 and 13.4.7, respectively). For the CNNs, we used the corresponding version of the Capsule-Forensics network using feature aggregation instead of the dynamic routing algorithm, the multi-task learning network [30], the XceptionNet version used in FaceForensics++ work [36], and the EfficientNet network [44]. Among them, the multi-task learning network is a generative classifier while the rest are discriminative classifiers. For the multi-task learning network, in addition to ground-truth labels, segmentation masks

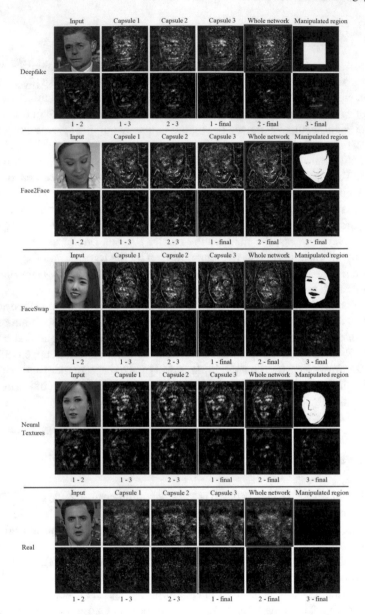

Fig. 13.5 Activation of three capsules and entire Capsule-Forensics network (columns 2, 3, 4, and 5, respectively) on images created using deepfake [3] (row 1), Face2Face [46] (row 3), FaceSwap [36] (row 5), and Neural Textures [45] (row 7) methods and on a real image. Column 6 shows the manipulated regions corresponding to the manipulated images in column 1. The first three columns of rows 2, 4, 6, 8, and 10 show the differences between the activations of capsules 1 and 2, 1 and 3, and 2 and 3 on the corresponding row above, respectively. The three last columns in order show the differences between the activations of capsules 1, 2, and 3 and the activation of the whole network

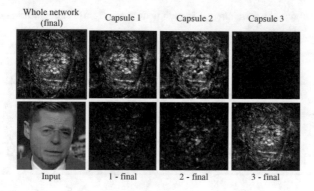

Fig. 13.6 Example case in which one capsule did not work correctly. First row shows activation of whole network and of three capsules. Second row from left to right shows input image and differences between activation of each capsule and of whole network. Although capsule 3 failed to detect manipulated image, final result was correct due to agreement between other two capsules

of the manipulated regions are needed for training. When testing, since segmenting manipulated regions is beyond the scope of this work, we used only its encoder part to perform binary classification. For XceptionNet, we modified its fully connected layer and trained it in two phases. For EfficientNet [44], which recently received a high score in the Deepfake Detection Challenge, we used the B4 version (denoted as EfficientNet-B4) which requires an input size of 380 × 380 pixels. The larger versions (B5, B6, and B7) require larger inputs and have more parameters, making it impossible to train them on a single-GPU machine.

For simplicity, we used only multi-class classification to compare the original setting in our previous work [32] with the new setting in this work. For the remaining experiments, we tested only binary classification. Except for the one discussed in Sect. 13.4.7, all the evaluations were for performance on seen attacks.

13.4.1   Datasets

We used videos from the FaceForensics++ dataset [36], supplemented with the Google DFD dataset [1]. We used all three levels of compression (none, moderate, and high) and mixed them together to make multiple compression datasets for our experiments. For training, we used version 1 of the FaceForensics++ dataset including original videos and three corresponding manipulated videos created by deepfake [3], Face2Face [46], and FaceSwap [36] methods. For testing, two scenarios were used: seen attacks and unseen attacks. For seen attacks, we used a test set from version 1 of the FaceForensics++ dataset. For unseen attacks, we used test videos created using Neural Textures [45] (unseen method), which was added in

Table 13.1 Configuration of training, validation, and test sets from FaceForensics++ dataset version 1 (for seen attacks) [36]

Type	Training set	Validation set	Test set
Real	720×3 vids $72,000 \times 3$ imgs	140×3 vids $1,400 \times 3$ imgs	140×3 vids $1,400 \times 3$ imgs
Deepfake	720×3 vids $72,000 \times 3$ imgs	140×3 vids $1,400 \times 3$ imgs	140×3 vids $1,400 \times 3$ imgs
Face2Face	720×3 vids $72,000 \times 3$ imgs	140×3 vids $1,400 \times 3$ imgs	140×3 vids $1,400 \times 3$ imgs
FaceSwap	720×3 vids $72,000 \times 3$ imgs	140×3 vids $1,400 \times 3$ imgs	140×3 vids $1,400 \times 3$ imgs

Table 13.2 Configuration of test sets for unseen attacks created using Neural Textures method [45] and Google DFD dataset [1]

Type	Neural textures (unseen method)	Google DFD dataset (unseen data)
Real	0 vids 0 imgs	140×3 vids $1,400 \times 3$ imgs
Fakes	358×3 vids $3,580 \times 3$ imgs	$3,065 \times 3$ vids $30,650 \times 3$ imgs

version 2 of the FaceForensics++ dataset, and the entire Google DFD dataset [1] (unseen data).

We took the first 100 frames of the input video for the training set and the first 10 frames for the validation and test sets. FaceForensics++ dataset version 1 (for seen attacks) was divided into a training set, a validation set, and a test set, as shown in Table 13.1. The test sets for unseen attacks are shown in Table 13.2.

13.4.2 Metrics

We used four metrics in our evaluation:

- Classification accuracy $= \frac{TP+TN}{TP+TN+FP+FN}$, where TP, TN, FP, and FN are true positive, true negative, false positive, and false negative, respectively.
- Equal error rate (EER): common value when false positive rate (FPR) equals false negative rate (FNR). FPR $= \frac{FP}{N}$ (number of false positives divided by number of negatives). FNR $= \frac{FN}{P}$ (number of false negatives divided by number of positives).
- Half total error rate (HTER): HTER $= \frac{FPR+FNR}{2}$.
- Attack presentation classification error rate (APCER): "proportion of attack presentations using the same PAI species incorrectly classified as bona fide presentations in a specific scenario."[1]

---

[1] ISO/IEC 30107-3 definition. Accessed at https://www.iso.org/obp/ui/#iso:std:iso-iec:19989:-1: ed-1:v1:en:term:3.1.

The thresholds used to determine whether the classification outputs were real or fake were selected on the basis of the EERs calculated for the development sets.

13.4.3 Effect of Improvements

In the first experiment, we measured the effectiveness of the improvements introduced here: larger input size, more primary capsules, and dropout in the dynamic routing algorithm. Since Capsule-Forensics is not limited to binary classification, we also evaluated its multi-class classification ability by changing the number of output capsules, from "Real" and "Fake" capsules to "Real," "Deepfake," "Face2Face," and "FaceSwap" capsules. This modification is obvious and did not require substantial changes to the network architecture.

As shown in Table 13.3, using larger images improved performance substantially as expected. The effect of random noise was limited. In our previous work [32], most of the training sets were small, so random noise made a substantial contribution. In this work, we used the first 100 frames instead of the first 10 for the training set, so the set was ten times larger. Although the random noise did not result in improvement in all cases, it still played an important role in reducing the HTER when combined with dropout and increased the accuracy of multi-class classification. Increasing the number of primary capsules also helped improve performance. The combination of all three improvements achieved the best performance for both binary and multi-class classification. We refer to this combination as "new setting" in Table 13.3 to distinguish it from the "original setting" (the setting used in our previous work [32]).

13.4.4 Feature Extractor Comparison

The feature extractor is an important part of the Capsule-Forensics network (block **A** in Fig. 13.3). Rather than training a simple CNN from scratch along with the other parts of the network, as is done in the traditional capsule network approach [39], we used part of a pretrained CNN (trained on the ImageNet dataset [37]). We selected three commonly used extractors as candidates:

- VGG-19 [41]: used from the beginning until the third max pooling layer.
- ResNet-50 [16]: used from the beginning until the end of the "conv3_x" layer.
- XceptionNet [11]: used from the beginning until the end of the first block of its "middle flow."

In addition to evaluating these candidates, we evaluated a simple CNN with three convolutional layers as the feature extractor, like the ones used in conventional capsule networks. The CNN was trained along with the other parts of the Capsule-Forensics network. In addition, we also fine tuned the pretrained feature extractors

Table 13.3 Performance of Capsule-Forensics with original [32] and new settings introduced here

Input size	No. of capsules	Random noise	Dropout	Binary classification accuracy (%)	Binary classification HTER (%)	Multi-class classification accuracy (%)
Original setting [32]:						
128 × 128	3	No	No	87.45	15.41	85.89
128 × 128	3	Yes	No	88.57	15.35	87.12
New setting:						
300 × 300	3	No	No	89.88	11.28	87.51
300 × 300	3	Yes	No	90.86	11.29	87.54
300 × 300	10	No	No	91.61	11.52	88.51
300 × 300	10	Yes	No	91.32	12.07	89.98
300 × 300	3	No	Yes	91.33	12.37	89.19
300 × 300	3	Yes	Yes	91.19	11.93	88.44
300 × 300	10	No	Yes	92.17	10.70	90.51
300 × 300	**10**	**Yes**	**Yes**	**92.00**	**10.64**	**91.22**

(indicated by "FT" after their names) to check whether fine-tuning helps improve overall performance. We tested the extractors on both the original and new settings except for the simple CNN. It was tested on only the original setting since training it on the new setting would consume a much greater amount of memory and take much longer. The results are shown in Table 13.4.

All the extractors performed better using the new setting. Fine-tuning did not help much when using the new setting. Besides reducing memory usage and shortening training time, using pretrained feature extractors resulted in better performance than using a CNN extractor trained from scratch. These results support our hypothesis that using a pretrained feature extractor contributes to the superiority of our Capsule-Forensics network.

The ResNet-50 based feature extractor has the smallest number of parameters, making it about ten times smaller than the VGG-19 and XceptionNet ones. The VGG-19 extractor with the new setting achieved the highest classification accuracy and had the lowest HTER. For dealing with seen manipulations, if performance is more important than the number of parameters, VGG-19 is the best choice. Otherwise, ResNet-50 is more suitable.

Table 13.4 Performance (in %) of feature extractors with and without fine-tuning (FT) with both original and new settings

Feature extractor	Training accuracy	Test accuracy	Test HTER	No. of parameters
Original setting [32]:				
Simple CNN	98.97	83.36	25.42	371,712
VGG-19	99.81	88.57	15.35	2,325,568
VGG-19 FT	99.54	90.08	12.49	2,325,568
ResNet-50	99.60	88.21	16.09	225,344
ResNet-50 FT	99.69	87.45	13.60	225,344
XceptionNet	99.58	85.52	19.10	2,720,736
XceptionNet FT	99.45	85.41	18.91	2,720,736
New setting:				
VGG-19	99.83	**92.00**	**10.64**	2,325,568
VGG-19 FT	99.63	90.98	13.40	2,325,568
ResNet-50	99.17	90.59	14.60	**225,344**
ResNet-50 FT	99.69	90.14	14.94	225,344
XceptionNet	99.79	90.42	13.35	2,720,736
XceptionNet FT	99.84	91.39	10.85	2,720,736

13.4.5   Effect of Statistical Pooling Layers

In another experiment, we compared the performance and size of two versions of the Capsule-Forensics network: one using and one not using a statistical pooling layer for each primary capsule (block **B** in Fig. 13.3). Previous work [31, 35] suggested that using a statistical pooling layer is effective for detecting computer-generated images. For the version without statistical pooling layers, we replaced the 1D convolutional layers with 2D ones and added an adaptive average pooling layer at the end of each primary capsule. We hypothesized that the statistical pooling layer helps filter out unnecessary information, i.e., information that is not relevant to deepfake detection. Therefore, using a statistical pooling layer in each primary capsule helps reduce feature size and improve performance. Moreover, reducing the feature size results in a smaller routing matrix, which uses less memory and computation power. We used the VGG-19 feature extractor in this experiment. The results are shown in Table 13.5.

With both the original and new settings, using statistical pooling layers greatly improved classification accuracy and reduced the HTER for the seen test set. Moreover, using them reduced the number of parameters by 400%. These results support our hypothesis that using statistical pooling layers contributes to the superiority of our Capsule-Forensics network. An interesting observation from the results is that the number of parameters was independent of the input size (128×128 in the original setting and 300×300 in the new setting). This is because both the statistical and adaptive average pooling layers were designed to deal with variations in input size.

Table 13.5 Performance (in %) with and without statistical pooling (SP) layer in primary capsules for both original and new settings with VGG-19 feature extractor. (Number of parameters does not include number for feature extractor.)

Settings	Test accuracy	Test HTER	No. of parameters
Original setting [32]:			
With SP layer	88.57	15.35	1,571,070
Without SP layer	83.51	15.78	6,689,280
New setting:			
With SP layer	92.00	10.64	1,571,070
Without SP layer	87.70	11.65	6,689,280

13.4.6 Capsule-Forensics Network Versus CNNs: Seen Attacks

In a third experiment, we compared the performance of the dynamic routing algorithm used in the Capsule-Forensics network with that of traditional feature aggregation (block **C** in Fig. 13.3). The VGG-19 feature extractor was used in both cases. We also evaluated the performance of the multi-task learning network [30], the XceptionNet network, and the EfficientNet-B4 network [44]. It is important to note that this version of XceptionNet differs from the one used in our feature extractor (Sect. 13.4.4), which was pretrained on the ImageNet dataset [37], with only part of it used. Since the training dataset was imbalanced (the number of fake samples was three time the number of real samples), we additionally evaluated the effect of using a weighted softmax function during training. The experiment results are shown in Table 13.6.

The effect of using a weighted softmax function is not clear. Since the dataset was not heavily imbalanced, this result is reasonable. Although having the smallest number of parameters, the multi-task learning network had the worst performance. The dynamic routing algorithm helped the Capsule-Forensics network achieve higher performance, especially with the new setting. The numbers of parameters for the Capsule-Forensics network and the corresponding CNN using feature aggregation were almost the same, whereas the numbers for the EfficientNet-B4 and the XceptionNet networks were about 4.5 to 5.3 times larger. Moreover, the test accuracy of the Capsule-Forensics network and the Efficient-B4 network was almost the same. The large input size of the EfficientNet-B4 network (380×380 vs 300×300) might be the reason for its lower HTER.

In addition to the results on the mixed compression test set shown in Table 13.6, we also broke it down into three compression levels, as shown in Table 13.7. There were no substantial differences between the performances of Capsule-Forensics, Xception-Net, and EfficientNet-B4. Their performances were degraded from no compression to moderate compression to high compression. With their average accuracy about 84%, detecting highly compressed deepfake videos was still challenging when most of the deepfake artifacts were erased by the compression algorithm. Capsule-Forensics and

Table 13.6 Performance (in %) of Capsule-Forensics using dynamic routing algorithm, its corresponding CNN using the traditional feature aggregation approach, and the other baselines on seen attacks. Number of parameters is for entire network, including feature extractor

Settings	Test accuracy	Test HTER	No. of parameters
Original setting [32]:			
Dynamic routing	88.57	15.35	2,796,889
Feature aggregation	86.26	15.15	2,798,059
New setting:			
Dynamic routing	**92.00**	10.64	**3,896,638**
Feature aggregation	91.82	11.51	3,903,328
Multi-task learning [30]	73.08	26.30	148,200
XceptionNet [36]	90.73	9.91	20,811,050
EfficientNet-B4 [44]	**92.82**	**8.67**	17,552,202
Using weighted softmax:			
Dynamic routing	**92.21**	10.91	**3,896,638**
Feature aggregation	91.75	10.68	3,903,328
XceptionNet [36]	91.83	10.14	20,811,050
EfficientNet-B4 [44]	91.49	**8.64**	17,552,202

Table 13.7 Performance (in %) of Capsule-Forensics and other classifiers at three levels of compression on the FaceForensics++ dataset.

Detector	No compression		Moderate compression		High Compression	
	Accuracy	HTER	Accuracy	HTER	Accuracy	HTER
Capsule-Forensics	97.27	3.87	94.62	6.42	84.11	21.64
Multi-task learning [30]	81.12	17.80	69.23	25.94	68.86	35.19
XceptionNet [36]	96.12	4.80	92.82	7.60	83.25	17.33
EfficientNet-B4 [44]	98.37	2.50	95.50	4.88	84.96	18.62

EfficientNet handled the moderately compressed deepfake videos quite well, with only about 3% degradation in accuracy compared with the uncompressed ones.

Using the Capsule-Forensics network can save a large amount of memory and computation power compared with the amounts used by CNNs while maintaining high performance even for compressed videos. This is important for applications integrating a presentation attack detector into an Internet of things or a handheld device that does not have powerful hardware to prevent unauthorized facial authentication. The Capsule-Forensics network demonstrated it effectiveness against this kind of attack [32].

Table 13.8 Performance (in %) of three versions of Capsule-Forensics network, two versions of the corresponding CNN, and other baselines on unseen attacks. Number of parameters is for **entire network**, including feature extractor

Detectors	Neural Textures		Google DFD dataset		No. of parameters
	Accuracy	APCER	Accuracy	HTER	
Capsule-Forensics (VGG-19)	24.33	75.67	44.51	40.29	3,896,638
Capsule-Forensics (ResNet-50)	**37.93**	**62.07**	**64.98**	40.89	**1,796,414**
Capsule-Forensics (XceptionNet FT)	31.38	68.62	55.73	38.30	4,007,673
Feature aggregation (VGG-19)	28.81	71.19	58.09	38.70	3,903,328
Feature aggregation (ResNet-50)	24.00	76.00	62.48	37.70	1,803,104
Multi-task learning [30]	**44.69**	**55.31**	**78.74**	42.21	**148,200**
XceptionNet [36]	26.79	73.21	47.29	40.37	20,811,050
EfficientNet-B4 [44]	31.55	68.45	58.63	**34.23**	17,552,202

13.4.7 Capsule-Forensics Network Versus CNNs: Unseen Attacks

Detecting unseen attacks is a difficult problem in deepfake detection, especially for machine-learning-based detectors. When the data distribution changes, the learned features, and decision boundaries are usually no longer correct. Furthermore, large networks with a large number of parameters tend to memorize the training data, especially when the data amount is small. We expected that the Capsule-Forensics network can be better generalized than large networks thanks to the statistical pooling operation and dynamic routings of the primary capsules. To test this, we performed one last experiment in which we tested the detectors on a challenging unseen manipulation method, Neural Textures [45]. It is unlike any of the methods normally used to create seen datasets. We also tested the detectors on a different large deepfake dataset, the Google DFD dataset. We evaluated three new versions of the Capsule-Forensics network with different feature extractors (VGG-19, ResNet-50 (lightweight) and fine-tuned XceptionNet) and with two versions of a CNN using feature aggregation (with VGG-19 and ResNet-50 feature extractors), the multi-task learning network [30], the XceptionNet network [36], and the EfficientNet-B4 network [44].

As shown in Table 13.8, all the detectors performed poorly on the Neural Textures method, with APCERs greater than 50%. The three best detectors on seen attacks (Capsule-Forensics using VGG-19, XceptionNet, and EfficientNet-B4—which are discriminative classifiers) had the worst performances on this method. The multi-task

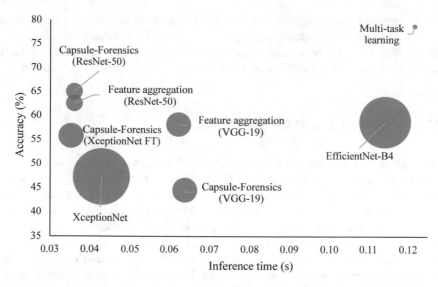

Fig. 13.7 Comparison between several versions of Capsule-Forensics network and CNNs for classification accuracy, inference time, and model size on Google DFD dataset [1]

learning network (which is a generative classifier) achieved the best results, followed by the lightweight Capsule-Forensics network using the ResNet-50 feature extractor. The performances of all detectors were slightly better on the Google DFD dataset. The Capsule-Forensics network using ResNet-50 again had the second highest accuracy, below the multi-task learning network. Since the multi-task learning network was specially designed to deal with unseen attacks, it was able to beat all the other detectors. However, its drawback is poor performance on seen attacks, as seen in the previous section.

Figure 13.7 shows a comparison on the classification accuracy, inference time (for one image), and model size of all detectors on the Google DFD dataset [1]. All tests were done using a NVIDIA DGX Station machine. The Capsule-Forensics network using the ResNet-50 feature extractor and its corresponding CNN using feature aggregation had the second smallest sizes and were the second fastest detectors. They were a bit slower than the Capsule-Forensics network using the XceptionNet feature extractor. Due to the design of the VGG-19 network, detectors using it as the feature extractor have the longest inference times (about twice the shortest times). The XceptionNet-based detector had the largest size but had limited detection accuracy. The EfficientNet-B4-based detector and the multi-task learning detector were the two slowest ones. It is important to note that we measured only the inference time of the encoder part of the multi-task learning detector for the binary classification task. Although it has fewer parameters than the other detectors, some memory-related operations slowed it down.

Although having limited performance on unseen attacks, this experiment demonstrated that the Capsule-Forensics network is better able to detect deepfakes than

CNNs. Between the two versions of the Capsule-Forensics network, if performance on seen attacks is more important, using VGG-19 as the feature extractor is the better choice. If performance on unseen attacks is more important, or a lightweight and fast network is needed, using ResNet-50 as the feature extractor is the better choice.

13.5 Conclusion and Future Work

Our experiments demonstrated that the Capsule-Forensics network is better able to detect deepfakes than conventional CNNs. Its use of a pretrained feature extractor, statistical pooling layers, and a dynamic routing algorithm enables it to achieve better performance with fewer parameters than corresponding CNNs. Furthermore, it has better performance than other discriminative classifiers on unseen manipulations, although further improvement is needed. Visualization of the activation of each capsule enables the learned features to be analyzed. These promising results and the understanding gained from the analysis should lead to further research on and development of capsule networks, not only for digital forensics but also for many other applications.

Future work includes enabling the Capsule-Forensics network to use temporal information to detect fake videos and improving its generalizability (in other words, reducing the gap between discriminative classifiers and generative classifiers). Moreover, deepfake datasets mostly contain images and videos containing only one or two people. In reality, deepfake methods can be applied to a crowd; therefore, deepfake detection in the wild is also an important research direction.

Acknowledgements This work was partially supported by JSPS KAKENHI Grants JP16H06302, JP18H04120, JP21H04907, JP20K23355, and JP21K18023 and by JST CREST Grants JPMJCR18A6 and JPMJCR20D3, including the AIP challenge program, Japan.

13.6 Appendix

This appendix presents a simple example of the dynamic routing algorithm shown in Algorithm 1 with three ($m = 3$) primary capsules $\mathbf{u}^{(i)} \in \mathbb{R}^k$, $i = 1..3$ and two ($n = 2$) output capsules $\mathbf{v}^{(j)} \in \mathbb{R}^l$, $j = 1..2$. All equations are written out in full.

There are three routing matrices corresponding to the three primary capsules, each represented by

$$\widehat{\mathbf{W}}^{(i)} = \mathbf{W}^{(i)} + \mathbf{N} \ \forall i$$

$$= \begin{bmatrix} w_{1,1}^{(i)} & w_{1,2}^{(i)} & \cdots & w_{1,k}^{(i)} \\ w_{2,1}^{(i)} & w_{2,2}^{(i)} & \cdots & w_{2,k}^{(i)} \\ \vdots & \vdots & \ddots & \vdots \\ w_{l,1}^{(i)} & w_{l,2}^{(i)} & \cdots & w_{l,k}^{(i)} \end{bmatrix} + \begin{bmatrix} n_{1,1} & n_{1,2} & \cdots & n_{1,k} \\ n_{2,1} & n_{2,2} & \cdots & 2,k \\ \vdots & \vdots & \ddots & \vdots \\ n_{l,1} & n_{1,2} & \cdots & n_{l,k} \end{bmatrix},$$

with $\widehat{\mathbf{W}}^{(i)} \in \mathbb{R}^{l \times k}, \mathbf{W}^{(i)} \in \mathbb{R}^{l \times k}, \mathbf{N}^{(i)} \in \mathbb{R}^{l \times k}, \mathbf{N}^{(i)} \sim \mathcal{N}(0, 0.01)$.

The next steps are to process $\mathbf{u}^{(i)}$ to form $\widehat{\mathbf{u}}^{(i)}$:

$$\widehat{\mathbf{u}}^{(i)} = \begin{bmatrix} \widehat{u}_1^{(i)} \\ \widehat{u}_2^{(i)} \\ \vdots \\ \widehat{u}_l^{(i)} \end{bmatrix} = \widehat{\mathbf{W}}^{(i)} \text{squash}(\mathbf{u}^{(i)}) = \begin{bmatrix} \widehat{w}_{1,1}^{(i)} & \widehat{w}_{1,2}^{(i)} & \cdots & \widehat{w}_{1,k}^{(i)} \\ \widehat{w}_{2,1}^{(i)} & \widehat{w}_{2,2}^{(i)} & \cdots & \widehat{w}_{2,k}^{(i)} \\ \vdots & \vdots & \ddots & \vdots \\ \widehat{w}_{l,1}^{(i)} & \widehat{w}_{l,2}^{(i)} & \cdots & \widehat{w}_{l,k}^{(i)} \end{bmatrix} \text{squash} \left(\begin{bmatrix} u_1^{(i)} \\ u_2^{(i)} \\ \vdots \\ u_k^{(i)} \end{bmatrix} \right),$$

with $\mathbf{u}^{(i)} \in \mathbb{R}^k, \widehat{\mathbf{u}}^{(i)} \in \mathbb{R}^l$.

$$\widehat{\mathbf{u}}^{(i)} \leftarrow \text{dropout}(\widehat{\mathbf{u}}^{(i)}).$$

Then, two matrices $\mathbf{B}^{(1)}, \mathbf{B}^{(2)} \in \mathbb{R}^{l \times 3}$ corresponding to the two output capsules are initialized:

$$\mathbf{B}^{(j)} = \begin{bmatrix} b_{1,1}^{(j)}) & b_{1,2}^{(j)} & b_{1,3}^{(j)} \\ b_{2,1}^{(j)}) & b_{2,2}^{(j)} & b_{2,3}^{(j)} \\ \vdots & \vdots & \vdots \\ b_{l,1}^{(j)}) & b_{l,2}^{(j)} & b_{l,3}^{(j)} \end{bmatrix} = \begin{bmatrix} 0 & 0 & 0 \\ 0 & 0 & 0 \\ \vdots & \vdots & \vdots \\ 0 & 0 & 0 \end{bmatrix}.$$

For r iterations do:

$$\mathbf{C}^{(j)} = \begin{bmatrix} c_{1,1}^{(j)} & c_{1,2}^{(j)} & c_{1,3}^{(j)} \\ c_{2,1}^{(j)} & c_{2,2}^{(j)} & c_{2,3}^{(j)} \\ \vdots & \vdots & \vdots \\ c_{l,1}^{(j)} & c_{l,2}^{(j)} & c_{l,3}^{(j)} \end{bmatrix} = \begin{bmatrix} \text{softmax}(b_{1,1}^{(j)}, b_{1,2}^{(j)}, b_{1,3}^{(j)}) \\ \text{softmax}(b_{2,1}^{(j)}, b_{2,2}^{(j)}, b_{2,3}^{(j)}) \\ \vdots \\ \text{softmax}(b_{l,1}^{(j)}, b_{l,2}^{(j)}, b_{l,3}^{(j)}) \end{bmatrix}, \mathbf{C}^{(j)} \in \mathbb{R}^{l \times 3}.$$

$$\mathbf{s}^{(j)} = \begin{bmatrix} s_1^{(j)} \\ s_2^{(j)} \\ \vdots \\ s_l^{(j)} \end{bmatrix} = \begin{bmatrix} c_{1,1}^{(j)} \\ c_{2,1}^{(j)} \\ \vdots \\ c_{l,1}^{(j)} \end{bmatrix} \odot \begin{bmatrix} \widehat{u}_1^{(1)} \\ \widehat{u}_2^{(1)} \\ \vdots \\ \widehat{u}_l^{(1)} \end{bmatrix} + \begin{bmatrix} c_{1,2}^{(j)} \\ c_{2,2}^{(j)} \\ \vdots \\ c_{l,2}^{(j)} \end{bmatrix} \odot \begin{bmatrix} \widehat{u}_1^{(2)} \\ \widehat{u}_2^{(2)} \\ \vdots \\ \widehat{u}_l^{(2)} \end{bmatrix} + \begin{bmatrix} c_{1,3}^{(j)} \\ c_{2,3}^{(j)} \\ \vdots \\ c_{l,3}^{(j)} \end{bmatrix} \odot \begin{bmatrix} \widehat{u}_1^{(3)} \\ \widehat{u}_2^{(3)} \\ \vdots \\ \widehat{u}_l^{(3)} \end{bmatrix}$$

($\odot$ represents element-wise multiplication).

$$\mathbf{v}^{(j)} = \begin{bmatrix} v_1^{(j)} \\ v_2^{(j)} \\ \vdots \\ v_l^{(j)} \end{bmatrix} = \text{squash}(\mathbf{s}^{(j)}).$$

$$\mathbf{B}^{(j)} \leftarrow \mathbf{B}^{(j)} + \begin{bmatrix} \widehat{\mathbf{u}}^{(1)} & \widehat{\mathbf{u}}^{(2)} & \widehat{\mathbf{u}}^{(3)} \end{bmatrix} \odot \mathbf{v}^{(j)}$$

$$= \begin{bmatrix} b_{1,1}^{(j)} & b_{1,2}^{(j)} & b_{1,3}^{(j)} \\ b_{2,1}^{(j)} & b_{2,2}^{(j)} & b_{2,3}^{(j)} \\ \vdots & \vdots & \vdots \\ b_{l,1}^{(j)} & b_{l,2}^{(j)} & b_{l,3}^{(j)} \end{bmatrix} + \begin{bmatrix} \widehat{u}_1^{(1)} v_1^{(j)} & \widehat{u}_1^{(2)} v_1^{(j)} & \widehat{u}_1^{(3)} v_1^{(j)} \\ \widehat{u}_2^{(1)} v_2^{(j)} & \widehat{u}_2^{(2)} v_2^{(j)} & \widehat{u}_2^{(3)} v_2^{(j)} \\ \vdots & \vdots & \vdots \\ \widehat{u}_l^{(1)} v_l^{(j)} & \widehat{u}_l^{(2)} v_l^{(j)} & \widehat{u}_l^{(3)} v_l^{(j)} \end{bmatrix}.$$

Finally, return $\mathbf{v}^{(j)}$.

Figure 13.4 is a visualization of $\mathbf{C}^{(2)}$, where $l = 4$.

References

1. Contributing data to deepfake detection research. https://ai.googleblog.com/2019/09/contributing-data-to-deepfake-detection.html. Accessed 24 Sept 2019
2. Dexter studio. http://dexterstudios.com/en/. Accessed 01 Sept 2019
3. Terrifying high-tech porn: Creepy 'deepfake' videos are on the rise. https://www.foxnews.com/tech/terrifying-high-tech-porn-creepy-deepfake-videos-are-on-the-rise. Accessed 17 Feb 2018
4. Afchar D, Nozick V, Yamagishi J, Echizen I (2018) MesoNet: a compact facial video forgery detection network. In: International workshop on information forensics and security (WIFS). IEEE
5. Agarwal S, Farid H, Gu Y, He M, Nagano K, Li H (2019) Protecting world leaders against deep fakes. In: Conference on computer vision and pattern recognition workshops (CVPRW), pp 38–45
6. Alexander O, Rogers M, Lambeth W, Chiang JY, Ma WC, Wang CC, Debevec P (2010) The digital emily project: Achieving a photorealistic digital actor. IEEE Comput Graph Appl 30(4):20–31
7. Averbuch-Elor H, Cohen-Or D, Kopf J, Cohen MF (2017) Bringing portraits to life. ACM Trans Graph
8. Bahadori MT (2018) Spectral capsule networks. In: International conference on learning representations (ICLR)
9. Bappy JH, Simons C, Nataraj L, Manjunath B, Roy-Chowdhury AK (2019) Hybrid lstm and encoder-decoder architecture for detection of image forgeries. IEEE Trans Image Process
10. Bayar B, Stamm MC (2016) A deep learning approach to universal image manipulation detection using a new convolutional layer. In: Workshop on information hiding and multimedia security (IH&MMSEC). ACM
11. Chollet F (2017) Xception: deep learning with depthwise separable convolutions. In: Conference on computer vision and pattern recognition (CVPR). IEEE
12. Cozzolino D, Poggi G, Verdoliva L (2017) Recasting residual-based local descriptors as convolutional neural networks: an application to image forgery detection. In: Workshop on information hiding and multimedia security (IH&MMSEC). ACM

13. Dolhansky B, Bitton J, Pflaum B, Lu J, Howes R, Wang M, Ferrer CC (2020) The deepfake detection challenge dataset. arXiv preprint arXiv:2006.07397
14. Fridrich J, Kodovsky J (2012) Rich models for stage analysis of digital images. IEEE Trans Inf Foren Sec
15. Fried O, Tewari A, Zollhöfer M, Finkelstein A, Shechtman E, Goldman DB, Genova K, Jin Z, Theobalt C, Agrawala M (2019) Text-based editing of talking-head video. In: International conference and exhibition on computer graphics and interactive techniques (SIGGRAPH). ACM
16. He K, Zhang X, Ren S, Sun J (2016) Deep residual learning for image recognition. In: Conference on computer vision and pattern recognition (CVPR), pp 770–778
17. Hinton GE, Krizhevsky A, Wang SD (2011) Transforming auto-encoders. In: International conference on artificial neural networks (ICANN). Springer
18. Hinton GE, Sabour S, Frosst N (2018) Matrix capsules with EM routing. In: International conference on learning representations workshop (ICLRW)
19. Huang G, Liu Z, Van Der Maaten L, Weinberger KQ (2017) Densely connected convolutional networks. In: Conference on computer vision and pattern recognition (CVPR), pp 4700–4708
20. Jiang L, Li R, Wu W, Qian C, Loy CC (2020) Deeperforensics-1.0: A large-scale dataset for real-world face forgery detection. In: Conference on computer vision and pattern recognition (CVPR)
21. Karras T, Laine S, Aila T (2019) A style-based generator architecture for generative adversarial networks. In: Conference on computer vision and pattern recognition (CVPR), pp 4401–4410
22. Kim H, Garrido P, Tewari A, Xu W, Thies J, Nießner M, Pérez P, Richardt C, Zollhöfer M, Theobalt C (2018) Deep video portraits. In: International conference and exhibition on computer graphics and interactive techniques (SIGGRAPH). ACM
23. Kingma DP, Ba J (2015) Adam: a method for stochastic optimization. In: International conference on learning representations (ICLR)
24. Korshunov P, Marcel S (2018) Speaker inconsistency detection in tampered video. In: European signal processing conference (EUSIPCO). IEEE, pp 2375–2379
25. Korshunov P, Marcel S (2019) Vulnerability assessment and detection of deepfake videos. In: International conference on biometrics (ICB)
26. Li L, Bao J, Zhang T, Yang H, Chen D, Wen F, Guo B (2020) Face x-ray for more general face forgery detection. In: Conference on computer vision and pattern recognition (CVPR), pp 5001–5010
27. Li Y, Chang MC, Farid H, Lyu S (2018) In ictu oculi: Exposing AI generated fake face videos by detecting eye blinking. arXiv preprint arXiv:1806.02877
28. Li Y, Yang X, Sun P, Qi H, Lyu S (2020) Celeb-df: A large-scale challenging dataset for deepfake forensics. In: Conference on computer vision and pattern recognition (CVPR), pp 3207–3216
29. Liu A, Wan J, Escalera S, Jair Escalante H, Tan Z, Yuan Q, Wang K, Lin C, Guo G, Guyon I et al (2019) Multi-modal face anti-spoofing attack detection challenge at cvpr2019. In: Conference on computer vision and pattern recognition workshops (CVPRW), pp 0–0
30. Nguyen HH, Fang F, Yamagishi J, Echizen I (2019) Multi-task learning for detecting and segmenting manipulated facial images and videos. In: International conference on biometrics: theory, applications and systems (BTAS). IEEE
31. Nguyen HH, Tieu NDT, Nguyen-Son HQ, Nozick V, Yamagishi J, Echizen I (2018) Modular convolutional neural network for discriminating between computer-generated images and photographic images. In: International conference on availability, reliability and security (ARES). ACM
32. Nguyen HH, Yamagishi J, Echizen I (2019) Capsule-forensics: Using capsule networks to detect forged images and videos. In: International conference on acoustics, speech and signal processing (ICASSP). IEEE, pp 2307–2311

33. Nirkin Y, Keller Y, Hassner T (2019) Fsgan: Subject agnostic face swapping and reenactment. In: International conference on computer vision (ICCV). IEEE
34. Ozbulak U (2019) Pytorch cnn visualizations. https://github.com/utkuozbulak/pytorch-cnn-visualizations
35. Rahmouni N, Nozick V, Yamagishi J, Echizen I (2017) Distinguishing computer graphics from natural images using convolution neural networks. In: International workshop on information forensics and security (WIFS). IEEE
36. Rössler A, Cozzolino D, Verdoliva L, Riess C, Thies J, Nießner M (2019) Faceforensics++: learning to detect manipulated facial images. In: International conference on computer vision (ICCV)
37. Russakovsky O, Deng J, Su H, Krause J, Satheesh S, Ma S, Huang Z, Karpathy A, Khosla A, Bernstein M, Berg AC, Fei-Fei L (2015) ImageNet Large scale visual recognition challenge. Int J Comput Vis
38. Sabir E, Cheng J, Jaiswal A, AbdAlmageed W, Masi I, Natarajan P (2019) Recurrent convolutional strategies for face manipulation detection in videos. In: Conference on computer vision and pattern recognition workshops (CVPRW), pp 80–87
39. Sabour S, Frosst N, Hinton GE (2017) Dynamic routing between capsules. In: Conference on Neural Information Processing Systems (NIPS)
40. Selvaraju RR, Cogswell M, Das A, Vedantam R, Parikh D, Batra D (2017) Grad-cam: visual explanations from deep networks via gradient-based localization. In: International conference on computer vision (ICCV). IEEE, pp 618–626
41. Simonyan K, Zisserman A (2015) Very deep convolutional networks for large-scale image recognition. In: International conference on learning representations (ICLR)
42. Suwajanakorn S, Seitz SM, Kemelmacher-Shlizerman I (2017) Synthesizing obama: learning lip sync from audio. ACM Trans Graph
43. Szegedy C, Liu W, Jia Y, Sermanet P, Reed S, Anguelov D, Erhan D, Vanhoucke V, Rabinovich A (2015) Going deeper with convolutions. In: Conference on computer vision and pattern recognition (CVPR), pp 1–9
44. Tan M, Le Q (2019) Efficientnet: rethinking model scaling for convolutional neural networks. In: International conference on machine learning (ICML), pp 6105–6114
45. Thies J, Zollhöfer M, Nießner M (2019) Deferred neural rendering: image synthesis using neural textures. In: Computer graphics and interactive techniques (SIGGRAPH). ACM
46. Thies, J, Zollhofer, M, Stamminger, M, Theobalt, C, Nießner, M (2016) Face2Face: real-time face capture and reenactment of RGB videos. In: Conference on computer vision and pattern recognition (CVPR). IEEE
47. Tripathy S, Kannala J, Rahtu E (2019) Icface: interpretable and controllable face reenactment using gans. arXiv preprint arXiv:1904.01909
48. Vougioukas K, Center SA, Petridis S, Pantic M (2019) End-to-end speech-driven realistic facial animation with temporal gans. In: Conference on computer vision and pattern recognition workshops (CVPRW), pp 37–40
49. Wang SY, Wang O, Owens A, Zhang R, Efros AA (2019) Detecting photoshopped faces by scripting photoshop. In: International conference on computer vision (ICCV). IEEE
50. Xi E, Bing S, Jin Y (2017) Capsule network performance on complex data. arXiv preprint arXiv:1712.03480
51. Xiang C, Zhang L, Tang Y, Zou W, Xu C (2018) Ms-capsnet: a novel multi-scale capsule network. IEEE Signal Process Lett 25(12):1850–1854
52. Zagoruyko S, Komodakis N (2016) Wide residual networks. In: British machine vision conference (BMVC). BMVA
53. Zakharov E, Shysheya A, Burkov E, Lempitsky V (2019) Few-shot adversarial learning of realistic neural talking head models. arXiv preprint arXiv:1905.08233

54. Zhou P, Han X, Morariu VI, Davis LS (2017) Two-stream neural networks for tampered face detection. In: Conference on computer vision and pattern recognition workshop (CVPRW). IEEE
55. Zhou P, Han X, Morariu VI, Davis LS (2018) Learning rich features for image manipulation detection. In: Conference on computer vision and pattern recognition (CVPR), pp 1053–1061

Chapter 14
DeepFakes Detection: the DeeperForensics Dataset and Challenge

Liming Jiang, Wayne Wu, Chen Qian, and Chen Change Loy

Abstract Recent years have witnessed exciting progress in automatic face swapping and editing. Many techniques have been proposed, facilitating the rapid development of creative content creation. The emergence and easy accessibility of such techniques, however, also cause potential unprecedented ethical and moral issues. To this end, academia and industry proposed several effective forgery detection methods. Nonetheless, challenges could still exist. (1) Current face manipulation advances can produce high-fidelity fake videos, rendering forgery detection challenging. (2) The generalization capability of most existing detection models is poor, particularly in real-world scenarios where the media sources and distortions are unknown. The primary difficulty in overcoming these challenges is the lack of amenable datasets for real-world face forgery detection. Most existing datasets are either of a small number, of low quality, or overly artificial. Meanwhile, the large distribution gap between training data and actual test videos also leads to weak generalization ability. In this chapter, we present our on-going effort of constructing DeeperForensics-1.0, a large-scale forgery detection dataset, to address the challenges above. We discuss approaches to ensure the quality and diversity of the dataset. Besides, we describe the observations we obtained from organizing DeeperForensics Challenge 2020, a real-world face forgery detection competition based on DeeperForensics-1.0. Specifically, we summarize the winning solutions and provide some discussions on potential research directions.

L. Jiang · C. C. Loy (✉)
S-Lab, Nanyang Technological University, Jurong West, Singapore
e-mail: ccloy@ntu.edu.sg

L. Jiang
e-mail: liming002@ntu.edu.sg

W. Wu · C. Qian
SenseTime Research, Beijing, China
e-mail: wuwenyan@sensetime.com

C. Qian
e-mail: qianchen@sensetime.com

© The Author(s) 2022
C. Rathgeb et al. (eds.), *Handbook of Digital Face Manipulation and Detection*,
Advances in Computer Vision and Pattern Recognition,
https://doi.org/10.1007/978-3-030-87664-7_14

14.1 Introduction

Face swapping has become an emerging topic in computer vision and graphics. Indeed, many works [1, 4, 6, 41, 53, 76] on automatic face swapping have been proposed in recent years. These efforts have circumvented the cumbersome and tedious manual face editing processes, hence expediting the advancement in face editing. At the same time, such enabling technology has also sparked legitimate concerns on its potential for being misused and abused. The popularization of "DeepFakes" on the Internet has further set off alarm bells among the general public and authorities, in view of the conceivable perilous implications. Accordingly, countermeasures to safeguard against these photorealistic fake videos become a dire need to be in place promptly, especially innovations that can effectively detect videos that have been manipulated.

Although academia and industry have contributed several effective face forgery detection methods [54, 56, 63, 64, 93, 99], some challenges could still exist. First, current face manipulation advances can produce high-fidelity fake videos, making forgery detection challenging. Besides, the generalization capability of most existing detection models is poor, particularly in *real-world* scenarios where the media sources and distortions are unknown. Meanwhile, the DeepFakes techniques will keep evolving in the future. The better face editing quality will render forgery detection more challenging, entailing the increasing importance of the model generalization.

In this chapter, we present our on-going efforts to address the challenges above. The primary difficulty in overcoming these challenges is the lack of amenable datasets. Working toward forgery detection, various groups have contributed datasets (*e.g.*, FaceForensics++ [81], Deep Fake Detection [13], and DFDC [23, 24]) comprising manipulated video footages. The availability of these datasets has undoubtedly provided essential avenues for research into forgery detection. Nonetheless, the aforementioned datasets fall short in several ways. Videos in these datasets are either of a small number, of low quality, or overly artificial. Understandably, these datasets are inadequate to train a good model for effective forgery detection in real-world scenarios. This is particularly true when current advances in human face editing are able to produce more photorealistic videos than the ones in these datasets. On another note, we observe a high similarity between training and test videos, in terms of their distribution, in certain works [57, 81]. Their actual efficacy in detecting real-world face forgery cases, which are much more variable and unpredictable, remains to be further elucidated.

We believe that forgery detection models can only be enhanced when trained with a dataset that is exhaustive enough to encompass as many potential real-world variations as possible. To this end, we propose a large-scale dataset, named DeeperForensics-1.0 [41], consisting of 60, 000 videos with a total of 17.6 million frames for real-world face forgery detection. The main steps of our dataset construction are shown in Fig. 14.1. We set forth three yardsticks when constructing this dataset: (1) *Good quality.* The dataset shall contain the videos that are more realistic

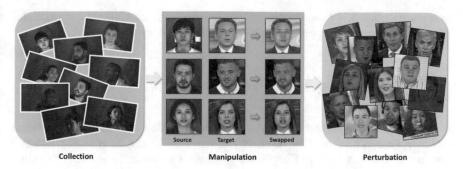

Source Target Swapped

Collection Manipulation Perturbation

Fig. 14.1 DeeperForensics-1.0 is a new large-scale dataset for *real-world* face forgery detection

and closer to the state-of-the-art DeepFakes video distributions. (Sections 14.3.1 and 14.3.2) (2) *Large scale.* The dataset shall be made up of a large number of video sets. (Section 14.3.3) (3) *High diversity.* There shall be sufficient variations in the video footages (*e.g.*, compression, blurry, and transmission errors) to match those that may be encountered in the real world (Sect. 14.3.3).

The major challenge in the preparation of this dataset is the lack of good-quality video footages. Specifically, most publicly available videos are captured under an unconstrained environment resulting in large variations, including but not limited to suboptimal illumination, large occlusion of the target faces, and extreme head poses. Importantly, the lack of the official informed consents from the video subjects precludes the use of these videos, even for non-commercial purposes. On the other hand, while some videos of manipulated faces are deceptively real, a larger number remains easily distinguishable by human eyes. The latter is often caused by model negligence toward appearance variations or temporal differences, leading to preposterous and incongruous results.

We approach the aforementioned challenge from two perspectives. (1) Collecting fresh face data from 100 individuals with informed consents (Sect. 14.3.1). (2) Devising a novel end-to-end face swapping method, DeepFake Variational Auto-Encoder (DF-VAE), to enhance existing videos (Sect. 14.3.2). In addition, we introduce diversity into the video footages through the deliberate addition of distortions and perturbations, simulating real-world scenarios. The DeeperForensics-1.0 dataset also features a hidden test set, containing manipulated videos that achieve the high deceptive ranking in user studies. The hidden test set is richer in distribution than the publicly available training set, suggesting a better real-world forgery detection setting.

Using the introduced DeeperForensics-1.0 dataset, we organized the Deeper-Forensics Challenge 2020 [40] with the aim to advance the state of the art in face forgery detection. Participants in this challenge were expected to develop robust and generic methods for forgery detection in real-world scenarios. This chapter also covers details of the DeeperForensics Challenge 2020, including the platform, evaluation metric, timeline, participants, results, *etc*. The winning solutions of top-3 entries are included. We present discussions to take a closer look at the current status and possible future development of real-world face forgery detection.

14.2 Related Work

In this section, we provide an overview of the current status of relevant studies *w.r.t.*DeepFakes detection. The taxonomy of these works can be generally grouped into four paradigms, namely DeepFakes generation methods, DeepFakes detection methods, DeepFakes detection datasets, and DeepFakes detection benchmarks.

14.2.1 DeepFakes Generation Methods

The popularization of DeepFakes videos is attributed to the rapid development of generative models. Existing state-of-the-art generative models are mainly built on deep neural networks [26, 33, 48, 50, 74], showing impressive capability in capturing high-level latent representations of visual data and synthesizing new images. Two popular categories of generative models for face manipulation are auto-encoders (AE) [33, 50] and generative adversarial networks (GAN) [26].

The vanilla AE [33] reconstructs images, aiming at learning latent codes in an unsupervised manner, typically for dimensional reduction and feature learning. Auto-encoders have been widely used to generate images since the development of variational auto-encoders (VAE) [49, 50]. Extensive well-known off-the-shelf face manipulation software are based on auto-encoders, *e.g.*, DeepFakes [4] and DeepFace-Lab [1, 76]. These methods tend to learn the identity information for face manipulation through the reconstruction process. However, they usually fit the specific domain and cannot scale to multiple identities. The manipulation method DF-VAE [41] for the DeeperForensics-1.0 dataset is based on variational auto-encoders. DF-VAE is an end-to-end many-to-many face swapping method, which considers style matching and temporal continuity for video manipulation.

Another category of generative models is GAN [26, 67, 79], where a generator tries to fool a discriminator by refining the synthesized images continuously until the discriminator fails to perceive them as fakes. GAN has been extensively applied in face generation [43–45], image-to-image translation [17, 38, 39, 42, 104], style transfer [36, 59], and semantic image synthesis [39, 42, 60, 75, 95]. For face manipulation, the open-source DeepFakes software, faceswap-GAN [6], is a typical GAN-based method. It exploits adversarial losses to the denoising auto-encoder and applies attention mechanisms to improve the clarity of the swapped faces. ReenactGAN [97] introduced the notion of boundary latent space for robust many-to-one face reenactment. Some recent GAN-based innovations were designed in the more challenging face manipulation context, *e.g.*, subject agnostic [72] and occlusion aware [53].

14.2.2   DeepFakes Detection Methods

The development of face forgery detection approaches is constantly evolving along with the advancement of face manipulation techniques. One of the early forgery detection methods is [103]. They proposed a two-stream network for forgery detection. The initial system was trained to detect facial expression manipulations. Later on, MesoNet was proposed in [10]. They introduced two different networks composed of few layers in order to focus on the mesoscopic properties of the images. This method was originally tested in their private database and has been proved to be an effective approach in the FaceForensics benchmark [81]. A temporal-aware framework for automatic fake video detection was discussed in [28]. They leveraged the benefits of both convolutional neural networks (CNN) and recurrent neural networks (RNN). They integrated them into a single framework and averaged the results for evaluation.

More recent forgery detection approaches mainly considered different artifacts introduced during face manipulation. Some methods were based on visual artifacts, *e.g.*, face warping artifacts [56], dissonance of saturation [65], discrepancy between the face and its context [73], region-based artifacts [87], and temporal inconsistencies [91]. Some approaches considered noises from generative models, *e.g.*, GAN fingerprints [100], convolutional traces [27], and frequency-domain clues [78]. Others exploited physiological signs as an important forgery detection basis. They utilized eye blinking [55], head poses [99], heart rate [32], and emotions [68] as important cues for effective face forgery detection.

Real-world face forgery detection, in which video sources and distortions are highly unconstrained and unpredictable, remains less explored. Some studies [16, 54, 83, 93] have started to consider the model generalization issue for forgery detection, which is crucial for real-world face forgery detection. The design of the DeeperForensics-1.0 dataset [41] and the DeeperForensics Challenge 2020 [40] aims to offer a benchmark and platform for a more systematic study about this problem.

14.2.3   DeepFakes Detection Datasets

Building a dataset for forgery detection requires a huge amount of effort on data collection and manipulation. Early forgery detection datasets comprised images captured under highly restrictive conditions, *e.g.*, MICC_F2000 [11], Wild Web dataset [101], and Realistic Tampering dataset [52].

Due to the urgent need for video-based face forgery detection, some research groups have devoted their efforts to create video forensics datasets. UADFV [99] contained 98 videos, *i.e.*, 49 real videos from YouTube and 49 fake ones generated by FakeAPP [7]. DeepFake-TIMIT [51] manually selected 16 similar looking pairs of people from VidTIMIT [82] database. For each of the 32 subjects, they generated about 10 videos using low-quality and high-quality versions of faceswap-

GAN [6], resulting in a total of 620 fake videos. Celeb-DF [57] included 408 YouTube videos, mostly of celebrities, from which 795 fake videos were synthesized. FaceForensics++ [81] is the first large-scale face forensic dataset that consisted of 4,000 fake videos manipulated by four methods (*i.e.*, DeepFakes [4], Face2Face [86], FaceSwap [5], and NeuralTextures [85])), as well as 1,000 real videos from YouTube. Afterward, Google joined FaceForensics++ and contributed Deep Fake Detection [13] dataset with 3,431 real and fake videos from 28 actors. Recently, Facebook invited 66 individuals and built the DFDC preview dataset [24], which comprised 5,214 original and tampered videos with three types of augmentations.

To build the DeeperForensics-1.0 dataset, we invite 100 actors and collect high-resolution (1920 × 1080) source data with these actors showing various poses and expressions under different illuminations. 3DMM blendshapes [14] are taken as a reference to supplement some exaggerated expressions. We obtain consents from all the actors for using and manipulating their faces. A newly proposed end-to-end face swapping method (*i.e.*, DF-VAE) is exploited to improve the generated video quality. Besides, seven types of perturbations at five intensity levels are applied to simulate real-world scenes better. The dataset also includes a mixture of distortions to a single video. In total, the DeeperForensics-1.0 dataset contains 60,000 high-quality videos with 17.6 million frames.

14.2.4 DeepFakes Detection Benchmarks

The FaceForensics benchmark [81] is a popular benchmark for facial manipulation detection. The benchmark included six image-level face forgery detection baselines [10, 12, 18, 19, 25, 80]. The FaceForensics benchmark added several distortions to the videos by converting them into different compression rates. The benchmark did not include different perturbation types or a mixture of them. Celeb-DF [57] also provided a face forgery detection benchmark including seven methods [10, 18, 56, 64, 70, 99, 103] trained and tested on different datasets. In the aforementioned benchmarks, the test set usually shares a similar distribution with the training set. Such an assumption may inherently introduce biases and render the detection methods impractical for face forgery detection in real-world settings with much more diverse and unknown fake videos.

The DeeperForensics-1.0 benchmark features a challenging hidden test set with manipulated videos achieving high deceptive scores in user studies. The hidden test set is richer in distribution than the publicly available training set to better simulate the real-world distribution. The benchmark includes the entries submitted to the DeeperForensics Challenge 2020. The top-3 challenge winning solutions in this benchmark are elaborated on in Sect. 14.4.5. Temporal information—a significant cue for video forgery detection besides the single-frame quality—has been considered. In addition, readers are referred to [41] for more video-level forgery detection baselines [15, 30, 34, 89, 92] in the DeeperForensics-1.0 benchmark.

14.3 DeeperForensics-1.0 Dataset

This section introduces the DeeperForensics-1.0 dataset [41]. The dataset consists of 60, 000 videos with 17.6 million frames in total, including 50, 000 collected source videos and 10, 000 manipulated videos. Toward building a dataset that is suitable for real-world face forgery detection, DeeperForensics-1.0 is designed with the careful consideration of *quality*, *scale*, and *diversity*. In Sects. 14.3.1 and 14.3.2, we discuss the details of data collection and methodology (*i.e.*, DF-VAE) to improve the quality of data. In Sect. 14.3.3, we show our approaches to increase the scale and diversity of samples.

14.3.1 Data Collection

Source data is the first factor that highly affects *quality*. Taking results in Fig. 14.2 as an example, the source data collection increases the robustness of our face swapping method to extreme poses, since videos on the Internet usually have limited head pose variations.

We refer to the identity in the driving video as the "target" face and the identity of the face that is swapped onto the driving video as the "source" face. Different from previous works, we find that the source faces play a more critical role than the target faces in building a high-quality dataset. Specifically, the expressions, poses,

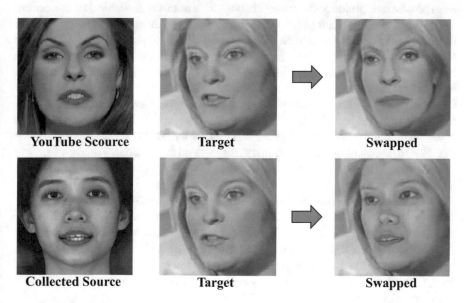

| YouTube Scource | Target | Swapped |

| Collected Source | Target | Swapped |

Fig. 14.2 Comparison of face swapping results using an in-the-wild YouTube video or the collected video as source data, with the same manipulation method and setting

Fig. 14.3 Diversity in identities, poses, expressions, and illuminations in the collected source data of DeeperForensics-1.0

and lighting conditions of source faces should be much richer in order to perform robust face swapping. The data collection of DeeperForensics-1.0 mainly focuses on source face videos. Figure 14.3 shows the diversity in different attributes of the collected source data.

We invite 100 paid actors to record the source videos. Similar to [13, 24], we obtain consents from all the actors for using and manipulating their faces to avoid the portrait right issues. The participants are carefully selected to ensure variability in genders, ages, skin colors, and nationalities. We maintain a roughly equal proportion *w.r.t.* each of the attributes above. In particular, we invite 55 males and 45 females from 26 countries. Their ages range from 20 to 45 years old to match the most common age group appearing on real-world videos. The actors have four typical skin tones: *white*, *black*, *yellow*, and *brown*, with ratio 1:1:1:1. All faces are clean without glasses or decorations.

A professional indoor environment is built for a more controllable data collection. We only use the facial regions (detected and cropped by LAB [96]) of the source data; thus, the background is neglected. We set seven HD cameras from different angles: front, left, left-front, right, right-front, oblique-above, and oblique-below. The resolution of the recorded videos is high (1920 × 1080). The actors are trained in advance to keep the collection process smooth. We request the actors to turn their heads and speak naturally with eight expressions: neutral, angry, happy, sad, surprise, contempt, disgust, and fear. The head poses range from −90° to +90°. Furthermore, the actors are asked to perform 53 expressions defined by 3DMM blendshapes [14] (see Fig. 14.4) to supplement some extremely exaggerated expressions. When performing 3DMM blendshapes, the actors also speak naturally to avoid excessive frames that show a closed mouth.

In addition to expressions and poses, we systematically set nine lighting conditions from various directions: uniform, left, top-left, bottom-left, right, top-right, bottom-right, top, and bottom. The actors are only asked to turn their heads under the uniform illumination, so the lighting remains unchanged on specific facial regions to avoid many duplicated data samples recorded by the cameras set at different angles. In total, the collected source data of DeeperForensics-1.0 comprise over 50, 000 videos with around 12.6 million frames.

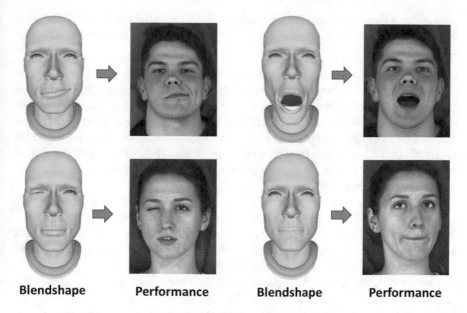

Fig. 14.4 Examples of 3DMM blendshapes and the respective collected source data in DeeperForensics-1.0

14.3.2 DeepFake Variational Auto-Encoder

To improve the *quality* of manipulated data in DeeperForensics-1.0, we consider three key requirements in formulating a high-fidelity face swapping method: (1) The method should be generic and scalable to generate a large number of videos with high quality. (2) The problem of face style mismatch caused by the appearance variations should be addressed. Some failure cases in existing datasets are shown in Fig. 14.5. (3) Temporal continuity of generated videos should be taken into consideration.

Based on the aforementioned requirements, we propose DeepFake Variational Auto-Encoder (DF-VAE), a learning-based face swapping framework. DF-VAE con-

Fig. 14.5 Examples of style mismatch problems in several existing face forensics datasets

sists of three main parts, namely a structure extraction module, a disentangled module, and a fusion module. The details of DF-VAE framework are introduced in this section.

Disentanglement of structure and appearance. The first step of DF-VAE method is face reenactment—animating the source face with similar expression as the target face, without any paired data. Face swapping can be considered as a subsequent step of face reenactment that performs fusion between the reenacted face and the target background. For the robust and scalable face reenactment, we should disentangle the structure (*i.e.*, expression and pose) and appearance (*i.e.*, texture, skin color, *etc.*) representations of a face. This disentanglement is difficult since the structure and appearance representations are far from independent.

Let $\mathbf{x}_{1:T} \equiv \{x_1, x_2, ..., x_T\} \in X$ be a sequence of source face video frames, and $\mathbf{y}_{1:T} \equiv \{y_1, y_2, ..., y_T\} \in Y$ be the sequence of corresponding target face video frames. We first simplify our problem and only consider two specific snapshots at time t, x_t, and y_t. Let $\tilde{x}_t$, $\tilde{y}_t$, d_t represent the reconstructed source face, the reconstructed target face, and the reenacted face, respectively.

Consider the reconstruction procedure of the source face x_t. Let s_x denote the structure representation and a_x denote the appearance information. The face generator can be depicted as the posteriori estimate $p_\theta(x_t | s_x, a_x)$. The solution of our reconstruction goal, marginal log-likelihood $\tilde{x}_t \sim \log p_\theta(x_t)$, by a common variational auto-encoder (VAE) [50] can be written as follows:

$$\log p_\theta(x_t) = D_{KL}\left(q_\phi(s_x, a_x | x_t) \,\|\, p_\theta(s_x, a_x | x_t)\right) \\ + L(\theta, \phi; x_t), \tag{14.1}$$

where q_ϕ is an approximate posterior to achieve the evidence lower bound (ELBO) in the intractable case, and the second RHS term $L(\theta, \phi; x_t)$ is the variational lower bound *w.r.t.* both the variational parameters ϕ and generative parameters θ.

In Eq. (14.1), we assume that both s_x and a_x are latent priors computed by the same posterior x_t. However, the separation of these two variables in the latent space is rather difficult without additional conditions. Therefore, DF-VAE employs a simple yet effective approach to disentangle these two variables.

The blue arrows in Fig. 14.6 demonstrate the reconstruction procedure of the source face x_t. Instead of feeding a single source face x_t, we sample another source face x' to construct unpaired data in the source domain. To make the structure representation more evident, we use the stacked hourglass networks [69] to extract landmarks of x_t in the structure extraction module and get the heatmap $\hat{x}_t$. Then we feed the heatmap $\hat{x}_t$ to the Structure Encoder E_α, and x' to the Appearance Encoder E_β. We concatenate the latent representations (small cubes in red and green) and feed it to the Decoder D_y. Finally, we get the reconstructed face $\tilde{x}_t$, *i.e.*, marginal log-likelihood of x_t.

Therefore, the latent structure representation s_x in Eq. (14.1) becomes a more evident heatmap representation $\hat{x}_t$, which is introduced as a new condition. The unpaired

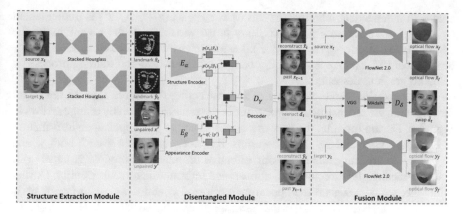

Fig. 14.6 The main framework of DeepFake Variational Auto-Encoder (DF-VAE). In training, we reconstruct the source and target faces in blue and orange arrows, respectively, by extracting landmarks and constructing an unpaired sample as the condition. Optical flow differences are minimized after reconstruction to improve temporal continuity. In inference, we swap the latent codes and get the reenacted face in green arrows. Subsequent MAdaIN module fuses the reenacted face and the original background resulting in the swapped face

sample x' with the same identity $w.r.t.x_t$ is another condition, being a substitute for a_x. Equation (14.1) can be rewritten as a conditional log-likelihood:

$$
\begin{aligned}
log\, p_\theta \left(x_t | \hat{x}_t, x' \right) = D_{KL} \left(q_\phi \left(z_x | x_t, \hat{x}_t, x' \right) \| p_\theta \left(z_x | x_t, \hat{x}_t, x' \right) \right) \\
+ L \left(\theta, \phi; x_t, \hat{x}_t, x' \right).
\end{aligned}
\tag{14.2}
$$

The first RHS term KL-divergence is non-negative, we get the following:

$$
\begin{aligned}
\log p_\theta \left(x_t | \hat{x}_t, x' \right) &\geq L(\theta, \phi; x_t, \hat{x}_t, x') \\
&= \mathbb{E}_{q_\phi(z_x|x_t,\hat{x}_t,x')} \left[-\log q_\phi \left(z_x | x_t, \hat{x}_t, x' \right) + \log p_\theta \left(x_t, z_x | \hat{x}_t, x' \right) \right],
\end{aligned}
\tag{14.3}
$$

and $L(\theta, \phi; x_t, \hat{x}_t, x')$ can also be written as follows:

$$
\begin{aligned}
L \left(\theta, \phi; x_t, \hat{x}_t, x' \right) = &- D_{KL} \left(q_\phi \left(z_x | x_t, \hat{x}_t, x' \right) \| p_\theta \left(z_x | \hat{x}_t, x' \right) \right) \\
&+ \mathbb{E}_{q_\phi(z_x|x_t,\hat{x}_t,x')} \left[\log p_\theta \left(x_t | z_x, \hat{x}_t, x' \right) \right].
\end{aligned}
\tag{14.4}
$$

We let the variational approximate posterior be a multivariate Gaussian with a diagonal covariance structure:

$$
\log q_\phi \left(z_x | x_t, \hat{x}_t, x' \right) \equiv \log \mathcal{N} \left(z_x; \mu, \sigma^2 \mathbf{I} \right),
\tag{14.5}
$$

where $\mathbf{I}$ is an identity matrix. Exploiting the reparameterization trick [50], the non-differentiable operation of sampling can become differentiable by an auxiliary variable with independent marginal. In this case, $z_x \sim q_\phi \left(z_x | x_t, \hat{x}_t, x'\right)$ is implemented by $z_x = \mu + \sigma \epsilon$ where ϵ is an auxiliary noise variable $\epsilon \sim \mathcal{N}(0, 1)$. Finally, the approximate posterior $q_\phi(z_x | x_t, \hat{x}_t, x')$ is estimated by the separated encoders, Structure Encoder E_α and Appearance Encoder E_β, in an end-to-end training process by standard gradient descent.

We discuss the whole workflow of reconstructing the source face. In the target face domain, the reconstruction procedure is the same, as shown by orange arrows in Fig. 14.6. During training, the network learns structure and appearance information in both the source and the target domains. It is noteworthy that even if both y_t and x' belong to arbitrary identities, our effective disentangled module is capable of learning meaningful structure and appearance information of each identity. During inference, we concatenate the appearance prior of x' and the structure prior of y_t (small cubes in red and orange) in the latent space, and the reconstructed face d_t shares the same structure with y_t and keeps the appearance of x'. DF-VAE framework allows concatenations of structure and appearance latent codes extracted from arbitrary identities in inference and permits *many-to-many face reenactment*.

In summary, DF-VAE is a conditional variational auto-encoder [49] with robustness and scalability. It conditions on two posteriors in different domains. In the disentangled module, the separated design of two encoders E_α and E_β, the explicit structure heatmap, and the unpaired data construction jointly force E_α to learn structure information and E_β to learn appearance information.

Style matching and fusion. To fix the obvious style mismatch problems as shown in Fig. 14.5, we adopt a masked adaptive instance normalization (MAdaIN) module in DF-VAE. We place a typical AdaIN [35] network after the reenacted face d_t. In the face swapping scenario, we only need to adjust the style of the face area to match the original background. Therefore, we use a mask m_t to guide AdaIN [35] network to focus on style matching of the face area. To avoid boundary artifacts, we apply Gaussian Blur to m_t and get the blurred mask m_t^b.

In our face swapping context, d_t is the content input of MAdaIN, and y_t is the style input. MAdaIN adaptively computes the affine parameters from the face area of the style input:

$$\text{MAdaIN}(c, s) = \sigma(s)\left(\frac{c - \mu(c)}{\sigma(c)}\right) + \mu(s), \tag{14.6}$$

where $c = m_t^b \cdot d_t$, $s = m_t^b \cdot y_t$. With the low-cost MAdaIN module, we reconstruct d_t again by Decoder D_δ. The blurred mask m_t^b is used again to fuse the reconstructed image with the background of y_t. At last, we get the swapped face $\overline{d}_t$.

The MAdaIN module is jointly trained with the disentangled module in an end-to-end manner. Thus, by a *single* model, DF-VAE can perform *many-to-many face swapping* with obvious reduction of style mismatch and facial boundary artifacts (see Fig. 14.7 for the face swapping between three source identities and three target identities). Even if there are multiple identities in both the source domain and the target domain, the quality of face swapping does not degrade.

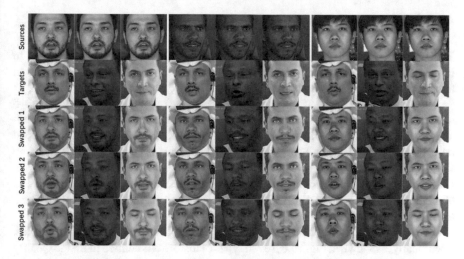

Fig. 14.7 Many-to-many (three-to-three) face swapping by a *single* model with obvious reduction of style mismatch problems. This figure shows the results between three source identities and three target identities. The whole process is end-to-end

Temporal consistency constraint. Temporal discontinuity of the fake videos generated by certain face manipulation methods leads to obvious flickering of the face area, making them easy to be spotted by forgery detection methods and human eyes. To improve temporal continuity, DF-VAE lets the disentangled module learn temporal information of both the source face and the target face.

For simplification, we make a Markov assumption that the generation of the frame at time t sequentially depends on its previous P frames $\mathbf{x}_{(t-p):(t-1)}$. We set $P = 1$ to balance quality improvement and training time.

To build the relationship between a current frame and previous ones, we further make an intuitive assumption that the optical flows should remain unchanged after reconstruction. We use FlowNet 2.0 [37] to estimate the optical flow $\tilde{x}_f$ *w.r.t.* $\tilde{x}_t$ and x_{t-1} and x_f *w.r.t.* x_t and x_{t-1}. Since face swapping is sensitive to minor facial details which can be greatly affected by flow estimation, we do not warp x_{t-1} by the estimated flow like [94]. Instead, we minimize the difference between $\tilde{x}_f$ and x_f to improve temporal continuity while keeping stable facial detail generation. To this end, we propose a new temporal consistency constraint, which can be written as follows:

$$L_{temporal} = \frac{1}{CHW} \|\tilde{x}_f - x_f\|_1, \tag{14.7}$$

where $C = 2$ for a common form of optical flow.

We only discuss the temporal continuity *w.r.t.* the source face in this section. The case of the target face is the same. If multiple identities exist in one domain, temporal information of all these identities can be learned in an end-to-end manner.

14.3.3 Scale and Diversity

The extensive data collection and the introduced DF-VAE method are designed to improve the *quality* of manipulated videos in the DeeperForensics-1.0 dataset. In this section, we mainly discuss the *scale* and *diversity* aspects.

The DeeperForensics-1.0 dataset contains 10, 000 manipulated videos with 5 million frames. We take 1, 000 refined YouTube videos collected by FaceForensics++ [81] as the target videos. Each face of our collected 100 identities is swapped onto 10 target videos; thus, 1, 000 raw manipulated videos are generated directly by DF-VAE in an end-to-end process. Thanks to the scalability and multimodality of DF-VAE, the time overhead of model training and data generation is reduced to 1/5 compared to the common DeepFakes methods, with no degradation in quality. Thus, a larger scale dataset construction is possible.

To enhance diversity, we apply various perturbations existing in real scenes. Specifically, as shown in Fig. 14.8, seven types of distortions defined in Image Quality Assessment (IQA) [58, 77] are included. Each distortion is divided into five intensity levels. We apply random-type distortions to the 1, 000 raw manipulated videos at five different intensity levels, producing a total of 5, 000 manipulated videos. Besides, an additional of 1, 000 robust manipulated videos are generated by adding random-type, random-level distortions to the 1, 000 raw manipulated videos. Moreover, in contrast to other datasets [13, 51, 57, 81, 99], each sample of another 3, 000 manipulated videos in DeeperForensics-1.0 is subjected to a mixture of more than one distortion (examples shown in Fig. 14.8). The variety of perturbations improves the *diversity* of DeeperForensics-1.0 to approximate the data distribution of real-world scenarios better.

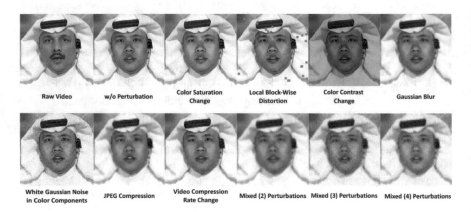

Fig. 14.8 Seven types of perturbations and the mixture of two (Gaussian blur, JPEG compression) / three (Gaussian blur, JPEG compression, white Gaussian noise in color components) / four (Gaussian blur, JPEG compression, white Gaussian noise in color components, color saturation change) perturbations in DeeperForensics-1.0.

14.3.4 Hidden Test Set

Several existing benchmarks [57, 81] have demonstrated high-accuracy face forgery detection results using their proposed datasets. However, the sources and imposed distortions of DeepFakes videos are much more variable and unpredictable in real-world scenarios. Due to the huge biases introduced by a close distribution between the training and test sets, the actual efficacy of these studies [57, 81] in detecting real-world face forgery cases remains to be further elucidated.

An indispensable component of DeeperForensics-1.0 is its introduced hidden test set, which is richer in distribution than the publicly available training set. The hidden test set suggests a better real-world face forgery detection setting: (1) Multiple sources. Fake videos in the wild should be manipulated by different unknown methods; (2) High quality. Threatening fake videos should have high quality to deceive human eyes; (3) Diverse distortions. Different perturbations should be taken into consideration. The ground truth labels are hidden and are used on the host server to evaluate the accuracy of detection models. The hidden test set will evolve by including more challenging samples along with the development of DeepFakes technology.

Overall, DeeperForensics-1.0 is a new *large-scale* dataset consisting of over 60, 000 videos with 17.6 million frames for real-world face forgery detection. *Good-quality* source videos and manipulated videos constitute two main contributions of this dataset. The *high-diversity* perturbations applying to the manipulated videos enhance the robustness of DeeperForensics-1.0 to simulate real scenes. The dataset has been released, free to all research communities, for developing face forgery detection and more general human-face-related research.[1,2]

14.4 DeeperForensics Challenge 2020

In this section, we detail the DeeperForensics Challenge 2020 on real-world face forgery detection, which aims at soliciting innovations to advance the state of the art in DeepFakes detection. The challenge uses the DeeperForensics-1.0 dataset introduced above, and the model evaluation is performed online on the current version of the hidden test set. Participants are expected to devise robust and generic methods for forgery detection in real-world scenarios. The challenge results constitute an essential part of the DeeperForensics-1.0 benchmark. We describe the detailed challenge information and summarize the winning solutions to take a closer look at the current status and possible future development of real-world face forgery detection.

---

[1] GitHub (dataset and code): https://github.com/EndlessSora/DeeperForensics-1.0.

[2] Project page: https://liming-jiang.com/projects/DrF1/DrF1.html.

14.4.1 Platform

The DeeperForensics Challenge 2020 is hosted on the CodaLab platform[3] in conjunction with ECCV 2020, the second Workshop on Sensing, Understanding, and Synthesizing Humans.[4] The online evaluation is conducted using Amazon Web Services (AWS).[5]

First, participants register their teams on the CodaLab challenge website. Then, they are requested to submit their models to the AWS evaluation server (with one 16 GB Tesla V100 GPU for each team) to perform the online evaluation on the hidden test set. When the evaluation is done, participants receive the encrypted prediction files through an automatic email. Finally, they submit the result file to the CodaLab challenge website.

14.4.2 Challenge Dataset

The DeeperForensics Challenge 2020 employs the DeeperForensics-1.0 dataset [41] that was proposed in CVPR 2020. The detailed information of this dataset has been provided in Sect. 14.3. The evaluation of the challenge is performed online on the current version of the hidden test set (Sect. 14.3.4).

All the participants using the DeeperForensics-1.0 dataset should agree to its Terms of Use [9]. They are recommended but not restricted to train their algorithms on DeeperForensics-1.0. The use of any external datasets should be disclosed and follow the Terms of Use.

14.4.3 Evaluation Metric

Similar to Deepfake Detection Challenge (DFDC) [2], the DeeperForensics Challenge 2020 uses the binary cross-entropy loss (BCELoss) to evaluate the performance of face forgery detection models:

$$\text{BCELoss} = -\frac{1}{N} \sum_{i=1}^{N} \left[y_i \cdot \log\left(p\left(y_i\right)\right) + \left(1 - y_i\right) \cdot \log\left(1 - p\left(y_i\right)\right) \right], \quad (14.8)$$

where N is the number of videos in the hidden test set, y_i denotes the ground truth label of video i (fake: 1, real: 0), and $p\left(y_i\right)$ indicates the predicted probability that video i is fake. A smaller BCELoss score is better, which directly contributes to a

---

[3] Challenge website: https://competitions.codalab.org/competitions/25228.

[4] Workshop website: https://sense-human.github.io/index_2020.html.

[5] Online evaluation website: https://aws.amazon.com.

higher ranking. If the BCELoss score is the same, the one with less runtime will achieve a higher ranking. To avoid an infinite BCELoss that is both too confident and wrong, the score is bounded by a threshold value.

14.4.4 Timeline

The DeeperForensics Challenge 2020 lasted for nine weeks—eight weeks for the *development phase* and one week for the *final test phase*.

The challenge officially started at the ECCV 2020 SenseHuman Workshop on August 28, 2020, and it immediately entered the development phase. In the development phase, the evaluation is performed on the *test-dev* hidden test set, which contains 1, 000 videos representing general circumstances of the full hidden test set. The *test-dev* hidden test set is used to maintain a public leaderboard. Participants can conduct four online evaluations (each with 2.5 h of runtime limit) per week.

The final test phase started on October 24, 2020. The evaluation is conducted on the *test-final* hidden test set, containing 3, 000 videos (also including test-dev videos) with a similar distribution as test-dev, for the final competition results. A total of two online evaluations (each with 7.5 h of runtime limit) are allowed. The final test phase ended on October 31, 2020.

Finally, the challenge results were announced in December 2020. In total, 115 participants registered for the competition, and 25 teams made valid submissions.

14.4.5 Results and Solutions

Among the 25 teams who made valid submissions, many participants achieve promising results. We show the final results of the top-5 teams in Table 14.1. In the following subsections, we present the winning solutions of top-3 entries.

Table 14.1 Final results of the top-5 teams in the DeeperForensics Challenge 2020. The runtime is shown in seconds.

Ranking	TeamName	UserName	BCELoss↓	Runtime↓
1	Forensics	BokingChen	0.2674	7690
2	RealFace	Iverson	0.3699	11368
3	VISG	zz110	0.4060	11012
4	jiashangplus	jiashangplus	0.4064	16389
5	Miao	miaotao	0.4132	19823

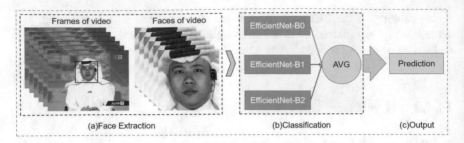

Fig. 14.9 The framework of the first-place solution in the DeeperForensics Challenge 2020

- **Solution of First Place**

As shown in Fig. 14.9, the method designed by the champion team contains three stages, namely Face Extraction, Classification, and Output.

Face Extraction. They first extract 15 frames from each video at equal intervals using VideoCapture of OpenCV. Then, they use the face detector MTCNN [102] to detect the face region of each frame and expand the region by 1.2 times to crop the face image.

Classification. They define the prediction of the probability that the face is fake as the face score. They use EfficientNet [84] as the backbone, which was proven effective in the Deepfake Detection Challenge (DFDC) [2]. The results of three models (EfficientNet-B0, EfficientNet-B1, and EfficientNet-B2) are ensembled for each face.

Output. The final output score of a video is the predicted probability that the video is fake, which is calculated by the average of face scores for the extracted frames.

Implementation Details. The team employs EfficientNet pre-trained on ImageNet as the backbone. They select EfficientNet-B0, EfficientNet-B1, and EfficientNet-B2 for the model ensemble. In addition to DeeperForensics-1.0, they use some other public datasets, *i.e.*, UADFV [99], Deep Fake Detection [13], FaceForensics++ [81], Celeb-DF [57], and DFDC Preview [24]. They balance the class samples with the down-sampling mode. The code of the champion solution has been made publicly available.[6]

– *Training*: Inspired by the DFDC winning solution, appropriate data augmentation could contribute to better results. As for the data augmentation, the champion team uses the perturbation implementation in DeeperForensics-1.0 [8] during training. They only apply the image-level distortions: color saturation change (CS), color contrast change (CC), local block-wise (BW), white Gaussian noise in color components (GNC), Gaussian blur (GB), and JPEG compression (JPEG). They randomly mix up these distortions with a probability of 0.2. Besides, they also try other data

---

[6] https://github.com/beibuwandeluori/DeeperForensicsChallengeSolution.

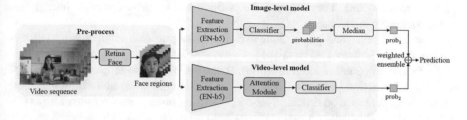

Fig. 14.10 The framework of the second-place solution in the DeeperForensics Challenge 2020

augmentation [3], but the performance improvement is slim. The images are resized to 224 × 224. The batch size is 128, and the total training epoch is 50. They use AdamW optimizer [62] with initial learning rate of 0.001. Label smoothing is applied with a smoothing factor of 0.05.

– *Testing*: The testing pipeline follows the three stages in Fig. 14.9. They clip the prediction score of each video in a range of [0.01, 0.99] to reduce the large loss caused by the prediction errors. In addition to the best BCELoss score, their fastest execution speed may be attributed to the use of the faster face extractor MTCNN and the ensemble of three image-level models with fewer parameters.

- **Solution of Second Place**

Face manipulated video contains two types of forgery traces, *i.e.*, image-level artifacts and video-level artifacts. The former refers to the artifacts such as blending boundaries and abnormal textures within image, while the latter is the face jitter problem between video frames. Most previous works only focused on artifacts in a specific modality and lacked consideration of both. The team in the second place proposes to use an attention mechanism to fuse the temporal information in videos and further combine it with an image model to achieve better results.

The overall framework of their method is shown in Fig. 14.10. First, they use RetinaFace [22] with 20% margin to detect faces in video frames. Then, the face sequence is fed into an image-based model and a video-based model, where the backbones are both EfficientNet-b5 [84] with NoisyStudent [98] pre-trained weights. The image-based model predicts frame by frame and takes the median of probabilities as the prediction. The video-based model takes the entire face sequence as the input and adopts an attention module to fuse the temporal information between frames. Finally, the per-video prediction score is obtained by averaging the probabilities predicted by the above two models.

Implementation Details. The team implements the proposed method via PyTorch. All the models are trained on 8 NVIDIA Tesla V100 GPUs. In addition to the DeeperForensics-1.0 dataset, they use three external datasets, *i.e.*, FaceForensics++ [81], Celeb-DF [57], and Diverse Fake Face Dataset [21]. They used the official splits provided by the above datasets to construct the training, validation, and test sets. They balance the positive and negative samples through the down-sampling technique.

– *Training*: The second-place team uses the following data augmentations: RandAugment [20], patch Gaussian [61], Gaussian blur, image compression, random flip, random crop, and random brightness contrast. They also employ the perturbation implementation in DeeperForensics-1.0 [8]. For the image-based model, they train a classifier based on EfficientNet-b5 [84], using binary cross-entropy loss as the loss function. They adopt a two-stage training strategy for the video-based model. In stage-1, they train an image-based classifier based on EfficientNet-b5. In stage-2, they fix the model parameters trained in stage-1 to serve as face feature extractor and introduce an attention module to learn temporal information via nonlinear transformations and *softmax* operations. The input of the network is the face sequence (*i.e.*, 5 frames per video) in stage-2, and only the attention module and classification layers are trained. The binary cross-entropy loss is adopted as the loss function. The input size is scaled to 320×320. The Adam optimizer [47] is used with a learning rate of 0.0002, $\beta_1 = 0.9$, $\beta_2 = 0.999$, and weight decay of 0.00001. The batch size is 32. The total number of training epochs is set to 20, and the learning rate is halved every 5 epochs.

– *Testing*: They sample 10 frames at equal intervals for each video and detect faces by RetinaFace [22] as in the training phase. Then, the face images are resized to 320×320. Test-time augmentation (TTA) (*e.g.*, flip) is applied to get 20 images (10 original and 10 flipped), which are fed into the network to get the prediction score. They clip the prediction score of each video to $[0.01, 0.99]$ to avoid excessive losses on extreme error samples.

● **Solution of Third Place**

Similar to the second-place entry, the team in the third place also utilize the poor temporal consistency in existing face manipulation techniques. To this end, they propose to use a 3D convolutional neural network (3DCNN) to capture spatial-temporal features for forgery detection. The framework of their method is shown in Fig. 14.11.

Implementation Details. First, the team crops faces in the video frames using the MTCNN [102] face detector. They combine all the cropped face images into a face video clip. Each video clip is then resized to $64 \times 224 \times 224$ or $64 \times 112 \times 112$. Various data augmentations are applied, including Gaussian blur, white Gaussian noise in color components, random crop, random flip, *etc*. Then, they use the processed video clips as the input to train a 3D convolutional neural network (3DCNN) using the cross-entropy loss. They examine three kinds of networks, I3D [15], 3D ResNet [29], and R(2+1)D [90]. These models are pre-trained on the action recognition datasets, *e.g.*, kinetics [46]. In addition to DeeperForensics-1.0, they use three external public face manipulation datasets, *i.e.*, the DFDC dataset [23], Deep Fake Detection [13], and FaceForensics++ [81].

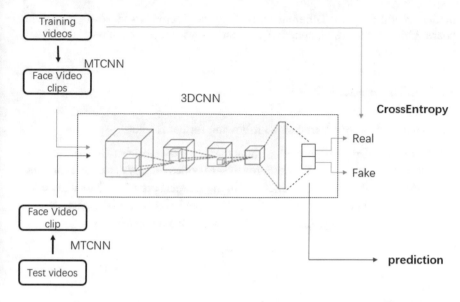

Fig. 14.11 The framework of the third-place solution in the DeeperForensics Challenge 2020

14.5 Discussion

In this chapter, we have introduced a new large-scale dataset named DeeperForensics-1.0. The dataset facilitates the research of face forgery detection in real-world scenarios. We have also presented several methods that consider different potential aspects in developing a robust face forgery detection model. Winning solutions of the DeeperForensics Challenge 2020 have achieved promising performance.

In summary, there are three key points inspired by these methods that could improve real-world face forgery detection. (1) Strong backbone. Backbone selection for a forgery detection model is important. The high-performance winning solutions are based on state-of-the-art EfficientNet. (2) Diverse augmentations. Applying appropriate data augmentations may better simulate real-world scenarios and boost the model performance. (3) Temporal information. Since the primary detection target is the fake videos, temporal information can be a critical clue to distinguish the real from the fake.

Despite the promising results, we believe that there is still much room for improvement in the real-world face forgery detection task. (1) More suitable and diverse data augmentations may contribute to a better simulation of real-world data distribution. (2) Developing a robust detection method that can cope with unseen manipulation methods and distortions is a critical problem. At this stage, we observe that the model training is data-dependent. Although data augmentations can help improve the performance to a certain extent, the generalization ability of most forgery detection models is still poor. (3) Different artifacts in the DeepFakes videos (*e.g.*, checkerboard Artifacts and fusion boundary artifacts) remain rarely explored.

14.6 Further Reading

Interested readers are referred to the following further readings:

- [41] for more detailed information about the DeeperForensics-1.0 dataset and more detection baselines in the DeeperForensics-1.0 video forgery detection benchmark.
- [40] for more detailed information about the DeeperForensics Challenge 2020.
- [23, 31, 57, 81] for other closely related DeepFakes detection datasets.
- [66, 71, 88] for surveys on DeepFakes creation and detection.

References

1. DeepFaceLab https://github.com/iperov/DeepFaceLab. Accessed 20 Aug 2019
2. Deepfake Detection Challenge. https://www.kaggle.com/c/deepfake-detection-challenge. Accessed 15 Feb 2020
3. Deepfake detection (DFDC) solution by selimsef https://github.com/selimsef/dfdc_deepfake_challenge. Accessed 30 Oct 2020
4. DeepFakes https://github.com/deepfakes/faceswap. Accessed 16 Aug 2019
5. FaceSwap https://github.com/MarekKowalski/FaceSwap. Accessed 18 Aug 2019
6. faceswap-GAN https://github.com/shaoanlu/faceswap-GAN. Accessed 16 Aug 2019
7. FakeAPP https://www.fakeapp.com. Accessed 25 July 2019
8. Perturbation implementation in DeeperForensics-1.0 https://github.com/EndlessSora/DeeperForensics-1.0/tree/master/perturbation. Accessed 30 Oct 2020
9. Terms of use: DeeperForensics-1.0 dataset https://github.com/EndlessSora/DeeperForensics-1.0/blob/master/dataset/Terms_of_Use.pdf. Accessed 21 May 2020
10. Afchar D, Nozick V, Yamagishi J, Echizen I (2018) Mesonet: a compact facial video forgery detection network. In: Proceedings of the IEEE international workshop on information forensics and security
11. Amerini I, Ballan L, Caldelli R, Del Bimbo A, Serra G (2011) A sift-based forensic method for copy-move attack detection and transformation recovery. IEEE Trans Inf Forensics Secur 6:1099–1110
12. Bayar B, Stamm MC (2016) A deep learning approach to universal image manipulation detection using a new convolutional layer. In: Proceedings of the 4th ACM workshop on information hiding and multimedia security
13. Blog GA Contributing data to deepfake detection research. https://ai.googleblog.com/2019/09/contributing-data-to-deepfake-detection.html. Accessed 25 Sep 2019
14. Cao C, Weng Y, Zhou S, Tong Y, Zhou K (2013) FaceWarehouse: a 3D facial expression database for visual computing. IEEE Trans Visualization Comput Gr 20:413–425
15. Carreira J, Zisserman A (2017) Quo vadis, action recognition? a new model and the kinetics dataset. In: Proceedings of the IEEE conference on computer vision and pattern recognition

16. Chai L, Bau D, Lim SN, Isola P (2020) What makes fake images detectable? understanding properties that generalize. In: Proceedings of the european conference on computer vision
17. Choi Y, Choi M, Kim M, Ha JW, Kim S, Choo J (2018) StarGAN: unified generative adversarial networks for multi-domain image-to-image translation. In: Proceedings of the IEEE conference on computer vision and pattern recognition
18. Chollet F (2017) Xception: deep learning with depthwise separable convolutions. In: Proceedings of the IEEE conference on computer vision and pattern recognition
19. Cozzolino D, Poggi G, Verdoliva L (2017) Recasting residual-based local descriptors as convolutional neural networks: an application to image forgery detection. In: Proceedings of the 5th ACM workshop on information hiding and multimedia security
20. Cubuk ED, Zoph B, Shlens J, Le QV (2020) RandAugment: practical automated data augmentation with a reduced search space. In: Proceedings of the IEEE conference on computer vision and pattern recognition workshops
21. Dang H, Liu F, Stehouwer J, Liu X, Jain AK (2020) On the detection of digital face manipulation. In: Proceedings of the IEEE conference on computer vision and pattern recognition
22. Deng J, Guo J, Ververas E, Kotsia I, Zafeiriou S (2020) RetinaFace: Single-shot multi-level face localisation in the wild. In: Proceedings of the IEEE conference on computer vision and pattern recognition
23. Dolhansky B, Bitton J, Pflaum B, Lu J, Howes R, Wang M, Ferrer CC (2020) The deepfake detection challenge dataset. arXiv preprint arXiv:2006.07397
24. Dolhansky B, Howes R, Pflaum B, Baram N, Ferrer CC (2019) The deepfake detection challenge (DFDC) preview dataset. arXiv preprint arXiv:1910.08854
25. Fridrich J, Kodovsky J (2012) Rich models for steg analysis of digital images. IEEE Trans Inf Forensics Secur 7:868–882
26. Goodfellow I, Pouget-Abadie J, Mirza M, Xu B, Warde-Farley D, Ozair S, Courville A, Bengio Y (2014) Generative adversarial nets. In: Proceedings of the advances in neural information processing systems
27. Guarnera L, Giudice O, Battiato S (2020) Deepfake detection by analyzing convolutional traces. In: Proceedings of the IEEE conference on computer vision and pattern recognition workshops
28. Güera D, Delp EJ (2018) Deepfake video detection using recurrent neural networks. In: Proceedings of the IEEE international conference on advanced video and signal based surveillance
29. Hara K, Kataoka H, Satoh Y (2017) Learning spatio-temporal features with 3D residual networks for action recognition. In: Proceedings of the IEEE international conference on computer vision workshops
30. He K, Zhang X, Ren S, Sun J (2016) Deep residual learning for image recognition. In: Proceedings of the IEEE conference on computer vision and pattern recognition
31. He Y, Gan B, Chen S, Zhou Y, Yin G, Song L, Sheng L, Shao J, Liu Z (2021) ForgeryNet: A versatile benchmark for comprehensive forgery analysis. In: Proceedings of the IEEE conference on computer vision and pattern recognition
32. Hernandez-Ortega J, Tolosana R, Fierrez J, Morales A (2021) DeepFakesON-Phys: deepfakes detection based on heart rate estimation. In: Proceedings of the AAAI conference on artificial intelligence workshops (2021)
33. Hinton GE, Salakhutdinov RR (2006) Reducing the dimensionality of data with neural networks. Science 313:504–507
34. Hochreiter S, Schmidhuber J (1997) Long short-term memory. Neural Comput 9:1735–1780
35. Huang X, Belongie S (2017) Arbitrary style transfer in real-time with adaptive instance normalization. In: Proceedings of the IEEE international conference on computer vision
36. Huang X, Liu MY, Belongie S, Kautz J (2018) Multimodal unsupervised image-to-image translation. In: Proceedings of the European conference on computer vision
37. Ilg E, Mayer N, Saikia T, Keuper M, Dosovitskiy A, Brox T (2017) Flownet 2.0: Evolution of optical flow estimation with deep networks. In: Proceedings of the IEEE conference on computer vision and pattern recognition

38. Isola P, Zhu JY, Zhou T, Efros AA (2017) Image-to-image translation with conditional adversarial networks. In: Proceedings of the IEEE conference on computer vision and pattern recognition
39. Jiang L, Dai B, Wu W, Loy CC (2020) Focal frequency loss for image reconstruction and synthesis. In: Proceedings of the IEEE international conference on computer vision
40. Jiang L, Guo Z, Wu W, Liu Z, Liu Z, Loy CC, Yang S, Xiong Y, Xia W, Chen B, Zhuang P, Li S, Chen S, Yao T, Ding S, Li J, Huang F, Cao L, Ji R, Lu C, Tan G (2021) DeeperForensics Challenge 2020 on real-world face forgery detection: methods and results. arXiv:2102.09471
41. Jiang L, Li R, Wu W, Qian C, Loy CC (2020) DeeperForensics-1.0: a large-scale dataset for real-world face forgery detection. In: Proceedings of the IEEE conference on computer vision and pattern recognition
42. Jiang L, Zhang C, Huang M, Liu C, Shi J, Loy CC (2020) TSIT: a simple and versatile framework for image-to-image translation. In: Proceedings of the european conference on computer vision
43. Karras T, Aila T, Laine S, Lehtinen J (2017) Progressive growing of GANs for improved quality, stability, and variation. arXiv:1710.10196
44. Karras T, Laine S, Aila T (2019) A style-based generator architecture for generative adversarial networks. In: Proceedings of the IEEE conference on computer vision and pattern recognition
45. Karras T, Laine S, Aittala M, Hellsten J, Lehtinen J, Aila T (2020) Analyzing and improving the image quality of StyleGAN. In: Proceedings of the IEEE conference on computer vision and pattern recognition
46. Kay W, Carreira J, Simonyan K, Zhang B, Hillier C, Vijayanarasimhan S, Viola F, Green T, Back T, Natsev P et al (2017) The kinetics human action video dataset. arXiv:1705.06950
47. Kingma DP, Ba J (2014) Adam: a method for stochastic optimization. arXiv:1412.6980
48. Kingma DP, Dhariwal P (2018) Glow: generative flow with invertible 1x1 convolutions. In: Proceedings of the advances in neural information processing systems
49. Kingma DP, Mohamed S, Rezende DJ, Welling M (2014) Semi-supervised learning with deep generative models. In: Proceedings of the advances in neural information processing systems
50. Kingma DP, Welling M (2013) Auto-encoding variational bayes. arXiv:1312.6114
51. Korshunov P, Marcel S (2018) Deepfakes: a new threat to face recognition? assessment and detection. arXiv:1812.08685
52. Korus P, Huang J (2016) Multi-scale analysis strategies in PRNU-based tampering localization. IEEE Trans Inf Forensics Secur 12:809–824
53. Li L, Bao J, Yang H, Chen D, Wen F (2020) FaceShifter: towards high fidelity and occlusion aware face swapping. In: Proceedings of the IEEE conference on computer vision and pattern recognition
54. Li L, Bao J, Zhang T, Yang H, Chen D, Wen F, Guo B (2020) Face x-ray for more general face forgery detection. In: Proceedings of the IEEE conference on computer vision and pattern recognition
55. Li Y, Chang MC, Lyu S (2018) In ictu oculi: exposing ai created fake videos by detecting eye blinking. In: Proceedings of the IEEE international workshop on information forensics and security
56. Li Y, Lyu S (2018) Exposing deepfake videos by detecting face warping artifacts. arXiv:1811.00656
57. Li Y, Yang X, Sun P, Qi H, Lyu S (2019) Celeb-DF: a new dataset for deepfake forensics. arXiv:1909.12962
58. Lin KY, Wang G (2018) Hallucinated-iqa: No-reference image quality assessment via adversarial learning. In: Proceedings of the IEEE conference on computer vision and pattern recognition
59. Liu MY, Breuel T, Kautz J (2017) Unsupervised image-to-image translation networks. In: Proceedings of the advances in neural information processing systems
60. Liu X, Yin G, Shao J, Wang X, Li H (2019) Learning to predict layout-to-image conditional convolutions for semantic image synthesis. In: Proceedings of the advances in neural information processing systems

61. Lopes RG, Yin D, Poole B, Gilmer J, Cubuk ED (2019) Improving robustness without sacrificing accuracy with patch gaussian augmentation. arXiv:1906.02611
62. Loshchilov I, Hutter F (2019) Decoupled weight decay regularization. In: Proceedings of the international conference on learning representations
63. Masi I, Killekar A, Mascarenhas RM, Gurudatt SP, AbdAlmageed W (2020) Two-branch recurrent network for isolating deepfakes in videos. In: Proceedings of the european conference on computer vision
64. Matern F, Riess C, Stamminger M (2019) Exploiting visual artifacts to expose deepfakes and face manipulations. In: Proceedings of the IEEE winter applications of computer vision workshops
65. McCloskey S, Albright M (2019) Detecting gan-generated imagery using saturation cues. In: Proceedings of the IEEE international conference on image processing
66. Mirsky Y, Lee W (2021) The creation and detection of deepfakes: a survey. ACM Comput Surveys 54:1–41
67. Mirza M, Osindero S (2014) Conditional generative adversarial nets. arXiv:1411.1784
68. Mittal T, Bhattacharya U, Chandra R, Bera A, Manocha D (2020) Emotions don't lie: a deepfake detection method using audio-visual affective cues. arXiv:2003.06711
69. Newell A, Yang K, Deng J (2016) Stacked hourglass networks for human pose estimation. In: Proceedings of the european conference on computer vision
70. Nguyen HH, Fang F, Yamagishi J, Echizen I (2019) Multi-task learning for detecting and segmenting manipulated facial images and videos. arXiv:1906.06876
71. Nguyen TT, Nguyen CM, Nguyen DT, Nguyen DT, Nahavandi S (2019) Deep learning for deepfakes creation and detection: a survey. arXiv:1909.11573
72. Nirkin Y, Keller Y, Hassner T (2019) FSGAN: subject agnostic face swapping and reenactment. In: Proceedings of the IEEE international conference on computer vision
73. Nirkin Y, Wolf L, Keller Y, Hassner T (2020) Deepfake detection based on the discrepancy between the face and its context. arXiv:2008.12262
74. Van den Oord A, Kalchbrenner N, Espeholt L, Vinyals O, Graves A et al (2016) Conditional image generation with PixelCNN decoders. In: Proceedings of the advances in neural information processing systems
75. Park T, Liu MY, Wang TC, Zhu JY (2019) Semantic image synthesis with spatially-adaptive normalization. In: Proceedings of the IEEE conference on computer vision and pattern recognition
76. Petrov I, Gao D, Chervoniy N, Liu K, Marangonda S, Umé C, Jiang J, RP L, Zhang S, Wu P et al (2020) DeepFaceLab: a simple, flexible and extensible face swapping framework. arXiv:2005.05535
77. Ponomarenko N, Jin L, Ieremeiev O, Lukin V, Egiazarian K, Astola J, Vozel B, Chehdi K, Carli M, Battisti F et al (2015) Image database TID2013: peculiarities, results and perspectives. Signal Process Image Commun 30:57–77
78. Qian Y, Yin G, Sheng L, Chen Z, Shao J (2020) Thinking in frequency: face forgery detection by mining frequency-aware clues. In: Proceedings of the european conference on computer vision
79. Radford A, Metz L, Chintala S (2015) Unsupervised representation learning with deep convolutional generative adversarial networks. arXiv:1511.06434
80. Rahmouni N, Nozick V, Yamagishi J, Echizen I (2017) Distinguishing computer graphics from natural images using convolution neural networks. In: Proceedings of the IEEE workshop on information forensics and security
81. Rössler A, Cozzolino D, Verdoliva L, Riess C, Thies J, Nießner M (2019) FaceForensics++: learning to detect manipulated facial images. In: Proceedings of the IEEE international conference on computer vision (2019)
82. Sanderson C (2002) The vidtimit database. Tech. rep, IDIAP
83. Sun K, Liu H, Ye Q, Liu J, Gao Y, Shao L, Ji R (2021) Domain general face forgery detection by learning to weight. In: Proceedings of the AAAI conference on artificial intelligence

84. Tan M, Le Q (2019) EfficientNet: rethinking model scaling for convolutional neural networks. In: Proceedings of the international conference on machine learning
85. Thies J, Zollhöfer M, Nießner M (2019) Deferred neural rendering: image synthesis using neural textures. arXiv:1904.12356
86. Thies J, Zollhofer M, Stamminger M, Theobalt C, Nießner M (2016) Face2face: real-time face capture and reenactment of rgb videos. In: Proceedings of the IEEE conference on computer vision and pattern recognition
87. Tolosana R, Romero-Tapiador S, Fierrez J, Vera-Rodriguez R (2021) Deepfakes evolution: analysis of facial regions and fake detection performance. In: Proceedings of the international conference on pattern recognition workshops
88. Tolosana R, Vera-Rodriguez R, Fierrez J, Morales A, Ortega-Garcia J (2020) Deepfakes and beyond: a survey of face manipulation and fake detection. Inf Fusion 64:131–148
89. Tran D, Bourdev L, Fergus R, Torresani L, Paluri M (2015) Learning spatiotemporal features with 3D convolutional networks. In: Proceedings of the IEEE international conference on computer vision
90. Tran D, Wang H, Torresani L, Ray J, LeCun Y, Paluri M (2018) A closer look at spatiotemporal convolutions for action recognition. In: Proceedings of the IEEE conference on computer vision and pattern recognition
91. Trinh L, Tsang M, Rambhatla S, Liu Y (2021) Interpretable and trustworthy deepfake detection via dynamic prototypes. In: Proceedings of the IEEE winter conference on applications of computer vision
92. Wang L, Xiong Y, Wang Z, Qiao Y, Lin D, Tang X, Van Gool L (2016) Temporal segment networks: towards good practices for deep action recognition. In: Proceedings of the european conference on computer vision
93. Wang SY, Wang O, Zhang R, Owens A, Efros AA (2020) CNN-generated images are urprisingly easy to spot...for now. In: Proceedings of the IEEE conference on computer vision and pattern recognition
94. Wang TC, Liu MY, Zhu JY, Liu G, Tao A, Kautz J, Catanzaro B (2018) Video-to-video synthesis. arXiv:1808.06601
95. Wang, T.C., Liu, M.Y., Zhu, J.Y., Tao, A., Kautz, J., Catanzaro, B.: High-resolution image synthesis and semantic manipulation with conditional GANs. In: Proceedings of the IEEE Conference on Computer Vision and Pattern Recognition (2018)
96. Wu W, Qian C, Yang S, Wang Q, Cai Y, Zhou Q (2018) Look at boundary: a boundary-aware face alignment algorithm. In: Proceedings of the IEEE conference on computer vision and pattern recognition
97. Wu W, Zhang Y, Li C, Qian C, Loy CC(2018) ReenactGAN: learning to reenact faces via boundary transfer. In: Proceedings of the European conference on computer vision
98. Xie Q, Luong MT, Hovy E, Le QV (2020) Self-training with noisy student improves ImageNet classification. In: Proceedings of the IEEE conference on computer vision and pattern recognition
99. Yang X, Li Y, Lyu S (2019) Exposing deep fakes using inconsistent head poses. In: Proceedings of the IEEE international conference on acoustics, speech and signal processing
100. Yu N, Davis LS, Fritz M (2019) Attributing fake images to GANs: learning and analyzing GAN fingerprints. In: Proceedings of the IEEE international conference on computer vision
101. Zampoglou M, Papadopoulos S, Kompatsiaris Y (2015) Detecting image splicing in the wild (web). In: Proceedings of the IEEE international conference on multimedia & expo workshops
102. Zhang K, Zhang Z, Li Z, Qiao Y (2016) Joint face detection and alignment using multitask cascaded convolutional networks. IEEE Signal Process Lett 23:1499–1503
103. Zhou P, Han X, Morariu VI, Davis LS (2017) Two-stream neural networks for tampered face detection. In: Proceedings of the IEEE conference on computer vision and pattern recognition workshops
104. Zhu JY, Park T, Isola P, Efros AA (2017) Unpaired image-to-image translation using cycle-consistent adversarial networks. In: Proceedings of the IEEE international conference on computer vision

Chapter 15
Face Morphing Attack Detection Methods

Ulrich Scherhag, Christian Rathgeb, and Christoph Busch

Abstract Morphing attacks pose a serious threat to face recognition systems, especially in the border control scenario. In order to guarantee a secure operation of face recognition algorithms in the future, it is necessary to be able to reliably detect morphed facial images and thus be able to reject them during enrolment or verification. This chapter provides an overview of morphing attack detection algorithms and metrics to measure and compare their performance. Different concepts of morphing attack detection are introduced and state-of-the-art detection methods are evaluated in a comprehensive cross-database experiments considering various realistic image post-processings.

15.1 Introduction

Facial recognition systems have been found vulnerable to Morphing Attacks (MAs). In these attacks, the facial images of two (or more) individuals are combined (morphed) and the resulting morphed facial image is then presented during registration as a biometric reference. If the morphed image is accepted, it is likely that all individuals that contributed to the morphed facial image can be successfully authenticated against it. Morphing attacks thus pose a serious threat to facial recognition systems, in particular in scenarios where the reference image is often provided in printed form by the applicant. The vulnerability of facial recognition systems to face MAs is already well known [5, 29]. Many different approaches for Morphing Attack Detection (MAD)

U. Scherhag
iCOGNIZE GmbH, Dietzenbach, Germany
e-mail: ulrich.scherhag@icognize.de

C. Rathgeb (✉)
secunet Security Networks, Essen, Germany
e-mail: christian.rathgeb@secunet.com

C. Busch
Hochschule Darmstadt, Darmstadt, Germany
e-mail: christoph.busch@h-da.de

© The Author(s) 2022
C. Rathgeb et al. (eds.), *Handbook of Digital Face Manipulation and Detection*,
Advances in Computer Vision and Pattern Recognition,
https://doi.org/10.1007/978-3-030-87664-7_15

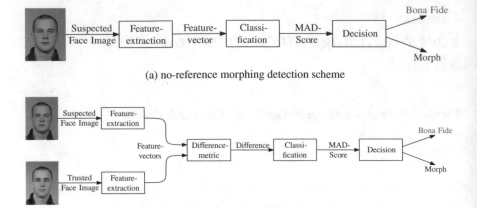

(a) no-reference morphing detection scheme

(b) differential morphing detection scheme

Fig. 15.1 Categorisation to no-reference and differential morphing attack detection scheme

have been proposed in the scientific literature. For a comprehensive survey on published morphing attack detection methods the interested reader is referred to [29, 31]. An automated detection of morphed face images is vital to retain the security of operational face recognition systems. According to [25], MAD systems can be divided into two categories: no-reference or single image MAD and reference-based or differential MAD. The corresponding scheme for single image MAD is shown in Fig. 15.1a.

The image to be analysed is passed to the MAD system. First, features are extracted, based on which a classifier decides whether the presented image is a morph or bona fide. The single image MAD scheme can be used during enrolment as well as during verification.

Differential MAD can be used in scenarios where another image, a Trusted Live Capture (TLC), is available in addition to the suspected morph. For example, during verification in an Automated Border Control (ABC) gate, when the probe image is acquired in addition to the extracted reference image from the electronic travel document (suspected morph). The schematic process of differential MAD is depicted in Fig. 15.1b. In general, the same features are extracted from both provided images. These are compared according to a fixed metric and the classifier uses this difference to decide if the suspected morph is a morph or bona fide. This method has the advantage that the additional information of the TLC is used for the decision. However, it should be noted that in real scenarios TLCs are usually acquired in semi-supervised environments, e.g. border gate, and therefore may show a lower quality and higher variance compared to the suspected images.

This bookchapter is organised as follows: Sect. 15.2 briefly discusses related works on MAD. Section 15.3 describes the considered MAD pipeline. The used database is described in Sect. 15.4. MAD methods are presented in Sect. 15.5 and evaluated in Sect. 15.6. Finally, a summary is given in Sect. 15.7.

15.2   Related Works

In recent years, numerous approaches for the automated detection of MAs have been presented. The majority of works is based on the single image scenario. The single image MAD approaches can be categorised into three classes: texture descriptors, e.g. in [20, 24, 26], forensic image analysis, e.g. in [23, 32], and methods based on deep neural networks, e.g. in [7, 21]. These differ in the artefacts they can potentially detect. A brief overview is given in Table 15.1.

Differential MAD can be categorised into approaches that perform a biometric comparison directly with the two facial images, e.g. in [30], and algorithms that attempt to reverse the (potential) morphing process, e.g. in [6, 16]. In the former category, features from both face images, the potentially morphed facial image and the probe image, are extracted and then compared. The comparison of the two feature vectors and the classification as bona fide comparison or MA is usually done using machine learning techniques. By specifically training these procedures for the recognition of MAs, they can—in contrast to facial recognition algorithms—learn to recognise specific patterns within the differences between the two feature vectors for these attacks. This has already been demonstrated for features derived from general purpose texture descriptors. While training a deep neural network from scratch in order to learn discriminative features for MAD requires a high amount of training data, pre-trained deep networks can be employed. The second type of differential MAD procedure aims at reversing the morphing process in the reference image ("de-morphing") by using a probe image. If the reference image was morphed from two images and the probe image shows a person contributing to the morph (the attacker), the face of the accomplice would ideally be reconstructed, which would be rejected in a subsequent comparison with the probe image using biometric face recognition; if, on the other hand, a bona fide reference image is available, the same subject should still be recognisable after the reversal of a presumed morph process with the probe image, and thus the subsequent comparison of the facial recognition process should be successful.

Despite promising results reported in many studies, the reliable detection of morphed facial images is still an open research task [14]. In particular, the generalis-

Table 15.1   Categories of singe image MAD approaches and analysed artefacts

Category	Analysed artefacts
Texture descriptors	Smoothened skin texture, ghost artefacts/ half-shade effects (e.g. on pupils, nostrils), distorted edges, offset image areas
Forensic image analysis	Sensor pattern noise, compression artefacts, inconsistent illumination or colour values
Deep-learning approaches	All possible artefacts learned from a training dataset

ability and robustness of the published approaches could not yet be proven while some results are hardly comparable and comprehensible. The vast majority of publications use internal databases of the respective research groups for training and testing [27]. In addition, different evaluation metrics are used in the publications. Since most implemented MAD procedures are not made publicly accessible, comparative independent evaluation of the detection performance is difficult. First efforts towards benchmarking MAD algorithms have been made in [15, 22]. Furthermore, most publications only use images from a single database and morphs generated with a single algorithm for training and testing, so that the generalisation capability of the methods cannot be assessed across different databases and morphing methods. In publications on differential MAD, the comparison images used often show a low variance with respect to poses, facial expressions and illumination and are usually produced shortly after the reference image—in real scenarios such as border control, a much higher variance is to be expected. In addition, many studies neglect the probable application of image post-processing techniques by an attacker, such as subsequent image sharpening, and the print-scan transformation [14].

15.3 Morphing Attack Detection Pipeline

The individual modules of the pipeline considered for MAD algorithms are illustrated in Fig. 15.2. The pipeline consists of the following 4 steps: data preparation, feature extraction, feature preparation, and classifier training.

15.3.1 Data Preparation and Feature Extraction

For most feature extractors it is necessary to pre-process the face image beforehand. The result of feature extractors depends on the resolution of the analysed image, requiring a normalisation of the image size. Especially with the TLCs, variances in position and pose may occur, which can be corrected by the data preparation. In addition, it is useful, for example, for texture-based feature extractors, to crop the image to the relevant facial area, ensuring that no information from the background influences the feature vector.

Depending on the feature extractor selected and the configuration, the obtained feature vector will contain different information, information not contained in the

Fig. 15.2 Design of MAD pipeline

feature vector is not available to the algorithms in the further process. For example, if a basic Local Binary Patterns (LBP) histogram is calculated, the feature vector will not contain any spatial information. If, despite the use of LBP histograms, spatial information is to be included in the feature vector, the image to be analysed can be divided into cells, a histogram can be calculated for each cell and the resulting histograms can be concatenated. Thus, spatial information in resolution of the cells can be preserved, however, the length of the feature vector increases accordingly.

15.3.2 Feature Preparation and Classifier Training

Once the feature vectors have been created, they have to be prepared for the training of the classifier. For example, many classifiers only accept one-dimensional input data, requiring multi-dimensional characteristics to be prepared accordingly. Further, for differential MAD algorithms, this module combines the feature vectors of the suspected morph and the TLC. The choice of the combination method is arbitrary but determines the length of the resulting feature vector as well as the contained information. Most classifiers require normalised data for optimal training, thus feature normalisation may be required.

In the last module classifiers are trained on basis of the previously prepared feature vectors. In order to achieve the best possible separation of the feature vectors into classes, appropriate classifiers and parameters have to be chosen. The optimal classifier and parameters depend on the information in the respective feature vectors.

15.4 Database

The face image database used in this work is based on the publicly available FERET [19] and FRGC [18] face image databases. The creation of the database requires 3 categories of images: bona fide reference images, morph input images, and TLC images. The bona fide reference images correspond to an unaltered passport image and should meet the corresponding quality criteria. The morph input images are used in pairs for the morphing process. These should be of passport image quality as well. For the selection of the images in passport image quality, the guidelines standardised in ISO/IEC 19794-5 [8] were followed. Consequently, only images with a closed or minimally opened mouth and a neutral facial expression or a slight smile were included. Images with reflecting glasses were discarded. The class of TLC images corresponds to live recordings, for example, at an ABC gate. Therefore, the images should not be of a controlled, high quality, as this cannot be expected from semi-supervised capturing. For this class, all images not classified as suitable for passport photos in the above pre-selection can be considered. Thus, these images may contain variations in sharpness, lighting, facial expressions, pose, etc.

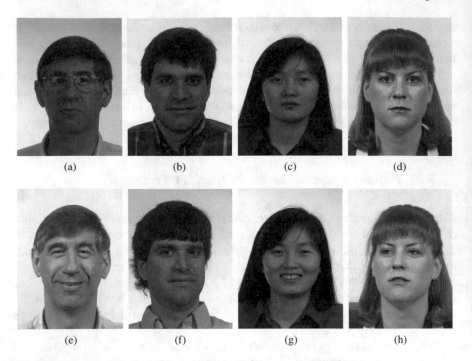

(a) (b) (c) (d)

(e) (f) (g) (h)

Fig. 15.3 Examples of reference and grey scale TLC images for FERET

Table 15.2 Composition of the database resulting from the image pre-selection

Database	Subjects	Male	Female	Bona fide	Morph input	TLC
FERET	530	330	200	530	530	791
FRGC	533	231	302	984	964	1726

The partitioning of the images into the classes *passport image quality* and *TLC quality* was carried out manually. In the FERET subset, mainly different facial expressions and slight rotations in the pose are included, examples are given in Fig. 15.3. In the FRGC subset, the variances are more significant. In addition to different facial expressions, different backgrounds, illuminations and focuses of the images can be observed, examples are shown in Fig. 15.4.

Based on the two pre-sorted classes, the images are divided into three categories: bona fide reference images, morph input images and TLC images. In order to create realistic scenarios, the time of capture between the passport images and the probe images is maximised as far as possible on the basis of the databases. Due to the large differences in the number of images per subject between the databases, different protocols are used for both databases. The composition of the resulting database is listed in Table 15.2.

(a)   (b)   (c)   (d)

(e)   (f)   (g)   (h)

Fig. 15.4 Examples of reference and grey scale TLC images for FRGC

15.4.1   *Image Morphing*

In order to enable the database to be used for evaluating the generalisability of
MAD algorithms towards differing morphing algorithms, four different morphing
algorithms are applied to construct the database, hereafter referred to as FaceFusion,[1]
FaceMorpher,[2] OpenCV and UBO Morpher:

- **FaceFusion** is a proprietary morphing algorithm. Originally being an iOS app,
  an adaptation for Windows which uses the 68 landmarks of Dlib and Delaunay
  triangles was applied. After the morphing process, certain regions (eyes, nostrils,
  hair) of the first face image are blended over the morph to hide artefacts. Optionally,
  the corresponding landmarks of upper and lower lips can be reduced as described
  in [12] to avoid artefacts at closed mouths. The created morphs have a high quality
  and low to no visible artefacts. An example is shown in Fig. 15.5b.
- **FaceMorpher** is an open-source implementation using Python. In the version
  applied for this work, the algorithm uses STASM for landmark localisation. Delaunay triangles, which are formed from the landmarks, are warped and blended. The

---

[1] www.wearemoment.com/FaceFusion.

[2] https://github.com/alyssaq/face_morpher.

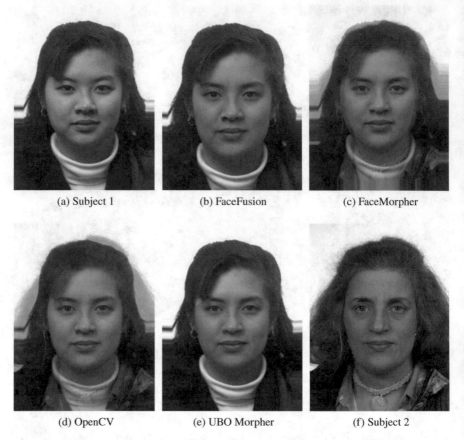

(a) Subject 1   (b) FaceFusion   (c) FaceMorpher

(d) OpenCV   (e) UBO Morpher   (f) Subject 2

Fig. 15.5 Examples of morphing face images **a** and **f** using all four algorithms (**b**)–(**e**)

area outside the landmarks is averaged. The generated morphs show strong artefacts in particular in the area of neck and hair. An example is shown in Fig. 15.5c.

- **OpenCV** is a self implemented morphing algorithm derived from "Face Morph
  Using OpenCV".[3] This algorithm works similar to FaceMorpher. Important differences between the algorithms are that for landmark detection Dlib is used instead
  of STASM and that for this algorithm landmarks are positioned at the edge of the
  image, which are also used to create morphs. Thus, in contrast to FaceMorpher,
  the edge does not consist of an averaged image, but like the rest of the image, of
  morphed triangles. However, strong artefacts outside the face area can be observed,
  which is mainly due to missing landmarks. An example is shown in Fig. 15.5d.
- **UBO Morpher** is the morphing tool of University of Bologna, as used, e.g. in [6].
  This algorithm receives two input images as well as the corresponding landmarks.
  Dlib landmarks were used in this work. The morphs are generated by triangulation,

---

[3] www.learnopencv.com/face-morph-using-opencv-cpp-python.

Table 15.3 Number of comparisons per post-processing in the resulting database

Database	Genuine Comp. Bona Fide Comp.	Impostor comparisons	Morph comparisons	Bona fide samples	Morph samples
FERET	791	418,966	791	530	529
FRGC	3,298	1,695,086	3,246	984	964

warping and blending. To avoid artefacts in the area outside the face, the morphed face is copied to the background of one of the original images. Even if the colours are adjusted, visible edges may appear at borderline of the blended areas. An example is shown in Fig. 15.5e.

The morph input images are used to create the morphs. Morph pairs were formed in a way to keep the ratio between morphs and bona fide images in balance. Two parameters, namely, sex and whether the subject wears glasses, are taken into account for the construction of the morph pairs. Morphing subjects of different sexes usually results in morphs with unnatural appearance. The creation of morphs with subjects of different sex are not to be expected in the real scenario, thus they are excluded from the database. Furthermore, it has been found, that if two subjects wearing glasses are morphed, the resulting morph contains double glasses. To avoid this kind of artefacts, morph pairs are formed with at most one subject wearing glasses.

The morph pairs are formed within one face database, in order to enable a clear separation of datasets during training and evaluation. Due to the different number of morph input images per subject in both databases, different protocols are defined. With each morphing tool morphs were created from all available morph pairs. The morphs were created with a blending and warping factor of 0.5. However, due to the automatic improvement processes of FaceFusion and UBO Morpher, the morphs created by these algorithms are not symmetrical.

The properties of the resulting database are listed in Table 15.3. For the evaluation of differential MAD algorithms the number of bona fide comparisons and morph comparisons is relevant, for single image MAD algorithms the number of bona fide samples and morph samples, respectively. The values given are per post-processing, quadrupling the actual number of passport images contained in the database.

15.4.2 Image Post-Processing

The passport images (morph and bona fide) and the TLC images are post-processed in a different way. The TLC images are converted to greyscale, as some camera systems used at border control are only providing monochrome images. Since the morphing algorithms produce different, and sometimes recognisable, outputs, for example, by partially normalising the images, all passport images (including the bona fides) are

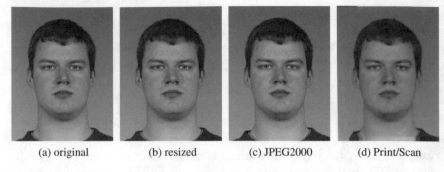

| (a) original | (b) resized | (c) JPEG2000 | (d) Print/Scan |

Fig. 15.6 Examples of an original image and the three post-processing types

normalised. This also prevents from over-fitting to artefacts not present in a real scenario, such as different image sizes between morphs and bona fides. During the normalisation process, images are scaled to 960×720 pixels, resulting in a face region of 320×320 pixels.

Depending on the process by which the facial image is inserted into the passport, various post-processing steps are performed on the image. To reflect the realistic scenarios, the database contains four different post-processing chains for all passport photographs (Fig. 15.6):

- **Unprocessed**: The images are not further processed. In the text below referred to as *NPP* (no post-processing). This serves as baseline.
- **Resized**: The resolution of the images is reduced by half, reflecting the average size of a passport image. This pre-processing corresponds to the scenario that an image is submitted digitally by the applicant.
- **JPEG2000**: The images are resized by half and then compressed using JPEG2000, a wavelet-based image compression method that is recommended for EU passports [4]. The setting is selected in a way that a target file size of 15KB is achieved. This scenario reflects the post-processing path of passport images if handed over digitally at the application desk.
- **Print/Scan–JPEG2000** The original images (uncompressed and not resized) are first printed with a high quality laser printer (*Fujifilm Frontier 5700R Minlab on Fujicolor Crystal Archive Paper Supreme HD Lustre photo paper*) and then scanned with a premium flatbed scanner (*Epson DS-50000*) with 300 dpi. A dust and scratch filter is then applied in order to reduce image noise. Subsequently, the images are resized by half and then compressed to 15 KB using JPEG2000.[4] This scenario reflects the post-processing path of passport images if handed over at the application desk as a printed photograph.

---

[4] Due to the glossy print, the scans exhibit a visible pattern of the paper surface, which is only partly removed by the dust and scratch filter and results in stronger compression artefacts than for scans of glossy prints.

15.5 Morphing Attack Detection Methods

Different types of MAD methods are considered in a single image and differential scenario. According to the previously described MAD pipeline, these use a similar pre-processing and the same classification. For the feature extraction step different types of texture descriptors are employed, including traditional algorithms as well as gradient-based methods. In addition, deeply learned features are used.

15.5.1 Pre-Processing

In the pre-processing, face images are normalised by applying suitable scaling, rotation and padding/cropping to ensure alignment with respect to the eyes' positions. Precisely, facial landmarks are detected applying the *dlib* algorithm [11] and alignment is performed with respect to the detected eye coordinates with a fixed position and an intra-eye distance of 180 pixels. Subsequently, the normalised images are cropped to regions of 160×160 pixels centred around the tip of the nose.

15.5.2 Feature Extraction

For the feature extraction step, three types of descriptors are considered: texture descriptors, gradient-based descriptors, as well as descriptors learned by a deep neural network.

Texture Descriptors: During the creation of morphed facial images, the morphing process introduces changes into the image that can be used to detect said images. In particular, these changes are reflected by faulty regions, such as overlapping landmarks, which result in incorrectly distorted triangles, as shown in Fig. 15.7a. Another error common to automated morphing algorithms is artefacts in the eye region, which is particularly prone to errors due to the high contrast provided by shadows and wrinkles, and the difficult detection of the iris. An example of artefacts in the eye region is given in Fig. 15.7b. Furthermore, ghost artefacts can be caused by landmarks that are too few or too poorly positioned. This happens frequently in the area of the neck or hair, as visualised in Fig. 15.7c. In order to be able to map this kind of image changes in feature vectors, texture descriptors can be used. In this work, the suitability of LBP [1] and Binarized Statistical Image Features (BSIF) [10] for detecting these artefacts is investigated.

By calculating the classical LBP histogram obtained from 3 LBP patches, any local information contained in the image is discarded. To preserve local information, the LBP image can be divided into cells, subsequently a histogram is calculated for each cell. As a result, the length of the feature vector multiplies by the number of cells, but spatial information is obtained in resolution of the cell division. An inevitable correlation exists between cell division, patch size, image size and the resulting histogram. The finer the cell division and the larger the patch, the fewer values can be calculated per cell and the sparser the histogram. As the resolution increases, the number of values per cell increases as well. For the applied patch sizes and the region of 160×160 pixels, a subdivision into 4×4 cells has shown to be appropriate, thus it is implemented in addition to the LBP calculation without cell division.

As a further texture descriptor, BSIF is used. As for LBP, it has been shown that the use of larger BSIF patches results in more robust systems, but using smaller BSIF patches results in significantly higher performance [28]. In order to allow a better comparison to BSIF with a patch size of 3×3 pixels with 8 filters are used. The resulting feature vector is of length 256. Also, to ensure comparability, the same configuration as for LBP of division into 4×4 cells is implemented.

Gradient-based Descriptors: Histograms of Oriented Gradients (HOG) [2, 13] represents a gradient-based descriptor. For HOG, the definition of the parameters influences the result of the histogram calculation, as well as the length and content of the feature vector. In order to achieve a robust and general applicable HOG extraction, recommended standard parameters[5] are applied, namely 9 orientations, 8×8 pixels per cell (which corresponds to 20×20 cells for regions of 160×160 pixels), and 3×3 cells per block, resulting in a feature vector of length 26,244.

Deep Features: Machine learning algorithms, especially Deep Convolutional Neural Networks (D-CNN), can be used to extract statistically significant features from images in addition to hand-crafted feature extractors. The difficulty of this approach is the dependence of the information represented in the extracted features on the nature of the training data used to train the feature extractor. If the wrong training data is chosen, this might cause an over-fitting of the feature extractor, resulting in very good results on known data, which, however, cannot be reproduced in a real use case on unknown data. In order to avoid this effect, only D-CNN pre-trained for face recognition are applied in this thesis. These networks have been trained to extract representative features from facial images, without containing morphed facial images in the training process, thus implicitly preventing an over-fitting to artefacts of a specific morphing algorithm. In the implemented MAD pipeline the feature extractors of three different face recognition systems are used, which are described in more detail in the following sections.

In the MAD pipeline the existing implementation[6] of the authors of [3] is utilised. In contrast to the previously mentioned methods, here the images are

---

[5] The standard parameters are derived from the documentation of the used HOG implementation: https://scikit-image.org/docs/dev/api/skimage.feature.html.

[6] The corresponding source code can be found at: https://github.com/deepinsight/insightface.

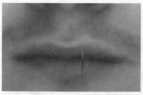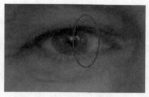

(a) Example of errors intro- (b) Example of errors in eye re- (c) Example of errors in hair reduced by incorrectly distorted gion   gion
triangles

Fig. 15.7 Example of errors introduced by incorrect morphing

normalised using MTCNN and scaled to 112×112 pixels, prior to training or
feature extraction. The authors offer several pre-trained models, in this pipeline
the model *LResNet50E-IR,ArcFace@ms1m-refine-v1* is chosen, since, according
to the authors, it achieves the most stable performance on the tested databases. The
architecture of the selected network is, as the name suggests, a residual network
comprised of 50 layers. A residual network is characterised by shortcut connections between different layers, allowing the output of a previous layer (residuals)
to be processed as input on subsequent layers, simplifying the computationally
expensive training of very deep CNN.

15.5.3 Classification

In a single image MAD system, the detector processes only the suspected reference
image. For this detection approach, the extracted feature vectors are directly analysed. In contrast, in the differential detection systems, a trusted live capture from
an authentication attempt serves as additional source of information for the detector. This information is utilised by estimating the vector *differences* between feature
vectors extracted from processed pairs of images. Specifically, an element-wise sub-
traction of feature vectors is performed.

Support Vector Machines (SVMs) with Radial Basis Function (RBF) kernels
are used to distinguish between bona fide and retouched face images. In order to
train SVMs, the *scikit-learn* library [17] is applied. Since the feature elements of
extracted feature vectors are expected to have different ranges, data-normalisation is
employed. Data-normalisation turned out to be of high importance in cross-database
experiments. It aims to rescale the feature elements to exhibit a mean of 0 and a
standard deviation of 1. At the time of training, a regularisation parameter of $C = 1$
and a kernel coefficient Gamma of $1/n$ is used, where n represents the number of
feature elements.

15.6 Experiments

To compare different MAD algorithms with each other, uniform evaluation methods and metrics are essential. For the evaluation of the vulnerability of face recognition systems against MAs, different metrics have been introduced in previous publications, e.g. [25], which will not be described further. To evaluate the performance of MAD algorithms, each comparison is considered individually, since each morph has to be detected separately. For this reason, the metrics defined in ISO/IEC 30107-3 [9] for the performance reporting of presentation attacks can be used, namely, Attack Presentation Classification Error Rate (APCER) and Bona Fide Presentation Classification Error Rate (BPCER), which are defined as follows [9]:

- **APCER**: proportion of attack presentations using the same PAI species incorrectly classified as bona fide presentations in a specific scenario.
- **BPCER**: proportion of bona fide presentations incorrectly classified as presentation attacks in a specific scenario.

In an effective MAD system, the resulting MAD scores of MA and bona fide samples should be clearly separable. For overlapping MAD score distributions, a trade-off between security (low APCER) and high throughput (low BPCER) has to be found by setting a corresponding decision threshold. The Detection Equal Error Rate (D-EER) reflects the error rates in a single operating point where the APCER is equal to the BPCER. Hereafter the D-EER will be used for measuring the performance of MAD methods.

15.6.1 Generalisability

In the first experiment, the generalisability of MAD methods across heterogeneous data sources in analysed. To this end, the MAD methods based on LBP and BSIF texture descriptors are evaluated in a single image and a differential scenario. On the one hand, this is done for a split of the FRGC dataset into a training and test set. On the other hand, the entire FRGC dataset is used for training while testing is performed on the FERET dataset. Obtained results are summarised in Table 15.4. It can be observed that D-EER values significantly increase in case the data source is unknown. This holds for both, the single image and differential scenario when using LBP and BSIF for the feature extraction. That is, MAD algorithms may overfit to certain data sources which underlines the importance of evaluating MAD methods in cross-database experiments. In all of the following experiments, the FRGC database will be used during the training stage and testing is performed on the FERET dataset.

Table 15.4 Influence of unknown data sources on MAD methods

Training		Test		Single image		Differential	
Database	Morphing algorithm	Database	Morphing algorithm	LBP (%)	BSIF (%)	LBP (%)	BSIF (%)
FRGC-Train	OpenCV	FRGC-Test	OpenCV	5.2	3.5	3.9	4.7
FRGC	OpenCV	FERET	OpenCV	22.4	20.1	28.8	18.1

15.6.2   Detection Performance

In the next experiment, the suitability of all feature extractors for MAD is investigated. Here, training is conducted on low quality morphs (FaceMorpher and OpenCV) while the testing is done on high quality morphs (FaceFusion, UBO Morpher) in order to obtain a more challenging scenario. Table 15.5 summarised the three best performing MAD methods in the single image and differential scenario (best results marked bold). For the single image scenario, the most competitive results are achieved when using HOG for feature extraction. However, obtained D-EERs are still rather high, i.e. reliable MAD appears more challenging in the single image scenario. In contrast, for the differential MAD methods significantly lower D-EER can be obtained. In particular, for the use of deep features D-EER values below 3% are achieved. Note, that deep features have not been found suitable for the single image MAD. Hence, it can be concluded that deep features are highly suitable for differential MAD which has also been reported in [15, 30]. Focusing on single image MAD more elaborated feature extractors are required to better distinguish between bona fide and morphed face images.

Table 15.5 Performance of MAD algorithms

Training	Test	Single image			Differential		
Morphing algorithm	Morphing algorithm	LBP (%)	BSIF (%)	HOG (%)	LBP (%)	HOG (%)	Deep features (%)
FaceMorpher	FaceFusion	31.01	30.76	**24.05**	24.30	19.37	**2.71**
	UBO morpher	26.71	28.99	**19.75**	19.62	15.70	**2.58**
OpenCV	FaceFusion	26.20	31.01	**23.92**	22.41	18.73	**2.71**
	UBO morpher	24.05	28.61	**20.63**	19.11	15.70	**2.71**

15.6.3 Post-Processing

Eventually, the influence of considered image post-processings on the used MAD methods is estimated. Here, training is performed on the original images and testing on post-processed ones. It was found that resizing has negligible impact on MAD performance of the considered methods. Table 15.6 summarises the impact of image compression using JPEG2000 for the best performing single image and differential MAD approach. Focusing on the best single image MAD based on HOG, a significant increase of D-EER values can be observed. This means image compression negatively impacts this single image MAD algorithm. Due to the compression, artefacts which have been learned to distinguish morphed images from bona fide images might vanish which is particularly the case for the used JPEG2000 algorithm. In contrast, deep features turn out to be robust to image compression. This is the case since these are extracted by a face recognition model which has been trained to extract discriminative face representations which are highly robust to such post-processings.

Finally, the impact of printing and scanning on the MAD performance is evaluated. Corresponding results are summarised in Table 15.7. Again, a significant drop in the detection performance can be observed for the single image MAD method based on HOG. The artefacts introduced by the printing and scanning process increase the D-EER to a large extent. However, the differential MAD algorithm based on deep features maintains detection performance for printed and scanned images.

Table 15.6 Influence of image compression on MAD methods

Morphing algorithm		Single image	Differential
Training	Test	HOG	Deep features
FaceMorpher	FaceFusion	28.2% (+4.1)	3.0% (+0.3)
	UBO morpher	27.3% (+7.6)	3.1% (+0.5)
OpenCV	FaceFusion	31.9% (+8.0)	2.7% (+-0)
	UBO morpher	31.0% (+10.4)	2.7% (+-0)

Table 15.7 Influence of printing and scanning on MAD methods

Morphing algorithm		Single image	Differential
Training	Test	HOG	Deep features
FaceMorpher	FaceFusion	34.1% (+10)	1.3% (-1.4)
	UBO Morpher	36.6% (+16.8)	3.2% (+0.6)
OpenCV	FaceFusion	53.4% (+29.5)	1.4% (-1.3)
	UBO Morpher	37.1% (+19.5)	3.1% (+0.4)

15.7 Summary

MAs pose a high security risk to modern facial recognition systems in particular for border control. To counteract this, reliable methods for MAD must be developed. Various research groups from the fields of image processing and biometrics have recently published scientific papers on this topic, and several publicly funded research projects are currently dealing with this problem. However, research in this field is still in its infancy and does typically not address the variance of the image data available in border control scenarios. The development of MAD approaches that are effective and robust in real-world scenarios will require a considerable amount of future research as well as close collaborations with border guard agencies.

The majority of the MAD methods published so far—in particular the single image MAD methods—aim at the detection of artefacts that can easily be avoided, e.g. clearly visible ghost artefacts, double compression artefacts and changed image noise patterns. Further, usually face images are taken from a single data source, i.e. face image database. Hence, reported detection rates tend to be over-optimistic. MAD approaches are, like any classification task, susceptible to over-fitting to training data. When evaluating MAD approaches, images of which source and properties differ from those of the training data, i.e. images from other databases and morphs created with other techniques should be employed. In case of unknown MAs, i.e. face images stem from different data sources and were created with unknown morphing algorithms, the detection performance of MAD methods may significantly drop, as shown in this work. Further, it was shown that post-processing steps applied to reference images like printing/scanning and strong image compression may cause drastic drops in the detection performance at least for single image MAD, since artefacts caused by morphing vanish in the post-processed reference. In contrast to many published works on MAD (see [29, 31]), the results reported in this work are supported by external evaluations conducted in [15, 22].

In contrast, research should focus on the development of MAD methods that detect artefacts that are difficult to avoid. While the detection performance for differential MAD based on deep features showed promising results in the experiments of this work, the used datasets might not fully reflect real-world scenarios. For border control scenarios, MAD techniques need to be robust against print-scan transformations, resizing and strong compression of reference images. Similarly, in the case of differential MAD, considerable variance of illumination, background, pose, appearance (hair, beard, glasses, etc.) and ageing (up to 10 years for passports) can be expected in probe images. In order to be applicable to these scenarios, MAD approaches should be trained and evaluated on images exhibiting these characteristics.

Acknowledgements This research work has been partially funded by the German Federal Ministry of Education and Research and the Hessian Ministry of Higher Education, Research, Science and the Arts within their joint support of the National Research Centre for Applied Cybersecurity ATHENE.

References

1. Ahonen T, Hadid A, Pietikäinen M (2004) Face recognition with local binary patterns. Springer, Berlin, pp 469–481
2. Dalal N, Triggs B (2005) Histograms of oriented gradients for human detection. In: Proceedings of the 2005 computer society conference on computer vision and pattern recognition (CVPR)
3. Deng J, Guo J, Xue N, Zafeiriou S (2019) Arcface: additive angular margin loss for deep face recognition. In: Proceedings of the 2019 computer vision and pattern recognition (CVPR)
4. Commission European (2018) EU-eMRTD specification. Technical report, European Commission
5. Ferrara M, Franco A, Maltoni D (2014) The magic passport. In: Proceedings of the 2014 international joint conference on biometrics (IJCB). IEEE
6. Ferrara M, Franco A, Maltoni D (2018) Face demorphing. IEEE Trans Inf Forensics Secur 13(4):1008–1017
7. Ferrara M, Franco A, Maltoni D (2021) Face morphing detection in the presence of printing/scanning and heterogeneous image sources. IET-Biometrics, pp 1–13
8. ISO/IEC JTC1 SC37 Biometrics (2011) Information technology–Biometric data interchange formats–Part 5: face image data
9. ISO/IEC JTC1 SC37 Biometrics (2017) Information technology–biometric presentation attack detection–part 3: testing and reporting. ISO ISO/IEC IS 30107-3:2017, International Organization for Standardization, Geneva, Switzerland
10. Kannala J, Rahtu E (2012) BSIF: binarized statistical image features. In: Proceedings of the 21st international conference on pattern recognition (ICPR), pp 1363–1366
11. King DE (2009) Dlib-ml: a machine learning toolkit. J Mach Learn Res 10:1755–1758
12. Makrushin A, Neubert T, Dittmann J (2017) Automatic generation and detection of visually faultless facial morphs. In: Proceedings of the 12th international joint conference on computer vision, imaging and computer graphics theory and applications (VISIGRAPP). SCITEPRESS - Science and Technology Publications
13. McConnell RK (1986) Method of and apparatus for pattern recognition
14. Merkle J, Rathgeb C, Scherhag U, Busch C, Breithaupt R (2019) Face morphing detection: issues and challenges. In: Proceedings of the international conference on biometrics for borders (ICBB)
15. Ngan M, Grother P, Hanaoka K, Kuo J (2020) Face recognition vendor test (FRVT) part 4: Morph-performance of automated face morph detection. Technical report, National Institute of Standards and Technology (NIST)
16. Ortega-Delcampo D, Conde C, Palacios-Alonso D, Cabello E (2020) Border control morphing attack detection with a convolutional neural network de-morphing approach. IEEE Access 8:92301–92313
17. Pedregosa F et al (2011) Scikit-learn: machine learning in Python. J Mach Learn Res (JMLR) 12:2825–2830
18. Phillips PJ, Flynn PJ, Scruggs T, Bowyer KW, Chang J, Hoffman K, Marques J, Min J, Worek W (2005) Overview of the face recognition grand challenge. In: Proceedings of the 2005 computer society conference on computer vision and pattern recognition (CVPR). IEEE
19. Phillips PJ, Wechsler H, Huang J, Rauss PJ (1998) The FERET database and evaluation procedure for face-recognition algorithms. Image Vision Comput 16(5):295–306
20. Raghavendra R, Raja KB, Busch C (2016) Detecting morphed face images. In: Proceedings of the 8th international conference on biometrics theory, applications and systems (BTAS). IEEE
21. Raghavendra R, Raja KB, Venkatesh S, Busch C (2017) Transferable deep-CNN features for detecting digital and print-scanned morphed face images. In: Proceedings of the 2017 conference on computer vision and pattern recognition workshops (CVPRW). IEEE
22. Raja K, Ferrara M, Franco A, Spreeuwers L, Batskos I et al (2020) Morphing attack detection - database, evaluation platform and benchmarking. IEEE Trans Inf Forensics Secur
23. Scherhag U, Debiasi L, Rathgeb C, Busch C, Uhl A (2019) Detection of face morphing attacks based on PRNU analysis. IEEE Trans Biom Behav Identity Sci (T-BIOM), pp 1–16

24. Scherhag U, Kunze J, Rathgeb C, Busch C (2020) Face morph detection for unknown morphing algorithms and image sources: a multi-scale block local binary pattern fusion approach. IET-Biomet pp 1–11
25. Scherhag U, Nautsch A, Rathgeb C, Gomez-Barrero M, Veldhuis RMJ, Spreeuwers L, Schils M, Maltoni D, Grother P, Marcel S, Breithaupt R, Raghavendra R, Busch C (2017) Biometric systems under morphing attacks: assessment of morphing techniques and vulnerability reporting. In: Proceedings of the 2017 international conference of the biometrics special interest group (BIOSIG). IEEE
26. Scherhag U, Ramachandra R, Raja KB, Gomez-Barrero M, Rathgeb C, Busch C (2017) On the vulnerability of face recognition systems towards morphed face attacks. In: Proceedings of the 5th international workshop on biometrics and forensics (IWBF). IEEE
27. Scherhag U, Rathgeb C, Busch C (2018) Performance variation of morphed face image detection algorithms across different datasets. In: Proceedings of the 6th international workshop on biometrics and forensics (IWBF). IEEE
28. Scherhag U, Rathgeb C, Busch C (2018) Towards detection of morphed face images in electronic travel documents. In: Proceedings of the 13th workshop on document analysis systems (DAS). IAPR
29. Scherhag U, Rathgeb C, Merkle J, Breithaupt R, Busch C (2019) Face recognition systems under morphing attacks: a survey. IEEE Access 7:23012–23026
30. Scherhag U, Rathgeb C, Merkle J, Busch C (2020) Deep face representations for differential morphing attack detection. IEEE Trans Inf Forensics Secur (TIFS), pp 3625–3639
31. Venkatesh S, Ramachandra R, Raja K, Busch C (2021) Face morphing attack generation detection: a comprehensive survey. IEEE Trans Technol Soc, pp 1–1
32. Zhang LB, Peng F, Long M (2018) Face morphing detection using fourier spectrum of sensor pattern noise. In: Proceedings of the 2018 international conference on multimedia and expo (ICME). IEEE

Chapter 16
Practical Evaluation of Face Morphing Attack Detection Methods

Luuk Spreeuwers, Maikel Schils, Raymond Veldhuis, and Una Kelly

Abstract Face morphing is a technique to combine facial images of two (or more) subjects such that the result resembles both subjects. In a morphing attack, this is exploited by, e.g., applying for a passport with the morphed image. Both subjects who contributed to the morphed image can then travel using this passport. Many state-of-the-art face recognition systems are vulnerable to morphing attacks. Morphing attack detection (MAD) methods are developed to mitigate this threat. MAD methods published in literature are often trained on a limited number of or even a single dataset where all morphed faces are created using the same procedure. The resulting MAD methods work well for these specific datasets, with reported detection rates of over 99%, but their performance collapses for face morphs created using other procedures. Often even simple image manipulations, like adding noise or smoothing cause a serious degradation in performance of the MAD methods. In addition, more advanced tools exist to manipulate the face morphs, like manual retouching or morphing artifacts can be concealed by printing and scanning a photograph (as used in the passport application process in many countries). Furthermore, datasets for training and testing MAD methods are often created by morphing images from arbitrary subjects including even male-female morphs and morphs between subjects with different skin color. Although this may result in a large number of morphed faces, the created morphs are often not convincing and certainly don't represent a best effort attack by a criminal. A far more realistic attack would include careful selection of subjects that look alike and create high quality morphs from images of these subjects using careful (manual) post-processing. In this chapter we therefore argue that for robust evaluation of MAD methods, we require datasets with morphed images created using a large number of different morphing methods, including

L. Spreeuwers (✉) · M. Schils · R. . Veldhuis · U. Kelly
University of Twente, Enschede, Netherlands
e-mail: l.j.spreeuwers@utwente.nl

R. . Veldhuis
e-mail: r.n.j.veldhuis@utwente.nl

U. Kelly
e-mail: u.m.kelly@utwente.nl

© The Author(s) 2022
C. Rathgeb et al. (eds.), *Handbook of Digital Face Manipulation and Detection*,
Advances in Computer Vision and Pattern Recognition,
https://doi.org/10.1007/978-3-030-87664-7_16

351

various ways to conceal the morphing artifacts by, e.g., adding noise, smoothing, printing and scanning, various ways of pre- and post-processing, careful selection of the subjects and multiple facial datasets. We also show the sensitivity of various MAD methods to the mentioned variations and the effect of training MAD methods on multiple datasets.

16.1 Introduction

A morphed face image is a combination of two or more face images, created in a way that all contributing subjects are verified successfully against the morphed image. Suppose A' and B' are images of two distinct subjects A and B, shown in Fig. 16.1a and b. With face morphing, the two images are combined to create attack sample M, see Fig. 16.1c. If we perform identification tasks with state-of-the-art facial recognition software, a good morph will generate high comparison scores between morph M and templates of subjects A and B. It is obvious that face morphing poses a severe threat to all processes where face recognition is used to establish the identity of subjects, as first reported in [4]. Also human face recognition is vulnerable, as reported by Robertson et al. [15].

Automated morphing attack detection can be the solution to this problem. The morphing process leaves certain traces in the morphed image because the image is locally stretched or compressed and the images are combined. In high quality morphs, these textures differences are not visible to humans. Automated morphing attack detection scenarios can be subdivided into two types; morphing attack detection with or without a sample as reference. The scenario with reference sample means that apart from the morphed image, also an image of one of the original contributing subjects is available, which in principle makes morphing attack detection simpler. In this research we primarily address automated morphing attack detection without reference sample.

Many of the published methods for face morphing attack detection are developed and tested using a single dataset with morphed and bona fide samples and often good detection results are reported. However, the use of a single dataset and therefore a single, specific way to generate morphed images, may result in a morphing attack detection method that works well only for this specific type of face morphing. An example is morphing attack detection based on so-called double JPEG compression detection—detection of artifacts that occur because the morphed images are created from JPEG compressed images and compressed again when they are stored. Such a method will fail to detect morphed images if they are stored uncompressed.

The aim of this chapter is to demonstrate evaluation of morphing attack detection methods using single datasets and cross dataset testing and sensitivity to several simple morphing disguise techniques. It is based on research at the University of Twente, Netherlands, published in [18, 19].

In the remainder of this chapter, first a brief overview of some related work on face morphing attack detection is presented. Next, the creation of 4 datasets with morphed

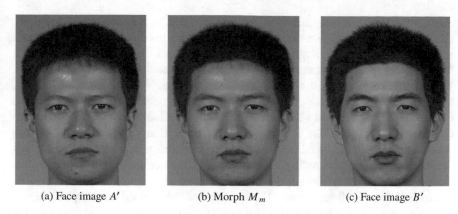

(a) Face image A' (b) Morph M_m (c) Face image B'

Fig. 16.1 Bona fide face samples (left and right) and manual face morph (center). Images from FRGC [11]

face images is described that are used to train and test morphing attack detection methods. Multiple datasets are required to investigate cross dataset performance of morphing attack detection. Subsequently, a morphing attack detection method based on Local Binary Patterns (LBP) and a Support Vector Machine (SVM) is presented which will be used as a representation of morphing attack detection methods that are trained using a dataset with morphed and bona fide images. Next, two approaches to disguise morphing: adding nose and scaling images are presented for which we will investigate morphing attack detection robustness. Then, experiments and results are presented concerning within and cross dataset performance of morphing attack detection and robustness against morphing disguise and the effect of selection of faces that look alike. Finally, conclusions are presented.

16.2   Related Work

In order to evaluate the performance of morphing attack detection methods, the following metrics were introduced in ISO/IEC 30107-3 [2]:

Attack Presentation Classification Error Rate (APCER) Proportion of attack presentations incorrectly classified as bona fide presentations.

Bona Fide Presentation Classification Error Rate (BPCER) Proportion of bona fide presentations incorrectly classified as presentation attacks.

A bona fide sample refers to a non-morph and an attack sample refers to a morph. The trade-off between APCER and BPCER can be represented in a Detection Error Trade-Off (DET)-curve and also Equal Error Rates (EER) can be reported.

Currently, much published work on face morphing attack detection is based on textural feature classifiers, e.g., LBP features or features obtained using Convolutional Neural Networks, followed by an SVM classifier or other, see, e.g., [13, 20]. Tested on single datasets of morphed face images good results are reported in literature. Creation of good datasets with morphed face images is one of the most important steps in the development of reliable face morphing attack detection methods. In [13] 450 morphed faces are created manually from a dataset comprised of 110 subjects. The face region is detected with Viola Jones detection. Various features like LBP, LBQ, 2DFFT (Fourier Transform) and BSIF filters are extracted. The combination of BSIF [6] with 7×7 and 12bit and SVM yields an Attack Presentation Classification Error Rate (APCER) of 1.73%. The dataset of 450 morphs was split into three subsets; training, testing, and validation. A problem with the dataset however is that these sets are not split according to the original 115 subjects. This means a morph in the training set may share a contributing subject with a morph in the test or validation set. In [17] the experiments from [13] are repeated, but instead the morphing attack detection process at a passport control is simulated by printing and scanning the face images. Morphing attack detection performance was analyzed before and after printing and scanning. It is found that printing and scanning images add noise and granularity, causing a loss in morphing attack detection performance. The dataset was split into training and testing sets without overlapping subjects. The reported performances are in the order of 40% BPCER at 10% APCER.

Apart from the various ways to split data in training and test sets, there are also various methods to create morphed images. The most popular method is based on the detection of landmarks in faces, triangularization, and warping of the triangles. More details are provided in Sect. 16.3. But there are various ways to define the landmarks and triangulation and each of them leads to small differences in the created morphs. It is also possible to create morphs manually using graphical software or to manually or automatically post-process the created morphs. Again this leads to variations in the types of morphs. Finally, also deep-learning methods for creation of face morphs are being developed, again leading to different types of morphs, see, e.g., [3].

In the next sections, it will be demonstrated that using only a single dataset for training and testing, even though it may be split into disjunct sets for training and testing, may lead to far too optimistic performance results. If the morphing attack detection methods are evaluated using datasets with morphed faces that were created using a different procedure or the images are manipulated by, e.g., adding some noise, the performance tends to be much worse.

16.3   Creation of Morphing Datasets

For experiments with morphing attack detection a large number of face morph images is required. We use automated morphing algorithms to quickly generate morphs. The dataset is split in a part for training and a part for testing with no overlap in subjects.

16.3.1   Creating Morphs

Various ways exist to create morphed face images. Nowadays, much research concentrates on the use of Generative Adversary Networks (GANs) for this purpose. However, the simpler landmark-based approaches still result in higher quality morphs. Therefore in this chapter, we chose this method to create morphs.

To create a face morph, the first step is to extract landmarks from both face images. For manual morphing the landmarks can be selected by hand, for automated morphing we use an existing landmark localisation algorithm. For morphing it is critical to know which parts in the image of one contributing subject correspond to the parts of another. Therefore it is vital that landmarks are accurately extracted, if they are placed incorrectly, it can lead to extremely poor morphs. There are several landmark localisation algorithms available. We found that STASM [10] and DLIB [7] result in high quality morphs. Figure 16.2a shows STASM landmarks on a face sample A'. A triangular mesh is defined over the landmarks using Delaunay Triangulation [8] (Fig. 16.2b). Now each triangle can be related to its corresponding triangle from the other contributing image. The triangles are morphed toward average triangles located in the final morph M_a using an affine transformation.

A blending value α defines the weight of contribution of the involved subjects. There are various ways of selecting α: we can set $\alpha = 0.5$ so that both subjects contribute equally to the morph or face recognition software can be used to set α so that the morph generates approximately the same comparison score for both contributing subjects. If the morph should resemble one of the subjects more than the other (the passport application is considered more critical than the use of the passport for automated border control), α can be set to a value of, e.g., 0.3 or 0.7.

The automatically generated morphs normally suffer from artifacts near the boundaries of the face and around the eyes, nose and mouth, because of the lim-

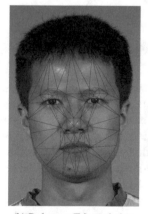

(a) STASM Landmarks   (b) Delaunay Triangulation

Fig. 16.2 Initial steps of the morphing process (images from FRGC [11])

Table 16.1 Characteristics of the datasets, resolution is given in pixels Inter Eye Distance (IED)

Dataset	Resolution IED (pix)	Morph train images	Bona fide train images	Morph test images	Bona fide test images
FRGC	129	500	150	500	150
ARF	177	500	150	500	100
Feret Color	177	750	250	750	250
Feret Gray	60	500	200	500	200

ited number of landmarks. In our research on morphing attack detection, we only used the inner part of the face.

When creating morphed face images, it is vital to save them in a lossless format like ".png" to ensure the morphing attack detection methods do not detect compression artifacts.

16.3.2 Datasets

We created four datasets with images of different quality and properties, originating from different facial datasets: FRGC [11], ARF [9], Feret color and Feret gray [12].

An overview of the created datasets with information on resolution (Inter Eye Distance, IED), number of training and testing images is given in Table 16.1.

Note that the resolution of the Feret Gray dataset is much lower than the resolution of the other datasets. This may impact morphing attack detection performance. Care was taken to use different subjects for each of the subsets: Morph Train, Non-Morph Train, Morph Test and Non-Morph Test. For all morphs, we used $\alpha = 0.5$ for the blending factor.

16.4 Texture-Based Face Morphing Attack Detection

To demonstrate the effects of within and cross dataset testing and concealing morphing artifacts, we chose a simple example of a trained texture-based morphing attack detection method. Even though BSIF filters perform better in literature, we chose to use LBP to extract features as it is not trained and shows results close to that of BSIF. With the use of landmarks the face region as shown in Fig. 16.3a is extracted and resized to a fixed size. The face region is cut off at the top of the eyebrows and somewhat below the mouth. With this region we ensure that the sides of the face which often contain obvious morphing artifacts are not present in the face image. We convert the image to gray scale and apply histogram equalization, enhancing image contrast (Fig. 16.3b). Using the FRGC dataset we performed a parameter sweep for

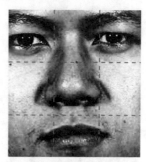

(a) Original cropped face   (b) Gray, histogram equalised
                                             cropped face

Fig. 16.3 Region of interest for LBP operator, the dashed lines show the areas for which local LBP histograms are obtained

LBP parameters: uniform/non-uniform LBP, number of neighbors n and radius r. We find that uniform LBP features with "standard" parameters, $(n = 8, r = 1)$ and a 3×3 histogram result in a good performance. Increasing the number of histograms; e.g., 4×4 or 5×5 layout, only slightly increases the performance but also the dimensionality of the feature space increases. We therefore decided to use the "standard" parameters. For uniform LBP, a single histogram contains 59 feature values, which means for a 3×3 layout the feature space has 531 dimensions. The SVM classifiers are trained on between 650 and 1,000 samples.

16.5   Morphing Disguising

As pointed out earlier, often morphing attack detection methods are trained on a single dataset with morphed images. This may result in a morphing attack detection method that only detects a certain property of the morphing creation process. If the morphing creation process is slightly disturbed, these methods will fail.

Here, we investigate two simple ways to disguise the morphing process: adding Gaussian noise to the image and rescaling. In the first approach, a small amount of Gaussian noise is added to the image, masking certain noise characteristics of the morphing process that a morphing attack detection method may have learnt. The noise is kept small, such that to the human eye it is barely noticeable, see Fig. 16.4.

In the second approach, the image is down-scaled using a scaling factor s and then up-scaled again to its original resolution. In this way, some of the higher spatial frequencies are lost also masking the typical noise characteristics of morphed images. Examples of down-up scaled images are shown in Fig. 16.5. Again the manipulation is barely noticeable to the human eye.

Another way to hide the artifacts of face morphing is to print the photograph on paper and next scan it to obtain a digital photograph again. This is still common

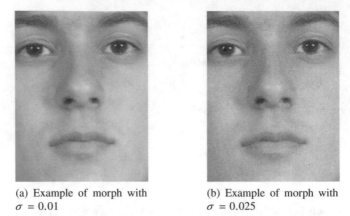

(a) Example of morph with   (b) Example of morph with
σ = 0.01   σ = 0.025

Fig. 16.4 Morphs with added Gaussian noise. The gray level range of the image is 0.1

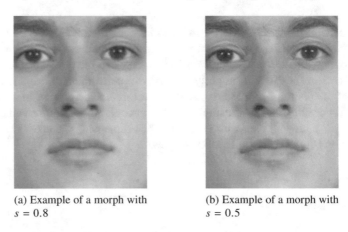

(a) Example of a morph with   (b) Example of a morph with
s = 0.8   s = 0.5

Fig. 16.5 Down-up scaled morphs to disguise morphing

practice for passport application in many countries, where the photographer prints the photograph and the subject brings the printed photograph to the municipality to apply for a new passport. The printed photograph is scanned in order to obtain a digital representation that is stored in the chip of the passport and is printed on the passport data page. The effect of printing and scanning has been thoroughly investigated in [5], where a significant decrease in morphing attack detection performance is reported. If the morphing attack detection methods are also trained on printed and scanned photographs, the performance improves again but is still significantly lower that on digital-only images. The effect is very comparable to the effects of adding noise and scaling we demonstrate in Sect. 16.6.

16.6   Experiments and Results

In order to demonstrate the impact of a number of the described factors on the performance of the LBP/SVM morphing attack detector, we present the following experiments:

1. Within dataset performance
2. Cross dataset performance
3. Mixed dataset performance
4. Robustness against additive Gaussian noise
5. Robustness against down-up scaling
6. Selection of similar subjects

16.6.1   Within Dataset Performance

With this experiment we investigate if the morphing attack detection method we used performs in line with the results reported in literature. Furthermore, we use the performance as a baseline to compare the results of the other experiments with.

For each of the datasets listed in Table 16.1 the SVM of the morphing attack detector was trained on features extracted from the training set and the morphing attack detection was determined using the test set.

The results are shown in the form of a DET-curve in Fig. 16.6. We can observe that the performance for 3 of the 4 datasets is similar (EER 2.5–5%), while for the low resolution Feret Gray set the results are poorer (EER = 17%). The reason for the poorer results is likely that the image quality (resolution) of the Feret Gray dataset is significantly lower.

The EER for the various datasets is shown in the top of Table 16.2. The MAD methods trained on the different datasets are called LBP-SVM1-LBP-SVM4.

The performance on the other datasets is in line with results reported in literature (EER = 1.7% in [13]).

16.6.2   Cross Dataset Performance

Next the cross dataset morphing attack detection performance is determined. In this experiment the SVMs are trained using the binary pattern features of the one dataset and tested using the test set of another dataset. The experiments were only conducted for the FRGC and ARF datasets and the results are shown in the middle part of Table 16.2.

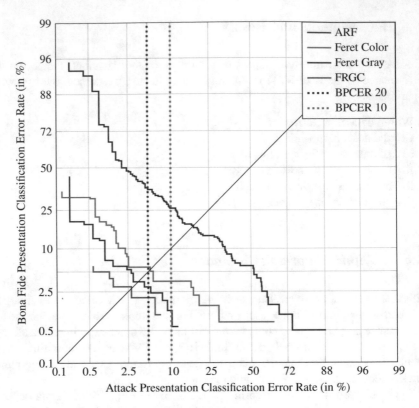

Fig. 16.6 DET-curve of LBP experiments on all datasets

Table 16.2 MAD performance reported as EER for within, cross and mixed dataset testing for various datasets

MAD method	Training set	Test set	Test proc.	EER (%)
LBP-SVM1	FRGC	FRGC	Within	2.5
LBP-SVM2	ARF	ARF	Within	3
LBP-SVM3	Feret Color	Feret Color	Within	5
LBP-SVM4	Feret Gray	Feret Gray	Within	20
LBP-SVM1	FRGC	ARF	Cross	80
LBP-SVM2	ARF	FRGC	Cross	79
LBP-SVM5	FRGC+ARF	FRGC+ARF	Mixed	35

The cross dataset performances were much worse than the within dataset performances, suggesting that indeed the morphing attack detector learnt features very specific for the dataset it was trained on: the EER of the LBP-SVM1 and LBP-SVM2 methods increases to 80% resp. 79%.

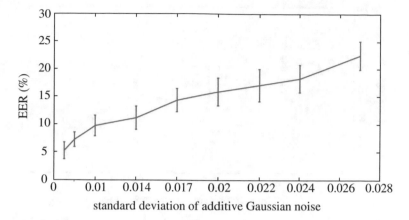

Fig. 16.7   Morphing attack detection performance for added Gaussian noise

16.6.3   Mixed Dataset Performance

In this experiment the SVMs are trained using 50% of both of the datasets FRGC and ARF and tested using the test set of both datasets. The results are given at the bottom of Table 16.2. The EER for this mixed test set is equal to 35%.

The mixed dataset performance is better than the cross dataset performances, suggesting that if multiple datasets are used for training, the morphing attack detector becomes more robust. The performance is still much worse than the within dataset performance, though.

16.6.4   Robustness Against Additive Gaussian Noise

In this experiment, we add Gaussian noise to the morphed images in order to disguise artifacts generated by the morphing process. The standard deviation of the noise was varied from 0.004 to 0.027, where the gray level range was normalized to 0.1. Only within dataset performance is reported.

The results are depicted in Fig. 16.7. We can observe that for small σ of the noise, the EER of the morphing attack detection is still around 5%, close to the baseline experiment. When the noise increases, the EER increases to above 20% for $\sigma = 0.027$. Note that even this noise will not be observed by human inspection, so it seems morphing artifacts can quite successfully be disguised by adding a bit of noise to the morphed images.

The experiments were done several times for different divisions of the data in training and test sets. The error bars show the minimum and maximum EER values obtained.

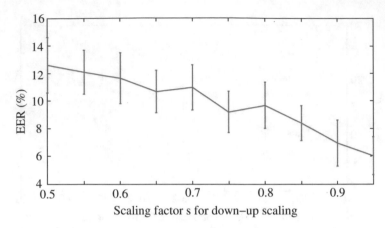

Fig. 16.8 Morphing attack detection performance for down and up scaling with scaling factor s.

16.6.5 Robustness Against Scaling

In this experiment, the original face images are first down-scaled with a factor s and then up-scaled again to their original resolution. In this way, some fine detail, i.e., high spatial frequency information is lost. Since morphing also influences (high) frequency contents of the face images, it is likely that traces caused by morphing can be obscured by this down-up scaling of the image. We investigated the impact on the morphing attack detection performance for a scaling range of $s = 0.5.0.95$. Only within dataset performance is reported.

The results are depicted in Fig. 16.8. We can observe that for $s = 0.95$, i.e., hardly any high frequency information is lost, the EER of the morphing attack detection is still around 5%, close to the baseline experiment. When the down scaling factor is lower, the EER increases to above 12% for $s = 0.5$. Note that even for this scaling factor, the difference to the original image will not be observed by human inspection, so it seems morphing artifacts can successfully be disguised by down-up scaling as well.

The experiments were done several times for different divisions of the data in training and test sets. The error bars show the minimum and maximum EER values obtained.

16.6.6 Selection of Similar Subjects

For this experiment, we created two sets of morphed faces. For the first set, arbitrary images were used to create morphs without paying attention to the similarity between the subjects. Indeed, even morphs between male and female subjects occur in this

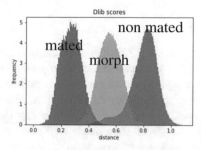 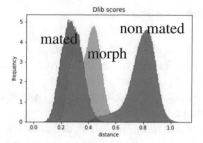

Fig. 16.9 Distance score distributions of morphs of arbitrary subjects (left) and of subjects selected on their resemblance (right). The distance scores of the latter are much closer to those of bona fide images

dataset. For the second set, the subjects used to create morphs were selected in such a way that gender matched and according to the DLIB face recognition system [1] they are reasonably similar. In Fig. 16.9 the distance scores of mated comparisons (2 images of the same subject), non-mated comparisons (two different subjects) and morph comparisons (a morph with an image of one of the contributing subjects) are depicted. The DLIB face recognition system decides that two images originate from the same subject if the distance score is below 0.6. In Fig. 16.9 on the left it can be seen that for morphs from arbitrary subjects about 70% of the morphs are accepted as genuine images, while for the morphs created from subjects selected on their resemblance, nearly all morphs are accepted (Fig. 16.9 right). Of course, criminals will attempt to create as good morphed face images as they can, thus the 2nd scenario is much more likely in practice. Therefore, it is important that morphing attack detection systems should not only be evaluated using morphs created using various different morphing methods, but also with morphs created from carefully selected similar subjects representing a criminals best effort to create high quality face morphs, see, e.g., [16].

16.7 The SOTAMD Benchmark

A very good attempt at creating a versatile benchmark for morphing attack detection methods was developed in the framework of the European SOTAMD (State Of The Art of Morphing attack Detection) project [14]. It includes morphed images created using 7 different morphing algorithms with various post-processing methods including manual post-processing for part of the dataset. In addition it includes printed and scanned bona fide and morphed images using several print and scan protocols. The subjects used to create morphs were selected based on various criteria including facial recognition scores and human observation. In [14] several morphing attack detection algorithms are tested. On the hardest tests, all these algorithms fail to provide acceptable results, which demonstrates the great challenge of reliable morphing attack detection.

16.8   Conclusion

Face morphing, the combination of two face images of distinct subjects into one image that resembles both subjects, poses a serious threat to face recognition. In several publications it is claimed that reliable morphing attack detection is possible. We noticed that often morphing attack detection methods are developed and tested using a single dataset with morphed face images. In this chapter we show that this results in morphing attack detection that only works well for a single type of morph or dataset. Using a LBP/SVM based morphing attack detection method that performs well on a single dataset (around 2% EER), we show that for cross dataset testing, the performance collapses resulting in an EER as high as 80%. Experiments with mixed datasets suggest that morphing attack detection can be made more robust if trained on multiple datasets. In addition, we show that the morphing artifacts that are used as features for detection can be obscured by simple image manipulations like adding Gaussian noise or down-up scaling the morphed images. The EER for within dataset detection increased from below 5% to above 20% for adding noise and above 12% for down-up scaling. In both cases the manipulation was almost invisible to the human observer.

We therefore argue that morphing attack detection methods should be tested extensively on multiple datasets obtained from different sources and morphing methods and a range of image manipulations. Furthermore, they should be tested on morphed face images that were created from similar subjects rather than arbitrary subjects and carefully post-processed in order to mimic a criminal's best effort at creating high quality facial morphs.

References

1. http://dlib.net/face_recognition.py.html
2. Information technology-biometric presentation attack detection-part 3: Testing and reporting, jtc 1/sc 37. ISO/IEC FDIS 30107-3:2017 (2017)
3. Damer N, Saladié AM, Braun A, Kuijper A (2018) Morgan: recognition vulnerability and attack detectability of face morphing attacks created by generative adversarial network. In: 2018 IEEE 9th international conference on biometrics theory, applications and systems (BTAS), pp 1–10. https://doi.org/10.1109/BTAS.2018.8698563
4. Ferrara M, Franco A, Maltoni D (2014) The magic passport. In: IEEE international joint conference on biometrics, pp 1–7. https://doi.org/10.1109/BTAS.2014.6996240
5. Ferrara M, Franco A, Maltoni D (2019) Face morphing detection in the presence of printing/scanning and heterogeneous image sources. CoRR arXiv:1901.08811
6. Kannala J, Rahtu E (2012) Bsif: binarized statistical image features. In: Proceedings of the 21st international conference on pattern recognition (ICPR2012), pp 1363–1366
7. King DE (2009) Dlib-ml: a machine learning toolkit. J Mach Learn Res 10:1755–1758
8. Lee DT, Schachter BJ (1980) Two algorithms for constructing a delaunay triangulation. Int J Comput Inf Sci 9(3):219–242. https://doi.org/10.1007/BF00977785.
9. Martinez AM, Benavente R (1998) The AR Face Database. Tech. rep, CVC
10. Milborrow S, Nicolls F (2014) Active shape models with SIFT descriptors and MARS. VISAPP

11. Phillips PJ, Flynn PJ, Scruggs T, Bowyer KW, Chang J, Hoffman K, Marques J, Min J, Worek W (2005) Overview of the face recognition grand challenge. In: Proceedings of the 2005 IEEE computer society conference on computer vision and pattern recognition (CVPR'05), vol 1. IEEE Computer Society, Washington, DC, USA (2005), pp 947–954. https://doi.org/10.1109/CVPR.2005.268

12. Phillips PJ, Wechsler H, Huang J, Rauss PJ (1998) The feret database and evaluation procedure for face-recognition algorithms. Image Vis Comput 16(5):295–306

13. Raghavendra R, Raja KB, Busch C (2016) Detecting morphed face images. In: 2016 IEEE 8th international conference on biometrics theory, applications and systems (BTAS), pp 1–7. https://doi.org/10.1109/BTAS.2016.7791169

14. Raja K, Ferrara M, Franco A, Spreeuwers L, Batskos I, De Wit F, Gomez-Barrero M, Scherhag U, Fischer D, Venkatesh S, Singh JM, Li G, Bergeron L, Isadskiy S, Ramachandra R, Rathgeb C, Frings D, Seidel U, Knopjes F, Veldhuis R, Maltoni D, Busch C (2020) Morphing attack detection-database, evaluation platform and benchmarking. IEEE Trans Inf Forensics Secur 1–1. https://doi.org/10.1109/TIFS.2020.3035252

15. Robertson D, Kramer R, Burton A (2017) Fraudulent id using face morphs: experiments on human and automatic recognition. PLoS One 12(3). https://doi.org/10.1371/journal.pone.0173319

16. Röttcher A, Scherhag U, Busch C (2020) Finding the suitable doppelgänger for a face morphing attack. In: 2020 IEEE international joint conference on biometrics (IJCB), pp 1–7. https://doi.org/10.1109/IJCB48548.2020.9304878

17. Scherhag U, Raghavendra R, Raja KB, Gomez-Barrero M, Rathgeb C, Busch C (2017) On the vulnerability of face recognition systems towards morphed face attacks. In: 2017 5th international workshop on biometrics and forensics (IWBF), pp 1–6. https://doi.org/10.1109/IWBF.2017.7935088

18. Schils M (2017) Towards a structured approach for face morphing detection. University of Twente, Master EE Biometrics and Computer Vision

19. Spreeuwers L, Veldhuis R, Schils M (2018) Towards robust evaluation of face morphing detection. In: 2018 26th European signal processing conference, EUSIPCO 2018, European signal processing conference. IEEE, United States, pp 1027–1031. https://doi.org/10.23919/EUSIPCO.2018.8553018. http://www.eusipco2018.org/. (26th European Signal Processing Conference, EUSIPCO 2018, EUSIPCO ; Conference date: 03-09-2018 Through 07-09-2018)

20. Wandzik L, Kaeding G, Vicente-Garcia R (2018) Morphing detection using a general- purpose face recognition system. In: 26th European signal processing conference, EUSIPCO 2018, Roma, Italy, 3–7 Sept 2018. IEEE, pp 1012–1016. https://doi.org/10.23919/EUSIPCO.2018.8553375.

Chapter 17
Facial Retouching and Alteration Detection

Puspita Majumdar, Akshay Agarwal, Mayank Vatsa, and Richa Singh

Abstract On the social media platforms, the *filters* for digital retouching and face beautification have become a common trend. With the availability of easy-to-use image editing tools, the generation of altered images has become an effortless task. Apart from this, advancements in the Generative Adversarial Network (GAN) leads to creation of realistic facial images and alteration of facial images based on the attributes. While the majority of these images are created for fun and beautification purposes, they may be used with malicious intent for negative applications such as deepnude or spreading visual fake news. Therefore, it is important to detect digital alterations in images and videos. This chapter presents a comprehensive survey of existing algorithms for retouched and altered image detection. Further, multiple experiments are performed to highlight the open challenges of alteration detection.

17.1 Introduction

Social media platforms have become the new source of information, and millions of images and videos are uploaded and shared on these platforms on a daily basis.

P. Majumdar performed the experiments and analyzed the results. A. Agarwal helped in writing the chapter. All authors have reviewed and updated the chapter

P. Majumdar
Puspita Majumdar IIIT-Delhi, Delhi, India
e-mail: pushpitam@iiitd.ac.in

A. Agarwal
Akshay Agarwal SUNY, University at Buffalo, Buffalo, NY, USA
e-mail: aa298@buffalo.edu

M. Vatsa
Mayank Vatsa IIT Jodhpur, Jodhpur, India
e-mail: mvatsa@iitj.ac.in

R. Singh (✉)
Richa Singh IIT Jodhpur, Jodhpur, India
e-mail: richa@iitj.ac.in

© The Author(s) 2022
C. Rathgeb et al. (eds.), *Handbook of Digital Face Manipulation and Detection*,
Advances in Computer Vision and Pattern Recognition,
https://doi.org/10.1007/978-3-030-87664-7_17

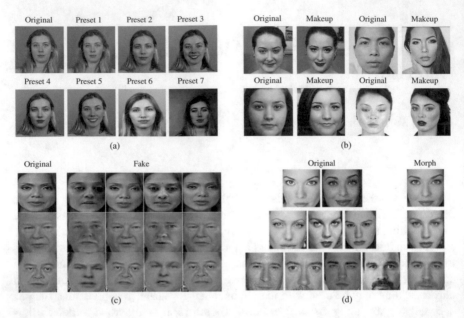

Fig. 17.1 Samples of different facial alterations. **a** Retouching **b** Makeup **c** DeepFakes, and **d** Morphing

While uploading images or sharing them among individuals, the face images are generally retouched/altered to make them look more beautiful or appealing due to the fascination toward few societal factors such as fair complexion and flawless skin [1]. As shown in Fig. 17.1, these alterations can either be in the form of simple retouchings such as removal of pimples, age spots, and wrinkles to complex alterations such as *morphing* or *deepfake* that change the geometric properties.

In cosmetic industries, facial retouching/alteration is commonly used to sell beauty products by making the seller (model) look more appealing in advertisements. These advertisements convey the wrong information of obtaining a flawless appearance upon using their beauty products, which in turn mislead people to use their beauty products. Digitally retouched images can also adversely affect the mindset of the general population and can lead to mental stress [57]. It negatively affects the self-esteem of the viewers by trying to follow the societal norm of pleasant appearance. This leads to body dissatisfaction amongst women and sets unrealistic expectations among them, which leads to various psychological and sociological issues. To cope with the situation, some countries have enacted the "Photoshop Law" to label retouched advertisement photos as retouched [48].

The effect of retouching on face recognition algorithms cannot be ignored. Several countries require hard copy of photographs on identification documents such as driver's license and passports. Generally, people digitally retouch their images and use the prints for application. These images are used to create the identification documents and may serve as an enrollment image to be matched with real-time query images of a subject. The real-time original images, when matched with enrolled retouched images, degrade the identification performance [9, 53].

Apart from digital retouching, alterations on face images can be in the form of (i) morphing, (ii) attribute modification via GANs, and (iii) deepfakes. In morphing, a new face image is generated using the information available from two or more source face images to conceal own identity or gain the identity of others [5, 44, 60]. GANs based techniques alter the local or global facial attribute of the input face images [32, 33]. In deepfakes, altered videos are generated by face swapping or facial reenactment techniques [56]. With the availability of online tools and apps for performing these alterations flawlessly and effortlessly, anyone can create altered samples.

The effect of altered images in facial recognition algorithms and their use for spreading fake news is a major concern. It is shown that morphed images significantly reduce the performance of face recognition algorithms, including commercial systems and deep neural networks-based models [23, 44]. Their adverse effect can be seen in the application of automatic border access through e-passport. Generally, while issuing e-passports, a hard copy of the photograph is required. The user can provide the morphed photograph to fool both human examiner and automatic face recognition algorithms. Apart from this, spreading fake news using deepfakes is a serious challenge. For example, deepfakes [55] can be used to create fake videos that show celebrities in pornographic content by generating an individual's face that closely matches with another face in the video. Fake videos of Mr. Barack Obama were widely circulated on the Internet [64]. Often, generative models are used for creating such content and can be done in real-time by swapping faces along with their facial expressions [70]. The problem becomes severe when these altered images/videos are presented as evidence in the courts or are used during political campaigns. It is therefore important to detect the altered face images [10, 32, 33, 54].

The outline of this chapter is as follows. Section 17.2 discusses the literature of different algorithms proposed for the detection of retouched and altered images. This section further provides the details of the databases proposed for retouching and alteration detection. A thorough experimental evaluation of the performance of existing algorithms to detect retouched and altered images in cross-domain/manipulation settings is discussed in Sect. 17.3. In Sect. 17.4, we highlight the open challenges that require the attention of the research community and focused research efforts, followed by the conclusion in Sect. 17.5.

17.2 Retouching and Alteration Detection—Review

In the literature, researchers have proposed different techniques for detecting facial retouching and alterations. While retouching is done for an appealing appearance without any ill intent, alterations such as morphing and face swap are generally

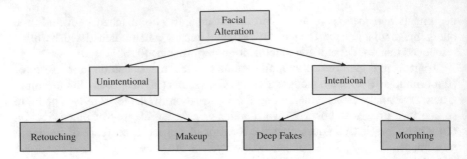

Fig. 17.2 Categorization of facial alterations into unintentional and intentional adversary

done with malicious intent. Therefore, as shown in Fig. 17.2, we have segregated the literature into unintentional and intentional adversary detection. In the following subsections, we discuss the algorithms proposed for the detection of retouched and altered images, followed by the details of the publicly available databases for the same.

17.2.1 Digital Retouching Detection

Retouching on facial images can be performed digitally using easy-to-use image editing tools or physically by applying facial makeups. Retouching is done for beautification purposes, generally, without any malicious intent and can be categorized as *unintentional adversary*. However, due to the adverse effect of self-acclaimed ideal face complexion and an appealing appearance by retouching of face images on social media applications, countries such as Israel, UK, and USA [25, 63, 65] have enacted laws to regulate the use of retouched images. For the strict adhesion of such laws, the successful detection of digitally retouched images is important. To facilitate research in this direction, researchers have proposed different algorithms to create retouched images and analyzed their effect on face recognition algorithms, followed by designing different algorithms for its detection.

In 2011, Kee et al. [36] proposed an amalgamation of photometric and geometric features for an effective retouching of face and body images. Later, Ferrara et al. [22, 23] evaluated the impact of face retouching or beautification on commercial and handcrafted features based face recognition algorithms. In the earlier work, Ferrara et al. [23] have performed multiple levels of beautification and studied its impact on the equal error rate (EER) of the commercial face recognition systems. It is shown that even with the slight beautification, the EER of the system changes by ∼2%, whereas heavy retouching can increase the EER by ∼17%. In 2016, Bharati et al. [9] created one of the largest databases both in terms of the number of subjects and type of retouching mediums. The performance of commercial face recognition systems is evaluated on the proposed database. The authors have reported a difference of ∼7.50% and ∼11% in the rank-1 recognition performance of the commercial system and openBR [37], respectively. Further, an algorithm is proposed for detecting retouched images using face patches as input in the deep Boltzmann machine (DBM) for feature extraction and support vector machine (SVM) for binary classification. Experiments are performed on two databases and the proposed algorithm achieved an overall accuracy of 87.10% on the ND-IIITD database and 96.20% on the Celebrity database. These preliminary works highlight the challenges of recognizing retouched face images. Bharati et al. [10] have further created a demography-based retouched face database. The database contains subjects belonging to different gender groups and ethnicity. The authors have also proposed a retouching face detection algorithm based on supervised autoencoder. The experiments are performed with both seen and unseen demographic ethnicity in the training and testing sets. The Caucasian demographic subset yields the lowest detection performance even under seen demographic experimental setting. The performance of the detection algorithm is at-least 2% lower under unseen demographic experimental scenario than the seen demographic scenario. Jain et al. [33] have used the softmax probabilities as the features in the SVM classifier for retouched face detection. Recently, the authors [32] have proposed a multi-level hierarchical framework for the detection of original and altered images. Altered images are further classified into retouched and GANs generated images. Rathgeb et al. [54] have proposed a differential detection approach based on the assumption that while detecting a retouched image, a counter trusted original image is also available. Three difference vectors are computed using texture features, facial landmarks, and featured from deep neural networks. A support vector machine classifier is trained on each difference vector, and a weighted fusion is performed for decision. A critical drawback is the assumption of the availability of the trusted source and its characteristics. While the previous works performed the binary classification of original and retouched images, a recent work by Wang et al. [68] have proposed a framework to first perform the retouching detection and later suggested a possible undo operation to develop the unaltered image. For binary classification dilated residual network is trained using heavy data augmentation techniques. On the detected manipulated images, optical flow field is calculated for measuring the pixel warping effect.

Another related field to digital retouching is facial cosmetics or makeup, i.e., physical retouching. According to multiple market reports, the business of cosmetics is growing exponentially. For example, the US market growth is at the rate of CAGR of 2.47% from the year 2015 to 2020 [67]. Makeups drastically alter the facial appearance of a person and are applied to various facial regions such as eyes, skin, and lip. Similar to digital retouching, makeups also affect the performance of face recognition algorithms. Several researchers have shown the impact of facial makeup in the performance degradation of face recognition algorithms, including commercial systems [18, 29, 62, 69]. To counter the impact of facial makeup on recognition, several algorithms have been proposed to detect makeup images. Chen et al. [12] have utilized the SVM and AdaBoost classifier trained on the fusion of shape and color features for detecting makeup images. Kose et al. [38] proposed an ensemble-based technique, and Liu et al. [42] have used the entropy information combined with SVM for makeup image detection. Kotwal et al. [39] have utilized the intermediate layer features of deep convolutional neural network (CNN) for age-induced makeup detection. The authors have also proposed a new facial makeup database with both male and female individuals. It is shown that the age-induced makeup can significantly degrade the performance of face recognition network, namely LightCNN [72]. Apart from the simple classification of images as with and without makeup, research works have also been proposed for the removal of makeup to obtain non-makeup images. Cao et al. [11] have proposed a generative adversarial network, namely, bidirectional tunable de-makeup network (BTD-Net) for makeup removal. Arab et al. [6] have proposed a two-level defense against the makeup-based alteration. In the first level, images are first detected for makeup or non-makeup. Later, the makeup removal algorithm is proposed utilizing Cycle generative adversarial network (Cycle GAN) [74]. The authors have shown a significant improvement in the rank-1 face matching accuracy through their makeup removal technique, surpassing several existing algorithms, including BTD-Net. Rathgeb et al. [53] presented a survey of the impact of beautification on face recognition algorithms and different detection techniques.

17.2.2 Digital Alteration Detection

Digital alterations, including morphing, GANs based alterations, and deepfakes are performed with malicious intent and fall under the category of the *intentional adversary*. With the advancements in computer vision and deep learning algorithms, digitally altering/manipulating an image/video has become an easy task. Altered/manipulated images raise serious concerns when used for illegal access, spreading fake news during political campaigns, or as evidence in court. This has attracted the attention of the research community, and several algorithms have been proposed for the generation and detection of altered images. Agarwal et al. [5] have prepared a large scale video-based face swap database using Snapchat. Face swap is an alteration technique in which more than one individual can share a single identity. The authors have shown the vulnerabilities of commercial face recognition systems, and mobile unlocking algorithms against face swapped images. A novel feature descriptor is also proposed to highlight the minute inconsistencies near eyes, nose, and mouth regions. The feature descriptor is then fed into the SVM classifier for binary classification. Other types of alterations include the creation of a new face image by blending multiple faces based on the measurement of facial landmarks [13, 58, 71]. The detection and blending of facial landmarks are performed using different algorithms. In an early attempt to secure the face recognition algorithms against such alterations, researchers have proposed different image features based detection algorithms [34, 59, 61]. Recent detection algorithms against such alterations are based on the characteristics of facial landmarks, head pose [3, 73] and

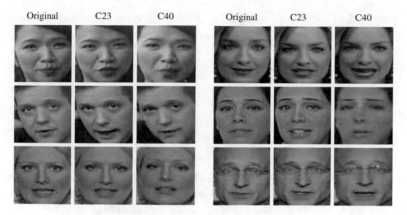

Fig. 17.3 Illustrating the difference between the compressed and uncompressed frames extracted from the original videos of the FaceForensics++ dataset [56]

eye blinking [35]. For detecting GANs based alterations, Jain et al. [32] proposed a three-level hierarchical network, Digital Alteration Detection using Hierarchical Convolutional Neural Network (DAD-HCNN). The proposed network not only distinguishes altered images from original ones but also classifies the images generated using different models of GANs.

With the advancement of generative adversarial networks (GANs), the generation of face swapping and morphing became an easy task. GANs lead to the generation of high resolution manipulated face images such as deepfakes. In deepfakes, the face of a person in a video is swapped with another person (face swapping), or someone's expression is animated over the person in the video (facial reenactment). Face swapping techniques can be broadly divided into two groups: *(i) computer graphics-based techniques* and *(ii) deep neural network-based techniques*. Computer graphics techniques are based on detecting facial landmarks and merging these landmarks for the generation of swapped faces. Deep neural network-based techniques automatically identify the pose and other related information for swapped face generation. To motivate research toward the detection of deepfakes, Facebook has recently organized the Deepfake Detection Challenge (DFDC) [19]. Rossler et al. [56] have proposed one of the largest databases (FaceForensics++) covering different manipulation types generated using computer graphics-based techniques and GANs. The videos in the proposed database are available in three different qualities. Figure 17.3 shows the difference between the compressed and uncompressed frames extracted from the original videos. Authors have evaluated the performance of existing alteration detection algorithms and deep CNN models on the FaceForensics++ database. It is found that XceptionNet [14] outperformed existing algorithms. It is observed that the detection of altered, compressed videos are challenging than uncompressed videos. Dang et al. [17] have proposed an attention-based network utilizing the features of CNN networks for fake detection. Kumar et al. [40] have utilized the patch-based ResNet architecture for the detection of face manipulation videos. Recently, Ciftci et al. [15]

have proposed to use biological signals for fake detection. However, the detection algorithms developed to filter out the manipulated videos are itself observed to be vulnerable against different alterations [3, 4, 27, 31]. This demands the need for the development of robust fake detection algorithms. A detailed survey on deepfakes is given in [47, 66].

17.2.3 Publicly Available Databases

Researchers have proposed multiple facial retouching and deepfake databases to encourage research toward detection of altered images. The following discusses the details of the databases proposed in the literature for retouching and deepfake detection.

Facial Retouching Databases

Bharati et al. [9] have prepared one of the largest database, the ND-IIITD database, covering seven presets of retouching. Different preset variations are applied using professional software, namely, Portraitpro Studio Max [50]. Retouching is applied to important facial landmark regions such as eyes, lips, nose, and skin texture. Also, relevant retouching operations are applied based on the gender of a person. For example, in preset-1, some of the characteristics of retouching applied to females include skin blush, smooth lips, eyes blue, and nose shorten. For males, the characteristics of retouching include pulp lips, nose slim, shorten wrinkles, and forehead-sculpt. The database contains original images of 325 identities of UND-B [24], on top of that, seven presets are applied for the generation of a variety of retouched face images. In total, the database contains 2600 original and 2275 retouched face images. The authors also created a Celebrity database by downloading images from the Internet. Images pairs labeled with retouched and non-retouched are used to create the database. The database contains 330 images belonging to 165 celebrities. Later, Bharati et al. [10] developed a demography based retouched face database using two tools, namely, BeautyPlus [8] and Potraitpro Studio Max [50]. The database contains subjects belonging to two gender groups, male and female, and three ethnicities, Indian, Chinese, and Caucasian. In total, the database contains 1200 original and 2400 retouched images. Recently, Rathgeb et al. [52] proposed a retouched face database with 800 retouched and 100 original images. Retouched images are created using five different mobile apps. Table 17.1 summarizes the details of the existing facial retouching databases.

DeepFake Databases

In 2017, Agarwal et al. [5] proposed SWAPPED—Digital Attack Video Face database. The database is prepared using Snapchat that swaps/stitches two faces to create fake videos. The database contains 129 real and 612 fake videos of 110

Table 17.1   Details of existing facial retouching databases

Database	Images		Subjects		Retouching Tool
	Real	Retouched	Male	Female	
ND-IIITD [9]	2600	2275	211	114	PortraitPro Studio Max
Celebrity [9]	165	165	25	140	Unknown (Online Sources)
MDRF [10]	1200	2400	300	300	BeautyPlus and Potraitpro Studio Max (v12)
Rathgeb et al. [52]	100	800	50	50	Multiple Mobile Apps

and 31 subjects, respectively. Li et al. [41] proposed the UADFV database with 49 real and 49 fake videos. The database is created using FakeApp mobile application. A large scale database, namely, FaceForensics++ is proposed by Rossler et al. [56]. The database contains 1000 real videos (downloaded from YouTube). Different manipulation techniques are applied to the real videos to generate 4000 fake videos. The database contains four different subsets of manipulated videos that are generated using (i) computer graphics-based techniques and (ii) learning-based techniques. Computer graphics-based techniques include *FaceSwap (FS)* and *Face2Face (F2F)* while learning-based techniques include *DeepFakes (DF)* and *NeuralTextures (NT)*. Each of the manipulation methods requires the source and target videos for the generation of fake/altered videos. FaceSwap utilizes facial landmarks for the generation of a 3D shape model and swaps the facial regions by minimizing the difference between the landmarks in the source and target subject. Post-processing is required to smoothen out the blended regions and for color correction. While FaceSwap blends two faces together, the Face2Face method transfers the expression from the source video to the target video. Therefore, the swapped videos generated using FaceSwap contains the identity of both source and target subjects while the target identity is preserved in Face2Face. DeepFakes is an autoencoder based manipulation technique with a shared encoder that is trained to reconstruct the source and target faces. GAN loss is applied in the NeuralTextures method, and the mouth region is altered. This method relies on tracked geometry for effective manipulation of the expression at the mouth region. Later, a more advanced version of the database is released with more realistic settings of the real-world scenario [28]. By utilizing 363 real videos of 28 paid actors, 3068 deepfake videos are generated. Both the above databases cover the videos in three different qualities: (i) uncompressed (raw), (ii) low compression with quantization factor set to 23 (high quality), and (iii) high compression with quantization factor set to 40 (low quality). Li et al. [43] presented a large scale DeepFake video dataset, termed CelebDF, with high-quality DeepFake videos of celebrities. The fake videos are generated using an advanced version of face swap algorithms. The dataset contains a total of 590 real and 5639 fake videos. Recently, Facebook

Table 17.2 Details of existing deepfake databases

Database	Real		Fake	
	Videos	Source	Videos	Source
SWAPPED [5]	129	Real-time	612	Snapchat
UADFV [41]	49	Youtube	49	FakeApp
FaceForensics++ [56]	1000	Youtube	4000	FaceSwap, Face2Face, NeuralTexture, DeepFake
DeepFake Detection [28]	363	Real-time	3068	DeepFake
Celeb-DF [43]	590	Youtube	5639	DeepFake
DFDC [20]	21154	Actors	102000	DeepFake
WildDeepFake [75]	3805	Online	3509	DeepFake (Online)

has released the Deepfake Detection Challenge (DFDC) [20] database. It is one of the largest databases containing more than 100,000 fake videos of 3426 actors. Zi et al. [75] created the WildDeepfake database by collecting images from the Internet. Table 17.2 summarizes the details of the existing deepfake databases.

17.3 Experimental Evaluation and Observations

In the literature, algorithms proposed for detecting retouched and deepfake images have shown high accuracy when the models are trained on a specific type of alteration and evaluated on similar alterations. For instance, Jain et al. [33] have proposed a convolutional neural network framework for retouching detection by training the framework on retouched and original images. The proposed framework is evaluated on the ND-IIITD database. As reported in Table 17.3, the framework achieved more than 99% accuracy. Similarly, in [56], we observe that existing algorithms perform well when the models are trained on a specific type of manipulation (Table 17.4). Here, the authors used the FaceForensics++ database for detecting manipulated images.

The high performance of deep learning models to detect retouched and altered images (Tables 17.3 and 17.4) in the same domain/manipulation settings indicate that deep models are able to learn distinguishable features when the distribution of the evaluation dataset is similar to the training dataset. In other words, high performance is observed when the training of deep models is done with some apriori knowledge about the type of alterations performed on the images. However, in a real-world scenario, it is not practical to assume such apriori knowledge. Therefore, in this chapter, we highlight the challenges of retouching and alteration detection in a real-world cross train-test alteration detection scenarios (i.e., when trained on one and test on another).

Table 17.3 Classification accuracy (%) for retouching detection on the ND-IIITD database and comparison with existing reported results in literature [33]

Algorithm	Accuracy
Kee and Farid [36]	48.80
Bharati et al. [9] (Unsupervised DBM)	81.90
Bharati et al. [9] (Supervised DBM)	87.10
Jain et al. [33] (Thresholding)—(64, 64, 3)	99.70
Jain et al. [33] (SVM)—(64, 64, 3)	99.42
Jain et al. [33] (Thresholding)—(128, 128, 3)	99.48
Jain et al. [33] (SVM)—(128, 128, 3)	99.65

- **Cross-domain**: Detecting altered images belonging to different domains (retouched and manipulated).
- **Cross manipulation**: Detecting images generated using different types of manipulations.
- **Cross ethnicity**: Detecting altered images belonging to different ethnicities.

Multiple experiments are performed to evaluate the performance of deep models for retouching and alteration detection in the above three experimental settings. Experiments are performed using two state-of-the-art deep models, namely, ResNet50 [30] and XceptionNet [14]. Two popular databases from the literature, namely, ND-IIITD face retouching database and FaceForensics++ database, are used for the experiments. We have also used the IndianForensics database [46] for the cross ethnicity experiment. Figure 17.4 shows some sample images of the databases. Protocols to perform the experiments and the implementation details are discussed below:

Experimental Protocol and Implementation Details: For the experiments, the ND-IIITD database is divided into non-overlapping training and testing sets with 50% subject-wise partitioning corresponding to each retouched and original preset [9]. Training sets of all the presets are combined to create a single training set. Similarly, all the testing sets are merged together into a single testing set. For the FaceForensics++ database, pre-defined protocol is followed for training, validation, and testing partitioning [56]. The IndianForensics database [46] is divided into 50% train-test splits for the experiments. Videos of the FaceForensics++ and IndianForensics databases are divided into frames. 10 frames per video are extracted, and the results are reported using frame based accuracy.

Pre-trained ResNet50 and XceptionNet models are fine-tuned by adding two fully connected dense layers of 512 dimensions after the final convolutional layer. Models are trained using Adam optimizer for 20 epochs with a batch size of 32. For the initial 10 epochs, the learning rate is set to 0.0001 and reduced by 0.1 after every 5 epochs. Frames are extracted from the videos of the FaceForensics++ database and resized to 128×128 resolution. The images of the ND-IIITD database are also resized to 128×128 resolution. All the experiments are performed under TensorFlow 2.0

Table 17.4 Classification accuracy (%) of manipulation-specific forgery detectors on the FaceForensics++ database (from [56])

	No Compression				Compressed 23				Compressed 40			
	DF	F2F	FS	NT	DF	F2F	FS	NT	DF	F2F	FS	NT
Steg. Features + SVM [26]	99.03	99.13	98.27	**99.88**	77.12	74.68	79.51	76.94	65.58	57.55	60.58	60.69
Cozzolino et al. [16]	98.83	98.56	98.89	**99.88**	81.78	85.32	85.69	80.60	68.26	59.38	62.08	62.42
Bayar and Stamm [7]	99.28	98.79	98.98	98.78	90.18	94.93	93.14	86.04	80.95	77.30	76.83	72.38
Rahmouni et al. [51]	98.03	98.96	98.94	96.06	82.16	93.48	92.51	75.18	73.25	62.33	67.08	62.59
MesoNet [2]	98.41	97.96	96.07	97.05	95.26	95.84	93.43	85.96	89.52	84.44	83.56	75.74
XceptionNet [14]	**99.59**	**99.61**	**99.14**	99.36	**98.85**	**98.36**	**98.23**	**94.50**	**94.28**	**91.56**	**93.70**	**82.11**

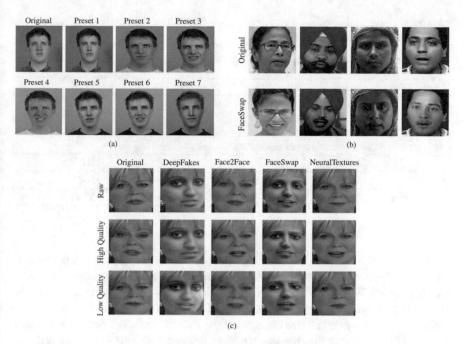

Fig. 17.4 Sample images of the **a** ND-IIITD [9] **b** IndianForensics [46], and **c** FaceForensics++ [56] databases

environment on a DGX station with Intel Xeon CPU, 256 GB RAM, and four 32 GB Nvidia V100 GPU cards.

17.3.1 Cross-Domain Alteration Detection

The aim of these experiments is to evaluate the generalizability of deep models to detect altered images across different domains. In these experiments, models trained on the ND-IIITD database are separately evaluated on the four face manipulation subsets of the FaceForensics++ database (Deepfakes, Face2Face, FaceSwap, and NeuralTextures), and vice versa. Experiments are performed on the uncompressed subsets of the FaceForensics++ database to maintain uniformity with respect to the compression factor of the images in both the databases. Compression introduces artifacts that pose additional challenges to the detection algorithms. Therefore, to solely analyze the challenges due to unseen alterations across different domains, the compression factor of the images is kept consistent during the experiments.

Table 17.5 shows the classification accuracy of deep models trained on different manipulation types of the FaceForensics++ database and evaluated on the ND-IIITD

Table 17.5 Classification accuracy (%) of the models trained on the FaceForensics++ database and evaluated on the ND-IIITD database

	DF	F2F	FS	NT
ResNet50	49.95	49.95	48.59	50.21
XceptionNet	56.22	49.86	46.23	52.89

Table 17.6 Classification accuracy (%) of the model trained on the ND-IIITD database and evaluated on different manipulation types of the FaceForensics++ database

	DF	F2F	FS	NT
ResNet50	50.43	50.18	50.11	50.54
XceptionNet	53.50	52.00	48.68	53.11

database. It is observed that the models do not perform well and yield almost random accuracy for retouching detection. Models trained on FaceSwap achieve the lowest accuracy of 48.59% and 46.23%, with ResNet50 and XceptionNet, respectively. The classification accuracy of the model trained on the ND-IIITD database and evaluated separately on different subsets of the FaceForensics++ database is shown in Table 17.6. Similar to the previous scenario, it is observed that deep models do not perform well in cross-domain settings. The degradation in performance is due to the effect of the domain shift from the training set to the evaluation set.

17.3.2 Cross Manipulation Alteration Detection

To observe the performance of deep models for unseen manipulation detection, experiments are performed on the FaceForensics++ database. This experiment is performed to analyze the robustness of deep models by training them on a specific manipulation type and evaluating on others. We have used four subsets of manipulated videos (with different quality levels) of the FaceForensics++ database for the experiments. Training and evaluation of the models are performed on a fixed quality level. For example, models trained on the uncompressed videos of a specific manipulation type are evaluated on the uncompressed videos of other manipulation types.

Table 17.7 shows the classification performance of deep models for unseen manipulation detection. It is observed that most of the models do not perform well in cross manipulation detection settings. Interestingly, there is minimal effect of compression observed on the performance of deep models. Rather in some cases, it is observed that the performance of deep models on the compressed videos is better than uncompressed videos. For instance, models trained on FaceSwap (FS) when evaluated on DeepFakes (DF) achieves 58.57% and 61.89% accuracy using ResNet50 and XceptionNet, respectively, on high compressed videos (compressed 40), while these models achieve 50.82% and 51.00% accuracy on uncompressed videos. It is our assertion

Table 17.7 Classification accuracy (%) of the models trained on a specific type of manipulation and evaluated on others of the FaceForensics++ database

Trained on		No Compression			Compressed 23			Compressed 40		
		F2F	**FS**	**NT**	**F2F**	**FS**	**NT**	**F2F**	**FS**	**NT**
DF	ResNet50	53.54	49.46	58.57	51.18	50.04	51.71	54.04	53.75	52.86
	XceptionNet	56.36	49.64	63.57	51.86	49.93	54.07	53.36	55.64	52.89
		DF	**FS**	**NT**	**DF**	**FS**	**NT**	**DF**	**FS**	**NT**
F2F	ResNet50	58.11	50.75	51.57	55.79	52.18	50.79	58.86	53.32	54.25
	XceptionNet	63.11	51.18	51.61	59.96	51.68	52.86	58.96	52.96	54.25
		DF	**F2F**	**NT**	**DF**	**F2F**	**NT**	**DF**	**F2F**	**NT**
FS	ResNet50	50.82	53.07	50.00	51.04	52.32	50.18	58.57	51.36	50.29
	XceptionNet	51.00	52.39	49.93	52.36	53.61	48.96	61.89	51.64	51.00
		DF	**F2F**	**FS**	**DF**	**F2F**	**FS**	**DF**	**F2F**	**FS**
NT	ResNet50	86.89	56.68	49.39	74.43	56.39	48.04	61.29	60.11	52.32
	XceptionNet	91.32	67.00	49.75	76.68	58.57	48.61	61.89	61.50	50.79

that instead of learning the discriminative features to distinguish manipulated videos from original ones, the models are learning the compression artifacts in compressed videos for discrimination. Therefore better performance is achieved for low-quality videos. It is also important to observe that the models trained on NeuralTextures (NT) achieves high accuracy when evaluated on DeepFakes (DF), while the opposite is not true. This raises several questions about the kind of information learned by deep models for discrimination. All these observations open new research threads toward developing sophisticated algorithms for unseen manipulation detection. It further emphasizes the importance of the interpretability of deep models for a better understanding of the obtained results.

17.3.3   Cross Ethnicity Alteration Detection

To observe the fairness of detection algorithms, experiments are performed on the FaceForensics++ and IndianForensics databases, to analyze the performance of deep models in cross ethnicity settings. The IndianForensics database contains 200 original and 234 fake videos of Indian people. Fake videos are created by face swapping using FSGAN [49]. Experiments are performed by training the models on the IndianForensics database and evaluating on FaceSwap manipulated videos of the FaceForensics++ database and vice versa. The aim of these experiments is to evaluate the performance of detection algorithms across Indian and non-Indian ethnicities. Figure 17.5 shows the classification accuracy for the same. ResNet50 and XceptionNet models trained on the IndianForensics database yield an accuracy of 39.29% and 39.79%, respectively, on detecting FaceSwap manipulated videos of the FaceForensics++ database. On the other hand, models trained on the FaceForensics++

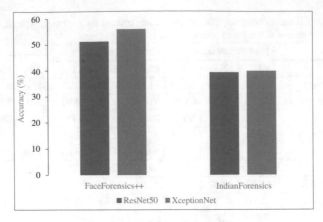

Fig. 17.5 Classification accuracy (%) of the models trained on the IndianForensics database and evaluated on the FaceForensics++ database and vice versa

database yields an accuracy of 51.35% and 55.95% on the IndianForensics database corresponding to ResNet50 and XceptionNet, respectively. The low detection accuracy indicates the effect of ethnicity on the performance of detection algorithms. A similar effect of ethnicity on the alteration detection algorithms has been recently shown by Mehra et al. [46].

17.4 Open Challenges

To develop robust alteration detection algorithms/systems which can be deployed in the real world, we believe that the challenges discussed below require the attention of the research community.

Generalizability of Detection Algorithms Across Different Domains: Retouching and deepfakes are different types of facial alterations that belong to different domains of adversaries (unintentional and intentional). In the literature, various algorithms/deep models have been proposed for their detection, and high performance is achieved by training them separately, either for the task of retouching detection or deepfakes detection. However, as mentioned in the previous section, in a real-world scenario, the apriori knowledge of the type of alteration is not available. It is possible that the images in the evaluation dataset are altered using some other image editing tools and techniques which are not seen during the training process. The experiments performed to evaluate the generalizability of deep models for cross-domain alteration detection indicate that deep models do not perform well for detecting altered images belonging to different domains of adversaries. Therefore, it is important to develop generalizable algorithms that could handle the effect of domain shift between different types of alterations.

Robustness of Detection Algorithms Across Different Types of Manipulations: Manipulations are performed using different computer vision-based techniques, learning-based techniques, and using simple mobile applications. Due to the ease of creating manipulated images/videos, social media platforms are now flooded with altered content. With the advancement of technology, different types of manipulated images are created on a daily basis and shared through social media platforms. It is therefore important that the detection algorithms deployed on these platforms must detect the altered images generated using new techniques. In a real-world scenario, it is impractical to regularly update the deployed models with new types of manipulated images/videos. Thus, the detection algorithms/models should be robust to unseen manipulations as well.

Effect of Ethnicity on Detection Algorithms: Fairness in model predictions with respect to different demographic groups or protected attributes (such as gender and race) is important for the trustability and dependability of deep learning algorithms [23, 42]. Therefore, in a real-world scenario, the detection algorithms must be fair across different demographic groups. In other words, the performance of detection algorithms/deep models should be equal across different demographic groups. Experiments performed to detect altered images in cross ethnicity settings indicate that the performance of deep models degrades significantly when the altered images belong to different ethnicities. This highlights the need for sophisticated detection algorithms to overcome the challenges of cross ethnicity effect.

17.5 Conclusion

Face image alterations have a very diverse usage, ranging from beautification, to getting unauthorized access, to even spreading fake news. Based on the intent, alterations can be broadly classified into two categories: unintentional manipulations which include makeup and retouching/beautification, and intentional manipulations which includes deepfakes. Both these alterations significantly degrade the performance of face recognition algorithms and have several adverse effects when used with malicious intent. In this chapter, as the first contribution, we have provided a comprehensive survey of the literature toward these manipulations. For both the alterations, a summary of the relevant databases and detection techniques is provided. The survey can help the research community to progress in the field of altered image detection and to develop secure face recognition algorithms/systems.

The second contribution of this chapter aims at highlighting the open challenges in facial alteration detection. In the literature, the detection algorithms are generally evaluated by training and testing under the same domain (for instance, same alteration type), and the algorithms have shown high detection accuracy. In this chapter, we showcase more diverse usage of the algorithms and performed several experiments to evaluate the performance of two state-of-the-art deep convolutional network models under those challenging unseen alteration detection settings. It is found that the models that reported high accuracy for seen alteration settings failed miserably under unseen alteration settings. We assert that the challenges discussed in this chapter and the experimental results will help the research community in building robust and generalizable detection algorithms deployable in the real world.

Acknowledgements R. Singh and M. Vatsa are partially supported through a research grants from MeitY, and MHA, Government of India. P. Majumdar is partly supported by DST INSPIRE Ph.D. Fellowship. M. Vatsa is also partially supported through Swarnajayanti Fellowship by the Government of India.

References

1. 68 percent of adults edit their selfies before sharing them with anyone. https://fstoppers.com/mobile/68-percent-adults-edit-their-selfies-sharing-them-anyone-95417. Accessed 29 January 2021
2. Afchar D, Nozick V, Yamagishi J, Echizen I (2018) Mesonet: a compact facial video forgery detection network. In: IEEE international workshop on information forensics and security (WIFS), pp 1–7
3. Agarwal S, Farid H, Gu Y, He M, Nagano K, Li H (2019) Protecting world leaders against deep fakes. In: CVPR workshops, pp 38–45
4. Agarwal A, Sehwag A, Vatsa M, Singh R (2019) Deceiving the protector: fooling face presentation attack detection algorithms. In: IEEE international conference on biometrics (ICB), pp 1–6
5. Agarwal A, Singh R, Vatsa M, Noore A (2017) Swapped! digital face presentation attack detection via weighted local magnitude pattern. In: IEEE international joint conference on biometrics (IJCB), pp 659–665
6. Arab MA, Azadi Moghadam P, Hussein M, Abd-Almageed W, Hefeeda M (2020) Revealing true identity: detecting makeup attacks in face-based biometric systems. In: ACM international conference on multimedia, pp 3568–3576
7. Bayar B, Stamm MC (2016) A deep learning approach to universal image manipulation detection using a new convolutional layer. In: ACM workshop on information hiding and multimedia security, pp 5–10
8. Beautyplus. https://www.beautyplus.com/. Accessed 29 January 2021
9. Bharati A, Singh R, Vatsa MBowyer KW (2016) Detecting facial retouching using supervised deep learning. IEEE Trans Inform Forensics Secur 11(9):1903–1913
10. Bharati A, Vatsa M, Singh R, Bowyer KW, Tong X (2017) Demography-based facial retouching detection using subclass supervised sparse autoencoder. In: 2017 IEEE international joint conference on biometrics (IJCB), pp 474–482
11. Cao C, Lu F, Li C, Lin S, Shen X (2019) Makeup removal via bidirectional tunable de-makeup network. IEEE Trans Multimedia 21(11):2750–2761
12. Chen C, Dantcheva A, Ross A (2013) Automatic facial makeup detection with application in face recognition. In: 2013 international conference on biometrics (ICB), pp 1–8
13. Choi D, Hwang C (2011) Image morphing using mass-spring system. In: International conference on computer graphics and virtual reality, pp 156–159
14. Chollet F (2017) Xception: deep learning with depthwise separable convolutions. In: IEEE conference on computer vision and pattern recognition, pp 1251–1258
15. Ciftci UA, Demir I, Yin L (2020) Fakecatcher: detection of synthetic portrait videos using biological signals. IEEE transactions on pattern analysis and machine intelligence
16. Cozzolino D, Poggi G, Verdoliva L (2017) Recasting residual-based local descriptors as convolutional neural networks: an application to image forgery detection. In: ACM workshop on information hiding and multimedia security, pp 159–164

17. Dang H, Liu F, Stehouwer J, Liu X, Jain AK (2020) On the detection of digital face manipulation. In: IEEE/CVF conference on computer vision and pattern recognition, pp 5781–5790
18. Dantcheva A, Chen C, Ross A (2012) Can facial cosmetics affect the matching accuracy of face recognition systems? In: IEEE fifth international conference on biometrics: theory, applications and systems (BTAS), pp 391–398
19. Deepfake Detection Challenge. https://deepfakedetectionchallenge.ai
20. Dolhansky B, Bitton J, Pflaum B, Lu J, Howes R, Wang M, Ferrer CC (2020) The deepfake detection challenge dataset. arXiv preprint arXiv:2006.07397
21. Dwork C, Hardt M, Pitassi T, Reingold O, Zemel R (2012) Fairness through awareness. In: Proceedings of the 3rd innovations in theoretical computer science conference, pp 214–226
22. Ferrara M, Franco A, Maltoni D (2016) On the effects of image alterations on face recognition accuracy. In: Face recognition across the imaging spectrum, pp 195–222. Springer
23. Ferrara M, Franco A, Maltoni D, Sun Y (2013) On the impact of alterations on face photo recognition accuracy. In: International conference on image analysis and processing, pp 743–751
24. Flynn PJ, Bowyer KW, Phillips PJ (2003) Assessment of time dependency in face recognition: An initial study. In: International conference on audio-and video-based biometric person authentication, pp 44–51
25. French law on photoshopped images. https://www.huffpost.com/entry/france-photoshop-models-law$_$n$_$59d0dcc6e4b05f005d34c309. Accessed 29 January 2021
26. Fridrich J, Kodovsky J (2012) Rich models for steganalysis of digital images. IEEE Trans Inform Forensics Secur 7(3):868–882
27. Gandhi A, Jain S (2020) Adversarial perturbations fool deepfake detectors. In: IEEE international joint conference on neural networks (IJCNN), pp 1–8
28. Google AI, contributing data to deepfake detection research. https://ai.googleblog.com/2019/09/contributing-data-to-deepfake-detection.html. Accessed 29 January 2021
29. Guo G, Wen L, Yan S (2013) Face authentication with makeup changes. IEEE Trans Circuit Syst Video Technol 24(5):814–825
30. He K, Zhang X, Ren S, Sun J (2016) Deep residual learning for image recognition. In: IEEE conference on computer vision and pattern recognition, pp 770–778
31. Hussain S, Neekhara P, Jere M, Koushanfar F, McAuley J (2021) Adversarial deepfakes: Evaluating vulnerability of deepfake detectors to adversarial examples. In: IEEE/CVF winter conference on applications of computer vision, pp 3348–3357
32. Jain A, Majumdar P, Singh R, Vatsa M (2020) Detecting GANs and retouching based digital alterations via DAD-HCNN. In: IEEE/CVF conference on computer vision and pattern recognition workshops, pp 672–673
33. Jain A, Singh R, Vatsa M (2018) On detecting GANs and retouching based synthetic alterations. In: 2018 IEEE 9th international conference on biometrics theory, applications and systems (BTAS), pp 1–7
34. Jassim S, Asaad A (2018) Automatic detection of image morphing by topology-based analysis. In: IEEE European signal processing conference (EUSIPCO), pp 1007–1011
35. Jung T, Kim S, Kim K (2020) Deepvision: Deepfakes detection using human eye blinking pattern. IEEE Access 8:83144–83154
36. Kee E, Farid H (2011) A perceptual metric for photo retouching. Natl Acad Sci 108(50):19907–19912
37. Klontz JC, Klare BF, Klum S, Jain AK, Burge MJ (2013) Open source biometric recognition. In: IEEE sixth international conference on biometrics: theory, applications and systems, pp 1–8
38. Kose N, Apvrille L, Dugelay JL (2015) Facial makeup detection technique based on texture and shape analysis. In: IEEE international conference and workshops on automatic face and gesture recognition (FG), vol 1, pp 1–7
39. Kotwal K, Mostaani Z, Marcel S (2019) Detection of age-induced makeup attacks on face recognition systems using multi-layer deep features. IEEE Trans Biometr Behav Identity Sci 2(1):15–25

40. Kumar P, Vatsa M, Singh R (2020) Detecting face2face facial reenactment in videos. In: IEEE/CVF winter conference on applications of computer vision, p. 2589–2597
41. Li Y, Chang MC, Lyu S (2018) In ictu oculi: Exposing ai generated fake face videos by detecting eye blinking. In: IEEE international workshop on information forensics and security
42. Liu KH, Liu TJ, Liu HH, Pei SC (2015) Facial makeup detection via selected gradient orientation of entropy information. In: IEEE international conference on image processing (ICIP), pp 4067–4071
43. Li Y, Yang X, Sun P, Qi H, Lyu S (2020) Celeb-df: a large-scale challenging dataset for deepfake forensics. In: IEEE/CVF conference on computer vision and pattern recognition, pp 3207–3216
44. Majumdar P, Agarwal A, Singh R, Vatsa M (2019) Evading face recognition via partial tampering of faces. In: IEEE/CVF conference on computer vision and pattern recognition workshops, pp 11–20
45. Majumdar P, Chhabra S, Singh R, Vatsa M (2020) Subgroup invariant perturbation for unbiased pre-trained model prediction. Frontiers Big Data 3:52
46. Mehra A, Agarwal A, Vatsa M, Singh R (2021) Detection of digital manipulation in facial images (student abstract). In: AAAI conference on artificial intelligence
47. Mirsky Y, Lee W (2021) The creation and detection of deepfakes: a survey. ACM Comput Surv (CSUR) 54(1):1–41
48. New Israeli law bans use of too-skinny models in ads. https://cnn.it/1mNTiY1. Accessed: 9 February 2021
49. Nirkin Y, Keller Y, Hassner T (2019) FSGAN: Subject agnostic face swapping and reenactment. In: Proceedings of the IEEE/CVF international conference on computer vision, pp 7184–7193
50. Portrait pro21. https://www.anthropics.com/portraitpro/. Accessed 29 January 2021
51. Rahmouni N, Nozick V, Yamagishi J, Echizen I (2017) Distinguishing computer graphics from natural images using convolution neural networks. In: IEEE workshop on information forensics and security, pp 1–6
52. Rathgeb C, Botaljov A, Stockhardt F, Isadskiy S, Debiasi L, Uhl A, Busch C (2020) Prnu-based detection of facial retouching. IET Biometrics 9(4):154–164
53. Rathgeb C, Dantcheva A, Busch C (2019) Impact and detection of facial beautification in face recognition: an overview. IEEE Access 7:152667–152678
54. Rathgeb C, Satnoianu CI, Haryanto N, Bernardo K, Busch C (2020) Differential detection of facial retouching: a multi-biometric approach. IEEE Access 8:106373–106385
55. Reddit bans deepfake porn videos. http://www.bbc.com/news/technology-42984127. Accessed 9 February 2021
56. Rossler A, Cozzolino D, Verdoliva L, Riess C, Thies J, Nießner M (2019) Faceforensics++: learning to detect manipulated facial images. In: IEEE/CVF international conference on computer vision, pp 1–11
57. Russello S (2009) The impact of media exposure on self-esteem and body satisfaction in men and women. J Interdisciplinary Undergrad Res 1(1):4
58. Sadu C, Das PK (2020) Swapping face images based on augmented facial landmarks and its detection. In: IEEE region 10 conference (TENCON), pp 456–461
59. Scherhag U, Budhrani D, Gomez-Barrero M, Busch C (2018) Detecting morphed face images using facial landmarks. In: International conference on image and signal processing, pp 444–452
60. Singh R, Agarwal A, Singh M, Nagpal S, Vatsa M (2020) On the robustness of face recognition algorithms against attacks and bias. In: AAAI conference on artificial intelligence, vol 34, pp 13583–13589
61. Spreeuwers L, Schils M, Veldhuis R (2018) Towards robust evaluation of face morphing detection. In: IEEE european signal processing conference (EUSIPCO), pp 1027–1031
62. Sun Y, Ren L, Wei Z, Liu B, Zhai Y, Liu S (2017) A weakly supervised method for makeup-invariant face verification. Pattern Recogn 66:153–159
63. Supermodels without photoshop: Israel photoshop law. https://www.ibtimes.com/supermodels-without-photoshop-israels-photoshop-law-puts-focus-digitally-altered-images-photos. Accessed 29 January 2021

64. Suwajanakorn S, Seitz SM, Kemelmacher-Shlizerman I (2017) Synthesizing obama: Learning lip sync from audio. ACM Trans Graph 36(4):95:1–95:13

65. The self esteem act. https://www.dailymail.co.uk/femail/article-2048375/Self-Esteem-Act-US-parents-push-anti-Photoshop-laws-advertising.html. Accessed 29 January 2021

66. Tolosana R, Vera-Rodriguez R, Fierrez J, Morales A, Ortega-Garcia J (2020) Deepfakes and beyond: a survey of face manipulation and fake detection. Inform Fusion 64:131–148

67. United states beauty and personal care products. https://www.mordorintelligence.com/industry-reports/united-states-cosmetics-products-market-industry. Accessed 29 January 2021

68. Wang SY, Wang O, Owens A, Zhang R, Efros AA (2019) Detecting photoshopped faces by scripting photoshop. In: IEEE/CVF international conference on computer vision, pp 10072–10081

69. Wang S, Fu Y (2016) Face behind makeup. In: AAAI conference on artificial intelligence, vol 30

70. Watch a man manipulate George Bush face in real time. https://bit.ly/2wVgNN4. Accessed 9 February 2021

71. Wu J (2011) Face recognition jammer using image morphing. Boston Univ., USA, Tech. Rep. ECE-2011

72. Wu X, He R, Sun Z, Tan T (2018) A light cnn for deep face representation with noisy labels. IEEE Trans Inform Forensics Secur 13(11):2884–2896

73. Yang X, Li Y, Lyu S (2019) Exposing deep fakes using inconsistent head poses. In: IEEE international conference on acoustics, speech and signal processing (ICASSP), pp 8261–8265

74. Zhu JY, Park T, Isola P, Efros AA (2017) Unpaired image-to-image translation using cycle-consistent adversarial networks. In: IEEE international conference on computer vision, pp 2223–2232

75. Zi B, Chang M, Chen J, Ma X, Jiang YG (2020) Wilddeepfake: a challenging real-world dataset for deepfake detection. In: 28th ACM international conference on multimedia, pp 2382–2390

Part IV
Further Topics, Trends, and Challenges

Chapter 18
Detecting Soft-Biometric Privacy Enhancement

Peter Rot, Peter Peer, and Vitomir Štruc

Abstract With the proliferation of facial analytics and automatic recognition technology that can automatically extract a broad range of attributes from facial images, so-called *soft-biometric privacy-enhancing techniques* have seen increased interest from the computer vision community recently. Such techniques aim to suppress information on certain soft-biometric attributes (e.g., age, gender, ethnicity) in facial images and make unsolicited processing of the facial data infeasible. However, because the level of privacy protection ensured by these methods depends to a significant extent on the fact that privacy-enhanced images are processed in the same way as non-tampered images (and not treated differently), it is critical to understand whether privacy-enhancing manipulations can be detected automatically. To explore this issue, we design a novel approach for the detection of privacy-enhanced images in this chapter and study its performance with facial images processed by three recent privacy models. The proposed detection approach is based on a dedicated attribute recovery procedure that first tries to restore suppressed soft-biometric information and based on the result of the restoration procedure then infers whether a given probe image is privacy enhanced or not. It exploits the fact that a selected attribute classifier generates different attribute predictions when applied to the privacy-enhanced and attribute-recovered facial images. This **pre**diction **m**ismatch (PREM) is, therefore, used as a measure of privacy enhancement. In extensive experiments with three popular face datasets we show that the proposed PREM model is able to accurately detect privacy enhancement in facial images despite the fact that the technique requires no supervision, i.e., no examples of privacy-enhanced images are needed for training.

P. Rot (✉) · V. Štruc
Faculty of Electrical Engineering, University of Ljubljana, Tržaška cesta 25,
1000 Ljubljana, Slovenia
e-mail: peter.rot@fe.uni-lj.si

V. Štruc
e-mail: vitomir.struc@fe.uni-lj.si

P. Peer
Faculty of Computer and Information Science, University of Ljubljana, Večna pot 113,
1000 Ljubljana, Slovenia
e-mail: peter.peer@fri.uni-lj.si

C. Rathgeb et al. (eds.), *Handbook of Digital Face Manipulation and Detection*,
Advances in Computer Vision and Pattern Recognition,
https://doi.org/10.1007/978-3-030-87664-7_18

18.1   Introduction

Recent advances in computer vision, machine learning, and artificial intelligence have pushed the capabilities of automated recognition technology far beyond of what was possible only a few years ago [1–4]. Using state-of-the-art recognition techniques it is possible today to reliably link facial images to individuals and to infer a wide variety of (soft-biometric) attributes, such as gender, age, ethnicity, kin relations, or even health-related attributes, from images captured in less than ideal conditions [5–8]. These advances have made it possible to deploy face recognition technology across a number of application domains ranging from security, border control, and criminal investigations to entertainment, mobile gadgets, social media, autonomous driving, or even health services [9]. While the outlined developments have brought about many societal benefits, increased security, and made a multitude of everyday tasks considerably more convenient, the increased proliferation of face recognition techniques also resulted in privacy concerns related to the possible (mis)use of biometric (facial) data.

Driven by these concerns, a considerable amount of research is currently looking at privacy mechanisms that can provide a trade-off between the utility of the data for facial analytics on the one hand, and the privacy of individuals, on the other [10–13]. To comply with GDPR's minimization principle,[1] facial analytics needs to limit the processing of information only to what is necessary in relation to the key utility of the system. For instance, in face verification systems, where the key utility is to validate an identity claim and user consent is typical only given for this specific use case, automatic inference of potentially sensitive soft-biometric information should not be possible. Nevertheless, recent research shows [14] that a multitude of sensitive information can still be extracted from the data processed within common face verification systems. This information can potentially be misused, without user's consent for other purposes (i.e., function creep) such as automatic targeted advertising, user profiling, or discrimination.

Existing mechanism used for ensuring privacy with facial images are usually based on deidentification technology [15, 16]. Such technology aims to conceal (suppress, remove, or replace) potentially sensitive visual information in images with the goal of privacy protection and can broadly be categorized into two distinct groups: (*i*) techniques that target identity, and (*ii*) techniques that focus on soft-biometric information. Solutions from the first group are useful for privacy protection when sharing visual data captured by third parties on various services, e.g., Google StreetView, where people may appear in the captured data, or when analyzing surveillance footage to protect the privacy of innocent bystanders. Solutions from the latter group also referred to as *deidentification techniques for soft-biometric identifiers* [15, 17] or (more recently) *soft-biometric privacy-enhancing techniques* [10, 18] are relevant, e.g., in the context of social media, where people are in general willing to share their

---

[1] GDPR Data Minimization Principle: https://ico.org.uk/for-organisations/guide-to-data-protection/guide-to-the-general-data-protection-regulation-gdpr/principles/data-minimisation/#data_minimisation.

images online with friends and families, but typically object to privacy intrusions (e.g., targeted ads) facilitated by automatic processing of the uploaded images. In such settings, soft-biometric privacy-enhancing techniques (or soft-biometric privacy models) that try to manipulate facial images in a way that makes automatic extraction of facial attributes, such as age, gender, or ethnicity, challenging but preserves the visual appearances of the input images as much as possible are highly desirable. Such techniques are also at the heart of this chapter.

While a number of soft-biometric privacy models have been proposed in the literature over the years, many still rely (to some extent) on the concept of *privacy through obscurity*, where (improved) privacy protection is ensured as long as the privacy-enhanced images are processed in the same way as all others. If a potential adversary launches a reconstruction attack and tries to recover the suppressed attribute information, the privacy protection may be rendered ineffective [19]. It is, therefore, critical to understand to what extent privacy enhancement can be detected. If an adversary is able to detect that an image has been tampered with, he/she may use specialized analysis tools, manual inspection, or other more targeted means of inferring the concealed information. The *detectability* of privacy enhancement is, hence, a key aspect of existing privacy models that to a great extent determines the level of privacy protection ensured by privacy-enhanced images in real-world settings. However, despite its importance and implications for the deployment of soft-biometric privacy models in real-world applications, this issue has not yet been explored in the open literature.

In this chapter we try to address this gap and present a study centered around the task of detecting image manipulations caused by soft-biometric privacy models. Our goal is (i) to assess whether privacy enhancement can be detected automatically, and as a result (ii) to provide insight into privacy risks originating from such detection techniques. To facilitate the study, we develop a novel detection approach that uses a super-resolution based procedure to first recover suppressed attribute information from privacy-enhanced facial images and then exploits the PREdiction Mismatch (PREM) of an attribute classifier applied to facial images before and after attribute recovery to flag privacy-enhanced data. The proposed approach is evaluated in extensive experiments involving three recent privacy models and three public face datasets. Experimental results show that PREM is not only able to detect privacy enhancement with high accuracy across different data characteristics and privacy models used, but also that it ensures highly competitive results compared to related detection techniques from the literature.

In summary, we make the following key contributions in this chapter:

- We introduce, to the best of our knowledge, the first technique for the detection of soft-biometric privacy enhancement in facial images. The proposed technique, called PREM, measures the Kullback–Leibler divergence between the predictions of a soft-biometric attribute classifier applied to facial images before and after attribute recovery. As we discuss in the chapter, PREM (i) exhibits several desirable characteristics, (ii) requires no examples of privacy-enhanced images for training, and (iii) is applicable under minimal assumptions.

- We show, for the first time, that it is possible to detect privacy-enhanced facial images with high accuracy across a number of datasets and privacy models, suggesting that the *detectability* of privacy-related image tampering techniques represents a major privacy risk.
- We demonstrate the benefit of designing PREM in a learning-free manner through comparative experiments with a related detection technique from the literature.

The rest of the chapter is structured as follows: Sect. 18.2 provides relevant background information, presents an overview of the state-of-the-art in soft-biometric privacy-enhancing techniques, and elaborates on the importance of detecting face manipulations caused by privacy enhancement. Section 18.3 describes PREM and discusses its characteristics. Section 18.4 presents the experimental setup used for the evaluation of the proposed detection approach and discusses results and findings. Section 18.5 concludes the chapter with a discussion of the key findings and directions for future work.

18.2 Background and Related Work

This section provides background information on the topic of soft-biometric privacy enhancement and reviews relevant prior work. A more comprehensive review of the broader field of visual privacy and advances in the area of privacy protection with facial images is presented in some of the excellent recent surveys on these topics, e.g., [10, 15, 17, 20, 21].

18.2.1 Problem Formulation and Existing Solutions

Soft-biometric privacy enhancement can formally be defined as follows: given an original face image, $I \in \mathbb{R}^{w \times h}$, where w and h are the image width and height in pixels, and a soft-biometric attribute classifier ξ_a, where

$$\xi_a : I \mapsto \{a_1, a_2, \dots, a_N\}, \tag{18.1}$$

and the attribute labels $\{a_i\}_{i=1}^{N}$ correspond to classes $\{C_1, C_2, \dots, C_N\}$, the goal of soft-biometric privacy enhancement, ψ, is to generate privacy-enhanced images,

$$I_{pr} = \psi(I) \in \mathbb{R}^{w \times h}, \tag{18.2}$$

from which ξ_a cannot correctly predict the class labels a_i. Because the goal of ψ is to conceal selected soft-biometric information from automatic classification techniques without significantly altering the visual appearance of the images for human observers, an additional constrained is commonly considered when designing ψ, that is, that the privacy-enhanced images *have to be* as close as possible to the originals, i.e., $I_{pr} \approx I_{or}$, in terms of some target objective, for example, the Mean Squared Error (MSE) or Structural Similarity (SSIM). The goal of this constraint is to preserve the utility of the data after privacy enhancement, e.g., to ensure that the privacy-enhanced images can be shared with friends and family on the web, while making unsolicited automatic processing infeasible.

From a conceptual point of view, existing soft-biometric privacy-enhancing techniques can be categorized into the following two groups depending on whether they try to induce:

- **Misclassifications**: Solutions from the first group typically rely on adversarial perturbations (and related strategies) and enhance privacy by inducing misclassifications, i.e., $\xi_a(I_{pr}) \neq \xi_a(I_{or})$, where an incorrect attribute class label is predicted from I_{pr} with high probability.
- **Equal class probabilities**: Solutions from the second group most often rely on (input-conditioned) synthesis models that enhance privacy by altering image characteristics in such a way that equal class posteriors are generated by the considered attribute classifier ξ_a given a privacy-enhanced image I_{pr}, i.e., $p(C_1|I_{pr}) \approx p(C_2|I_{pr}) \approx \cdots \approx p(C_N|I_{pr})$.

18.2.2   Soft-Biometric Privacy Models

A considerable amount of research has been conducted on the topic of soft-biometric privacy over recent years [12, 13, 18, 22–25]. Mirjalili and Ross [26], for instance, presented a privacy-enhancing technique that suppresses gender information in face images. The technique applies Delaunay triangulation over prominent facial landmarks to represent input faces as a set of triangles. In the next step, the texture within these triangles is modified in such a way that a targeted gender classifier produces unreliable classification results, while the original texture appearance is preserved as much as possible. The authors showed that such an approach leads to image perturbations that efficiently suppress gender information but have only a minimal impact on visual appearance and in turn on verification accuracy.

Another approach to soft-biometric gender privacy was presented in [27]. Here, the authors proposed a so-called Semi-Adversarial Network (SAN) that utilizes *conditional image synthesis* to suppress gender information in facial images. SAN models represent convolutional auto-encoders that are trained in an adversarial setting using two discriminators, where the first aims to enforce gender privacy and the second tries to retain verification accuracy (i.e., image similarities). The results reported by the authors show that the SAN model is able to obscure a high degree of gender information in facial images, while retaining the utility of the data for biometric verification purposes. An extension of this work was also presented later with the goal of improving the generalization capabilities of the initial SAN to unseen classifiers [23]. The main idea of the extended FlowSAN model is to utilize multiple

SAN transforms successively with the aim of making the privacy enhancement less dependent on a single target (gender) classifier. FlowSAN models were shown to offer better generalization capabilities than the simpler one-stage SANs, while still offering a competitive trade-off between privacy protection and utility preservation.

To make SAN models applicable beyond the (binary) problem of gender privacy, Marialli et al. [12] proposed PrivacyNet [12], an advanced SAN model based on the concept of Generative Adversarial Networks (GANs). Different from previous techniques aimed at soft-biometric privacy, PrivacyNet was demonstrated to be capable of privacy enhancement with respect to multiple facial attributes, including race, age and gender. PrivacyNet, hence, generalized the concept of SAN-based privacy enhancement to arbitrary combinations of soft-biometric attributes. The SAN-family of algorithm falls into the second group of techniques discussed above and tries to induce equal class probabilities with the considered attribute classifiers.

A misclassification-based approach to privacy enhancement of k facial attributes via adversarial perturbations (k-AAP) was introduced by Chhabra et al. in [11]. The approach aims to infuse facial image with so-called adversarial noise with the goal of suppressing a predefined set of arbitrary selected facial attributes, while preserving others. k-AAP is based on the Carlini Wagner L2 attack [28] and achieves promising results with attribute classifiers that were included in the design of the adversarial noise. The approach results in image perturbations (for most images) that are efficient at obscuring attribute information for machine learning models but are virtually invisible to a human observer. However, similarly as the original version of SAN, k-AAP does not generalize well to arbitrary classifiers. The idea of flipping facial attributes using adversarial noise was also explored in [22] where the authors investigated the robustness of facial features perturbations generated by the Fast Gradient Sign Method (FGSM) method [29].

While the techniques reviewed above try to manipulate facial images to ensure soft-biometric privacy, recent research is also looking at techniques that try to modify image representation and suppress attribute information at the representation (or feature) level [13, 18, 30–32]. However, such techniques are based on different assumptions and relevant mostly in the context of biometric systems. In this work we, therefore, focus only on the more general topic of image-level soft-biometric privacy enhancement.

18.2.3 Detecting Privacy Enhancement

When evaluating soft-biometric privacy-enhancing techniques, the literature typically focuses on performance and the level of privacy protection the techniques can offer. Other aspects are commonly of less interest and, as a results, are significantly less explored. This leads to several interesting research questions, e.g., *To what extent can privacy enhancement be detected? Is it possible to flag facial images that have been tampered with by privacy-enhancing techniques?* While a considerable body of work has been presented in the literature to detect traditional image tampering, e.g., [33–35], existing detection methods have mostly been investigated within the digital forensics community. The problem of detecting privacy enhancement, on the other hand, has not yet been explored in the literature. Because some privacy models are based on adversarial perturbations, this problem is also partially related to adversarial-attack detection techniques [36–40]. However, since soft-biometric privacy enhancement also includes synthesis-based methods, data hidding solutions and a wide variety of other approaches [10], the problem of detecting such image modifications is considerably broader. In the remainder of the chapter, we present our solution to the problem of privacy enhancement detection, which relies on a simple attribute recovery procedure.

18.3   Tampering Detection Through Prediction Mismatch (PREM)

In this section we now describe the proposed approach for detecting privacy enhancement (or tampering) in facial images. We focus on gender experiments in this chapter, but the proposed approach is general and can be applied to arbitrary soft-biometric attributes.

18.3.1   PREM Overview

Soft-biometric privacy enhancement aims to introduce minute changes into facial images in such a way that the predictions of a selected attribute classifier become unreliable, while the original appearance of the facial images is preserved as a much as possible. As a result, existing soft-biometric privacy models commonly add (targeted) high-frequency components to the input images, which are imperceivable to human observers, but adversely affect the performance of automatic recognition techniques. Based on these characteristics, we design a detection technique in this chapter that tries to identify images that were tampered with by soft-biometric privacy models.

The main idea of our detection technique is illustrated in Fig. 18.1. At the core of the technique is an attribute recovery procedure, $\chi(\cdot)$, that tries to restore suppressed attribute information from the given input image I. For unaltered facial images a selected soft-biometric attribute classifier ζ is expected to produce similar predictions before and after attribute recovery. For tampered images, on the other hand, a mismatch is expected between the predictions generated from the input image I and the corresponding attribute-recovered version I_{re}. This **PRE**diction **M**ismatch (PREM) can then be exploited for detecting privacy enhancement. Details on PREM are provided in the following section.

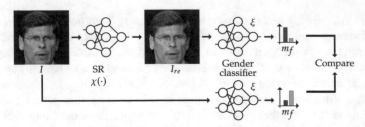

Fig. 18.1 Overview of the proposed PREM techniques for the detection of soft-biometric privacy enhancements in facial images. At the core of the detection technique is a super-resolution (SR) based procedure that aims to restore suppressed attribute information. PREM exploits the mismatch between the predictions of a selected attribute (*gender* in this work) classifier generated from the original and attribute-recovered images to detect privacy enhancement. PREM is *learning-free* and, hence, requires no examples of privacy-enhanced images

18.3.2   Super-Resolution for Attribute Recovery

To restore soft-biometric attributes from privacy-enhanced facial images, we consider a simple super-resolution (or hallucination[2]) approach. Super-resolution can be seen as a special type of restoration approach that selectively adds specific details (high-frequency components) to low-resolution input images. Because the high-frequency details are added in a selective manner based on learnt correspondences between pairs of low- and high-resolution facial images, images subjected to super-resolution are in essence remapped to a higher resolution, which impacts image characteristics, including those infused by privacy enhancement. The use of super-resolution for attribute recovery is further motivated by its success in mitigating the impact of adversarial noise, which is also used as a privacy-enhancing mechanism by some of the existing privacy models.

   We propose a straight-forward two-step procedure to remove the effect of privacy enhancement on the appearance and characteristics of facial images—see Fig. 18.2 for an illustration. In the first step, the input image, $I_{pr} \in \mathbb{R}^{w \times h}$ is downscaled by a factor s, i.e.,

$$I_{pr}^{(s)} = f_s(I_{pr}), \tag{18.3}$$

where $f_s(\cdot)$ is a simple bilinear down-sampling function conditioned on s and $I_{pr}^{(s)} \in \mathbb{R}^{w_s \times h_s}$ is the downscaled image with $w_s < w$ and $h_s < h$. This down-sampling step acts as a low-pass filter that removes high-frequency information from the image and is, therefore, expected to impact (high-frequency) image artifacts introduced by the privacy models the most. In the second step, the procedure then restores the

---

[2] Note that single image super-resolution techniques are referred to as face hallucination methods when applied to facial images. This term illustrates the fact the high-frequency components are hallucinated by the super-resolution model during up-sampling [41–43].

Fig. 18.2 Overview of the proposed approach to attribute recovery through super-resolution (SR). The privacy-enhanced image, I_{pr} is first downscaled to remove high-frequency components introduced by the privacy models. High-frequency components are then selectively added back into the restored image, I_{re}, through a super-resolution model

downscaled image to its original size (w× h) and recovers semantically meaningful image details (with attribute information) through super-resolution-based upscaling, i.e.,

$$I_{re} = h_s(I_{pr}^{(s)}) \in \mathbb{R}^{w \times h}, \tag{18.4}$$

where h_s is a super-resolution model that upscales images by a factor of s. The high-frequency information that is lost with the down-sampling procedure is, to a certain degree, reconstructed with the super-resolution model, such that the output image is similar to the input. However, as illustrated in Fig. 18.2 the super-resolved image is typically slightly smoother and contains hallucinated image details.

We denote the presented attribute recovery procedure as $\chi : I_{pr} \mapsto I_{re}$ and use the state-of-the-art C-SRIP model from [43] for our implementation. Here, I_{re} stands for the attribute-recovered images, shown on the right side of Fig. 18.2. We note at this point, that the described recovery procedure is model agnostic, so any super-resolution model could be used instead of C-SRIP with similar results. C-SRIP was selected for our implementation because of its state-of-the-art performance and the fact that it is publicly available.

18.3.3 Measuring the Prediction Mismatch

As suggested above, the proposed PREM detection technique exploits the fact that for privacy-enhanced images, I_{pr}, a selected attribute classifier ξ generates different posterior probabilities $p(C_k|I_{pr})$ than for images subjected to the presented super-resolution based attribute recovery procedure, $p(C_k|I_{re})$. Because we consider the task of detecting privacy enhancements aimed at suppressing gender information in facial images, similarly to [18, 23, 44, 45], the classes C_k are defined as $C_k \in \{C_m, C_f\}$, where m denotes the male and f the female class. However, we note that in general the same conceptual solution could be applied to arbitrary attribute classes C_k. By comparing the posteriors, $p(C_k|I_{pr})$ and $p(C_k|I_{re})$, it is possible

---

Algorithm 1: Detecting soft-biometric privacy enhancement with PREM

Input: Input probe image I
Output: Detection score τ

1 Implement attribute recovery procedure χ based on SR model h_s—Eqs. (18.3) and (18.4);
2 Attempt attribute recovery: $I_{re} = \chi(I)$;
3 Use ξ for classification over I and I_{re};
4 Calculate detection score $\tau = D_{SKL}$—Eq. (18.5);
5 Determine whether I is tampered based on τ;

---

to determine whether an image has been tampered with or not. In this work we utilize a symmetric version of the Kullback–Leibler divergence [46] to compare the distributions generated by the attribute classifier, i.e.,

$$D_{SKL}(p,q) = D_{KL}(p\|q) + D_{KL}(q\|p), \tag{18.5}$$

where

$$D_{KL}(p\|q) = \sum_{x \in \mathcal{X}} (p(x) - q(x)) \log\left(\frac{p(x)}{q(x)}\right), \tag{18.6}$$

where $p = p(C_k|I_{pr})$, $q = p(C_k|I_{re})$, $\mathcal{X} = C_k$. To facilitate the detection of soft-biometric privacy enhancement (or tampering), D_{SKL} is used as a detection score τ in our experiments. A decision whether the probe image I was tampered with or not can be made based on the value of τ. D_{SKL} is in general bounded by $[0, \infty]$, where a value of 0 indicates that there is no difference between distributions.

18.3.4 PREM Summary and Characteristics

A high-level summary of the proposed PREM detection technique is given in Algorithm 1. The techniques have several desirable characteristics, i.e.,

- **Training free detection**: Unlike competing techniques for image tampering detection, PREM is training-free and does not require any examples of privacy-enhanced images for training. PREM relies solely on the fact that the output of a (in this case gender) classifier changes after attribute recovery compared to the output produced with the original face image. Thus, the detection scheme is expected to work, across a wide range of privacy enhancement techniques as long as they are based on the same assumptions, i.e., minimal changes in appearance compared to the original images.
- **Complementarity to supervised detection techniques**: While the task of detecting privacy enhancement in facial images is new, there are related tampering-detection techniques that could be adopted for this task. Because these techniques

typically rely on supervision [40, 47], PREM provides complementary information that can be combined with supervised techniques to further improve performance.

- **Generality**: The concept exploited by PREM is not limited to the described super-resolution based recovery approach and can be implemented with any techniques that is able to restore suppressed soft-biometric attributes. Thus, PREM can easily accommodate more advance recovery schemes and is expected to benefit from future advances in this problem area.

18.4   Experiments and Results

The experiments, presented in this section, aim at (i) evaluating the extent to which soft-biometric privacy enhancement can be detected, (ii) analyzing the performance of PREM in blue comparison to alternatives from the literature, (iii) exploring the complementarity of PREM and competing detection techniques, and (iv) providing insight into the behavior of the technique and its limitations. As emphasized earlier, we focus on privacy-enhancing techniques that are trained to suppress *gender information*, which is also the most frequent attribute considered in the literature when studying soft-biometric privacy models [18, 23, 44, 45].

18.4.1   Datasets and Experimental Setup

We use three publicly available face datasets for the experiments, i.e., Labeled Faces in the Wild (LFW) [48], MUCT [49], and Adience [50]. The datasets come with the necessary attribute labels (for gender in this case) and contain facial images captured in unconstrained settings and in a wide variety of imaging conditions—a few examples are shown in Fig. 18.3. Additionally, the datasets are commonly used in research on soft-biometric privacy enhancement, e.g., [12, 18, 23, 30]) and are, therefore, also selected for this work.

To have a consistent starting point for the experiments, all images are roughly aligned, so that faces are approximately centered. Next, the facial region is cropped to exclude background pixels and finally, the images are rescaled to a standard size of 224×224 pixels. Because gender classifiers are needed to train the soft-biometric privacy models, one such classifier ζ is trained for each dataset using a gender-balanced set of training images, i.e., around 5700 for LFW, 10400 for Adience and 3600 for MUCT. A separate set of images from each dataset is reserved for the testing stage. This testing set does not overlap in terms of subjects with the training data.

(a) LFW examples   (b) MUCT examples   (c) Adience examples

Fig. 18.3 Example images from the three datasets used in the experimental evaluation. The datasets were captured in challenging and diverse (real world) imaging conditions posing a significant challenge to both privacy enhancement as well as detection techniques

18.4.2 Utilized Privacy Models

We implement three recent soft-biometric privacy models for the experiments, i.e., the k-AAP approach from [11], the FGSM-based method from [51] and the FlowSAN technique from [23]. FlowSAN can in general be implemented with different trade-offs between the level of attribute suppression ensured and the preserved utility of the facial images. We, therefore, consider two different model variants in our experiments: *(i)* one with a sequence of three SAN models (i.e., FlowSAN-3), and *(ii)* one with a sequence of five SAN models (i.e., FlowSAN-5). The selected techniques are utilized for the evaluation because of their state-of-the-art performance and the fact that they rely on different privacy mechanisms. A few examples of the impact of the privacy models on the visual appearance of selected facial images are presented in Fig. 18.4. Note that the models result in visually different image manipulations. While the appearance of the images processed with the adversarial techniques k-AAP and FGSM is very close to the originals, the FlowSAN models introduce larger changes. However, these changes also help with the robustness of the models with respect to unseen gender classifiers. We note that the appearance of the FlowSAN enhanced images in Fig. 18.4 is a direct consequence of the design of the FlowSAN models, which can be implemented to provide a trade-off between visual quality and privacy protection—larger degradations ensure better privacy protection, while higher quality images result in lower levels of privacy.

18.4.3 Implementation Details

Gender classifiers. A VGG16 model architecture [52] is used to implement the gender classifiers ζ needed for the privacy enhancement. We adapt a pretrained VGGFace2 [53] for gender classification by replacing the original softmax layer

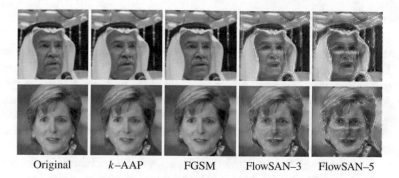

| Original | k–AAP | FGSM | FlowSAN–3 | FlowSAN–5 |

Fig. 18.4 Impact of the privacy models on the visual appearance of facial images. The adversarial methods (k-AAP and FGSM) introduce only minor changes, whereas the FlowSAN models generated more pronounced appearance differences—note that these models are designed to be robust to unseen classifiers, which is not the case with the adversarial techniques

Table 18.1 Values of hyper-parameters utilized for the implementation of the selected soft-biometric privacy models

Model	Strategy	Parameters
k-APP	Fixed parameters	#Max iter.: 20, Learn. rate: 0.01, Init. const.: 1, 000
FGSM	Value search	Range: [0.9–0.51], #Epochs: 200, Epsilon: 0.5
FlowSAN	Two versions	#SANs in sequence: 3 and 5

with a two-class softmax. The models are then learned by fine tuning the last two layers using the Adam optimizer with a learning rate of 0.001, momenta $\beta_1 = 0.9$ and $\beta_2 = 0.999$ and an ϵ value of 10^{-7}. For the FlowSAN models several such classifiers are trained using different configurations of training data, as suggested in [54].

Super-resolution model. To implement the attribute recovery procedure, the C-SRIP[3] [43] super-resolution model is selected. The model is trained on the Casia WebFace dataset [55]. For the recovery procedure, χ, images are first resized from the original size of 224×224 to 64×64 pixels and then subjected to the super-resolution model to upsample the images back to the initial image resolution.

Privacy models. The three soft-biometric privacy models selected for our experiments, k-AAP, FGSM and FlowSAN (FlowSAN-5) rely on several hyper-parameters. These are selected based on preliminary experiments and the suggestions made by the authors of the models. Table 18.1 provides a summary on the hyper-parameters used in the experiments.

---

[3] C-SRIP: https://lmi.fe.uni-lj.si/en/research/fh/.

18.4.4 Results and Discussions

PREM Evaluation. In the first series of experiments, we analyze the performance of PREM with respect to the detection of privacy-enhanced images. To this end, we use a gender-stratified test set of 698 privacy-enhanced and 698 original images for each privacy model (k-APP, FGSM, FlowSAN-3 and FlowSAN-5) and each dataset considered in the experiments. We partition the test images into 4 disjoint data splits, over which we report results. Because privacy enhancement detection is framed as a two-class classification problem in this work, we report results graphically in terms of Received Operating Characteristics (ROC) curves and quantitatively in the form of the Area Under the ROC Curve (AUC). The 4 data splits are also utilized to generate confidence intervals for the ROC curves.

Figure 18.5 shows the average ROC curves and corresponding confidence intervals for this first experimental series. Because the performance differences across different privacy models are small, the curves are presented on a semi-log scale for better visualizations. AUC scores of the experiments are reported in Table 18.2. As can be seen, PREM achieves almost ideal detection performance for all privacy models on the LFW and MUCT datasets and with average AUC scores of 0.629 for k-AAP, 0.858 for FGSM, 0.775 for FlowSAN-3 and 0.793 for FlowSAN-5 also performs well on Adience. The slightly weaker results on Adience are a consequence of the challenging imaging characteristics present in the dataset and are in line with observations made in the open literature [18], where different models (addressing various tasks) perform worse on this dataset.

Comparison with Competing Models. Note again that the task of detecting soft-biometric privacy enhancement in facial images has not been explored widely in the

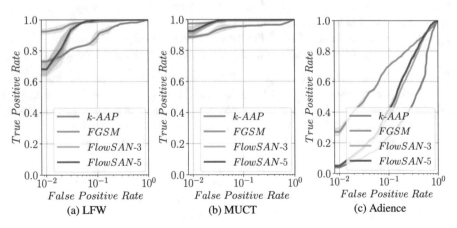

Fig. 18.5 ROC curves generated for the privacy enhancement detection experiments with the proposed PREM detection approach: **a** on LFW, **b** on MUCT and **c** on Adience. Note that the detection of the privacy enhancement is more successful on the LFW and MUCT, than on Adience, which is a highly challenging face dataset captured in real-world settings

Table 18.2 AUC scores ($\mu \pm \sigma$) generated in the detection experiments. The learning-free (black-box) PREM technique is compared against the recent (supervised) T-SVM approach to adversarial-attack detection from [40]. Results are reported for white-box as well as black-box settings

Priv. Model	Dataset	PREM (ours)	White-box	Black-box		Combined (ours)
			T-SVM	T-SVM (A)[†]	T-SVM (B)[‡]	
k-AAP	LFW	0.957 ± 0.005	0.984 ± 0.007	0.743 ± 0.013	0.984 ± 0.007	0.946 ± 0.020
	MUCT	0.965 ± 0.005	0.534 ± 0.021	0.727 ± 0.030	0.534 ± 0.021	0.939 ± 0.024
	Adience	0.629 ± 0.007	0.541 ± 0.007	0.604 ± 0.008	0.541 ± 0.007	0.638 ± 0.008
FGSM	LFW	0.989 ± 0.003	0.955 ± 0.011	0.894 ± 0.013	0.921 ± 0.016	0.988 ± 0.006
	MUCT	0.989 ± 0.003	0.852 ± 0.012	0.858 ± 0.015	0.552 ± 0.030	0.985 ± 0.007
	Adience	0.858 ± 0.003	0.624 ± 0.009	0.595 ± 0.016	0.471 ± 0.014	0.831 ± 0.013
FlowSAN-3	LFW	0.987 ± 0.002	1.000 ± 0.000	1.000 ± 0.000	0.997 ± 0.002	0.996 ± 0.004
	MUCT	0.993 ± 0.001	1.000 ± 0.000	1.000 ± 0.000	0.524 ± 0.020	1.000 ± 0.000
	Adience	0.775 ± 0.002	1.000 ± 0.000	1.000 ± 0.000	0.609 ± 0.005	0.986 ± 0.003
FlowSAN-5	LFW	0.988 ± 0.001	1.000 ± 0.000	1.000 ± 0.000	0.998 ± 0.001	0.996 ± 0.004
	MUCT	0.994 ± 0.001	1.000 ± 0.000	1.000 ± 0.000	0.531 ± 0.018	1.000 ± 0.000
	Adience	0.793 ± 0.011	1.000 ± 0.000	1.000 ± 0.000	0.563 ± 0.005	0.988 ± 0.003

[†] T-SVM trained on FlowSAN-5 and training data from LFW
[‡] T-SVM trained on k-AAP and training data from LFW

literature. However, because privacy enhancement techniques share some characteristics with adversarial attacks, we select the recent state-of-the-art transformation-based detection technique T-SVM from [40] as a baseline for the experiments and compare it to the proposed PREM approach. T-SVM utilizes a combination of the discrete wavelet transform (DWT) and the discrete sine transform (DST) to represent input images and relies on a support vector machine (SVM) for privacy enhancement detection. As such, it requires training data to be able to distinguish between original and privacy-enhanced images. We, therefore, consider two distinct experimental settings in the evaluations to compare PREM and T-SVM, i.e.,

- **White-box setting**: In this setting, unfiltered access to all privacy models is assumed. Thus, T-SVM is trained separately for each privacy model using corresponding training images. The training part of LFW (i.e., around 5700 images) is utilized to learn the detection model and the test part of LFW, MUCT and Adience is used for the evaluation.
- **Black-box setting**: In this setting, access to some privacy-enhanced images is assumed, but not to images of all considered privacy models. As a result, T-SVM needs to generalize to unseen privacy models when trying to detect tampering. Two different detection models are considered in the experiments. The first, T-SVM (A), is trained for the detection of FlowSAN-5 enhanced images and only on data from LFW. The second, T-SVM (B), is trained for detecting k-AAP based enhancement, again only on LFW. Both models are tested on all datasets and with all privacy models.

The results in Table 18.2 shows that in the white-box scenario T-SVM is comparable to PREM on LFW in terms of AUC scores for k-AAP and FGSM, but significantly worse on the MUCT and Adience datasets. This observation suggests that despite access to privacy-enhanced training images for all privacy models, the performance of T-SVM is affected by the data characteristics, which is much less the case with the proposed *learning-free* PREM technique. For the experiments with the FlowSAN models, T-SVM offers ideal detection performance on all three datasets. PREM, on the other hand, is very competitive on the images from LFW and MUCT, but performs weaker on images from the Adience dataset. The presented results suggest that the generalization ability of the white-box T-SVM technique is below PREM despite access to privacy-enhanced training examples for each privacy model, which are not required for PREM.

When examining the AUC scores for the black-box setting, we see that T-SVM performs somewhat weaker than in the white-box scenario. T-SVM (A), trained with FlowSAN-5 processed images, is still able to ensure ideal detection performance for both FlowSAN variants on all three experimental datasets, but is less competitive with images enhanced with k-AAP and FGSM. For these privacy models the detection performance of T-SVM (A) drops slightly behind the white-box T-SVM and considerably behind PREM. T-SVM (B), trained with k-AAP images of LFW, is the least competitive and only able to match the performance of PREM for a few selected cases involving LFW. These results clearly demonstrate the added value of training-free privacy enhancement detection, where the detection performance is not affected by the available training data, which otherwise considerably affects the generalization capabilities of the detection techniques.

Combined Privacy Enhancement Detection. In the previous section we demonstrated that PREM is able to detect privacy enhancement in facial images with high accuracy. We also observed that the competing method, T-SVM, is highly competitive on images where PREM performed weaker, e.g., with the FlowSAN models on Adience. In this section, we, therefore, try to make use of the best of both worlds and explore whether a combination of the two detection approaches can further improve results. To make the experimental setup as challenging as possible, we assume a black-box experimental setting for T-SVM (marked T-SVM (A) in Table 18.2) and train it with LFW images processed by FlowSAN-5. We then consider this model with all other (unseen) privacy models and all three datasets.

Given an input face image I, both PREM and T-SVM produce a detection score, $\tau_{prem}(I)$ and $\tau_{tsvm}(I)$, that is utilized to make a decision on whether images were tampered with or not. Since the two detection models are independent, we combine the computed detections scores using a product fusion rule of the following form:

$$\tau = \tau_{prem}^{\beta} \cdot \tau_{tsvm}^{1-\beta}, \tag{18.7}$$

where τ stands for the combined detection score and β represents a parameter that balances the relative contribution of the two scores and is set to $\beta = 0.5$ in this work.

The detection results for the combined approach are presented on the right part of Table 18.2. As can be seen, the combination of the detection scores leads to a comparable detection performance to PREM for k-AAP and FGSM on images from the LFW and MUCT datasets. Here, PREM convincingly outperformed T-SVM in the comparative evaluation and the combined approach is able to match PREMs AUC score with these privacy models. For privacy enhancement with the FlowSAN models, the combination of the detection techniques again performs comparable to the better performing of the two individual models on all experimental datasets. Here, the combined detection approach achieves close to perfect performance (also on Adience) and further improves on the initial capabilities of PREM, which was the weaker of the two detection models on this dataset.

Overall, the results suggest that the combination of PREM and T-SVM is beneficial for the detection of privacy enhancement and contributes toward more robust performance across different privacy models and data characteristics. The conceptual differences between PREM and T-SVM allow the combined approach to capture complementary information for the detection procedure and produce more reliable detection scores across all experiments.

Visual analysis. In the last part of our evaluation, we conduct a qualitative analysis and investigate what data characteristics cause PREM to fail. A few examples of face images, where PREM generated errors at a decision threshold that ensures equal error rates (EERs) with the ROC curves from Fig. 18.5 is presented in Fig. 18.6. Here, images in the top row correspond to cases where PREM failed to detect privacy enhancement. As can be seen, these images contain visible image artifacts that cannot be recovered using the super-resolution in based attribute recovery procedure, resulting in minimal changes in the gender predictions and subsequently misdetections. Images in the bottom row represent examples that have been classified as being privacy enhanced but in fact represent original unaltered faces. In most cases,

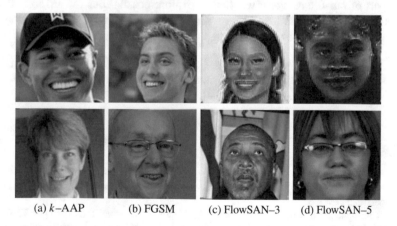

    (a) k–AAP   (b) FGSM   (c) FlowSAN–3   (d) FlowSAN–5

Fig. 18.6 Visual examples of misdetections produced by PREM at a decision threshold corresponding to the equal error rate (ERR) on the ROC curves from Fig. 18.5. Images in the top row correspond to cases where PREM failed to detect the privacy enhancement and images in the bottom row correspond to examples incorrectly flagged by PREM as being privacy enhanced. Example results are reported for all privacy models considered in the experiments

these images are of poorer quality (due to blur, noise, etc.) and get improved by our attribute recovery procedure. As a result, the output of the gender classifier changes sufficiently to incorrectly classify the images as being privacy enhanced.

18.5 Conclusion

In this chapter we studied the problem of soft-biometric privacy enhancement and explored to what extent such privacy enhancement can be detected. To facilitate the study we designed a novel approach for the detecting privacy enhancements in facial images, called PREM. We evaluated PREM with three recent privacy enhancement techniques and three experimental datasets. Our experimental results showed that PREM was able to detect privacy enhancement with across all considered privacy models and facial images of very different characteristics. These findings have considerable implications for future research in privacy enhancement, e.g.,

- If privacy enhancement can be detected, the flagged images may be processed with alternative means and more elaborate analysis techniques. This type of processing could invalidate the effect of privacy enhancement.
- Privacy-enhancing techniques need to come with privacy guarantees to ensure that even after detection, privacy-enhanced images may not be misused. This points to the need for formal soft-biometric privacy models [10] that allow to quantify the level of privacy ensured. Such models have been considered with deidentification techniques [56] but have not yet been explored in the literature for soft-biometric privacy solutions.

As part of our future work, we plan to explore possibilities toward formal soft-biometric privacy models that address some of the challenges outlined above and offer privacy protection even if subjected to advanced means of processing.

Acknowledgements This research was supported in parts by the ARRS Research Project J2-1734 "Face Deidentification with Generative Deep Models", ARRS Research Programmes P2-0250 (B) "Metrology and Biometric Systems" and P2-0214 (A) "Computer Vision".

References

1. Guo G, Zhang N (2019) A survey on deep learning based face recognition. Comput Vis Image Understand 189:1–37
2. Ross A, Banerjee S, Chen C, Chowdhury A, Mirjalili V, Sharma R, Swearingen T, Yadav S (2019) Some research problems in biometrics: the future beckons. In: International conference on biometrics (ICB), pp 1–8
3. Križaj J, Peer P, Štruc V, Dobrišek S (2019) Simultaneous multi-descent regression and feature learning for facial landmarking in depth images. Neural Comput Appl, pp 1–18
4. Batagelj B, Peer P, Štruc V, Dobrišek S (2021) How to correctly detect face-masks for COVID-19 from visual information? Appl Sci 11(5):1–24

5. Berthouze N, Valstar M, Williams, A, Egede J, Olugbade T, Wang C, Meng H, Aung M, Lane N, Song S (2020) Emopain challenge 2020: multimodal pain evaluation from facial and bodily expressions. In: IEEE conference on automatic face and gesture recognition (FG)
6. Puc A, Štruc V, Grm. K (2021) Analysis of race and gender bias in deep age estimation models. In: 28th European signal processing conference (EUSIPCO), pp 830–834
7. Gonzalez-Sosa E, Fierrez J, Vera-Rodriguez R, Alonso-Fernandez F (2018) Facial soft biometrics for recognition in the wild: Recent works, annotation, and cots evaluation. IEEE Trans Inform Forensics Secur (TIFS), 13(8):2001–2014
8. Robinson JP, Shao M, Wu Y, Liu H, Gillis T, Fu Y (2018) Visual kinship recognition of families in the wild. IEEE Trans Pattern Anal Mach Intell (TPAMI) 40(11):2624–2637
9. Rattani A, Derakhshani R (2018) A survey of mobile face biometrics. Comput Electr Eng 72:39–52
10. Meden B, Rot P, Terhörst P, Damer N, Kuijper A, Scheirer W, Ross, A Peer P, Štruc. V (2021) Privacy-enhancing face biometrics: a comprehensive survey. Under Rev
11. Chhabra S, Singh, R Vatsa M, Gupta G (2018) Anonymizing k-facial attributes via adversarial perturbations. International joint conferences on artificial intelligence (IJCAI)
12. Mirjalili V, Raschka S, Ross A (2020) PrivacyNet: semi-adversarial networks for multi-attribute face privacy. IEEE Trans Image Process (TIP), 29:9400–9412
13. Morales A, Fierrez J, Vera-Rodriguez R, Tolosana. R (2020) SensitiveNets: learning agnostic representations with application to face images. IEEE Trans Pattern Anal Mach Intelli (TPAMI)
14. Philipp PT, Fährmann D, Damer N, Kirchbuchner F, Kuijper A (2020) Beyond identity: what information is stored in biometric face templates? In: 2020 IEEE international joint conference on biometrics (IJCB), pp 1–10
15. Ribarić S, Ariyaeeinia A, Pavesić N (2016) De-identification for privacy protection in multimedia content: a survey. Signal Process: Image Commun 47:131–151
16. Meden B, Malli RC, Fabijan S, Ekenel HK, Štruc V, Peer P (2017) Face Deidentification with generative deep neural networks. IET Signal Process 11(9):1046–1054
17. Garfinkel SL (2015) De-identification of Personal Information. National Institute of standards and technology (NIST)
18. Bortolato B, Ivanovska M, Rot P, Križaj J, Terhörst P, Damer N, Peer P, Štruc V (2020) Learning privacy-enhancing face representations through feature disentanglement. In: IEEE international conference on automatic face and gesture recognition (FG)
19. Rot P, Peer P, Struc V (2021) PrivacyProber: assessment and detection of soft–biometric privacy-enhancing techniques. Under Rev, 1–18
20. Winkler T, Rinner B (2014). Security and privacy protection in visual sensor networks: a survey. ACM Comput Surv 47(1)
21. Padilla-López JR, Chaaraoui AA, Flórez-Revuelta F (2015). visual privacy protection methods: a survey. Expert Syst Appl 42(9):4177–4195
22. Rozsa A, Günther M, Rudd EM, Boult T (2019) Facial attributes: accuracy and adversarial robustness. Pattern Recogn Lett 124:100–108
23. Mirjalili V, Raschka S, Ross A (2019). FlowSAN: privacy-enhancing semi-adversarial networks to confound arbitrary face-based gender classifiers. IEEE Access 7:99735–99745
24. Terhörst P, Damer N, Kirchbuchner F, Kuijper A (2019) Unsupervised privacy-enhancement of face representations using similarity-sensitive noise transformations. Appl Intell, 1–18
25. Terhörst P, Huber M, Damer N, Rot P, Kirchbuchner F, Struc V, Kuijper A (2020) Privacy evaluation protocols for the evaluation of soft-biometric privacy-enhancing technologies. In: International conference of the biometrics special interest group (BIOSIG)
26. Mirjalili V, Ross A (2017) Soft biometric privacy: retaining biometric utility of face images while perturbing gender. In: International joint conference on biometrics (IJCB), pp 564–573
27. Mirjalili V, Raschka S, Namboodiri A, Ross A (20108) Semi-adversarial networks: convolutional autoencoders for imparting privacy to face images. In: International conference on biometrics (ICB), pp 82–89
28. Carlini N, Wagner D (2017) towards evaluating the robustness of neural networks. In: IEEE Symposium on security and privacy (SP), pp 39–57

29. Goodfellow I, Shlens J, Szegedy C (2015) Explaining and harnessing adversarial examples. In: International conference on learning representations
30. Terhörst P, Riehl K, Damer N, Rot P, Bortolato B, Kirchbuchner F, Štruc V, Kuijper A (2020) PE-MIU: a training-free privacy-enhancing face recognition approach based on minimum information units. IEEE Access
31. Terhörst P, Huber M, Damer N, Kirchbuchner F, Kuijper A (2020) Unsupervised enhancement of soft-biometric privacy with negative face recognition. arXiv preprint arXiv:2002.09181
32. Roy PC, Boddeti VN (2019). Mitigating information leakage in image representations: a maximum entropy approach. In: IEEE conference on computer vision and pattern recognition (CVPR), pp 2586–2594
33. Zheng L, Zhang Y, LL Thing V (2019) A survey on image tampering and its detection in real-world photos. J Vis Commun Image Represent 58:380–399
34. AP da Costa K, Papa JP, Passos LA, Colombo D, Del Ser J, Muhammad K, de Albuquerque VHC (2020) A critical literature survey and prospects on tampering and anomaly detection in image data. Appl Soft Comput
35. Meena KB, Tyagi V (2019) Image forgery detection: survey and future directions. In: Data, engineering and applications, pp 163–194. Springer
36. Nowroozi E, Dehghantanha A, Parizi RM, Choo KR (2020) A survey of machine learning techniques in adversarial image forensics. Comput Secur
37. Bulusu S, Kailkhura B, Li B, Varshney P, Song D (2020) Anomalous example detection in deep learning: a survey. IEEE Access 8:132330–132347
38. Wang X, Li J, Kuang X, Tan Y, Li J (2019) The security of machine learning in an adversarial setting: a survey. J Parallel Distrib Comput 130:12–23
39. Chakraborty A, Alam M, Dey V, Chattopadhyay A, Mukhopadhyay D (2018) Adversarial attacks and defences: a survey. CoRR, abs/1810.00069
40. Agarwal A, Singh R, Vatsa M, Ratha NK (2020) Image transformation based defense against adversarial perturbation on deep learning models. IEEE transactions on dependable and secure computing (TDSC)
41. Baker S, Kanade T (2000) Hallucinating faces. In: IEEE international conference on automatic face and gesture recognition (FG), pp 83–88
42. Grm K, Pernuš M, Cluzel L, Scheirer WJ, Dobrisek S, Štruc V (2019) Face hallucination revisited: an exploratory study on dataset bias. In: IEEE conference on computer vision and pattern recognition workshops (CVPR)
43. Grm K, Scheirer WJ, Štruc V (2020) Face hallucination using cascaded super-resolution and identity priors. IEEE transactions on image processing (TIP), 29:2150–2165
44. Othman A, Ross A (2014) Privacy of facial soft biometrics: suppressing gender but retaining identity. In: European conference on computer vision (ECCV), pp 682–696. Springer
45. Terhörst P, Damer N, Kirchbuchner N, Kuijper A (2019) Suppressing gender and age in face templates using incremental variable elimination. In: International conference on biometrics (ICB), pp 4–7
46. Johnson D, Sinanović S (2001) Symmetrizing the Kullback-leibler distance. IEEE Transactions on information theory (IT)
47. Mustafa A, Khan SH, Hayat M, Shen J, Shao L (2019) Image super-resolution as a defense against adversarial attacks. IEEE Trans Image Process (TIP), 29:1711–1724
48. Huang GB, Ramesh M, Berg T, Learned-Miller E (2007) Labeled faces in the wild: a database for studying face recognition in unconstrained environments. Technical Report 07-49, University of Massachusetts, Amherst
49. Milborrow S, Morkel J, Nicolls F (2010) The MUCT landmarked face database. Pattern recognition association of South Africa. http://www.milbo.org/muct
50. Eidinger E, Enbar R, Hassner T (2014) Age and gender estimation of unfiltered faces. IEEE Trans Inform Forensics Secur (TIFS), 9(12):2170–2179
51. Chatzikyriakidis E, Papaioannidis C, Pitas I (2019) Adversarial face de-identification. In: IEEE international conference on image processing (ICIP), pp 684–688

52. Simonyan K, Zisserman A (2015) Very deep convolutional networks for large-scale image recognition. CoRR, abs/1409.1556
53. Cao Q, Shen L, Xie W, Parkhi OM, Zisserman A (20108) VGGFACE2: a dataset for recognising faces across pose and age. In: IEEE international conference on automatic face and gesture recognition (FG), pp 67–74
54. Mirjalili V, Raschka S, Ross A (2018) Gender privacy: an ensemble of semi adversarial networks for confounding arbitrary gender classifiers. IEEE international conference on biometrics theory, applications and systems (BTAS), pp 1–10
55. Yi D, Lei Z, Liao S, Li SZ (2014) Learning face representation from scratch. CoRR abs/1411.7923, 2014
56. Meden B, Emeršič Ž, Štruc V, Peer P (2018) k-Same-Net: k-anonymity with generative deep neural networks for face deidentification. Entropy 20(1):1–24

Chapter 19
Face Manipulation Detection in Remote Operational Systems

Marc Michel Pic, Gaël Mahfoudi, Anis Trabelsi, and Jean-Luc Dugelay

Abstract In this chapter, we present the various categories of Face Manipulation and their use within different remote operational systems. We then use the example of remote identity document onboarding systems to illustrate how each category can be used in practice to compromise such a system. After a definition of the different Face Manipulation categories and the common algorithms used to produce them, we go through the various manipulation detection algorithms and common image and video forgery datasets. We then introduce some known counter-forensics methods that can be used by an attacker to avoid detection. Knowing the detection methods and the counter-forensic, we present how we can build up a safer system by using the correct methods at the correct time. But also how knowledge about the tampering process could be used to design the user experience to make the systems harder to compromise. We complete this review by the standardisation effort and legal aspect on the matter. And we conclude by discussing the remaining challenges and perspectives for better use of nowadays detection methods in practical usage.

19.1 Introduction

The worldwide crisis of 2020 due to the COVID-19 pandemic changed our day-to-day interaction significantly. It confirms the global trend of generalising the use of remote operations, and we believe that this trend will continue in the coming years.

M. M. Pic (✉) · G. Mahfoudi · A. Trabelsi
SURYS, Bussy-Saint-Georges, France
e-mail: m.pic@surys.com

G. Mahfoudi
e-mail: g.mahfoudi@surys.com

A. Trabelsi
e-mail: a.trabelsi@surys.com

J.-L. Dugelay
EURECOM, Biot, France
e-mail: jean-luc.dugelay@eurecom.fr

© The Author(s) 2022
C. Rathgeb et al. (eds.), *Handbook of Digital Face Manipulation and Detection*,
Advances in Computer Vision and Pattern Recognition,
https://doi.org/10.1007/978-3-030-87664-7_19

413

Many remote technologies are heavily based on facial recognition, but also on the more general behaviour and context analysis such as liveness challenges or even verifying if a person is wearing a medical face mask. For those operational systems, the ability to detect Face Manipulation is essential. We can classify those systems into three main categories and many subcategories.

The first category is the systems with a direct Face Recognition need such as Automated identity authentication like Automated Border Controls (ABCs) at Airports and Remote face authentication systems. The second category is systems using Indirect Face Recognition. Those would be used for tracking individuals across one or many acquisition devices or detecting an individual in a specific area. The last category would be the Face Behaviour Analysis Systems. Those aim at verifying that a specific attended action/behaviour is performed by an identified person anddetecting an unexpected action/behaviour linked to a specific person or to detect actions/behaviours in the context of a group of people.

In this chapter, we will illustrate the common kind of face manipulation and the ways of securing an operational system against those. For the sake of clarity, we will look at those attacks within the context of a remote identity document and person acquisition scenario. Even though this does not fully embrace the many aspects of the different remote operational systems, it will allow us to give a practical example of all types of forgeries and means to secure such applications.

We will start by introducing a typical remote identity document onboarding system and explain which part is most likely to be attacked. We will discuss about the different types of Facial Manipulation attacks and how they fit into our particular system. We will then give a definition of each attack and present the common technologies and methods to create those forgeries. After, we will present common face manipulation detection methods and more general image manipulation detection algorithms. We will also introduce datasets used to study those attacks and to train the detection algorithms. Then, we will discuss some typical counter-forensic methods and how one can design his/her system to reduce the chances of forgeries. Finally, we will conclude with a discussion of the remaining challenges and perspectives for better use of nowadays detection methods in practical usage.

19.2 Remote Identity Document Onboarding

For the rest of this article, we will place ourselves within the framework of a generic remote identity document onboarding system. A brief overview of such a system is given in Fig. 19.1. We can see that such systems are made of two main steps. First, the user is asked to take a picture/video of his/her ID document. Then, he is asked to take a picture/video of himself/herself. The challenges for the system are then multiple. It must first authenticate the ID documents. Then, it must verify that the user is the owner of the document. Once all the verification steps are passed, the systems store user information such as name and age. But also a picture of the user that will later be used to authenticate him/her again when needed.

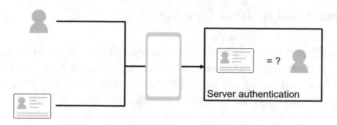

Fig. 19.1   Generic Remote identity document onboarding system

Table 19.1   Attacks and associated scenario

	Non-biometric	Face swapping	Face morphing	De-identification
Live attack	X	X		X
Portrait attack		X	X	X

In such a scenario, an attacker could have three main **strategies**. He can try to perform some kind of identity theft. Helped by someone else, they can create a common biometry so the two people can later on share their identity. Or lastly, he could try to create and use a completely fake identity for privacy concern or other.

Whatever his goal, he can only attack one or both parts of the system, i.e. the portrait during the document acquisition or his biometry during his self-portrait acquisition. We will refer to this as **support**. We will call an attack during the self-portrait acquisition a Living Person Attack and an attack during the document acquisition a Portrait Attack.

Then, depending on his objective, he will apply one or many of the four main **categories** of Face Manipulation. The Non-Biometric Face manipulation, Face Swapping, Face Morphing or Face De-Identification.

In the case of remote identity document onboarding, Non-Biometric Face manipulation would typically be used to fool liveness challenges. Face Swapping would serve in case of identity theft and might be used either for a Living Person Attack or a Portrait Attack. Face Morphing would be employed to create a shared biometry, which is typically used during a Portrait Attack. And finally, De-identification would be used to create a synthetic identity for both a Living Person Attack and a Portrait Attack. The manipulation and their associated supports are summed up in Table 19.1.

In the next section, we will give a more precise definition of each attack and the common algorithms used to perform them.

19.3   Face Manipulation Algorithms

Here, we will first give a description of each category of attacks and give general uses cases for each. Even though those attacks are conceptually different, nevertheless they all target the face area, they are inherently based on the same tampering algorithm. We will give a brief overview of the best-known tampering methods.

19.3.1   Categories of Attacks

Non-biometric manipulation

As stated, we observed an increasing used in systems such as the remote identity document onboarding. Those systems imply some face-related controls (e.g. face recognition behaviour). We define the non-biometric manipulations as any manipulation of the face that does not alter biometric traits.

The first application of such manipulations takes place during liveness detection. Liveness detection is often defined as the verification that the person in front of the camera is indeed alive and interacting voluntarily. We wish to detect attempts of fooling the systems with attacks such as photo presentation, screen presentation and mask presentation. But also that the person is not forced to perform actions by someone. Typical liveness challenges include eye-blinking, smile, head movements, etc. Recent examples have shown the importance of such detection. It is possible to create synthetic eye-blinking digitally without having to alter any biometric traits of an individual.

When a proof of action or inaction is needed, such manipulations can also be involved. For example, within the context of the COVID-19 crisis, verifying that a taxi driver wore a medical mask was necessary to allow him to drive a customer. Such verification is not at all related to the biometry, but can suffer from a non-biometric manipulation. When managing a large fleet, one might be the subject of attacks.

Those manipulations may not be as severe as identity theft or other. Though it is important to acknowledge those as they are easy to achieve and can lead to more problematic issues.

Face Swapping

Face swapping is a well-known technique that consists of the replacement of someone's face in an image or a video. There exist two main kinds of face swapping. It can either be applied on a portrait or to a live acquisition of a person [1].

The first case is what is usually called Face swapping and is typically used to perform an identity theft. Applying it to a portrait does not reduce its usage to images only. On Fig. 19.2, an example of a real-time face swapping is given for id document

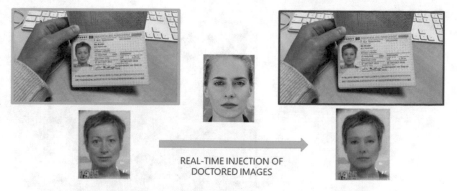

Fig. 19.2 Video Replacement of the portrait picture thanks to inverse fit swapping

Fig. 19.3 An example of deepfake by face reenactment. From left to right: target actor, pilot actor, reenacted actor

portrait within a video stream. Face swapping is often realised with classical methods [2] but can also use some more advanced deep learning techniques [3]. More details will be given in Sect. 19.3.2.

When applied on a live acquisition of a person, Face swapping is often referred to as Face Reenactment. The idea behind face reenactment is to animate a target face according to a video of a source actor or with a given set of expressions. In a sense, it can be used to perform non-biometric manipulation. Here, we are interested in the specific case where an attacker would reenact the face of someone else.

Face swapping on a still portrait or using Face reenactment is mostly used to perform identity theft. It is a very versatile manipulation as it can be applied at different stages of an operational system (Fig. 19.3).

Face Morphing

As described earlier, one can decide to perform a complete face replacement which is commonly called a Face Swap. It is important to consider a face swapping as a subset of a more general attack often called a face morphing.

Fig. 19.4 Morphing with various α_b and α_l (genuine images from [6])

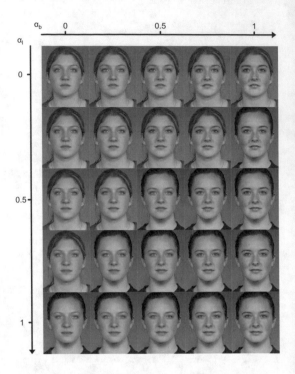

When performing a face swap, the attacker completely replaces the facial area. In a Face Morph Attack, two parameters are introduced to both control the blending factor α_b of the two faces but also a deformation factor α_l that aims at averaging the two face shapes. By adding control over α_b and α_l, it enables to exploit a flaw in common face recognition software. This attack was introduced in ref. [4] where it was shown that using $\alpha_b = 0.5, \alpha_l = 0.5$ allows producing a composite face that can later be used to authenticate two people using the same ID document. Later, it has been shown in ref. [5] that α_b seems to have a more significative impact on various face recognition systems. Figure 19.4 illustrates the effect of varying (α_b, α_l) couples.

In general, we assume that the face morphing can be produced before being printed and scanned back to a digital format to hide any traces of manipulation. In a typical remote onboarding scenario, it is important to keep in mind that those attacks exist. In particular, if we intended to use the photo to later authenticate the user.

Face De-identification

The rapid development of GANs (see Sect. 19.3.2) has led to more advanced face manipulation methods.

One good example is the advance in face de-identification methods which consist in removing some or all biometric traits of an individual. Those came from an

Fig. 19.5 From left to right, original identity, covering, blurring, pixelization, d-id

increasing concern about privacy as biometric authentication methods are becoming more common, but also from new regulations such as the General Data Protection Regulation (GDPR).

Three common methods were used before the introduction of the GAN-based face manipulation, i.e. masking, blurring and pixelization [7]. An example of each of those approach is given in Fig. 19.5.

Masking consists of covering the face with a graphic object (e.g. smiley) or a plain colour. Blurring and pixelization use simple filtering applied to the face area (e.g. Gaussian blur). These de-identification methods are simple and effective but come with some limitations. Firstly, the destructive approach produces an unpleasing result. Secondly, it is possible to partially reverse some of those methods [8] (e.g. de-blurring, de-pixelization and de-noising). And finally, these techniques do not allow suppressing specific characteristics (e.g. age and ethnicity). More sophisticated methods, using GANs, solve these problems. In ref. [9], the authors have been able to completely suppress a source face biometry while preserving the visual aspect of a face. The de-identified face is neither identifiable by a human nor by facial recognition algorithms. Their method allows to automatically de-identify a face in a video in real time. Using this technique, it is also possible to modify or remove biometric characteristics such as the age [10], gender or ethnicity.

19.3.2   Common Face Manipulation Algorithms

Landmark-based face manipulation

Even though deep learning-based face manipulation algorithm performs extremely well, there is still use cases where a more classical method is appropriate. One advantage of classical methods is that they do not need training data and can most of the time produce convincing results in real time.

Landmark-based methods usually come down to three simple steps. First, a face detection algorithm is applied. Then salient face features, often called landmarks, are extracted. And finally, the manipulation is performed.

In general, classical face manipulation algorithms used common landmark detection techniques like [11]. In such cases, those methods would only be used in simple

2D cases, i.e. fixed portrait tampering. More advanced methods exist to perform 3D face alignment. In general, classical face manipulation algorithm used common landmark detection techniques like [11]. In such cases, those methods would only be used in simple 2D cases, i.e. fixed portrait tampering. More advanced methods exist to perform 3D face alignment. They rely on a 3D mask synthesis which offers very good results. They are particularly well suited to be applied to images and also videos. One of the earliest methods [12] proposed to replace the face with a 3D model. This 3D face is then edited to modify facial expressions. However, it was not possible to make a real-time facial reenactment at that time. Newer methods yield dense 3D alignment in real time such as [13–15]. In [16], the authors have successfully developed a facial reenactment system that allows editing a face in the video in real time with a simple camera. They first detect facial expressions in a source and the target video. Then, they generate a 3D model of the face of both the target and the source video. Next, they transfer the facial expressions from the source to the target 3D model. Finally, they blend the 3D model on the target video. This produces very convincing results. Today, it is also possible to give life to a still image [17] by transferring facial expressions from a pilot video and optionally the voice.

At the time of writing, those more advanced methods tend to be much more difficult to implement. Because of that, AI-based methods are usually preferred for their ease of use. And thanks to the numerous existing face databases, many powerful methods have been proposed.

AI-Based Face Manipulation

With recent advances in generative models (Variational Auto Encoders (VAEs) and Generative Adversarial Networks)GANs)), Deep learning-based face manipulation has received a lot of attention. In particular, with the apparition of the popular deepfakes. The term deepfake is a portmanteau word composed of the "deep" to refer to "deep learning" and the word fake. The inventor of deepfake is an Internet user under the pseudonym "deepfake". He was inspired by a paper that proposed a method to modify the environment of a video [18], and he applied it to faces. In this paper, Liu et al. built a framework that uses VAEs and GANs to apply modifications on each frame of a video.

The DeepFakes allow exchanging in a fast, automatic and realistic way a face in a video. Nowadays, the term deepfake is also used to designate more generally a "hyper-realistic" falsification of a video or audio signal.

The biggest danger is that it does not require special technical skills to make a deepfake unlike the more complex landmark-based method. Nor is it necessary to master complicated software. Today, anyone can make a deepfake.

The first deepfake method only used VAEs to replace a face in a video. A deepfake based on auto-encoders consists of using two auto-encoders and crossing the decoders. An auto-encoder is a type of neural network used to reconstruct an image from compressed information (called latent space) of the same image. In order to build a deepfake, it is necessary to train one of the auto-encoders with images of faces of a first individual and to train the other auto-encoder with images of the second individual. Then, once the training phase is complete, the decoders are swapped to force the reconstruction of another face from the latent space. One of the important points in this method of deepfake generation is that both auto-encoders need to share the same encoder during the training stage.

But thanks to the various advances in GANs, in particular since the well-known SyleGAN [19] introduced by NVDIA research team, many deep facial forgery methods are now based on this technology rather than on VAEs.

A deepfake based on GANs used the neural networks introduced in 2014 by Ian Goodfellow [20]. In the same spirit as auto-encoders, a GAN is made of two distinct parts, a generator G and a discriminator D. In the case of deepfake generations, the role of the generator is to synthesise a video capable of deceiving the discriminator, and the role of the discriminator is to determine whether the content proposed by the generator is authentic or not.

Most recently, the authors of [21] were even able to remove the needs of the GAN to be trained on a specific individual. Rather, they trained their network to animate a single photo according to a source video. This last advance simplified even further the sequence of processing attached to the creation of deepfakes for non-experts.

19.4 Detecting Face Manipulation

In many practical applications, it is possible to control some parts of the acquisition process. Whether we can directly control the acquisition device or only access the incoming streaming for the said device, it is important to look at the problematic of Face Manipulation detection as a subset of image manipulation detection.

This does not mean that specialised detection should not be considered but rather that they should be completed with additional methods. In this section, we will introduce the common Face Manipulation detection method along with some more general Image Manipulation detection algorithms.

We will also talk about how much the control of the acquisition device and the definition of the User Interface can play a significant role in the detection of image tampering.

19.4.1 Face Specific Methods

When we do know that the acquired media will contain a human face, ignoring face-specific tampering detection method would be rather unwise.

Knowing that the acquired face cannot be considered as genuine, there exist many methods that aim at exposing digital tapering. We will consider two main categories, first the methods looking for weaknesses in the manipulation process and secondly the methods that try to expose physical inconsistencies.

Deepfake Detection Methods

With the increasing creation of deepfakes, many detection methods have been pro-posed. In the literature, there are mainly three categories of deepfake detection meth-ods: based on physiological analysis, based on image texture analysis and based on automatic detection with artificial intelligence. As part of the physiological analysis, Li et al. [22] observed some inconsistencies in the eye blinking in a deepfake video. Using a Long-term Recurrent Convolutional Network (LCRN), they successfully detected deepfake videos. In ref. [23], the authors determine whether a video is a deepfake or not by analysing inconsistencies in head position. For detection methods based on image or texture analysis, the authors mainly look for inconsistencies in the optical flow [24] or the presence of artefacts [25]. Finally, approaches purely based on a detection using artificial intelligence pass the frames of a video through neural networks. The neural networks can be recurrent neural networks [26], 3D convolutional networks [27], recurrent networks or an ensemble of them. Kumar et al. [28] proposed a method dedicated to detect videos to which face reenactment has been applied using [16]. They proposed an ensemble of 5 ResNets trained to identify noise patterns or artefacts. Despite very good results and robustness at different lev-els of video compression, their method cannot be used in real time. Megahed et al. have described a method [29] for detecting face reenactment manipulations based on Histogram of Oriented Gradient and SVM. Unfortunately, because of the significant diversity of the different ways to generate a deepfake, it is very difficult to develop a method suitable to detect all possible types of deepfake videos. Some methods have been proposed to detect both deepfakes by face swapping and deepfakes by face reenactment. In ref. [30], the authors trained two convolutional neural networks to detect both swapped face videos and reenacted face videos. Despite encouraging results, their methods are dependent on the training database and, therefore, do not work very well on unseen types of deepfakes. In ref. [31], the authors also propose a method based on deep learning to automatically detect deepfakes by looking at the facial regions. Their method is robust to different levels of compression. However, it is also very dependent on the training database. A model able to detect with a high level of accuracy a type of deepfake can easily be fooled by a deepfake that has been generated with another method. In addition to the variety of deepfakes generation methods that make it difficult to generalise detection techniques, it is also impor-tant to consider that the models must be robust to adversarial attacks. Indeed, in ref. [32], it has been shown that it is possible to easily deceive a detector by injecting an adverse noise into a video.

19.4.2   Face Agnostic Methods

Image forensic can be divided into two main categories, i.e. active and passive image forgery detection. In passive image forgery detection, we have to authenticate an image without any knowledge of the digital media. Whereas active forgery detection has access to at least a partial information about the image provenance and leverage that knowledge to authenticate the media.

One can intuitively understand how active forgery detection is preferred as we can pinpoint very specific properties of the image to assess its authenticity. As mentioned earlier, in practical cases, we often have some controls on the acquisition device. This can be used to our advantage as we can somewhat impose some constraints on the acquired media to go from passive forgery detection to active forgery detection.

This allows us to add many layers of authentication on top of the previously mentioned face-specific detection methods and build a more confident prediction about the image integrity.

Camera-based methods

The first category of image manipulation detection algorithm is based on the characteristics and steps involved in the creation process of a digital image. A brief overview of the acquisition pipeline is given in Fig. 19.6. Light passes through the lenses before reaching the camera sensor. Sensors are not perfectly manufactured and small defects can be used as fingerprints of a particular sensor. A widely known fingerprint for camera model identification is the Photo Response Non Uniformity (PRNU) which was first introduced in ref. [33]. A sufficient number of images from one camera (about 50) allows us to produce a fingerprint which can then be used to assess if an image comes from a specific camera. In some cases, the PRNU has further been used to locate the digital tampering by searching for partial mismatch of the fingerprint [34, 35].

Common camera sensors first separate the lights using what is called a Colour Filter Array (CFA). This filter generally separates the information into three channels (typically red, green and blue) which are later on interpolated to produce the full-size image. This whole operation is known as image demosaicing. This operation tends to leave correlation between the final pixels which can be used to detect digital forgeries by locating the CFA grid and type. Because one sensor can only use one specific CFA, the detection of portions of an image with either a misaligned CFA or a mismatching type can inform of the presence of a digital tampering [36, 37].

Once the acquisition pipeline is complete, a final image pixel z can be roughly modelled as

$$z = x + \eta \tag{19.1}$$

where x was the true pixel value corrupted by some noise η. In reality, more elaborate models than Eq. 19.1 are used such as [38] when x is corrupted by various noises and processes. Typical noise sources are the so-called shot noise (due to the way light reaches the sensor) and read noise due to amplification, quantification, etc. On top of that, different post-processing such as gamma correction or compression would further corrupt the observed pixel x.

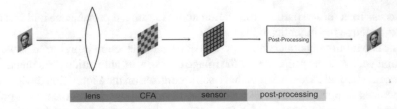

Fig. 19.6 Simplified acquisition pipeline

Whatever the noise model used, one can make the assumption that the counterfeit will not be able (or will not try) to reproduce a consistent noise across the image. Many methods aim at exposing those inconsistencies [39].

Few other methods focus on other artefacts such as inconsistencies in chromatic aberrations [40] and inconsistent camera response function [41, 42].

Pixel-based methods

Another class of image manipulation detection methods is the pixel-based method. Instead of targeting parts of the acquisition pipeline, those methods rather try to target some parts of the tampering process.

In fact, there exist a few common tampering categories: Image splicing where an element from one image is inserted into another image; copy-Move where elements are duplicated within a single image; object-removal where objects are removed from an image (typically using inpainting algorithms).

While producing a forged image, a digital artist often uses a combination of those types of forgery and produce what we usually call a compositing.

Because the digital artist most likely wants his/her compositing to be convincing, he would use various techniques and post-processing to reach his goal. Think of the production of a deepfake. As we mentioned, CNNs tend to produce blurry results. A counterfeit might then want to enhance the quality of his deepfake by applying a sharpening filter. Such post-processing is performed by the widely used DeepFaceLab software for instance. Whatever the processing use, it will leave traces.

Most of the time, the detection of splicing forgeries relies on camera-based methods. In fact, in such forgeries, a large portion of the image may carry a significant difference with respect to intrinsic camera properties. It is not unreasonable to suppose that the spliced part might have gone through several post-processing such as sharpening and Gaussian blurring. In those cases, some methods [43, 44] aim at exposing those post-processing as a trace of image forgery.

For copy-move forgery, camera-based methods tend to be ill-suited as the duplicated element will share most of the initial image properties. For this reason, there exist many algorithms targeting copy-move forgery directly [45]. One challenge of copy-move forgery detection is the presence of Similar but Genuine Object (SGO). In the case of SGO, most algorithms tend to produce a high false positive rate [46]. This becomes a strong issue in the case of remote ID onboarding as pictures of ID documents contain many SGO. This has been addressed by a few previous papers [47, 48] and has yet to be further developed with more work and more datasets.

Object-removal is a more specific attack and is less studied in the state of the art. One reason is that most object-removal forgeries are performed either with direct copy move or with inpainting algorithms, because current professional software tends to use exemplar-based inpainting algorithms. Thus, object-removal can often be detected with copy-move detection methods, but there exists research focussing especially on Object-Removal [49, 50].

Format-Based Methods

The last category of image forgery detection algorithm is the format-based method. Those algorithms make neither particular assumption on the acquisition pipeline nor on the tampering process. Rather they aim at authenticating the format of a given media.

In a system such as Fig. 19.7 (see Sect. 19.5.2), the acquisition pipeline is controlled.

By assuming the acquisition process is secure, the authentication of the media can be reduced to specify a check on the format properties. For instance, if the media was a JPEG image sent with a quality factor of 95, one could verify that this property did not change. One advantage of format-based methods is that they have proved to be extremely effective and have been well studied.

For images, several approaches have been proposed for JPEG images. It is possible with state-of-the-art methods to verify various properties such as the JPEG quality factor [51] or the presence of a double compression [52]. While less studied, methods for analog video formats exist too.

19.4.3   Datasets

In this section, we will introduce the most common image and video tampering datasets for both Face Manipulation and general tampering detection.

Images Datasets

A list of common image tampering datasets is given in Table 19.2. This table is far from being exhaustive and thus illustrates the wide availability of datasets. In particular since 2019, three extremely large datasets (PS-Battles [53], DEFACTO [54] and IMD2020 [55]) have been publicly released containing all kinds of forgeries that should allow researchers to properly evaluate, train or test their forensic algorithms.

On the other hand, there exist only a few datasets that are face specific. In 2017, the FaceSwap dataset was released containing only face swap manipulations. They used two different methods to develop the dataset. The Biometix datasets, released in 2017, contained 1082 Face Morphing based on the FERET face dataset. In the

Table 19.2 Image and face manipulation datasets and information

Dataset	Manipulation	Size
Columbia gray and colour [56]	Splicing	1092
MICC F220 and F2000 [57]	Copy-move	810
Casia v1 and v2 [58]	Splicing, copy-move	6044
COVERAGE [46]	Copy-move	100
Biometix [59]	Face morphing	1082
FaceSwap [60]	Face swapping	1,927
PS-Battles [53]	All	102,028
DEFACTO [54]	All	229,000
IMD2020 [55]	All	72000
OpenMFC2020 [61]	All	16,000

DEFACTO dataset, about eighty thousand face morphing are available. Apart from those, we could cite the DSI-1 dataset for completeness, but it only contains about 25 tampered images.

Even though most splicing detection methods are applicable to Face Manipulation detection, we believe that more specific datasets would help in the development of more specific methods.

Video Datasets

In contrary to image forgery datasets, there exist only a few general video tampering datasets. Some common datasets are given in Table 19.3. We believe that this is due to the extremely large degrees of freedom when compressing a video that make it difficult to produce a dataset that would suit everyone's needs. Often, researcher ends up crafting their own dataset depending on the feature they use.

Thanks to the initiative of the NIST, researchers now have access to a dataset of about 1500 tampered video.

If we lack general-purpose video forgery datasets, many video datasets dedicated to the detection of deepfake forgeries have been proposed. This imbalanced could be explained by the dangers they represent against biometric authentication systems but also by the fact that deepfake detection algorithms often operate blindly. Thus,

Table 19.3 General video tampering datasets

Dataset	Manipulation	Size
SULFA [62]	Copy-move	10
MTVFD [63]	Copy-move, splicing, frame swapping	30
OpenMFC2020 [61]	Various	1,500

Table 19.4 Deepfakes Datasets and informations

Dataset	Fake videos	Real videos	Identity	Methods	Augmentation
UADFV	49	49	49	1	–
DeepfakeTIMIT	640	320	43	2	–
FaceForensics++	4000	1000	–	4	2
Google DFD	3000	363	28	5	–
Celeb-DFD	5639	890	59	1	–
Deeper	1000	59000	100	1	7
DFDC	104500	23654	960	5	19

the large degree of freedom when creating the forgeries is considered as part of the problem and the detection method should be able to work in all scenarios.

To the best of our knowledge, we count seven large datasets of deepfakes (Table 19.4). The most important and recent database is the one attached to the Deepfake Detection Challenge (DFDC) [64]. The Deepfake Detection Challenge is an international competition, launched in December 2019, to help the scientific community to develop new techniques to detect deepfakes. The competition closes at the end of March 2020, and the winning solution achieved an accuracy score of 82%.

19.5 Counter-Forensics and Countermeasures

19.5.1 Counter-Forensics

We described many different tampering detection approaches. In a way, all those methods implicitly assume that the attacker will perform a naive tampering which in turn will leave many traces.

Though it is not unreasonable to assume so, it is important to also consider cases where the attacker will try his/her best to hide traces of his forgery. This can go from simply correcting incorrect EXIF metadata to directly target detection methods described in Sect. 19.4.2.

For example, in ref. [65], the authors propose a method to suppress the PRNU of an image and to replace it with the one of another camera. In ref. [66], the authors showed that it was possible to mislead CFA-based algorithms. Other approaches try to hide the forgery at the compression level such as [67], and some methods even target specific forgeries such as [68].

Regarding face-specific methods, rapid advances in the realistic rendering of deepfakes and GAN-based facial forgeries are strongly connected to the progress of methods for detecting such contents. But as each new detection method reveals a "weakness" in the synthesised content, it is then rapidly fixed in order to hide the forged image or video from detection.

First counter-forensic has corrected physical or physiological inconsistencies by adding, in the case of deepfakes, a natural eye blink that was missing and in the general case of face swapping, correcting the orientation of the face in relation to the head. They also adjusted inconsistencies in colour, brightness or artefacts that can randomly appear on a GAN-generated image.

Another powerful counter-forensic is the use of adversarial attacks. An adversarial attack consists of adding a computed noise imperceptible to the human eye into the image. This noise has a big impact on deep learning-based detectors [69]. Based on this approach, several methods have been proposed to make a deepfake video recognised as an original video by deep learning-based deepfake detectors [70, 71]. The authors of [32] have successfully generated a single adversarial attack that misled three different deepfake detectors.

19.5.2 Countermeasures

Here, we will take a more macroscopic look at typical remote identity document verification systems and discuss how one would use the methods described in Sect. 19.4.2 to ensure the integrity of the end media.

We will consider two main scenarios. In the first case, we have access to the acquisition device and can somewhat control it as in Fig. 19.7. The captured media is then sent over the network to some servers that will later have to authenticate it.

In the second scenario Fig. 19.8, we have no knowledge about the acquisition device. A server simply receives a media that needs to be authenticated. In that case, it is still possible by design to impose some constraints on the media such as the format and size.

Controlled acquisition device

Whenever possible, it is always preferred to have some sort of control over the acquisition process. The reason is that active detection methods are arguably more effective than completely passive approaches.

In particular, within the scenario of Fig. 19.7, it is possible to use every single category of detection algorithms described earlier which allows for a more reliable decision.

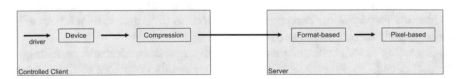

Fig. 19.7 Controlled acquisition pipeline

Fig. 19.8 Uncontrolled
acquisition pipeline

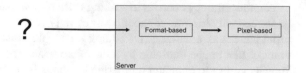

In such a case, we can assume that the attacker can perform his/her tampering during three different stages. The first option is to attack the stream at the earliest stage of the acquisition pipeline, i.e. at the driver level. Any electronic component of a system is controlled by a piece of software called a driver. In the case of a camera, the role of the driver would be to directly control the sensor to retrieve the raw image data. It would then apply every basic image processing needed to pass forward a readable RGB image, i.e. demosaicing, camera response function and some basic noise filtering.

If the image is altered at the driver level and unless there is a known watermarking algorithm used at a hardware level, camera-based detection algorithms are the way to go. In fact, at this stage, the image is supposed to directly come from the sensor and thus must fulfil some models such as the uniqueness of the CFA, a precise model of the sensor noise and so on. As for every method, false positives are possible. But repeated tampering detection by multiple methods at this stage must imply a deeper analysis at a later stage of the system.

After passing the drivers, we receive an RGB-like image. The client is now in charge of sending the media to a distant server. Because we should not assume the network channel to be safe, as it could be subject to a man-in-the-middle attack, for instance, it is then the last opportunity to inject knowledge on the media before sending it on the network. Think of applying a specific JPEG/MPEG compression adding a specific watermark, etc. which will later be used to enhance the format-based detection method for instance.

Once the media has reached the server and after applying format-based method to verify the last known properties of the image. Pixel-based and more face-specific methods can now be used to further confirm any previous detection that might have occurred. It is fine to use such methods at the very end of the pipeline as they often assume nothing about the properties of the acquisition device nor the format used in case of a compression.

One major advantage of having control over the acquisition device is also the possibility to interact with the user in some cases such as remote KYC. In that scenario, it is possible to ask the user to perform actions in order to make the tampering process harder. Suppose we ask the user to capture his ID document. We know that the ID photo is a potential target for a counterfeit. We also know that to alter the photo in real time, a precise detection of the face and some landmarks is needed. One challenge of both face and landmark detection is the presence of an occluding element in the face. Asking the user to hide part of the photo at some point might make the automatic tampering algorithm to fail which could cause visible artefacts.

Another strategy consists in making difficult the manipulation creation. This can be applied only in some contexts. Ruiz et al. [72] proposed a method based on adversarial attacks as a defense. By adding a specific noise in the image, they are able to make that image unusable by a deepfake generator. In that sense, having a good knowledge of the common tampering methods is necessary to develop more challenging user experiences for a counterfeit.

Uncontrolled acquisition device

As already mentioned, having control over the acquisition stage is preferable. It is not always possible though and one might have to accept media from an unknown source as in Fig. 19.8. But it does not mean that such a system must accept anything as an input.

First of all, imposing a specific format for the incoming media is mandatory as this already allows the use of specific format-based methods. Also, if the quality of the media is sufficient enough, the blind camera-based method can still be applied. As already pointed out, pixel-based methods are always a good option as they are most of the time blind detections.

Unlike the controlled case, one should keep in mind that the counterfeit has all the needed time to try and hide his/her manipulation. It is, thus, reasonable to assume that he/she will try to apply as many counter-forensic methods as he/she can make every decision algorithm less reliable.

As for the controlled case, asking the user to send pictures or video with specific constraints (e.g. hiding part of the face) is a good idea, even though in this scenario the counterfeit will have the time to correct visible artefacts.

A general rule of thumb for both scenarios would be to impose as many constraints as possible to ensure that only really experienced counterfeit will be able to fool the system.

Preventive Measures

When the context allows conceiving the initial ID document in order to prevent specifically digital attacks on the portrait, different countermeasures can be taken to facilitate the detection of manipulations. First strategies can be related to the addition of semi-fragile watermarks [73] in the content, which will disappear during an image manipulation and thus trigger a detection. The second category of strategies is to secure the image thanks to cryptographic seal, based on perceptual hashes [74, 75].

19.6 Reference Framework, Standardisation and Legal Aspects

Growing usage of remote identification generates growing types of frauds and growing needs for a safer environment. New regulations are emerging.

In France, a new reference framework, named PVID, describes the recommendations to remotely acquire the identity of someone [76]. In its preliminary version, it forbids limiting the control only to still images to authenticate a person. Rather, the authentication must be performed based on a video stream. It also requires a hybrid approach with both human and machine checks. This reference framework is planned to be included in the French implementation of the E-IDAS, giving it a European impact. PVID is supposed to be published in April 2021. It would probably impose constraints on resolution, frame rate and perhaps bandwidth of the transmitted video and will forbid any disruption of the video stream. It also imposes a double verification process involving parallel humans and machines.

In Europe, the security Agency ENISA has published in February 2021 an analysis of the Remote ID Proofing [77], in which they describe remote verification in several cases with or without a human operator and in the context of a video acquisition to prevent manipulation. They based their work on the 2018 document of German BSI [78] which precise clearly the threats and attacks, but also the condition of success of attacks.

In order to qualify the solutions proposed by vendors, some dedicated laboratories begin to appear to test the capacities of manipulation detectors, with private large sets of software or hybrid attacks. Comparable methodologies, tools and datasets are clearly required in the next years to insure a global level of security against face manipulations.

19.7 Conclusions

With the worldwide crisis of 2020 due to the COVID-19, we observed significant adoption of remote technologies. We believe that this trend will continue and that many systems will need to be able to confidently authenticate their end-users which will come with an increasing use of face and behaviour recognition software.

In the meantime, the deepfakes visual quality has Improved, and in the future, the deepfakes will be even more realistic by correcting all the imperfections they still include. Nowadays, deepfakes are mainly used to create adult content or entertainment videos. However, we believe that in the next few years, deepfakes will be the most used way for attacking facial recognition systems. With those evolving technologies, the creation of a forged media stream is becoming easier every day.

We must anticipate the use of those powerful technologies against any operational system based on face and behaviour recognition software. Thus, the detection of those tampered media is becoming increasingly important.

In this chapter, we introduced the four common Face Manipulation categories. We described how each of these methods could be used against an operational system. We focussed our attention on the example of a remote system for identity document verification. It is an interesting use case as it gives many opportunities for an attacker to fool the system. We also gave a brief overview of many detectors specific to faces, general image manipulation detection methods but also some datasets for image and video tampering detection. Then we introduced a few common counter-forensics methods, but also countermeasures to increase the overall system reliability whether the acquisition device is controlled or not. Finally, we discussed standardisation and legal aspects covering such systems.

As of today, the detection of deepfakes and other attacks is far from being solved. Looking at the bright side, we saw that many detection algorithms already exist. Even though none of those can fully operate in a completely blind manner, most of them can be used in a more active approach. This requires the overall system to be carefully designed. A proper combination of all those tools may give powerful insights about a given media integrity. We believe that most of the time, some constraints over the media properties can be imposed. Completely blind detection algorithms are welcomed but should not prevail. We encourage researchers to develop a more formal definition of operational systems and to imagine precise lifecycles of digital media. This would allow the development of more specific datasets, detection methods and interpretability of such methods. This in turn would be extremely beneficial as it would help to close the gap between theoretical research and operational applications.

We believe that Face Manipulation Detection must be included in the pipeline of required processing for any official document. It could be organised in a way similar to the ICAO Picture Compliance test for instance. We also recommend the standardisation of the tests and the methodologies to measure the efficiency of the Face Manipulation Detection algorithms in order to obtain fair and efficient comparison between vendors. This standardisation effort needs to take into account the various strategies, contexts and goals described here, in order to define meaningful metrics.

References

1. Tolosana Ruben, Vera-Rodriguez Ruben, Fierrez Julian, Morales Aythami, Ortega-Garcia Javier (2020) Deepfakes and beyond: a survey of face manipulation and fake detection. Inf Fusion 64:131–148
2. Bitouk D, Kumar N, Dhillon S, Belhumeur P, Nayar S (2008) Face swapping: automatically replacing faces in photographs. In: SIGGRAPH 2008
3. Korshunova I, Shi W, Dambre J, Theis L (2017) Fast face-swap using convolutional neural networks. In: Proceedings of the IEEE international conference on computer vision, pp 3677–3685

4. Ferrara M, Franco A, Maltoni D (2014) The magic passport. In: IEEE international joint conference on biometrics. IEEE, pp 1–7
5. Ferrara M, Franco A, Maltoni D (2019) Decoupling texture blending and shape warping in face morphing. In: 2019 international conference of the biometrics special interest group (BIOSIG)
6. Phillips PJ, Flynn PJ, Scruggs T, Bowyer KW, Chang J, Hoffman K, Marques J, Min J, Worek W (2005) Overview of the face recognition grand challenge. In: 2005 IEEE computer society conference on computer vision and pattern recognition (CVPR'05), vol. 1. IEEE, pp 947–954
7. Korshunov P, Araimo C, De Simone F, Velardo C, Dugelay JL, Ebrahimi T (2012) Subjective study of privacy filters in video surveillance. In: 2012 IEEE 14th international workshop on multimedia signal processing (MMSP). IEEE, pp 378–382
8. Ruchaud Natacha, Dugelay Jean-Luc (2016) Automatic face anonymization in visual data: are we really well protected? Algorithms and Systems, In Image Processing
9. Gafni O, Wolf L, Taigman Y (2019) Live face de-identification in video. In: 2019 IEEE/CVF international conference on computer vision (ICCV). IEEE, pp 9377–9386
10. Antipov G, Baccouche M, Dugelay JL (2017) Face aging with conditional generative adversarial networks. In: 2017 IEEE international conference on image processing (ICIP). IEEE, pp 2089–2093
11. Kazemi V, Sullivan J (2014) One millisecond face alignment with an ensemble of regression trees. In: Proceedings of the IEEE conference on computer vision and pattern recognition. IEEE, pp 1867–1874
12. Vlasic D, Brand M, Pfister H, Popovic J (2005) Face transfer with multilinear models. In: SIGGRAPH 2005
13. Cao Chen, Hou Qiming, Zhou Kun (2014) Displaced dynamic expression regression for real-time facial tracking and animation. ACM Trans Graph (TOG) 33(4):1–10
14. Jeni LA, Cohn JF, Kanade T (2015) Dense 3d face alignment from 2d videos in real-time. In: 2015 11th IEEE international conference and workshops on automatic face and gesture recognition (FG), vol 1. IEEE, pp 1–8
15. Thies Justus, Zollhöfer Michael, Nießner Matthias, Valgaerts Levi, Stamminger Marc, Theobalt Christian (2015) Real-time expression transfer for facial reenactment. ACM Trans. Graph. 34(6):183–1
16. Thies J, Zollhöfer M, Stamminger M, Theobalt C, Nießner M (2016) Face2face: real-time face capture and reenactment of rgb videos. In: 2016 IEEE conference on computer vision and pattern recognition (CVPR). IEEE, pp 2387–2395
17. Averbuch-Elor H, Cohen-Or D, Kopf J, Cohen MF (2017) Bringing portraits to life. ACM Trans Graph (TOG) 36:1–13
18. Liu MY, Breuel T, Kautz J (2017) Unsupervised image-to-image translation networks. In: NIPS
19. Karras T, Laine S, Aila T (2019) A style-based generator architecture for generative adversarial networks. In: Proceedings of the IEEE/CVF conference on computer vision and pattern recognition. IEEE, pp 4401–4410
20. Goodfellow I, Pouget-Abadie J, Mirza M, Xu B, Warde-Farley D, Ozair S, Courville A, Bengio Y (2014) Generative adversarial networks. arXiv:1406.2661
21. Siarohin A, Lathuilière S, Tulyakov S, Ricci E, Sebe N (2020) First order motion model for image animation. arXiv:2003.00196
22. Li Y, Chang MC, Lyu S (2018) In ictu oculi: exposing ai created fake videos by detecting eye blinking. In: 2018 IEEE international workshop on information forensics and security (WIFS). IEEE, pp 1–7
23. Yang X, Li Y, Lyu S (2019) Exposing deep fakes using inconsistent head poses. In: ICASSP 2019-2019 IEEE international conference on acoustics, speech and signal processing (ICASSP). IEEE, pp 8261–8265
24. Amerini I, Galteri L, Caldelli R, Del Bimbo A (2019) Deepfake video detection through optical flow based cnn. In: 2019 IEEE/CVF international conference on computer vision workshop (ICCVW). IEEE, pp 1205–1207
25. Li Y, Lyu S (2019) Exposing deepfake videos by detecting face warping artifacts. arXiv:1811.00656

26. Guera D, Delp EJ (2018) Deepfake video detection using recurrent neural networks. In: 2018 15th IEEE international conference on advanced video and signal based surveillance (AVSS). IEEE, pp 1–6
27. Lima O, Franklin S, Basu S, Karwoski B, George A (2020) Deepfake detection using spatiotemporal convolutional networks. arXiv:2006.14749
28. Kumar P, Vatsa M, Singh R (2020) Detecting face2face facial reenactment in videos. In: 2020 IEEE winter conference on applications of computer vision (WACV). IEEE, pp 2578–2586
29. Megahed A, Han Q (2020) Face2face manipulation detection based on histogram of oriented gradients. In: 2020 IEEE 19th international conference on trust, security and privacy in computing and communications (TrustCom). IEEE, pp 1260–1267
30. Afchar D, Nozick V, Yamagishi J, Echizen I (2018) Mesonet: a compact facial video forgery detection network. In: 2018 IEEE international workshop on information forensics and security (WIFS). IEEE, pp 1–7
31. Rossler A, Cozzolino D, Verdoliva L, Riess C, Thies J, Nießner M (2019) Faceforensics++: learning to detect manipulated facial images. In: Proceedings of the IEEE/CVF international conference on computer vision. IEEE, pp 1–11
32. Neekhara P, Dolhansky B, Bitton J, Ferrer CC (2020) Adversarial threats to deepfake detection: a practical perspective. arXiv:2011.09957
33. Lukas J, Fridrich J, Goljan M (2006) Digital camera identification from sensor pattern noise. IEEE Trans Inf Forensics Secur 1(2):205–214
34. Chierchia Giovanni, Poggi Giovanni, Sansone Carlo, Verdoliva Luisa (2014) A bayesian-mrf approach for prnu-based image forgery detection. IEEE Trans Inf Forensics Secur 9(4):554–567
35. Korus Paweł, Huang Jiwu (2016) Multi-scale analysis strategies in prnu-based tampering localization. IEEE Trans Inf Forensics Secur 12(4):809–824
36. Ferrara Pasquale, Bianchi Tiziano, De Rosa Alessia, Piva Alessandro (2012) Image forgery localization via fine-grained analysis of cfa artifacts. IEEE Trans Inf Forensics Secur 7(5):1566–1577
37. Le N, Retraint F (2019) An improved algorithm for digital image authentication and forgery localization using demosaicing artifacts. IEEE Access 7:125038–125053
38. Thai TH, Retraint F, Cogranne R (2015) Generalized signal-dependent noise model and parameter estimation for natural images. Signal Process 114:164–170
39. Pan X, Zhang X, Lyu S (2011) Exposing image forgery with blind noise estimation. In: Proceedings of the thirteenth ACM multimedia workshop on multimedia and security. IEEE, pp 15–20
40. Johnson MK, Farid H (2006) Exposing digital forgeries through chromatic aberration. In: Proceedings of the 8th workshop on multimedia and security. IEEE, pp 48–55
41. Hsu Yu-Feng, Chang Shih-Fu (2010) Camera response functions for image forensics: an automatic algorithm for splicing detection. IEEE Trans Inf Forensics Secur 5(4):816–825
42. Chen C, McCloskey S, Yu J (2017) Image splicing detection via camera response function analysis. In: Proceedings of the IEEE conference on computer vision and pattern recognition. IEEE, pp 5087–5096
43. Cao G, Zhao Y, Ni R, Yu L, Tian H (2010) Forensic detection of median filtering in digital images. In: 2010 IEEE international conference on multimedia and expo. IEEE, pp 89–94
44. Cao G, Zhao Y, Ni R, Kot AC (2011) Unsharp masking sharpening detection via overshoot artifacts analysis. IEEE Signal Process Lett 18(10):603–606
45. Christlein Vincent, Riess Christian, Jordan Johannes, Riess Corinna, Angelopoulou Elli (2012) An evaluation of popular copy-move forgery detection approaches. IEEE Trans Inf Forensics Secur 7(6):1841–1854
46. Wen B, Zhu Y, Subramanian R, Ng TT, Shen X, Winkler S (2016) COVERAGE-A novel database for copy-move forgery detection. In: 2016 IEEE international conference on image processing (ICIP). IEEE, pp 161–165
47. Li Yuanman, Zhou Jiantao (2018) Fast and effective image copy-move forgery detection via hierarchical feature point matching. IEEE Trans Inf Forensics Secur 14(5):1307–1322

48. Mahfoudi G, Morain-Nicollier F, Retraint F, Pic MM (2019) Copy and move forgery detection using sift and local color dissimilarity maps. In: 2019 IEEE global conference on signal and information processing (GlobalSIP). IEEE, pp 1–5

49. Zhang Dengyong, Liang Zaoshan, Yang Gaobo, Li Qingguo, Li Leida, Sun Xingming (2018) A robust forgery detection algorithm for object removal by exemplar-based image inpainting. Multimed Tools Appl 77(10):11823–11842

50. Mahfoudi G, Morain-Nicolier F, Retraint F, Pic MM (2020) Object-removal forgery detection through reflectance analysis. In: 2020 IEEE international symposium on signal processing and information technology (ISSPIT) (ISSPIT-2020), virtual

51. Retraint F, Zitzmann C (2020) Quality factor estimation of jpeg images using a statistical model. Digital Signal Process 103:102759

52. Farid H (2009) Exposing digital forgeries from jpeg ghosts. IEEE Trans Inf Forensics Secur 4(1):154–160

53. Heller S, Rossetto L, Schuldt H (2018) The ps-battles dataset-an image collection for image manipulation detection. arXiv:1804.04866

54. Mahfoudi G, Tajini B, Retraint F, Morain-Nicolier F, Dugelay JL, Pic MM (2019) DEFACTO: image and face manipulation dataset. In: 2019 27th European signal processing conference (EUSIPCO). IEEE, pp 1–5

55. Novozamsky A, Mahdian B, Saic S (2020) IMD2020: a large-scale annotated dataset tailored for detecting manipulated images. In: Proceedings of the IEEE/CVF winter conference on applications of computer vision workshops. IEEE, pp 71–80

56. Hsu Y-F, Chang SF (2006) Detecting image splicing using geometry invariants and camera characteristics consistency. In: 2006 IEEE international conference on multimedia and expo. IEEE, pp 549–552

57. Amerini Irene, Ballan Lamberto, Caldelli Roberto, Del Bimbo Alberto, Serra Giuseppe (2011) A sift-based forensic method for copy-move attack detection and transformation recovery. IEEE Trans Inf Forensics Secur 6(3):1099–1110

58. Dong J, Wang W, Tan T (2013) Casia image tampering detection evaluation database. In: 2013 IEEE China summit and international conference on signal and information processing. IEEE, pp 422–426

59. Biometix dataset. https://www.linkedin.com/pulse/new-face-morphing-dataset-vulnerability-research-ted-dunstone. Last Accessed 22 Feb 2021

60. Zhou P, Han X, Morariu VI, Davis LS (2017) Two-stream neural networks for tampered face detection. In: 2017 IEEE conference on computer vision and pattern recognition workshops (CVPRW). IEEE, pp 1831–1839

61. Guan H, Kozak M, Robertson E, Lee Y, Yates AN, Delgado A, Zhou D, Kheyrkhah T, Smith J, Fiscus J (2019) MFC datasets: large-scale benchmark datasets for media forensic challenge evaluation. In: 2019 IEEE winter applications of computer vision workshops (WACVW). IEEE, pp 63–72

62. Qadir G, Yahaya S, Ho AT (2012) Surrey university library for forensic analysis (sulfa) of video content. In: IET conference on image processing (IPR 2012). IEEE, pp 1–6

63. Al-Sanjary OI, Ahmed AA, Sulong G (2016) Development of a video tampering dataset for forensic investigation. Forensic Sci Int 266:565–572

64. Dolhansky B, Bitton J, Pflaum B, Lu J, Howes R, Wang M, Canton Ferrer C (2020) The deepfake detection challenge dataset. arXiv:2006.07397

65. Villalba LJ, Orozco AL, Corripio JR, Hernandez-Castro J (2017) A PNRU-based counter-forensic method to manipulate smartphone image source identification techniques. Future Gener Comput Syst 76:418–427

66. Chuang WH, Wu M (2012) Robustness of color interpolation identification against anti-forensic operations. In: International workshop on information hiding. Springer, pp 16–30

67. Stamm MC, Tjoa SK, Lin WS, Liu KR (2010) Undetectable image tampering through jpeg compression anti-forensics. In: 2010 IEEE international conference on image processing. IEEE, pp 2109–2112

68. Amerini Irene, Barni Mauro, Caldelli Roberto, Costanzo Andrea (2013) Counter-forensics of sift-based copy-move detection by means of keypoint classification. EURASIP J Image Video Process 2013(1):1–17
69. Szegedy C, Zaremba W, Sutskever I, Bruna J, Erhan D, Goodfellow I, Fergus R (2014) Intriguing properties of neural networks. CoRR. arXiv:1312.6199
70. Hussain S, Neekhara P, Jere M, Koushanfar F, McAuley J (2020) Adversarial deepfakes: evaluating vulnerability of deepfake detectors to adversarial examples. arXiv:2002.12749
71. Carlini N, Farid H (2020) Evading deepfake-image detectors with white- and black-box attacks. In: 2020 IEEE/CVF conference on computer vision and pattern recognition workshops (CVPRW). IEEE, pp 2804–2813
72. Ruiz N, Bargal SA, Sclaroff S (2020) Disrupting deepfakes: adversarial attacks against conditional image translation networks and facial manipulation systems. In: ECCV workshops 2020
73. Lee CF, Shen JJ, Hsu FW (2019) A survey of semi-fragile watermarking authentication. In: Jeng-Shyang P, Akinori I, Pei-Wei T, Lakhmi CJ (eds) Recent advances in intelligent information hiding and multimedia signal processing. Springer International Publishing, Cham, pp 264–271
74. Pic MM, Ouddan A (2017) Photometrix^{TM}: a digital seal for offline identity picture authentication. In: European intelligence and security informatics conference (EISIC). IEEE
75. Pic MM, Mahfoudi G, Trabelsi A (2019) A phygital vector for identity, robust to morphing. In: Digital document security (DDS2019)
76. Référentiel d'exigences pvid (v1.0). https://www.ssi.gouv.fr/uploads/2020/11/anssi_pvid_referentiel_exigences-v1.0.pdf. Last Accessed 22 Feb 2021
77. Remote id proofing. https://www.enisa.europa.eu/publications/enisa-report-remote-id-proofing/at_download/fullReport. Last Accessed 22 Feb 2021
78. Technical guideline tr-03147 assurance level assessment of procedures for identity verification of natural persons. https://www.bsi.bund.de/SharedDocs/Downloads/EN/BSI/Publications/TechGuidelines/TR03147/TR03147.pdf. Last Accessed 22 Feb 2021

Chapter 20
Promises, Social, and Ethical Challenges with Biometrics in Remote Identity Onboarding

Katrin Laas-Mikko, Tarmo Kalvet, Robert Derevski, and Marek Tiits

Abstract Issuance of identity documents has commonly relied on face-to-face customer onboarding. Checking a person's physical presence and appearance has been an essential part of identity enrolling procedures to avoid the risk of identity forgery. Yet, several weaknesses, including face morphing attacks, have been identified in document issuing processes. In the context of the COVID-19 pandemic, increasing international mobility, and a greater focus on user convenience, established onboarding rules and procedures have been disrupted. Solutions are being sought which would eliminate the barriers that stem from physical distance while offering at least equal or even better onboarding processes than in-person identity verification. Recently, novel remote onboarding solutions have appeared on the market. They vary from human-assisted video identification procedures to biometric-based automated verification procedures. The main social and ethical issues with biometrics in remote identity onboarding are (1) the risk of harming integrity of personal identity and misuse of it; (2) the risk of privacy invasion and function creep; (3) ethical issues that are raising from algorithmically driven actions and decisions; and (4) public perception and social acceptance of technology. These non-technical requirements need to be addressed in developing identity verification technologies based on biometrical algorithms and security techniques.

K. Laas-Mikko
SK ID Solutions AS, Pärnu mnt 141, Tallinn, Estonia
e-mail: katrin.laas-mikko@skidsolutions.eu

T. Kalvet (✉) · R. Derevski · M. Tiits
Institute of Baltic Studies, Lai 30, 51005 Tartu, Estonia
e-mail: tarmo@ibs.ee; tarmo.kalvet@taltech.ee

R. Derevski
e-mail: robert@ibs.ee

M. Tiits
e-mail: marek@ibs.ee; marek.tiits@taltech.ee

T. Kalvet · M. Tiits
Department of Business Administration, Tallinn University of Technology (TalTech), Ehitajate tee 5, 19086 Tallinn, Estonia

Advances in Computer Vision and Pattern Recognition,
https://doi.org/10.1007/978-3-030-87664-7_20

437

20.1 Introduction

Information and the concept of the "digital society" is the driving force for change in the twenty-first century. Throughout this process, the advancement of technology is a fundamental part of it and serves as a catalyst to enable a wide spectrum of new and unique opportunities. Digitalisation is ubiquitous and takes a prominent role in our daily lives. It can even be described as a "post-digital world" where digital solutions are entirely bound up with our everyday lives and becomes inseparable [1]. In an unprecedented "fourth revolution" of automation and digitalisation, which includes the rise of such spheres as artificial intelligence (AI), virtual reality, the Internet of Things (IoT) or big data analytics [2, 3], things that seemed to be as something from science fiction just some decades ago (smartphones, internet or virtual reality) are normal and essential part of our daily life today [1].

The advancement of technology promises enormous changes in the future. For instance, in the field of communication "we are rapidly reaching a point where computational algorithms can create nearly any form of human communication that is, for all intents and purposes, indistinguishable from reality" [4]. Some scholars even go as far as to state that soon, hundreds of billions of devices might be communicating with the internet [3], which is many times more than the entire human population. Technology has also redefined what is considered possible and what the boundaries are between physical and digital. Let us take digital nomads, for instance, who embark on various forms of remoteness and use digital opportunities as a mediator between technology and infrastructure [1, 5]. This digital lifestyle demonstrates that it has never been easier to travel and work; where one could find themselves working from a laptop in a coffee shop today and from a co-working space in another country a week later [5].

With the increasing availability of different tools, forgery has also become massive and widespread. As Boneh et al. have argued "the barrier to entry for manipulating content has been lowering for centuries. Progress in machine learning is simply accelerating the process" [4]. With the development of digital technology, the ability to forge or manipulate data—including biometrics technology and its realism—develops as well. In fact, there are hundreds of different technologies and programmes available to forge or manipulate data. These can be spoofing attacks, adversarial attacks or digital manipulation attacks [6]. Similarly, the topics of digital security have become the cornerstone for further development of the information society. Identity theft has become a significant concern for individuals, organizations, and businesses and has directed all relevant stakeholders to work on secure digital identity solutions.

Until recently, government-issued identity documents, including strong electronic identity which serves as a means for authentication or electronic signature, have been exclusively issued as a part of a face-to-face customer onboarding process. Checking a person's physical presence has been an essential part of identity enrolling procedures to avoid the risk of identity forgery. Yet, several weaknesses, including face morphing attacks (digital image alterations), have been identified in document issuing processes. With synthetic media and artificial intelligence generated, like 'deep fakes', it is becoming increasingly difficult to identify a true identity from a fake one. Various approaches are being applied to tackle this, including taking the identity document photo in the application office, i.e., live enrolment. Even this is a break with tradition for many countries and entails a sizeable overhaul in the public sector, which can be reluctant to change and often lacks the necessary formal methods that ensure a smooth transition. Behind the successful implementation of live enrolment is proper risk management: covering technological, political, and organizational risks, but also understanding cultural differences, potential ethical challenges and addressing them [7].

It has also been suggested that in improving identity management and identity documents, the focus should be primarily on breeder documents that generally lack standardised and security features and are generally considered to be a weak link in the government-issued identity documents chain. The introduction of biometric data to the breeder documents or introduction of centralized biometric identity databases would be technically feasible for establishing a stronger link between the birth certificate and the respective document holder. As another solution, it has also been suggested to issue identity cards instead of birth certificates to newborns immediately from birth. This can be implemented relatively quickly, avoiding the costs of development, international standardization and introduction of a completely new (breeder) document. Again, the collection and processing of biometric data are clearly subject to ethical and societal concerns, especially when the collection and use of infants' biometric data is concerned [8].

Furthermore, increasing international mobility, the COVID-19 pandemic, and a greater priority on user convenience poses a significant challenge to the established onboarding rules and procedures. This is especially true when it comes to issuing a national electronic identity or opening bank accounts internationally. A silver bullet is being sought—the remote customer onboarding and identity verification solutions— which would eliminate the barriers that stem from a physical distance while offering at least equal or better onboarding processes than face-to-face identity verification with the physical presence of a person.

In this chapter, we research the requirements of the different use-cases of remote identity verification solutions for identity onboarding, including the main risks and challenges from ethical, societal and privacy perspectives. We hypothesise that automated identity verification technologies based on biometric algorithms that ensure a person's presence and vital state, while also protecting one's identity through advanced security techniques, are key elements for a secure and reliable remote solution. However, next to developing technically superior solutions, there are also non-technical requirements to ensure the accuracy of the claimed identity presented during the identity onboarding process, such as the user's context-awareness of the person who is enrolled via the remote solution, the trustworthiness of identity provider, and the social and ethical issues.

After the current introductory section, the chapter will establish the need for remote identity verification based on the rapid spread of identity theft and people's expectations. In section three, the emergence of remote biometric identity verification technologies is discussed, and use cases are introduced. These are then discussed from the perspectives of ethics, privacy and societal acceptability in section four. The chapter concludes with the discussion and conclusions.

20.2   Identity Theft and the Emerging Need for Remote Identity Verification

20.2.1   Risks and Societal Implications of Identity Theft

Obtaining someone else's personal information or identity document (ID), such as an identity card or passport, is where identity fraud begins, and it is becoming increasingly popular [9, 10]. With a stolen identity, the fraudster can effectively become someone else, allowing them to access the victim's financial or other accounts, access communications, set up new contracts, or present false information to the authorities. This is not only a violation of privacy but may bring about substantial financial and/or legal consequences to the victim. Evidence is also available on the associated major social and psychological impacts [9, 11].

In our earlier research [11, 12], it has been concluded that roughly 25–30% of the population of Austria, France, Germany, Italy, Spain, and United Kingdom have experienced some form of attempted or confirmed misuse of personal information over the period of 2013–2015. Only 10% of these cases were detected before personal information was actually taken. Thus, around 100 million citizens were forced to take extra steps to protect their identity during a 3-year period in the EU. Almost half of them had to do so more than once, as they experienced multiple incidents. As a result of the misuse of personal information, close to 40 million EU citizens have experienced significant personal consequences, such as debt collectors contacting them, problems with their family or friends, being denied a new service, having to face legal problems, etc.

The total value of the money, goods or services obtained by criminals from 2013 to 2015 was roughly 12–16 billion euros in the EU. This is, however, only the "consumer side". From the misuse of personal information, various institutional actors, e.g., financial or health insurance institutions, are likely to have incurred additional financial losses that are unknown to the individuals and, therefore, not reflected in this study [11, 12]. For instance, in the United States of America, Internal Revenue Service has estimated that it paid 4 billion euros in fraudulent identity theft refunds in filing season 2013, while preventing fraudulent refunds of 18 billion euros (based on what they could detect) [13]. It is within reason than to assume that, given the above example, the rough financial cost of identify in Europe reflects only the tip of the iceberg.

Other studies such as those commissioned and co-operated on by the United States Department of Justice and the Bureau of Justice Statistics [14, 15] have studied identity theft issues in recent years and confirm the scale and growth of the problem.

Javelin's 2020 Identity Fraud Study concludes that total identity fraud reached 15 billion euros in 2019 while criminals are targeting smaller numbers of victims and inflicting damage that is more complex to prevent or remediate. The research states that "the type of identity fraud has drastically changed from counterfeiting credit cards to the high-impact identity fraud of checking and savings account takeover. At a time when consumers are feeling financial stress from the global health and economic crisis, account takeover fraud and scams will increase" [16].

Eurobarometer survey on cyber security from 2020 [17] is also reflecting raising concerns: as compared to the study from 2017 [18], less Europeans feel they can protect themselves sufficiently against cybercrimes (59%, down from 71% in 2017). Three key concerns are related to falling victim to the bank card or online banking fraud (67%), the infection of devices with malicious software or identity theft (both 66%), and 6% of the respondents have actually experienced identity theft 2017–2019 [17].

20.2.2   The Need for Remote Biometric Identity Verification

Based on the increasing sophistication of attacks and the number of actual cases of identity theft, the need for strong electronic identity is especially clear in online services. The following three key arguments are developed: (1) on the importance of the strong electronic identity solutions, (2) on the importance and acceptance of the biometric solutions and (3) on the emerging need for remote identity onboarding methods.

First, earlier research has shown that the public has little trust in the security of popular Internet services, such as e-mail or Facebook [19]. Widespread misuse of Internet accounts, bank accounts and credit cards does not foster trust in these services. However, the personal experience with the attempted abuse or misuse of personal information does not lead to the decline of confidence in government issued identity documents. Confidence in government issued electronic identity cards and passports remains very high [20, 21] and is likely to be because the misuse of government issued identity documents remains infrequent in citizens' view as compared to other forms of identity fraud.

Government issued electronic identity solutions for online transactions are, thus, an obvious choice for bolstering security of Internet services and broadening the use of electronic authentication and signatures both in public and private applications. Furthermore, front-runner countries' experience in the widespread acceptance of electronic identity documents, such as Estonia, shows that mobile ID can serve as a convenient and secure alternative to more traditional electronic identity cards. In fact, the majority of the users of mobile ID seldom turn back to their electronic identity card when online authentication on Internet or electronic signature is required.

Furthermore, people who have experienced misuse of personal information are more likely to prefer identity documents that are more difficult to misuse, e.g., when lost or stolen. Victims of the misuse of personal information are also more likely to accept modern forms of online authentication, such as electronic identity cards or mobile ID, including in combination with fingerprints or other biometrics.

Second, the importance and acceptance of biometric solutions have increased considerably, and such technologies should be preferred in identification solutions. The direct aim of biometric technology (which includes biometric identifiers like face and fingerprints) is to enhance the reliability of identification. Biometrics is a tool used to identify and reliably confirm an individual's identity based on physiological or behavioural characteristics (or a combination of both) that are unique to a specific human being. Since biometrics provides a close link between the physical person and identity credential, e.g., a government issued identity document, it is considered a strong form of identification technology [21].

Biometric identification can be applied and regarded as part of a more extensive security system for identity management in a restricted security environment or system (e.g., an eBank) to distinguish one person from another and decide whether the specific person has access rights to the environment. It can also be used within broader security systems to ensure legal access to a state or area, such as the Schengen area. Thus, the use of biometrics in border guard solutions can be used to identify illegal immigrants or people who have been blacklisted as international criminals or terrorists.

The use of biometrics has the potential to raise the effectiveness and trust level in transactions, procedures and systems where the verification or identification of a person is necessary. Use of biometric traits, for example fingerprints or faces, ensures with high probability that the person identified is the person he or she claims to be and thus can be reliably related to his or her rights, entitlements, actions and responsibilities. In other words, biometric "data" does not need to be remembered and kept somewhere in secret, as a human's biometric features cannot be forgotten or lost [22, 23]. This, in turn, can create more conventional and more reliable alternative to traditional authentication methods, such as passwords.

However, the reliability of identities and identity documents depends largely on the overall security of the issuing process, from the person's registration in the support system (e.g., information system managing identity issuance) to the overall organisation of the issuance. Every link in this trust chain must be secure. If it emerges, for example, that a passport (including its chip) is technically difficult to forge, criminals will look for more easily exploitable weak spots such as issuance process, corrupt officials or information system weaknesses in order to forge an identity.

Biometrics as a form of identity technology has many advantages over traditional means of identification like personal identification numbers (PIN), passwords or token-based approaches. It is difficult to forge or duplicate a person's biometric trait; as such, it can prevent identity theft or rule out the use of several identities by a single individual. Also, biometric identification is more convenient compared to other identification tools or methods, since biometrics is 'what you are'—and therefore always at hand [24]. But because of this connection there are also considerable risks related to the use of biometrics (see more in section three). Nevertheless, each biometric characteristic (and the method used to capture it) has strengths and weaknesses regarding their universality, uniqueness, permanence, collectability, performance, acceptability and circumvention [24]. Therefore, often multi-modal biometrical systems are considered. For example, ePassports and some of the electronic identity cards combine face and fingerprints. Also, not every biometric approach is suitable for every implementation context. Some higher security processes would require authoritative identity source against enrolled biometrics to be verified (for example enrolled facial image against some register or reliable identity document). For some biometrics enrolment must take place in a controlled and secure environment using special equipment that is not available for normal user (enrolling fingerprints and sending to service provider, for example, or iris scan). Some biometrics is also under special legal protection, where its enrolment and use are legally restricted (fingerprints in some countries, for example).

Third, we would argue that there is clear need for remote identification methods for identity onboarding. Until recently, government issued electronic identity documents, but also electronic identity means or electronic signature certificates on the highest security level have been exclusively issued based on the physical face-to-face customer onboarding.

However, increasing international mobility and greater priority on user convenience, but also the COVID-19 pandemic, challenge the established onboarding rules and procedures. This is especially true when it comes to issuing electronic identity or opening bank accounts internationally. A silver bullet is being sought (the remote customer onboarding and identity verification solutions), which would eliminate the barriers that stem from physical distance, while offering at least equal or even better onboarding processes in comparison to face-to-face identity verification with physical presence of a person.

Novel remote onboarding processes have recently appeared on the market; they vary from human-assisted video identification procedures to biometric-based automated verification procedures. Earlier research has concluded that a considerable aspect in successful implementation of biometric technology is public trust and acceptability. Generally speaking, distrust among citizens regarding the technology, be it deployment difficulties, inconvenience, false acceptance rates or else, lowers the general trust in that technology among individuals but also state agencies deploying that technology [20, 21].

20.3 Remote Biometric Identity Onboarding Technologies

20.3.1 Emergence of Biometric Remote Identity Onboarding

There are several modalities for issuing identity documents in operation in Europe. In some of the countries, specialised passport offices of the national government provide identity documents to citizens. In other countries, regional or local governments issue documents. At the more detailed organisational level, there is even more of a variability in enrolment approaches, e.g., whether the enrolment of document data takes place on the site of document issuing authority or remotely, live or not live, under different levels of supervision (attended, semi-attended, automated controlled or uncontrolled), with centralised or decentralised data storage, professional or non-professional acquisition of biometric data, by capturing a single modality or multiple biometric modalities in the same session, with a data processing system developed by the public administration or by a private company.

Traditionally, professional photographers have been put in charge of capturing the facial images, which were then handed as print-out or digital file to the issuer of identity documents. However, this approach is prone to unwanted morphing of facial images. Therefore, live or semi-live by an official or in an official photo-booth that is located in a controlled environment have become preferable. But, there is an increasing need to allow also for completely remote enrolment, including the capture of the facial image and the data from the previously issued identity document.

In 2020, European Union Agency for Cybersecurity (ENISA) conducted a research mapping down identity verification practices used in different European countries for identity onboarding. ENISA concluded that identity onboarding technologies could be divided into several categories: "onsite with the operator, video with the operator, remote automatic, electronic identification means, certificate based and combined" [25]. The first, second, and the final onboarding categories listed above require a real time presence by both the verifier and the applicant, which can be challenging to organise when performing identification procedures on a daily basis (i.e., banking). The remaining three methods—remote automatic, based on the electronic identification means and certificates—are representing solutions that can be used remotely and at the convenience of the person.

Traditional identity checking methods have their obvious shortcomings. Most notably, physical identity checks require that the person checking the identity and the applicant must be present at the same place. This is a requirement that can prove "complicated, time consuming, and given the recent pandemic crisis even dangerous for health-related reasons" [25]. Contrastingly, remote verification solutions like remote verification by AI based on facial biometrics (often labelled "selfie-id"), electronic authentication methods (fingerprint scanners on phones) or certificate-based solutions (electronic signatures) makes it easier to identify the person and prove their physical existence but without any requirement of physical presence at an official enrolment station.

Hence, the significance of remote identity proofing methods for identity onboarding is increasing, especially in cross-border applications in Europe and elsewhere. The ENISA study found that 23 of 30 trust service providers (TSP) surveyed already used remote identity proofing methods as a part of their services in 2020. The most widely used method (used by 11 TSPs) is the remote method with a verifying operator (typically based on synchronous audio–video call) while the second most popular option involves electronic identification means, incl. notified electronic identification schemes. Remote automatic processes based on AI processing of the applicant's picture (selfie) and a picture of ID is recorded for four TSPs. As such, it demonstrates the wide interest of TSPs and companies in using remote proofing methods and the increasing interest towards this field. This is further illustrated by Fig. 20.1 where it could be seen that remote identity proofing is already allowed and practiced in extensive number of the EU member states. TSPs indicated to extend the number of remote identity proofing methods or introduce new ones; six TSPs plan to offer remote automatic identification based on AI [25].

What is currently missing is a unified approach and common regulatory framework in terms of remote identity verification. The absence of commonly accepted practices has resulted in a situation where different initiatives emerge across countries which share some common elements but also numerous differences that can lead to challenges related to the disjointed nature of remote identification policies. As such, even though the remote identity verification technologies are becoming more popular, the importance of cross-country recognition and legislation together with technical know-how and uniformity in methods and practices across the countries might help to strengthen and advance the development of a synchronized and secure

Fig. 20.1 Geographical map of the remote identity proofing practice for any (regulated) purpose [25]

remote identity verification solutions. Key to solving some of these challenges lies not just on public and private sector cooperation, but also on interoperability between governments issued electronic identity systems and private sector electronic identities [26].

Financial sector is generally considered as frontrunner in digital transformation and in the development of electronic services. For example, banks have been historically identified as the 'informal' leaders of the Estonian software industry and have generated overall trust towards ICT due to their successful implementation of internet banking services [27, 28]. Financial sector is also currently one of the prominent fields where cross-border identification solutions are being sought, as the need for having bank accounts in many countries and onboarding international clients in the twenty-first century is growing. A few years ago, financial institutions started to onboard new customers remotely in non-face-to-face processes. This takes place both on the domestic level as well as across the national borders using commercial identity verification solutions. The mobile payment apps, such as Wise, Revolut or Monzo, exemplify a hot arena for remote customer onboarding that builds on (live) facial images and on the government issued identity documents. The biometric identify verification technologies acquired by the financial institutions to help them verify the identity of their customers *en masse* and with a higher accuracy than a human operator could offer. But of course, the challenges that the banks face are broader than just identity checks and include such aspects as credit referencing, address verification, employment checks, income verification etc. Thus, the need for cross-border solutions for remote identity verification solutions makes financial sector one of the main domains where novel technological solutions are pioneered (like using blockchain, decentralised identity networks, "trusted events", non-standard identity sources, etc.) [26].

ETSI, the European standardisation organisation, has ongoing activities regarding standardizing identity proofing for the trust services (issuing e-signature and e-seal certificates). ETSI has prepared new standard for policy and security requirements for trust service components providing identity proofing of trust service objects [29]. There is the expectation that this standard would be of use not only for trust services but also for other means of electronic identity (which are usually issued by state authorities) and for the financial sector, especially for anti-money laundering (AML) and know your customer (KYC) processes. This calls for synchronising identity proofing area more widely, including physical identity verification and remote identification.

Typically, remote identification solutions rely on biometric verification, unless a new identity is based on an already issued electronic identity that can be verified during the onboarding either by the means of on-line authentication or qualified electronic signature. Biometric verification that takes place during the remote enrolment process assumes the existence of an authoritative source that a newly issued (secondary) identity could be based on. In the absence of such possibility, a more thorough process would be required for the identification of the person (analogue of refugee identification process for example), while risk of creating a new double identity cannot be completely avoided.

The almost only biometric characteristic that can be viably used for remote identification is the facial image. It is a universal and accessible means that allows for enrolment of identity in an environment that is not strictly controlled; it is compatible with accessible primary authoritative sources (e.g., travel documents, databases) and is a mature technology with presentation attack detection mechanisms.

Other biometric data, such as fingerprints or eye iris image, are not suitable for enrolment to create the new identity for a person in uncontrolled remote environment, as there is no suitable reference data available from authoritative sources, the access to such sources is restricted by the law or undesirable from ethics and privacy points of view. Thence, other biometric characteristics beyond face images are only usable in multimodal applications, e.g., fingerprints can replace a PIN code as a part of access control.

Last but not the least, putting the biometrics based remote identification solutions into use assumes the existence of high-level presentation attack detection methods and a security system that is in regular re-assessment and improvement in terms of the detection of new attack-vectors and mitigation of emerging risks. In other words, on-going enhancement of the face morphing and other presentation attack detection methods is absolutely crucial.

20.3.2 Biometric Remote Identity Onboarding Technologies

Based on two above-mentioned studies [25, 26], the main methods regarding remote biometric identity verification technologies for identity onboarding could be approached as follows:

First, **human assisted video identity verification** is, for the time being, perhaps the most popular onboarding method. The method is similar to face-to-face onboarding, except that the presence of applicant is not physical, but the communication takes place through a secure audio and video communication channel. In this process, a human operator carries out the person's identity verification in a similar way compared to the physical process, i.e., checks if the national identity document is authentic and valid, reads/copies data from this document, and compares visually, if the facial image from identity document against the face of the applicant. The operator plays the central role and makes decision about verification match and whether to issue a new identity to the applicant.

The main weakness of this method is that operator alone may not be able to detect document forgeries, image, or video forgeries, etc. without the assistance of a specialised software, as advanced presentation attacks are impossible to detect with a "bare human eye". Also, this case physical MRTD-s are used, forged documents detection is easier and document integrity controls are more advanced with eMRTD-s. This can potentially be software assisted where a software is used for checking the authenticity of the document and for verifying whether the person who visible in a live video session is a high-probability match with the facial image in document. In this way, extra steps can be taken to ensure that the video session is not manipulated and attacked.

The second method for identity verification is **automated remote identity verification solutions** that base their decisions solely on machine-learning systems. The process is conducted and guided by a dedicated software application that carries out automated steps of data collection and comparison without operator's intervention. Usually, the onboarding starts with reading/capturing identity document of applicant, i.e., picture or video of identity document. Thereafter, facial verification takes place by taking a short video of the applicant and comparing the live facial image in a video against the portrait photo in the identity document. On the back end, this includes security checks against a presentation attack by checking liveness of person, etc.

When the validation and security checks are satisfied, an automatic system decides whether to issue a new identity or to cancel the issuance. An automatic system does not mean that there could not be monitoring and alerting system, where if there is suspicious activity or uncertain events the human operator can intervene and decide what to do. Here, the biometrical verification system and supporting presentation attack detection systems play a crucial role as they must ensure that this particular person is the same person as he or she presents. Also, the identity document and its authenticity are very important as it is usually the only trustworthy and widely recognised source against which the identity of the applicant can be compared. But for automated purposes, not every identity document is suitable and sufficiently secure, only documents that comply to ICAO 9303 standard for biometrically enabled Machine-Readable Travel Document (eMRTD) meet such expectations. Usually, eMRTD includes facial image, fingerprint (optionally) and/or iris images and also provides data authenticity and integrity controls (PKI based passive and active authentication).

The weakness of this method lies primarily in whether the solution can be manipulated by attackers (phishing). Therefore, the applicant's awareness is crucial—whether she or he understands the context of transaction and purpose for which his/her data are collected and used. Security measures shall be implemented in such a way that the presentation attack or phishing adversary could not easily assume the context of the transaction and the purpose for which the applicant's data would be used.

Third, **combined video identity verification**. Identity verification tasks are carried out mainly by machine learning systems based on biometrical verification (in development for France and Spain eID-s). Combined method is defined as mixing video session, where the main verification functions are carried out by AI and machine learning systems and assisted by a human operator who interacts where necessary or to make a final decision to issue an identity. The human operator can understand and can check the person's motivation and awareness for this procedure. This method addresses weaknesses from the previous alternatives and is suitable in the context where other measures are not appropriate.

The main objective of combined methods is to bind the applicant's biometric data with the biometric data contained in government-issued identity document (as a trustworthy source) and make sure that the claimed identity and captured live biometric data match with different security measures. Here, "liveness" of the person participating in the onboarding process and his/her awareness of identity verification context (for which purposes identity verification is carried out) are as important as in previous methods.

The remote identity onboarding solutions require electronic identity solutions that can be handed over remotely (for example mobile phone application and server or cloud-based solutions) or physical carrier of electronic identity can be delivered in secure way so that only rightful person can receive and activate the identity token. For reading eMRTD-s, NFC reader enabled mobile phones are needed. Thus, it means that availability of these kind of remote solutions are limited with certain technical capabilities and enabling technologies.

Remote identity onboarding use-cases where the newly created identity will be used for further transactions and where physical presence of applicant is usually needed are (1) banks issuing authentication means for online banking customers or providing access to e-merchants customers using electronic wallet; (2) public authorities or identity providers for issuing e-identity means (for authentication) in public or private services; and (3) trust service providers for issuing e-signature certificates and/or devices. Use cases for single electronic transactions that need in-person or remote onboarding verification include the opening a bank account (AML and KYC requirements) and signing agreements which would normally require the physical presence of a person.

Today there are professional remote identity onboarding providers which offer video interviews, identity document check (both physical and digital), enrolment of biometric characteristics and biometric verification (with presentation attack measures) services. The largest providers are offering tailor-made customer solutions and/or service packages, concentrating on a specific service, like biometrics enrolment and verification or digital identity document check which will be integrated and orchestrated together within some remote identity verification service solution.

Also, mixed use-cases exist where trust service providers perform remote identity verification and linked to a specific bank customer. The main similarity for these different solutions is the biometric characteristics that are used, like facial biometrics and the recognition task itself. This type of solution is 1:1—meaning one-to-one biometrical verification; matching a biometric sample (video-selfie) with biometric reference data from a trusted source like a digital identity document (eMRTD) to prove a person's claim about his or her identity.

20.4 Ethics, Privacy and Societal Acceptability of Biometric Identity

20.4.1 Risks and Main Ethical Issues

In order to weigh values, assessing and identifying relevant risks (to values) and benefits of technology, defining the context is important [30, 31]. According to [30] and [32], technology can be viewed on different levels of abstraction: as a high-level socio-technical system (for example, technologies like biometrics, cloud computing, affective computing), as an artefact (hardware or smaller scale technical items, for example RFID chip) or at the level of applications of technology. The latter includes the use of technologies (and artefacts) for particular purposes and in specific settings/technical configurations (for example ePassport, specific solutions as for example smart (automated) CCTV for the identification of abnormal behaviour or specific kind of remote identity onboarding solutions). A particular high-level technology or artefact can raise different risks and ethical issues depending on the context and its application [30].

As we have seen from the use-cases above, the main functionality of remote identification solutions is to onboard the new identity for issuing e-identification/authentication means or e-signature devices for transactions to access certain systems (bank systems, specific e-service environments) and e-services or to perform single e-transactions. Identity verification of a person is based on face biometrics or theoretically may be based on other biometrical characteristics such as fingerprints or iris biometrics.

Biometrical characteristics are used mainly either for the purpose of establishing a subject's identity ("who is the person") or for verification/authentication ("is this the person who he claims to be?") in various information systems, but sometimes also to monitor abnormal activities and intentions using behavioural biometrical characteristics to profile a person [33].

Thus, there are two main ways of biometric comparison. The first is biometric *verification,* a one-to-one process in which the face of the authenticator/user is compared to the existing model. The second one is *identification*, which is a one-to-many process of comparing the authenticator's data to many existing samples in the database and seeking for the match [22]. The latter is more complex procedure as it involves not just authenticating the user, but also verifying the identity of the user. In both cases, biometric interaction starts from *enrolment* process when the initial biometric sample is constructed. This serves as a biometric template which is then stored in the database and is taken as a basis for *matching*, which takes place when the user scans biometric data in the future for recognition. This results in a *matching score* which is produced to reflect the level of similarity between the sample and the biometrics of authenticator [22].

So far, remote identity onboarding solutions have focused mainly on linking a person's data to his or her claimed identity. Thus, the aim is to make sure whether a person is who she or he claims to be by comparing biometrical data *one-to-one*.

This biometric recognition task and its possible privacy impact or consequences are less invasive than in the case of co-called *one-to-many* identification where person is searched from the crowd, databases or checklist and from the systems that use behavioural biometrics to monitor, detect, or profile a person based on some traits or behaviour pattern which may expose malicious intentions or dangerous activities (carrying explosives, etc.). Thus, different kinds of biometrical recognition tasks must be distinguished, since they entail different kind of security and privacy risks, and ethical considerations.

The main risk groups that are related to remote identity onboarding solutions are (1) falsified evidence, where the applicant applies for a false identity by using a forged document, or a manipulated video or photo, etc.; (2) identity theft, where applicant uses genuine evidence, which belongs actually to a different person; (3) phishing, where the attacker tries to get private or sensitive information with social engineering skills and pretends to be a trusted source/party to ultimately take over the identity of another person. The first two first risks groups are also addressed by European Telecommunications Standards Institute [29].

These risk groups/risks can have many risk sources including, technical system vulnerabilities or presentation attack detection system weaknesses, weak identity evidence with poor quality, to malicious social engineering, insider with malintent, brute force attacks, etc. Additionally, risks such as data leaks, data loss, or data integrity problems may cause consequences like identity misuse because of exposed identity data, and a user's rejection or discrimination etc. Also, unbalanced biometric dataset for biometric verification or identification testing, poor image quality etc. can increase the risk of a user´s rejection, discrimination, or accusations depending on the use-case. Possible consequences are discussed in the next sub-chapters about ethical values.

Regarding biometric identity verification for identity onboarding, the severity of consequences or harm are dependent on the use-case, including where and for which purposes biometric onboarding or use is implemented. If the use-case of onboarding is related to the single transaction—for example to sign some legal contract—then the practical consequence is limited with financial damage and privacy breach. However, if identity onboarding is for issuing certificates for authentication or electronic signature, then it would cause far-reaching identity damage, privacy breach, financial consequences or other problems for the person and critical reputational damage for the service provider.

Based on these above-mentioned risks and possible harms, the main ethical and social issues that will be raised in remote onboarding solutions case are (1) harming integrity of personal identity and misuse of it; (2) privacy and function creep; (3) ethical issues that are raising from algorithmically driven actions and decisions; and (4) public acceptance of technology.

20.4.2   Integrity of Practical Identity

Biometrics includes an individual biometric feature in the form of a physiological or anatomical attribute or distinctive behaviour that reflects "What I am" [29]. Biometrical information is representing and defining the person—his/her "informatized" body [34], or embodied identity. When we link personal information as name and some other kind of identifiers to the biomedical or "embodied" information— the practical identity of a person is created. This practical identity is included into identity systems and identity data processing activities.

When we talk about the risks for identity manipulation, the integrity the person's practical identity is in danger because through this practical identity and identity verification he/she is not proving his/her identity claim only but also or his/her rights, entitlements, ownership, and benefits. In case of remote identity onboarding solutions, new electronic identity will be issued based on biometrical verification. Your identity and corresponding data brings new entitlements, benefits, and/or rights, i.e., access to e-services and social benefits. The central component of the practical identity concept is the idea of an autonomous or self-determining person who is held accountable for his/hers reasons, motives, and actions. "If someone else engages in manipulation of a person's identity, that person is not fully able to use his own rights and entitlements; in the worst case, someone else will do this in their stead" [33]. As discussed above, identity theft can be severely damaging to a person, creating financial, legal, social, and psychological problems.

Biometric data are irreversible—they cannot be revoked because biometric traits are unique. If such data is copied and forged or confused, the data owner will have great difficulty proving that he or she is unconnected to the instances of use of the data or that identity is not created by themselves. At the same time, in the remote identity onboarding process context, the main objective of biometric verification is again to mitigate risks of identity loss and identity theft so that no one can pass him- or her-self off as someone else and thereby make use of the rights, entitlements and benefits belonging to another individual.

Therefore, regarding remote identity onboarding solutions, the security and integrity measures play a crucial role for detecting identity forgery or theft, or other vulnerabilities that might compromise the identity and the trust of those kind of identity systems. That presumes from the service provider a mature risk and a security management system.

20.4.3   Privacy and Function Creep

The recent studies have shown that the loss or violation of privacy as a result of potential data leaks and data disclosure, identity theft, misuse of personal data, and other risks remain the main ethical and social concerns in terms of using biometrics.

There are several privacy definitions; thus, it is important to define how it is used in the context of this chapter. Here, the privacy normative conception is used and can be described as limited to the 'sphere' surrounding the person, within which that person has the right to control access to himself or herself. Privacy is further defined as "the person's right to decide to what extent other persons can access and use information concerning him or her, and who those persons are who have access to his or her physical body; those who access and use physical/intimate space surrounding the person" [35].

Privacy is mostly regarded as instrumental value because it protects other values or interests of a person. The most favoured theoretical argument is that privacy protects a more fundamental value that of individual autonomy [36–38]. The modern concept of privacy implies respect for the autonomy of a person. In the field of scientific research, this is connected with the moral and legal claim for informed consent before intervention in other people's lives and the person's right to the self-identification that forms the core of a person's autonomy [33]. Also, [39] and [40] discuss privacy, individual value of autonomy and value of privacy in social construction of relationships and interaction. Steeves and Regan suggest that "/…/ privacy is an inherently social practice that enables social actors to navigate the boundary between self/other and between being closed/open to social interaction" [39].

How does this definition of privacy fit into the identity onboarding solution and biometrical data processing context? Mainly it means that biometrical data must be collected and used with a person's clear and informed consent, and this consent is basically autonomous act of a person to authorize data processing in the scope and on aims presented to the person. Thus, it means that presenting the transaction context to the person and clearly stating the conditions of data processing are crucial. Data processed without consent generally occurs when the party obtaining data forgets to ask for consent, and data are disclosed because of data leakage, hacker re-used some vulnerability to get personal data or even gains access to the person's data through hacking. These examples constitute a form of privacy loss as the person did not authorized the data processing activity. Also, as privacy is the instrumental value—the breach of privacy usually results in consequences from inconvenience of leaked biometrical images, until serious practical identity loss—where someone else is using your identity, accessing, and stealing your property, savings etc.

There is one special kind of privacy breach—namely "function creep". In short, function creep is the situation where someone's personal data (including biometric data) is used by the government or another data-processing body beyond the scope for which it was initially intended and informed to the person [20, 21]. It is important to understand that what this situation entails is not just the violation of privacy by the authorities but also their abuse of rights and exercising more power than they were granted. This can have social repercussions meaning that it could not be guaranteed that the databases of biometrics possessed by the state or service provider will be used solely for identity verification purposes as initially intended. For instance, the lack of transparency in processing biometric data means that the state or service provider could use it for covert mass-surveillance and identification of suspects [20, 21], profiling and etc. This sort of privacy loss is related with value of self-determination and right to not be discriminated.

Privacy is not an absolute value but one that varies between individuals and cultures especially when it comes into contact with other values. In practice people routinely face trade-offs and balancing acts such as privacy vs. security (e.g., at airports) or convenience like regarding remote identity onboarding solutions. According to [41] privacy is a complex decision problem—subjective perceptions of threats and potential damages, psychological needs, and actual personal returns all play a role in affecting decisions to protect or to share personal information. However, Acquisti and Grossklags refer to problems in privacy valuation: incomplete and asymmetric information about privacy-related contexts, risks and outcomes of trade-offs and inconsistent decisions (due to uncertainty and limited knowledge about future events, people's behaviour, emotional judgements etc.), which may result in a dichotomy between attitudes and actual behaviour [41]. Also, people may not really have alternative choices for using technologies, services, etc. which may jeopardize their privacy (but not necessarily) [20].

Remote identity onboarding solutions are generally designed to soften the consequences of a crisis (as COVID-19) or to offer connivance services instead of processes where a person might have to travel hundreds of kilometres to get the desired or needed electronic identity token. At the same time, providers of identity boarding solutions recognize that there is a need for identity security monitoring to compare biometrical data not only 1:1 for creating a new identity but also matching identity with already known adversaries etc. Also, as we saw above, remote identity onboarding solutions are vulnerable to attacks against enrolment and verification of biometrical data or presented evidence, thus a system of presentation attack detection security control must be built up. To ensure transparency and trustworthiness of data processing, the context awareness checks and informed consent must be at the core of privacy policies. To this end, data protection laws and information security best practices must be followed.

20.4.4 Ethical Issues Raising from Algorithmically Driven Actions and Decisions

Kloppenburg and Van der Ploeg, prominent scholars in the surveillance studies and biometrics have conceptualised the nature of biometrics in terms of bodily differences and automated discrimination. They point out normative assumptions of biometric recognition that everybody has unique bodily characteristics and at the same time people in essence are similar, thus the human bodily features are defined into the range of different human features. The "normalized" bodily features are defined and built into algorithms, systems or equipment. Bodily differences and automated discrimination appear in multiple ways as for example with demographic distributions in a training set for tuning algorithms, quality of images, setting thresholds for false negatives and positives etc. [42]. Hidalgo also points out that "interestingly, the use of learning and training sets, as well as the obscurity of deep learning, makes algorithms similar to humans by providing them with a form of culturally encoded and hard-to-explain intuition" [43].

Indeed, a large-scale performance test about demographic effects was made by the National Institute of Standards and Technology (NIST) in 2019 [44]. The overall conclusion was that there is empirical evidence for the existence of demographic differentials in most evaluated face recognition algorithms. But different algorithms perform differently, the most equitable also rank among the most accurate. Regarding identity verification (1:1), the main findings in this report suggest that for false positives, using higher quality photos rates are highest in the case of West and East African and East Asian people, and lowest in Eastern European individuals. With smaller impact, they found false positives to be higher in women than in men, also elevated in elderly and in children. For explanation that false positives may present security concerns, as this means that people with the wrong identity may pass identity verification. At the same time regarding 1:N, this would mean that for false positives, the person may be placed on some kind of "list"; which could lead to false accusations or a banned travel status. High quality false negatives are higher among Asian and American Indians, but African and Caribbean people, especially older people, false negatives triggered by lower quality border crossing images are higher. For those impacted by false negatives, this would mean wrongful rejection at border crossings and more inconvenience. Although the goal of the study was not to explore the causes and effects, it was noted that testing algorithms from different regions it seems to refer to the need for demographically more diverse training data [44].

As mentioned previously, in the case of remote identity onboarding solution biometrical recognition task 1:1 biometrical verification is used. For the person who is rejected as a false negative, it may bring some inconveniences, as he or she will be not allowed to get digital identity from distance and must go to the physical customer service point if alternative onboarding services are not available. Certainly, it does not foster digital inclusion in the e-society. Tolerance ranges are not usually open and obvious, which makes societal scrutiny also difficult [45].

False positives also play a crucial role in remote identity onboarding solutions. Weak algorithms or racial and sex biased solutions can accidentally associate a person with the wrong identity and issue a new identity. This then leads back to the integrity of a person's practical identity and how it can be misused.

Another issue concerns the automatic machine-learning and AI based decisions about human proceedings and actions. What are the contexts and situations where purely machine judgments are adequate in rational and moral sense and in which context should the human operator assist? Of course, biometrical recognition systems are very limited in their functions and decision power, there are moral implications embedded into algorithms and automated decisions (as discrimination), but it is hard to see the moral agent behind it. An interesting study was conducted 2018 by NIST researchers compared the performance of automated identification software to human participants who were identifying people using biometric verification and highly challenging image pairs. The conclusion was that the best face recognition algorithms worked in the range of the best humans: professional forensic facial examiners. However, optimal face identification was achieved only when humans and machines worked in collaboration [46].

Nevertheless, there is question how to control the quality of automated decisions in operation and who carries the responsibility if automated decisions has serious consequences, such as false identity or identity misuse.

20.4.5 Public Acceptance of Technology

One of the possible barriers for introducing new technologies is the risk that they will not be accepted by the users. To our knowledge there are no studies specifically on the acceptance of biometrics in remote identity onboarding available. However, one can learn from other studies undertaken on related biometric technologies.

Large scale biometrical systems were introduced in Europe with implementing the so-called ePassports. And, already since their introduction of ePassports, scholars have concluded that insufficient public information on the objectives of the utilisation of ePassports and eIDs and their rapid adoption without public discussion can escalate public fears and create a trust deficit.

Our own studies confirm an absence of public information regarding the functions of ePassports and biometric impacts of their implementation. In particular, many people seem to lack information regarding the role of biometrics, ePassports and their functioning. In other words, how are ePassports meant to make our life easier and in what ways are they more effective than traditional identification methods? How are they meant to increase our security? The unclear reasoning behind implementation of new solutions has a negative impact on their acceptability and may raise questions about their relevance [20]. An important aspect in successful implementation of biometric technology is public trust and acceptability. Generally speaking, distrust among citizens regarding the technology, be it deployment difficulties, inconvenience, false acceptance rates or else, lowers the general trust in that particular technology among individuals but also state agencies deploying that technology [20, 21].

Tiits et al. have also analysed public perceptions on a number of potential future uses of ePassports and related data. It is found that the majority of the general public also agrees with public entities using passport photos for identity checks. The public is, however, less willing to accept the government making use of fingerprints and even less so other biometric applications in making identity checks. The majority of respondents are, in fact, against the use of fingerprints or eye iris images in the case of low security services that do not require strong authentication of a person. The acceptability of private businesses making use of biometrics for identity checks follows largely the above pattern, even though acceptance levels are lower than for public authorities [20, 21]. However, since the study was published, the use of biometrics has become wider in consumer level devices and we expect the wider approval of facial images by the public, as has happened with the fingerprint images.

The study concluded with several recommendations which are valid for increasing the acceptance of the biometrics in remote identity onboarding. It was concluded that the number of people who are uninformed or undecided about various aspects of ePassports and their use, remains high. The expected benefits and risks of ePassports have received only limited attention in the public media sphere in most of the countries and more public debate is needed. However, increasing awareness on the technical aspects of ePassports will not necessarily lead to higher acceptance among the future generations of ePassports. What the public expects is that the benefits of specific uses of ePassports are clear, and, most importantly, proper technological and organisational measures are in place to secure that privacy is maintained and that the use of personal data is limited only to the purposes originally stated. It was also confirmed that the acceptability of technology is context-dependent and a function of a trade-off between expected benefits and perceived risks (costs). This is where earlier experience becomes crucial. The research shows that if people accept the use of advanced biometrics, such as fingerprints or eye iris images in one scenario, they are more willing to accept them in others. Thus, the successful pathway to greater acceptability for the use of advanced biometrics in ePassports should start from the introduction of perceivably high-benefit and low-risk applications [20, 21].

20.5   Discussion and Conclusions

Until recently, government-issued identity documents, including strong electronic identity, which serves as a means for authentication or electronic signature, have been exclusively based on face-to-face customer onboarding. Checking a person's physical presence has been an essential part of identity enrolling procedures to avoid the risk of identity forgery. Yet, several weaknesses, including face morphing attacks, have been identified in document issuing processes. With synthetic media and artificial intelligence generated 'deep fakes', it is becoming increasingly difficult to tell apart a true identity from a fake one. So, with the increasing availability of data manipulation tools, forgery has also become massive and widespread. Hence, identity theft has become a growing concern for individuals, organisations, and businesses and has directed all the stakeholders to work on secure digital identity solutions. Thereby, the establishment of a trustworthy (electronic) identity, the fight against identity theft and privacy protection have become the cornerstones for further development of the society.

Furthermore, increasing international mobility, the COVID-19 pandemic, and greater priority on user convenience poses a significant challenge to the established onboarding rules and procedures. This is especially true when it comes to issuing a national electronic identity or opening bank accounts internationally. A solution is being sought—the remote customer onboarding and identity verification solutions— which would eliminate the barriers that stem from a physical distance while offering at least equal or better onboarding processes than face-to-face identity verification with the physical presence of a person.

Biometrics is only reliable link for binding together identity evidence and the real person that can be presented through a video-session. Face biometrics is used and seems to be a suitable biometric option from different perspectives. The use of such biometrics has the potential to raise the effectiveness and trust level in transactions, procedures, and systems where the verification or identification of a person is necessary. Also, biometric identification is considered more convenient compared to other identification tools or methods. Recently, novel remote onboarding solutions have appeared on the market; they vary from human-assisted video identification procedures to biometric-based automated verification procedures. The almost only biometric characteristic that can be viably used for remote identification is the facial image. It is a universal and accessible means that allows for enrolment of identity in an environment that is not strictly controlled; it is compatible with accessible primary authoritative sources (e.g., travel documents, databases) and mature technology with presentation attack detection mechanisms exists. However, putting the biometrics based remote identification solutions into use assumes the existence of high-level presentation attack detection methods and a security system that is regularly assessed and improved in terms of the detection of new attack-vectors and mitigation of emerging risks. In other words, on-going enhancement of the face morphing and other presentation attack detection methods is absolutely crucial.

We have analysed different use-cases of remote identity verification solutions for identity onboarding, main risks, and challenges from ethical, societal and privacy perspectives. Automated identity verification technologies based on biometrical algorithms and security techniques to ensure a person's genuine presence and aliveness identifying presentation, deepfake replay, and other similar attacks are key elements for a secure and reliable remote solution. In addition, other non-technical requirements for the reliability of the claimed identity presented during the identity onboarding process—user's context-awareness while the person is enrolled via remote solution, the trustworthiness of identity provider, etc.—must be not underestimated and shall be addressed as well.

Regarding biometrical identity verification for identity onboarding severity of consequences or harm is dependent on the use-case, where and for which purposes biometric onboarding or use is implemented. If the use-case of onboarding is related to the single transaction, then the practical consequence is limited with financial damage and privacy breach. However, if identity onboarding is for issuing certificates for authentication or electronic signature, then it would cause far-reaching identity damage, privacy breach, potential financial harm, and other problems for a person and critical reputational damage for the service provider.

The main social and ethical issues with biometrics in remote identity onboarding are (1) the risk of harming integrity of personal identity and misuse of it; (2) the risk of privacy invasion and function creep; (3) ethical issues that are raising from algorithmically driven actions and decisions; and (4) public perception and social acceptance of technology. In the case of integrity of person's identity, during the identity theft or loss more than privacy will be harmed, the person could be refused access to services, lose control over their identity, and face damages which are done in their name.

Regarding privacy and function creep, the main issues are related to remote onboarding solutions where a person's data are used without his or her authorisation. In these cases, how the data is leaked—whether it be from a data leak or unsecure service, hackers (adversaries), or vulnerable data systems—is not as important as what the consequences were. For example, differences in consequences and harm i.e., financial harm or adverse consequences manifesting from the takeover of a person's identity. In case of remote systems using biometric recognition, it may be temptation to perform one-to-many matching for profiling, blacklisting etc., which could go beyond the data processing purposes authorized by and communicated to the persons.

Algorithmical decisions and actions refer to situations where a person who is rejected as a false negative may suffer from an inconvenience at the very least. As an example, he or she may be refused from remote onboarding for new digital identity and may be referred to go to the physical customer service point where an alternative face-to-face onboarding service is available. Likewise, false positives are a crucial risk factor in remote identity onboarding solutions. Overly loose algorithms or racially or gender biased solutions may associate a person erroneously to a wrong identity or assign a new identity to the wrong person altogether.

Finally, it is important to understand and address the potential public acceptance issues. The end goal to be to support activities that increase the awareness of the benefits and risks for using technologies and methodologies for biometric identification. This is particularly important regarding the benefits of specific uses of biometrics in remote identity onboarding and ensuring to the would-be users that the proper technological and organisational measures are in place to secure that privacy is maintained and that the use of personal data is limited only to the purposes originally stated.

These non-technical concerns and risks need to be addressed in developing identity verification technologies based on biometrical algorithms and security techniques. At the same time, introduction of such innovative solutions puts challenges to public administrations.

The absence of a unified approach, common regulatory framework and commonly accepted practices has resulted in a situation where different initiatives emerge across countries which share some common elements but also numerous differences that can lead to challenges related to interoperability. It is recommended to share between the EU member states (and beyond) the technical know-how, but also how social and ethical risks have been managed.

Acknowledgements This research was funded by the European Commission, grant number 883356—Image Manipulation Attack Resolving Solutions (iMARS).

References

1. Dufva T, Dufva M (2019) Grasping the future of the digital society. Futures 107:17–28
2. Tsekeris C (2018) Industry 4.0 and the digitalisation of society: curse or cure? Homo Virtual 1(1)4–12
3. Helbing D (2015) The automation of society is next: how to survive the digital revolution. Create space independent publishing platform
4. Boneh D, Grotto AJ, McDaniel P, Papernot N (2019) How relevant is the turing test in the age of sophisbots? IEEE Secur Priv 17(6):64–71
5. Nash C, Jarrahi M, Sutherland W, Phillips G (2018) Digital nomads beyond the buzzword: defining digital nomadic work and use of digital technologies. Lect Note Comput Sci Conf 2018:1–10
6. Dang H, Liu F, Stehouwer J, Liu X, Jain AK (2020) On the detection of digital face manipulation. In: 2020 IEEE/CVF conference on computer vision and pattern recognition (CVPR), pp 5780–5789
7. Kalvet T, Karlzén H, Hunstad A (2018) Live enrollment for identity documents in europe: the cases of Sweden, Norway, Kosovo, and Estonia. J Democr Open Gov 10(2):53–73. https://doi.org/10.29379/jedem.v10i2.517
8. Kalvet T, Tiits M, Laas-Mikko K (2019) Public acceptance of advanced identity documents. In: Ojo A, Kankanhalli A, Soares D (eds) Proceedings of the 11th international conference on theory and practice of electronic governance. Galway, Ireland, pp 429–432. https://doi.org/10.1145/3209415.3209456
9. Akdemir N (2021) Coping with identity theft and fear of identity theft in the digital age. In: López Rodríguez AM, Green MD, Kubica ML (eds) Legal challenges in the new digital age. Leiden, Koninklijke Brill NV, pp 176–197
10. Reyns BW (2018) Identity-related crimes. In: Reichel R, Randa R (eds) Transnational crime and global security. Praeger Security International, 161–179
11. Kalvet T, Tiits M, Ubakivi-Hadachi P (2019) Risks and societal implications of identity theft. In: Chugunov A, Misnikov Y, Roshchin E, Trutnev D (eds) Electronic governance and open society: challenges in Eurasia: 5th international conference, EGOSE 2018. St. Petersburg, Russia, Revised Selected Papers. Springer, 14–16 Nov 2018
12. Tiits M, Ubakivi-Hadachi P (2016) Societal risks deriving from identity theft. EKSISTENZ D9.2. Tartu: Institute of Baltic Studies
13. U.S. Government Accountability Office (2014) Identity theft: additional actions could help IRS combat the large, evolving threat of refund fraud. Report to congressional requesters, GAO, 14–633. https://www.gao.gov/assets/670/665368.pdf
14. Harrell E (2015) Victims of identity theft, 2014. Bureau of justice statistics. https://www.bjs.gov/content/pub/pdf/vit14.pdf
15. Oudekerk B, Langton L, Warnken H, Greathouse SM, Lim N, Taylor B, Welch V (2018) Building a national data collection on victim service providers: a pilot test. Bureau of justice statistics. https://www.ncjrs.gov/pdffiles1/bjs/grants/251524.pdf
16. Javelin (2020) Identity fraud study: genesis of the identity fraud crisis. https://www.javelinstrategy.com/coverage-area/2020-identity-fraud-study-genesis-identity-fraud-crisis
17. Kantar (2020) Europeans' attitudes towards cyber security. Special Eurobarometer 499. https://ec.europa.eu/commfrontoffice/publicopinion/index.cfm/survey/getsurveydetail/instruments/special/surveyky/2249#p=1&instruments=special&yearFrom=1974&yearTo=2017&surveyKy=2249
18. TNS Opinion & Social (2017) Europeans' attitudes towards cyber security. Special Eurobarometer 464a. https://ec.europa.eu/commfrontoffice/publicopinion/index.cfm/Survey/getSurveyDetail/instruments/special/yearFrom/1974/yearTo/2017/surveyKy/2171
19. Tiits M, Ubakivi-Hadachi P (2015) Common use patterns of identity documents. EKSISTENZ D9.1. Institute of Baltic Studies, Tartu
20. Tiits M, Kalvet T, Laas-Mikko K (2014) Analysis of the epassport readiness in the EU. FIDELITY deliverable 2.2. Institute of Baltic Studies, Tartu

21. Tiits M, Kalvet T, Laas-Mikko K (2014) Social acceptance of epassports. In: Brömme A, Busch C (eds) Proceedings of the 13th international conference of the biometric special interest group. IEEE Darmstadt

22. Buciu I, Gacsadi A (2016) Biometrics systems and technologies: a survey. Int J Comput Commun Control 11(3):315–330

23. Liljander A (2019) Attitudes towards biometric authentication technologies between cultures: acceptance in Finland and Brazil. Information systems, master's thesis, University of Jyväskylä

24. Jain AK, Bolle R, Pankanti S (1996) Biometrics. Personal identification in networked society. Boston, MA, Springer

25. European Union Agency for Cybersecurity (2021) Remote id proofing. Analysis of methods to carry out identity proofing remotely. https://www.enisa.europa.eu/publications/enisa-report-remote-id-proofing

26. European Commission (2019). Report on existing remote on-boarding solutions in the banking sector: Assessment of risks and associated mitigating controls, including interoperability of the remote solutions, Brussels: directorate-general for financial stability. Financial Services and Capital Markets Union. https://europa.eu/!rj88wv

27. Kalvet T (2012) Innovation: a factor explaining e-government success in Estonia. Electron Gov 9(2):142−157

28. Kalvet T, Aaviksoo A (2008) The development of eservices in an enlarged EU: egovernment and ehealth in Estonia. Office for Official Publications of the European Communities. Luxembourg

29. European Telecommunications Standards Institute (2020). Electronic signatures and infrastructures (ESI); policy and security requirements for trust service components providing identity proofing of trust service subjects. Draft ETSI TS 119 461 V0.0.5 (2020–12). https://docbox.etsi.org/esi/Open/Latest_Drafts/Draft%20ETSI-TS-119-461-v0.0.5.pdf

30. Stahl BC, Heersmink R, Goujon P, Flick C, Hoven van den J, Wakunuma KJ, Ikonen V, Rader M (2010) Identifying the ethics of emerging information and communication technologies: an essay on issues, concepts and method. Int J Tech 1(4)

31. Nissenbaum H (2010) Privacy in context. Technology, policy, and the integrity of social life. Stanford University Press, Stanford, California

32. Brey PAE (2012) Anticipating ethical issues in emerging IT. Eth Inf Tech 14(4)

33. Sutrop M, Laas-Mikko K (2012) From identity verification to behaviour prediction: ethical implications of second-generation biometrics. Rev Policy Res 29(1)

34. Ploeg I (2003) Biometrics, and the body as information: normative issues of the socio-technical coding of the body. In: Lyon D (ed) Surveillance as social sorting: privacy, risk, and digital discrimination. Routledge, London, New York

35. Laas-Mikko K, Sutrop M (2016) How Do violations of privacy and moral authonomy threaten the basis of our democracy? In: Delgado A (ed) Technoscience and citizenship: ethics and governance in the digital society. Springer, Cham, Switzerland

36. Gavison R (1980) Privacy and the limits of law. Yale Law J 89

37. Kupfer J (1987) Privacy, autonomy, and self-concept. Am Philos Q 24

38. Rössler B (2005) The value of privacy. Polity Press, Cambridge

39. Steeves V, Regan P (2014) Young people online and the social value of privacy. J Inf Commun Eth Soc 12(5)

40. Rössler B, Mokrosinska D (2013) Privacy and social interaction. Philos Soc Crit 39(8)

41. Acquisti A, Grossklags J (2007) What can behavioral economics teach us about privacy? In: Acquisti A, Gritzalis S, Di Vimercati S, Lambrinoudakis C (eds) Digital privacy: theory, technologies, and practices. Auerbach Publications

42. Kloppenburg S, Van der Ploeg I (2018) Securing identities: biometric technologies and the enactment of human bodily differences. Sci Cult 29(2)

43. Hidalgo C (2021) How humans judge machines. MIT Press, Cambridge

44. Grother P, Ngan M, Hanaoka K (2019) Face recognition vendor test (FRVT). Part 3: demographic effects. https://nvlpubs.nist.gov/nistpubs/ir/2019/NIST.IR.8280.pdf

45. Lyon D (2008) Biometrics, identification and surveillance. Bioethics 22(9)

46. Phillips PJ, Yates AN, Hu Y, Hahn CA, Noyes E, Jackson K, Cavazos JG, Jeckeln G, Ranjan R, Sankaranarayanan S, Chen JC, Castillo CD, Chellappa R, White D, O'Toole A (2018) Face recognition accuracy of forensic examiners, superrecognizers, and face recognition algorithms. PNAS 115 (24)

Chapter 21
Future Trends in Digital Face Manipulation and Detection

Ruben Tolosana, Christian Rathgeb, Ruben Vera-Rodriguez, Christoph Busch, Luisa Verdoliva, Siwei Lyu, Huy H. Nguyen, Junichi Yamagishi, Isao Echizen, Peter Rot, Klemen Grm, Vitomir Štruc, Antitza Dantcheva, Zahid Akhtar, Sergio Romero-Tapiador, Julian Fierrez, Aythami Morales, Javier Ortega-Garcia, Els Kindt, Catherine Jasserand, Tarmo Kalvet, and Marek Tiits

Abstract Recently, digital face manipulation and its detection have sparked large interest in industry and academia around the world. Numerous approaches have been proposed in the literature to create realistic face manipulations, such as DeepFakes and face morphs. To the human eye manipulated images and videos can be almost indistinguishable from real content. Although impressive progress has been reported in the automatic detection of such face manipulations, this research field is often

The original version of this chapter has been revised: Acknowledgement section has been updated. The correction to this chapter is available at https://doi.org/10.1007/978-3-030-87664-7_22

R. Tolosana (✉) · R. Vera-Rodriguez · S. Romero-Tapiador · J. Fierrez · A. Morales · J. Ortega-Garcia
Universidad Autonoma de Madrid, Madrid, Spain
e-mail: ruben.tolosana@uam.es

R. Vera-Rodriguez
e-mail: ruben.vera@uam.es

S. Romero-Tapiador
e-mail: sergio.romerot@uam.es

J. Fierrez
e-mail: julian.fierrez@uam.es

A. Morales
e-mail: aythami.morales@uam.es

J. Ortega-Garcia
e-mail: javier.ortega@uam.es

C. Rathgeb · C. Busch
Hochschule Darmstadt, Darmstadt, Germany
e-mail: christian.rathgeb@h-da.de

C. Busch
e-mail: christoph.busch@h-da.de

considered to be a *cat and mouse game*. This chapter briefly discusses the state of the art of digital face manipulation and detection. Issues and challenges that need to be tackled by the research community are summarized, along with future trends in the field.

21.1 Introduction

Over the last couple of years, digital face manipulation and detection has become a highly active area of research. This is demonstrated through the increasing number of workshops in top conferences [1–5], international projects such as MediFor and the recent SemaFor funded by the Defense Advanced Research Project Agency

L. Verdoliva
University of Naples Federico II, Naples, Italy
e-mail: verdoliv@unina.it

S. Lyu
University at Buffalo, Buffalo, USA
e-mail: siweilyu@buffalo.edu

H. H. Nguyen
The Graduate University for Advanced Studies, Hayama, Japan
e-mail: nhhuy@nii.ac.jp

J. Yamagishi · I. Echizen
National Institute of Informatics, Chiyoda City, Japan
e-mail: jyamagis@nii.ac.jp

I. Echizen
e-mail: iechizen@nii.ac.jp

P. Rot · K. Grm · V. Štruc
University of Ljubljana, Ljubljana, Slovenia
e-mail: peter.rot@fe.uni-lj.si

K. Grm
e-mail: klemen.grm@fe.uni-lj.si

V. Štruc
e-mail: vitomir.struc@fe.uni-lj.si

(DARPA), and competitions such as the Media Forensics Challenge (MFC2018)[1] launched by the National Institute of Standards and Technology (NIST), the Deep-fake Detection Challenge (DFDC)[2] launched by Facebook, and the recent Deeper-Forensics Challenge.[3]

Face manipulation techniques can erode trust in digital media through fake news and the spread of misinformation [6]. With the big impact of social networks on our daily life, disinformation can be easily widespread and influence the public opinion [7]. Its targets can be individuals, economy, or politics [8]. Manipulated videos have already been used to create political tensions, and the technology enabling their creation is being considered as a threat by various governments [9].

Motivated by those facts, researchers have proposed various techniques to detect digital face manipulations in the recent past [10, 11]. In addition, public databases have been made available and first benchmarks have been conducted by different research groups [12–17], proving the high potential of the latest manipulation detectors. Nonetheless, a reliable detection of manipulated face images and videos is still considered an unsolved problem. It is generally conceded that digital face manipulation detection is still a nascent field of research in which numerous issues and challenges have to be addressed in order to reliably deploy such methods in real-world applications.

This chapter concludes the book providing an overview of open issues and challenges in the field of digital face manipulation and detection. Limitations of state-of-the-art methods are pointed out and potential future research direction toward advancing both fields are summarized, including promising application areas as well as novel use-cases. Moreover, legal and societal aspects of digital face manipulation and detection are discussed, such as the legality and legitimacy of the use of the manipulation detection or the potentially conflicting right to "one's own image", among others.

A. Dantcheva
Inria Sophia Antipolis, Biot, France
e-mail: antitza.dantcheva@inria.fr

Z. Akhtar
State University of New York Polytechnic Institute, Utica, USA
e-mail: akhtarz@sunypoly.edu

E. Kindt
Universiteit Leiden, Leiden, Netherlands
e-mail: els.kindt@kuleuven.be

E. Kindt · C. Jasserand
KU Leuven, Leuven, Belgium
e-mail: catherine.jasserand@kuleuven.be

T. Kalvet · M. Tiits
Institute of Baltic Studies and TalTech, Tallinn, Estonia
e-mail: tarmo@ibs.ee

M. Tiits
e-mail: marek@ibs.ee

---

[1] https://www.nist.gov/itl/iad/mig/media-forensics-challenge-2018.

[2] https://www.kaggle.com/c/deepfake-detection-challenge.

[3] https://competitions.codalab.org/competitions/25228.

Listing currently unsolved problems in the field, this chapter is intended to serve as a starting point for new researchers in the field.

The remainder of this chapter is organized as follows: Sect. 21.2 briefly describes the current state of the art in face manipulation together with public available databases. The most relevant issues with respect to the detection of face manipulations are discussed in Sect. 21.3. In Sect. 21.4, future research directions and application areas are summarized. Subsequently, Sect. 21.5 discusses societal and legal aspects of face manipulation and detection. Finally, a summary is given in Sect. 21.6.

21.2 Realism of Face Manipulation and Databases

21.2.1 State of the Art

Face manipulation techniques have been improved significantly in the last years as discussed in Part II of the book. State-of-the-art techniques are able to generate fake images and videos that are indistinguishable to the human eye [10, 11, 18]. However, when considering automatic end-to-end manipulation techniques, the visual quality is not always stable and it depends severely on different aspects [17, 19–21]. Figure 21.1 shows some weaknesses that limit the naturalness and facilitate fake detection. We highlight next some of the most critical aspects:

- **Face detection and segmentation**, which is not 100% accurate [22, 23]: this problem becomes worse when input images or videos are in bad quality, e.g., bad lighting condition, noisy, blurry, or low resolution.
- **Blending manipulated faces into the original image or video**: although there have been improvements in the blending algorithms [19], artifacts at the edges of the manipulated and original regions still exist in many cases. In addition, mismatch between these two regions (e.g., lighting condition, skin color, or noise) can degrade the realism of the manipulated images/videos, making them easier to be detected.
- **Low-quality synthesized faces**: while progress has been made here thanks to Generative Adversarial Networks (GAN), for example, through the recent StyleGAN2 model [24] that is able to generate non-existent faces with high resolution, editing with such models through GAN inversion techniques is time consuming and computationally demanding. This computational complexity also hinders development of high-resolution video manipulation techniques. Basic techniques often generate low-resolution face images, typically between 64×64 and 256×256 pixels as discussed in Chap. 4 of the book.
- **Temporal inconsistencies along frames**: this is of special importance in face manipulations such as Audio-to-Video as discussed in Chap. 8 of the book: Are there any relationships between audio and other facial features such as eyes, teeth, and even head movements? Techniques based on 3D pose and expression could further benefit this research line [25].

Fig. 21.1 Weaknesses of automatic end-to-end face manipulations that limit the naturalness and facilitate fake detection

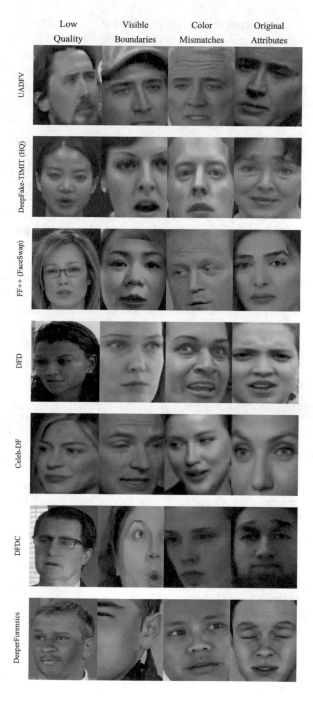

Apart from the aspects commented before, it is also interesting to highlight that most face manipulation techniques are currently focused only on the visual quality at pixel level [10, 11], to the best of our knowledge. Biological aspects of the human being should be also taken into account in the manipulation process, e.g., blood circulation (heart rate) and eye blink rate could be automatically extracted from the faces to detect whether the video is real or fake [26, 27], as discussed in Chap. 12.

21.2.2 Missing Resources

Although new public databases are being released recently, these generally lack diversity and include low-quality videos. Specifically, for image databases, GAN-based models have been proved to be very effective in creating realistic faces, but these are usually generated with one model (e.g., StyleGAN2 [24]) with one specific set of parameters [28–30]. Video databases, on the other hand, are plagued with low-quality synthesis results, exhibiting visible blurring or boundary artifacts. As a result, it is easy for current fake detectors to over-adapt to the specific characteristics of the generation method and artifacts. In addition, high-accuracy fake detection performances on databases containing significant fraction of low-quality videos will not be representative for the performance in real life.[4] To make the detection more challenging, databases need to improve on the types and variants of the generation models, post-processing steps, codecs, and compression methods, as well as adversarial attacks.

Furthermore, current databases are still small and monotonic compared with those in other areas like image classification or speech, e.g., ImageNet [31] or Vox-Celeb2 [32]. One of the largest databases, the DFDC dataset [12], only has 128,154 videos with less than 20 types of manipulation methods. Moreover, most databases only contain one or two subjects in an image or video except the recently released Face Forensics in the Wild (FFIW) database [33], and they are easily perceived (not a small subject in a crowd). It is also interesting to highlight that none of the databases contain manipulated or synthesized speech except the DFDC, but its manipulation is simple and is hard to be considered as "fake".

Finally, it is important to highlight two more missing resources in face manipulation: (i) the generation of manipulated face databases based on 3D manipulation techniques [34], and (ii) the generation of multimodal manipulated face databases as current ones are only focused on the manipulation of either audio or face visual information [35, 36].

---

[4] https://www.youtube.com/channel/UCKpH0CKltc73e4wh0_pgL3g.

21.3 Limitations of Face Manipulation Detection

21.3.1 Generalizability

The vast majority of existing face manipulation detection techniques have been evaluated only on known types of face manipulations or on a single database [10, 11]. In other words, the published empirical results showed performances of detectors under same train and test manipulation type/database. However, their performances usually drop significantly when evaluated under cross-manipulation setting (where train and test sets are not from the same manipulation type or database) [12, 19, 37, 38]. Therefore, reported detection performance rates are over-optimistic.

Tackling the unknown emerging face manipulations is still a key challenge [30, 39]. In fact, generalization of detection techniques is crucial in attaining dependable accuracy in real-life scenarios. It is agreed upon researchers that face manipulation and detection is well described as a *cat and mouse game*, where improvements in one area trigger improvements in the other.

The generalization capabilities of existing detectors are still an open issue that is difficult to address with today's (mostly supervised) solutions. An evident example of this *generalization problem* was demonstrated by the recent Deepfake Game Competition (DFGC) [40], held in conjunction with the 2021 edition of the International Joint Conference on Biometrics (IJCB 2021[5]). The competition had multiple rounds of submissions, where participants first designed DeepFake detectors based on the training data provided by the organizers and then contributed novel DeepFake generation techniques to test the detectors. With most developed detection techniques, the performance deteriorated quickly with the introduction of novel DeepFakes not seen during training.

Beyond being able to generalize, it is important that current methods are robust to possible post-processing steps. In fact, media assets often undergo a number of not malicious operations, such as compression and resizing [41], that occurs every time they are uploaded over a social network or made available on a website. Now these operations tend to weaken the forensic traces and above all cause a misalignment between training and test data that can make the learning-based detectors not properly work [11]. Similar problems are also seen in other related areas, for example, Presentation Attack Detection (PAD) [42–45], which despite decades of research, issues with cross-dataset performance and robustness to unseen attacks is still a major issue of even the most advanced solutions.

---

[5] http://ijcb2021.iapr-tc4.org/.

21.3.2 Interpretability

Until now, very few studies have attempted to explore the interpretability and trust-worthiness aspects of face manipulation detectors [46]. Many detection methods, particularly those based on deep neural networks, generally lack explainability owing to the black box nature of deep learning techniques. The fake detectors presently label a face sample with a fakeness probability score, occasionally detection confidence is provided, but little insight about such results is provided beyond simple numerical scores. It would be more beneficial to describe why a detector predicts a specific face as real or manipulated. For instance, which face parts are believed to be forged and where the detector is looking for label prediction [17]. For human, it is vital to comprehend and trust the opinion of a fake detector—however, the human expert operates at the end of the processing chain and therefore wants to understand the decision. A numerical score or label not corroborated with decent reasoning and insights cannot be accepted in some critical applications like journalism or law enforcement, among others.

Furthermore, it is not easy to characterize the intent of a face manipulation. So far, learning-based detectors cannot distinguish between malicious and benign processing operations. For example, it is impossible to tell if a change of illumination was carried out only for the purpose of enhancement or to better fit a swapped face in a video. In general, characterizing the intent of a manipulation is extremely difficult and it will become even harder with the spread of deep learning-based methods in almost all the enhancement operations. In fact, how can a face manipulation detector realize that GAN content generated for super-resolution is acceptable while GAN content that modify a face attribution is not? In a world where most of the media are processed using deep learning-based tools, it is increasingly likely that something be manipulated, and the key to forensic performance is learning the intent behind a manipulation. A good forensic detector should be able to single out only malicious manipulations on faces, by leveraging not only on the single media but looking at the context and including all other related media and textual information.

21.3.3 Vulnerabilities

State-of-the-art detection methods make heavy use of deep learning, i.e., deep neural network models serve as the most popular backbone. Such approaches can suffer severely from the adversarial attacks as some recent works suggested [47–49]. Although real-world fake detectors may cope with various degradations like video/image noise, compression, etc., they can be vulnerable to adversarial examples with imperceptible additive noises [47, 50]. Prior studies have demonstrated that detectors based on neural networks are most susceptible to adversarial attacks [51]. Unfortunately, it has been noticed that all existing methods seem to fail against adversarial attacks, even the accuracy of some fake detectors is reduced to 0% [51].

Beyond adversarial attacks, it is worth observing that every detection algorithm should take into account the presence of an adversary to fool it. In fact, by relying on the knowledge of the specific clues exploited by a face manipulation detector, one can make it not work anymore. For example, if an adversary knows that the algorithm exploits the presence of the specific GAN fingerprints that characterize synthetic media, then it would be possible to remove them [30] and also to insert real fingerprints related to modern digital cameras [52]. Overall, researchers should be always aware about the two-player nature of this research and design a detector robust also to possible targeted attacks.

21.3.4 Human Capabilities

Detecting high-quality face manipulations by humans is already a highly challenging tasks, especially if the subject is not versed in this area. While researchers working on face manipulation are still often able to spot giveaways with the current generation of manipulation techniques, it is expected that this will change in the near future. Although humans have a limited capability to detect high-quality face manipulations, they are usually better at detecting manipulation patterns with little prior knowledge. Thus, they can still be included in the forensic applications' decision-making. Human in the loop systems will lead us to a better reliable detection of high-quality face manipulations. As the quality of digital face manipulation is improving so quickly, it might not be possible to detect them solely based on human visual inspection without an in-depth analysis of image characteristics. Two recent studies [53, 54] have shown that humans cannot reliably distinguish images generated by advanced GAN technologies from pristine images. The average accuracy turned out to be around 50% (coin tossing) for untrained observers, increasing to just 60% for trained observers with unlimited analysis time [54]. In ref. [53], experiments reveal that the realism of synthetic images even surpasses those of real images (68% for synthetic images versus 52% for real ones).

Fooling machines, on the other hand, is more challenging as long as examples of face manipulations are available for supervised training, which does not always simulate real-life scenarios.

21.3.5 Further Limitations

Standards in the field of face manipulation and detection represent the common rules for assembling, evaluating, storing, and sharing samples and detectors' performances. There are no international standards yet, although some inceptive efforts have been made toward this [21]. There is a strong need for standardized frameworks, which should be composed of protocols and tools for manipulation generation and detection, common criteria, and open platforms to transparently analyze systems against benchmarks. Such standardized frameworks will help operators and consumers of digital media to generate, evaluate, configure, or compare face manipulation and detection techniques.

21.4 Face Manipulation and Detection: The Path Forward

21.4.1 Application Areas for Face Manipulation

Face manipulation techniques could mark a milestone in many different application areas in the near future. We summarize next and in Fig. 21.2 some potential applications:

- **Movie industry**: it is a simple and cheap way to do animations compared with traditional computer graphics techniques.[6] With some improvements in terms of quality and resolution, we can foresee that DeepFakes will revolutionize the movie industry, for example, allowing dead actors to act again and to speak seamlessly many languages, enhancing expressions, as well as allowing new settings and takes (e.g., 3D views anytime, without expensive equipment).
- **Social networks and entertainment**: there already exist several startups focusing on building funny animations from still images using lip sync technology, e.g., Avatarify,[7] Wombo.ai,[8] DeepNostalgia.[9]
- **Privacy protection**: face manipulation techniques could conceal certain attributes of the subject from human observers or automatic techniques. For example, face de-identification techniques aim to make identity inference from images and video impossible by altering key facial properties [55, 56], and soft-biometric privacy-enhancing techniques [57] try to modify image characteristics to make it difficult to automatically infer potentially sensitive attribute information from facial images, e.g., age, gender, or ethnicity. These techniques could be very valuable, among others, to replace faces of subjects or witnesses who wish to conceal their identity in fear of prosecution and discrimination.
- **e-Commerce**: face attribute manipulations could further benefit the retail sector, for example, through popular applications such as FaceApp.[10] Consumers could use this technology to try on a broad range of products such as cosmetics and makeup, glasses, or hairstyles in a virtual and user-friendly environment.
- **e-Learning**: face manipulation techniques could enhance the process of remote education of children/students in many different scenarios, for example, swapping teacher's face with their parents as it is proved that familiarity enhances the rate of learning. Similarly, videos of historical figures could be generated, allowing

---

[6] https://www.youtube.com/watch?v=dHSTWepkp_M&t=76s.

[7] https://avatarify.ai/.

[8] https://www.wombo.ai/.

[9] https://www.myheritage.com/deep-nostalgia.

[10] https://www.faceapp.com/.

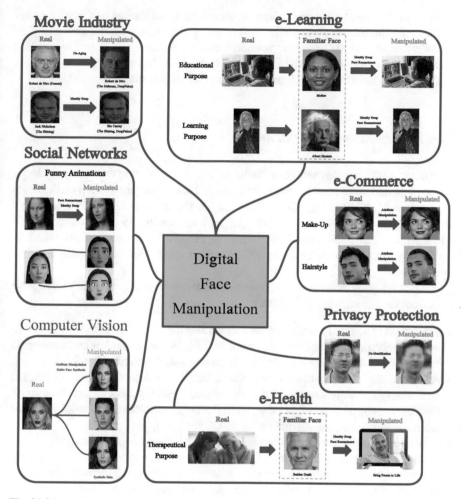

Fig. 21.2 Application areas of the face manipulation technology

students to learn about the topics in a more interactive way, generating more appealing learning scenarios.

- **e-Health**: bring a person to life using face manipulation techniques could be very valuable for therapeutic purposes, allowing patients to express their feelings and get over hard situations, e.g., sudden deaths.
- **Computer vision**: due to the nature of contemporary machine learning models (which are notoriously data hungry), larger and larger datasets are needed for training and ensuring competitive performance. A common, but questionably practice established by the computer vision community in recent years, is to address this demand for data collecting large-scale datasets from the web. However, no consent is obtained for such collections and the generated datasets are often associated with

privacy concerns. Using synthetic data, generated from images of a small number of consenting subject and state-of-the-art manipulation techniques, may be a possibility to address the need for the enormous amount of data required by modern machine learning models and comply with existing data protection regulations, such as General Data Protection Regulation (GDPR) of the European Union.

21.4.2 Promising Approaches

Fake detection technology will continue improving in the coming years. One evidence is that more and more publications have appeared in the last years in top conferences such as AAAI, CVPR, and ICCV. However, as the face manipulation technology will also improve simultaneously, we may still not see highly reliable detectors in a near future, especially those that can handle unseen face manipulations, which is currently one of the most challenging limitations of the detectors as discussed in Sect. 21.3.

Several research directions can be pursued to improve the generalization problem of current face manipulation detectors:

- We expect to see more interest in **one-class learning** models, commonly used in the anomaly and novelty detection literature [58, 59]. Such models learn from real examples and do not require examples of manipulated data to train fake detectors. As a result, they are expected to generalize better for the detection of novel (unseen) face manipulation techniques. Of course, such detection techniques come with their own set of problems that range from data representation and model design to learning objectives, among others.
- **Online learning** is also one promising way to deal with generalization [60]. Unfortunately, current databases are not optimal to conduct online learning research. Therefore, focusing on making better databases and applying online learning can be done together to improve face manipulation detection in the future.
- Recent studies suggest that no single feature/characteristic is adequate to build effective and robust detectors of face manipulations. On the other hand, many successful real-life machine learning solutions are based on **ensemble models** that fuse results from individual types of features or detectors and are calibrated for stronger collective performance [61, 62]. The most notable example is the recent fake detectors presented in the DeepFake Detection Challenge [12].
- Similar to the previous point, **multimodal approaches**, which are able to fuse multiple detection strategies including artifact analysis, identity-aware detection, as well as contextual information such as accompanying text, audio, and origin of data. Multimodal approaches also increase the interpretability and hence the understanding of the reasoning of deep neural networks [63].
- More recently, **identity-aware detection** mechanisms have been proposed which do not learn to detect specific artifacts but rather learn features of a subject [64].

However, such schemes additionally require reference data resulting in a differential detection approach [65, 66].

Apart from the promising fake detection approaches listed above, researchers working on the topic of face manipulation could incorporate mechanisms that intentionally include imperceivable elements (watermarks) into the manipulated images/videos in order to make the detection easier [67, 68]. While such idea does not address the general problem of detecting face manipulations, it could set the bar for adversaries higher and make sharing face manipulation techniques (with legitimate use cases) with the research community less challenging.

Finally, face manipulation techniques could also improve privacy protection [69]. Research on privacy-enhancing techniques is increasingly looking at formal privacy schemes, such as k-Anonymity [70, 71] or ϵ-differential privacy [72, 73], which provide formal (mathematically proven) guarantees about the privacy levels ensured. We expect to see novel algorithms around these concepts in the near future.

21.5 Societal and Legal Aspects of Face Manipulation and Detection

Face manipulation brings an array of complex legal issues. There is no comprehensive legislation on the use of manipulated images, yet several aspects are already regulated in various countries. It should hence not surprise that the development of new manipulation technology and the detection thereof also leads to new issues and questions from a legal perspective which deserve further research.

If it is used to mislead, manipulated images can cause significant harm to the individuals they falsely portray. They can cause emotional distress and reputational damage. The victims of these fake images can try to find relief through torts and criminal laws. Beyond individuals, these digitally altered images can also affect society at large. The problem is that viewers are most of the time not aware that these images are not genuine. In some countries, altered (body) images used for commercial purposes (such as the fashion industry) need to be labeled. More generally, legislative proposals in several countries try to tackle the transparency issue by imposing an obligation to inform users that they interact with AI-generated content (such as DeepFakes). Besides this aspect, manipulated face images might also be subject to copyright protection. But only the photographer of the original images can benefit from it and object to their use without his or her authorization. On the other side, the subjects might benefit from image, publicity, and privacy rights for the alteration of their images without their consent. The rules are different from one country to another. In some jurisdictions, they will be balanced with individuals' freedom of speech (that could allow them to alter these images). But not every use of altered face images is intended to be malicious. Indeed, they can be very beneficial to some industries (such as entertainment or healthcare as discussed in Sect. 21.4.1). Therefore, it is very challenging to tackle the complexity of the use of digitally manipulated face images with a single piece of legislation while technically it would be possible to apply cryptographic techniques to ensure the integrity and authenticity of image data. Finally, there is room to investigate the rules applicable to the digital alteration of the face images for research purposes.

Focusing on face manipulation, one shall keep in mind that in several countries individuals have a right to "one's own image". This implies that individuals are entitled to control their representation and the reproduction of their images, especially face, to the outside world. In an increasingly digitized world, these individuals may also choose to protect their digital images, for example, to prevent profiling. Detecting manipulations, based on this right to control your own image by protecting it, should not have adverse effects for these individuals, unless there is a clear legal rule that this would be forbidden for legitimate reasons, e.g., on identity documents. The potential conflict between this specific right to "one's own image" and other needs, e.g., of public authorities deserves further discussion and debate, based on researched arguments.

All new digital technology used in a societal context raises inevitably new questions, also from the legal side. The reasons why digital technologies are often under close review also by the regulator is that such technologies may change existing (power) relations and affect prior balances once established, for example, when investigating crime or when spreading news information.

Once the manipulation technologies are more widely used, for Example, for spreading fake news over digital platforms, the owners of such platform will face the need for a delicate exercise of assessing whether and removing any information was manipulated. This exercise risks to collide with some fundamental principles in democratic societies, such as the right of freedom of speech, but also the rights to respect for privacy and data protection. For instance, there are currently several proposals for the regulation of digital content on platforms, including an EU Commission's proposal of a Digital Services Act, setting a common set of rules on obligations for so-called intermediaries offering digital services. These services would include video messages, which could be manipulated as to the identities of the actors therein, leading to identity theft or spreading false information.

In case manipulation detection methods are used by public authorities competent for preventing, investigating, detecting, or prosecuting criminal offences this shall be done in a lawful and fair manner. While these are broad concepts, case law further explains how to apply these concepts. Lawfulness refers to the need—in accordance with the rule of law principle—to adopt adequate, accessible, and foreseeable laws with sufficient precision and sufficient safeguards whenever the use of the detection technology, which may be considered as a part of or sub process to, e.g., for face recognition, could interfere with fundamental rights and freedoms. When used for forensics, explainability of the algorithms used, also in court, will be high on the agenda. Fairness points to the need for being transparent about the use of the technology. Furthermore, it is obvious that the use of the detection methods should be restricted to well-defined legitimate purposes, such as, e.g., preventing illegitimate migration or detecting identity fraud. From an organizational point, one should also know that decisions purely and solely based on automated processing, producing adverse legal effects or significantly effecting subjects, are prohibited, unless authorized by law, and subject to appropriate safeguards, including at least human oversight and intervention. Again, according technical solutions to assure the authenticity of data would need to be implemented as a prerequisite.

As argued in Chap. 20, the risk of harming integrity of personal identity and misuse of it as well as the risk of privacy invasion and function creep represent major issues. In the case of integrity of subject's identity, during the identity theft or loss more than privacy will be harmed, the subject could be refused access to services, lose control over their identity, and face damages which are done in their name.

Regarding privacy and function creep, the main issues are related to solutions where a subject's data are used without his or her authorisation. In these cases, how the data is leaked—whether it is from a data leak or insecure service, hackers (adversaries), or vulnerable data systems—is not as important as what the consequences were [74, 75].

The absence of a unified approach, common regulatory framework, and commonly accepted practices has resulted in a situation where different initiatives emerge across countries which share some common elements but also numerous differences that can lead to challenges related to interoperability. It is recommended to share between countries next to technical know-how additionally how social and ethical risks have been and are being managed.

Lastly, it is important to note that face manipulation techniques are also expected to have positive impact on society and economy. For instance, face manipulation techniques can help to address privacy issues through privacy-enhancing techniques, they facilitate the training of machine learning models with synthetic data (without images scrapped from the web), they can help with sustainability by facilitating virtual fitting rooms for the beauty and fashion industries and drive economic development with (high added value) mobile e-commerce, entertainment, and social media applications.

21.6 Summary

This concluding chapter has given an overview of different unsolved issues in (and surrounding) the research field of digital face manipulation and detection. It summarizes the opinions of several distinguished researchers from academia and industry of different backgrounds, including computer vision, pattern recognition, media forensics as well as social and legal research, regarding the future trends in said field. Moreover, this chapter has listed various avenues which should be considered in future research and, thus, serves as good reference point for researchers working in the area of digital face manipulation and detection.

This research work has been funded by

- The German Federal Ministry of Education and Research and the Hessian Ministry of Higher Education, Research, Science and the Arts within their joint support of the National Research Center for Applied Cybersecurity ATHENE.
- The ARRS Research Project J2–1734 "Face deidentification with generative deep models", and ARRS Research Programs P2–0250 (B) "Metrology and Biometric Systems" and P2–0214 (A) "Computer Vision".
- PRIMA (H2020-MSCA-ITN-2019-860315), TRESPASS-ETN (H2020-MSCA-ITN-2019-860813), DATAFACE (H2020-MSCA-IF-2020-895978), BIBECA (MINECO/FEDER RTI2018-101248-B-I00), REAVIPERO (RED2018-102511-T), and COST CA16101 (MULTI-FORESEE).
- The Defense Advanced Research Projects Agency (DARPA) and the Air Force Research Laboratory (AFRL) under agreement number FA8750-20-2-1004. The U.S. Government is authorized to reproduce and distribute reprints for Governmental purposes notwithstanding any copyright notation thereon. The views and conclusions contained herein are those of the authors and should not be interpreted as necessarily representing the official policies or endorsements, either expressed or implied, of DARPA and AFRL or the U.S. Government.
- The PREMIER project, funded by the Italian Ministry of Education, University, and Research within the PRIN 2017 program and by a Google gift.
- The European Commission, grant number 883356—Image Manipulation Attack Resolving Solutions (iMARS).
- The Cybersecurity Initiative Flanders, Strategic Research Program (CIF).

References

1. Barni M, Battiato S, Boato G, Farid H, Memon N (2020) MultiMedia forensics in the wild. In: International conference on pattern recognition
2. Biggio B, Korshunov P, Mensink T, Patrini G, Rao D, Sadhu A (2019) Synthetic realities: deep learning for detecting AudioVisual fakes. In: International conference on machine learning
3. Gregory S, Cristian C, Leal-Taixé L, Christoph B, Hany F, Matthias N, Sergio E, Edward D, McCloskey S, Isabelle G, Arslan B, Justus T, Luisa V, Hugo Jair E, Christa S, Andreas R, Jun W, Davide C, Guo G (2020) Workshop on media forensics. In: Conference on computer vision and pattern recognition
4. Kiran R, Naser D, Cunjian C, Antitza D, Adam C, Hu H, Raghavendra R (2020) Workshop on Deepfakes and presentation attacks in biometrics. In: Winter conference on applications of computer vision
5. Verdoliva L, Bestagini P. Multimedia forensics. In: ACM multimedia
6. Citron D (2019) How DeepFake undermine truth and threaten democracy. https://www.youtube.com/watch?v=pg5WtBjox-Y
7. Allcott Hunt, Gentzkow Matthew (2017) Social media and fake news in the 2016 election. J Econ Perspect 31(2):211–36
8. Suwajanakorn Supasorn, Seitz Steven M, Kemelmacher-Shlizerman Ira (2017) Synthesizing obama: learning lip sync from audio. ACM Trans Graph 36(4):1–13

9. Kietzmann J, Lee LW, McCarthy IP, Kietzmann TC (2020) Deepfakes: Trick or Treat? Bus Horiz 63(2):135–146
10. Tolosana Ruben, Vera-Rodriguez Ruben, Fierrez Julian, Morales Aythami, Ortega-Garcia Javier (2020) DeepFakes and beyond: a survey of face manipulation and fake detection. Inf Fusion 64:131–148
11. Verdoliva Luisa (2020) Media forensics and DeepFakes: an overview. IEEE J Sel Top Signal Process 14:910–932
12. Dolhansky B, Bitton J, Pflaum B, Lu J, Howes R, Wang M, Ferrer CC (2020) The DeepFake detection challenge (DFDC) dataset. arXiv:2006.07397
13. Jiang L, Li R, Wu W, Qian C, Loy CC (2020) DeeperForensics-1.0: a large-scale dataset for real-world face forgery detection. In: Proceedings of the IEEE/CVF conference on computer vision and pattern recognition
14. Raja K, Ferrara M, Franco A, Spreeuwers L, Batskos I, Gomez-Barrero FD, Scherhag U, Fischer D, Venkatesh S (2020) In: Singh JM, Li G, Loïc B, Sergey I, Raghavendra R, Christian R, Dinusha F, Uwe S, Fons K, Raymond V, Davide M, Christoph B (eds) Evaluation platform and benchmarking. IEEE transactions on information forensics and security, morphing attack detection-database
15. Rössler A, Cozzolino D, Verdoliva L, Riess C, Thies J, Nießner M (2018) FaceForensics: a large-scale video dataset for forgery detection in human faces. arXiv:1803.09179
16. Rössler A, Cozzolino D, Verdoliva L, Riess C, Thies J, Nießner M (2019) FaceForensics++: learning to detect manipulated facial images. In: Proceeding of the IEEE/CVF international conference on computer vision
17. Ruben Tolosana, Sergio Romero-Tapiador, Julian Fierrez, and Ruben Vera-Rodriguez. Deep-Fakes Evolution: Analysis of Facial Regions and Fake Detection Performance. In *Proc. International Conference on Pattern Recognition Workshops*, 2020
18. Mirsky Yisroel, Lee Wenke (2021) The Creation and Detection of Deepfakes: A Survey. ACM Computing Surveys 54(1):1–41
19. Li Y, Yang X, Sun P, Qi H, Lyu S (2020) Celeb-DF: a large-scale challenging dataset for DeepFake forensics. In: Proceeding of the IEEE/CVF conference on computer vision and pattern recognition
20. Scherhag Ulrich, Rathgeb Christian, Merkle Johannes, Breithaupt Ralph, Busch Christoph (2019) Face recognition systems under morphing attacks: a survey. IEEE Access 7:23012–23026
21. Venkatesh S, Ramachandra R, Raja K, Busch C (2021) Face morphing attack generation & detection: a comprehensive survey. In: IEEE transactions on technology and society
22. Zhang S, Chi C, Lei Z, Li SZ (2020) Refineface: refinement neural network for high performance face detection. In: IEEE transactions on pattern analysis and machine intelligence
23. Zhou Y, Liu D, Huang T (2018) Survey of face detection on low-quality images. In: Proceedings of the IEEE international conference on automatic face & gesture recognition, pp 769–773
24. Karras T, Laine S, Aittala M, Hellsten J, Lehtinen J, Aila T (2020) Analyzing and improving the image quality of StyleGAN. In: Proceedings of the IEEE/CVF conference on computer vision and pattern recognition
25. Deng Y, Yang J, Chen D, Wen F, Tong X (2020) Disentangled and controllable face image generation via 3D imitative-contrastive learning. In: Proceedings of the IEEE/CVF conference on computer vision and pattern recognition
26. Ciftci UA, Demir I, Yin L (2020) Fakecatcher: detection of synthetic portrait videos using biological signals. In: IEEE transactions on pattern analysis and machine intelligence
27. Hernandez-Ortega J, Tolosana R, Fierrez J, Morales A (2021) DeepFakesON-Phys: DeepFakes detection based on heart rate estimation. In: Proceedings of the 35th AAAI conference on artificial intelligence workshops
28. Gragnaniello D, Cozzolino D, Marra F, Poggi G, Verdoliva L (2021) Are GAN generated images easy to detect? A critical analysis of the state-of-the-art. In: Proceedings of the IEEE international conference on multimedia and expo

29. Marra F, Gragnaniello D, Verdoliva L, Poggi G (2019) Do GANs leave artificial fingerprints? In: Proceeding of the IEEE conference on multimedia information processing and retrieval
30. Neves Joã C, Tolosana Ruben, Vera-Rodriguez Ruben, Lopes Vasco, Proenca Hugo, Fierrez Julian (2020) GANprintR: improved fakes and evaluation of the state of the art in face manipulation detection. IEEE J Sel Top Signal Process 14(5):1038–1048
31. Deng J, Dong W, Socher R, Li LJ, Li K, Fei-Fei L (2009) ImageNet: a large-scale hierarchical image database. In: Proceedings of the IEEE/CVF conference on computer vision and pattern recognition
32. Chung JS, Nagrani A, Zisserman A (2018) VoxCeleb2: deep speaker recognition. arXiv:1806.05622
33. Zhou T, Wang W, Liang Z, Shen J (2021) Face forensics in the wild. In: Proceedings of the IEEE/CVF conference on computer vision and pattern recognition
34. Pang Min, He Ligang, Kuang Liqun, Chang Min, He Zhiying, Han Xie (2020) Developing a parametric 3D face model editing algorithm. IEEE Access 8:167209–167224
35. Giachanou A, Zhang G, Rosso P (2020) Multimodal multi-image fake news detection. In: Proceedings of the IEEE international conference on data science and advanced analytics
36. Singhal S, Kabra A, Sharma M, Shah RR, Chakraborty T, Kumaraguru P (2020) Spotfake+: a multimodal framework for fake news detection via transfer learning. In: Proceedings of the AAAI conference on artificial intelligence
37. Du M, Pentyala S, Li Y, Hu X (2020) Towards generalizable Deepfake detection with locality-aware AutoEncoder. In: Proceedings of the ACM international conference on information & knowledge management
38. Nguyen HH, Fang F, Yamagishi J, Echizen I (2019) Multi-task learning for detecting and segmenting manipulated facial images and videos. In: Proceedings of the IEEE international conference on biometrics theory, applications and systems
39. Cozzolino D, Thies J, Rössler A, Riess C, Nießner M, Verdoliva L (2018) ForensicTransfer: weakly-supervised domain adaptation for forgery detection. arXiv:1812.02510
40. Peng B, Fan H, Wang W, Dong J, Li Y, Lyu S, Li Q, Sun Z, Chen H, Chen B et al (2021) DFGC 2021: a DeepFake game competition. arXiv:2106.01217
41. Rathgeb C, Bernardo K, Haryanto NE, Busch C (2021) Effects of image compression on face image manipulation detection: a case study on facial retouching. IET Biom 10
42. Galbally Javier, Marcel Sebastien, Fierrez Julian (2014) Biometric anti-spoofing methods: a survey in face recognition. IEEE Access 2:1530–1552
43. Marcel S, Nixon MS, Fierrez J, Evans N (2019) Handbook of biometric anti-spoofing, 2nd edn
44. Ramachandra Raghavendra, Busch Christoph (2017) Presentation attack detection methods for face recognition systems: a comprehensive survey. ACM Comput Surv 50(1):1–37
45. Tolosana Ruben, Gomez-Barrero Marta, Busch Christoph, Ortega-Garcia Javier (2019) Biometric presentation attack detection: beyond the visible spectrum. IEEE Trans Inf Forensics Secur 15:1261–1275
46. Trinh L, Tsang M, Rambhatla S, Liu Y (2021) Interpretable and trustworthy DeepFake detection via dynamic prototypes. In: Proceedings of the IEEE/CVF winter conference on applications of computer vision
47. Carlini N, Farid H (2020) Evading Deepfake-image detectors with white-and black-box attacks. In: Proceedings of the IEEE/CVF conference on computer vision and pattern recognition workshops
48. Gandhi A, Jain S (2020) Adversarial perturbations fool Deepfake detectors. In: Proceedings of the international joint conference on neural networks
49. Huang Y, Juefei-Xu F, Wang R, Xie X, Ma L, Li J, Miao W, Liu Y, Pu G (2020) FakeLocator: robust localization of GAN-based face manipulations via semantic segmentation networks with bells and whistles. arXiv:2001.09598
50. Huang R, Fang F, Nguyen HH, Yamagishi J, Echizen I (2020) Security of facial forensics models against adversarial attacks. In: Proceedings of the IEEE international conference on image processing

51. Hussain S, Neekhara P, Jere M, Koushanfar F, McAuley J (2021) Adversarial Deepfakes: evaluating vulnerability of Deepfake detectors to adversarial examples. In: Proceedings of the IEEE/CVF winter conference on applications of computer vision
52. Cozzolino D, Thies J, Rössler A, Nießner M, Verdoliva L (2021) SpoC: spoofing camera fingerprints. In: Proceedings of the IEEE/CVF conference on computer vision and pattern recognition workshops
53. Lago F, Pasquini C, Böhme R, Dumont H, Goffaux V, Boato G (2021) More real than real: a study on human visual perception of synthetic faces. arXiv:2106.07226v1
54. Nightingale Sophie J, Agarwal Shruti, Härkönen Erik, Lehtinen Jaakko, Farid Hany (2021) Synthetic faces: how perceptually convincing are they? Vision Sciences Society (VSS) meeting, In Proc
55. Meden Blaž, Emeršič Žiga, Štruc Vitomir, Peer Peter (2018) k-same-net: k-anonymity with generative deep neural networks for face deidentification. Entropy 20(1):60
56. Meden B, Mallı RC, Fabijan S, Ekenel HK, Štruc V, Peer P (2017) Face deidentification with generative deep neural networks. IET Signal Process 11(9):1046–1054
57. Mirjalili Vahid, Raschka Sebastian, Ross Arun (2019) FlowSAN: privacy-enhancing semi-adversarial networks to confound arbitrary face-based gender classifiers. IEEE Access 7:99735–99745
58. Giovanni C, Luisa P, Verdoliva D (2019) Extracting camera-based fingerprints for video forensics. In: Proceedings of the IEEE/CVF conference on computer vision and pattern recognition workshops
59. Perera P, Oza P, Patel VM (2021) One–class classification: a survey, pp 1–19. arXiv:2101.03064
60. Hoi SC, Sahoo D, Lu J, Zhao P (2021) A comprehensive survey. Neurocomputing, Online Learning
61. Dong Xibin, Zhiwen Yu, Cao Wenming, Shi Yifan, Ma Qianli (2020) A survey on ensemble learning. Front Comput Sci 14(2):241–258
62. Sagi O, Rokach L (2018) Ensemble learning: a survey. Wiley Interdiscip Rev Data Min Knowl Discov 8(4)
63. Montavon G, Binder A, Lapuschkin S, Samek W, Müller KR (2019) Explainable AI: interpreting, explaining and visualizing deep learning, vol 11700. Springer Nature
64. Cozzolino D, Rössler A, Thies J, Nießner M, Verdoliva L (2021) ID-reveal: identity-aware DeepFake video detection. arXiv:2012.02512
65. Rathgeb C, Satnoianu C-I, Haryanto NE, Bernardo K, Busch C (2020) Differential detection of facial retouching: a multi-biometric approach. IEEE Access 8:106373–106385
66. Scherhag U, Rathgeb C, Merkle J, Busch C (2020) Deep face representations for differential morphing attack detection. In: IEEE transactions on information forensics and security
67. Hsu LY, Hu HT (2020) Blind watermarking for color images using EMMQ based on QDFT. Expert Syst Appl 149
68. Khare P, Srivastava VK (2021) A secured and robust medical image watermarking approach for protecting Iitegrity of medical images. Trans Emerg Telecommun Technol 32(2)
69. Terhörst P, Huber M, Damer N, Rot P, Kirchbuchner F, Struc V, Kuijper A (2020) Privacy evaluation protocols for the evaluation of soft-biometric privacy-enhancing technologies. In: 2020 International conference of the biometrics special interest group (BIOSIG), pp 1–5
70. Newton EM, Sweeney L, Malin B (2005) Preserving privacy by de-identifying face images. IEEE Trans Knowl Data Eng 17(2):232–243
71. Sweeney Latanya (2002) K-anonymity: a model for protecting privacy. Int J Uncertain Fuzziness Knowl-Based Syst 10(5):557–570
72. Croft WL, Sack JR, Shi W (2019) Differentially private obfuscation of facial images. In: Proceedings of the international cross-domain conference for machine learning and knowledge extraction
73. Dwork C (2008) Differential privacy: a survey of results. In: Proceedings of the international conference on theory and applications of models of computation
74. Tiits Marek, Kalvet Tarmo, Mikko Katrin-Laas (2014) Analysis of the e-passport readiness in the EU. Institute of Baltic Studies, Technical report, Tartu

75. Tiits M, Kalvet T, Mikko K-L (2014) Social acceptance of e-passports. In: Proceedings of the international conference of the biometrics special interest group

Correction to: Future Trends in Digital Face Manipulation and Detection

Ruben Tolosana, Christian Rathgeb, Ruben Vera-Rodriguez,
Christoph Busch, Luisa Verdoliva, Siwei Lyu, Huy H. Nguyen,
Junichi Yamagishi, Isao Echizen, Peter Rot, Klemen Grm, Vitomir Štruc,
Antitza Dantcheva, Zahid Akhtar, Sergio Romero-Tapiador, Julian Fierrez,
Aythami Morales, Javier Ortega-Garcia, Els Kindt, Catherine Jasserand,
Tarmo Kalvet, and Marek Tiits

Correction to:
Chapter 21 in: C. Rathgeb et al. (eds.), *Handbook of Digital*
Face Manipulation and Detection, **Advances in Computer**
Vision and Pattern Recognition,
https://doi.org/10.1007/978-3-030-87664-7_21

The original version of the book was inadvertently published with incorrect acknowledgement (21.6 Summary) in this chapter 21, which has now been corrected as in below:

PRIMA (H2020-MSCA-ITN-2019-860315), TRESPASS-ETN (H2020-MSCA-ITN-2019-860813), DATAFACE (H2020-MSCA-IF-2020-895978), BIBECA (MINECO/FEDER RTI2018-101248-B-I00), REAVIPERO (RED2018-102511-T), and COST CA16101 (MULTI-FORESEE).

The book and the correction chapter have been updated with the change.

The updated version of this chapter can be found at
https://doi.org/10.1007/978-3-030-87664-7_21

Index

© The Editor(s) (if applicable) and The Author(s) 2022
C. Rathgeb et al. (eds.), *Handbook of Digital Face Manipulation and Detection*,
Advances in Computer Vision and Pattern Recognition,
https://doi.org/10.1007/978-3-030-87664-7

483

Printed in the United States
by Baker & Taylor Publisher Services